SIGNS, STREETS, AND STOREFRONTS

SIGNS, STREETS, AND STOREFRONTS

A HISTORY OF ARCHITECTURE AND GRAPHICS ALONG AMERICA'S COMMERCIAL CORRIDORS

MARTIN TREU

THE JOHNS HOPKINS UNIVERSITY PRESS
BALTIMORE

© 2012 Martin Treu
All rights reserved. Published 2012
Printed in the United States of America on acid-free paper
9 8 7 6 5 4 3 2 1

The Johns Hopkins University Press
2715 North Charles Street
Baltimore, Maryland 21218-4363
www.press.jhu.edu

Library of Congress Cataloging-in-Publication Data

Treu, Martin, 1957–
   Signs, streets, and storefronts : a history of architecture and graphics along America's commercial corridors / Martin Treu.
     p. cm.
   Includes bibliographical references and index.
   ISBN 978-1-4214-0494-3 (hdbk. : alk. paper) — ISBN 1-4214-0494-X (hdbk. : alk. paper)
   1. Signs and signboards—United States. 2. Roadside architecture—United States.
3. Cultural landscapes—United States. I. Title.
   HF5841.T74 2012
   659.13'42—dc23   2011047322

A catalog record for this book is available from the British Library.

Special discounts are available for bulk purchases of this book. For more information, please contact Special Sales at 410-516-6936 or specialsales@press.jhu.edu.

The Johns Hopkins University Press uses environmentally friendly book materials, including recycled text paper that is composed of at least 30 percent post-consumer waste, whenever possible.

Book design by Kimberly Glyder

For Margaret Broske,
    Thelma Nopoulos, and Dee Dee

Contents

ix   **ACKNOWLEDGMENTS**

3   **INTRODUCTION**

12   **CHAPTER 1.** THE MAKING OF MAIN STREET
         Transformation and Invention on the Commercial Frontier, 1700s–1899

48   **CHAPTER 2.** THE GREAT BLIGHT WAY
         Electricity and Reform from Main Street to City Center, 1900–1917

80   **CHAPTER 3.** VISIONS AND VELOCITY
         The Expansive Age of the Automobile, 1918–1928

116   **CHAPTER 4.** SIGN AS STOREFRONT
         America Discovers Modernism, 1929–1945

194   **CHAPTER 5.** LANDSCAPES OF MORE AND LESS
         Consequences of Commercial Freedom and Restraint, 1946–1964

250   **CHAPTER 6.** REDISCOVERING MAIN STREET
         Retrenchment, Repair, and Reinvention, 1965–2010

311   **CONCLUSION**

323   **NOTES**

365   **ESSAY ON SOURCES**

375   **INDEX**

         COLOR PLATES FOLLOW PAGE 212

Acknowledgments

I BEGAN TO APPRECIATE SIGNS and architecture at a very early age. The neon-lit marquees overhead on North St. Claire Street in my home town of Toledo created a virtually continuous ceiling of light that warmed and welcomed my family in, what seemed to me, an otherwise dark and overwhelming downtown. The sublime silhouette, after dark, of the old Grand Pavilion and Coliseum at Cedar Point amusement park was both haunting and exciting to me. These striking buildings and graphics left lasting impressions about place and poetry even before I entered school. While I was still quite young and receptive, my parents took me south to Sarasota, Florida, and drove me through the magic neon gateway of the North Tamiami Trail, with its glowing seahorses, flamingos, and hibiscus flowers. It was clear that we had arrived somewhere exotic, somewhere completely different from the humdrum of home.

My love for buildings and iconography led to a life in architecture and graphics. At Stanford University, as part of my design curriculum, I took a series of photography classes and snapped a carefully composed photograph of the marquee of the then-decrepit Stanford Theatre in Palo Alto. Unwittingly, I began the journey of documenting the commercial corridor and its many features, a long passage that would lead, eventually, to this book. I still appreciate the guidance of my Stanford professors Leo Holub, Robert Parker, Matt Kahn, and Jan Molenkamp. At the University of Virginia, I began to understand the American Landscape in terms of gradations of artifice between rural and urban. Basic principles became clear to me: context is key to understanding any element; space is as significant as solid; and the street is both path and place. For this and much more, I thank especially Robin Dripps, Lucia Phinney, Carroll William Westfall, and Richard Guy Wilson.

I began to document Main Streets and old commercial highway development out of sheer passion for the subject and because I realized that change was rapid—many things were being lost quickly. I also detected that much of this loss was not simply natural attrition as businesses moved on or signs decayed. The speed of destruction was due, in large part, to aggressive new legislation. This urged me on to explore and document as much as I could. Eventually, I turned to the Graham Foundation for Advanced Studies in the Fine Arts to help me in this endeavor, and I am forever grateful that it deemed my subject worthy.

The vast scope of this book required enormous amounts of travel; hence there are many who helped me along the way. Historians and writers to whom I owe thanks include John Maciuika and Alan Hess. Mary Means and Kennedy Lawson Smith, both, at one time, leaders of the National Main Street Center at the National Trust for Historic Preservation, were generous with their insights and details regarding the early years of the program. I am also grateful to Norman Mintz, another pioneer in the Main Street movement, and Scott Day. Of the many leaders of the state Main Street centers, I'd like to thank Ron Frantz and Tim Reinders in particular. At the National Park Service, Beth Savage, Michael Auer, Rebecca Shiffer, and Audrey Tepper were of great assistance many times over many years. At the Society for Commercial Archeology, Betsy Jackson and Sarah Speare were both helpful and encouraging. Pete Philips deserves special recognition for providing guidance through his groundbreaking PAS memo, which helped me to assist in creating an ordinance for the protection of landmark signs in Sarasota. His regular column for the Society for Commercial Archeology, over many years, has helped its readers to better appreciate and understand historic signs.

Key institutions provided essential information that was specific to individual sites or revealed broad historical trends. For their generosity with time and ideas, I owe special thanks to Julie Tozer at the Avery Library, Columbia University; Kurt Helfrich at the University Art Museum, University of California, Santa Barbara; and Dawn Hugh, at the Historical Museum of Southern Florida. Chicago eventually became my de facto base of operations as I explored the country, and the Chicago History Museum revealed its treasure trove of information about the city and the nation. Robert Medina, rights and reproductions coordinator, guided me through the vast photographic archive with tremendous skill and knowledge. He was endlessly generous with excellent suggestions and unlimited support; I owe him extraordinary thanks for lifting this book up to a higher level. Recognition is also due to Lesley Martin, Debbie Vaughan, Elizabeth Patterson, Thomas Guerra, and Erin Tikovitsch. I received additional help in Chicago from Lorna Donley and Pat Bakunas of Special Collections at the Chicago Public Library and University of Illinois, Chicago, respectively. I spent a great deal of time at the Ryerson and Burnham Libraries, Art Institute Chicago; Regenstein Library, University of Chicago; and Newberry Library. I thank the staff of each for their assistance and patience.

Hundreds of other libraries and institutions across the country proved essential for my research, including many small-town archives too numerous to list; acknowledging these repositories of information, I would like to thank, in no particular order, Kelly Haigh at University of California, Los Angeles, Special Collections; Dace Taube, at University of Southern California Special Collections; Sally McKay at Getty Research Institute; Jen Cohlman at Smithsonian Cooper-Hewitt, National Design Museum; Lynn Catanese, Hagley Museum and Library; Melanie Bower, Museum of the City of New York; Laura Stalker, Huntington Library; Elizabeth Terry, Library of Congress; Richard J. Sklenar, Theatre Historical Society of America; and Debra Gust, Curt Teich Postcard Archives. My appreciation is also extended to the staff of the research center at the Wolfsonian–Florida International University in Miami Beach and the Ohio Historical Society.

From east to west, my gratitude is endless. There are many city planners, preservationists, historical society archivists, foundation directors, mayors, librarians, architects, and citizens who helped me to establish a familiarity with many special commercial corridors and an understanding of how they evolved over time. This list includes, but is far from limited to the following: in New York, Elaine Lustig; in Providence, Rhode Island, William McKenzie ("Mack") Woodward, Clark Schoettle, Thomas Deller, Ted Sanderson, Jason Martin, Arnold B. ("Buff") Chase Jr., Christopher Ise, and Malcolm Grear; in Guilford, Connecticut, George Kral, Joel Helander, and Russ Campaigne; in Reading, Pennsylvania, Andrew Miller and Jeff McGraw; in Philadelphia, Len Davidson; in Baltimore, Mary Markey; and in Wildwood, New Jersey, Jack Morcy. Moving south, I extend acknowledgments to, in New Orleans, Charles Tonetti, Hilary S. Irvin, and John Magill; in Charleston, South Carolina, Karen Emmons, Philip Overcash, Linda Bennett, and Alice Tellis-Critikos; in Staunton, Virginia, William Frazier, Kathleen Frazier, and Frank Strassler; in Savannah, Stephanie Jackel; in Williamsburg, Carl Lounsbury; in Orlando, Jodi Rubin; in Miami, Jean-Francois Lejeune, Thomas Mooney, and Shannon McCartt; in Tallahassee, Michael Zimney; and in Sarasota, Lorrie Muldowney, Jeff LaHurd, Frank Folsom Smith, and Clarence Eng. Crossing up and over to the heartland, I express gratitude, in Chicago, to Tim Samuelson, Paul Petraitis, Ledell Edwards, Laura Jones, and Cindy Roubik; in Springfield, Illinois, to Michael Jackson; in Findlay, Ohio, to Paulette Weiser; in Bryan, Ohio, to Tom Voigt, Douglas Johnson, Dan Yahraus, and Jane Kelly; in Bowling Green, Ohio, to Jean Geist; in Sidney, Ohio, to Barbara Dulworth and Cindy Stangle; in Columbus, Ohio, to William Hoy; in Cincinnati, to Anne Shepherd and Jeff Russ; in Niles, Michigan, to Lisa Croteau and Donna Ochenryder; in Redwood Falls, Minnesota, to Gary Revier and Beth Anderson; in Buffalo Lake, Minnesota, to Tammy Almich and Connie Kottke; in Grinnell, Iowa, to Dorrie Lalonde, Gordon Canfield, David Danforth, Jim Ramsey, and Bill Menner; in Albia, Iowa, to Dave Johnson, Michael Judge, Jim King, and Raymond Davis; in Carroll, Iowa, to Douglas Burns and Art Neu; and in Oklahoma City, to Sam Teague. Finally, heading west, I would like to thank George Kramer, of Ashland, Oregon. On my travels, I was assisted generously in Albuquerque, by Mary Pietsch Davis, Sandy Fish, and Doug Crandell; in Ontario, California, by Cathy Wahlstrom, Melanie Mullis, and Kelly Zackmann; in Redlands, California, by Nathan Gonzales, Larry Burgess, Robert Dahlquist, and Manuel Baeza; in Monrovia, California, by Barbara Lynch and Ili Lobaco; in Pomona, California, by Michael Schowalter, Malcolm Oliver, and Mickey Gallivan; in Pasadena, by Jeff Cronin, Sue Mossman, Marsha Rood, and John Andrews; in Santa Barbara, by Lee Goodwin, Michael Redman, Mary Louise Day, Jake Jacobus, David Davis,

Jan Hubbell, and Louise Boucher; and in Los Angeles, by Eldon C. Davis, Chris Nichols, and my dear friend, the amazing John English.

A very special nod is due to those who have worked extensively in the sign business and were kind enough to sit with me while I asked a few thousand questions. Affectionately, to me, they are known as the sign guys. They represent a vast group of craftsmen, designers, and businessmen through history whose collective story has barely been told. For sharing with me, I thank Keith Knecht, Ray Quiel, Wayne Heath, Ken Millar, Bob Behounek, Bob Hunterford, Joseph Woodard, Warren Kinsey, Robert Kinsey, John Ruggles, Jim McNabb, Roger Schwartzbauer, Lyle Hanzal, Gerald Poblocki, Billy ("Mac") Teague, Charles Stofel, Bill Marquet, Bob Galler, and Billy Meskel. This book owes a great deal to these gentlemen and their predecessors in the field. It is also particularly indebted to the kindness, generosity, and endless patience of the great folks at ST Media Group, *Signs of the Times* magazine, and the American Sign Museum, above all, Wade Swormstedt and Tod Swormstedt.

I am indebted to Robert J. Brugger at the Johns Hopkins University Press for his patience and faith, through my years of great sickness, when it looked like I would never be able to see this enormous project through to completion. There was a great gulf between beginning and end, but he was motivated to move ever onward. I would also like to express appreciation to Glenn Perkins and Kenny Marotta for their skillful polish and tremendous care in seeing that everything worked, connected, and made sense.

I am also most beholden to friends and colleagues who, ages ago, helped me to secure financial support for the earliest studies that led to this book and provided lodging and useful suggestions along the way; they include, most especially, Dana Gluckstein, Michael Dieden, George Penniman, Anne Lacouture Penniman, and Bill Hutchins. Michael McDonough and Tristan Farnan Alexander journeyed with me across the map many times over, mile after mile, year after year, eager to discover and patient as saints. They were dream companions for these journeys. When I was on my own, their encouragement continued to keep me fueled and centered. Michael has read many, many versions of the manuscript and always come to me with enthusiasm and clarity. He has been an essential touchstone and practically deserves credit as co-author. My mother, Diane, wanted so much to see this book in print; she was another champion for my work. How I wish she could have made it to the end. I thank her with all my heart for her love and support. Lastly, but with tremendous affection and gratitude, I thank my beloved Rob for calling me his beautiful genius and recharging my confidence when I needed it most. He shared me with the work for a long, long time, kept me calm, and urged me on. The project drew us together, revealed a bond of mutual love for the subject, a great gift to me that began one fine day in the research library.

SIGNS,
STREETS, AND
STOREFRONTS

Introduction

THE OLD NEON SIGN for the Flamingo Colony Motel in Sarasota, Florida, featuring a tall neon flamingo wrapping its sinewy neck up and over letters stacked vertically on a streamlined pylon, was sent to the scrap-metal heap in 1986. Along with a rakishly angled porte cochere, the sign established a real sense of style for what was otherwise a rather modest motel strip. Reflected in the pool, the neon vision once lured weary travelers off the hot two-lane highway and into a miniature Eden of cool bliss (see plate 1). The Flamingo Colony sign had been one of the more highly crafted and artistic of the graphic landmarks from the golden age of American highway travel, the late 1940s through early 1960s. It stood along the Tamiami Trail, which for decades was the main north-south automobile route through Sarasota.[1] The fate of the flamingo became commonplace along the trail in the 1980s and 1990s, as countless vintage signs gave way to simple, plastic-faced substitutes (fig. 1). Significant artifacts of old Sarasota disappeared, and the city suffered a pronounced loss of character. This book explores the nature of the signage Americans once put up and now have lost, as well as the architecture that it embellished, calling for a fuller appreciation of what remains on our older commercial corridors.

No one can deny the extent of this loss—all over the country. Sarasota, a small, gulfside city on the highway linking Tampa and Miami, for many years had attracted tourists and retirees—as either a way station or a destination. After a long drive from Ohio or New York, after coursing through swampy savannah and scrub jungle, one arrived in Sarasota to encounter a sudden and dramatic concentration of neon signage. This dense succession of graphics came courtesy of the local lodging industry. The signs offered tourists a multitude of paradisiacal visions. Besides the Flamingo Colony, visitors were enticed by the Pink Cloud, the Alamanda, the Sapphire Shore, and the Tropical Terrace, to name just a few. Feathery palms swayed over neatly mowed motel lawns; moss-draped live oaks formed a shady backdrop for the motel complexes on both sides of the road. Six-foot neon seahorses and tropical birds beckoned to drivers at dusk. The evocative motel names often appeared in large, loose script, a languorous look that contributed to the resort-like atmosphere. In smaller lettering, the words *ice* and *air-conditioning* were usually placed lower on the signs, just above the hot car hoods that covered radiators still hissing after the day's long drive. The signs were not intrusively tall, and the motel buildings were modest versions of residential types: individual cabins or multiunit ranch-house forms.

The collection of neon signs that lined Sarasota's Tamiami Trail defined both a long shaft of space and a distinctive and memorable place, an effect destroyed today by the removal of the old signs. The close and regular spacing of

(opposite) Figure 1

The new sign for the Flamingo Colony Motel (designer unknown), in same location as shown in color plate 1 (inset). Designed to make use of the maximum area limit stated in the municipal code, this new sign replaced the amortized neon sign in the late 1980s.

PHOTO BY AUTHOR, 1992.

Figure 2

The new sign for the Publix Market, North Tamiami Trail, Sarasota, Florida. The Publix chain eventually replaced the old neon lettering and removed the neon cascade in all store locations (see plate 2). Its goal was to modernize with a new corporate logo and to meet tougher sign code requirements. The company decided not to take advantage of Sarasota's historic sign ordinance, which would have permitted it to maintain the store's original graphics and architectural details.

PHOTO BY AUTHOR, 1991.

the signs on both sides of the roadway created a virtual colonnade leading into town—especially at night, when most other roadside distractions disappeared in the darkness. The bright intensity of the signs and their great number contributed to a sense of enclosure on the road. Their character and form established a unique sense of place. The rich texture of the sign materials, along with the exotic images and names rendered in neon, transformed a mere roadway into a glorious gateway of light and wonderful shapes. The signs immediately and emphatically established Sarasota's identity as a semitropical winter haven, lush with possibilities for escape from the everyday world up north.

By contrast, their replacements were generic rectangular acrylic light boxes, pole-mounted at virtually the same height from one to the next. Each new sign was so small and high that it contributed little to defining the edge of the street. Gone were the neon outlines of tropical flora and fauna. All words, the new signs offered no pictures or anything to pique the imagination. By the 1990s, the entrance to Sarasota could just as easily have been to anywhere.

The transformation of the Tamiami Trail extended past the pole and pylon motel signs at road's edge to include the loss of the dazzling all-neon facade of

the Publix Market (see plate 2). In the late 1980s, the porcelain enamel lettering scaled to fill the elaborate, symmetrical facade was removed; the newly bleak, neon-free facade was marked on one end only with a small acrylic-faced logo panel and modest lettering. The fully electric Publix Markets facades, designed and built in the 1950s and 1960s for the Florida-based grocery chain, were almost as ambitious as the facade of the Stardust hotel in Las Vegas. In the center of the long frontage for each store were abstract shapes, like gigantic, inverted Cadillac fins, flanking a central pylon of animated, cascading white neon—known in the company as the "waterfall." In midcentury, such showmanship seemed appropriate, perhaps even essential, for buildings pushed back from the street by large parking lots. In previous decades, such markets had been located right on the sidewalk. The Publix facade was a powerful example of what architect Robert Venturi would call a "decorated shed" and writer Tom Wolfe would identify as "electrographic architecture."[2] The graphics and architectural design of the building front were so inextricably combined that removal of the original neon was tantamount to full demolition. With the new signage, the facade appeared blank and off-center (fig. 2). Instead of the integrated identity of the original design, the new company logo appeared merely pasted on. The alteration of the Publix was the coup de grace in the visual denuding of the Tamiami Trail in Sarasota.

The courthouse square in Bryan, Ohio, offers another example of a commercial place that locals purposefully transformed in the late twentieth century. In this case, the town rapidly removed many of its signs and peeled off materials that covered original brick storefronts. Until the late 1970s, when legislation forced these changes to its commercial streetscapes, Bryan looked like many other prosperous county seats in the Midwest. For more than one hundred years, citizens in town and farmers from throughout the county had flocked to this regional commercial center. Commercial buildings—stores, restaurants, and a movie house—lined all four sides of the square. The business signs evolved slowly, over time. From the late 1880s to the early 1900s, generous fabric canopies came down every morning by means of hand cranks. Each awning identified its proprietor in big letters painted on the broad sweep of the canvas. Wood and metal signs were attached to the fascias and cornices of buildings or spanned entire upper facades between rows of windows. Since the nineteenth century, most businesses also had signs that were fastened perpendicular to the building facades. These "projecting" signs were located at various heights over the sidewalk, and several reached all the way out to the edge of the street.

By the 1950s, the original brick and wood storefronts had been covered by newer materials, and electric versions of the projecting and flush-mounted signs, in a vast range of sizes, materials, lettering styles, and heights, had replaced the old painted signs. The scale of the new projecting signs ranged from being roughly the same as those of the early 1900s to some that were significantly larger. Over the course of several decades, the old storefronts and facades had been modified—some of them, several times. The changes ranged from minor sign updates to major, multistory applications of modernizing materials that unified several individual buildings with blank, windowless skins of textured metal and vast, script lettering. Schatzer's Jewelers, on a prominent corner of the square, had a stainless-steel blade sign from the 1950s, with a neon diamond and flamboyant diagonal supports. Ringer's Drugs had a porcelain enamel sign projecting from between second-story windows. These and many other such signs survived until the late 1970s, when they suddenly disappeared, along with many of the facade and storefront revisions from the 1920s through 1960s. Upper-story windows, once covered over, have gradually reappeared since the 1970s. Brick is once again the dominant facing of the square, and slim, new signs are all wall-mounted and of uniform size, location, and color.

The changes, enforced or strongly encouraged by the city, have delivered a quasi-historic look to the square. With the shinier mid-twentieth-century material removed from most facades, the buildings present a wall around the square of brown, terra cotta, and white. The purge of a half-century of commercial accretions has meant that some smaller-scale, highly crafted additions were lost along with the cruder, large-scale cover-ups. The black Vitrolite storefront of Hallock Realty, with its silver art deco details, was demolished. Stough's Paint Store lost its streamlined porcelain enamel storefront, where both canopy and facade were fluidly integrated with the design of the projecting sign, rendered with the same colors, materials, and rounded corners (fig. 3). The absence of all the projecting signs that once hung over the sidewalk had a significant impact on the pedestrian scale of the town. It eliminated a feeling of enclosure overhead that was once emphasized at night when the neon and bulb signs created a virtual canopy of light and warmth over the sidewalk.

The transformations of Sarasota's Tamiami Trail and Bryan's courthouse square typify changes that have occurred on suburban roadways and in urban centers across the United States. On commercial strips, the exuberant, first-generation suburban signs of the post–World War II period—and their variety of form, scale, and location—have given way to a series of compact acrylic lightboxes on poles, most of them approximately the same size and elevation from the ground. Commercial buildings on the strip have become increasingly anonymous boxes. Along many such corridors, a series of strip mall signs meet the eye, each identifying anything from four to forty-four tenants in a collective graphic grid and appearing as instantly legible as a full page of text from a book. In some communities, the entrance corridor is defined by a series of discreet, ground-mounted signs virtually camouflaged by elaborate green landscaping.

Many older commercial thoroughfares—Main Streets everywhere—have been scrubbed down to their original nineteenth-century veneers, unsullied by history, shining as if just built. The historic buildings are often impeccably restored. Simple gold-leaf lettering appears in windows, and conservative graphics are discreetly flush-mounted above entrances. But the dense variety of

 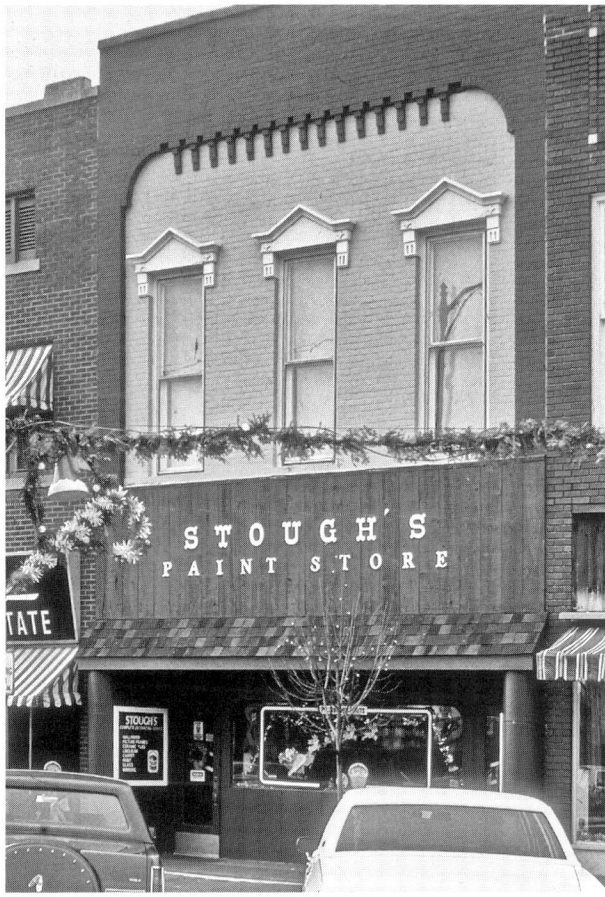

commercial signs and storefronts that had accumulated in the streetscapes over many years, showcasing the creativity and ambitions of craftspeople and proprietors, has been stripped away. Layers of history have been purged. Often, the newer, more "polite" signs appear more decorative than functional—as if only tourists, and not local citizens, walked the streets. Returned to their "historic" appearances, most of these restored and rehabilitated traditional centers have a look that is unprecedented. History was never this tidy.

How do we account for this transformation? Research indicates that toughened public policy explains much, if not most, of the destruction of early- and mid-twentieth-century signage and the ensuing uniformity in new signs. This was forced change, not loss through attrition or change of business. Although tighter budgets have encouraged many businesses to replace the expensive repair costs of neon with the ease of acrylic sign maintenance, radically reductive new legislation introduced in the 1970s explains more destruction than has previously been acknowledged. The story of commercial architecture and storefronts is more complex, as Main Street has in large part merely responded to shifting public taste, as well as to government advice and incentive, in order to

Figure 3

Stough's Paint Store, Lynn Street, Bryan, Ohio, in the 1940s and circa 1978. The fluid visual integration of the streamline moderne, porcelain enamel storefront and projecting sign—a modernization to the original facade—was destroyed when an academic group proposed removal of material seen to conflict with the original building front.

COURTESY OF THE BRYAN DEVELOPMENT CORPORATION.

survive. The strip, in turn, has responded to restrictive codes and market forces to become more muted, more economical.³

A new paradigm for our conception of a sign could lead to a better and fuller understanding of the contribution signs have made through history and their value today. If we were to consider a sign not simply as an advertisement but as an element of urban design that contributes to the character, scale, and identity of a street, we might have a richer understanding of what makes a good city. If we were also to consider a graphic as an element of an architectural composition or a feature essential to a building's identity, perhaps we would better understand what a building can do.⁴ Although many signs may be admired as curious or beautiful artifacts in isolation, their meaning and importance cannot be fully gathered without studying them in context. Divorcing signs from their onsite roles makes it all too easy to trivialize them or dismiss them as mere clutter. The context is physical, cultural, and most especially temporal, changing with the times. As cultural geographer Peirce F. Lewis has said, artifacts of past times "were not seen to be 'inefficient' or silly by the people who made them, or caused them to be made. To understand [these] objects, we must try to understand the people who built them—our cultural ancestors—in their cultural context, not ours." For a moment, at least, we must suspend our own judgments. In his guide to reading cultural landscapes, Lewis presents a series of axioms for seeing the landscape, and he stresses observation in geographic context, which means resisting the temptation to trim away potentially unattractive neighboring buildings and tangles of telephone wires. We learn little by making monuments of single artifacts, be they edifices or beautifully crafted porcelain enamel neon signs.⁵

To reevaluate business signs requires a parallel study of commercial buildings and storefronts. The commercial corridor is an integrated system of advertisements and anchors, a balance between highlighted individuals and regular, flowing, connected community. Illuminated projections often contrast with rhythmic, continuous walls. Traditionally, signs assumed the lion's share of the promotional side of this symbiosis. In the early nineteenth century, in principle if not in practice, signs conformed to tight, regular spaces just above display windows. But very early in the development of the commercial corridor, it was apparent that advertisers would strive to make their graphics unique in size, shape, placement, and quantity. Buildings, in contrast, remained anchored to the sidewalk, their first floors of relatively equal height. For a time, signs could speak as buildings could not. Architects and builders acknowledged the public's limited tolerance for novelty in building design, and economy often dictated form and detail. Eventually, a growing disparity between rooflines revealed how much the corridor could accommodate variety and the impulse to stand out within the crowd. The visual interrelationships among sign, storefront, and building would change radically over the years. At times the role of visual lead would shift from sign to architecture; at times it would be difficult to distinguish the one from the other.

Commercial architecture has historically depended on graphics to identify both a building's use and its inhabitant.[6] Before the development of specific commercial building types in the 1800s, a sign may have been the only visual element to differentiate a residence from a store or tavern. Houses were often converted into businesses simply by the placement of a wooden graphic hanging on a post and a few minor modifications to the building interior. Later in the 1800s, as the classic multistoried Main Street commercial building developed, with its increased glass frontage at ground level for the storefront, signs were essential to distinguish one business from another along the sidewalk. At ground level, the regular rhythm of windows and piers provided a relatively neutral "background" for individual graphic identity and expression. As businesses moved out into the open space of the suburbs in the twentieth century, builders were free to employ unique architectural forms to identify commercial structures, leaving signs with reduced responsibility for garnering attention and distinguishing one business from the next. However, by the end of the twentieth century, as commercial architecture became blank, flexible, inexpensive shells of air-conditioned space, signs once again were a very important element in communicating identity, even if that identity was often already established through other media. A logo sign for the regional bank or the local Home Depot transforms a generic and variable branch building or big-box warehouse into a specific and familiar place.

Interacting since the settlement of the colonies, four interest groups have contributed to the rich American tradition of business signs working in concert with commercial building facades. First, an advertiser's (or business owner's) taste and budget directed signage efforts and created effective storefronts. The advertiser's goal was to make the business noticeable and enticing. Often this led to plentiful, exuberant graphics and richly embellished building surfaces. Competition drove advertisers to increase the visuals over time. For a period, trademark architecture worked as an effective "sign" to help identify chain businesses.

Second, sign technology and manufacturing techniques became an increasingly important variable, especially during the twentieth century with the advent of electric lighting, which included the development of neon. The character of bulb or neon illumination inspired designers and allowed them to create new sign images and forms. New building materials also played a part in this development. The manufacturers of glass, porcelain enamel, and sheet metal and storefront framing manipulated the look of Main Street and the commercial strip, constantly encouraging new looks that employed more of their products. Their campaigns to update the appearance of commercial corridors produced promotional material of every description that ballyhooed "modern" design and advanced technologies. Colorful and seductive advertisements appeared in sign and architecture trade journals.

The potential customer provided a sometimes unpredictable third element in the equation. He or she represented the traveling target whose attention the signs aimed to reach out and grab. Once, the customer's pace simply equaled the speed of a walking person or horse. After the 1910s, customers in many settings raced past retail shops in automobiles, too quickly to read much more than a few words. Signs and architecture needed to be distinctive, even garish, to catch the customer's fleeting attention. At about this same time, many customers, acting as aesthetic progressives, decried "excessive" or "inappropriate" signage, describing it as an "eyesore." Out of this sentiment came attempts to control signage through various local ordinances. Members of both the progressive and City Beautiful movements proposed sign limitations in the same way that they called for effective street lighting, buried telephone lines, and improved roadways. These efforts lapsed during the Great Depression, World War II, and the period of exuberance and prosperity that followed in the 1950s. Eventually a great reaction set in; by the 1970s, preservationists, in their zeal to show off old commercial architecture to best advantage, revealed a prejudice against historic signs.

Finally, we must understand the designer as another independent variable, someone who generated forms based on need but also on an aesthetic sensibility developed by experience and education. Early on, the designer (as well as the advertiser) was responsible for the development of the first true sign and commercial architecture types. The designer was perhaps merely a builder in these early years, responding to need, materials, and recent precedent. Later, the designer (as architect or graphic specialist) attempted to integrate sign and building visually, a goal driven by aesthetics and a professional urge to reform the randomness and clutter of the commercial landscape. Modernism carried appeal because it seemed to entice the customer with something new. The look and philosophy of the movement also preferred to purge design of unnecessary ornament and to rethink the shop as an efficient machine for selling. From the 1940s through 1960s, the shopping mall emerged from a desire among design leaders to reform the perceived chaos of the entire commercial corridor, to impose order on it.

As a reflective look backward, this volume aims to shine the spotlight on creative commercial design that, in many cases, has been demolished or is threatened. Thousands of key features of the American capitalist landscape have come and gone without documentation or much discussion. Signs clearly require something closer to the attention that historians give to architecture. The effort to preserve historic buildings across the United States has benefited from many years of careful documentation, analysis, and rethinking of the field of architectural history. Only recently has commercial architecture received much attention, but as a serious subject for study, it is still largely overlooked and underappreciated. Only a short shelf of books and journal articles have comprehensively addressed the most common commercial buildings—the ones that were to be found on small-town Main Streets and the highways into town. Signs have barely been considered seriously since architect Robert Venturi's breakthrough work in the late 1960s and the wise words of cultural geographer J. B. Jackson, beginning in the 1950s.[7] With this book, I approach the daunting task of providing a comprehensive, insightful examination of an often-neglected yet major element of the American landscape—with the hope that such an effort will encourage new support for the preservation of historic signs and time-honored patterns for sign design and placement. I also make an attempt to address both the "high-style" design of storefronts and buildings by leading architects and the "low-style" signs and storefronts of sign crafters and contractors without academic backgrounds or big budgets. As an examiner of cultural landscapes, Paul Groth reminds us that "ordinary, everyday landscapes are worthy of study . . . Everyday experience is essential to the formation of human meaning."[8] This material is worthy of a comprehensive history, something that ties a great many loose threads together, recognizing graphics as major contributors to the common places we remember from the past and those that we experience in the present, each day.

Chapter 1
THE MAKING OF MAIN STREET
TRANSFORMATION AND INVENTION ON THE COMMERCIAL FRONTIER, 1700s–1899

BY THE MID-1700S, Duke of Gloucester Street in Williamsburg, Virginia, presented a tension between urban and rural, between community and individual, that would define the American commercial thoroughfare for many years to come. Although this capital was hardly typical of Main Streets that formed in the American colonies, it revealed these primary forces well—forces one could see manifest in new ways as the country grew. This tension was inherited from England, where continental baroque city-planning initiatives by architects such as Christopher Wren, requiring dense settlement around grand public spaces, were offset by a tendency to give each dwelling or privately developed neighborhood its own exterior space, whether it was a lot behind a house or a small communal square surrounded by terrace housing. This duality reflected shifts in political power, away from the monarchy and into the hands of Parliament and its citizens. As England's former colonies reached westward, individuality increasingly came to define the look of city streets. Legislation in America would evolve to protect property rights for the individual, as a rule, protecting the lone citizen's desires when the needs of the community were perceived as overreaching. This explains, in large part, why America's commercial buildings would eventually become as randomly singular as their owners' personalities, and why signs would shout in a variety of shapes and sizes from every conceivable location.

English settlement in North America was characterized from the start by a strong preference, even yearning, for the rural over the urban. This proclivity was driven in part by the rapid growth of London and subsequent decline of the traditional agrarian countryside in England. Founders like William Penn in Pennsylvania and the Puritans of New England were wary of the corruptive influences of the city. The Puritans decried the city as a place where commerce led to personal aggrandizement; their beginnings in this country were focused on God and community. New England and Pennsylvania were conceived as low-density landscapes patterned after those occupied by the gentry in the mother country. Even by the late eighteenth century, Thomas Jefferson expressed a preference for an agrarian nation. Inland settlement in seventeenth-century New England was not in dense villages but in scattered agricultural communities that came to be known as "towns," in local parlance. These were, by definition, geometrically bounded areas, ideally six miles to the side, with farmsteads spread loosely beyond a meetinghouse that acted as a hub. Penn envisioned his new city of Philadelphia—his "green country town"—as a series of deep 800-foot-wide lots along a 15-mile stretch of the Delaware River. When he could not acquire enough riverfront land to implement this ambitious scheme, he commissioned a plan with four parks and a central square regularly spaced in a grid of mostly acre and half-acre lots bisected by wide streets. Purchases of rural Pennsylvania land were automatically tied to ownership of a lot in the city. Savannah's founders also believed in the power of the rural countryside; the regular pattern of public squares, and the systematic granting of a garden and farm lot with each town lot—all physically contiguous with the town center—was planned to cleanse the city of its potentially negative traits. Houses were purposefully placed at some distance from each other.[1]

Eventually, rural and communal settlement attributes gave way to the realities of urban growth and individual self-betterment. As trade increased and populations surged, Pennsylvania and New England gave birth to villages and towns of increasing concentration. New England town centers, once modest gatherings of a few buildings around the meetinghouse (resembling encampments, according to a contemporary observer), first experienced relatively dense growth around the common (the old meetinghouse lot) beginning in the federal period.[2] Only then was the classic image of the inland New England village

finally established, with residential structures, located near each other but rarely contiguous, often placed into commercial use. The towns that developed rapidly in eastern Pennsylvania and Maryland during the eighteenth century were decidedly more urban. Pennsylvania towns mimicked the streets of London, with brick row houses built cheek-by-jowl, without setbacks. These towns were conceived as urban establishments from the start, even those established with only a handful of buildings. They were places created for commerce.[3]

In contrast to the rural ideals that originally shaped settlements in the Northeast, Williamsburg was conceived as a true city, a place of high artifice. The Virginia capital was to be a cultural outpost in a colony that was quite sparsely settled. The decision was a very conscious injection of "urban" patterns into a landscape of farms and random-looking crossroads villages. Despite that lofty aim, the town revealed the nature of its rural context at many turns. Its materials were not as consistently polished as the brick and stucco facades of London or the towns of Pennsylvania, nor were its street edges as tightly defined. In Williamsburg today we can see past and future, collective and individual, urban

Figure 4

Duke of Gloucester Street (buildings roughly 1711–80), Colonial Williamsburg, Virginia. A balance of urban and rural design features developed in this colonial capital, with a wide, dramatically axial street lined with relatively humble buildings marked by signs on posts (rather than signs consistently hanging from facades as in European urban centers).

PHOTO BY AUTHOR, 2002.

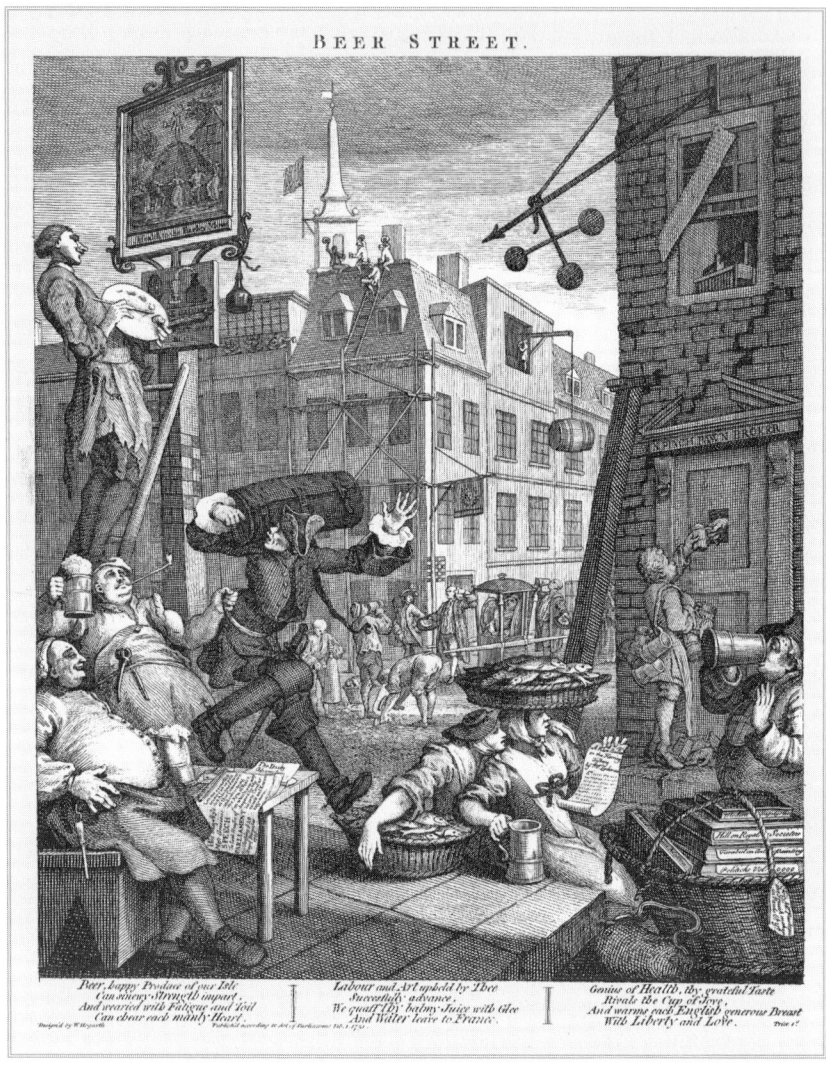

Figure 5
William Hogarth, *Beer Street* (1751). The classic vertical inn sign was usually depicted in rural or semirural settings by eighteenth-century painters and engravers in England.
© TRUSTEES OF THE BRITISH MUSEUM.

and rural—in balance—through the town's layout, architecture, and signs (fig. 4). The primary thoroughfare was as broad and straight as some of the grand, royal streets of Europe. Governor Francis Nicholson established the baroque plan, involving one major and one minor axis, in the early 1700s. The city's signs were hung on posts erected in front of one- and two-story buildings for businesses along streets that mixed residential and commercial uses. Many of the structures along Duke of Gloucester Street would have been equally at home in the countryside: they were basically domestic in form and therefore not especially urban. Most were residences and turned their gables away from the street, assuming a lower profile. All of the buildings with gables facing the street were shops; this simple change of orientation was a primary step in the transformation of what was basically domestic into something more public and commercial. The tavern buildings, with roof ridge lines running parallel to the street, were essentially the same as taverns along lonely rural highways and were not fundamentally different from houses.[4] Weakly, they contributed to the sense of containment that such an ambitious avenue required at its edges. The buildings lining Duke of Gloucester Street did not share common walls but were separated by sometimes wide spaces. The relatively humble buildings appeared little like their taller, stone counterparts in London, where a continuous street wall was maintained, building after building.

Signs on posts, like those in Williamsburg, were rare in central London. William Hogarth's mid-eighteenth-century illustrations depict such business identifications only in newer communities on London's edge or in fully rural locations. Most of his images of urban locations showed signs hanging from building facades on narrow streets. In other drawings from that time, too, signs hung directly from facades on broader streets and squares. Both types existed in Williamsburg. Along Duke of Gloucester Street, one encountered post-mounted signs planted a few feet in front of tavern buildings, out in the public right-of-way; at the same time, merchant signs hung directly on shop fronts.

In its transition from a nation of lonely rural outposts to one of rapidly growing, densely developed market towns, America consistently represented the individual in built form. The early tavern was necessarily dominated by its signpost, which was an essential marker for identifying a business in a structure that could otherwise be confused for a home. As cities expanded, the development of a specific commercial building type led, by the mid-1800s, to relatively uniform architecture. This uniformity required signs to represent the individual, singling out each entity among many. As the nineteenth century progressed, commercial buildings became increasingly flamboyant and distinct, and builders used height and profuse ornamentation to make their structures leap out from the continuous street elevation. As the architecture rippled with eye-catching features and facades, with solid walls increasingly replaced by glass, there were fewer and fewer places for graphics to appear. Signs were therefore forced to compete for visual attention in inventive, sometimes excessive, new ways—and often in novel new locations.

Early History: Urbanizing the Rural for Town Commerce

Commercial architecture and shop signs of the American colonies can be traced primarily to England. The classic "vertical" inn sign of Virginia and the New England states, which welcomed weary guests from afar, dominated William Hogarth's urban setting in *Beer Street* (1751), one of his most famous images (fig. 5). In principle, the vertical inn sign was a painting hanging within a frame (metal in Hogarth's image, most often wooden in the colonies). Sign paintings depicted an icon or set of icons that combined to convey the name of the establishment. Icon signs were a part of a tradition imported from Europe that dated back at least to the Middle Ages. Because few people could read, symbols or pictures were necessary. Newspaper advertisements would sometimes advise their literate patrons to find an entertainment establishment "at the sign of the Red Lion," at the "sign of the Sun," or the "sign of the anchor." Rebus signs were also popular, summoning the sound of the proprietor's name with pictures (e.g., three cocks for Cox or a horse fording a stream for Horsford).[5]

Because of the simple domestic appearance of the country inn or "ordinary" of colonial America, the sign communicated its public function. Without such a feature, a traveler might mistake the structure for just another pitched-roof house. Colonial law in Connecticut mandated that inn signs be clear: "Every person licensed for Common Entertainment shall have some suitable Signe set up in the view of all Passengers for the direction of Strangers where to go, where they may have entertainment; and such as shall have no Signe by the first of September 1673 shall pay a fine."[6] A traveler's observation from the 1780s revealed how a sign's distinct form advertised not only the existence of a business but a particular type of enterprise: "The taverns in the country are recognizable, even at a distance, by a sort of gallows arrangement, which stands out over the road and exhibits the patron of the house."[7]

Here was a sign type strongly suitable to the vast spaces of America, to its nature as a land where people were often on the move. This clear landmark was not unlike the cloverleaf signs of the late twentieth century, the small corporate rectangles on tall posts, luring the travel-weary from the interstate highway. The eighteenth-century vertical signs typically advertised inns or taverns along country roads, where travelers would stop on long journeys, horses would be changed on stagecoach routes, and farmers could gather from their distant fields and homesteads. But as the nature of American settlement changed, and people concentrated more and more in villages and towns, the local inn was increasingly found on the green, the square, or the budding Main Street. Engravings by John Warner Barber and Henry Howe in the 1830s and 1840s illustrate many examples of how the rural vertical or post sign was imported from the countryside into the village center (fig. 6). To our eyes, such markers for the local inn may appear striking in appearance, disproportionate in scale, spires of commerce floating alone in public space, competing for attention with the steeple of the meetinghouse or church. But they were, indeed, most welcoming to outsiders.[8]

The importance of a tavern to a village or any sort of settlement cannot be overemphasized. It may have been the first outpost of civilization on a lonely road. It was usually the first commercial establishment in any community, the only place to do enough business to require a central location. It served many functions, and that versatility was very necessary in small communities. In New England's embryonic town centers, before a permanent meetinghouse was built, the tavern was sometimes used for church services. It was usually placed next to the meetinghouse, providing a more informal site for gatherings of all kinds. Court was sometimes held in taverns. Eventually, the "town house" (or town hall) was the place for such activities. In large market towns, like Philadelphia, the tavern became the focus of men's daily activities. Where one street corner

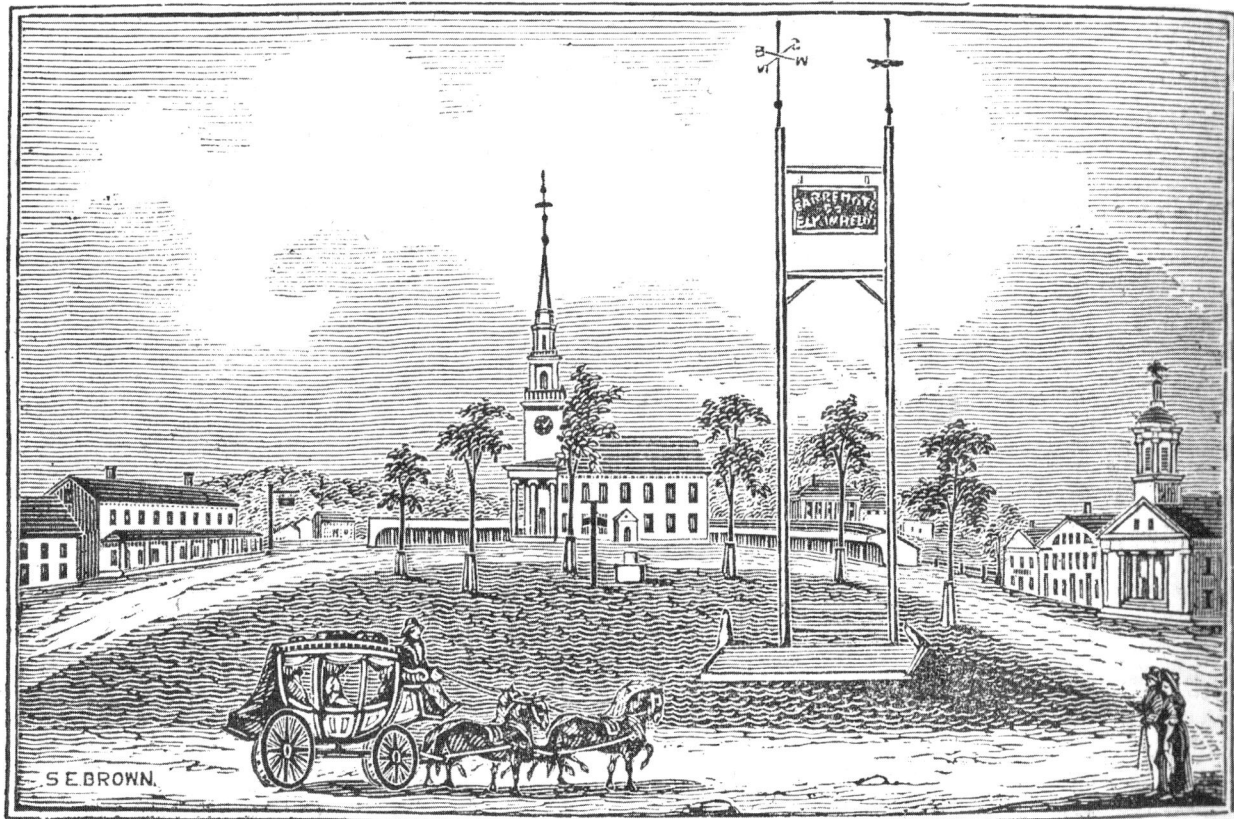

Figure 6

Sign for the Barre Hotel, as seen from porch of same, looking across village common, Barre, Massachusetts, in 1839. The conspicuous scale of many inn and tavern signs John Warner Barber depicted in his travels through the Northeast indicated they were major features in towns frequently consisting of loose collections of individually distinctive buildings.

JOHN WARNER BARBER, *HISTORICAL COLLECTIONS: BEING A GENERAL COLLECTION . . . RELATING TO THE HISTORY AND ANTIQUITIES OF EVERY TOWN IN MASSACHUSETTS* (1840), 554. REPRODUCTION COURTESY OF THE NEWBERRY LIBRARY, CHICAGO, F844.069.

was like another due to the city's grid layout, taverns and tavern signs created a sense of order.[9]

The details of a tavern's vertical sign often served to link it visually to the building and enterprise that was advertised. The frame around the painted image that provided the icon distinctive to each tavern sometimes served this purpose. It often suggested the welcoming interior of the inn or tavern. The turned wooden posts and the pediment that made up the frame were not only architectural features but also direct borrowings from doorway pediments and the backs, posts, and crest rails of early eighteenth-century "great chairs."[10]

An obvious potential model for America's urban commercial thoroughfare might have been London's Cheapside, the city's busiest and most highly regarded street for shopping during the eighteenth century. An engraving from 1750 of this broad thoroughfare illustrates a multitude of finely painted signs in an intensely urban space. These signs were hung on fine wrought-iron supports out over the heads of the pedestrians walking along the edge of the great thoroughfare, close to the merchants. There was a notable homogeneity to the architecture that defined the street wall, with rather plain-fronted buildings of four to five stories. The signs, too, appeared to be approximately the same size, varying only in shape, and they were located on each building front at approximately the same level. This consistency was striking. The more common context for

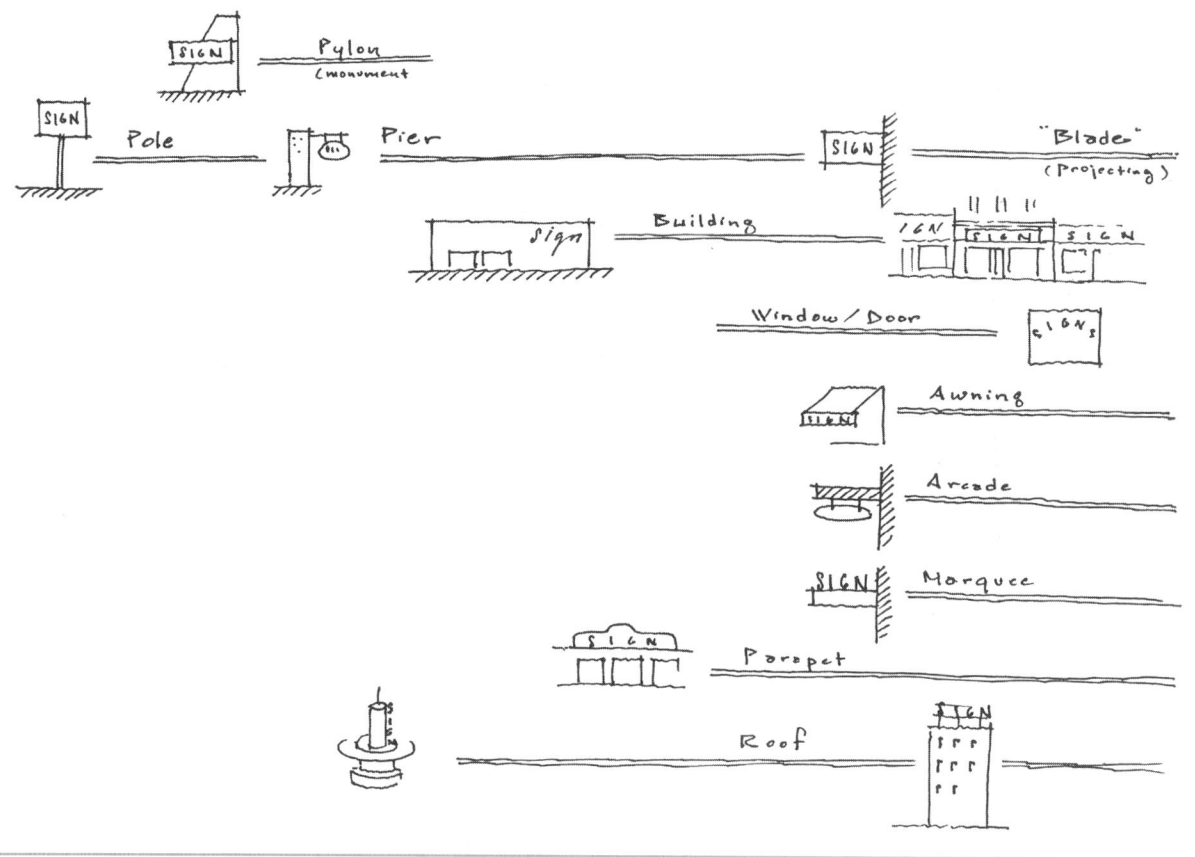

RURAL   **URBAN**

Figure 7

Transect of sign types, from rural to urban. The basic transition from rural post sign to urban wall sign, as American cities grew in the late eighteenth and early nineteenth centuries, reversed in the mid-twentieth century as development began to favor rural or suburban locations.

DRAWN BY AUTHOR.

the hanging sign was the narrow street, illustrated by Hogarth and others. Even the earliest shops, still open-fronted, had hanging signs to help establish presence and mark individuality within a maze of merchants. The hanging sign was mandated in tighter urban locations, where the post of a vertical sign would be impossible due to space limitations.

The streets of medieval London were dotted with other types of signs, identifications more ancient than the painted panel, which can be dated to the late 1400s. The development of the shop and its sign, in history, actually began once the closed, concessionary system of the guilds, which excluded competition and advertising, came to an end. Any remarkable object that happened to stand before a tavern was readily interpreted as a sign.[11] Most often, the early signs of London were three-dimensional models of the image to be represented. Thus, the simple mortar and pestle was hung in enlarged sculptural form above a druggist's shop, the sugarloaf—another simple form—for the grocer, and the enlarged shoe for the cobbler.[12] Louis-Sébastien Mercier's *Tableau de Paris* (1783) tells us of ridiculously great object signs: "spurs as large as a wheel, gloves big enough to house a three year old babe."[13]

The fascia sign, where identification was established with a board running the full width of the shop above the display windows, came into its own after legislation in London in 1762 prohibited hanging signs. This was critical to the development of what later came to be understood as the traditional shop front.[14] But in America, other forces were at work to make this sign type more common, and to merge what had formerly been a freestanding artifact with the surface of the commercial building.

In the towns and cities of the United States, there emerged in the early nineteenth century a progression from a rather rural, domestically influenced architecture that was adapted to commerce to a new architecture and sign type that became wholly commercial and urban. Although founding fathers such as Thomas Jefferson had hoped America could develop as a largely rural nation, it had, due to market and industrial forces, become a country that revolved around towns and cities. The urban population in the United States jumped from 6 percent in 1800 to 20 percent by 1860.[15] The change to a new, truly urban commercial building type had the effect of uniting sign and building. No longer was the sign a separate object on a post. By the mid-1800s, sign and building would be less "figural" and more "ground." Increasingly, commercial America was becoming a nation of front-gabled and flat-roofed structures built in series along the street edge, identified by flush-mounted graphics (fig. 7).

The first step in the urbanizing of the American commercial sign came when the wall or fascia sign began to supplant the post sign long associated with the rural inn. This happened as early as the 1820s. By 1850, all Connecticut inns still operating had replaced their earlier signs.[16] During a brief transitional period, the vertical painted panel sign became a horizontal rectangle or oval frame with two to three lines of text, set off by nonfigural decoration.[17] The next step was the loss of the sign's illustrative or representational element, making it completely reliant on text for communication. With this change, it became even more horizontal. An engraving of Fourth Street in Philadelphia from 1800 by William Russell Birch and Thomas Birch shows the post sign in transition (fig. 8). On long, projecting poles, horizontal sign panels were thrust out to the edge of the planked sidewalks; vertical posts supported their ends. Instead of sitting independently, the sign structure was now engaged with the building. As late as the late nineteenth century, such signs could still be seen in newly founded towns or on the frontier's edge. The next step in the urbanization of the sign in America was the true projecting sign, which often consisted of a hanging plaque on a cantilevered support. This was a sign type common in early-eighteenth-century Europe, where street space was at a premium and projections were necessarily modest. The most urban of signs were those painted or mounted directly on building facades, flush instead of projecting. Such signs became quite popular by the mid-nineteenth century in America, even though the wider streets of the new nation did not require them.

Literacy in America had increased; iconographic signs were no longer required for effective identification. Offsite ownership, space leasing, and shorter-lived businesses may also partially explain the change to verbal signs; identification could be altered with greater ease. The nature of business identity had also evolved since the late eighteenth century. Village Hotel and American House had replaced the Red Lion and the Anchor.[18] The American commercial enterprise had become a more efficient, less sentimental machine, urged on with an eye for economy and efficiency. There was also a need to communicate more plainly and loudly against growing competition in an increasingly urban setting.

The transition from rural to urban was less direct in the evolution of commercial architecture. In towns settled prior to the nineteenth century, buildings built on main streets and public squares were domestic in form, even if used

Figure 8
Fourth Street, Philadelphia, in 1799. The somewhat hybrid signs shown along this corridor illustrate the post sign in transition from freestanding rural artifact to physically engaged urban (or hanging) identification.
ENGRAVING BY WILLIAM RUSSELL BIRCH AND THOMAS BIRCH. THE PRINT AND PICTURE COLLECTION, FREE LIBRARY OF PHILADELPHIA.

commercially.[19] In growing mercantile cities of the East, spotty construction along potentially commercial thoroughfares gave way in the late eighteenth and early nineteenth century to continuous development, with individual domestic structures lined up end to end, composing a "row." Roof ridgelines were parallel to the street, maintaining a time-honored domestic profile. In the Mid-Atlantic states, constituting these rows was the central hall or "I-house" unit, with chimney wall at both ends (a form borrowed from northern Europe and the British Isles). It became the building block of Main Street, according to historian Richard Francaviglia.[20] This row phenomenon was particularly noticeable in cities like Philadelphia and Baltimore. During this period of urbanization, the standards of the community outweighed the presence of the individual, as little in the architecture and urban layout identified the distinct proprietor. The sign thus played an essential role in differentiating a residence from a business and telling one business from the next (see plate 3).

For many years, domestic architecture, though not ideally suited to continuous street elevations, was nevertheless employed for commercial buildings in cities like Boston, New York, and Philadelphia, where buildings were placed tightly side by side. Slight alterations made these buildings suited to greeting customers. The Lamb Tavern in Boston (early eighteenth century), for example, provided an entrance loggia, a space "carved out" of the otherwise solid corner of the gambrel-roofed structure.[21] A framed sign panel with a painted lamb was thrust over the street on a simple board. In rural states like Virginia, stores retained the same vocabulary as domestic architecture up through the first quarter of the nineteenth century, but simple alterations permitted them to be business-ready.[22] The Prentis printing store in Williamsburg (1739) was accommodated in a building built to function commercially, one of the earliest store structures still extant in America. The store was a variation on the basic house, with the gable turned to the street, a central door, and flanking, slightly oversized windows. Such fenestration eventually came to characterize the earliest shops in Virginia.[23] By the late eighteenth and early nineteenth century, stores were often marked with large bow windows of small glass panes and simple signboards at the fascia level. In a few decades, the ground floors of most commercial buildings were opened dramatically to the street with large areas devoted to a grid of glass panes. Architectural historian Richard Longstreth identifies the architectural phenomenon of a building with a predominantly transparent (business) first floor below a more solid (residential) upper floor as the "two-part commercial block," a key element of the American Main Street.[24]

Even the side-row house type of Charleston, South Carolina, could be modified for commercial purposes (fig. 9). Though urban in its relationship to the street, the side-row maintained a degree of rural character due to the open "garden" space typically placed at its side even in densely developed sections of town. In its purest form, a simple I-shaped, multistoried, gable-ended structure was positioned so that its short side faced the street, flush to the sidewalk. This formal front along with a high garden wall helped to maintain the urban character of the street. A solid front with a door was often applied to the street end of the otherwise open piazza, or porch, which divided house from side garden. This door provided entrance to the residence. The business entrance was located on the main body of the house, where large windows flanked a door centered on the short, street elevation.[25] In principle, each house had two entrances: business and private.

By the 1830s, the Greek Revival style was transforming public and commercial architecture. The gables of buildings built in this style typically faced the street and were fashioned as large pediments, outlined with heavy cornice moldings. This design approach transformed what was once an ordinary feature of a building into something stronger and grander, recalling classical Greek temples. Although often employed for houses of the relatively wealthy, the greatest impact of the Greek Revival style (1825–1860) was in institutional and commercial architecture. Its use along Main Street brought the potential for reasserting the presence of the individual over the community. Instead of a row of buildings with ridgelines parallel to the street, the thoroughfare was punctuated, as of the 1830s, with powerful pediments.

The town of Guilford, Connecticut, like many in the East, offered examples of domestic buildings employed in the services of commerce, as well as newer, purpose-built commercial buildings that retained certain domestic features. Several eighteenth-century frame houses around the green were modified in the late nineteenth century with larger first-floor windows for business. A Greek Revival structure at 9 Boston Street (1858) operated, successively, as a store, a grocery, a bank, and a hardware store. The second story served as an apartment. Sometime in the late 1880s, the first-story cornice and fascia were altered to cantilever with bracket supports as an open porch in order to shield enlarged display windows in the original facade. Later, this porch was enclosed and employed for even grander display purposes. On the green in Lebanon, Connecticut, an elaborate, richly ornamented, Palladian second-story window transformed what would otherwise have been a domestic wood-clad building (1885) into something far more public. In this case, the second story was created as a meeting hall for the local grange society that built the structure to include a cooperative store on the first floor. The inflated scale of the structure also implied importance, if not community use. Of the structures scattered widely along Lebanon's elongated green, the building was one of very few that were used commercially.

The commercial centers of New England, developed earlier in the nineteenth century than those of Midwestern towns, were composed primarily of more domestic, precommercial or protocommercial buildings. In smaller towns of the Northeast whose growth was arrested by changes in industry or transportation, one can still see relatively simple, pitched-roof structures placed irregularly around or near the town common. Some—but rarely all—were used for businesses at some point. Several stores were updated in the late nineteenth

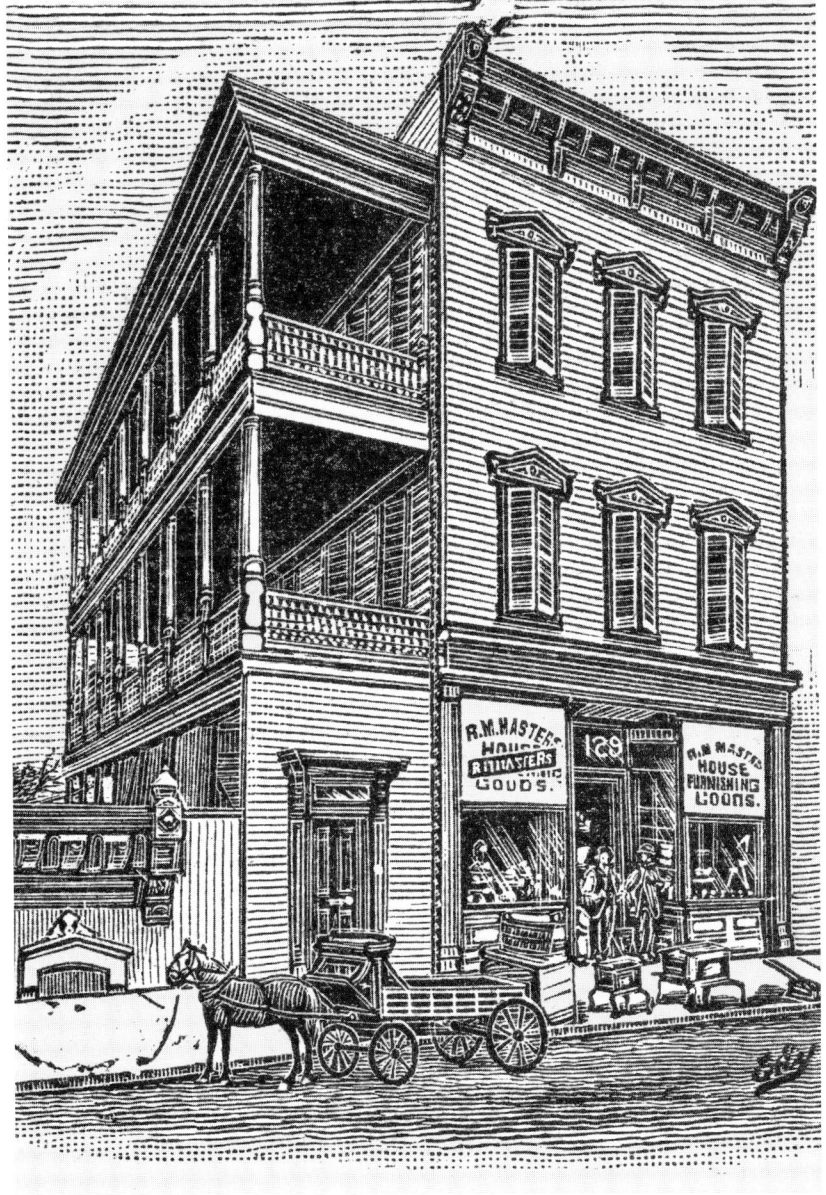

Figure 9

Side row house, Charleston, South Carolina. This form of house is especially suitable for operation as both business and residence, as the door to the commercial enterprise can be placed directly on the street, situated squarely in the center of the building facade, surrounded by display glass. The residential entrance begins to the side of the facade, leading to yet another door located down the length of the piazza and side garden, well off the street.

ANDREW MORRISON, THE CITY OF CHARLESTON AND THE STATE OF SOUTH CAROLINA (1889), 91. REPRODUCTION COURTESY OF SPECIAL COLLECTIONS, UNIVERSITY OF VIRGINIA LIBRARY (F277.C4 M6 1889).

century with the addition of porches or larger ground-floor windows. Some of these structures were moved to their present sites from elsewhere and reoriented with their gable ends turned toward the street or common. The rural inclination of these New England towns is reflected in the relatively sparse placement of buildings around the common. Often large in scale, in proportion to population, these commons did not require efficient settlement. Although upper floors were often used residentially, store proprietors sometimes constructed their homes next to their stores instead of living above their shops. Town commons were then, and are today, typically surrounded by a mixture of shops and houses,

Figure 10

Public Square, Newark, Ohio, in 1846. Compared to the view of the central space of Barre, Massachusetts (fig. 6), and other New England town centers during the same period, commercial and governmental centers of Ohio were more ordered and regular. Buildings lined up, with few gaps, along the straight edges of square plazas, with ridgelines corresponding.

HENRY HOWE, *HISTORICAL COLLECTIONS OF OHIO* . . . (1889), 327. REPRODUCTION COURTESY OF THE NEWBERRY LIBRARY, CHICAGO, F892.421.

the latter often called into the service of commerce periodically over nearly two centuries of occupation.

Due to their later settlement, Midwestern towns, influenced in part by the commerce-driven density and focus of Pennsylvanian and mid-Atlantic towns, tended to segregate business compactly along particular streets.[26] Buildings butted up against each other, even in the early years of community growth, with common height and ridgeline following the street. A comparison of village and town centers in the New England and Midwestern states, illustrated in engravings produced in the 1830s and 1840s by John Warner Barber and Henry Howe, demonstrates a pronounced difference in regularity and density of buildings between the two regions (fig. 10). In the earliest years of development, there were, however, some important similarities between the Midwest and New England; the pronounced contrast would come later. In their formative years, a mixture of houses and stores surrounded the courthouse squares in places like Bryan, Ohio, just as they did the commons of New England. Just barely settled in the 1840s, around the time that many central Massachusetts towns had reached their peak of development, Bryan's square eventually progressed to the next stage of commercial evolution. Bryan's Main Street, which ran along its courthouse square, was originally the site of several modest two-story wood-frame structures whose gable ends were oriented toward the square. It appears that a two-story, brick, Greek Revival building with a substantial white pediment replaced one of these around 1853, once the real boom began and following a fire on this block. By around 1870, however, this building had been replaced by a new structure with a flat roof, parapet front, tall narrow windows, and a first floor that was almost fully taken up by windows. Other such structures, all recently built and all in brick, soon flanked it. Bryan's square and Main Street reached their peak at the time that a task-specific American commercial architecture had evolved. The edge around the square was entirely composed of brick commercial buildings presenting a continuous wall to the street.

In contrast, a town like Barre, Massachusetts, with a population similar to that of Bryan in the mid- and late nineteenth century, had a somewhat ragged, albeit dense, edge of commercially used structures along only one side of its common (fig. 11). Appearing solid from an oblique angle, it was actually composed of a procession of distinct, gable-ended structures dating from the 1830s and earlier. Over time, these buildings, originally with distinct gaps between them, were united with side additions and common porches, all in frame construction. As in many New England towns, Guilford's few buildings dedicated to commerce in the early nineteenth century were scattered among residences rather than concentrated along a particular stretch of street. By the twentieth century, the number of stores increased dramatically, and they began crowding out residences along two sides of the community green. As of the 1920s, these two sides of the green, which were part of the alignment of the important Boston Post Road, were almost exclusively business. Of New England towns, only those that continued to grow substantially in the late 1900s would be updated with brick, pedimented structures like those common everywhere in the Midwest and West. Guilford's green received a sprinkling of these, due in large part to its popularity as a summer destination. Other towns in the interior of Massachusetts, like Templeton, which were bypassed by industrial-age wealth, were never updated with later-nineteenth-century commercial buildings. They presented nothing remotely like solid edges along their commons; spotty arrangements of buildings, predominantly domestic in form and use, scattered around often immense public spaces.[27]

Figure 11

East side of common, Barre, Massachusetts, circa 1900. The unusually solid edge to this New England common was nevertheless primarily made up of buildings individually distinct in profile (most pre-1850), with gables facing the street. The rest of the common was bordered by freestanding structures often widely spaced—the norm in many villages of the region, relatively unaltered by industrial-age development.

COURTESY OF MS. LUCY ALLEN.

Designed for Main Street: Task-Suited Commercial Architecture and Signage

Although a strictly commercial building did not emerge as an American architectural type until the early nineteenth century, the mercantile building as a distinct form had been developing for many years prior to that in England and Europe. In medieval days wares simply were placed on the ground or in stands, booths, and carts.[28] By the seventeenth century, most shops were still open-fronted and stall-like; the traditional house-and-shop relationship, in which the craftsman or shopkeeper lived above or behind the showroom or workplace but did not own it, had also been established.[29] Show windows were widespread by the 1750s, at least among the better shops such as those along Cheapside in London. The ground floor was made as open as possible by substituting a massive bressumer (or beam) borne on strong supports for load-bearing walls.[30]

The parapet-fronted, flat-topped building led to the future of commercial architecture in America: it was custom-designed and task-specific. It could be two stories or four; in other words, its height could be varied somewhat without suffering comparisons to historical laws of proportion. As long as it was crested with a suitable cornice, it looked complete. And proportions mattered little when buildings such as this were built flush alongside others. Towns and cities in America were growing quickly, and the flexible, modest commercial architecture that started to appear in great quantity suited them perfectly. The fully evolved commercial building type had a flat or simple sloped roof concealed behind a parapet front. The flat roof provided tremendous flexibility, allowing the building to extend the full length of a deep, narrow lot or to expand laterally along the street front as necessary. It also allowed rooftop rainwater to drain to the back of the site instead of on adjoining buildings or on the sidewalk. The parapet front disguised the modesty of the roof while increasing the dignity and presence of the building with additional height. Wall signs on the front of the building were given increased area and a key location via the enlarged upper facade. The parapet on a one-story building was called a "false front" because it rose so much higher than the true structure behind it. As historian Vincent Scully and architect Robert Venturi have pointed out, the false front enhanced the urban character of the street in the most fragile of settlements.[31] Commercial buildings with false fronts appeared in great numbers from the mid-1800s onward.[32]

Richard Longstreth contends that by the mid-nineteenth century, uniform characteristics in the architecture of the commercial districts from town to town were abundant: "Were one to simply look at unidentified photographs, it would be difficult to tell whether an emporium constructed about 1860 was located in Boston, Philadelphia, Louisville, St. Louis, New Orleans, or San Francisco... Even if the architectural dialects were different, the underlying grammar was much the same."[33] A major explanation for this homogeneity was a uniformity of lot size, and the narrow configuration of the lot. The grid system of the National Land Ordinance of 1785 had led almost universally to subdividing the standard commercial lot to approximately twenty-five feet in width and one hundred feet in depth.[34] The speculative nature of building also helped explain this sameness within each town and from one town to the next. By midcentury, the designs for buildings outside the great Eastern cities were now often produced by builders and untrained artists armed with increasingly accessible trade journals and style books; architects were not essential. Just a few years later, the look of the buildings on Main Street could easily be determined with the use of drawings in newspaper advertisements or lumberyard catalogs as guides. Such easy, universal sources stimulated repetition from town to town. This phenomenon was especially traceable in a state such as Iowa, which was settled from east to west, the western half of the state being established from the 1850s on, once rail became the dominant form of long-haul transportation.[35]

Railroads had an enormous effect on the urbanization of America and on commercial architecture, hastening a transformation catalyzed by the availability of mass-produced building materials. Although many towns in the Ohio and Mississippi river valleys had been settled in the 1830s or earlier, they experienced their first real growth after the railroads arrived in the 1850s. The railroads were famous for creating towns from scratch. Architectural and cultural historian Carole Rifkind asserts that in the United States the railroad was the greatest town builder of all.[36] It drove the rate of construction and determined the materials and even the methods for building more powerfully than any other landowner, population movement, or architect. In 1850, the Illinois Central Railroad received the first federal land grant, which led to its establishing stations approximately every ten miles along its route.[37]

Railroads changed the way buildings were constructed, making available even on the frontier standardized machine-cut lumber, inexpensive pressed materials, and prefabricated architectural parts from across the nation and beyond. Eastern Iowa's initial growth had been before the railroad; its buildings had been constructed primarily of native timber and handmade bricks. Relatively treeless western Iowa, settled after the railroad crossed the state, benefited from the presence of lumber mills in Muscatine and Chicago.[38] The railroads made balloon-frame construction, and thus a much lighter architecture, possible by bringing milled lumber and machine-made nails so affordably to any town with rail access. Railroads also provided transport for simulated stone products, available beginning in the 1860s, and the new, affordable plate glass produced in the United States since the Civil War. Most of all, the railroads hastened a homogeneity of design and the speed at which towns emerged.

During his first visit to America, in 1841, Charles Dickens was struck by the newness of everything he saw. So much was being built so quickly, especially in the commercial centers of towns. The typical American urban area was certainly a far cry from London's stone, stucco, and brick, soiled by smoke from

coal fires. Of Boston, he wrote: "The air was so clear, the houses so bright and gay; the signboards were painted in such gaudy colors; the gilded letters were so very golden; the bricks were so very red; the stone was so very white; the blinds and area railings were so very green; the knobs and plates upon the street doors so marvelously bright and twinkling; and all so slight and unsubstantial in appearance—that every thoroughfare in the city looked exactly like a scene in a pantomime."[39] And of Worcester, Massachusetts, he continued, bemused: "All of the buildings looked as if they had been built and painted that morning... In the keen evening air, every sharp outline looked a hundred times sharper than ever."[40]

The English author's observations could just as easily have been applied to lower King Street in Charleston, South Carolina, where a great many buildings were erected between 1830 and 1850. King Street was one of the city's primary commercial thoroughfares in the mid-nineteenth century, gaining dominance over the course of the next hundred years. Running from north to south through the urban core, it effectively operated as Charleston's "Main Street." One after another of its commercial buildings offered a simple street-facing elevation. The typical commercial structure of Charleston was composed of three bays and three stories, with a flush brick or stucco facade. None of the fussy ornament or projections of the Victorian period had yet been developed. Straightforward stone lintels defined windows. An attic "story" just below the cornice presented a series of slim, horizontal openings that aligned with the windows below; each was filled with a decorative, cast-iron grill.

One full commercial block facing the courthouse square in Bryan, Ohio, was erected almost entirely during the 1860s by various builders who seemed to be in agreement about creating a continuity of surface and design. Although the streetscape presented a variety of building heights and window-head configurations, it nevertheless offered a satisfying homogeneity. This was achieved via window size and proportion, consistent use of red brick, and—because this was early in the period now commonly referred to as the Italianate—muted surface undulation. Pilasters, if articulated at all, were subtly defined. The limited variety in architectural detail during this decade was created, for instance, with a minor sawtooth or bracket corbelling near the cornice. Such visual embellishments, however, were nothing compared to the ornamental gymnastics of the decades to come (see plate 4).

By the 1840s, a developing specialization in merchants and stores required something to distinguish one enterprise from another. Increased product availability and growing cities meant that general merchandisers were splitting into shops with greater focus. The row of almost homogeneous storefronts required signs to identify the nature and character of each business.

The most basic location for a sign was on the fascia, the continuous panel that crossed the full width of the store, above the shop windows; it coincided with the deep structural beam that bore the load of the wall above the glazed

(opposite) *Figure 12*
Park Row, nos. 11–21, New York City, in 1896. A hierarchy of messages was discernible even for buildings that seemed at first glance to be overwhelmed by signs.
COLLECTION OF THE NEW-YORK HISTORICAL SOCIETY.

opening. In architectural history, the term *fascia* was used in reference to the architrave portion of the classical entablature, the part believed to represent the lintel that spanned columns in the primitive hut on which the Greek temple was based. The projecting trim located directly above the fascia of a shop front was called the cornice, another component of the classical entablature (not to be confused with the cornice that "caps" the building at roof level). In Roman times, the frieze was often carved with lettering to denote the identity or purpose of the building. The frieze and the stepped fascia of the architrave were simplified into a single component in the new visual economy of the nineteenth century commercial facade. Often no more than twelve to eighteen inches deep, this slim space, usually just called the fascia, carried painted lettering that identified the proprietor and/or the type of business conducted on premises.[41]

Commercial architecture and advertising both contributed to the design development of business signs. The letterforms for fascia signs were often stretched horizontally in order to make the best use of this wide but relatively slim space (which was often less in height than in classical precedent). In this way, the sign was molded and conditioned by the architecture, which in turn was responding to the limitations of space and the efficiencies afforded by such innovations as steel structural members. Graphic developments also had an influence. Prior to 1900, the sign painter had few resources for lettering styles

Figure 13

Carter's Corner, near Courthouse Square, looking northwest on North Main Street, Bryan, Ohio, in 1870. The projecting plank sign, a type somewhere between rural post sign and urban fascia sign, was often associated with nascent towns on the frontier, where patrons from the countryside were often unfamiliar with local businesses.

WILLIAMS COUNTY (OHIO) PUBLIC LIBRARY PHOTOGRAPHIC ARCHIVES, 1989.08.3.

or guidance in the technical requirements of the field. He learned his skill as an apprentice. However, one or two printed resources were also available to assist or inspire him, though the extent of their availability is uncertain. One small book, published in Boston in 1842, displayed key sign painter alphabets.[42] In 1875, A. P. Boyce published a manual that probably enjoyed wide circulation, emphasizing technique and practical matters.[43] Sign makers lacking such sources might refer to newspaper advertisements or rely on posters heralding traveling shows or patent medicines. The visual saturation of these exceptionally creative paper advertisements—achieved with a wide variety of type styles in a full range of sizes—may explain, in part, the eventual spread of lettering over the face of commercial buildings. In this case, the printed media indirectly transformed the appearance of the American commercial street.

The availability of increasingly larger and more affordable pieces of glass had a major impact on storefront design and on sign placement. Until the 1830s, a grid of mullions segmented the shop window into small squares, due to the cost and technical limitations of spun "Crown" glass, which had first appeared in the shops of London's New Exchange in 1667. Mass-produced German sheet glass bridged the gap between 1832 and midcentury, when relatively cheap plate glass first became available in the United States. As of the late 1830s, four-by-eight-foot sheets of imported glass were to be found on some of the storefronts along New York's Broadway. But after the Civil War, when sheet glass began to be widely produced in America, just about any merchant could obtain large plates of it, and the storefront truly opened up to the outside.

The canvas awning was often a major secondary location for business identification. In the early 1800s, an awning-like feature, or canopy, was an improvised structure consisting of timber or cast-iron posts and angled wooden rafters with canvas. After the Civil War, iron-plumbing pipe lightened the frame and permitted ornate, cantilevered supports that eased the removal of fabric from time to time. Operable awnings, including the roller type, which arrived in the late 1800s, permitted daily lowering and retraction. The extreme slope of early awnings permitted major graphics to be applied. A decrease in slope, with the advent of transom glass around 1900, moved graphics to the valence.[44]

The slim sign fascia and awning valence were often insufficient to identify a store in an era of mounting competition. Commercial graphics spread everywhere on a building's surface. In some cases, the upper facade and cornice were covered with lettering that identified businesses located above street level, but often these elevated graphics also served to advertise the primary business on the ground floor. In 1841 Dickens had marveled at how the upper stories were "covered with boards and inscriptions . . . various symbols and devices, almost covering the whole front."[45] By 1868, when the Trinity Building in New York City was documented in a photograph, it carried a virtual skin of painted signboards and carved wooden letters advertising the businesses operating within. By the late 1900s, it was typical to find horizontal sign panels painted to the full width of the facade, placed between rows of windows, story by story. Sometimes this ladder of lettering was capped at the building's cornice with a figural parapet sign.

A hierarchy of facade signs on business structures was established during the nineteenth century. To borrow from architect Robert Venturi's terminology, a system of signs ranging from the "heraldic" to the "informational" appeared from the top of the commercial building to the bottom (fig. 12). The heraldic sign, which honored the proprietor with suitably scaled fanfare, was meant to gain a customer's attention from afar and lure him closer. This category included a sign at the crest of the building (ranging from an ornate parapet graphic to a modest "false front" sign), and the sign along the fascia, at street level. The heraldic sign on the upper part of the building was commonly figural, taking on a curved or unique shape, sometimes projecting from the building's surface. Informational signs supplied support or supplemental information, such as the "what," "when," and "how much," often appearing on or between windows and at doorways.

Even as these new facade-based signs appeared in urban areas, rural sign types could still be found in abundance in the late nineteenth century. One could find modified examples of the freestanding traditional inn sign, located on posts at the edges of sidewalks from the short Main Street of Lanesboro, Minnesota, to King Street in Charleston, South Carolina. These were relatively rare compared to the "board arm," or horizontal, projecting sign, which was the more urban version of this tradition. In some cases, the length of a street bristled with wide, occasionally crude, signs of this kind. Most were supported with narrow pieces of iron pipe at the edge of the boardwalk or sidewalk, but some were true, cantilevered signs (fig. 13). All of these projecting signs reached out to grab the attention of people unfamiliar with the merchants of a town. The signs' messages were usually generic and familiar: American House, City Hotel, or General Store. They could be found in towns on the edge of the frontier but also in municipalities back East, bringing a piece of the countryside into the city.[46]

The false front sign was another popular way to identify businesses in the earliest days of a developing community. This type was a major graphic applied to an extended form of parapet that often created the illusion of greater height than a building actually possessed. Born of acute need and limited resources, the false front worked efficiently to create visual dominance and a sense of spatial containment along the street, in contrast to the wide-open landscape of the frontier. It resulted from an urge to establish something substantial in a tenuous community (fig. 14). Most false fronts were wood framed and could be constructed rapidly during a town's formative years; they would be replaced by brick structures of greater architectural presence as soon as resources permitted. These new buildings rarely offered the ample graphic area that the older falsefronts presented to the street. To the builders of second-generation Main Street edifices, architectural flamboyance, even prestige, often became more important than boastful business identification.

Facade Conflict: Competition between Architecture and Signs

The late nineteenth century was a time when individualism spoke loudly in built form; building design became more ornate, even theatrical, and novelty increasingly was employed to gain attention. Even in a modest county seat such as Bryan, Ohio, the shift from the previous decades was noticeable. Pilasters that were once gently placed regularly between windows on relatively smooth walls gave way to boldly segmented facades with deep shadows. Multiple levels of wall surface were created with inventively shaped inset panels arranged around windows. The surface of a building bumped in and out. Windows were noticeably larger than they had been a generation earlier. From approximately 1870 on, builders placed elaborate, highly sculptural hoods over the window heads—stepped, peaked, keyed, or of a more exotic shape. Each building, though still similar in scale and proportion to its neighbor, seemed to strive in some way to

Figure 14

False fronts (circa 1880s), Medicine Bow, Wyoming. An exaggerated extension of the facade plane past the roofline, the false front resulted from an urge to establish something substantial and urban in a community built quickly on the edge of the frontier.

PHOTO BY ARTHUR ROTHSTEIN, 1940. LIBRARY OF CONGRESS, PRINTS AND PHOTOGRAPHS DIVISION, FSA/OWI COLLECTION, LC-USF 34-29619-D.

be unique. This was the subtle beginning of a greater trend. Such architectural articulation precluded upper-story signage. There was less and less space available to append a sign in any but the most awkward of fashions.

Over some forty years during the mid-nineteenth century, street elevations displayed marked increases in visual complexity and verticality. Drawings of the same blocks of Chestnut and Market Streets in Philadelphia, spanning this period, show an evolution from basic pitched roofs and ridgelines running parallel to the street, above simple, flat-fronted facades punctured by basic windows (fig. 15). By the 1850s, two- and three-story buildings were being replaced with five and six stories, the architecture becoming more articulated with pilasters, cornices, and elaborate, figural parapets. Window grids and small panes of glass were replaced with single sheets. Apertures above the street grew taller, and proportionally narrower. More and more signs were placed well above the first floor, many of them incorporated in parapets at the building crests. By the

1870s, the architecture was progressively more eclectic and ornamented, with windows sometimes assuming exotic shapes. Signs were placed in increasingly creative locations.

Commercial architecture of the 1870s and 1880s demonstrated an affection for surface ornament and roofline flourishes. Cornices became much heavier, with elaborate brackets and, in some cases, peaked parapets breaking through continuous horizontal entablatures, forming small dormer windows or creating special panels to display the dates of construction or the names of building owners. On some buildings, small pinnacles were added at intervals along the cornice, betraying the era's fascination with the Gothic. Tiny Redwood Falls, Minnesota, which did not have a store until 1865 or the railroad until 1878, was built up almost entirely during this indulgent, eclectic period. Redwood Falls was not an unusually prosperous town, but one would not know that from looking at the complex, lacy Gothic filigree on the crest of its Philbrick building (1886), which was perhaps the most elaborate of several highly ornamented buildings (fig. 16). Although the brickwork of the facade may not have been particularly fancy, the cornice was absolutely saturated with decorative brackets and corbels. This was an enthusiastic mixture of Gothic church detailing with secular Renaissance features, a casual eclecticism encouraged by the growing bounty of images in print, prefabricated components available by catalog, and the delivery of materials via railroad.

Technological advances such as cast- or pressed-metal forming made increasingly elaborate commercial facades possible. From the 1870s to the 1910s, cast-iron elements could be purchased through catalogues. In addition, hardware shops in many towns boasted "tin shops," which were dedicated to the sale of cornices and window hoods. The mechanization of stone and wood cutting further added to the wealth of options available to the builder of commercial structures.[47]

A look at an engraving made of one commercial block on State Street in Chicago in the 1880s reveals how business signs sometimes interacted with the new architectural agitation (fig. 17). The identifying signs are barely squeezed into the small space remaining between bands of windows. They are fastened to the building's surface, no longer truly flush, as they sometimes overlapped windows and spanned projecting pilasters. It was rare to see a sign at the roofline of a building—there was too much architecture competing for attention there. The first-floor fascia, traditionally reserved for signs, was now a rare refuge for business identity. The fascia sign became larger than the (reduced) fascia space itself. In some cases the sign was clumsily fastened, angled forward, overlapping the fascia's ornate cornice. In December 1884, one Minneapolis architect publicly complained that too many buildings were being "bedecked and bedazzled with every manner of projections and gee-gaws, any kind of trash, so that it be a 'new style'—God save us!"[48] That same year, a similar lament appeared in a Minneapolis newspaper: "You will find in most of the business blocks lately erected in St.

(opposite) *Figure 15*
400 block, Chestnut Street, Philadelphia, Pennsylvania, north side, in 1851 and 1880. A comparison of the appearance of the same block across thirty years reveals the transformation of commercial architecture from one of relative simplicity to ornate eclecticism. (TOP) JULIO H. RAE, RAE'S PHILADELPHIA PICTORIAL DIRECTORY AND PANORAMIC ADVERTISER (1851), PLATE 7. COURTESY OF THE ATHENAEUM OF PHILADELPHIA. (BOTTOM) DEWITT C. BAXTER, THE BAXTER PANORAMIC BUSINESS DIRECTORY, 2ND SET (1880). COURTESY OF THE ATHENAEUM OF PENNSYLVANIA.

Paul that certain one-idea styles have been followed in but few circumstances. As a rule, there is a mixture and sometimes you will see the plain Gothic, the arch French, the Romanesque, and the Queen Anne all combined to produce a unique and striking effect."[49]

By the end of the nineteenth century, the sign industry had introduced a decorative approach that was every bit as ornate as the architecture of the period. Chipped-glass signs were elaborate yet concentrated panels that were often applied over old painted fascia signs or fastened in drum form, vertically at the street corner or at a recess in front of the entrance door. Their sparkling effect was achieved by pitting the glass surface with the aid of strong glue and by masking the part of the sign that was not to be chipped. Rawson & Evans (New York and Chicago) was the largest producer of this type of business identification. These signs were the result of a buildup of competition between businesses for the customer's attention and between sign companies for new clients. They were also a product of competition between signs and increasingly frenetic architecture for the attention of the passerby. As signs' space on the building surface decreased, their intensity increased. The graphic layout of such signs was usually as elaborate as the reflective finish technique, employing script-type styles, curved baselines, and scroll borders.

Broadly stated, the more elaborate signs of the late nineteenth century were as eclectic and highly ornamental as the architecture of the period. Most

Figure 16

Philbrick Block (1886), Redwood Falls, Minnesota, circa 1890, circa 1967, and in 2005. Commercial buildings of the 1880s were particularly ornate (LEFT). Primary settlement of Redwood Falls occurred during this period, and its streets were lined with elaborate cornices. By the 1950s, owners often updated the vertical proportions of older buildings (MIDDLE), removing cornice ornament and leaving behind plain, flat parapets more suitable to modernism. They also reduced tall display windows, less needed thanks to electric lighting, to create a more horizontal building appearance. During the 1970s and 1980s, more window area was filled in partly to improve energy conservation. Ultimately the original buildings were completely obscured (RIGHT), with upper windows fully filled and painted out to appear as solid wall. Second-story space became unrentable as old commercial buildings competed with vast, new, one-story structures built away from the town centers.

LEFT, MIDDLE: COURTESY OF GARY REVIER.
RIGHT: PHOTO BY AUTHOR, 2005.

Figure 17
State Street, Chicago Loop, circa 1878. As commercial building facades became more ornamented, finding suitable places to fasten signs became more and more difficult.
COURTESY OF THE CHICAGO HISTORY MUSEUM, i61995.

facade signs were, however, relatively simple due to the severe limitations of space, though they may have been great in number and cleverly located. Many were basically a line or two of lettering, economically rendered with little ornamentation. But other signs, such as hanging panels, window signs, and drum signs at corners and in doorways, were less limited in space and warranted great detail due to the closer proximity of the viewer. These signs primarily employed compositions of rectangles, curvaceous shields, arches, and "folded-ribbon" banners. Some consisted of free-floating script, finished with an emphatic return swash for greater visual punch. The best signs of the period contrasted large plain areas with focused zones of intense ornamentation, not unlike Louis Sullivan's approach in architecture. But unlike Sullivan, all sign makers of the late nineteenth century felt free to borrow generously from past styles—the Gothic, baroque, and Roman classical. In some instances, styles were combined. When highly talented designers did this carefully, convincing compositions could result, but in lesser hands, the end products were often chaos and clutter.

Architecture became increasingly hostile to wall signs near the end of the nineteenth century, perhaps most especially with the popularity of cast-iron wall systems. Storefronts and building fronts of cast-iron presented surfaces that were all rippling columns, ornament, and glass. Daniel Badger first proposed and installed a cast-iron storefront in 1842. The compressed strength of cast iron made it a viable substitute for bulkier masonry, allowing more light to enter the interior. This new system also made use of the new, grander dimensions of plate glass. The rather ingenious kit of parts, sent to the site packed in straw, included tall, fluted iron columns with grooves for Badger's patented roll-down shutters (which, when up, were hidden away in the cornice of the ground floor).[50] The contrast between nearby facades and the building fronts Badger, James Bogardus, and their contemporaries produced, was striking. Badger's fronts relied almost exclusively on the Venetian Renaissance for form and ornament, an architectural language that provided more opening within a solid wall area, thus radically lightening the appearance of the facade. By reducing the solid, opaque surface area of the building, the cast-iron designers nearly eliminated the space once dedicated to business advertisement. Badger's impact on American commercial construction was immense. His peak production began in the 1860s, with the nationwide spread of the railroads. By 1865, his company had produced 654 iron storefronts. His 1865 catalogue likely influenced the design of at least one building along many a Main Street. Cast iron's heyday would continue for the next two decades.[51]

One striking example of the change Badger and Bogardus brought about was illustrated in the *Historical Atlas of Berks County* (1876). Two adjacent building fronts on the 600 block of Penn Street in Reading, Pennsylvania, were of approximately the same width, but one facade was made of stone and the other of iron (fig. 18). The window area of the cast-iron front was more than double that of the masonry building, despite the equivalent square footage. Narrow applied pilasters, thin continuous sills, and finely applied ornament virtually dematerialized what little solid area remained of the iron front. In contrast, the ornament of the masonry building was applied only at the cornice and window heads—perhaps updating the look of an older structure. The designer of the iron front focused the application of ornament on the skin of the building, instead of at the upper cornice level, where more traditional masonry buildings concentrated decorative effect. This further served to lighten the cast-iron building's appearance in contrast to its stone neighbor. And as a result of all this facade energy, the only place remaining for the sign was on the canopy.

Despite its reputation for design simplicity and clarity, much of the work of the Chicago School offered little more room for signs than did contemporary eclectic architecture. Louis Sullivan's intricately integrated graphic identifications for his bank designs of the 1910s and 1920s were nowhere evident in his retail work for other businesses. His facade for the Krause Music Store (1922), in fact, almost perversely denied the opportunity for mounting a sign. The center of the storefront was occupied by a major vertical piece of ornament, and the space directly above the display windows scooped dramatically in from the sidewalk. All other surfaces rippled with ornament. Though it was much simpler, the design for the Van Allen department store in Clinton, Iowa (1912–14) employed ornament in conspicuous places as well, forcing all signage to be located oddly off center or mounted over glass. The same was true for the Schlesinger & Meyer department store (later Carson, Pirie, Scott).[52] Holabird & Roche's commercial building for Peter C. Brooks (aka the Flat Iron Arts Building, 1913), a three-story wedge in Chicago, was built in the age of the automobile, yet it offered no place for signs of a readable scale (fig. 19). The limited panel space above the shop windows was so decorated with glazed terra cotta that no sign of suitable

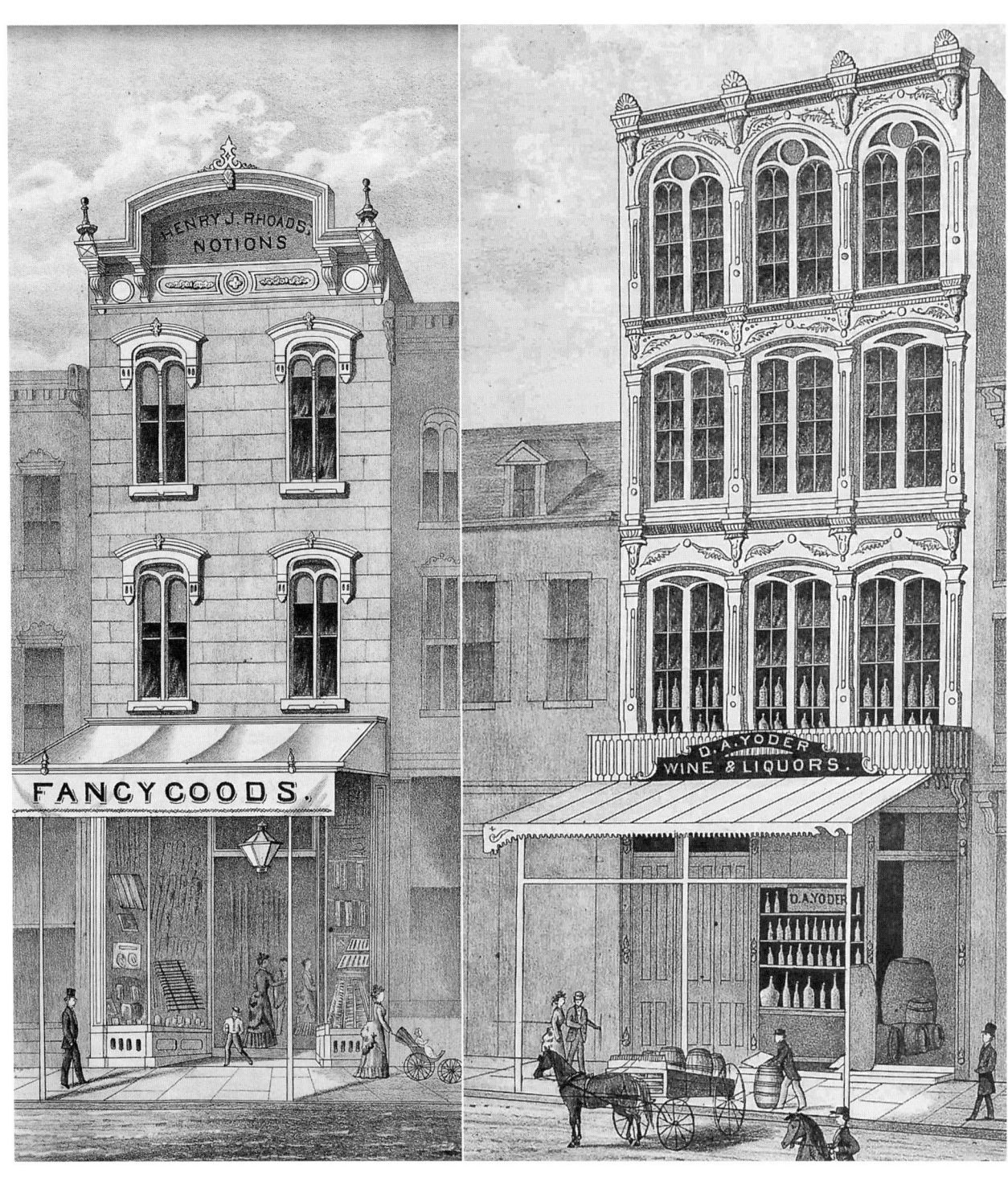

size was possible. Graphics eventually covered transom windows or projected away from the building's surface for visibility. The great proportion of glass on the structure, made possible by the steel frame, virtually eliminated space for advertising.

The conflict between building facades and storefront graphics of the late nineteenth century led some proprietors simply to cease trying to place signs in the discreet spots the architects had afforded them. Traditional locations, such as the fascia or parapet were too stingy for signs adequate to the competitive needs of the expanding city. In some cases, this condition led to increased graphic competition and extreme appearances. The facade of The Fair, a department store in Chicago, was saturated with graphics. The main building and the front and side walls of a one-story addition all were covered with a continuous skin of advertising. The parapets for both structures were an accumulation of graphic panels (fig. 20). The entire building could be read as a very busy poster. Many of the buildings, if not entire blocks, along Broadway in New York City, were also so covered with business graphics that architectural ornament seemed superfluous.

The projecting sign, which had proven popular for quick, easy recognition since the days of town-building along the American frontier, became even more necessary (in updated form) with the advent of the electric streetcar and the subsequent introduction of the automobile. Projecting signs had also proven necessary in the late 1800s as wall signs were forced off the facades of increasingly ornamented buildings, but now it was an issue of speed that demanded their use. Potential patrons in streetcars and automobiles would need time to encounter, read, select, and stop, which meant that signs had to be legible from greater distances. They needed to be larger and perpendicular to the surface of a building since they were first experienced at oblique angles down the street. The electric trolley was first successfully tested in service in Richmond, Virginia, in 1888. Almost overnight this means of conveyance spread as a popular means of transportation throughout the United States. By 1890, fifty-one cities had installed service and, by 1895, 850 lines were in operation. The new streetcars moved at a rapid twenty to forty miles per hour when unimpeded—quite a change from the horse car. Just a few years after electric streetcars became ubiquitous, the first automobiles began to appear in cities and towns. Roseland, Illinois, fifteen miles south of Chicago's Loop, had its first auto agent in 1903. Cars would make projecting signs even more necessary for quick-moving customers.

The streetscape of Roseland, like that of many communities and neighborhoods near central Chicago, was heavily influenced by streetcar and automobile. The new speed of connection to the Loop led to swifter development at the turn of the twentieth century than in previous periods, and to less investment per lot. New building in the heart of Roseland was much simpler than the elaborate gabled, turreted, two- and three-story buildings of blocks developed before 1890. In the early 1900s, many of the newly built structures were single story (fig. 21). The two-story buildings constructed during this period of increased mobility

(opposite) Figure 18
Two facades along the 600 block of Penn Street, Reading, Pennsylvania, in 1876. The use of cast iron (RIGHT) instead of masonry (LEFT), permitted a dramatic increase in the amount of glass and simplified the application of ornament.
NEW HISTORICAL ATLAS OF BERKS COUNTY PENNSYLVANIA (1876), 51. COURTESY OF THE HISTORICAL SOCIETY OF BERKS COUNTY.

Figure 19

Commercial building for Peter C. Brooks, aka the Flat Iron Arts Building (Holabird & Roche, 1913), Chicago. The steel frame permitted even greater area for glass than the cast iron front had. Although created well into the age of the automobile, the expanded fenestration plus the elaborate Chicago School ornament prevented the easy or natural application of signs that motorists could decipher.

PHOTO BY SIGMUND J. OSTY, 1966. COURTESY OF THE CHICAGO HISTORY MUSEUM, i61994.

were far simpler than their predecessors. Both one- and two-story commercial buildings were flat-fronted, with unornamented or modestly decorated parapet tops. Windows, too, were given little flourish, and there was significantly more glass on the second floor. The proportion of these second stories was greatly changed from that of the late nineteenth century; it was horizontal instead of vertical. Windows were wider, often bundled together, and the cornice or parapet was placed low over window heads. Electric signs stretched above parapets or projected from the slim space between windowsill and fascia. They often reached out all the way to the curb: illuminated, urbanized versions of the traditional, painted, projecting signs of the frontier. As the automobile increased in popularity and electricity propelled sign making to greater and greater elaboration, a shift in visual emphasis toward the sign would create unprecedented streetscapes and increasing calls to tame this new "beast."

During the course of the nineteenth century, both sign making and commercial building in America transformed from rural or residential forms to more urban ones. The increasing dominance of the market town in the United States and the need to form civilized outposts on the frontier (reproductions of the

city, with high density, a well-defined street edge, and a true sense of enclosure) drove this transition. The commercial building conformed to an efficient envelope with a flat roof, large front windows, and a sequence of rooms to accommodate merchant and merchandise. The commercial sign, once freestanding, conformed to this envelope and to the continuous commercial streetscape, up to a point. The post type of the traditional inn sign was abandoned, and in many cases business identification was painted directly on the building's skin or a board fastened tightly to the facade.

As the commercial building became increasingly uniform due to the proliferation of standard materials distributed by the railroads and common design ideas communicated through builders' catalogs and architectural pattern books, the location of the commercial sign became more varied and abundant. It spread itself over the entire skin of the building. The sign, in fact, became increasingly less standard than the buildings on which it was painted or fastened. Lettering became more ornate and varied due to the aggressive development of type

Figure 20

E. J. Lehmann's The Fair, Adams Street, Chicago, circa 1880s. This discount department store was an exaggerated example of building-as-sign, or sign-as-building, slathering graphics over surfaces instead of deferring to architectural ornament—an obvious move for a company noted for the scale of its advertisements in newspapers.
COURTESY OF THE CHICAGO HISTORY MUSEUM, i59563.

styles in print and the experimentation of sign painters in the field. This helped merchants to create some distinction along an otherwise potentially monotonous row of buildings.

Neither was the commercial sign confined physically to the building. Along many streets, the sign had retained a degree of physical independence from the building or business that it advertised because it projected free of the facade. Some Main Streets retained the tradition of the frontier settlement by continuing to place simple plank signs over the sidewalk. In many cities, these primitive projecting signs were upgraded to well-crafted graphics, but the principle was the same. The complex, more highly ornamented architectural surfaces of the latter part of the nineteenth century were physically more hostile to applied lettering. This encouraged the sign designer to create an even more independent graphic, for there seemed to be no place to put a sign on a commercial building, as ironic as that seemed. As the century progressed, architects gave buildings increasingly more fanciful shapes; structures became more figural as they rose above the norm and were less a part of the background. This was sometimes done in an effort to create identity architecturally, to be less dependent on a sign. Ironically, such designs encouraged the sign maker to create even more independent signs. By the turn of the century, new technologies brought electric light and greater speed of transport. The figural sign and the figural building would be ever more essential for quick identification in a demanding visual environment.

(opposite) Figure 21
Photographic panoramas showing sections of Michigan Avenue between 111th and 113th Streets, Roseland (Chicago), Illinois. The majority of these structures were built during the first decade of the twentieth century. The automobile was still a novelty, but more than a decade of fast and efficient streetcars had stretched development horizontally, making second stories optional.
PHOTO BY NELS O. LARSEN, 1927. PUBLISHED IN BILL STACHMUS, RON NIETUPSKI, BETTE KOOISTRA, MARIO AVIGNONE, AND PAUL PETRAITIS, *ROSELAND, THE GOLDEN YEARS: A PICTORIAL PRESERVATION OF MEMORIES* (1984), 2:XXXI–XXXIX. PERMISSION COURTESY OF BETTY JO PURVIS.

Chapter 2
THE GREAT BLIGHT WAY
ELECTRICITY AND REFORM FROM MAIN STREET TO CITY CENTER, 1900–1917

THE ERECTION, IN 1893, of the first modern electric signs for purely commercial purposes seemed timed for conflict. That same year, in Chicago, the World's Columbian Exposition opened. Its grounds were a virtual city so disciplined and harmonious—compared to the seemingly random commercialism of most American urban areas—that it inspired the City Beautiful movement. The electric sign appeared to satisfy a national desire to distinguish the individual from his neighbors, to shout above the visual noise of the rest of the street. But the exposition was a place where building height, materials, coloration, and architectural style were the result of a design consensus. It also demonstrated how electrical illumination could uniformly adorn buildings, if only in pure white light. In contrast, the first electric signs along Broadway in New York City used buildings merely as support, appearing as immense letters composed of red, blue, green, and white bulbs that flashed above the rooftops. These lights promoted products and travel destinations, not the businesses directly below them.[1]

By 1893, a variety of building styles and signs lined American commercial thoroughfares. Yet in some places, due to the speed of development or the need for swift replacement due to fires, there was remarkable homogeneity. Built on narrow lot frontages, each building facade helped define a continuous street wall; this architectural rhythm was established around midcentury, when windows and fascia boards were placed at the same height. By the 1890s, signs appeared to be everywhere in the commercial core of town—at all heights and sizes. Already in 1864, a Parisian visitor to New York City had reported to his readers "advertising is the indispensable adjunct of this great village fair [New York]. On every hand are floating banners, monstrous signs, and flamboyant decoration. Advertising matter extends into the street, onto the edge of the sidewalk between the gutter and the pedestrian's feet."[2] Indeed, by the end of the century, signs seemed to cling to every possible surface, an apparent communication chaos made worse by the inhospitable character of new facade design (fig. 22). This was an accumulation of decades of sign-making in a riot of strategies.

Flush-mounted, painted signs often began at a building's crest, above or below the cornice, and stepped down the facade between window levels. A jumble of smaller signs hung above shop windows, the larger of which were crowded with urgent invitations and identifications. Signs were painted directly on boards or fashioned with individually crafted wooden letters. And everywhere were awnings—long, heavy expanses of fabric, sloped as near to vertical as possible to carry yet more lettering. Conventional signs oriented parallel to the street were sometimes muted by a series of aggressive projecting signs, painted on board and supported at the edge of the sidewalk with posts. In November 1898 the *Chicago Daily Tribune* marveled at the confusion:

> In few parts of the city are overhead sideboards allowed, but [at Van Buren and Clark Street] they swing above the sidewalks in wildest profusion . . . The shopkeepers have not expended all their advertising energies upon the overhead signs, for the front walls and windows are plastered from end to end with advertisements just as seductive as those chronicled overhead. One can readily imagine the results produced by such myriads of hanging signs on a windy night. When stiff zephyrs from the lake sweep down Van Buren Street in stormy weather the signs join in a chorus of creaking and groaning that can be heard for blocks, far above the roar of the elevated trains which are constantly rumbling overhead.[3]

Electricity brought both solutions and problems to the commercial thoroughfare. Certainly, it benefited the sign industry, which was struggling with inhospitable architectural facades that left little space for a real graphic presence. Eventually, the facade conflict problem was mitigated by a few architects who anticipated the inclusion of signs as part of their comprehensive building designs. Movie theaters and automobile showrooms, two new commercial building types of the electrical age, especially reflected the coordinated efforts of sign designers and architects. The perceived chaos of all signs, particularly the new electric ones, prompted civic reformers to agitate against the laissez-faire momentum of construction and advertising, hoping to control signs or even ban them. But their efforts were countered by boosterism, especially in small towns, where Main Streets were being updated to resemble miniature Broadways and State Streets. Electric lighting offered corporations enormous power to alter the appearance of America's commercial thoroughfares.

Sign Evolution: Technological and International Influences on Design

As new buildings sported more ornamental facades, leaving little room for lettering, sign makers discovered a solution that suited the circumstances. The development of the small-scale electric sign ushered in a period when designers worried little about how to incorporate graphics with facade features like the

fascia. The electric graphic was not easily mounted flush to a building, due to its bulk, so it most often appeared as a projecting sign. Affordable versions for businesses first appeared around 1900. By 1906, the year that the Cincinnati-based *Signs of the Times* was launched, quickly becoming the industry's leading trade journal, there were some seventy-five thousand electric signs in the United States.[4] An article citing this abundance claimed, "There are many districts that show as many as eight large Edison electric signs within one block."[5] By 1910, Los Angeles boasted that almost one sign per day had been installed since the start of the Southern California Edison Company's electric-sign campaign almost a year earlier. By 1917, even Fort Dodge, Iowa, with a population of twenty-two thousand, claimed one sign lamp (or bulb) per capita.

The earliest electric signs in small towns were extraordinary novelties, magical and mysterious. A business in Guilford, Connecticut, installed that town's first electric sign in 1908 and provoked this response: "Fred Flagg, the new clothing merchant located in the former Henry Hale store, made another demonstration of enterprise on Monday evening when the glare of electric lights in front

Figure 22

Broadway at East 14th Street, New York City, circa 1910. In the nineteenth century, sign crafters used the entire building facade as an open field for identity and information, with painted panels and individually mounted wooden letters. By 1910, these signs had been joined by a multitude of electric signs.
RUDOLPH M. DE LEEUW, *BOTH SIDES OF BROADWAY, FROM BOWLING GREEN TO CENTRAL PARK, NEW YORK CITY* (1910), 304. COLLECTION OF THE MUSEUM OF THE CITY OF NEW YORK.

of his store attracted the attention of everybody in the vicinity. Mr. Flagg has erected a large sign across the sidewalk on both sides of which is gold leaf lettering, a very fine piece of work. Across the top of this are twelve 32-power lamps and when all are lighted the sign is visible for a long distance."[6]

Electrical and metalworking expertise was required to build electric signs. In 1901, Federal Sign System, the nation's first dedicated electric-sign company, was formed in Chicago; it grossed $100,000 in 1908 and $900,000 only three years later. Soon, several other companies, both new or expanded, joined the fledgling industry, including the Haller Machine Company, Chase Electric, and Thomas Cusak (all of Chicago), Valentine Electric (Atlantic City), Newark Sign, A & W Sign (Cleveland), and Strauss & Company (later Artkraft Strauss, New York City). These companies were equipped to meet the demand for increasingly large electric signs. Outside Wieboldt's department store in Chicago, for example, was one sign that measured twenty-five feet tall, and the Robinson-Schween department store in Hamilton, Ohio, had a sign that extended from the first floor to the fourth-floor roof. Federal Sign System increased its sign production significantly by requiring only a lease, rather than an outright purchase, thus enabling even a small business to acquire a potentially expensive new appliance. The demand for electric signs was becoming so intense that it was nearly impossible for the new, smaller manufacturers to keep up with orders.[7]

In 1906, *Signs of the Times* described most electric signs as consisting of a colored porcelain-enamel center panel surrounded by a border of lamps.[8] Within a few years, the small incandescent bulb was typically incorporated into the stroke of the sign lettering, and some sign "boxes" were elaborately contoured. The Wieboldt department store sign, constructed by Haller Machine Company in 1906, was shaped in imitation of the company's trademark, a unique trapezoidal form. Dazzlingly employed around the edge was the popular "crawling snake," a wiggling line illuminated with chaser effects.[9] From quite early on, signs incorporated illustration. A sign produced in 1906 for Shayne's Fine Furs of Chicago displayed a polar bear astride an oddly shaped iceberg emblazoned with the name of the business. In addition to its typical fascia signs of painted, wooden letters, the Atlantic and Pacific Tea Company chain sometimes mounted illuminated letter *T*'s as single-character, projecting signs. By decade's end, many dentists were advertising their presence with signs depicting a giant tooth, roots and all, ablaze with points of white light. Some signs were merely shield forms or simple geometric shapes, while others were meticulously representational.[10] Federal Sign System advertised an American flag made of steel, illustrated so that it appeared to be rippling and lit with appropriately colored bulbs. Even more impressive, by 1916, was the projecting sign by the Quehl Company for Bejach's Billiards, which displayed intricately designed and animated human figures rolling balls and shooting pool.

By 1917, the main commercial route through most American towns may have boasted one or two of these creative, sparkling displays, but most electric

52   Signs, Streets, and Storefronts

signs were simple black or dark-blue sign boxes often fastened clumsily over storefront fascias and tipped slightly forward to accommodate the projecting cornice trim. While segmented sign boxes might awkwardly follow the curve of a projecting cupola or bay window, electric signs were most often designed to project over the sidewalk, a twentieth-century update of the old-fashioned wooden swinging sign. As the century progressed, electric signs became increasingly vertical, sometimes reaching the full height of a building's upper level, and their lettering was large enough to be legible from a quickly passing electric trolley car or an automobile. Between 1906 and 1917, the number of electric signs on Salina Street in Syracuse, New York, increased tenfold, from six to sixty-two. All across America, urban areas were experiencing a similar phenomenon, the enthusiastic embrace of electric graphics.

A range of influences stimulated the imaginations of early-twentieth-century sign designers. In addition to the newspaper graphics and handbills that had inspired nineteenth-century sign painters on the frontier, there were now trade journals and reference and instructional books.[11] Classic manuals such as Frank Atkinson's *Art of Sign Painting* (1909), *Henderson's Sign Painter* (1906), and Fred Knopf's *Coast Manual of Lettering and Designs* (1907) provided examples of some of the country's best painted work.[12] For the most part, these books focused on the basics of lettering skills and graphic layout; a few explained such classic techniques as mirroring, frosting, and embossing. Although painted-sign guidelines might have seemed irrelevant in this dawning age of electric bulbs and heavy metal frames, the design principles were still applicable to the rising generation of sign crafters. In fact, these manuals revealed how timeless the older sign arts were and how they could flourish alongside the new technology. Corresponding with the nascent years of the electric sign industry, as well as the birth of *Signs of the Times*, was the sudden abundance of books on sign *painting*. Sign painters remained in high demand for many primary business identifications, all window and drum signs, all informational graphics, all interior signs and showcards, and most temporary promotional displays (such as those for the burgeoning motion picture industry). Despite the growth in use of illuminated letters for major business signs, stock dimensional wood letter manufacturers, such as industry leader Spanjer Brothers of Chicago and Newark, continued successfully in business for years to come.

Sign painters accomplished their basic training through apprenticeship—younger men learning from skilled practitioners on the job. After apprentices completed a specified number of years in the field, they would graduate to the level of journeyman. Unlike architectural training, which had replaced such time-honored pathways with university programs, this field adhered to a centuries-old tradition. Practice was seen as the route to technical and artistic development. By the early twentieth century, affordable publications and private trade schools became available to supplement this process of gaining technical and artistic proficiency, sometimes offering a competitive edge to sign shop

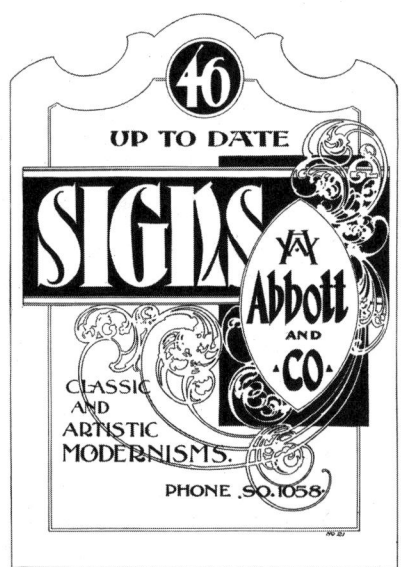

Figure 23

Design for drum sign (Frank H. Atkinson, 1909). In the earliest years of the twentieth century, several books and a new trade journal became available to influence aspiring sign crafters. FRANK H. ATKINSON, *ATKINSON SIGN PAINTING UP TO NOW: A COMPLETE MANUAL OF THE ART OF SIGN PAINTING* (1909), 93. REPRODUCTION COURTESY OF THE NEWBERRY LIBRARY, CHICAGO, H711.05.

applicants. C. J. Strong, owner and operator of the Detroit School of Lettering, published a series of mail-order manuals and pamphlets that addressed lettering and theory systematically. Other schools—some respected, some suspect—were created in cities nationwide. In some communities, unions would eventually force sign shops to grant apprentices time off to attend classes organized by union officials. However, whether in the field or in the classroom, instruction in the art of sign crafting placed emphasis on technical skills over design and layout.

Until about the late 1930s, American graphic art lagged behind that of Europe in terms of invention and economy of design. Ponderous text often diminished the effect of attractive advertising imagery in print. Primary reference sources such as *Henderson's Sign Painter* offered an endless array of graphic styles, including neoclassical, rococo, Gothic, American arts and crafts, and art nouveau lettering. Atkinson's book, reprinted several times over three decades, was a mix of the author's own designs and examples of work by others; at least half of these examples revealed a tendency to emphasize decoration (fig. 23). Clarity of design and communication often seemed secondary to the display of artistic bravado. Following the lead of these source books, American designers would either mimic the examples provided or combine what was already overdone or overwrought. The results were sometimes murky interpretations of their predecessors' work. To the immense credit of their makers, however, the signs of this period often revealed outstanding creativity and craftsmanship. Despite the abundance of ornament, many published examples displayed significant restraint and a knowing balance between silence and noise, the plain and the profuse. The books, published on the heels of Europe's art nouveau movement, included endlessly inventive lettering examples, including design variations in that style, and sophisticated takes on nineteenth-century lettering like Egyptian (sans-serif, in present-day terminology) and heavy slab serif. They also presented an abundance of novelty alphabets that pointed to the future, such as the multifaceted Broken Poster, a prescient example that now recalls art deco.

Signs of the Times was perhaps the best reference for the creation of electric signs, that portion of the industry growing at an astounding rate. This was a field in need of immediate guidance, with little history in manufacture and design upon which to draw. Regular columns addressed the potentials and pitfalls of designing with electric light. Journalists and sign professionals examined basic design principles and regularly reported on European advances in poster design, sign design, and, eventually, even architecture. By printing examples of imaginative new electric signs all over the United States, the magazine fostered both imitation and competition. It offered sales techniques, updates on new inventions and patents (of which there was a profusion during the industry's earliest years), and explanations of anti-sign legislation.

In 1910 *Signs of the Times* lamented that sign-painting quality was declining and that electric signs and patented prefabricated letters made of wood or metal were on the rise. "No more do you see the grand old New York Roman or Egyptian letter displayed on sign boards," the writer observed. "No more do you see attractive window work in gold, silver, pearl, etc. . . . most of the work shows the effect of hurry, with no general or apparent desire on the part of the sign painter to add to his reputation."[13] The article concluded by urging both sign designers and architects to make certain that signs were designed for the context in which they would be displayed—and that the context be designed to show them at their best.

Architects and Signs: Striving for Harmony in Commercial Facade Design

In the advice it offered to readers, *Signs of the Times* revealed the tension between sign and site—between the fanfare of the business sign, heralding the presence of an enterprise, and the artistic and civic responsibility for collective harmony that the design might help preserve along the street. In July 1906 contributor William Goltz encouraged sign companies to strive for the novel: "The sign should be entirely different in appearance from other signs in the same block. Some electric sign manufacturers have successfully taken it for granted in the past that the general public has not yet learned to consider this very important item, and they have been able to market, at very advantageous prices, large quantities of signs made up from stock letters of the same pattern and all furnished in the same colors."[14]

A year later, another *Signs of the Times* contributor, George Williams, approached the question quite differently. "The [sign] designer," he wrote, "should be familiar with the location proposed, the color surroundings, and the lines of the adjacent and prospective building and location, as well as the character of the business patronage of the client."[15] The word *location* here is significant. Increasingly, considerations of context were replacing random efforts at individuality. Almost ten years later, after countless ordinances against electric signs had been proposed or enacted across the nation, the magazine went a step further: "An electric sign designer should know something of architecture and have a knowledge of the different signs and periods of ornament . . . Almost all signs are used in conjunction with architecture, and it is here that a knowledge of architectural ornament and details is most useful. A design made in keeping with the architecture and the building on which it is used, the details, ornamentation and lettering true to the style, will be attractive and useful."[16]

At the same time, trade journals were encouraging architects to consider how appropriate graphics could enhance their commercial buildings. In 1912, *Architectural Record* published a twenty-page article, "Renaissance in Commercial Architecture," that featured examples for upscale shops such as Tiffany's, designed by eminent firms like Carrère & Hastings and Warren & Wetmore. Oddly, there was no mention of sign design, and in several photographs, identifying graphics were even missing from the shop fronts; in other photographs, the signs were so discreet that their effectiveness as advertisements or even identifications was questionable.[17] The probable explanation for this intentional oversight was that Fifth Avenue merchants waged a long-term battle with advertisers regarding large-scale signs placed on the upper-level walls and rooftops of New York's celebrated thoroughfare.

Signs of the Times articulately addressed architects' perceived antipathy to signage in the early twentieth century:

> Architects have uniformly harbored a prejudice against the specifications of electric signs upon buildings . . . The heterogeneous collection of signs plastered conspicuously over large surfaces, cramped confusedly in limited spaces and perched precariously at odd angles totally destroys the symmetry and grace of line that the architect has striven to maintain and refused to mar by the specification of electric signs . . . The tenant . . . would gladly have welcomed the architect's suggestion as to the harmonious kind of electric advertising on his particular building. However, the architect said, "No signs . . . " Unless [the architect] is totally blind to the march of events, he will see that his cooperation is needed not to aid the sign companies . . . as to preserve his artistic accomplishment and the beauty of the finished product.[18]

Criticism came directly from within the profession, too: "Architects are remiss when planning buildings of a certain type not to provide[,] as part of their external decoration, suitable frames for advertisements. The latter will be vastly improved if properly managed and will be used in any event," wrote a landscape architect in *Architectural Record* in 1912.[19]

Accomplished architects in smaller cities likewise avoided the "sign problem." In Staunton, Virginia, for example, the prolific T. J. Collins designed commercial buildings with little regard for the proprietor who needed to identify his enterprise. On most of Collins's facades, there was no natural place for a sign, not even in the customary fascia area above the shop windows. Even the facade and canopy of his New Theater (1913), designed late in his career, lacked a name. Collins did most of his work in the 1890s and early 1900s, when thrusting towers, columns, and projecting pediments characterized facades. Unless architects considered the particulars of signage in their designs, later add-on graphics from sign shops could well detract from their efforts. Collins's work dominated Staunton; his refusal to integrate signs into his structures established something of a precedent for the town.

Inspiring examples of how graphics could be smoothly integrated with facade design were abundant in early-twentieth-century Europe, where many architects embraced the graphic program of their storefronts and incorporated signs into their compositions. For example, in 1902, the Viennese architect Otto

Wagner designed the diminutive but impressive *Die Zeit* news-telegraph office with a metal-and-glass facade. It was more graphic than architectural, in the sense that the composition referred neither to traditional architectural forms nor to gravity, and lettering occupied approximately 20 percent of the facade. In 1907 and 1912, respectively, Adolf Loos designed the Kärntner Bar and the Manz Bookshop, both of which incorporated major signs illuminated from behind frosted or colored glass. At the bookshop, the informational sign, with its backlit opal-glass and strips to hold letters in place, somewhat resembled a modern-day movie theater marquee. It helped to establish the aesthetic of the entire store with a transom-level panel system whose lines continued inside the shop to define the interior. The Kärntner Bar, also known as the American Bar, featured a light box angled out over the narrow street, with stars and stripes from end to end.

Some of the finest early examples of signage integrated with architecture in America were in Chicago. One of the fifty-seven taverns in the city produced for the Schlitz Brewing Company, built on Southport Avenue in 1900, displayed the trademark Schlitz globe in unglazed terracotta, centered in a masonry gable and surrounded by a sunburst of bricks (see plate 5). By 1915, more examples of the marriage of sign and architecture were being published to inspire designers. The banks designed by the pathbreaking architect Louis Sullivan in the 1910s vividly demonstrated how to achieve this union. His Home Building Association structure in Newark, Ohio (1914–15), ranks among the most purely graphic of his works. The triangular element containing the firm's logo, "The Old Home," was linked to the edifice in several ways. It was an abstract representation of the ornamental flourish below it. The geometric shape fit well into a facade defined by rectangles. Sullivan linked this three-sided emblem to the rest of the surface with fine tendrils and other woven-in details. At some of Sullivan's other banks, such as the Peoples Savings & Loan Association (1916–18) in Sidney, Ohio, and Farmers & Merchants Union Bank (1919–20) in Columbus, Wisconsin, large, glazed terra-cotta frames for signs made of marble or tiles were part of larger compositions, all linked to the building whole.

The firm of another pioneering American architect, Daniel Burnham, created an integrated design for New York's Edison Building (1912), an example of what the architectural historian Richard Longstreth, from his study of composition types in commercial building facades, would call an "enframed window wall."[20] In this case, a large central portion of the facade was darkened and set back within a glazed terra-cotta frame continuous with the rest of the building's skin (fig. 24). A slim, elegant, and very tall projecting electric-sign box ran from the base of the dark rectangle to the crest of the building. Simple supports were regularly spaced up the side of the sign, pinning it cleanly to the building. Burnham's elaborate parapet sign for the May Company building in Cleveland (1912–14) was also beautifully unified with the architecture. By the early 1910s, more architects were considering identifying graphics in their designs. For instance,

the signs for the Kress chain of five-and-dime stores incorporated the company name into each architectural composition distinctively and ingeniously.[21]

With the growth of the motion-picture industry and the continued popularity of legitimate theater in the early twentieth century, some architects acknowledged that large-scale signs were an inescapable part of their design program. C. A. Brandenburgh's Museum in Philadelphia (architect unknown, c. 1890), whose surface was entirely covered in sign lettering, illustrated well how at least one theater lured potential customers off the street, although this was not typical of the day. The building also revealed, at an early stage, a conspicuous arched entrance, a feature that would be quite common in theater design through the 1920s.[22] Arches had figured prominently in American theater facades since the early 1800s. When inserted into a continuous commercial street wall lined with humble store entrances, the arch communicated that the entrance was something more extraordinary than a mere retail establishment. Arcaded entrances like that of Philadelphia's New Theatre (1822) evolved to become great single arches by the end of the century. For the Castle Square Theatre (Boston, 1894), the architect set a three-story triumphal arch between towers. B. F. Keith's New Theatre (Boston, 1897) employed arches more as ornament than opening, including a grand bowed parapet—in effect, using the historic form as a symbol or sign that meant "theater" to the public by this date. The novel identity created for New York's New Amsterdam Theater (Herts & Tallant, 1903) established an important design precedent, a powerful next step in the evolution of theater design. The bowed banner feature spanning the entrance beneath the grand arch demonstrated how seamlessly and dramatically a venue's identity could be integrated with the architecture, hinting at possibilities for development of the marquee sign in the future (fig. 25).

From the 1860s through the 1890s, opera houses featuring arches were built on Main Streets and courthouse squares across the country. Soon, for Americans everywhere, these arches came to identify entertainment venues. The town opera house, despite its rather formal and specific name, was often a very flexible venue, a place for gatherings, local recitals and speeches, and touring theater companies. Ground-level openings for access to these halls sometimes featured grand single arches, but in most cases, rentable storefronts defined the first floor. Tall arched windows on the second floor indicated where the auditorium was. Later, portico features or canopies identified these performance spaces, especially if films were shown there.

By 1910, movie attendance had grown to 10 million tickets sold per year, hastening an evolution in theater and theater-sign design. During the first decade of the twentieth century, cinemas enjoyed a brief golden age when sign and architecture appeared as one, designed by a single hand. The giant arched entrance figured prominently in these early designs, appearing very pronounced due to its application on relatively small-scale facades. In most cases, architects incorporated the names of these early cinemas above and around the curve of the great

(opposite) Figure 24
Edison Building (D. H. Burnham and Company, 1912), New York City. Burnham recognized the potential of incorporating the vertical projecting sign type into facade composition. This newly popular means of identifying business, stimulated by the burgeoning use of electric illumination, needed not be an afterthought.
ARCHITECTURAL RECORD (JULY 1915), 121. REPRODUCTION COURTESY OF RYERSON AND BURNHAM LIBRARIES, ART INSTITUTE OF CHICAGO.

(opposite) Figure 25 New Amsterdam Theatre (Herts & Tallant, 1903; altered), 42nd Street, New York City, in 1907. Although a grand arch often signified "theater" to passersby at this point in history, the canopy or marquee—here in its nascent stage—would eventually identify this type of business as the arch faded from use. This lavish canopy was well integrated with the design of the facade.
COLLECTION OF THE NEW-YORK HISTORICAL SOCIETY.

arches. For some, an icon worked more powerfully than any lettering. This was exemplified in such facades as the one created for Milwaukee's Butterfly Theater (August C. Willmanns, 1911) (fig. 26), where a great deal of the design credit must be given to the terra-cotta supply company in Chicago for creating such imaginative molds.[23] Great care was given to the design of each theater sign, integrating it for full visual effect with the entire facade for a triumphant whole by linking the style of lettering with the architectural ornament. In many cases, the building front, crest to base, was illuminated with incandescent bulbs, making the full facade, in effect, a sign. Eventually, as competition grew and theaters lined up alongside each other on key city streets, the vertical projecting sign made its appearance and subsequently dominated. In most cases, these graphics were unexceptional in design and bore little relationship to the architecture.

Hubris combined with growing competition and a need to fill theaters several times a day prompted some designers to create immense signs that were at stylistic odds with the buildings supporting them. The most obvious early example of this clash was seen on New York's lavish Rialto (Thomas Lamb, 1916), where the extravagant electronics mounted on the facade overwhelmed the architect's restrained neoclassical composition. From a ten-foot-diameter pinwheel of multicolored incandescent bulbs, placed directly over the canopy, electrically animated rockets shot toward the roof like fireworks. These triggered the lights for each letter, arranged along an immense curve above the pinwheel, and then caused an eagle, composed of electric bulbs at the parapet, to flap its wings against a background of illuminated flags.[24]

In 1917, one of the very first informational marquees—internally illuminated sign boxes extending out over the sidewalk—was unveiled. Created by Alfred Henry Jacobs as part of his design for the California Theatre (1917) in San Francisco, this marquee was fully ornamented in keeping with the Gothic style of the facade; it presented three lines of movie billing, with changeable letters of white opal-glass on a black background. The California was also notable for its unusually well-integrated identifying sign (fig. 27). Jacobs continued the fine tracery and vertical lines of the facade past the roof for an imaginative sign that seemed to emerge from the building below. This extended "parapet" sign borrowed directly from the pinnacled, perpendicular Gothic crest of the building but added fanciful flourishes of its own: spikes, tracery-like starbursts, and slim, vertical lettering—all perfectly consistent with the theater's architecture.

Another new commercial building type that required major graphics as part of the nature of its business developed during the first years of the new century. In 1910, *Architectural Record* praised the work of several celebrated architects—including Jarvis Hunt, Albert Kahn, Howard Shaw, and the firm of Holabird & Roche—who had contributed to the design of a new strip of automobile showrooms along South Michigan Avenue in Chicago. By solving the functional needs of this new building type, and applying ornament that fit the product being sold, these architects' efforts might herald "the crude beginnings

of a new architecture."²⁵ The showroom facades were two or three stories tall, employing a clean, utilitarian grid of glazing with openings large enough to light the interiors effectively and wide enough for vehicles to enter and exit easily. The terra-cotta and architectural details demonstrated a respect for this stretch of South Michigan Avenue, which had a reputation for refinement. The modest signs, many of which were designed by the architects, also seemed appropriate, according to the magazine article. But a period photograph reveals the true character of what eventually was termed Automobile Row: a panorama shows immense rooftop signs angled for the motorized shopper (fig. 28). The architects obviously did not design these gigantic graphics, almost the size of the buildings beneath them. The clumsy pig-iron supporting structures and generously scaled lettering stood in stark contrast to the otherwise tidy, new building elevations, which, like the earlier buildings on the street, were oriented to the pedestrian. Had these reputable professionals more aggressively addressed the novel requirements of this new business type, as well as the ample scale of the street, perhaps Automobile Row would have looked more fully designed for motorists. The photograph seems to forecast the character of future highway-strip development, when sign and architecture would often appear visually disconnected.²⁶

If the relationship of building and sign was often clumsy or discordant, what about the correlation of buildings to each other along the street? A sign by nature assumes the role of individualist competing for attention, but architecture was split between playing the obedient citizen—creating a degree of order along a potentially chaotic street—and being a sign of sorts, writ large. Like an advertisement, but composed of pilasters, windows, and cornices, the facade could be fashioned to appear rich, solid, or swanky as the case may require for clothiers, banks, or restaurants. The commercial street of the early twentieth century was even more eclectic than its counterpart in the late nineteenth. For one thing, more architectural styles had become common by this time, given the increased use of photography and easier access to journals. A grander assortment of facing materials and longer spans made possible by steel frames provided architects more opportunity to create the unique.

The north side of the courthouse square in Sidney, Ohio, illustrated well the design variety—and potential discord—of the period. A major fire in 1915 destroyed most of the block. Developers quickly filled in the large gaps with the taste of the times (fig. 29). Unlike whole blocks that were typically rebuilt with harmony, all at once, after fires destroyed them in the middle to late 1800s, the infill in Sidney demonstrated great visual diversity—variety characteristic of the early twentieth century. This was exaggerated in comparison with the structures that survived the fire in this same block. This whole side of the square stood in stark, eclectic contrast to the other sides, varied though they were. It was certainly dramatically different from the homogenous, red brick architecture around the courthouse square in towns like Bryan, Ohio. Two white, glazed terra-cotta commercial buildings in Sidney, swagged and decorated like wedding cakes,

(opposite) Figure 26
Butterfly Theater (August C. Willmanns, 1911; demolished), Milwaukee. Once early cinemas evolved past the primitive nickelodeon stage, architects rendered entire facades as advertisements, integrating sign, light, and ornament.
REPRODUCTION COURTESY OF THE WISCONSIN HISTORICAL SOCIETY.

sandwiched a bare-bones facade with wide, Chicago School windows. A narrow, petite, classical stone bank rested mausoleum-like on the other side of the alley. A building with an intricate glazing system, reminiscent of cast-iron storefronts, sat alongside an unadorned red brick building from 1854 that survived the fire. Building heights and proportions varied widely; the roof profile of the full block was irregular to say the least. What held this variety together was the consistent alignment of the facades to the sidewalk and a relative conformity in height of first floor cornices. Projecting signs and awnings provided more continuity from business to business than did the architecture, however. The signs were mostly straightforward electric boxes. Some, however, were incorporated into stained-glass treatment of the transoms. The architectural eclecticism on display on Poplar Street was hardly unique to Sidney.

New England provided other powerful examples of extreme variety along commercial streets in America. There, unassuming residential buildings of the colonial or federal period coexisted with purpose-built commercial structures of wholly different eras, presenting eclectic displays of orientation, profile, style, and materials. In this case, the reason for the diversity was less about the eclecticism of any one period and more about the long timeline of development. Early building in these towns was often spotty—more rural and less continuous or dense than development in Mid-Atlantic states and areas west. Later commercial infill between sparsely placed early buildings often explains the wild jumps in date. In Guilford, Connecticut, one- and three-story parapet-fronted, standard-issue American commercial structures (1902 and, eventually, 1935) were erected in between a modest, regionally specific, clapboard-skinned house from 1804 (with street-level windows slightly enlarged for trade) and a pair of robust Greek Revival store buildings from the 1850s. A brick, beaux-arts bank building finished off this chronologically assorted block in 1912. On the other commercially developed side of the green, simple frame houses from the late 1700s shared the street with a church from 1839 (modified heavily for commercial use

(opposite) *Figure 27*
The California Theatre / State Theatre (Alfred Henry Jacobs, 1917; demolished), San Francisco. In the hands of capable architects, theater signs could be organically related to architectural design. Here, the architect carried the lines of the facade up to an extended parapet for the identity, and the intricate ornament of the gothic style permitted a proper flourish that wove the ensemble together visually.
SAN FRANCISCO HISTORY CENTER, SAN FRANCISCO PUBLIC LIBRARY.

Figure 28
Automobile Row, South Michigan Avenue, Chicago. Although designed for the automotive age, which required a new approach to design that could visually register from afar, perhaps only the signs were fully effective in scale and orientation.
ARCHITECTURAL RECORD (APRIL 1910), 286. REPRODUCTION COURTESY OF RYERSON AND BURNHAM LIBRARIES, ART INSTITUTE OF CHICAGO.

Figure 29
East Poplar Street on Courthouse Square (1854, 1912–16, 1933), Sidney, Ohio. Although the greater part of the block was built within several years of a fire in 1915, it displays astonishing variety compared to blocks constructed under similar circumstances but in earlier decades. This diverseness attests to a penchant for eclecticism in commercial design during this period.
PHOTO BY AUTHOR, 2007.

with a porch) and a showy, wood-framed Italianate commercial structure that might have appeared more at home in San Francisco. In the 1920s, a stone and brick drugstore would join the parade. Despite the lack of uniformity among buildings in Guilford, Sidney, and similar places, it was the seemingly random design and placement of signs that was the focus of concern and reform on the business street.

Reform and Regulation: Civic Visions and the Struggle to Control the Streetscape

What motivated the reformers who tackled the perceived sign problems of the city? What colored their visions of what a good city should be? The civic-improvement efforts of the early twentieth century, including the celebrated—and sometimes derided—City Beautiful movement, aspired to improve the appearance of towns and cities.

Around the same time, an increasingly organized movement of political progressivism was emerging to illuminate and combat the various corruptions of city government that the laissez-faire capitalism of America's industrial revolution had fueled. Visionaries such as the novelist Edward Bellamy and the urban planner Ebenezer Howard generated ideas for future cities that would be far cleaner and more attractive than those of their own era. In his immensely popular utopian novel, *Looking Backward* (1888), Bellamy proposed both social and physical improvements. His fictionalized vision of Boston in the year 2000 was devoid of commercial signs; community stores were marked only with handsome statuary. Howard's plans for what he called "garden cities" were far more specific and included diagrams and instructions for execution. Howard envisioned a great communal shopping arcade where competition was severely regulated, thus eliminating copious signage. These paper proposals were not taken as true goals, but their appeal provided direction for many progressives to reduce the perceived clutter of American streets.[27] Equally compelling, and far more accessible, was the future as predicted by popular magazines like *King's Views of New York* and *Cassier's Monthly* (circa 1910) with covers featuring a multileveled metropolis of elevated train lines and sky-high pedestrian connections between skyscrapers. Such visions quickly filtered down to small towns like Staunton, Virginia, where a postcard montage of Beverley Street circa 1910 showed a monorail and several balloon-supported aircraft hovering above a bedlam of streetcars, bicycles, motorcycles, and hapless pedestrians. Other fantastic images inspired by the speculation of planners and futurists of the day for easing the congestion of the contemporary city included eclectic skylines of finials, domes, and cornices; yet signs, if they were shown at all, were subtly sketched in as discreet, continuous graphic bands over store windows.

Motivated by these ideals, civic activists attempted to restrain what they saw as the most offensive features of the existing city. They struggled to draft legislation that would regulate billboards and signs, which many regarded as symbolic of the effects of unrestrained capitalism. The streets of American cities and towns in 1910 were very different from those of 1893, when there had been virtually no limits placed on built advertisements. The installation, that year, of the first modern electric signs unleashed a revolutionary technology on the unsuspecting metropolis. By 1910, electric signs were rapidly changing the face of the cityscape, and reformers were keen to limit their dominance.

Larger signs and extended business frontage meant a dramatic change in the face of the commercial street. The advent of the electric streetcar in the 1890s, with its significant improvement in speed over its horse-drawn predecessor, permitted development to reach well past the old confines of the city. The extension of streetcar lines into virgin territory ushered in a new type of building suitable for rapid development: the taxpayer strip, a minimal one-story investment intended to cover expenses and bide time until the street or neighborhood matured and required a greater concentration of square footage in taller structures. One-story (and low, two-story) commercial buildings along major streets serviced new housing that spread in every direction; these were horizontal buildings for increasingly horizontal cities. The taxpayer and other one-story strip retail buildings were often marvels of decorative economy. At the turn of the twentieth century, buildings along Chicago's newly expanded grid of endlessly straight streets were crested with brick parapets adorned with simple, horizontal geometric patterns in brick relief or stone. Slightly more elaborate buildings were ornamented by terra-cotta panels cast with more complex designs inspired by the work of Louis Sullivan and others—mass-produced but affordable luxury ready made for rapid expansion (fig. 30). Strangely enough for structures built to suit streetcar development, unencumbered parapet space was rarely provided for flush wall signs. Soon this disparity mattered little, however, as progressively more signs were fastened to project from the facades, the better to be seen from a rapidly moving vehicle.

Electric signs of the early years were predominantly projecting ones, and for good reason. As facades incorporated more glass and ornament, there was less wall space for flush mounting of business identities. The cumbersome mechanics of electrical wiring and sockets required a depth in the sign frame that made it difficult to fasten the sign box flush to a façade, and because these signs required depth for the electrical chase, they could not be mounted easily within the modest area allotted to the traditional fascia. When electric signs were first fabricated in smaller cities and towns, they were, due to technical limitations, very simple oblongs. But in places such as Chicago, New York, Philadelphia, and St. Louis, electric signs were taking on increasingly unusual, even baroque shapes. A report from Memphis to *Signs of the Times* in 1910 was typically boastful: "Practically all of the live merchants have installed some sort of electric sign. A great many of the merchants who adopted electric sign advertising a few years ago, installing small signs, have recently installed much larger and better signs."[28]

The proliferation of ever-larger signs, combined with the visual power and dominance of electrical illumination, prompted mixed reactions. The general public tended to accept them as a positive visual indicator of progress. But many members of the middle and upper-middle classes had serious reservations. Occasionally, a member of the intelligentsia ventured a positive opinion. One Boston landscape architect, for example, praised the picturesque character of the electric signs on Scollay Square and cited their value as urban features. The magazine's editors dismissed these comments, expressed in a 1910 letter to *Architectural Record,* as heretical. They derided the landscape architect's praise for the view up Hanover Square, one that revealed the remarkable lights of the Star Theater, but agreed with his comment that "the immediate influence from examples of the kind offered by the theater is that advertising men have been far quicker to grasp the value of a conspicuous street terminal."[29] That same year, the new electrical marvels proved too much for the *New York Times:* "It is no longer considered sufficient to have signs, no matter of what size, that merely shine in various colors. Instead they must appear and disappear in alterations of brilliancy and darkness. This, by compelling attention instead of merely inviting it, is productive of mental irritation."[30]

On-site business signs were often lumped casually with billboards, even though they were fundamentally different in scale and location, and often made of different materials. Billboards were dismissed simply as "uglifiers of the landscape."[31] Disdain grew for any visual intrusion. Despite Broadway's heralded reputation as the nation's entertainment center, many New Yorkers felt that sign development along the "Great White Way" was moving too quickly by 1910. The scale and illumination of the signs had once blended "into a general effect of brightness and gayety," but no more.[32] Even as municipalities considered limitations or outright bans, encouraged by such champions of taste and public welfare as New York City's Municipal Art Society, the *Times* recognized that it was premature to seek such restrictions: "Some of the signs are gaudy and individually unattractive... [and] utterly commercial, but the spectacular effect in perspective is really beautiful."[33] And in regard to other locations in the city, another *Times* writer observed, recent legislation seemed questionable: "Not a few of [our correspondents] declare that the signs, instead of offending the eyes of the writers, add a pleasing variety and gayety to scenes that without them

Figure 30

Parapets of typical commercial strip buildings (1900–1912), Chicago. The placement of affordable mass-produced ornament often did not acknowledge the need to apply signs scaled and oriented to the motorist and streetcar rider.

PHOTOS BY AUTHOR, 2008.

would be dull and uninteresting. While these opinions prevail the courts can hardly be expected to sustain laws burdening signboard [i.e., billboard] advertisers with prohibition or even heavy taxes. Relief will only come when the dislike for this sort of advertising is so strong and so nearly general that disregard of it, instead of leading to increased trade, will cause a measurable diminution of the advertiser's business."[34]

Civic-reform groups such the Municipal Art Society were part of a widespread national movement to improve American towns and cities by encouraging citizen participation. Their ideology, originally articulated in the mid-nineteenth century, discouraged the forces of capitalism from dominating the rights of others. J. Horace McFarland, of the American Civic Association, denounced the growing use of large electric signs as "a form of special privilege and a violation of property rights." It was a privilege, McFarland contended, because as a citizen one had an obligation to erect the most beautiful and responsible structures possible when building on public right-of-ways. A tremendous expenditure of public money was required to build and maintain a handsome, efficient street; if an individual violated that effort in any way, McFarland believed, the city should limit or control that special privilege.[35]

Aside from the philosophical and diagrammatic inspiration that Edward Bellamy and Ebenezer Howard provided, American progressives were impressed by the commonplace civic improvements they had heard about or seen on the streets of Europe. European cities seemed as dynamic as any in the United States, yet they were far cleaner, better-administered, and more attractive entities whose growth and development were well controlled.[36] The unobstructed continuity of the architecture of the Rue de Rivoli in Paris, for example, appealed to Americans used to the wildly variable rooflines and building materials in their own cities. One preeminent civic-improvement reformer, Charles Mulford Robinson, likened a good street wall to a line of type: the letters need not be precisely the same height nor of exactly the same form, but "a line composed of such a mingling of exclamation points and periods as might well stand . . . for many a business street would be a total failure artistically."[37] After the city planner John Nolen studied the street-width-to-building-height ratios of European cities and then applied this knowledge to proposals for American towns, he concluded that there was no need for skyscrapers. Once architectural harmony had been so carefully achieved, why let the casual individualism of signs spoil the aesthetic effect?

> Civic art would have something to be proud of, if it could point to a modern business street the vista of which was unbroken by overhead banners or projecting signs . . . and on which, at the building lines there were harmonious facades of approximately even balcony and cornice heights, with no advertising above a certain reasonable limit, and below that all the signs so in harmony with the architecture as to seem a part of the structures, and beautiful and interesting; while above the chosen height there were

window announcements only, in gold leaf—self-contained, harmonious, and dignified.[38]

Robinson cited how Europe was leading the way regarding signs. In 1899 more than three hundred architects in London signed a petition for county council "begging action to repress the evils of monstrous letters and advertising." Several European cities prohibited roof-mounted signs outright. Others set restrictions instead. Robinson particularly admired Brussels, Belgium, for its 1895 municipal initiatives; during that year the city hosted an exposition of superior sign design and a sign-design competition. Both Paris and Brussels proposed that business signs should harmonize with architectural facades.[39]

Plans for a few town centers in the United States reflected European-influenced preferences of the civic-improvement leaders for picturesque, uncluttered streets, muted signs, and public amenities. Jarvis Hunt's 1910 proposal to redesign Wheaton, Illinois, and Howard Van Doren Shaw's 1916 plan for Market Square in Lake Forest, Illinois, presented handsome, if contrived, arrangements of rooflines, towers, and nonelectric signs that looked alien in early-twentieth-century America. Hunt's fantasy for radically rebuilding an average Midwestern town included only awning signs and the occasional wrought-iron standard with its hanging sign. Shaw proposed placing modest, mostly uniform signs only over display windows. Only Shaw's proposal was realized.

Such control over signs was in keeping with the philosophies of Bellamy and Howard, which downplayed the effects of competition. The ideal street for Charles Robinson—whose first guidebook to municipal improvement, *Modern Civic Art; or, The City Made Beautiful* (1903), was printed eleven times—was a street cleared of all physical and visual encumbrances. This meant the elimination of all signs projecting into the public concourse. Frank Koester, a prominent City Beautiful planner and designer, merely advised limiting how far a sign should be permitted to project. Neither man approved of roof-mounted signs. Robinson urged sign designers to compete using beauty rather than size and electricity when meeting a store's advertising needs.[40] He regarded the old symbol or rebus signs as visually economical and picturesque and believed that European crests of arms that served to identify families and long-established businesses should inspire unique trademarks for modern-day companies, replacing the excessive lettering that marred building facades.[41]

Strangely enough, the urban shopping arcade did not enjoy a resurgence of popularity in America following the publication of the ideas of Bellamy and Howard. The most notable arcades in the United States were those in Philadelphia (1827), Providence (1828), and Cleveland (1889). The concept of a highly controlled "streetscape," albeit under glass, appealed to many as a means of controlling architecture and, most especially, signs. Many continental arcades in Europe, however, permitted a wide range of shop sign shapes and sizes within their controlled spaces. London was one of the few cities where the owners insisted on uniform signs. This constraint was passed on to the arcade in Providence, the nation's oldest remaining. So a powerful precedent was set for extreme sign control in America at an early date. But arcades in Europe and America were created with private funds, and these followed the whim of the market. Progressives operated, by contrast, through public means, and focused on improving existing streets in America rather than creating new ones under glass.

Sign regulation, which has a long and complex history in America, has almost always depended on the extent of police power. The colonial assemblies and municipal legislative bodies of early New York, Philadelphia, Charleston, and other cities dictated the locations and kinds of materials to be used for constructing enterprises that might pose problems, such as fire hazards. In America in the late nineteenth century, only minimal restrictions were placed on outdoor advertising. In New York City, posters promoting patent medicines and quack doctors were illegal, but enforcement was erratic. It was also forbidden to post advertisements on city property—the rationale being that the city did not compete with private enterprise.[42] Growing antagonism against outdoor advertisements spurred the fledgling outdoor-sign industry to make its product more palatable. By the 1890s, the International Bill Poster Association, founded in 1872, had decreed how to standardize billboard size, mount them in steel structures whenever possible, establish leases, and safely maintain them.[43] Despite these new regulations, opposition toward billboards increased.

Court rulings that limited police power and state laws regulating what a municipality could—and could not—control hampered the containment of signs and billboards. In nineteenth-century parlance, to *police* meant to prevent actions that threatened public order, safety, or morals. By 1900, higher courts were examining how to interpret that mandate. Because the U.S. federal court system delegated the use of police power to the states, not to the cities, it was difficult to control urban signs and billboards.[44] Even when a municipality might be persuaded to limit its signs, the state was empowered to overrule such a decision.[45]

Once proposals for sign and billboard regulations began receiving civic support, just after 1900, courts often scrutinized the restrictions to determine if they were based on aesthetics or on considerations of health, safety, or morals. Civic-improvement leaders soon learned how to mask their true intent with language that addressed only those practical concerns. For example, they might propose an ordinance against offensively outsized signs by claiming that such objects were dangerous in gusty winds.

The struggle in the courts over how much a city could control the advertising in its streets was intense between 1907 and 1911. Thereafter, the issue was resolved—at least in principle—on a city-by-city basis. What turned the tide was the 1911 court ruling, in the case of *Gunning v. St. Louis,* in favor of a strict ordinance that regulated sign and billboard height, area, and setback from the street and imposed hefty permit fees on advertisers. The judge upheld the ordinance on the grounds that an offense of the eye was as odious as an offense to the nose or ears. He strengthened his argument that billboards were "inartistic and unsightly" by citing a litany of health and moral problems they created.[46] This new legitimacy for aesthetics probably encouraged civic leaders in Chicago and New York in their attempts to forbid, if not remove, all roof-mounted signs. Another major court decision in 1911—this one affecting roadside advertisements—also favored reform. Placing signboards on private property without the owner's written permission was now officially a misdemeanor, and anyone could destroy offending signs. At dawn on September 11, the day the restrictions on roadside signs became law, the Automobile Club of New York led a band of "sign smashers, equipped with shovels, axes, and ladders."[47]

Although far less publicized than the billboard brouhaha, legislation specific to on-site signs for businesses was an issue in the courts for years. Initially, state courts targeted projecting signs. For example, as early as the 1880s, Chicago building codes restricted them to a three-foot extension from a given wall and required a nine-foot clearance between the bottom of the sign and the sidewalk; any sign mounted above three stories had to be made of noncombustible materials. By 1903, the city's Municipal Art League called for the banishment of glaring store signs, especially those it previously had tolerated along State Street. The league voiced its disdain for "the advertising whirligigs and electric transparencies that make State Street look like a museum of atrocious things," and it pointed out how inspection fees, limits on proportion, and design competitions could help rein in such offending street graphics.[48]

Chicago's 1905 building code revealed a city at odds with itself over sign limitations. The code prohibited all projecting signs except for electric ones. By now there was grudging agreement that electric projecting signs, though far from ideal, were somewhat preferable to the older, painted signs. A January 1906 article in the *Chicago Daily Tribune* counted fifty-three hinged or chain-suspended traditional signs that swung, dangled, and creaked in the wind along a stretch of West Madison Street—despite the existence of a code prohibiting them.[49] This was particularly disturbing since several people recently had been injured when fierce winds caused such signs to fall on them. As a rule, electric signs did not endanger passersby; their electricity requirements rendered them far more substantial and solid, and usually they were securely fastened to the walls supporting them.

Whereas reformers such as Charles Mulford Robinson and Horace McFarland would not approve of the sometimes grotesque visual gimmicks incorporated in some electric signs, many businessmen and civic officials recognized how effectively these devices provided incidental, ambient lighting along commercial promenades, significantly enhancing the lighting afforded by municipal arc lights or the new incandescent streetlights.

Despite Chicago's tentative acceptance of electric signs in general, the increasing scale and garishness of these objects along State Street was an ongoing issue. By 1907, city commissioners demanded that all projecting electric signs be removed or refastened flush to the facades of the buildings they adorned. A headline in the *Chicago Daily Tribune* that September declared, "Rid State Street of Monster Signs; Electric Wigglers Disappear as Merchants Comply with Order Issued by City," and the accompanying article described how the street was changing as a result of the new ruling: "One of the most pretentious signs on the street that flashed red, white, and blue by turns at night, in front of the Lloyd Department Store, was hauled in yesterday by a corps of electricians with enough pulleys and ladders to wreck a building . . . Hillman's big electric sign that cut out a space of skyline about 4 by 16 feet has faded away . . . But the wiggly snakes that creep about the novel electric sign of Doctor N. Von Schill, 146 State Street, were on duty."[50] At least one writer for the same paper lamented this action as shortsighted:

> The all-knowing New Yorker who visits Chicago makes individual comparisons between the electric signs on Broadway and State Street. He doesn't know, however, that the lack of lights on this street is due to the esthetic taste of the more cultured west. Some months ago, an agitation was started by the State Street merchants upon whose artistic eyes these glaring lights grated, to have the signs that extended over the thoroughfare removed . . . Whatever may be said against the electric signs, it must be admitted that they light the streets of the city better than the regular lighting system does . . . Pass to a street where the electric sign is in evidence, and the effect is like noonday. Streets like Madison, Randolph, and Halsted on the west side have an air of life and even gaiety lacking in the streets devoid of such lighting. And the city gets the benefit.[51]

A photograph taken at night in 1910, three years after this change was made, shows State to be an almost somber venue at street level, rendered inconsequential by the parade of gigantic, electric rooftop advertisements. By this date, at least fifty U.S. cities had enacted ordinances limiting electric signs, yet they had done little to address roof-mounted, or "sky" signs. As a result, there was a profusion of both business signs and billboards on rooftops nationwide. The Fifth Avenue Association of New York City repeatedly decried this proliferation of electric rooftop signs, fearing "they will make Fifth Avenue look like the Midway of a world's fair." Fifth Avenue merchants, catering to a more privileged clientele, bemoaned the phenomenon on the pages of the *New York Times:* "We never found fault with outsiders using Fifth Avenue roofs for advertising signs until these signs became so large and flaring that they threatened, if they increased in size and number, to drive away our customers."[52] Compared with Chicago, which had already addressed sky signs with amendments to its building code between 1905 and 1909, New York's sign ordinance was quite limited at this time. In 1907 the city merely controlled the projection and clearance of signs; it had not yet established setback and height restrictions. In 1911 Chicago enacted legislation that banned electric rooftop signs altogether.

The previous year, Manhattan's superintendent of buildings protested when the owners of structures along Broadway distorted their rooftops and erected monstrous scaffolding in preparation for electrical displays. He joined the vice-president of the Municipal Art Commission in insisting they were not opposed to the actual displays but to what they referred to as "freak" building designs, adapted to generate additional income through advertising.[53] The City Beautiful planner Frank Koester was much less tolerant of signs; he despised the Great White Way and the poor example it set for the rest of America:

> In illumination, huge and glaring electric signs have been permitted to litter the roofs of buildings having any position of advantage, and with unexampled effrontery, to make night hideous with their intermittent flashings of recommendations of various articles of commerce and trade. All this is an excellent illustration of the small consideration private enterprise has for public interest when it is allowed to have its own way... This, the far-famed Great White Way, which might be more properly called a great blight way... all cities throughout the country, even to the smallest, are doing their best in imitation, strong in the belief that they are engaged in a most praiseworthy imitation.[54]

White Way, USA: The Enthusiasm for Bright Lights

In the 1910s, civic boosters in smaller American urban centers seemed intent on establishing scaled-down versions of New York's Great White Way along their Main Streets as a means of demonstrating their nationalism. This zeal was a manifestation of civic pride and showed a keen desire to capitalize on the growing automobile trade. The antibillboard, antisign concerns of big-city progressives seemed far less pressing than the need to build or update electricity plants and to organize and pay for overdue cosmetic improvements. The Great White Way served as a gilded goal, an ambitious aspiration. In the 1890s, Richard Harding Davis was one of many journalists who fueled enthusiasm for the glamour of Broadway by describing how, at night, "all the shop fronts are lighted, and the entrances to the theaters blaze out on the sidewalk like open fireplaces."[55] During the same era, the Scottish theater critic William Archer was as dazzled by Manhattan after dark as any small-town American might be: "At night... under the purple, star-lit sky, street life in the central region of New York is indescribably exhilarating. From Union Square to Herald Square, and even further up, Broadway and many of the cross streets flash out at dusk into the most brilliant illumination. Theaters, restaurants, stores, are outlined in incandescent lamps; the huge electric trolleys come sailing along in an endless stream, profusely jeweled with electricity; and down the thickly-gemmed vista of every cross street one can see the elevated trains, like luminous winged serpents, skimming through the air."[56]

The commercial and social center of most small American municipalities was generally, and simply, referred to as Main Street. It was the figurative face of every town. In Booth Tarkington's novel *The Gentleman from Indiana* (1902), the fictitious town of Plattville is a place where "only one street attained the dignity of a name—Main Street, which formed the south side of the square."[57] For many small-town occupants, Main Street was a piece of the wider world, imbued with enough activity and promise to kindle the imagination. One small figure in Plattville, Miss Tibbs, clung to the energy and excitement of this primary street, and her imaginings probably represented similar feelings in many other young residents: "When thirty or forty country people were scattered along the walks in front of the stores on Main Street, [Miss Tibbs] would [make] them appear as solid a phalanx as she could. Then she would murmur to herself, with the accent of soulful revel, 'The tangled streets,' and 'within the thronged city' or 'where the thronging crowds were swarming and the great cathedral rose' . . . She had never been beyond Carlow and the bordering counties in her life."[58]

Improving Main Street was a symbolic stride toward the future, an attempt to connect with life beyond the provinces. In the fall and spring, Plattville's Main Street was a river of mud—in summer, a mass of swirling dust. Around 1899, it was paved—rather early for small towns of the nation's interior.[59] Prosperity brought new stores to the square, a new bank of stone, and "then it was whispered, next affirmed, that . . . Main Street was to be asphalted. That was the end of the 'old days' of Plattville."[60] Hugh McVey, the protagonist of Sherwood Anderson's novel *Poor White* (1920), fled his rustic hometown for Burlington, somewhere east of the Mississippi, around 1890, and "for the first time he saw brick paved streets and street lighting with lamps. Although it was nearly ten o'clock at night when he arrived, people still walked about in the streets and many stores were open."[61] For McVey, this view of Main Street's improvements was a glimpse of what the world beyond offered, a landscape far removed from his humble beginnings.

Three major improvements were necessary to "civilize" the Main Streets of small-town America and convert them into provincial White Ways. First, the dirt surfaces of the street had to be paved. Second, the electric lighting had to be upgraded and attractively mounted. Third, electric signs needed to convey a sense of the community's prosperity, actual or anticipated. Roughly between 1900 and 1920 many small towns sought to achieve these goals. A journal aimed at urban progressives, beautifiers, planners, and even boosters, *The American City*, encouraged their efforts by reporting on the success of other municipalities and providing illustrations of streetlight poles, model public restrooms, and the like. Ideally, a visitor to any small town would be as enthused as the novelist Theodore Dreiser was upon his arrival in Fort Wayne, Indiana, in 1915: "We raced into the inescapable Main Street of the city . . . a thoroughfare so blazing with lights that I was much impressed. One would scarcely see more light on the Great White Way in New York."[62]

In his novel *Main Street*, Sinclair Lewis revealed the community boosterism behind the making of the small-town White Way, the anxious desire to put the hometown on the map: "Then, glory of glories, the town put in a White Way. White Ways were in fashion in the Middle west. They were composed of ornamented posts with clusters of high-powered electric lights along two or three blocks on Main Street. The *Dauntless* confessed: 'White Way Is Installed—Town Lit Up Like Broadway—Speech by Hon. James Blausser—Come On You Twin Cities—Our Hat Is In The Ring.'"[63]

Upgrading streets and road surfaces fostered community pride and stimulated trade with surrounding towns. The momentum to improve thoroughfares increased exponentially with the appearance of the earliest automobiles. In 1912 the *Staunton (Virginia) Spectator* reported on "the thirty-five separate bills that have been introduced to the United States Congress" for federal subsidy of highway improvements.[64] That same year, a proper state road was designated to run from Redwood Falls to Minneapolis, and Bryan, Ohio, committed to "modernize streets leading into town from each direction."[65]

Once streets were paved—and so no longer needed oiling—it was necessary to illuminate them. Initially, municipal street lighting depended on oil lamps and, later, gas lamps. Gas lighting, introduced in London in 1806, was the first street illumination most American towns and cities knew.[66] But some deemed it a luxury, as well as a fire hazard, and in many places it arrived after something of a wait. Charleston, South Carolina, saw its first gas streetlamps in 1819, but St. Paul did not install them until 1867, after two decades of rapid growth from humble beginnings. Bryan, Ohio, would not make the commitment to gas until 1879. In many towns, gas lighting was employed conservatively, during prescribed hours, and was not operated at all on moonlit nights.

Soon after Thomas Alva Edison set up the first electric-light power plant, on Manhattan's Pearl Street in 1882, the cold, bright light given off by arc lamps began glaring down on city streets. Minneapolis was among the first municipalities to install such illumination, positioning seven lamps along Washington Avenue, a downtown artery. By 1885, a thousand arc lamps lit Chicago streets, but gas lamps prevailed in the city's less-affluent neighborhoods for decades.[67] Eventually, the incandescent bulb replaced the arc light and provided a warmer, less glaring illumination. Among the most popular supports for the new incandescent lighting was the five-light post, with four white globes clustered just beneath a central globe. In the 1910s, a town lacking these or similar fixtures had not yet fashioned a true White Way.[68]

The lighting a municipality installed and maintained was only one factor necessary for imbuing Main Street with a White Way glow. Main Street boosters welcomed the contribution made by individual, electric business signs to the progressive appearance of the street as well as the effort to provide adequate lighting for lingering customers at night.[69] However, civic leaders in some communities—especially those familiar with the *American City* and the pronouncements of City Beautiful proponents—recognized the importance of monitoring their small-scale White Ways. The citizens of Meridian, Mississippi, appreciated the fact that, by 1911, their "infant Great White Way [was] getting to be a pretty big boy . . . We endeavor to have each sign embody something new in the way of flashing effect . . . it eliminates the possibility of monotony, and makes a street a matter of interest to the public."[70] But the city council of Fond du Lac, which in 1911 became the second community in Wisconsin to install a White Way, passed an ordinance to remove all signs extending more than four feet over the sidewalk. The city also provided incentives to each business that installed a new storefront.[71]

Not surprisingly, electric companies promoted the installation of electric signs in smaller towns and the outskirts of cities. Increased nighttime graphics required more kilowatt-hours and, therefore, meant greater profits. Some electric companies even subscribed to *Signs of the Times* in order to distribute thousands of free copies to merchants, who then could see what was being done elsewhere in America.[72] A monthly column in *Signs of the Times* was a virtual running advertisement for the industry; titled "America's Brightest and Busiest Streets," it highlighted a different town in each issue.

From the earliest days of electric companies, the 1890s, salesmen rented space on Main Street in order to display their signs and brilliant window dressings; they even offered free sign maintenance to stimulate sales.[73] In Muskogee, Michigan, the local gas and electric company made and gave to the city an electric welcome arch on Main Street, specifying that it be kept lit regularly for a period of years. Similar arches, erected above the White Ways of many towns and bearing slogans such as "Watch Wichita Win" and "Welcome to the Winter Capital of America," became rather common sights across the country during this time. Many companies set flat electrical rates and mounted elaborate sign campaigns in order to increase sales.[74] The Federal Sign Company, the nation's largest, was also in the electricity business. And some electricity producers, though independent of sign companies, worked closely with them, assisting whenever possible to secure contracts with merchants. A few electric companies even had offices or agents dedicated to the sign industry.

Big business clearly influenced the appearance of Main Street in the early twentieth century. Powerful electric companies had become aggressive, sending their forces directly to the decision makers, supplying incentives, and stimulating competition. Main Street would never be the same, as residents of small towns benefited from increased readership of newspapers and magazines and the swift rise of the automobile. Communities were now less isolated, and corporate opportunism fueled their drive to compete with one another. The result was commercial thoroughfares of light, burgeoning White Ways that stimulated the flow of big businesses to smaller towns for decades to come.

At the turn of the twentieth century, the arrival of electricity permanently and radically changed the way signs were manufactured and applied to buildings. Talented though many sign crafters of the era were, their best designs still resembled the mannered, ornate painted signs of the immediate past. Although electric signs required awkward boxed housings, extensive structural support, and copious wiring, a few surprisingly good creations emerged from this transitional period, thanks to both the sign fabricator and the building designer. Encouraged by articles in leading trade journals, a small number of architects addressed the obvious need to accommodate signs on their facades, and they provided brilliant examples of how a sign might not only coordinate with an architectural composition but also complement it. Unfortunately, the century's primary new commercial-building types—the movie theater and the automobile-sales showroom—reflected little of this inspiration in the long run. The earliest movie theaters offered the best examples of how sign and facade could be addressed creatively. But as the size of electric signs increased, architects tended to defer the graphic work, handing it off to others. Advertising requirements for an increasingly mobile public encouraged the installation of immense signs that overwhelmed the buildings to which they were attached, graphics designed and installed well after the buildings were completed. Collectively, the result was streets that were often visually defined by signs more than by buildings.

The counterforces of containment and growth characterize much of this era. The progressive effort to contain the proliferation and increasing scale of signs produced several small triumphs and defeats during the first decade of the century, defeats linked directly to judicial interpretation of the limits of police power. A major court decision in 1911 addressed the need to control what many perceived as an urban blight. But sometimes the goals for civic improvement in America at this time were contradictory. Small towns were eager to obtain those features that distinguished urban areas from the provinces. The so-called White Way phenomenon pitted one small town against the next for the honor of being symbolically connected with the glamour of Broadway. But once better roads and electrical current linked Main Street to the big city, it experienced both the benefits and the drawbacks of a closer relationship with the wider world.

Chapter 3
VISIONS AND VELOCITY
THE EXPANSIVE AGE OF THE AUTOMOBILE, 1918–1928

THE 1920S WAS A DECADE of tremendous exaggeration and desire to impress. The surging grandiosity of the advertising world was in large part responsible for this phenomenon; it seemed to permeate everything from conversation to the design of storefronts. Promotional illustrations in magazines became more lush even as ad copy grew in quantity. Lifestyles were advertised as much as products. Abundance spilled from outdoor billboards and newspaper promotions that linked a better life with the purchase of anything from cigarettes to automobiles to elaborate houses. The work of architects and sign designers paralleled this growing world of plenty with novel motifs and enormous scale. This strategy became increasingly necessary to wow the jaded passerby and satisfy clients who were responding to escalating competition.

New motion-picture palaces adorned with multistory vertical signs and exotic styles typified the extravagance, but even small commercial buildings were often lavishly embellished during this indulgent decade. Theater corporations like Fox Film and Chicago's Balaban and Katz were particularly adept at effectively promoting the extravagant design of movie palaces. Theater architecture and signs grew increasingly elaborate in the 1920s. Signs often reached extreme dimensions, and theaters bulged with new height and girth, far outgrowing their modest storefront forebears. Well-publicized archeological discoveries—like that of King Tutankhamen's tomb in Egypt and the ruins of the Maya in Central America and Mexico—fueled the use of exotic styles during this period. The cinema itself, however, was the most powerful force in acquainting patrons with the world of architectural possibilities.

Whole communities were known to adopt consistent, and often exotic, styles for their buildings in the 1920s. It was not the first instance in America for such coordination, but tremendous growth during this decade rendered perhaps the greatest number of examples. Sometimes the look proposed for Main Street was derived from community history, but occasionally it was wholly invented. This was not just a matter of civic pride or arbitrary taste but also a serious consideration of marketability. Older towns, such as Santa Barbara, California, and Santa Fe, New Mexico, could boast about their successes in weeding out undesirable development that did not contribute to a particular historic image. Some neighborhoods, such as the Fifth Avenue commercial corridor in New York City, battled successfully to eliminate objectionable signs that detracted from their self-image of gentility.

The increased speed of the automobile, combined with the noisy self-promotion that characterized the decade, gave rise to businesses that advertised themselves along highways and suburban commercial corridors. Buildings themselves were becoming more signlike. In some cases, corporate ownership and a trademarked architectural design resulted in a consistent look from location to location. In others, the increasing scale and distinctive form of the literal sign served to elevate the appearance of a business and render it quickly identifiable. Often, both factors merged to set the business apart from its neighbors. With the phenomenal growth of the gas station, competition within the industry and a need to appear less industrial led to the introduction of pleasingly exotic or formal architectural styles during this playful, boastful, exploitive decade.

Exotic Dreams, Extreme Scales: New Eclecticism and the Local Cinema

A description from Sinclair Lewis's *Babbitt* vividly sets the stage:

> At least once a week Mr. and Mrs. Babbitt and Tinka went to the movies. Their favorite motion-picture theatre was the Chateau, which held three thousand spectators and had an orchestra of fifty pieces which played Arrangements from the Operas and suites portraying a Day on the Farm, or a Four-alarm Fire. In the stone rotunda, decorated with crown-embroidered velvet chairs and almost medieval tapestries, parakeets sat on gilded lotos columns. With exclamations of "Well, by golly!" and "You got to go some to beat this dump!" Babbitt admired the Chateau. As he stared across the thousands of heads, a gray plain in the dimness, as he smelled good clothes and mild perfume and chewing-gum, he felt as when he had first seen a mountain and realized how very, very much earth and rock there was in it.[1]

During the 1920s, motion-picture theaters grew dramatically in scale and number. By early in the decade, the movie industry was already the nation's fourth largest. Americans spent a bit more than seven dollars a year to attend movies; ticket prices ranged between eleven and seventeen cents. One in six Americans went to the movies every day.[2] As urban theaters nationwide grew ever larger and more opulent, they came to be called "palaces," and many could accommodate some three thousand patrons.[3] The films shown in these lavish settings introduced audiences to fantastic locales and thus encouraged architects and designers to take bold steps in decorating interiors, lobbies, and exteriors.

Competition between architects and theater corporations during these frenzied building years led to imaginative design extremes. *More* was more during this boom period, and the success of print advertising, with its extravagant visuals and text, may have prompted theater owners to overload their building designs as well. Ads for movie palaces often trumpeted the architectural features of the edifice. An even greater lure, however, was the theater facade itself, which reminded people on the street that another world awaited them inside.

The sheer overload of design and iconography on display in theater facades of the 1920s was topped off by yet more advertising. Motion-picture exhibitors frequently hired sign painters to create temporary, large-scale displays that transported alluring images from the screen out into the cityscape. Some were display flats, or boards, wrapped around the first story of the theater, beginning at the exterior lobby under the marquee canopy. Hand-painted images of the faces and scenes from the film being promoted, along with lavish lettering for the title and stars' names, were featured on this broad canvas. Often the temporary displays reached far beyond the marquee and display cases to project out on the sidewalk or to envelope the upper building facade. At Manhattan's Criterion Theater, for example, the release of the 1925 Mary Pickford film *Dorothy Vernon of Haddon Hall* prompted a complete thematic recladding of the exterior walls of the corner site, covering most of the building's eclectic, Renaissance-revival-style five-story elevation; a false castle facade with Gothic windows and the star's name in ten-foot-tall Gothic letters enhanced the effect.

Even when they were not modified with dazzling, outsized graphics and temporary architectural embellishments, movie palaces of the 1920s enlivened the appearance of the city streets, to say the least. They were, in fact, architectural "events" because each one was remarkable in terms of both style and scale and was not at all like the average commercial building. Very early twentieth-century movie theaters were simply modified storefronts. Eventually, they became more elaborate, their facades frequently defined by a grand arch, heavy ornamentation, and plentiful electric illumination. By the 1920s, they often reached elevations of five or six stories, looming over adjacent commercial structures. Many theaters also occupied corner sites, an additional way of drawing visual attention. The potentially blank walls of these immense buildings were made more attractive by the imaginative placement of blind arches, inset panels, buttresses, and pilasters. Another feature that rendered movie theaters distinctive was the marquee. With its changeable backlit letters and exposed-bulb graphics, the illuminated marquee first appeared in the late 1910s. Tower features distinguished most of the Fox theaters on the West Coast, becoming almost a trademark with their extreme height or distinctive profiles relative to surrounding structures. Generally, these additions were unrelated to the interior space,

Figure 31

Ziegfeld Theater (Joseph Urban and Thomas Lamb, 1927; demolished), Sixth Avenue and 54th Street, New York City. Urban intended the facade to communicate the building's purpose vividly, and he designed a carefully integrated parapet sign to identify his patron. A conventional, nonintegrated roof sign was built instead (not shown).

RENDERING BY JOSEPH URBAN, 1926–27. JOSEPH URBAN PAPERS, RARE BOOK AND MANUSCRIPT LIBRARY, COLUMBIA UNIVERSITY.

serving instead as beaconlike signs, often bearing illuminated letters; some were brilliantly floodlit.

Motion-picture palaces were visually arresting not only because of their massive size and distinctive shapes but also because they displayed exotic styles and bizarre ornamentation. Theater designers were especially partial to the ornamentation of the Spanish baroque and rococo, as well as to seventeenth-century French and Italian styles. John Eberson, famous for his atmospheric, starlit interiors, created equally opulent theater exteriors, especially for corner sites. He often employed glazed domes and curvaceous parapets with sparkling terra-cotta tiles to create impressive street elevations.

Architects such as Eberson favored terra cotta—less costly and lighter than stone—because it permitted them to render lush detailing in an incredible array of colors. Fabrication involved pressing clay into forms offsite, so repeating ornamental motifs did not involve the heavy labor of craftsmen. Increased manufacture of this flexible sculptural and graphic surface material led to an eclectic range of iconography incorporated into the facades of commercial buildings. Winged tires adorned auto garages in place of classical cornice ornament, and elaborate bas-relief eagles watched from the upper corners of banks like gargoyles. Even the basic one-story taxpayer strip was lavished with ornament rendered in the glistening polychromatic material. Despite the creative potential for advertisement in terra cotta, business signs were rarely rendered in it. The one prominent exception was signs for banks—enterprises that by nature were less transitory, thus meriting the application of permanent signing to facades.

This unbridled emphasis on architectural and decorative indulgence fueled competition and provoked criticism. One skeptic even referred to the excesses as a "prostitution of architecture."[4] In his book *The Best Remaining Seats* (1961), Ben Hall documented theater-design one-upsmanship in New York City, beginning with the Regent Theater (1913, Thomas Lamb) up through the truly palatial Roxy (1927, W. W. Alschlager). The unlikely genesis of this competition was Lamb's early neoclassical conservatism, as demonstrated in his designs for the Strand (1914), the Rialto (1916), and the Capitol (1919); its culmination was the opulent Roxy. By the mid-1920s, public taste encouraged Lamb to attempt more creative, voluptuous work: "I noted a lessening in the response of the average patron to the charm of architectural backgrounds patterned after the works of the Adam Brothers. There was an underlying demand to do something more gay, more flashy... For this reason, I began to favor in my design an entirely different style, leaning toward the periods of Louis XVI and the very rich productions of the Italian Baroque style."[5] Lamb's response to public opinion is evident in his designs for Loew's Syracuse (1929) and 175th Street (1930) theaters, each suggestive of Asian exotica. Equally opulent in terms of their Far Eastern sculpture and imagery were the twin Fox theaters in Detroit and St. Louis (1928 and 1929, respectively), both designed by C. Howard Crane.

There were, of course, notable exceptions to excessively flamboyant theater design in the 1920s. One was the Ziegfeld Theater at Sixth Avenue and 54th Street in Manhattan, on which Thomas Lamb and Joseph Urban collaborated in 1927 (fig. 31). The primary facade was devoid of conventional ornament. Extra-wide, fluted pilasters supported a bowed cornice that held a stylized, stone representation of fabric or corded swags. The effect was an abstract, graphic evocation of the proscenium arch of a theater, with the fluted columns doubling as rippled side curtains. Above this "arch" was a pair of masks in profile, the iconic symbols of Tragedy and Comedy. For the top of the building, Urban fashioned a geometric sign that aligned perfectly with the window screen below; it spelled out ZIEGFELD, SHOW, and GIRL vertically in a tight matrix of letters, bracketed by the letter Z. This was a subtly integrated literal identity, but Urban probably thought of the building's facade as sign enough, as he had in his virtually letter-free storefront treatment for Bedell's. Praising the design as fresh and appropriate in *Architectural Record*, the architect Ely Jacques Kahn wrote, "The Ziegfeld theory, apparently, is that the kind of architecture that theatre owners

(opposite) Figure 32
Uptown Theatre (Rapp and Rapp, 1925), Broadway, Chicago. The owners of the theater, magnates Balaban and Katz, made certain that the enterprise was well advertised; the landmark signs could be seen from great distances, coming from the city center.
PHOTO BY FULTON-LAWSON, 1925. COURTESY OF THE CHICAGO HISTORY MUSEUM, i17085.

have produced for some years past is not necessarily the final word in design. The pathetic Adamesque creation . . . [and] Italian palaces in the latest interior decorator manner, need not be a steady diet."[6] Unfortunately, Urban's visually integrated sign rising from the parapet was never built. Instead, a more conventional pig-iron grid, with a changeable electric-bulb sign, was planted on the rooftop for the opening show. By the 1930s, when the theater was converted to a movie palace, a more elaborate vertical sign was fastened to the middle of the facade. The new roof sign, the heavy marquee below it, and the vertical sign in front advertised a different kind of business to a different market; the theater now offered more affordable tickets and required greater customer turnover. Subtlety, one might argue, was less appropriate when seats needed to be refilled around-the-clock.

From the mid-1910s, the primary way to identify major businesses, as well as theaters, was with vertical projecting signs. Originally, the vertical projecting sign was a means of enhancing a building's identity when either site limitations or city codes restricted the distances that horizontal signs could protrude. Sign companies in Toledo, Ohio, for example, lamented that city's limit of a four-foot extension from the building line, a ruling that forced 90 percent of signs to ascend a wall.[7] By the 1920s, vertical signs had become enormous. To vividly illustrate this point, the Chicago Theater on State Street, designed by the prolific movie palace architects Rapp and Rapp, supported a vertical sign that was seventy-four feet tall and seventeen feet wide. Built by the Thomas Cusak Company, it blazed with 2,874 bulbs and required special cantilevered construction for support. It was a rare exception to the city rules forbidding projecting signs on State Street. This monumental feature was placed off-center on an otherwise religiously symmetrical facade. Like other behemoth theater signs of that time, its purpose was to attract customers, not to enhance the architecture. The great sign attached to the facade of the Music Box Theater (Louis I. Simon, architect; White Way Sign, 1929), a scaled-down, neighborhood cinema in Chicago, was even larger in proportion to the architecture, and equally awkward and off-center (see plate 6).

Even the owners of smaller theaters succumbed to the perceived need to advertise with signs of enormous scale.[8] The Orpheum on State Street in Madison, Wisconsin (Rapp and Rapp, 1927), with a facade that was only three stories high, supported a sign that began at the roofline and continued up for a height equivalent to an additional four stories, an ambitious display requiring elaborate cantilevered support. Although it needed a less elegant gridded-steel support, an equally extreme sign was suspended above the roofline of Kansas City's Mainstreet Theater (1921). The only visible excuse for such an awkward connection was the scale of the structure's dome next to the sign.

Great vertical projecting signs were especially necessary to identify theaters that were visibly buried within tall office buildings and, therefore, lacked facades. Rapp and Rapp's Michigan Theater in Detroit (1926) had perhaps the largest such vertical sign, the scale of which may have been appropriate in the

Figure 33
Grand Lake Theatre (Reid Brothers, 1926), Grand and Lake Park Avenues, Oakland, California. A landmark in scale and placement, the sign (Theodore Wetteland) was the largest rotary contact sign west of the Mississippi.
PHOTO BY AUTHOR, 1993.

so-called Motor City, whose residents appreciated how large signs were required to grab the fleeting attention of motorists. The tremendous size of many such signs from this era, relative to human scale, bordered on the sublime.

Sign and architecture competed visually at Chicago's immense Uptown Theater (1925), one of Rapp and Rapp's most ambitious endeavors. There, the massive vertical facade of the multistory lobby with its immense arch was almost a sign unto itself (fig. 32). Nevertheless, Balaban and Katz, the Chicago-based theater corporation that owned the Uptown, insisted on a rooftop sign facing south toward the downtown Loop and the station for the elevated train. It also required a projecting sign the full height of the facade. Since the illuminated letters of the signs were suspended on an open metal grid, which significantly lightened the appearance of the facade sign, the scale of these signs did not entirely overwhelm the architecture; however, it did diminish the grandeur of the spectacular palace somewhat. The *Chicago Daily Tribune* proclaimed that "the radiance of the huge electric signs on the theatre . . . was reported to be visible over most of the north side."[9]

Despite the cascading fireworks electronically incorporated into the rooftop sign of Oakland, California's Grand Lake Theater (Reid Brothers, 1926), the graphics neither clashed nor competed with the architecture below (fig. 33). The sign suited the site and the building in scale, resting just above the half-rotunda feature the architects conceived for the corner. The theater name in lights also functioned as a significant landmark for the city at the intersection of Grand and Lake Park Avenues. Built as the largest rotary contact sign west of the Mississippi River, at seventy-two feet high, the sign was designed by Theodore Wetteland.

Increasingly impressive electrical displays in urban theater districts were creating virtual canyons of light. Even the brilliance of Chicago's State Street, dimmed by legislation enacted at the turn of the century, was once again dazzling local boosters:

> Electric signs are surely turning Chicago's downtown State Street into a white instead of a grey way the way it used to be right after dark, when the big stores had closed for the day and the center of things going on was transferred to Randolph Street, where the theatre lobbies blossomed out for the night . . . The first to really make a rift in the nightly darkness was the Chicago Theater . . . [and] Now the State-Lake.[10]

> They brag about the bright lights of Broadway, but there are more electric signs to the square mile in Chicago and suburbs than any other section of the country . . . As each great theatre goes up, the electric signs grow larger.[11]

Streets such as Chicago's State, Denver's Curtis, and Hennepin Avenue in Minneapolis were defined by solid walls of light, composed primarily of the full-facade vertical signs on movie theaters.

Realizing how disproportionate many outsized vertical signs were to their carefully orchestrated facades, a few theater architects attempted to reconcile building design with advertising graphics. And experts writing about theater design, such as R. W. Sexton, encouraged their efforts: "Electric signs . . . should be studied carefully as part of the architectural composition, for they are part of the architecture of the theatre in attaining its purpose as are the entrance doors and the ticket booth. A more careful study of these signs as architectural elements would tend to eliminate the unsightly signs which often obscure fine theatre fronts in which no allowance were made for such manner of display."[12]

Lewis Mumford, one of America's most influential writers on architecture and urban design, derided architects who did not consider electric graphics in their architectural design. Going a step further, in 1923, he encouraged architects to make these graphics the chief decorative motif of the facade, rather than apply lavish, historic stone and terra-cotta ornament.[13] It would be many years before such an achievement would be fully realized.

Several architectural firms demonstrated how carefully sign design could be integrated with theater design. In its creation of the Belasco Theatre (1926) in Los Angeles, the firm of Morgan, Walls & Clements produced one of the most refined examples, employing ornament derived from history. Its singular marquee design looked to the intense Churrigueresque ornament of the cornice. Applying such ornament to this canopy unified it with the building, as if it were truly an architectural feature and not an afterthought.

John Eberson produced some of the most successful and practical sign-and-building combinations of the 1920s. The resplendent, fan-like marquee of his Paradise Theater in Chicago (1927)—animated by 10,772 bulbs—matched the scale and opulence of the grand French Second Empire–style facade. It was not a literal continuation of the architectural detailing of the building, yet it almost seamlessly reflected the exuberant spirit of the structure. More carefully integrated was Eberson's facade and sign for the Loew's and United Artists theater collaboration in Louisville, Kentucky (1928). Here the architect created a symmetrically stepped parapet that rose to a point, thus reconciling the horizontal profile of the building with the towering vertical of the sign, which rested on a pedestal. The architect solved the visual puzzle presented by the age of the auto: how to visually combine the sign tower necessary for recognition from afar with the new, lower silhouette of most auto-age commercial buildings. In an article he wrote for a motion-picture exhibitors' publication in the late 1920s, Eberson included his sketches of possible designs. In each of these, impressively scaled towers served as both landmarks and identification, and all bore carefully coordinated giant vertical signs.

A few retail businesses attempted to compete with—or even learn from—the ambitious graphics of the motion-picture palaces. Some merely copied the cinemas by adding large, vertical projecting signs to the facades of otherwise less-than-extraordinary buildings. A few creative designers looked, with fresh eyes, at the nature of the American storefront in the age of electricity and designed the entire facade with light. For example, the entire upper elevation of a shoe store that opened in Cleveland in 1923 was covered with one large, electric graphic (fig. 34). The composition, installed by the Halter-Ragg Sign Company, consisted of a chaser frame defining the perimeter of the area, which contained two large illuminated bull's-eyes that each flashed "$5"; it filled a twenty-by-thirty-five-foot space with fifteen hundred lamps.[14] E. McKnight Kauffer, a celebrated expatriate graphic designer who often was critical of America's apparent reluctance to improve and modernize visual communication, would probably have approved of this example, as would Lewis Mumford, respected as a philosopher of technology. Kauffer's philosophy favored creative exploitation of the potential of design media: simple graphic forms and movement, as opposed to clumsy, elaborate illustrations.[15] The shoe-store sign succeeded, in part, because it had become the architecture, occupying all the space from the display windows to the crest of the parapet. The oscillating bull's-eyes were a form of ornament appropriate to the material, where the designer made no attempt to represent anything beyond basic bands of colored illumination.

Exotic architectural design was not limited to movie palaces during the 1920s. Spanish baroque or Spanish colonial revival styles were almost universally in vogue throughout the United States; they were incorporated in private residences and commercial enterprises such as restaurants, auto dealerships, and apparel shops. Part of the appeal of eclectic design was that it offered an element of escapism, just like motion pictures did. Spanish and Mediterranean styles were flexible, in that architects could seamlessly blend them with other exotic modes, such as Mexican, Moorish, North African, and Venetian, depending on slight twists in ornament or pattern. Deft manipulation of architectural flourishes could ease sudden jumps in facade profile demanded by the

Figure 34

Sign for Volkmor shoe store (Halter-Ragg Sign Company, 1923; demolished), Fourth Street, Cleveland, Ohio. The simply animated, bull's-eye graphics occupied the entire area usually given over to basic architectural ornament, effectively becoming sign-as-architecture. SIGNS OF THE TIMES (NOVEMBER 1923). COURTESY OF SIGNS OF THE TIMES.

transition from a low storefront entrance to the bulk of a theater auditorium. Since these styles were used to evoke quaint picturesque structures in foreign villages, architects had enormous freedom to employ them in compositions of visually disparate linked masses, including towers, arcades, and projecting balconies.

Alfred Alschuler, who designed many buildings along Chicago's commercial thoroughfares, was particularly adept at manipulating vaguely Mediterranean form and ornament to his purposes. His picturesque arrangements of open towers, arcades, and various window groupings effectively suggested the variety available at the businesses within—whether it was a restaurant, a clothier, or a grocery store (fig. 35). Alschuler's inventive elevations suggested, but did not imitate, the elaborate corner turrets and projecting bay windows of many commercial buildings of the 1880s, yet most of his structures did not even project out over the sidewalk. They were deceptively smooth, efficient building envelopes, contained by codes enforced to keep the sidewalks free from obstructions

Figure 35
Commercial Building (Alfred Alschuler, 1921; demolished), including Bull Dog and Whistle Restaurant, West Wilson Avenue, Chicago. The building was strictly contained in an envelope limited by straight urban property lines, but Alschuler agitated the composition with enough ornament to push the signs off of the building's surface.
PHOTO BY HARRY W. RUBLOFF, CIRCA 1921. COURTESY OF THE CHICAGO HISTORY MUSEUM, i61996.

and to protect the public right-of-way. However, the surfaces shimmered with glazed tiles, exotic patterns, and minor ornamentation.[16]

On the West Coast, the firms of Morgan, Walls & Clements and Marston, Van Pelt & Maybury were noted for the commercial structures they designed in Mediterranean and Spanish colonial styles, markedly different from Alschuler's approach in Chicago. Architect Stiles O. Clements favored large areas of plain stucco punctuated by sudden, elaborate bursts of Churrigueresque ornament placed around key doorways, windows, or corners. The marquee of the Belasco Theatre, designed by Clements's firm, was rendered with the same intense ornament, thus making it seem very much a part of the facade (fig. 36). Los Angeles architect Gordon B. Kauffman, with his design for Holmby Hall (1929), created a village-like, Caribbean/Spanish revival structure housing six stores as part of the Westwood Village business center that arose alongside the recently established University of California, Los Angeles, campus during the late 1920s. Large, plain surfaces were counterbalanced with an animated profile. The structure appeared as a bundle of different buildings rather than a single composition of pieces, and it lent the site a feeling of instant history, as if different builders had completed the construction over time.

Rarely did the architects of these eclectic, exotic commercial buildings in Chicago and Los Angeles address the critical issue of visually connecting their structures with signs. Unlike the Belasco example, many structures designed by Morgan, Wall, and Clements were identified boldly by electric graphics supported at the rooftop level, signs stylistically incompatible with the buildings below. Because they were placed atop industrial-looking pig-iron bases, these signs clashed with their sites' architectural aesthetic. Such signs had rapidly revealed themselves to be necessary for these building types in the 1920s, and architects knew they would be applied eventually. Reconciling such major rooftop structures and the historic building forms upon which they rested did not seem to be a priority of the time. Many of the more refined shops in Pasadena designed by Marston, Van Pelt & Maybury bore signs with gilded wooden letters fastened flush to the stucco over the arches of the display windows. The low roof edge over the arches squeezed the space for graphic identity so much that the resulting identifications were awkward and often too small for passing motorists. In Chicago, the projecting, electric signs on Alschuler's commercial buildings might be perceived as equally clumsy; they barely clung to the highly ornamented, sign-repellent facades.

A glimpse of the future, cloaked in the past, offered one solution for how to address this conflict between sign and architecture. Well outside of downtown Kansas City, developer J. C. Nichols created a romantic enclave of commercial and residential buildings in the Spanish colonial style. The Old World marketplace at the center of this brand-new development, known as Country Club Plaza, was a total design that employed carefully coordinated buildings, street fixtures, and landscaping for a full visual effect.[17] Business signs were severely restrained in scale and designed to uniform standards, thus eliminating the need to integrate each sign carefully with each building facade. Storefronts were unobtrusive, yet designed to give each merchant individual recognition and create a pleasing overall picturesque effect. Nichols was not the first to create a controlled commercial center, but he did lead the way to the future of shopping with the scale of his endeavor and the degree of control, which included arranging the merchant mix.

Yearning for Simpler Times: Defining and Protecting a Vision of Place

In the 1920s, many urban planners and architects favored styles that evoked a romantic past, and historical motifs appeared in both building and sign design. In extreme cases, whole towns were built to appear centuries old. In others, owners of establishments on commercial thoroughfares attempted to protect an image of gentility that was threatened by the rapid, transformative growth of the modern metropolis. City ordinances were enacted not only to protect the perceived charms of certain neighborhoods but also to lure prospective homebuyers and shoppers to them. There was a commercial advantage to the history and romance.

Santa Barbara, California, exemplified an American city that was transformed by a group of visionary community leaders who legislated their aesthetic goals. Photographs from the turn of the twentieth century show that a hodgepodge of two- and three-story Italianate commercial buildings, typical of almost any American town, originally lined State Street, the city's main thoroughfare. The tall, wood-post porches, forming an almost continuous shaded walkway, gave the street the character of the Old West depicted in Hollywood movies—certainly not the image for which the town would eventually become famous. Because unity was important to Santa Barbara's civic leaders, they sought to enforce a single municipal style.

In 1922, Allied Architects of Los Angeles submitted drawings to the city council showing how State Street might look once a uniform, Andalusian arcade extended the full length of a block of two- and three-story buildings. Nothing distinguished one business from another, except perhaps the small, discreet signs obscured within the shade of the arcade. In the drawings, only the subtle variety in the second- and third-story details—towers, unusual window shapes, and balconies—altered the uniformity of the harmonious streetscape. In an alternate proposal, the Community Drafting Room, an organization of local architects, suggested that there be far more play in building height, roof style, and shape of the arches. The Santa Barbara architect George Washington Smith and his design associate and chief delineator, Lutah Maria Riggs, proposed the most extreme scheme of all—with dramatically staggered rooftops, unconventional arch forms, generous balconies, street clocks, and even theater signs (fig. 37). All proposals demonstrated the arbitrary use of architectural embellishment for picturesque effect and not for establishing hierarchy or identity. Except for the marquee shown in one, graphics were severely restrained or nonexistent.

In the mid-1920s, Santa Barbara's Architectural Advisory Committee developed a plan for widening State Street by arcading sidewalks behind property lines; the goal was to establish a sort of conceptual unity. Santa Barbara's design leaders encouraged building owners to create arcaded loggias or porches throughout the old center. This simple strategy could have been effective in creating some sort of continuity woven through the variety of individual designs. Auto dealerships were fronted with long, plain single-story arcades supporting shed roofs or basic parapets; restaurants and gift shops were adorned with balconies above and arcades below (fig. 38). The effort was voluntary, property by property; in the long run, the city failed to create a continuous covered passageway.[18]

Figure 36

Belasco Theatre (Morgan, Walls & Clements, 1926; altered), Hill Street, Los Angeles, in 1926. The Belasco, like the neighboring Mayan Theatre by the same firm, contrasted intense bursts of ornament against large areas of plain stucco and a marquee visually united with this same ornament.
COURTESY OF THE HUNTINGTON LIBRARY, SAN MARINO, CALIFORNIA.

THE EXPANSIVE AGE OF THE AUTOMOBILE

To protect the aesthetic harmony of Santa Barbara against the commercial sign, civic leaders encouraged businesses to rusticate their signs, making them look vaguely historic or, at least, compatible with the simplicity of the white, stucco walls that predominated downtown. Ideally, proprietors would paint lettering directly on their buildings, fashion tasteful signs from wrought iron, or hang simple wooden plaques from suitably picturesque standards—also crafted from wrought iron. Obviously, electric signs would be inappropriate for a town with a pervasive Spanish colonial look. But despite the efforts of Santa Barbara's zealous aesthetic guardians, more than a few electric signs were installed on many of the new stucco-and-tile commercial buildings. Most were, however, modestly sized and sensibly scaled. One of the publications by the Advisory Architectural Committee revealed the city's approach to signs: "The appearance of many towns could be greatly improved by getting rid of undignified signs—the fire sale sign, the roof sign, the projecting sign. The attractiveness of Michigan Avenue and Fifth Avenue is due to the dignity of their signs fully as much as to the dignity of their buildings. The Architectural Advisory Commission is stressing *dignity of business signs* as an essential point in the erection of a beautiful city."[19]

In 1924 and 1925, comprehensive zoning and building ordinances were enacted for the city of Santa Barbara. In addition, the Board of Architectural Review, whose members included architects George Washington Smith and Carlton Winslow, was granted a form of veto power over proposed building plans.[20] Submissions rejected by the board were sent to the Community Drafting Room, where some of the city's best architects and designers assisted builders and business owners in adjusting their proposals according to the community's aesthetic master plan. With this help, design proposals generally won the approval of the Board of Architectural Review. Hoffmann described how this team of professionals sought a single vision: The Community Drafting Room "prepared suggestions for the harmonious treatment of whole block fronts: for stores, garages, . . . to conform to a style considered fitting for the region, yet strictly within the requirements and costs of the owner . . . Simple store signs were carefully designed and placed so that each would have its full value without destroying the appearance of its neighbors. This effect of block harmony . . . has been lost whenever even one, or a multiplicity of strong colored painted fronts and competing signs, have been introduced."[21]

Along with the work of talented designers and skillful reformers, another factor assured a swift and sweeping physical reshaping of Santa Barbara. An earthquake jolted the city on June 29, 1925. Conveniently enough for the reformers, the quake damaged most significantly those buildings that conformed least to the city's new self-image, such as the Greek Revival–style county courthouse built in 1872, while structures that already had been modified, emerged relatively unscathed. Civic leaders interpreted the aftermath of the temblor as a powerful

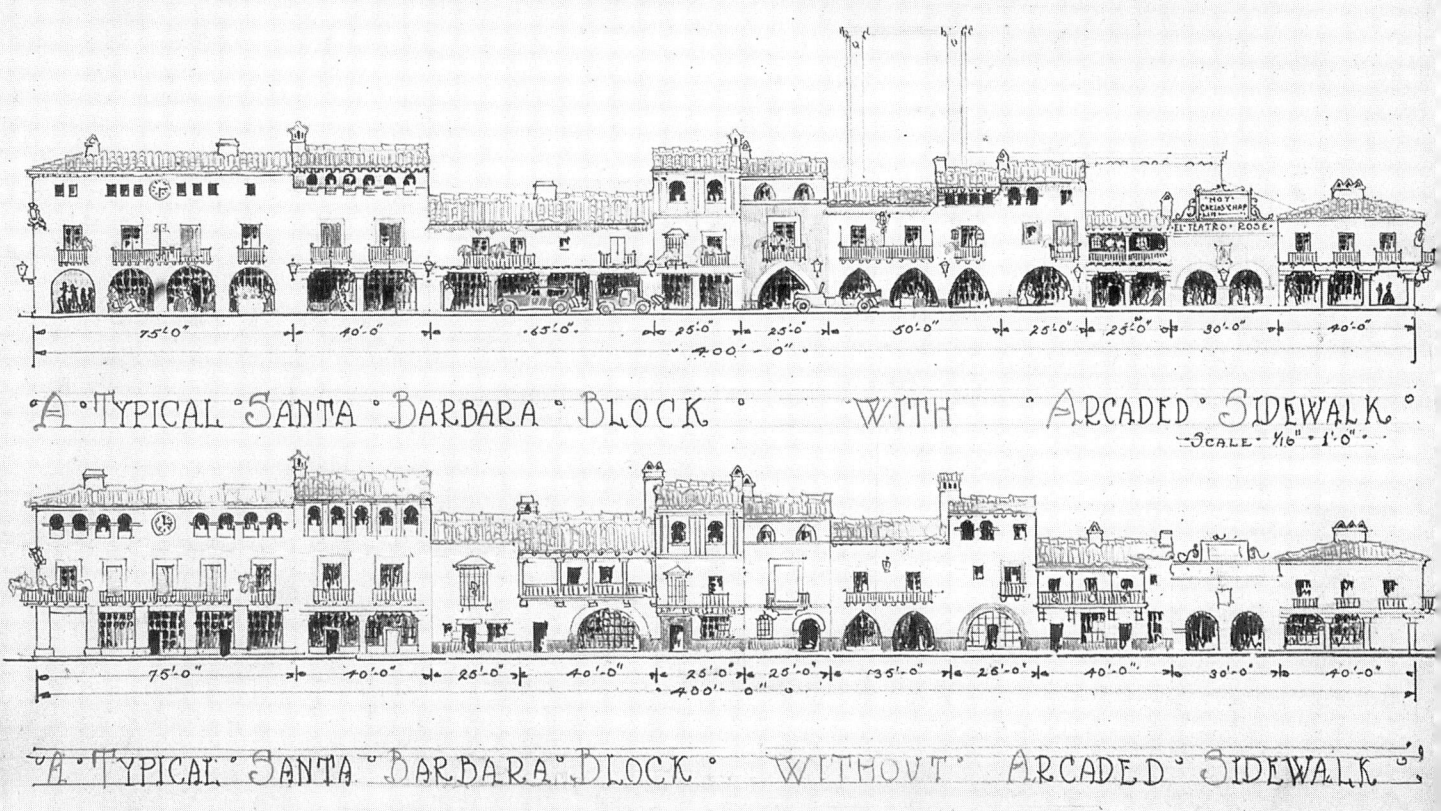

Figure 37
Proposal for State Street, Santa Barbara, California (George Washington Smith and Lutah Maria Riggs, circa 1925). Architect Smith's submission was but one of several concepts for "Hispanicizing" the old core of town and inspiring future development.
ARCHITECTURE & DESIGN COLLECTION, UNIVERSITY ART MUSEUM, UNIVERSITY OF CALIFORNIA, SANTA BARBARA.

sign that their city was on the right path and that their decisions regarding both the structure and decor of buildings were justified.

After the Board of Architectural Review was dissolved in 1926, the Plans and Plantings Committee became one of the most powerful civic voices influencing design. It sponsored a series of competitions to promote its Hispanic vision for the city. That year, Mary Craig, wife of the local designer James Osborne Craig, won second prize for an auto-repair garage plan she devised, while a furniture store by Murphy and Hastings won third. Granted, these were the accomplishments of some of the city's highly revered architects, but such honors proved that even modest structures could be handsome and contribute effectively to the city's improvement. The juries for these competitions looked for harmony of details, good proportions, the relation of the building to the setting, and an economical use of color. The committee paid particular attention to signs, feeling that "several structures of high architectural merit . . . could not be given their proper rating because both architectural features and detail had been obscured by over-sized or inharmonious commercial signs."[22] Lead reformer Pearl Chase noted the clumsy, disproportionate graphics displayed in many of the photographs taken for a survey of existing facades and signs conducted in the mid-1920s. Several older signs almost covered the entire space from the display windows to the crest of the parapet. The aesthetic monitors of Santa Barbara

Figure 38
Mihran Studio Building (Mihran, 1922; altered), East Carrillo, Santa Barbara, California. This example of the preferred style for Santa Barbara offered picturesque variety in a small commercial package and nonilluminated lettering in a vintage mode.
PEARL CHASE COLLECTION, DEPARTMENT OF SPECIAL COLLECTIONS, DAVIDSON LIBRARY, UNIVERSITY OF CALIFORNIA, SANTA BARBARA.

were ever vigilant against any hint of crass commercialism, determined to quash it before it could detract from their ideal city.

Santa Barbara's triumph at transforming itself intrigued and inspired civic reformers nationwide. They were, of course, charmed by the town's rather dreamy, romantic appearance, but they were equally impressed by the means and methods the community employed to remodel itself. The city's achievement was recognized by the Carnegie Foundation, which in 1922 awarded the Plans and Plantings Committee a multiyear grant to create a pilot project for civic improvement that would serve as a model for such endeavors by other cities.[23]

One stated goal of Santa Barbara's leaders was to encourage tourism, a necessity for a town with little industry. But such comprehensive work, and such careful publicizing of the town's success, also suggested a certain missionary zeal to help Americans everywhere to make their Main Streets magnificent. A town very much like Santa Barbara supplied Sinclair Lewis's *Main Street* protagonist, Carol Kennicott, with inspiration in her campaign to help Gopher Prairie make improvements.[24] Magazines targeted to many markets enthusiastically spread news of the city's success and allure. For example, the *Architectural Forum* called Santa Barbara, without qualification, "the best U.S. example of how architecture can be planned, influenced, and regulated."[25] Syndicated journalists wrote lengthy articles carried in newspapers and magazines across the country that extolled the city's charms and its residents' accomplishments; lavish illustrations accompanied many of these pieces. "We are a country too content with ugliness, and too individualistic to work together in a community," declared one writer. "Santa Barbara happened to have a body of citizens not content with ugliness and willing to work together."[26] After romancing the reader with seductive descriptions of arcades and hidden courtyards, freed from the clutter that was typical of American commerce, the writer claimed that other cities could follow Santa Barbara's lead if they, too, permitted diligent architectural review boards to scrutinize every plan affecting municipal improvement.

By the late 1920s, zoning laws directly or indirectly dictated streetscape aesthetics in most American cities. They segregated commercial development from residential, thus keeping electric signs away from homes, and they established limits for building heights and setbacks. Passage of the 1924 Federal Standard State Zoning Enabling Act resulted in the zoning of approximately eight hundred municipalities, including more than two-thirds of the nation's largest cities by the end of the decade.[27] Zoning had become an effective tool for individuals involved in the real estate market.[28] It was, after all, a constitutional exercise of "police power," and as such it had little, ostensibly, to do with aesthetics. Zoning and building codes existed to define the use of urban spaces and to establish limits on dimensions and materials in order to minimize the hazards of fire, structural collapse, and overcrowding. Some critics of the time, however, derided zoning as a mere tool for manipulating the value of real estate. Only about one-quarter of those cities with zoning ordinances in force had a comprehensive city plan.[29] They could clarify what they did not want (buildings too close together, smokestacks next to green lawns) but lacked a clear vision for what they *did* want.

Rebuilding core city districts—the dream of municipal leaders and architects at the turn of the twentieth century—began to seem impractical by the 1920s.[30] The critics Lewis Mumford and Clarence Stein railed against the aimless spread of the suburbs, and they continued to promote the establishment of limits on the growth of towns.[31] But as the quality of roads improved in response to the automobile boom, the debris of cities spread rapidly into their environs. As the magazine the *American City* lamented in 1928, "The beautiful roadsides are gone. Traveling through the state, one encountered a veritable automobile slum." To some, the solution was to zone these rural areas, thus preventing construction of a hot-dog stand or an auto-repair garage next to a private residence. If enacted, such legislation would preserve the appeal of the countryside by consolidating commercial development into regularly spaced intervals along the highway.[32]

In New York City, Fifth Avenue merchants won a major victory in their long-running battle against what they deemed the "commercial excess" that was threatening the main-stem thoroughfare's genteel character. Their specific targets in the 1910s and 1920s were electric rooftop and projecting wall signs. In 1916 the city passed an ordinance that banished all projecting electric signs along the avenue, from Washington Square to 110th Street, by the end of a five-year amortization period. As the date for full compliance neared, additional streets were added to the forbidden zone, including stretches of Madison Avenue and 34th and 57th Streets. The state supreme court upheld the ordinance on the grounds that "the multiplication of [illuminated] signs in this very busy section of the city easily can become an eyesore, a nuisance, and an improper use of air space."[33] Mention of the term *eyesore* revealed the subtle creep of aesthetics into legislative decisions previously limited to protecting citizens against physical threats or inconvenience.

Members of the Broadway Association were understandably nervous, anticipating that someday sign restrictions might dim the lights on the Great White Way. They challenged the court's decision, contending that such limits targeted some streets and not others. How was this a reasonable and equitable application of police power, free of aesthetic considerations and favoritism? Their argument led to a reversal of sorts: one week before the amortization period was up—on December 16, 1921—theaters were declared exempt from the sign limits.

The battle between the two forces continued for the rest of the decade.[34] Fifth Avenue merchants, their businesses identified by modestly scaled bronze lettering, faced a potential loss of customers if the character of their neighborhood was highjacked by outsized electric signs.[35] Not surprisingly, the association's determination to impose its notion of "good taste" prompted groups representing the threatened areas—including the Broadway Association, the Theatre Owners Chamber of Commerce, 42nd Street Property Owners and Merchants, and the Electrical Board of Trade—to retaliate. "It may not be generally known," one representative of the Electrical Board of Trade asserted, "but that holy of high-hatted citizens calling themselves the Fifth Avenue Association feel now that they should proceed to raise the rest of our metropolis to the lofty pinnacle of classy swank that Fifth Avenue exemplifies."[36]

Groups opposing the Fifth Avenue faction claimed the merchants association, with "delusions of dignity and grandeur," was imposing unfair restrictions on every small merchant within the radius of the vaunted avenue. They attempted to characterize the struggle as Goliath (the prosperous merchants) bullying David. In truth, the conflict was really between two giants, each trying to protect its own marketable identity. "Let us look into some of the side streets. Here the modest merchant gets a minute store at a price he can just about afford. He cannot dress up in bronze and marble finery. He must draw his trade by bright lights . . . and cheerful electric signs . . . Fifth Avenue says to him, 'Here, son, take down these signs you have; we've got big rents to pay here on the avenue. We can't afford to have you taking any of our customers away.'"[37]

Fifth Avenue was not the only major American "main street" that attempted to preserve its image during the 1920s. The city of Chicago sought to eliminate projecting electric signs altogether from certain streets. The move began as an effort to protect the newly created Wacker Drive along the Chicago River (completed in 1926), a delayed outcome of the ambitious Chicago Plan of 1909 that promoted civic beauty and efficiency. Once the commissioner of public works and the Municipal Art Commission achieved this goal, they turned their attention to the famous downtown Loop.[38] Omaha, Kansas City, Pasadena, and Boston also enacted some of the toughest sign ordinances in the nation, prompting many sign companies to comply and propose only wall-mounted graphics.[39]

Although the legislation appeared threatening in principle, signs mounted flat against a wall could often be just as large as those that projected. But because flush mounting somewhat limited sign creativity, and even scale, the restrictive laws potentially reduced profits.

By the 1920s, the sign business was to some extent becoming self-policing. It behooved the industry to prevent shoddy or tasteless installations, for such work served to lower standards (and, therefore, earnings). Well-written ordinances that were consistently enforced benefited all concerned, it claimed.[40] The industry bible, *Signs of the Times*, consistently advocated higher standards in outdoor advertising and the regulation of advertising in remote regions of natural beauty.[41] Although its attempts to rein in overly extravagant or unsuitable signage were not always successful, the journal continued to try improving sign design and sign-business practices. Sam Kamin, who wrote regularly for *Signs of the Times* and authored several books on the sign-making craft, addressed the issue of offensive projecting signs: "The utmost cooperation of all interested in the development of our industry is necessary in order to overcome threatening objections and prejudice against all forms of projecting signs. It behooves us, therefore, to do all we can to do away with all the so-called 'eye-sores' we find on our streets that we hear so much about. They really are hard to look at, cumbersome, junky signs, rusty hanging equipment, poorly erected—a menace, indeed, to public safety. No wonder architects and art leagues are up in the air and objecting against the erection of such 'eye-sores' on their carefully planned buildings."[42]

Signs of the Times writers, including Kamin, encouraged readers to simplify the lettering and graphics on their signs. This was a lesson learned from the advertising industry, which by the end of the 1920s was abandoning its longtime reliance on testimonials, ornate typefaces, and complex illustrations to get its messages across.[43] Researchers at the University of Wisconsin determined that viewers were more likely to remember pictures, not text, and that even the uneducated responded positively to visual unity, harmony, and proportionality.[44] *Signs of the Times* suggested that a sign with a clear and memorable picture was more effective than a whole street lined with text-based signs. A truly successful sign, contributor C. A. Atherton argued in the June 1923 issue, must first of all call for immediate action (Stop! Look! Buy!) and, second, must plant in the viewer's mind a striking and memorable image, something evocative of a particular feeling.[45] Another article in the same issue encouraged sign designers to see themselves not as painters of letters but as "store front advertisers."[46]

Although little had changed in terms of *style* until the late 1920s, sign scale and design had become more ambitious. *Signs of the Times* often featured complex sign designs with animated images in its pages. Signs were becoming text-heavy and unusual in contour, expanding beyond the basic vertical oblong.[47] Trade publications eventually encouraged sign painters and designers to simplify their work and to emulate print advertisers, who were beginning to replace word-burdened designs with spare and graceful images. It was difficult, however, to create pictures with lines composed of incandescent bulbs unless the graphic was enormous; the medium was not exactly fluid at the scale of the average sign. Although there were some stunning animated signs created in the first three decades of the twentieth century, particularly in New York's Times Square, these remained the exception. Designers across the country persisted in producing increasingly elaborate signs with archaic, decades-old ornamentation. Electric pictures, still rarely incorporated into the average sign, were usually additions rather than substitutions in sign composition. Like most architects of this period, sign designers seemed reluctant to depart from established modes and were inclined to add rather than subtract.[48]

Despite this apparent interest in rethinking the appearance of signs, those who designed them continued to clash with architects. Refining the shape or scale of a business graphic meant nothing if the sign was clumsily applied to a building, with little regard for the structure's architectural features. Sign professionals wished architects would make provisions in their designs "and thus make the sign part of the building, not an afterthought."[49] Architects countered that it pained them to see their facades covered, within weeks of completion "with all manner of heterogeneous signs hung in sketchy disregard of cornices, entablatures and the like."[50] In an attempt to reconcile the two sides, *Signs of the Times* suggested that sign designers make careful studies of the potential location for a sign, taking into consideration the architecture and color of the

Figure 39

Austin Automobile Company Showroom (architect unknown, 1927), East Colorado Boulevard, Pasadena, California. The unusual openness of this facade permitted better display of automobiles, yet the concentrated burst of Spanish plateresque ornament linked the building to California's idealized past and, most especially, the fashionable architecture of the city center.

PHOTO BY AUTHOR, 2006.

affected structure.[51] Unfortunately, few sign designers were trained well enough to execute such studies, nor was time to do so available to them. The conflict between architects and sign designers would not be resolved until the 1930s.

Design for Space and Speed: The Automobile and the Roadside

The phenomenal surge in automobile ownership and use in the 1920s profoundly affected architecture during those years. Rapidly increasing urban populations and the ease of commuting from outlying areas into city centers boosted land values. Outlying business districts became complete shopping hubs, almost miniature downtowns, complete with branch department stores and movie theaters.[52] The need for off-street parking and pull-in space led to discontinuous development along new commercial thoroughfares between centers. Parking spaces were available alongside, and sometimes even behind, new commercial structures.

In some cases, ornamentation on these buildings juxtaposed the minimal with the grandiose; a corner or entrance of an otherwise unremarkable structure might support an elaborate sign—an aesthetic flourish along an otherwise monotonous street wall. More elaborate features, true focal points or landmarks along a stretch of undistinguished edifices, were most successful in attracting motorists' attention. A triple-arched corner, evocative of a gateway to a hacienda, distinguished the Donahue Building at the busy Los Angeles intersection of Western Avenue and Wilshire Boulevard. A Cadillac dealership in Pasadena incorporated a similar architectural feature, although in this instance, the great curved parapet served as a signboard, identifying the name of the business.

On East Colorado Boulevard in Pasadena, a showroom designed by the Austin Company of California (1927) featured a distinctive, horizontally stretched arch of glass. At the apex, over the door, was a heavy burst of plateresque ornament with no visible means of support (fig. 39). This sudden visual flourish, which rose right up to the parapet, united this otherwise plain modern "box" with the nearby town center and its art deco and Spanish colonial architecture. Otherwise, the building was a harbinger of the future, in which more automobiles and more available land would prompt simpler one-story stretches of glass placed along ever-expanding roadways. The profusion of ornament at the center of this facade acted as a connotative "sign," communicating, in the most efficient manner possible, that this was a luxury business. The wide expanse of glass permitted unobstructed views of the automobiles to passers-by. This was a bold example of architectural history being contorted to the needs of the automobile. For all its advanced design, however, no provision was made for the addition of an electric sign to literally identify the business.

A craze for applying Tudoresque elevations to one- and two-story strip buildings presented architects with the challenge of reconciling vertically proportioned architecture with horizontal forms. One feature of this architec-

Figure 40

Goodman Shops Building (T. Beverley Kelm, 1922), West Sixth Street, Los Angeles. Even architectural styles with a bias for vertical proportions, like the Tudor, were stretched horizontally to suit the emerging automobile strip.

AMERICAN ARCHITECT—THE ARCHITECTURAL REVIEW (MAY 7, 1924), 457. REPRODUCTION COURTESY OF RYERSON AND BURNHAM LIBRARIES, ART INSTITUTE OF CHICAGO.

tural style, rooted in late-sixteenth-century England, particularly appealed to designers of twentieth-century commercial buildings: the enormous expanses of glass, exemplified in structures like Hardwick Hall in Derbyshire. The generous curving glass window located under a substantial brick gable of the Goodman Shops Building (T. Beverley Kelm, 1923) in Los Angeles permitted passing drivers to see inside the store easily (fig. 40). A three-story, late-nineteenth-century apartment building in the Lakeview neighborhood of Chicago received an auto-friendly update, with a commercial Gothic base applied as a new first-story facade. This 1920s renovation was merely a pseudo-historic skin, flush with the original structure at its more public side, but then this one-story Gothic "belt" thrust forward as a mass on its own, filling the small front yard on the side street with a retail addition. Several such one-story additions were added to two- and three-story residential structures in Chicago along key commercial corridors.

Some of the most auto-oriented commercial structures in the 1920s were grocery markets, especially those in Los Angeles, which were long, low, one-story edifices. Most were pushed back from the street, and many were placed around the perimeter of a quarter-circle of drive-up pavement. Architects often incorporated arches—arcades of sorts—along the lengths of these buildings to serve as stall openings for the various food vendors. This was a decade before the advent of the supermarket, which united several specialist shops like the greengrocer and the butcher. Towers, or towerlike features, often distinguished these buildings and were usually positioned for ideal visibility. Typically, roof signs identified the markets, but freestanding pole signs at the road's edge were also installed to catch the motorist's eye.[53] These graphics were not unlike the basic

Figure 41

Dyas Carleton Café building (Gable and Wyant, 1929; demolished), Wilshire Boulevard, Los Angeles. Freedom of space on a suburban lot permitted this auto-age composition to take on a more distinctive, functional form than would be permitted on a tight urban site. It was a harbinger of things to come.

PHOTO BY "DICK" WHITTINGTON STUDIO, CIRCA 1935. COURTESY OF JIM HEIMANN.

pole sign for the filling station, another business with off-street space for autos pushing buildings away from the street.

Commercial buildings increasingly became separate, figural entities, surrounded by space in the newly expanded city, instead of the zero-setback structures of the traditional commercial thoroughfare. The Dyas Carleton Café (Gable and Wyant, 1929) in Los Angeles applied traditional forms from Spanish architecture to a nontraditional layout and proportion (fig. 41). A squat, telescoped tower served as a distinctive landmark on the street corner and carried the primary sign; an inviting arcade communicated welcome and linked the tower to a shed-roofed entrance near parking. Consistent materials and style held together the rambling but balanced composition. The sign lettering was Old World instead of electric; it would undoubtedly please the Santa Barbara sign police. Despite its first impression as something from a hacienda in Mexico, this building was a creation of the motor age, a response to the freedom of space and the requirements of being identifiable from afar at high speed. Advanced enough in layout and massing to be from the 1930s or 1940s, although less sleek and blended, its forms were cloaked in materials and details that pleased the public of the 1920s.

The commercial landscape in America was becoming increasingly fragmented, a collection of pieces with little design or scale continuity. Development was often sporadic, leaving generous spaces between potential destinations for the motorist. More than an experience of space, it was an experience of images. Aldous Huxley captured the disorientation vividly, in fiction, with his description of an Englishman's arrival in Los Angeles—a rapid-fire sequence of visual and verbal non sequiturs:

Suddenly the car plunged into a tunnel and emerged into another world, a vast, untidy suburban world of filling stations and billboards, of low houses in gardens, of vacant lots and waste paper, of occasional shops and office buildings . . . The sunshine, slanting from behind them as they advanced, lit up each building, each sky sign and billboard as though with a spot-light . . .

EATS. COCKTAILS. OPEN NITES.

JUMBO MALTS.

DO THINGS, GO PLACES WITH CONSOL SUPER-GAS!

. . . The car sped onwards, and here in the middle of a vacant lot was a restaurant in the form of a seated bulldog, the entrance between the front paws, the eyes illuminated . . . The bulldog shot back into the past . . .

DRIVE IN FOR NUTBURGERS—whatever they were. He resolved at the earliest opportunity to have one. A nutburger and a jumbo malt . . .

CLASSY EATS. MILE HIGH CONES . . .

FINE LIQUORS.

TURKEY SANDWICHES . . .

Another zoomorph presented itself, this time a real estate agent's office in the form of an Egyptian sphinx . . . They turned to the right, sped past a Rosicrucian Temple, past two cat-and-dog hospitals [and] a School for Drum-Majorettes.[54]

Remarkable shapes and elaborate signs variously identified freestanding buildings along key thoroughfares such as Chicago's Lincoln Avenue at the northern edge of the city, and Wilshire Boulevard in Los Angeles. Cultural historian Chester H. Liebs termed this "quick-read architecture," visually distinctive roadside buildings designed to capture the motorist's attention. Some of these were created in the form of the product sold or as a symbol, representing the establishment's name. For the Toed Inn, built in Los Angeles, a giant froglike form was wrapped around a humble box-shaped diner. Liebs pointed out that these and numerous other fanciful examples of "representational giantism" harked back to the nineteenth century, when oversized watches, teapots, or teeth hanging above storefronts identified the nature of the businesses conducted within.[55] Contemporary examples of so-called mimetic, or programmatic, architecture were—and still are—the White Castle hamburger restaurants. Beginning business in the 1920s, owners of this venerable chain adopted a unique form of commercial architecture: a small-scale, crenulated, tower-like structure sheathed in white, glazed tile or brick. Even when buried midblock and surrounded by gray, stone office buildings, the singular white profile was identifiable and distinct from its surroundings.[56] The consistent architectural image worked as a sign to those already introduced to the chain.

(following spread) *Figure 42*
Ford Lunch (architect, sign company, and date unknown; demolished), Euclid Avenue and Holt Boulevard, Ontario, California, circa 1940. The modest original building was swallowed by graphics, making the entire structure an illuminated beacon along an important highway.
COURTESY OF THE ROBERT E. ELLINGWOOD MODEL COLONY HISTORY ROOM, ONTARIO CITY LIBRARY.

Commercial architects of the 1920s became keenly aware of the advertising power of a building's appearance and often proposed lavish, attention-grabbing exteriors but simple, generic interiors. Architectural writer and critic Reyner Banham used the phrase "functional building with fantastic garnish" to emphasize the difference between inside and out. One particularly striking example of this phenomenon was the Aztec Hotel in the southern California town of Monrovia (Robert B. Stacy-Judd, 1924).[57] An overscaled, cartoonlike appliqué of Mayan ornament covered a rather simple box of a building. A modest electric sign confirmed the name of the extravagantly encrusted structure. Another exuberant example of this type of building, what the architect and critic Robert Venturi called "the decorated shed"—that is, an unremarkable building sheathed with signs—was Ford Lunch (late 1920s). This twenty-four-hour café in Ontario, California, on the edge of the Mojave Desert east of Los Angeles, was a simple structure that was practically buried under electric sign bands, painted end panels, and vertical projecting signs (fig. 42). It served as a beacon for many, along the primary route, from desert to coastline, through the Inland Empire.

Effective identification of a commercial chain required distinctive and consistent graphics, especially if the architecture varied from site to site. As automobiles gave shoppers access to far more options, businesses competed for drivers' attention. One way to establish a distinctive identity was to adopt trademark signs. The Woolworth's five-and-dime-store chain was one of the first to establish such a visual identity in the 1880s; its sign was a wide, red fascia panel with gold lettering in an extended, serifed style.[58] Soon, most of the competition was using the red-and-gold color scheme for its own signs. The Kress Company, however, adopted a different look. Although the facades of its stores were unique from site to site, they were usually one of the most ornate buildings on the street and were built with a consistent buff or pale yellow brick. The company logo, rendered in glazed terra cotta or painted metal, was displayed creatively near the crest (see plate 7). It was difficult and expensive for chains to establish architectural consistency, particularly in areas where it might be necessary to remake facades on existing structures. Nonetheless, distinctive signs became more essential, especially in suburban locations, where many buildings were set back from the road.

Chains sometimes incorporated their signs as dominant graphic elements in newspaper and magazine advertisements. For example, the Sun Drug Company of southern California ran a series of ads in the 1920s featuring its electric sign and the tagline "the sign of Supreme Drug Store Service." The copy for one such ad read: "In Los Angeles, Long Beach, and Pasadena the cheery 'Sun' electric signs flash a hearty welcome to an ever-widening stream of satisfied customers. Whenever you see a 'Sun' sign you may enter the store assured of courteous, prompt, and helpful service."[59]

Corporate trademarks were the primary identifications for oil companies that had established their own chains of gasoline stations. Often the trademark *was* the sign—simply a graphic hoisted atop a pole at the street's edge. According to the historical geographers John A. Jakle and Keith A. Sculle, logos originally were attached to filling-station buildings, but starting around 1915, distinctive sign postings at the street also identified these businesses.[60] "An easily recognized trademark is more valuable than words," advised *Architectural Record* in 1930. "Lettering should therefore be limited to a minimum."[61] Members of the design community readily recognized the value of a sign that communicated clearly and efficiently. As one automobile-industry representative put it in a 1926 issue of *Signs of the Times:* "A standardized electric sign on our dealer's place of business will instantaneously identify that establishment as a place where Star cars may be purchased, serviced, or repaired. The standardized electric sign is the connecting link between all other forms of advertising and the dealer . . . The signs are made up in four different types to fit the various types of locations and to conform with local sign ordinances, but they have a general similarity."[62]

Beginning in 1927, Mrs. John D. Rockefeller Jr., the American Civic Association, and the Art Center of New York sponsored a series of national design contests, the purpose of which was to improve the appearance of gas stations and roadside refreshment stands.[63] This same group also produced and distributed a monthly publication to these businesses in order to enlighten them about the values of taste and restraint as they pertained to design. Oil companies responded to the reformers' concerns by altering the look of their gas stations, especially in residential neighborhoods. Some attempted to "domesticate" these structures with gables and brick, sometimes fashioning them as storybook houses; other stations were built to resemble classical temples, in an attempt to suggest park-like follies. The *New York Times* expressed subdued approval of these efforts: "The lowly filling station: . . . Its bright lights, bewildering by reason of their number, have been and still are the despair of city planners and beautifiers. But now the 'clothesline' type of structure is passing in favor of the dignified Southern Colonial and Early American style . . . Now to be acceptable to a neighborhood, the station[s] have some claim to beauty . . . What we call the 'clothesline' type of station, that is, the type with fluttering banners strung all over the place, is passing away. Dealers are becoming convinced that such confused advertising does not bring results."[64]

But domestication was often brushed aside for commercial exhibitionism. Literal signs were eventually restrained, but filling station buildings themselves became the showiest of signs. *Architectural Record* voiced dismay: "Greek sheet metal temples, Dutch windmills, Chinese Pagodas, miniature French Castles, and dreams of Spain and England, have been scattered generously along streets and highways . . . The doubtful value of these structures is the purely negative quality that they don't offend. But they have lost their individual character. They have not been permitted to be what they are."[65]

Included in the August 1922 issue of the *American City* was a handsome photograph of a filling station, glistening after a rain. Tall columns supported globe lights at the perimeter of the pull-in area, and a small, vaguely classical temple with a domed roof sat in the middle, the pump islands to the left and right; the caption read, "A Pleasing and Practical Service Station in New Haven." That same year, Beacon Oil (later, Standard Oil of New Jersey) had introduced its "Watertown prototype," a gas station resembling a six-sided, domed classical temple with a simple sign of vintage appearance hanging from a post with a metal standard.[66] The motive behind these corporate efforts was twofold: a combination of public relations and public service.

In July 1923 *American Architect and the Architectural Review* lampooned the proliferation of filling stations masquerading as less-commercial structures with a cartoon showing a motorist stopping to question a top-hatted pedestrian who stands in front of several small temples and statuary. "No, stranger," says the gentleman, "that isn't our public library. In fact, it doesn't even belong to the town! That is our new gas station. See that dome on the roof? I paid for that." But such fancy architectural appropriation did not always appease the neighborhood. In Nashua, Iowa, citizens protested when plans for a new gas station revealed that the building would resemble a famous local church. *American Architect* editorialized on what it deemed an insidious trend: Commercial architecture "has had . . . no compunction in appropriating to its use . . . architectural symbols that for centuries have stood for definite things. Should not this be a matter of great regret, and is it not worthy of the serious thought of architects? In their hands is placed the keeping of the great traditions of architecture, to be perpetuated for all time or to be debauched and cheapened . . . [Commercial architecture, and filling stations specifically] warrant their own symbolism . . . and should not be decked out in forms that for ages have represented civic and religious dignity."[67]

Another problem with filling-station aesthetics was the once chronic excess of signs surrounding and adorning the structures. Because the owners of many of the early stations had no affiliation to a single oil company, they advertised all sorts of products and services. Sinclair Lewis captured the visual chaos in his 1919 novel *Free Air:* "The Red Trail Garage, which is also, according to various signs, the agency for Teal Car Best at the Test, Stonewall Tire Service Station, Sewing Machines and Binders Repaired, Dr. Hostrum the Veterinarian every Thursday, Gas Today 27 cents."[68]

Throughout the 1920s and 1930s, architects explored how to eliminate reckless advertising fanfare around stations and yet communicate from afar the nature of the business and its brand name. One outstanding example, near Santa Barbara, was the Barnsdall–Rio Grande gas station designed by Morgan, Walls & Clements in 1929 as the flagship of two oil companies: a two-story stucco tower, topped by a lantern, served as both the station building and a dynamic landmark visible from the highway. With its barrel tiles and cornice detailing, it radiated a romantic Hispanic aura that appealed to tourists and recent émigrés to California who had preconceived images of the place from books and films.

The station name was emblazoned on a graphic band halfway up the tower, making this landmark feature a sign. In addition, a second, pole-mounted sign, fashioned to resemble a miniature oil derrick, was placed near the road's edge. The gas station was, in fact, located adjacent to the company's primary drilling field.[69]

Santa Barbara's zeal to make itself an ideal city spread to the highways that led into town and, specifically, to combating a surfeit of roadside billboards and businesses cluttered with signs and banners. Beginning in the late 1920s, the city's Plans and Plantings Committee periodically gave competitive awards to those gas stations that were least offensive visually. Judges considered the style and placement of signs, as well as the application of colors. In its promotional literature, the committee proudly acknowledged that its competition had a national impact, with several Eastern and Midwestern states using it as a model. Not surprisingly, the Barnsdall–Rio Grande station won an award from the committee, which declared that the grounds of the establishment were "finely kept," relatively "free from signs," and had "all possible plantings put in."[70]

Reformers, rural preservationists, and promoters of town identity were particularly offended by businesses that sought the attention of motorists by means of tasteless signs advertising (for example) tourist cabins, barbecue dinners, or souvenirs. Once again, Santa Barbara was held up as a model for civic improvement—this time because it campaigned to eliminate visual debris that detracted from the appearance of the main approaches to the city. Among Santa Barbara's most zealous reformers was Pearl Chase, who patrolled the highways and documented offensive structures and signs in order to subject them to public ridicule. The proactive stance of this city inspired other communities to take steps against unrestricted erection of signboards and filling stations. This often took the form of zoning along state highways to prevent the erection of outdoor billboards and piecemeal development such as refreshment stands and automotive services.[71]

Despite these efforts, signs termed unattractive or visually offensive proliferated along America's highways. Particularly noticeable were those posted to attract tourists seeking overnight lodgings. By 1926 more than fifty-three hundred "auto camps" existed; eight years later, that figure had tripled.[72] The earliest units were spartan because proprietors, fearful of damage and theft, were reluctant to invest much in their fledgling businesses. When oil companies urged the construction of up-to-date cabins alongside gas stations, many station operators purchased prefabricated cottages that were graced with domestic touches such as gabled roofs and flower boxes on windowsills.[73]

Too many roadside businesses survived by promising much and delivering very little. No doubt this was because many of the owners were farmers whose lands were now bounded by busy highways; they reasoned that a modest roadside business might deliver income more consistently than their crops did. Often these enterprises' decorative facades gave a misleading impression of what stood behind them. As cultural historian Daniel Bluestone observed, "The assemblage of signs created a commercial aesthetic obscuring the meager architecture; the forms and designs aimed to convey quickly a sense of plenty."[74] Or, as the novelist Sinclair Lewis wrote, "In most all these small towns you go into a place—well outside it's got a big fine illuminated electric sign with 'Eats' or something like that on it, so you think it's going to be a snappy up-to-date joint, but you get in and find it's run by some retired farmer and his daughter and the old woman."[75] The *New York Times* commented on this theme as well: "Some long-range motorists . . . they are rolling along and they hate to stop rolling. So the roadside is cluttered with beckoning signs by day and glittering with arresting lights by night. All the places of this type are alike as all the peas in a peck, from Maine to Florida, from New York to San Francisco."[76]

Early highway architecture and signs are perhaps best understood not by examining each artifact along the road but by considering them as a collective phenomenon. Certainly, motion was essential to the experience. In general, the highway was visually dazzling, even if the specific structures and signs were, more often than not, crass and tawdry. Beginning in the 1930s, America's automobile culture evolved, and with it the look of the landscape on either side of its highways. Little by little, the primitive would become professionalized.

American commercial architecture and signs of the 1920s were dramatically different from that of the past due to the influence of a surge in media consumption and skyrocketing use of the automobile. The cornucopia of images on the big screen, advertisements, and magazine articles encouraged a taste for the exotic at the same time that model cities like Santa Barbara were flaunting their successes in controlling excess. Meanwhile, affordable autos gave almost everyone access to new worlds, and architecture left the confines of the urban site, free to take on new forms.

The new motion-picture theaters grew to become anomalies along Main Street; they were no longer modified storefronts but true palaces, surging upward and outward, distinct and identifiable if only by girth and height. Most signs along America's commercial thoroughfares were still at odds with the buildings, especially the grandiose vertical electric signs for theaters and many major stores. They appeared to be designed for the scale of the street and the character and competition of the neighborhood rather than for the buildings to which they were attached. The signs were landmarks, visible from many blocks down the straight American streets. A few architects, like John Eberson, made successful early attempts to reconcile the great vertical sign with the theater front and increasingly heavy horizontal marquee. Signs of the 1920s, in most cases, had become an accretion of ideas and styles from previous decades rendered at greater and greater scale. They were eclectic composites, not unlike the great movie palaces.

Santa Barbara aimed for an ideal civic aesthetic, and its architects explored, in renderings, how whole streets could look with arcades and towers applied judiciously. There, city codes mandated a Hispanic appearance for all architecture in the old center, and highly publicized competitions promoted that look. On New York's Fifth Avenue, merchants chose to enforce an ideal image of their location, just as Santa Barbara did, but by eliminating the undesirable rather than encouraging participation in a specific design vision. They reinforced the concept of this important commercial corridor as a place, even as a political entity within the greater city, by legally excluding projecting and roof-mounted electric signs as "eyesores." Many cities across the country followed suit by banishing such signage outright.

By the end of the 1920s, commercial architecture, in many cases, was responding to the new speed and space that came with the growing use of automobiles. The decade was notable for its horizontality, for commercial buildings stretched to have maximum visual exposure along the road and convenient roll-up access. Architects and sign designers worked more aggressively and wisely to establish a consistent appearance for the signs and the architecture of chain businesses. Both building and lettering assumed a distinct, trademark look. Because of its unusually rapid development and awkwardly adolescent growth pains among commercial enterprises, the filling station was the greatest target for discussion and reform during the decade. Designers of stations faced the challenge of creating more efficient, less offensive identification on tiny buildings that were neither comically exotic nor inappropriately domestic.

The conflict between sign and architecture in an urban context, demonstrated in immense vertical signs and aggressive ornamentation on even modest commercial buildings, was resolved to some extent as development moved out to the vast reaches of the city's periphery. In suburbia, signs and architecture shared the same new space, space in which to stretch, even to leave the surface of the building, if necessary, as a pole sign (especially for filling stations). On the highway or suburban arterial, the commercial building was increasingly becoming the sign; that is, the architecture was no longer a neutral urban facade on which identity was affixed but rather a business-specific envelope that communicated name, if not purpose. Like the famous Western false-fronts, it was often more show than substance, a very thin layer between the public and private realm. The only difference was that the skin now often—although not always—contoured to three dimensions.[77] Although building design contributed progressively more to business identification, conventional signs remained essential, though rather clumsy, adjuncts to each site. Only in the 1930s would all the disparate pieces of commercial design be visually coordinated, if not physically unified.

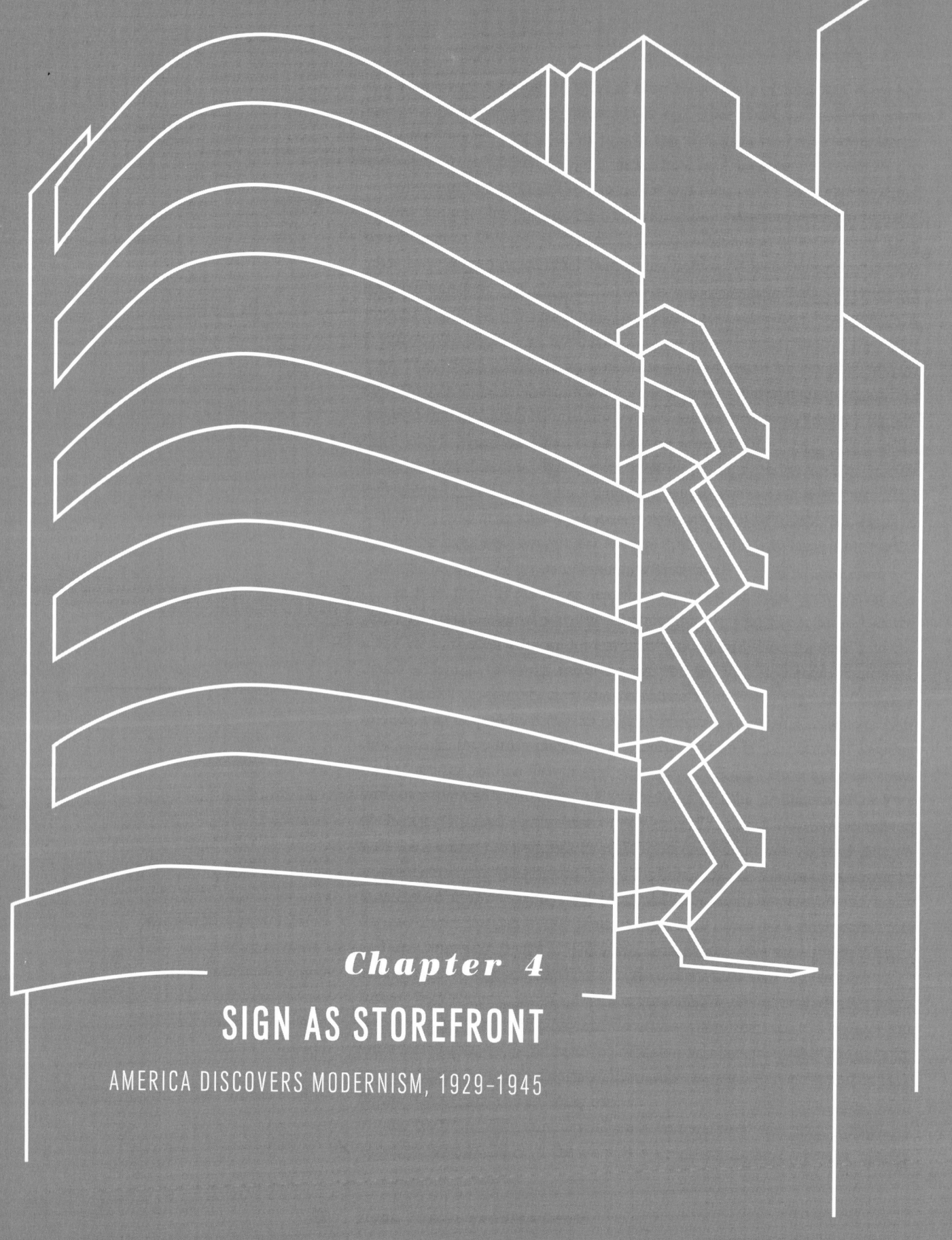

Chapter 4
SIGN AS STOREFRONT
AMERICA DISCOVERS MODERNISM, 1929–1945

IN THE 1930S, American architects and designers began to reconsider the purpose of the storefront and, as a result, radically altered its appearance. This stylistic evolution occurred during a period of increasing suburbanization, as the focus of commercial architecture shifted from confined urban sites and continuous street walls to undeveloped open spaces. Shop fronts of the nineteenth and early twentieth centuries relegated signs primarily to the fascia and parapet. But by the 1930s, designers carefully considered the advertising potential of the entire storefront or building facade. Eventually, they would manipulate those facades as one might strategically arrange the elements of a poster. Because architects were increasingly involved in sign design, they ensured that graphics coordinated with the size, placement, and style of the door and windows, as well as with the colors and textures of the facade. Trade journals and specialty books coached sign designers to be more aware of building design in their work. At times, a true visual continuity developed in facade design, uniting graphic and architectural elements in one continuous skin.

A subsequent development in storefront evolution was the reduction of the barrier between inside and outside. This design breakthrough began in urban locations, where storefronts lined up against the sidewalk. Designers sought to interrupt the once continuous plane of the street wall. What had been flat became figural. Distinctive parapets, major projecting signs, tower features, and freestanding showcases reached well beyond rooftops and out into the public passageway. Arcades—the covered exterior lobby spaces that permitted more store display windows leading up to the entrance door— became quite large, penetrating deep into stores. As retail establishments, restaurants, hotels, and theaters moved from the tight urban core to the open space of the suburbs and rural areas, commercial buildings became progressively more figural, taking on sometimes striking and memorable forms.

Four primary phenomena triggered these changes. The first was the unprecedented economic downturn of the 1930s, which prompted land values to nosedive. The overabundance of square footage in city centers resulting from investment splurges of the 1920s rendered many buildings valueless above their first floors. If any new construction was undertaken during the early years of the Great Depression, it was for single-story taxpayers. The focus, in general, turned to ground-floor retail frontage; remodeling existing first-floor facades generated the greatest return on an investment. Subtlety was not the order of the day when attempting to persuade customers that Main Street was still alive and worth visiting. The *National Real*

Estate Journal, and other trade publications, presented many before-and-after triumphs, quoting eye-popping leaps in rental rates to go with the eye-popping visual transformations.[1]

The next of the four phenomena prompting design changes was technological and economic in nature: the pressure generated by large American corporations eager to sell their building products during this period of economic stagnation. New or newly evolved, improved products like neon tubing, porcelain enamel, and an expanding palette of pigmented structural glass were promoted everywhere to pump up rents and retail sales. Advertisement claims such as "39% Occupancy to 72% with the help of Vitrolite" proved persuasive. The other two primary forces that generated sweeping visual change during the 1930s were design-based: the influence of commercial graphic and architectural experimentation from Europe and the emergence of the industrial designer in America. To emulate the holistic design of Europe, a new approach to creating innovative storefronts was essential. Designers of this period pushed past the boundaries traditionally assumed for their professions, a change that smoothed the lines between graphic and building design. Architects of the early twentieth century were adept at lettering and graphic layout—two basic sign-making skills that extended their artistic range beyond building design.

At the same time, there were forces reining in the potential exuberance of progressive graphic design. In the 1940s, architects, realizing their potential power to determine the appearance of signs placed on their buildings, began to propose uniform, muted graphics for small storefronts to reduce the perceived clutter of the commercial corridor. This became attractive especially with the rise of coordinated retail ensembles. Hard times also limited graphic development, as many businesses were forced to update old storefronts with modest new signs rather than full facade makeovers, leaving architects out of the picture. Sign makers, however, maintained a position of great importance on Main Street throughout this period.

Importing Integration: Learning from Modern European Shop Fronts

Although master architects such as Daniel H. Burnham and Louis Sullivan were skillfully integrating signs with facades as early as the 1910s, it was not until the late 1920s that American storefront designers truly began to reexamine the potential for unified storefronts. European influence stimulated this creative revolution. In the 1920s, French architects such as René Herbst published folios of inventive new European shop designs that would quickly inspire their American counterparts. The commercial savvy of Parisian designers and the city's spectacular imagery were both particularly impressive. Dutch architect Theo van Doesburg wrote of his impressions of the city to J. J. P. Oud in 1930: "Those who have not seen Paris at work have

Figure 43
Hotchkiss Automobile Dealership (Michon & Pigé, circa 1927; altered), Place de la Porte Champerret, Paris, circa 1929. In this influential early modern design, Michon & Pigé stretched the sign graphics the full width of the storefront, foreshadowing the streamline moderne aesthetic of the late 1930s.

RENÉ HERBST, *NOUVELLES DEVANTURES ET AGENCEMENTS DE MAGASINS*, 5TH SERIES (N.D.), PLATE 13. REPRODUCTION COURTESY OF RYERSON AND BURNHAM LIBRARIES, ART INSTITUTE OF CHICAGO.

a mistaken conception of the noise and movement and advertising...When I left Brussels and was riding in the tram in the dark to Gare du Midi, I was struck just as here by the tremendous role advertising plays in the cityscape ... The facades of the department stores are at present nothing but outside business cards, behind which the architectural picture is lost (which is just as well!)"[2]

Parisian design also impressed American designers. Ely Jacques Kahn, one of the most successful commercial architects in the United States during New York's skyscraper boom of the 1920s, was quoted about this trend in the *Architectural Forum:* "American design in architecture maintains the last bulwark of Classicism... [but in Europe] public interest in the latest design is keen; and Europe has quickly realized that there is profit in smart and forward-looking facades... Paris... in the shop at least, has maintained a leadership in smartness and brilliance that in turn has affected Germany and led to increased excellence... [These Paris shops]... seem alive, interesting, brilliant, chatty possibly... the exteriors have recently been rebuilt so as to obtain the advantages of large sheets of glass and interesting illumination."[3]

Two quotes by members of the American sign industry from *Signs of the Times* in the early 1930s reveal a similar admiration for new developments in Europe: "Sometimes European stores carry no exterior sign whatsoever, but the unique construction of the facade itself acts as a mute sign."[4] "The one characteristic that pleased me most when I first began to look closely at European electrical advertising was the great attention that is paid to making

(opposite) *Figure 44*
Kopp & Joseph Shop (A. Korn and S. Weitzmann, 1928; demolished), Berlin, circa 1929. Among the design advancements on display were the large expanse of glass and a display case that jutted out on to the sidewalk, both gestures eliminating the barrier between inside and out, and thus forecasting the thrust of storefront design in the 1940s.
MODERNE LADENBAUTEN (1928), 79. REPRODUCTION COURTESY OF RYERSON AND BURNHAM LIBRARIES, ART INSTITUTE OF CHICAGO.

Figure 45
André Hunebelle Glass Showroom (Lévêque, 1929; altered), Rue de la Boétie, Paris. This was one of the most influential early modern storefronts because of its architectural simplicity; its handsome, chaste, dimensional ribbon lettering style; and the generous scale of the graphics.
PHOTO BY THÉRÈSE BONNEY, 1929. COURTESY OF THE BANCROFT LIBRARY, UNIVERSITY OF CALIFORNIA, BERKELEY. REPRODUCTION COURTESY OF RYERSON AND BURNHAM LIBRARIES, ART INSTITUTE OF CHICAGO.

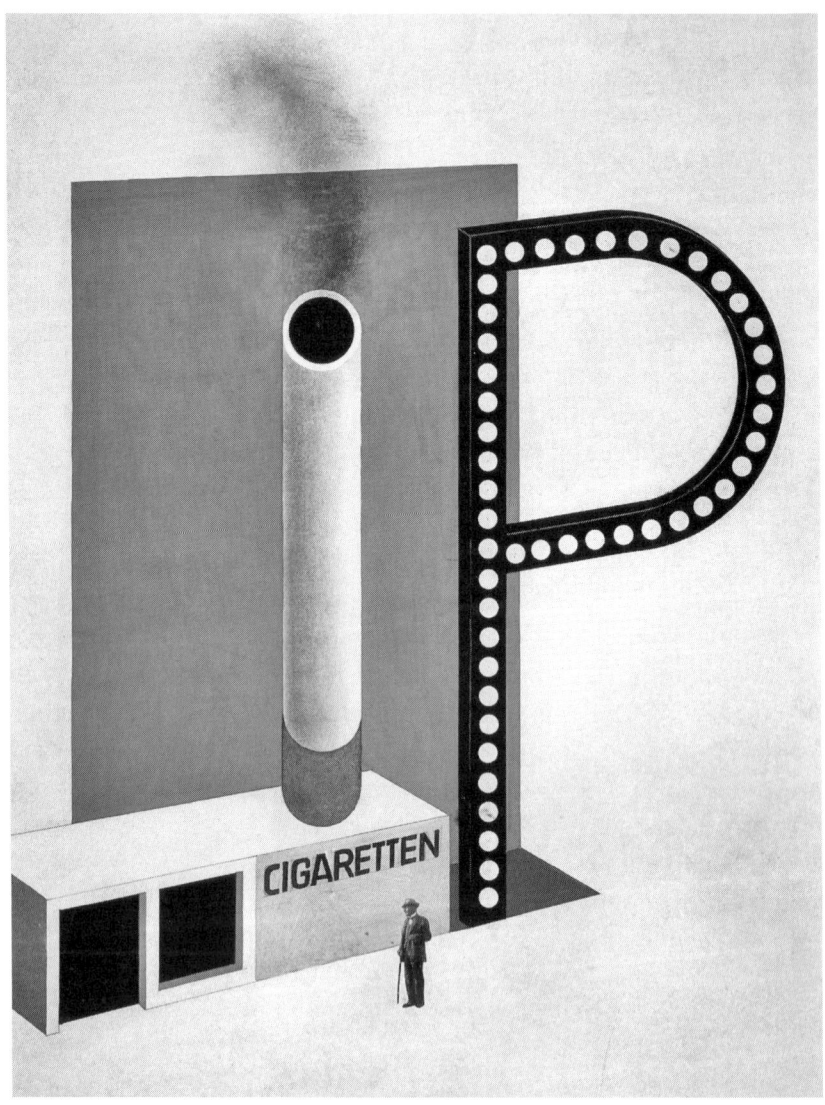

Figure 46

Design for kiosk to sell cigarette brand P (Herbert Bayer, 1924). With unashamed use of electricity, scale, and color, this bold, three-dimensional conceptual piece demonstrated well the European embrace of advertising and storefront design potential.

BAUHAUS-ARCHIV, BERLIN / ARTISTS RIGHTS SOCIETY (ARS), NEW YORK.

signs beautiful, individually different, and well finished. This characteristic is inherited from almost centuries of craftsmanship in the sign industry."[5]

European shop designers had blurred the line between what was the "sign" and what was the "architecture." Instead of merely adding the identification as an afterthought, the entire surface of the commercial establishment was one complete composition; no longer was lettering confined to its traditional location on the fascia board just above the shop windows. In fact, the slim fascia band, which had survived through the 1910s from classical architectural construction, almost disappeared from European shop front design by the mid-1920s. Instead, the identification of a business might appear anywhere on the surface of a commercial building. New business facades, often applied to existing urban buildings like thin skins on the lower stories, now extended well beyond the sills of the second-level windows. *Signs of the*

Times applauded how "the outstanding characteristic of electrical advertising in Europe is the simple and effective manner in which it blends with the exterior architecture."[6]

In their publications, French architects like René Herbst and L. P. Sézille emphasized Parisian work but also included some of the best examples from urban centers beyond France—particularly those from Germany, Holland, Belgium, and Czechoslovakia. Just one of many published examples of new retail design, the Hotchkiss auto dealership (Michon & Pigé, circa 1927) in Paris was remarkable for its squared and horizontally stretched lettering placed between graphic bands; these vertically compressed letters positioned near (though extending well beyond) the traditional location of old-fashioned fascia signs appeared as if they were almost supporting the load of the wall above. A silhouette of an automobile, stretched like the lettering, was the graphic on the lower band; the extreme horizontal proportion of the composition implied speed (fig. 43).[7] Pavilions for department stores had been the recipients of advanced design at the highly influential Exposition Internationale des Arts Décoratifs et Industriels Modernes in Paris in 1925; retail projects were major forerunners for the modern movement, providing plenty of copy for architecture and graphic journals.[8]

The American architectural and sign-trade press regularly reported on developments concerning Parisian and European commercial facades, as did General Electric's the *Magazine of Light*. J. J. P. Oud's Café de Unie (1924) in Rotterdam attracted particular attention because of its unique full-facade composition, unusual materials, and ample lettering. This was the most dramatic example yet of blurring the line between graphic and facade design, with lettering placed nowhere near the traditional fascia zone. In 1928, the *American Architect* highlighted the commercial architecture revolution in Europe, stressing the expanded use of glass in storefronts. The glass could be continuous from first story through second, or it might virtually wrap the full width of the store.[9] The Kopp & Joseph shop in Berlin by A. Korn and S. Weitzmann (1928) offered an extraordinary glass front with a display case that projected from within the enormous void of the shop entrance out into the street, by perhaps ten feet (fig. 44); *Architectural Record* published images of the shop in 1929, foreshadowing trends for extending the space of the store beyond its traditional boundaries, a movement that would begin in earnest in the United States in the 1940s. A few months earlier, the same journal enthusiastically described the Parisian glassware shop of André Hunebelle (by Lévêque), with its distinctive vertical sans-serif lettering composed of deep vertical strips of metal, with the sharp, thin edge facing forward (fig. 45). The article noted that the shop was striking because of the elongated letters.[10] Many designers emulated the ribbon lettering of André Hunebelle, making variations on this uncomplicated facade treatment elsewhere in Europe and eventually the United States.[11]

Europe offered not only a new look but also a new approach to design for Americans to follow. The English arts and crafts tradition, which emphasized the importance of a single person or a closely allied team controlling all facets of a project, influenced how European shop fronts were designed. Likewise, the Bauhaus movement, which originated in Germany, inspired continental and, eventually, American commercial architects and graphic designers to cross boundaries and approach all design comprehensively. Bauhaus graphic designer and architect Herbert Bayer was a perfect example of the multidisciplinary artist. In the mid-1920s, he designed a series of kiosks and commercial pavilions that appeared to embrace the spectacle of advertising, a novelty to high-style American designers, who typically shunned graphics. One kiosk advertised cigarettes with a giant three-dimensional reproduction of the product on the roof, alongside an equally immense trademark capital P in lights (fig. 46). Like his other creations, it was a minimalist composition of key icons with brightly colored panels. The Russian constructivists were also multidisciplinary artists who embraced graphic communication. They often incorporated signs and symbols in their sculptures, kiosks, and structures—but with the goal of communicating political messages, not commercial ones.[12] Nevertheless, their work received a great deal of coverage by the design press in America.

European influence came to America in a variety of ways. Many of America's most successful architects between the world wars were trained in Europe, specifically at the École des Beaux-Arts in Paris, where both drawing and the art of lettering were emphasized. Eventually, American architecture schools imported the structure and curriculum of the École. Architects who became commercially successful in America in the 1930s either had the good fortune of attending the École des Beaux-Arts in Paris directly (as did Stiles O. Clements of Los Angeles or Ely Jacques Kahn of New York) or studied at one of its American "offshoots," like Chicago's Armour Institute (later the Illinois Institute of Technology).[13] Other leading commercial architects in the United States during the 1930s had emigrated from Vienna, Berlin, or Zurich, where multidisciplinary design was common practice.

American architects who visited Europe grew confident of their graphic abilities and could compose persuasive presentation boards for their design critiques. Throughout the 1930s, *Architecture* magazine published extensive portfolios of architectural lettering and commercial signs—examples from the field intended to inspire and instruct. Within the pages of *Pencil Points*, readers would find articles devoted to the history of various typefaces and the rules for correct execution. *Architectural Record* carried similar pieces, although less frequently.

By the early 1930s, portfolios of lettering on buildings in the United States displayed in stateside architecture journals included many examples of the "European look." Some journals were also quick to publish examples from abroad. A 1930 issue of *Architectural Record* included specifications and drawings with dimensions and notes for the advanced signage shown in photographs. It was a veritable how-to for architects to jump in and get aggressively involved with lettering on storefronts, and it suggested the possibilities for the new medium of neon.[14] The sign industry, too, welcomed the novelty of new graphic and architectural forms, notable examples of which appeared in *Signs of the Times*.[15] Visually hungry American designers looked eagerly for guidance and reference as they attempted new layout techniques and advanced letterforms. In big cities, their inspiration might come by way of work completed locally by designers who had recently immigrated.[16] For most, new books on lettering and a steady stream of articles on the new look published in *Signs of the Times* delivered inspiration. Two of the most remarkable images presented in the trade journal were of posters by Austrians Joseph Binder, who immigrated to the United States in 1935, and Ernst Ludwig Franke, whose example suggested depth and dynamic movement with concentric airbrushed rings and angled, abstract figures. Of Binder's work, the magazine declared, "Every single line is well considered, every superfluous ornamentation avoided."[17] It is notable that even at this early date, the sign press had joined modernist architects in praising the banishment of "superfluous ornament."

By the late 1920s, American graphic designers were beginning to adopt features of the European style. Even rudimentary design manuals promoted the principles of European modernism. In a 1927 publication for the sign industry, *Modern Ornament and Design,* the American author wrote: "The arrangement of lettering in a design and the constructional appearance of the design as a whole are far more important than the exact construction of each individual letter or part ... Unity binds the various parts of a composition together in style and character; in other words, the grouping of all the elements should appear as one properly related mass."[18]

Other writers were now emphasizing the importance of dynamic layout and clarity in American commercial art. Rejecting the practice of including as much text and image in an advertisement as possible, the new approach stressed the benefits of white space. Graphics were now meant to flow, to be the result of a clear idea, rather than simply to be a list of points supplied by the client.[19] In the late 1920s, the modern approach slowly gained ground on several fronts: book design, editorial design for fashion and business magazines catering to the affluent, and promotional and corporate graphics. By the 1930s, many young Americans first saw modernistic design in the pages of *Advertising Arts* in their school libraries. Throughout the 1930s, the Museum of Modern Art gave respectability to the new look with a series of exhibitions. But America was a reluctant customer for modern design; even as the fresh movement became apparent, traditionalism in American graphics lingered.[20]

In 1940, the *Architectural Forum* proclaimed the preceding ten years the Design Decade, recognizing how important good design had been to saving the 1930s from economic ruin. It was a period that recognized the invaluable contributions of industrial designers such as Norman Bel Geddes, Raymond Loewy, Walter Dorwin Teague, Henry Dreyfuss, and Donald Deskey, who rethought commonplace objects. In many ways, these men were America's counterparts to the multidisciplinary, holistic designers of the Bauhaus. Although these professionals lacked the academic credentials of architects, the accomplishments of industrial designers eventually earned the respect of leaders in that field, as well as those designing graphics, fashion, and advertisements. Industrial designers' emphasis on surface appearance energized a movement in the 1930s to reconsider merchandising techniques. By conceiving of shops as machines for selling and as opportunities to expedite the process of acquiring goods and services, they prompted eventual changes in storefront design—specifically, the blending of sign and facade into a new and effective form of advertising.

Minimizing the difference between sign and facade in America was challenging. In the 1920s, signs had become increasingly cumbersome attachments to storefronts, and their awkward appearance suggested two disciplines—architecture and sign making—operating quite independently of each other. Now it was time for experts in both professions to work together. Their mission was obvious: "The greatest difficulty to the display designer is the gear-work which holds the display in place. This consists, in general cases, of guy wires, angle irons, conduits, etc. To do away with the appearance that the display was an afterthought and merely stuck on the building in any convenient spot, by providing a casing, in which the hanging appurtenances are concealed, is extremely effective."[21]

But merely hiding the unsightly electrical and structural works was hardly the entire solution. It was imperative that architects become more involved. In response to an article in the *American Architect* titled "Uncontrolled Signs Mar Buildings," an art director from an electrical-products company in Kansas City wrote, "The practice of the sign manufacturer to plaster his product upon buildings will continue until the architect gets wise to himself and calls on the proper type of sign men to help him with his problem... The present vogue of installing attractive and novel storefronts has given design-minded men a big play. Storefronts of today are enlarged displays, full of color and advertising value... Signs should be planned for from the beginning."[22]

Signs of the Times celebrated that architects had finally become sign conscious. Commercial architect Horace Ginsbern, later famous for his Chock Full o' Nuts coffee shops and Hanscom Bakeries in New York, wrote in the journal, "No longer does [the architect] regard the sign as a mere necessity to the store front, but he regards the effective display of the name of the store as an integral part of the store front design. A store front, properly designed, achieves good advertising value in merchandise display and name display within a unified design."[23]

The General Electric Company encouraged architects to employ lighting in their designs as often as possible, to create with light as they did with bricks and steel. "Fascia signs may be a part of the building façade or the shop front: projecting signs may grow gracefully from the wall: and roof signs may be made an integral and fitting crown. Usually in the past the architect has either been given no opportunity to participate in the design of the signs that are used on the building he erected, or has deliberately chosen to give no consideration to what has in our day become a necessary business facility."[24]

Several professional responsibilities were significantly redefined in the 1930s, setting the stage for increasingly comprehensive design. For example, the role of the "paste-up artist" had evolved into that of the "graphic designer," a specialist who, in addition to executing lettering and illustration, conceived of projects and oversaw their execution, start to finish. Similarly, the sign-shop "sketch artist" became, in many larger companies, the "sign designer," or even the "art director," an individual aesthetically sensitive to the necessity of beautifying buildings and working with the architecture.[25]

As a result of these changes in the 1930s, sign designers became involved in facade design. To promote collaboration between specialists, *Signs of the Times* urged architects to confer with sign-company art directors at the beginning of the design process.

Main Street Modernism: European Design in America

Buildings that reflected contemporary European architectural styles began to appear along the commercial corridors of major American cities in the late 1920s and early 1930s. Some of the first of these were created in Los Angeles by Austrian and German design émigrés J. R. Davidson, Rudolph Schindler, and Kem Weber. The *Los Angeles Times* referred to this phenomenon as "the invasion of the 1930 influence of modernism."

> A period of transition is apparent on every hand. The fancy seems to have struck the business section, especially, to be rid of the gingerbread type of structure that was the vogue forty years ago. In the principal business block of the city . . . every business structure on both sides of the block has undergone radical remodeling of front and general appearance during the last twelve months.[26]

Until the last two years the question "What is modern architecture?" troubled few heads on this Pacific Coast. But now, with raw-looking

(opposite) **Figure 47**
Maddux Air Lines office (Feil & Paradise and Jock Peters, 1928; demolished), South Olive Street, Los Angeles, circa 1929. This building is one of the earliest examples in the United States of engaging an entire facade for its advertising potential and designing each feature to coordinate to a unified and greater whole.
MOTT/MERGE COLLECTION, CALIFORNIA HISTORY SECTION, CALIFORNIA STATE LIBRARY.

monstrosities of form and color jumping up overnight on our very best buildings, the question is making itself heard on all sides.[27]

A modern storefront executed in downtown Los Angeles for Maddux Air Lines vividly demonstrated the early influence of modern European design on the West Coast (fig. 47). Created in 1928 by Feil & Paradise, a firm best known for its interior design, the one-and-a-half story structure located on Olive Street looked incongruous next to the taller and older buildings. Over the entrance was a large and vaguely cubistic pattern of rectangles, rendered in metal bars. The name of the business was spelled out in metal within this fragmented, modern grid. The entire composition was placed over frosted glass above the display windows and set within a square void in the smooth stucco facade. The asymmetrical stacking of rectangles in the metal graphic continued in relief and in paint on the stucco of the parapet above the glass. Details like the door handle carried the rectangular-metal-bar pattern down into the lower storefront. There was a conceptual unity to all parts, with continuity of pattern and form across the surface. At the upper right of the parapet, an airplane sculpted in relief emphasized the identity of the business, as if it were a corporate icon or a jazz-age version of the object sign of the Middle Ages. A projecting vertical electric sign, fastened near the plane, was the only jarring feature in that it recalled storefront designs of the 1920s with its somewhat awkward, angular attachment. Everything else about the building presaged the smooth continuity of the future.

J. R. Davidson produced considerably more modern commercial designs during this period in Los Angeles than Feil & Paradise did. His facade for the Hi-Hat Restaurant (1930), one of several storefronts he designed in the modern manner for a French Renaissance–style retail building by Morgan, Walls & Clements (1929) on Wilshire Boulevard, seamlessly connected modest vertical projecting signs at each end of an elaborate, modern fascia sign—the freestanding letters of which were backlit (fig. 48). Davidson unified the full-length sign with the windows below by making it subtly project over and around the window frame. His sign design was so successful that the owners retained it even when the restaurant was changed, years later, to Sardi's and then to Perino's. A store in downtown Los Angeles called the Fair copied the sign concept almost exactly. Two other Davidson commercial fronts from this period included the Bachelor's Men's Shop (1931) and the Laura Lee store (1932). For Bachelor's, Davidson used so much glass for the facade that the bulkhead (the threshold beneath the front display windows) was almost nonexistent. There was also no back wall to the window display, which opened the storefront considerably to the outside. This was a foreshadowing of the open-fronted trend in retail design of the 1940s. Simultaneous to this refined storefront work, Davidson prepared a remarkable proposal for a "drive-in curb" supermarket (1931), featuring an ambitious three-

Figure 48
The Hi-Hat Restaurant (J. R. Davidson, 1930; demolished), Wilshire Boulevard, Los Angeles. The architect fashioned not only the equivalent of a three-dimensional wall sign but also an integrated projecting vertical sign that could be spotted from down the street. The identity system was also part of the window framing—nothing appeared as if it were added at a later date.
ARCHITECTURAL RECORD (SEPTEMBER 1930), 237. REPRODUCTION COURTESY OF RYERSON AND BURNHAM LIBRARIES, ART INSTITUTE OF CHICAGO.

dimensional cage tower with neon letters. A massive, continuous, internally illuminated canopy/marquee stepped down from the parapet over the heads of entering customers; the market advertised its wares on this opal glass marquee as a cinema would its stars. This was an architect who relished the opportunity to identify his clients with graphics.

Where J. R. Davidson's storefront designs anticipated a look that would be increasingly in demand, those of Rudolph Schindler and Kem Weber were often so daringly experimental that only a few of their commercial projects were completed. As early as 1916, Schindler proposed an advanced concept for a series of Chicago commercial fronts that relied solely upon the graphic lettering in a continuous sign band to differentiate one establishment from the next. His facade for Sardi's (1932) in Hollywood was remarkable for the depth created with receding and projecting planes and the shadows formed by the bright California light (fig. 49). Unique lettering, angular and architectural, fitted perfectly in the grid of the plane that supported the marquee over the entrance. Schindler's design of a Vine Street location for the Lindy's restaurant chain, a proposal that was not ultimately realized (1932), foreshadowed the use of projecting "fins" and towers in the late 1930s and early 1940s to identify businesses from afar with integrated graphics. A series of stacked horizontal "speed lines" placed along the vertical sign served to unify the tower visually with the predominantly horizontal architecture below (fig. 50). Kem Weber worked successfully producing fairly restrained store exteriors for clients Barker Brothers and Sommer and Kaufmann, but he also explored exceptionally fluid, almost kinetic, street fronts for Paramount Studio sets and other unbuilt stores. Like Davidson, he took on the challenge of addressing the quickly evolving California drive-in building type—this time a restaurant—but the schemes remained only conceptual.[28]

During this same period, architects on the East Coast and in Chicago were also introducing European modernism to commercial corridors. In the late 1920s, the rich patterns and classical symmetry of French art deco characterized many East Coast business establishments without radically

Figure 49

Sardi's Restaurant (Rudolph Schindler, 1932; altered), Hollywood Boulevard, Hollywood, California, in 1933. Schindler carefully integrated a unique, architectural lettering style within the facade's module system. Though very graphic, the facade was truly a three-dimensional composition of planes at various levels and orientations.

RUDOLPH M. SCHINDLER COLLECTION, ARCHITECTURE AND DESIGN COLLECTION, UNIVERSITY ART MUSEUM, UNIVERSITY OF CALIFORNIA, SANTA BARBARA.

Figure 50
Proposal for Lindy's Restaurant on Vine Street, Los Angeles (Rudolph Schindler, 1932). A series of stacked horizontal "speed lines" placed along this early fin sign served to visually unify the tower with the predominantly horizontal architecture below.
RUDOLPH M. SCHINDLER COLLECTION, ARCHITECTURE AND DESIGN COLLECTION, UNIVERSITY ART MUSEUM, UNIVERSITY OF CALIFORNIA, SANTA BARBARA.

altering conventional architectural composition. Traditional symmetry continued to rule most storefront design for a time. Chain restaurants, such as automat Horn & Hardart in the early 1930s, presented facades that were almost theatrical—as flamboyant as many motion-picture palaces of the late 1920s, complete with marquees above the entrances. In 1930, the *Magazine of Light* praised one Philadelphia branch of Horn & Hardart for demonstrating an effective whole between sign, architectural lighting, and facade design.[29]

In New York, Viennese-born Joseph Urban excelled at designing fluid, progressive facades for theaters or storefronts. He also demonstrated a command of all aspects of design, a multidisciplinary talent often associated with the English arts and crafts movement or the Bauhaus.[30] Soon after immigrating to the United States in 1912, Urban began designing theaters for producer Florenz Ziegfeld.[31] His solution for the problematic exit staircases for the Reinhardt Theater (1927) was to convert them into unique ornamental features of the facade. Urban told the *American Architect* in 1928 that any modernist building should be "the sandwich board of the owner." In other words, the architecture itself could advertise a business or service. His design for Bedell's (1928), a women's clothing store on 34th Street in New York City, turned the entire front of the building into an extended window display. Instead of identifying the store by name, Urban chose to convey the nature and status of this retail enterprise by means of the building's shimmering facade, with its ornate nickel grill, and the products tastefully arranged behind glass.[32]

Urban's East Coast contemporaries designed large, plain facades of distinctive, often rich materials devoid of patterns and textures. Walter Dorwin Teague's Kodak showroom (1931) was notably simple in design. Teague suggested continuity between display area and the exterior lobby with a continuous lighted opal glass ceiling. Above the arcade entrance was the store's name in simple metal ribbon lettering on black granite.[33] The design simplicity of the extensively published Hunebelle glassware shop in Paris may have inspired Teague's design decisions. The Hunebelle store may also have influenced the similarly simple facade of the Loft Restaurant (Thompson & Churchill, 1929), in New York, which also placed large ribbon letters against a black marble background. The Loft facade was remarkable for its opal glass projecting signs that flanked the entrance, carefully integrated to tie in with the opal glass panels lined with chrome strips running over the display windows and placed on the ceiling of the entrance. J. R. Davidson's Hi-Hat in Los Angeles would incorporate similar blade sign features as part of its fully integrated facade. These architects were leaving nothing to chance; others would heap no last-minute wall or projecting signs onto their facades if they addressed all identity needs.

The New York architect Vahan Hagopian designed perhaps the most European and highly touted of the new, spare, modern storefronts of the eastern United States. The stores that he created for the London Character Shoe and A. S. Beck Shoes chains captured generous attention in the press. For the Newark store created for London Character Shoe, Hagopian employed the metal ribbon lettering popularized by the Hunebelle shop (fig. 51). The architect was also indebted to this European design in the way that his backlit lettering ran the full width of the display window and rested within a recessed panel that seemed almost a part of this aperture; thus, architectural and graphic features were fully united.[34] Hagopian added an important variation to this Parisian-style scheme, however; from a continuous illuminated canopy along the crest of the elevation, a cascade of neon poured down, spilling into the recessed entrance. This was a direct visual cue to lead the customer inside, almost as literally as a spotlit arrow might convey.

Commenting in 1930 on Hagopian's recently completed New York City, Brooklyn, and Newark facades for London Character Shoe, *Architectural Record* claimed "the lines of the 'poster,' an integral part of the design, lead the eye to the entrance."[35] This was a clear declaration that the storefront architect was using the tools of the advertising artist or graphic designer.

(opposite) **Figure 51** London Character Shoe Store (Vahan Hagopian, 1930; altered), Broad Street, Newark, New Jersey. Borrowing the deep ribbon lettering seen at the Hunebelle shop in Paris, Hagopian's frequently published shoe store quickly spread the European principals of design integration and full use of facade for advertising potential. ARCHITECTURAL RECORD (FEBRUARY 1930), 139. REPRODUCTION COURTESY OF RYERSON AND BURNHAM LIBRARIES, ART INSTITUTE OF CHICAGO.

Hagopian's Newark storefront was designed differently from the other two locations, but it shared key features and materials, like unpainted sheet aluminum facing, to unite the group as members of a family. Its six-inch-deep ribbon lettering made it unique, as the others were identified with flat, modernistic "Broadway"-style characters.[36] The Kinney's Shoes chain would soon spread this ribbon look to many cities in America, employing tall, back-lit letters of a thin profile (though not true ribbon letters) that also spanned the entire store width.[37]

Morris Lapidus's design for the Parisian Bootery (1928) on Manhattan's Fifth Avenue was another early example of how architecture could effectively draw customers into business establishments. The store's curved glass at the exterior lobby and eye-catching graphics would become hallmarks of this architect's style. Lapidus was particularly interested in creating sophisticated and powerful signage:

> Shortly after I began designing stores, I wandered into a bookstore that sold foreign magazines. I spotted one that gave me my first solid design element. The magazine was published in Germany and was called *Gebrauchsgraphik*. It was a magazine of graphics used for packaging, sign identification, and exhibits. It was like no magazine published in the United States. I immediately paid for a year's subscription and went on to receive this magazine for over ten years. I must admit that Europe was way ahead of us. I used the bold European graphics to create signs that identified my stores. My first little shoe store on Fifth Avenue used this type of lettering. Element number one in my store design became bold graphics.[38]

Designs by Lapidus would spread rapidly across America as he designed facades for the Mangel's clothing chain, working for the Ross-Frankel office beginning in 1930. The Mangel's storefronts usually carried all the way to the roof of the buildings in which they were housed, and large-scale lettering was carefully integrated with all other facade features.

The rapid growth of chain stores in America during the 1920s contributed significantly to the spread of modernism in commercial design during the 1930s. Chain stores could afford to invest in distinctive design by noted architects because the cost was distributed among many outlets. Building exact copies of trademarked facade design was rare at this time, however. Lapidus's work for Mangel's, for instance, was rarely duplicated verbatim from site to site. The architect experimented widely with variations on a particular look that incorporated bold squares and long bands of consistent colors; he even played around with the exact arrangement and relative scale of the unique lettering style chosen for the store. Facades for chains like Child's restaurant (architects John Corley Westervelt, William Van Alen,

and Dennison and Hirons, among others) and Schrafft's (architects Bloch and Hesse) eventually became consistently modern but individually unique, spreading the new look in design from the early 1930s. Consistent trademark lettering pulled the potentially disparate locations together as a family. At the same time, Raymond Loewy's design for Cushman's Bakery (1937) was eventually stamped out almost in duplicate for some 350 stores. A curved window and an antiseptic, white porcelain-enamel finish with gold trim created something of an icon, a building-as-logo that brought the streamlined modern look to many neighborhoods.[39]

Two architecture firms in Chicago were responsible for designing several of the most creative modern commercial buildings and storefronts in America, though neither spread modernism by way of chain duplication. One was Holabird & Root, whose storefront for the Walden Bookshop (1930)

Figure 52

Socatch Bakery and Walden Book Shop, Michigan Square Building (Holabird & Root, 1930; demolished), North Michigan Avenue, Chicago. Holabird & Root created inspired storefronts for the building it designed, including a frequently published facade for Walden Books. Instead of subsuming every store's identity to the building's restrained modernity, the firm explored a wide variety of possibilities for each business.

PHOTO BY HEDRICH-BLESSING, 1930. COURTESY OF THE CHICAGO HISTORY MUSEUM, HB-00346.

demonstrated the power of large-scale metal ribbon lettering.[40] Next to the bookstore, Holabird & Root covered the Socatch Bakery with a bold diagonal checkerboard of color that completely overwhelmed the subtle metal grid of lettering over the entrance glass (fig. 52). Only two years after its creation, a new tenant requested a less idiosyncratic design from the firm, indicating that American commerce was still somewhat averse to avant-garde design.

Another Chicago firm—that of George Fred Keck—created one of the most architecturally advanced retail structures in the nation. Its Miralago Ballroom building and shops (1930) on the city's North Shore was a freestanding retail strip with a flourish at one end, a functionally diverse yet visually cohesive commercial center (fig. 53). The first floor of store display windows was continuous glass, allowing the upper floor to appear as if it floated on pilotis, or slim columns (an effect reinforced by the cantilever at the end). On the second floor, a continuous ribbon-window of glass and coordinated panels, corresponding exactly to the height and placement of windows on the ballroom end, served to weave together the ensemble. The entrance to the ballroom was marked by projections forward and up from the lines established elsewhere. A vertical tower with a slim, integrated, projecting sign announced the building to motorists from a considerable distance. With its fully glazed, dematerialized first floor, ribbon windows above, crisp white stucco skin, and disciplined signage, the building might have well pleased the curators of the new show on International Style architecture at the Museum of Modern Art in New York.[41]

In 1932, architectural historian Henry-Russell Hitchcock and future architect Philip Johnson curated an exhibition for the Museum of Modern Art titled *The International Style: Architecture since 1922*, which included some key commercial projects. Their work placed judgment on both architecture and signs. Eventually various forms of this landmark project were displayed in thirty cities throughout the United States. Hitchcock and Johnson emphasized, by means of interpretive panels and brief captions, the importance of appropriate graphics on commercial buildings. This served as a call-to-arms for architects to recognize the critical role that signs played in design. In a volume the curators co-authored—also titled *The International Style: Architecture since 1922*—they noted the significance of absolute control and aesthetic unity: "The best architects give particular thought to matters of detail. Although they are incidentals, they require more than incidental attention. If there truly be a contemporary style of architecture, it must control these as well as larger matters . . . Careless architects leave details to chance, thus marring creditable work."[42]

Hitchcock and Johnson specifically advocated the creation of a harmonious relationship between architecture and signage. Although a sign could coexist with an architectural composition, it should remain at a certain physical remove and should avoid the appearance of applied ornamentation, the bane of modern architecture: "Clear unseriffed letter forms are most legible at a good scale and conform most harmoniously to the geometrical character of contemporary design. Letters set forward from the wall surface or in silhouette above a roof decorate a building without breaking up the wall surfaces . . . Script forms and fantastic placing may be justified for their effectiveness in advertising, but they are on the whole unarchitectural and best avoided."[43]

The authors cited three American commercial buildings that reflected or failed to reflect this new aesthetic: a Standard Oil service station in Cleveland, New York's McGraw-Hill Building (Raymond Hood, 1930), and Philadelphia's PSFS Building (Howe and Lescaze, 1929–32). They were harshly critical of the heavy glazed terra-cotta crown of signage on the McGraw-Hill tower but approved of the large red neon sign on the PSFS building since it was articulated as a separate piece of an overall composition of planes and cubes, and it stood free of the building mass (see plate 8). The curators lauded other sign designs for their subtlety, their respect for a building's materials

(opposite) Figure 53 Miralago Ballroom and Shops (George Fred Keck, 1930; demolished), Sheridan Road, Wilmette, Illinois. One of the purest examples of International Style principles applied to a commercial structure, this building might have received greater recognition had it not been demolished after only two years.
PHOTO BY WESLEY BOMAN, 1930. HISTORIC ARCHITECTURE AND LANDSCAPE COLLECTION (HALIC), RYERSON AND BURNHAM ARCHIVES, THE ART INSTITUTE OF CHICAGO. DIGITAL FILE #24475 ©THE ART INSTITUTE OF CHICAGO.

and architectural grid, and their adherence to the dictates of the International Style.

Hitchcock and Johnson were vehement in their warning against breaking up wall surfaces. This prompted some designers to follow the caveat to extremes. For example, in 1945, Walter Gropius, then head of the Harvard Graduate School of Design, conceived of a drugstore exterior that would be completely free of lettering. A sculptural element positioned in one of the exterior display cases of the proposed store was intended to communicate the store's identity at a glance. For another store, designed in 1944 by architect Pietro Belluschi, freestanding letters were placed above the roof edge. Perhaps in order to avoid interrupting the delicacy and purity of his vast glass front, Belluschi reduced the height of the lettering to a bare minimum and ran the words together in one long, continuous band that spanned the full width of the facade. He repeated the effect inside, just below the ceiling, around the perimeter of the store. It was, in effect, a sort of modern, abstract architectural frieze. It may have been the architect's plan that the store's contents, visible behind full glass, would be more effective than the graphics in communicating the purpose and basic identification of the store.

In dramatic contrast to the graphic restraint of the International Style, and its sometimes stark manifestations, *Signs of the Times* occasionally encouraged its readers to consider including more identifying graphics, often to the point of potential overload. Some of its writers and mentors urged discipline, outlining basic design principles and offering thoughtful examples. But often the most persuasive advice that it offered its readership was that *more* is more. Some columns in the sign journal began their argument in favor of more signs by explaining that the street climate in the United States was one of confusion and competition. Therefore the sign designer's work must stand out from all the rest. "The better the man, the more variety he gets in his design, the more alert he is for new, novel, and unusual layouts . . . In an electrical display [the buyer or owner] is more insistent on individuality, and he does not want a display made a la Henry Ford, simply because everyone has got one."[44]

One article in *Signs of the Times* mentioned no less than thirteen characteristics for an effective sign: motion, brightness, and color were the most crucial to making a sale.[45] Other articles stressed the importance of stimulating the imagination of the designer:

> Magazine advertisements, containers of all fancy goods, picture frames, jewelry, window trims and the like abound with ideas that can be used complete for electrical displays . . . Here is a recipe for a scrap-book for designs. Fifty *Saturday Evening Posts*, ten *Good Housekeepings*, jewelry catalogues . . . including locks, . . . catalogues of silverware dealers . . .[46]

If you want to get the latest . . . hunt up a modern skyscraper and go in and take a look around, then go outside and do the same thing. Take the outline of the building, remove all the windows and put in some letters and see if you don't have a design with class. Architectural magazines and architects' offices can supply plenty of ideas as to the latest modern trends.[47]

In addition to reading *Signs of the Times*, designers and fabricators sought professional counsel in various trusted guidebooks, many written by columnists for the magazine, whose advice they had come to know and trust.[48]

Few resources provided practical advice about designing for the new medium—the electric sign. Painted signs lent themselves easily to all kinds of decorative complexities, as long as the words were legible. Incandescent bulb signs, however, warranted an altogether different approach. There were

(previous spread) **Figure 54** Diorama of a modern city (1932), created by General Electric's lighting headquarters, Nela Park, Cleveland, Ohio. Aiming to show how illuminated facades and large-scale graphics could stimulate trade, this model also demonstrated how modern signs could be well integrated with architectural design.
AMERICAN ARCHITECT (MARCH 1932), 54. REPRODUCTION COURTESY OF RYERSON AND BURNHAM LIBRARIES, ART INSTITUTE OF CHICAGO.

obvious limitations to creating forms from points of light. The introduction of neon in the late 1920s provided a more fluid potential for sign design, but it presented a different set of limitations.

The first neon sign appeared in Los Angeles, at a Packard car dealership, as early as 1923. However, patent restrictions held by Georges Claude, the Frenchman who first created the long-life electrode for the medium, hindered the widespread use of neon for years. Claude's development of the electrode in 1915 had removed the final obstacle in the lengthy technical development of a practical, affordable luminous tube. In the 1920s, he attempted to sell General Electric an exclusive license in America, without success, and turned instead to selling territorial licenses to various smaller companies. Despite many illegal copies of the Claude technology across the nation, his monopoly prevented the 1920s from becoming the first true neon decade in America.[49]

Several other factors hindered modernization in American sign design: outmoded manuals and trade books, trade journals that preached mixed messages of restraint and harmony versus excess and novelty, and an apprentice or journeyman system that emphasized technical skills. H. C. Martin, one of the most creative contributors to *Signs of the Times*, lamented a certain laziness in his industry: "Stock, ready-cut layouts curb a workman's self-expression in developing his own ideas . . . The best service [they] can render the beginner is not to act as a prop for him to lean on, or as crutches, but rather to teach him to stand upon his own feet, to make him learn to walk for himself."[50]

Another *Signs of the Times* writer complained that the industry was stagnant in the early 1930s: "Aside from the greater brilliancy and the use of new colors, and the straightening of a few scrolls and a new line of stock ornaments, there is very little change [from a few years ago]. From the center of the sign, the left side and the right side are twin brothers; the copy is placed in a very systematic and orthodox manner; a border then encloses it and there are usually scrolls on the top and the bottom of the display; the border suddenly decides to be different and takes on a few jerks and twists, or there are a few dollars left and some scrolls of no particular design are thrown upon the display."[51]

There were, however, indications that at least a few designers were adopting a more modern approach to sign making: "In my department, I have installed an over-sized trash can which I reserve for a considerable number of sketches that are considered by our salesmen to be too modern for their prospects . . . I am pleasantly surprised to find that the percentage of such designs so discarded is becoming considerably smaller."[52]

In March 1932, the *American Architect* published an image of a city street and corner where all the buildings and signs were complementary instead of appearing haphazard. Created by General Electric's lighting headquarters near Cleveland, Nela Park, this dioramic model of an urban landscape was predominantly art deco in appearance, characterized by chevrons, exotic patterns, and symmetry (fig. 54). Although this effort was not as advanced as the best new work coming from Los Angeles or Chicago, its creators knew that their vision of the future would appeal to architects and potential clients. Letters on opal glass ran up the centerlines of towers or crested building tops. Well-integrated projecting signs, rare to nonexistent in America at this time, were pictured next to simple box-type electric signs hung in front of older buildings. There was even a theater, called the Ozark, with signs and a facade based closely on Oud's Café de Unie in Rotterdam. In every way, this model of modern design endorsed by a corporate giant confirmed that America would soon be seeing European modernism on Main Street.

Rescuing Main Street: Corporate Concepts, Competitions, and Incentives

In 1933, the European modernism that had appeared sporadically along a few commercial corridors in larger cities in the United States had its formal debut to all Americans at the world's fair in Chicago. The exposition, known as "A Century of Progress," met with mixed to poor reviews from the architectural press, but those writing for the sign industry deemed it a great success: "The forms you see on the 1933 World's Fair buildings are unlike any you have ever seen before. Don't be alarmed, the world is not coming to an end. It is living proof that the world is going on as usual, and that our creative artists are here translating contemporary life into new artistic form."[53]

At this world's fair, many company displays took the form of three-dimensional "advertisements" lining the avenues of the exposition. Each building was visually unique and stood alone as an architectural exclamation point. The pavilions were not designed, as they had been for the Chicago exposition of 1893, to harmonize visually. With their design strategies at the fair, America's big companies began to establish distinctive, trademark buildings and signs. Walter Dorwin Teague, who designed the memorable Texaco filling station prototype that was eventually installed coast to coast, enthused that "the designer's job will be a lot easier after the summer of 1933. The country will be full of new enthusiasm and littered with shattered complacencies. It will not be so difficult to be sensible."[54]

Somewhat ironically, a writer for *Signs of the Times* marveled at the design harmony of the fair, noting that all identifying signs on the buildings and exhibits conformed to the grander architectural scheme.[55] "Signs at the exposition are an incorporate part of the structures and displays...They are illuminated only by indirect lighting, thrown upon the letters from various

Figure 55
Second diorama of a modern city (1933), created by General Electric for A Century of Progress, Chicago. A far sleeker skyline than that imagined in fig. 54, this version demonstrated how quickly the relative fuss of art deco ornament and lettering was left behind.
MAGAZINE OF LIGHT (SUMMER 1933), COVER. COURTESY OF FISKE KIMBALL FINE ARTS LIBRARY, UNIVERSITY OF VIRGINIA.

angles or by illumination flooded against backgrounds behind the letters . . . Neon tube manufacturers will be impressed by the thousands of feet of tubing to illuminate the principal building."[56]

A new diorama of the city of the future, created by General Electric and displayed in the Electrical Building, graphically demonstrated how signs, lighting, and structure could complement each other—aesthetically and practically (fig. 55). This vision of what could be possible in the hands of capable designers making the most of new technology was a significant advance on the images published by the corporation just a year earlier. This was not 1932's hodge-podge of commercial styles borrowed from all over Europe, placed side by side. Instead, it was a sleek, harmonious, and spare adaptation of the International Style for commerce. Instead of decorated surfaces, it was all smooth intersecting planes, lines, and light. Graphic identity played a significant part in the composition of each building, if not the entire city skyline. As opposed to General Electric's earlier dioramas, this one was aimed at the consumer, not just architects and designers. It was created to be as tangible as possible, with great detail and up-to-date scale-model automobiles. To flesh out this vision, to make it seem real and attainable, General Electric presented a series of full-scale shop-front mock-ups, side by side. Each displayed large modern lettering and dominant, primary geometric shapes around which the designers created full-facade compositions. With storefronts illuminated so brilliantly, the signs seemed almost continuous with the glowing display windows.

Chicago's 1933 exposition advanced the use of neon, but only indirectly, by introducing ingenious ways to install continuous lighting behind letters as backlighting and along the profiles of architectural features.[57] Subtle sign illumination was the result of a directive from the Architectural Commission of the fair, which forbade the use of exposed bulbs and tubing; this governing body also restricted the location and size of signs. Lenox Lohr, the fair's general manager, proclaimed, "It was the belief of the Exposition that signs which are offensive or simply ugly, do not contribute to the box office, and may do actual harm."[58]

Much of the neon lighting at the fair was strictly architectural, in no way serving as direct advertisement. *Signs of the Times* marveled that "a cascade of mysterious green and blue light produced by a mile and a half of gaseous tubes [was] the unique illumination effect on the windowless walls of the Electrical Building." In his vast portfolio of designs for the fair (many unbuilt due to the downturn in the economy), industrial and theatrical designer Norman Bel Geddes exploited the medium to the fullest, stretching tubes along building tops, around perimeters, and up and down towers.[59] Other designers followed his lead. A single company—Federal Electric of Chicago—produced 23,000 feet of neon tubing for various buildings; the entire fair required thirty-five miles of the material.[60]

Many American sign designers were inspired by their experiences at the fair: "It is safe to assume that a large percentage of the customers of . . . signs or display manufacturer[s] will have witnessed the Chicago fair before the close of the season. They will carry home with them impressions of what they saw, and they will be inspired to apply as many of the innovations as possible to their own businesses."[61] "Its influence on color, architectural design, and lighting will be widely felt in the sign and outdoor advertising industry for some years to come."[62]

In contrast to the enthusiasm *Signs of the Times* expressed for the Chicago exposition was the skepticism of the architectural press. *Architect and Engineer* magazine, for example, questioned the brilliant color scheme applied boldly to all structures of the fair by Joseph Urban, obliterating architectural composition, to "hold the attention much as a billboard does."[63] The *Architect and Building News* agreed that it was clearly "three-dimensional poster work."[64]

In some cases, the claim that the corporate pavilions were simply three-dimensional advertisements was quite literally true. The Havoline structure, for instance, was a giant thermometer, intended to support company claims that its motor oil was "the best at all temperatures." Crane Plumbing built a de Stijl-inspired intersection of planes and towers that incorporated an immense shower that worked as a fountain. Nash Automobile presented a narrow glass tower that displayed a series of automobiles stacked one on top of the other like the letters of a major theater sign. The letters N-A-S-H at the tower's crest were necessary only to identify the brand, not the product. These distinct structures acted as temporary corporate icons, recognizable from a distance along the grand promenades of the fair. Though not established as consistently used, full-fledged trademarks, they were in some ways like the distinctive McDonald's original hamburger stands in the 1950s and 1960s, flanked by swooping golden arches—giant icons for the highway, easy-to-read "architecture" well suited for speeding automobiles.[65]

During the Great Depression, corporate America had a direct, even devious, campaign for Main Street's business, coordinated well with its slick consumer propaganda but aimed at those who made the final decisions regarding storefront materials: architects and designers. The suppliers of materials necessary for building storefronts were compelled to change America's commercial thoroughfares in significant ways—their livelihoods depended on it. Storefront catalogues had been responsible for the look of commercial thoroughfares since the middle 1800s, but now the makers of glass, cladding materials, and framing systems realized the potential for increasing sales in unprecedented ways. For example, advertisements by various suppliers of porcelain enamel, as well as myriad articles in architectural journals, helped propel a modest industry on its way toward exceeding over a million dollars in sales by 1936: "Porcelain enamel . . . has become identified with that which is up to date; in the simple meaning of the term, porcelain enamel is modern."[66] Certain companies were especially aggressive in promoting their materials as a means to realize change in Main Street's appearance—offering design guidance, publishing storefront ideas, and sponsoring elaborate competitions.

Aiding these efforts was the federal government's decision in 1935 to extend its FHA loan program so that businesses could borrow up to $50,000 (to be repaid monthly over a five-year period). The government aggressively tackled the decline in construction with a multipronged "modernize Main Street" program that included local offices for the promotion of building and modernizing, various advertising and publication campaigns, coordinated strategies with national manufacturers, and agreements with leading magazines for editorial coverage. Approximately two million stores, theaters, restaurants, and service stations in the United States could benefit from this program, which was calculated to stimulate sales in a stalled economy. The premise behind the effort was that something as seemingly superficial as a new look for commercial establishments would increase patronage and help the country as a whole.[67]

The momentum was already building at the grassroots level for revitalizing storefronts by the time that the U.S. government became involved. In communities nationwide, local business associations were urging merchants to improve the appearance of storefronts and fill empty display windows to downplay the toll the depression had taken. The growth of chain stores, and their resources for staying up-to-date, stimulated independent merchants into action with the belief that only by modernizing could their stores hope to recapture lost trade and compete.[68] "Paint-up-the-front" campaigns were proposed for many hard-pressed businesses unable to manage the capital outlay necessary for the new Federal Housing Authority (FHA) loan program.[69] The *Washington Post* advised that "Storefronts painted in bright, definite colors add distinction to the shop within and are easily remembered by passersby."[70] The 1930s saw the publication of books filled with before-and-after pictures—vivid illustrations of new and potentially profitable looks in commercial facade design. In *Modernizing Buildings for Profit* (1935), Kenneth Kingsley Stowell expressed the mindset of the time: "The importance of style and design in selling of all kinds has become increasingly apparent in recent years. Even Ford found that it was not sufficient to produce a car which would run at a lower price. It must also have an eye-appeal for the customer. The same is true for buildings and parts of buildings . . . Even a change of color in repainting may be enough to so change the atmosphere of a room, . . . that [it] will attract customers or tenants."[71]

Stowell's book, as well as articles such as "Modernize Main Street" in the *Architectural Forum*, provided architects and business owners with convincing case studies of how storefronts virtually unchanged since the turn-of-the-century could be modernized. Among many persuasive examples was a Piggly Wiggly grocery store created from two older shops in a one-story taxpayer strip. For $3,344.70, laborers had refinished the interior, removed the old cornice, clad the exterior in porcelain enamel, and fashioned a large sign with modern lettering glazed onto dark-blue panels.[72] A far more striking transformation, published in the same 1935 article, was the creation of a Hanscom Bake Shop by Horace Ginsbern (one of many storefronts designed by the architect for this chain in New York City) (fig. 56). For a cost of $2,000, Ginsbern reclad a humble nineteenth-century bakery facade with apple-green porcelain enamel trimmed with stainless steel, a look that certainly grabbed attention along a street of muted brick and weathered wood. The once-slim fascia sign was replaced with neon letters three times larger and a projecting sign of the same material as the continuous storefront skin. In other examples illustrated in the article, old bay windows and heavy parapets were scraped away and replaced with flush stone or stucco finishes detailed with subtle geometric patterns in minimal relief or high-contrast color combinations in tile or structural glass.[73]

The manufacturers of architectural materials that were essential for improving the look of America's Main Street reaped significant financial benefits. Few companies had more at stake with the potential success of a new look than General Electric, whose incandescent bulbs and neon tubes played a key role in facade remakes. In the 1920s, the company launched a multifaceted propaganda campaign to promote the advantages of embracing modern commercial design. Its lighting division distributed a publication to businesses and architects called the *Magazine of Light*. It focused on architecture and signs that employed light to the greatest effect and also offered the ideas of its experienced staff of design professionals.[74] The magazine published a profusion of rendered facade concepts with large-scale lettering as the dominant visual element, well integrated with other design features. In addition to extolling modernism in its trade journal, General Electric mounted traveling exhibits aimed at business leaders, architects, and designers. Years in advance of its major displays at Chicago's 1933-34 World's Fair, it also produced a series of full-scale model stores demonstrating new design possibilities for integrated signs and storefronts.[75] By the early 1930s, General Electric was aggressively advocating the use of as much illumination as possible in sign design. The intention was to blur the lines between roof sign, facade, light, and architecture, hence to spread the use of illumination. The company was especially partial to storefronts made entirely of glass—with generous use of back-lit opal glass above display windows and silhouetted modern lettering.[76]

Companies producing metal storefront systems, which had quickly made themselves essential to businesses since their debut around 1906, also played a major role in introducing modern design to commercial thoroughfares. Lavishly illustrated, full-page ad campaigns promoting the storefronts of manufacturers like Newmanco, Republic Steel, Brasco, Zouri, and industry leader Kawneer, had crowded the pages of publications like *Chain Store Age* since the 1910s. Advanced metal extrusion engineering made possible deep arcades and exterior lobbies in the early years of the twentieth century.[77] These manufacturers' advertisements in the 1920s sometimes demonstrated the possibility of including identifying graphics within the glass panels (or transom zone) above the entrance, an opportunity seldom explored by merchants until the 1930s. Ever searching for new ways to stimulate the updating of facades, these storefront companies jumped on the chance to promote the new look coming from Europe.[78] A rather sudden turn in design appeared in advertisements dating from 1929, a marked shift away from the relatively conservative schemes illustrated by these companies through the 1920s, with graphics and ornament that had changed little from 1900.

By 1930, storefront manufacturers were spreading the look of Europe in paid advertisements. Kawneer proudly touted its association with Holabird & Root in the creation of the Walden Book Shop. "The use of modern storefronts as a means of attracting greater crowds has become universal," claimed Kawneer, revealing how swiftly the change was coming about.[79] Kawneer offered its customers free booklets to stimulate modern design and stressed how the company's finesse for custom design could help chains develop a trademark look. By the middle 1930s, advertisements for Enduro, the "perfected stainless steel" from Republic Steel, promoted the company's association with Horace Ginsbern's novel work for the Hanscom Bake Shop chain. This manufacturer published countless ads illustrating storefront

Figure 56

Hanscom Bakery (Horace Ginsbern, circa 1935; demolished), New York City. Ginsbern adapted a consistent design to a wide variety of locations and site conditions, with striking color, horizontal panels of porcelain enamel and glass, and a trademark lettering style.
AMERICAN ARCHITECT (DECEMBER 1935), 70. REPRODUCTION COURTESY OF RYERSON AND BURNHAM LIBRARIES, ART INSTITUTE OF CHICAGO.

Figure 57
One of the competition submissions for modernizing shop fronts; printed in color and disseminated across America (Joseph M. Hirschman, 1935). By this time, architects across America had learned that the entire storefront, or even building front, could be considered a canvas for identity. They could assemble elements like lettering, window displays, and all sorts of graphic and architectural features as if they were parts of a poster.
LIBBEY-OWENS-FORD GLASS COMPANY, *52 DESIGNS TO MODERNIZE MAIN STREET WITH GLASS* (1935), 65.

framing, panel finishes, and signs—all in stainless steel—thus promoting complete, integrated storefront design.

Companies that manufactured pigmented structural glass also radically advanced modernism in American storefronts of the 1930s. The novelty of the material they produced, as well as its graphic potential, contributed greatly to their success. Pigmented structural glass was first developed around 1900, but it was not used on a building exterior until 1927.[80] Originally produced only in black and white, it eventually appeared in a rainbow of colors. Pigmented structural glass brought unprecedented color to Main Street, vibrant hues that would remain vibrant, covering brick and wood. The 1930 catalogue of one such product, Vitrolite, offered clever ways to design the sign and the surface immediately above display windows, focusing on patterns and color. A year or two later, the company's promotional material emphasized bolder graphics, examples of how modern lettering might be sandblasted into Vitrolite's surface or mounted with continuous metal standards across its shiny, polished face.[81]

In an aggressive, strategic effort to make use of the FHA's program and boost its engagement in the modernization of Main Street, the Libbey-Owens-Ford Glass Company (L-O-F) purchased the Vitrolite Company and launched a major promotional campaign for its new acquisition. The company recognized the value of collaborating with architects in order to influence their designs and their decisions regarding material specifications. L-O-F timed the purchase perfectly to make use of the new federal subsidy for commercial refurbishment, signed into law just as the glass company announced a major competition for architects across America to redesign Main Street, storefront by storefront.[82] Some three thousand architects, one-third of all those registered in the country, competed for prizes of up to $1,000 in each of four business categories: a food store, a drugstore, an apparel shop, and an automobile sales and service station. Their mandate was to address commercial design by types, revealing strategies that could be applied to storefronts everywhere. The jury included some of the most revered designers of the 1930s—Albert Kahn, John W. Root, and William Lescaze, among others. J. André Fouilhoux, who would soon design the Trylon and Perisphere for the 1939 New York World's Fair, chaired the jury. "This competition," the company predicted, "should have a far-reaching effect on raising the standards of store design, both through directing the interest of the designers to this field, and by providing merchants and dealers with a guide as to what an intelligent public taste will demand."[83]

The results of the competition were published in *Architectural Record*, several other trade journals, and a four-color book, *52 Designs to Modernize Main Street with Glass* (fig. 57).[84] The winning storefront proposals were striking not only for their brilliant color but also for the scale of lettering used for the identifying signs. This lettering was quite sophisticated and highly inventive. Approximately 20 to 50 percent of each facade, an area five to ten times the space allotted to the traditional signs that were being replaced, was allotted to such graphics. The entire building facade was incorporated into the graphic composition; designers paid no heed to the area once defined as the fascia, where signs were once confined, instead using large areas of bold colors as background to lettering placed in novel locations. In fact, the competition winners used no traditional architectural features in their facade designs, and the best compositions seemed to defy gravity—that is, no single element appeared to support another, from bottom to top, as was traditional in the past. The emphasis was unmistakably on surface: the sparkle of glass, the interaction of color, the visual balance of features like doorways and lettering. Windows were fashioned to appear as opaque as the Vitrolite; in most cases, nothing was visible beyond this "black" plane.[85] Also, the renderings submitted never indicated context, though real buildings and sites were given for remodeling (and shown in photographs in the competition publications). No upper floors or neighbors appeared in the drawings, as if the proposed businesses were surrounded by open, suburban space.

Although not quite as graphically ambitious as the winners on paper, the first-floor storefront for Fain's flooring in Providence, one of the many storefronts across America clearly influenced by this competition, presented a continuous glass surface: a red Vitrolite band above and clear glass below, spanning the entire storefront. The area devoted to the sign was significantly larger than the traditional fascia zone, and yet it was defined by horizontal bands much as the traditional fascia was (fig. 58). This ambitiously modern storefront was the result of modernizing the first floor of the Wayland Building (Charles Payton Hartshorn, 1874) in 1934 by Modern Industries. Though

Figure 58

Fain's Carpet and Rug Store (Modern Industries, 1934), North Main Street, Providence, Rhode Island. A vibrant example of the new look sweeping into smaller cities and towns and documented by the 1935 competition to modernize Main Street, this store shows a bold use of color, large-scale lettering, curves, and circles that were hallmarks of mid-1930s modernism.

PHOTO BY AUTHOR, 2007.

based in Providence, this turnkey firm designed and built fluidly integrated facades and interiors for businesses across the country (including coordinated logos, matchbook covers, and shopping bags), addressing the perceived need of the time to facelift for profit. Few examples built in the field in America during the 1930s were ever as fluid or expansive as those presented in *52 Designs to Modernize Main Street with Glass*, but this one came close.

Two years after the Vitrolite promotion, in 1937, the Pittsburgh Plate Glass Company (PPG) and the *Architectural Forum* magazine cosponsored a competition to encourage the use of glass in storefront design. In the early 1930s, the manufacturer organized tours to show architects and business owners how glass could enhance the appearance of commercial structures.[86] PPG was in fierce competition with L-O-F, and though it never managed quite as tight a tie-in to the FHA's modernizing campaign, it was at least slightly ahead by way of its ability to offer, in the year of the Main Street competition, a complete storefront system—including glass products and extruded metal framing.[87] The jury for this new competition, like that for Vitrolite, was stellar and included Harwell Hamilton Harris, Richard Neutra, Albert Kahn, industrial designer Donald Deskey, and the Miami architect Robert Law Weed.[88]

With his design for the Kitty Kelly shoe store chain (1937) on State Street in Chicago, Alfred Alschuler produced a defining example of how another novel architectural product, glass block, could be featured in a commercial facade (fig. 59).[89] This new glass product had been introduced to the public at the 1933–34 World's Fair in Chicago.[90] A four-story window of glass masonry dominated Alschuler's facade design for Kitty Kelly. Just over the first-floor display window, a Vitrolite band intersected the base of this vertical glass masonry feature. At this "crossing," the architect placed the sign for the store: dramatically compressed neon letters that filled this focal band perfectly. Many of the advertisements for Insulux, a glass-block product manufactured by Owens Illinois, featured pictures of this store. Alschuler also received a great deal of publicity with his corner building for Benson & Rixon menswear (1936) on State Street; in this facade, the architect was able to reveal the potential for glass block to turn corners dramatically and to become flush with the exterior wall surface (fig. 60). With these two major design feats alone, Alschuler demonstrated how glass block was the ideal material for the streamline age, where smooth surfaces and simplicity were prized over the articulation of parts. In Miami, architect Robert Fitch Smith pushed Alschuler's use of the product even further, extending glass block across the entire upper surface of his storefront for the National Cash Register showroom in Miami. The resulting three-story glass facade was particularly effective at night, when the three-dimensional metal letters resting on the canopy and the company logo above were silhouetted against the glowing interior.[91]

Despite these high-style applications, the use of glass block on America's Main Streets was mostly limited to continuous window bands of the material, which were evident on commercial structures nationwide. South Michigan Avenue in Roseland, Illinois—like many other Main Streets—was updated with several such buildings; two furniture stores were both given facelifts in the mid-1940s that featured ribbon windows of glass block. Haverty's furniture on King Street in Charleston, South Carolina, followed the lines of Alschuler's vertical Kitty Kelly store in Chicago. The blankness of these continuous skins of block or brick, the simplicity of the design idea, often motivated owners to add signs that ran right over the glass. Such unsympathetic signage was an ironic fallout of the streamline era, which otherwise demonstrated unprecedented sensitivity to integrating sign with architecture.

The Disappearing Storefront: From Streamlined Surface to the Open Facade

The media blitz generated by the glass companies' design competitions in the 1930s led, at first, to an emphasis on the surface of buildings and a disregard for projections. Commercial buildings and storefronts of this period extended to the edge of the lot line, as was traditional, with windows barely inset, and the graphics designed by architects rarely projected far beyond the streamlined surface. By the 1940s, these smooth building envelopes would give way to punctured surfaces, architectural forms stretched and grouped, and solid and void played off of each other.

Leading industrial designers of the 1930s, such as Henry Dreyfuss and Raymond Loewy, favored the straightforward, streamlined approach for many commercial buildings. Dreyfuss's widely published storefront for Western Union (1937)—basically an enormous graphic on frosted glass depicting a telegraph card—lacked the conventional curvature associated with his other work. Loewy's design for Cushman's Bakery certainly established a powerful precedent for keeping all things smooth and efficient. Another design that called attention to the skin of the building itself was the Trans-Lux Theater (Thomas Lamb, 1934) on Madison Avenue in New York City (fig. 61). Continuous bands of porcelain enamel wrapped tightly around the visible structural frame. These abutted the flush neon sign, which was yet another porcelain enamel panel; instead of pushing out over the sidewalk, as was conventional, this marquee was flush with the facade.

The publication in 1935 of *52 Designs to Modernize Main Street*, with its large-scale graphics and bold colors, influenced America's more prosperous commercial corridors almost immediately. Design emphasis was on surface, on two-dimensional effects. This was especially true in Miami Beach, where big graphic flourishes prevailed. The front facades of many of the city's three-story hotels boasted horizontal banding, vertical stripes and bas-reliefs in stucco, and graphic curves and painted circles (see plate 9). Neon emphasized many of these features. The hotel names were placed on continuous cantilevered stucco canopies over the first floor. The raised terraces that pushed out onto the sidewalk, suggesting a continuity of space between the open, glazed lobby and the outside, created a sense of depth for these otherwise flat buildings.

The ground-floor modernization of a sandwich shop on King Street in Charleston, South Carolina, revealed how superficial some makeovers of older buildings could be. In this instance, large, rounded windows from the streamline era replaced the neoclassical layering of entablature and column, which distinguished the original first story and the remaining stories above, where weight was visually transferred from top to bottom (fig. 62). The new storefront designs of the 1930s and 1940s were more graphically oriented, disregarding long-established architectural logic. In this case, the pilasters of the upper stories came down to "rest" on a cornice over a large opening that was given a novel form. For a more traditional nineteenth-century storefront—dominated by glass—a slim iron post, at minimum, would have provided support under the pilasters.[92]

By the late 1930s, *Signs of the Times* was regularly publishing ideas for full storefront design and encouraging the sign industry to expand its role

Figure 59

Kitty Kelly shoe store (Alfred Alschuler, 1937; altered), State Street, Chicago. With this powerful example of an architect incorporating graphics into facade design, Alfred Alschuler made bold use of glass block, a new tool for the modern architect.

PHOTO BY HEDRICH-BLESSING, 1937. COURTESY OF THE CHICAGO HISTORY MUSEUM, HB-04373B.

beyond the confines of the small, applied sign box. The subsequent leap that sign companies made into facade design demonstrated the graphic nature of commercial design at this time, where lettering, striping, pictures, portholes, and continuous bands of glass were arranged to greatest visual effect on what remained, basically, a flat surface (fig. 63).[93] Graphic and industrial designers such as Charles Oppenheimer, John Albright, and George F. Meyers created storefronts that basically followed in the steps of those generated for the 1935 "Modernize Main Street" competition sponsored by L-O-F, but they also began to address the third dimension in their work, treading more and more into the territory of architects. Some sign artists were particularly adept at integrating the vertical projecting sign with a full facade composition, making it an integral piece of a fluid whole. In the early 1940s, the sign industry began to publish compendia of proposed and recently completed storefronts created by sign designers.[94] Though many of these designers employed rounded corners, curved bulkheads, and stepped window displays in their storefront creations, their work explored the third dimension only minimally. Meyers, however, was a significant exception to this rule. Breaking the facade plane to include convincing spatial effects usually required the skills of architects, trained to think in terms of mass and volume.

Chicago architect Alfred Alschuler demonstrated prolifically how graphics could be inventively integrated with architectural composition emphasizing smooth, streamline building surfaces.[95] For his Buffalo, New York, store design for the W. T. Grant Company (1939), Alschuler made the sparest of designs, wrapping the corner site smoothly. The stacked ribbon windows emphasized the flow of the rich stone cladding. The design was deemed worthy enough to be included among the nineteen shops and stores selected for the Museum of Modern Art's *Guide to Modern Architecture*.[96] For the Grant stores created in Fort Worth (1939) and Milwaukee (1940), Alschuler revealed the store's identity as a sculptor might, by chiseling away at the surface of the wall. The sign was thus *of* the building, the result not of adding something but conceptually *removing* material—in this case, the counterspace around the letters (fig. 64). These signs were not only flush with the building's facade, they *were* the building facade.

By the 1940s, the perfect, smooth plane of the urban commercial building and storefront gave way to a surface of projections; the sign became in many instances the most visually disengaged of all the design elements. Sign canopies in wavelike forms and free-floating circular canopies at street corners distinguished Robert Fash's novel designs for Whelan Drugs in the late 1930s and early 1940s (fig. 65). The graphics rested on canopies that rippled and pushed away from the static wall surface, suggesting movement. Walls, canopies, and lettering remained a carefully coordinated whole, however, despite the subtle design independence given to each feature.[97] The General Motors mock street intersection visitors encountered at the end of their Futurama

(opposite) Figure 60

Benson & Rixon Company Building (Alfred Alschuler, 1936; altered), State Street, Chicago. Once more, Alschuler explored the design potential offered by glass block, this time with a building that would help to usher in the era of the streamline moderne, with its smooth, contoured building surface.

PHOTO BY HEDRICH-BLESSING, 1936. COURTESY OF THE CHICAGO HISTORY MUSEUM, HB-04358H.

AMERICA DISCOVERS MODERNISM

journey at the 1939 World's Fair in New York featured an immense, vertical sign on an otherwise smooth-cornered building. That same year, the May Company store opened on Wilshire Boulevard in Los Angeles. Designed by A. C. Martin and Samuel Marks, the building's rounded corner was like a tower of gold coins, a gleaming convex surface set off by a black concave frame with stacked lettering. The Albion Hotel in Miami Beach (Igor Polevitzky and T. Triplett Russell, 1939) was an exceptionally creative yet controlled example of how the smooth, continuous skin of the late 1930s was giving way to an ensemble of distinct pieces (see plate 10). The building recalled the round-cornered designs of Alschuler and others while anticipating the future, with elements that protruded in every direction. A row of sun canopies wrapped around windows on one elevation and a projecting glass-curtain-walled box punctured another, interrupting the otherwise smooth white stucco envelope of this corner building. A crown of radiating fins pushed up through the

Figure 61
Trans-Lux Theatre (Thomas Lamb, 1934; demolished), Madison Avenue, New York City. The continuous, unbroken building surface and flush marquee presented a major design shift by theater architect Lamb, whose designs from the late 1920s tended to be lavishly ornamented pastiches.
MICHAEL R. MILLER COLLECTION, THEATRE HISTORICAL SOCIETY OF AMERICA.

roof at the corner to support a sign, another breakaway from the contained, streamlined form.

The Julian Medical Building on Hollywood Boulevard (Morgan, Walls & Clements, 1934) was an earlier, anachronistic example of the streamlined building in which the architects "chafed at the bit," refusing to subordinate expressive, functional elements to a continuous skin (fig. 66). Concave curves both low and tall were placed directly behind the convex corner with its sign, elaborately marking the important intersection and enframing the graphic identity. The edges of these major verticals generated a series of vertical sun baffles on the western face, terminated by taller fins that marked the entrance to the second floor and served as vertical blade signs. The identity of the ground-floor tenant, Owl Drugs, rested on a canopy that wrapped around the corner just above the entrance. The architect created fin panels and insets in his composition to accommodate signs, even if he did not design the graphics

Figure 62
186 King Street (circa 1780s), Charleston, South Carolina. This 1940s first-floor modernization ignored the powerfully clear neoclassical organization of the facade, with columns aligned over columns, visually carrying weight from roof to foundation.
PHOTO BY LOUIS SCHWARTZ, CIRCA 1960S. COURTESY OF HISTORIC CHARLESTON FOUNDATION.

AMERICA DISCOVERS MODERNISM

(previous spread) **Figure 63** Neighborhood shopping center at Belmont, Lincoln, and Ashland Avenues, Chicago, circa 1955. An especially generous profusion of graphics marked this principal intersection as being distinct from the commercial streets leading up to it. In some cases, facades were defined by little more than large-scale lettering and basic graphic panels. COURTESY OF THE CHICAGO HISTORY MUSEUM, i50049.

himself. A building with such projections was so dramatically different from the typical, smooth-faced, streamlined corner building that one could imagine these pieces breaking away from the composition completely.

The Sontag Drugs building (1935) by Norstrom & Anderson on Wilshire Boulevard was a tight, modestly scaled assembly of rounded corners and squat towers held together by a horizontal band above the display windows (fig. 67). A dark, almost windowlike, void was created in the massing of solids on the south elevation, which served as a visual counterpart to the short tower nearer the entrance and a place for the trademark Sontag sign. This composition of solids and voids, of push and pull, prefigured the volumetric play of the 1940s. It was also an early step toward the figural architecture and independent sign structures of the 1950s.

The push and pull on the surface of commercial buildings led to a revolution of sorts in store design, beginning in the early 1940s, as architects emphasized the dynamic relationship of store interior to street. The impetus to do so was the perceived need to increase sales by removing all barriers between product and customer. The graphic advancements of the 1930s gave way to spatial strategy; three-dimensional design replaced two-dimensional concepts. In rethinking the role of storefronts in the 1940s, some designers actually scorned the superficial resurfacing of buildings popularized in the 1930s. The press expressed disdain for the naive notion that sleek new walls and attention-grabbing signs alone constituted significant change and improvement:

> The enthusiasm for modernity which followed World War I accepted little from the past. The mania was to be "new." The result was often sophomoric and monstrous. No one knows this better than those who invested money in this "Moderne" school of architecture. Now outdated, outmoded, and pitifully out of step with true modern expression, buildings so styled have suffered staggering depreciation in resale or use value.[98]

> It is evident that store design has made big strides forward. The distracting, eye-catching store "architecture" of ten years ago has been junked in favor of systemic study of consumer appeal in terms of display techniques, lighting, and mechanical equipment.[99]

Architects acknowledged that signs alone were not enough to lure customers to stores. Instead, they recognized the need to put the inside on the outside—that is, to pull the exterior lobby deeper into the store and push parts of the store out onto the sidewalk. Granted, this notion was not entirely new, but now designers sought to take the concept to a new level of development. Merchants had learned in the 1910s that deeper, larger exterior lobbies (or arcades, as they were also called) allowed shoppers to see more merchandise without entering the store. Once they had wandered off the sidewalk, browsers were likely to take the next step and proceed inside. The 1940s ushered in a fundamental design change—the removal of the back wall of the window display, which permitted shoppers to look deep into the store. To further minimize the barrier between inside and out, designers minimized the bulkhead, permitting display windows to extend from the ceiling nearly to the sidewalk. All-glass doors enhanced the sense of openness: "The entranceway must be so designed that there is no thought of a barrier in the customer's mind. He simply steps across that imaginary line into the store."[100] Because the entire storefront was now considered a display element, a subtle graphic should be incorporated into the composition.[101] With merchandise "doing more work" for pedestrians on Main Street, there was less need for signs to attract and inform potential pedestrian customers.

Figure 64

W. T. Grant Co. (Alfred Alschuler, 1939), Houston Street, Fort Worth, Texas, circa 1940. Alschuler revealed the store's identity as a sculptor might, by conceptually chiseling away at the surface of the wall, rendering the sign as if it were part of the building's flesh.

COURTESY OF THE CHICAGO HISTORY MUSEUM, i61997.

Not surprisingly, glass manufacturers aggressively promoted the movement to open storefronts. As early as 1937, the Libbey-Owens-Ford Glass Company hinted at a future beyond the flat graphics of many of the storefronts it published to promote use of its products. In color brochures created for architects, the company included images emphasizing three-dimensional applications of glass, where space continued fluidly from sidewalk to lobby or store interior (fig. 68). Then, in 1943, the company produced a lavishly illustrated book, *Visual Fronts,* to appeal directly to customers and architects alike. Most of the designs pictured eliminated so much solid wall, especially above the entrance, that the sign lettering almost seemed to float in space (fig. 69). In these retail designs, the ceiling/roof often pushed out beyond the common building line, and the glass membrane was pulled back toward the interior at an angle. Display cases were often continuous from outside to inside. In its ad campaigns for publications like *Chain Store Age* during the middle 1940s, L-O-F illustrated the rapid evolution toward the "Visual Front" by showing a sequence of storefronts dated 1900, 1935, and 194X. Even the look associated with the company's own product, Vitrolite—with its solid but brightly colored facades exemplified in the 1935 drawing—was sacrificed as passé to make way for the radical, new open front.[102]

In 1944 and 1945, Pittsburgh Plate Glass hired some of the most respected architects in the United States, including Eliel and Eero Saarinen, Pietro Belluschi, William Lescaze, Ely Jacques Kahn, and Walter Gropius, to propose examples of superior new retail design for urban sites. Nearly all of the resulting renderings portrayed double-height spaces with immense sheets of glass. Few renderings depicted any context; each could just as easily float on its own on some arterial road rather than line up with other such designs along Main Street or State Street. No upper stories were shown. Although a few of the participating architects included handsome lettered

Figure 65
Proposal for Whelan Drug Store, Vanderbilt Avenue, New York City (Robert Fash, 1944). Although a product of the streamline era, with its exceptionally smooth surface and gentle contours, this design also demonstrated the new movement to break the basic facade plane defined by the property line and push past the contained building envelope.
ARCHITECTURAL FORUM (OCTOBER 1944), 115. REPRODUCTION COURTESY OF RYERSON AND BURNHAM LIBRARIES, ART INSTITUTE OF CHICAGO.

identification, most paid only cursory attention to this element, incorporating letters that were so small, pale, or subtle as to be illegible. It appeared as if these famous modern architects had taken to extremes the graphic restraint and discipline Hitchcock and Johnson suggested in *The International Style*.

In the early 1940s, the Kawneer storefront company invited architects Ketchum, Gina & Sharp to remodel a full block of old commercial buildings along Main Street in Niles, Michigan, home of the company's plant; this new architectural firm was not ashamed to incorporate bold graphics. Store after store received the open-front treatment in the firm's 1944 proposal. Some of the buildings received full makeovers, from the ground level to the parapet, two stories up; others received only a first floor remodeling. In each case, all the old fascia signs were scrapped.[103] The architects proposed carving away the enclosed corner of the drugstore and rendered the building in perspective without any upper floors (fig. 70). Most of the storefront designs suggested a first story composed entirely of glass, with either a side wall or ceiling plane projecting beyond this glazing, like freestanding panels, out over the sidewalk. Free-floating display cases, some as low as coffee tables, rested in the voids between sidewalk and entrance. New wall sign lettering, significantly larger than the old and displaying great variety from business to business, announced the purpose of this design approach: to be accessible, appealing, and profitable.[104] These were machines for selling, as the Kawneer ads for that year trumpeted. In 1948, Ketchum had produced enough work to publish a book that included his many drawings for proposed stores that emphasized large, recessed lobbies and angled sign panels. In his work for individual stores, the architect stretched as a graphic designer, using scale and creative new lettering styles to particularly bold effect.[105] Kawneer maintained a relationship with Ketchum that lasted for most of the 1940s, publishing many double-page advertisements in *Chain Store Age* and journal articles heralding the open look that he espoused. Ketchum's storefront designs, including his love for creative lettering and graphics carefully integrated with the design whole, thus enjoyed constant media exposure.[106]

Morris Ketchum was one of several prominent designers working to alter the shape of America's retail landscape during the 1940s. For its 1940 issue dedicated to the "Design Decade," the *Architectural Forum* published Ketchum's earlier scheme set in an urban context, a "fundamental re-design of the conventional business block," which was far more radical than his eventual proposal for Niles.[107] Under an overhanging slab roof that covered an entire block, freely disposed all-glass storefronts angled randomly away from the sidewalk. Uniform, arcade-type signs were the only graphics to identify the businesses. Though the schemes stressed flexibility, the goal was to demonstrate design control, something that would prepare Ketchum for his shopping centers. Although Ketchum enjoyed manipulating large-scale lettering to create visual variety and stimulate sales, this project revealed an

(opposite) **Figure 66**
Julian Medical Building (Morgan, Walls & Clements, 1934; altered), Hollywood Boulevard, Los Angeles. This unusually ambitious and advanced design balanced the desire to articulate individual elements (a growing trend in the 1940s) with a desire to hold everything together with a continuous, curving facade skin (the prevailing modus operandi of the middle to late 1930s).
PHOTO BY MOTT STUDIOS, CIRCA 1935. MOTT / MERGE COLLECTION, CALIFORNIA HISTORY SECTION, CALIFORNIA STATE LIBRARY.

underlying need, most of all, to control the full effect of a design ensemble, whether graphics were muted or loud (see chapter 5 for more on Ketchum, his contemporaries, and control).

By the 1940s, the compositions of Morris Lapidus were so free-form that they threatened to break up the continuous wall of Main Street altogether. His radical design for Morris Jewelers (1941) in Wilkes-Barre, Pennsylvania, prompted *Architectural Record* to ask, "Where is the building line?" A wave-shaped sign canopy attempted to unify a dramatically angled side wall and a sculptural wall at the corner of a street; the result suggested the prow of an ocean liner. Lapidus focused his creative energy on removing the perceived barrier between the window shopper and the merchandise inside, including eliminating moldings around storefront windows and doors in an effort to make the glass "disappear."[108] Long a believer in the power of well-designed signs, Lapidus claimed in the 1940s that the entire storefront was "really a billboard, designed on the same principles as the poster."[109]

Victor Gruen produced ambitious retail designs, both graphically and spatially sophisticated, which also ruptured the continuous wall of the urban commercial corridor. For Grayson's ladies' ready-to-wear shop in Pasadena (Gruen and Krummeck, 1945), the flanking walls of the open-roofed arcade rippled and tapered, leading to a double-height entrance (fig. 71). Vertically extended, three-dimensional lettering crested an entrance that was blocked on axis by a free-floating exterior display case. Gruen and his firm designed eleven stores for Grayson's between 1940 and 1946, many of them with exceptionally tall openings and each unique. The Seattle store (1941) featured a four-story facade that scooped in one big curve down from the tall neon letters at the crest to the standard-height glass entrance doors as it moved deeper into the store. The vast space was generously lit at night. Other stores the firm designed also employed open-fronted height to great effect.[110] Along with generously scaled neon lettering, both in lush script and simple sans-serif forms, Gruen sometimes applied a continuous "ribbed" or "corduroy" skin of neon to his store canopies.

Donald Deskey, an industrial designer, produced several postwar storefront solutions for the Brunswick Sport Company (1944–46) that dramatically demonstrated how to "open up" a flat exterior and convert space above the entrance into effective advertising. One of his designs featured a rakishly angled sign above the entrance and a display case that seemed to burst forth from the lobby like a streamlined locomotive (fig. 72). At the end of the case, which was encircled with the word BILLIARDS, rested a replica of an enormous eight ball, dramatically lit from below. The novel scheme echoed mimetic architecture from the 1920s and 1930s, but in an innovative way, as part of an ambitious, elastic architectural massing.[111] Deskey, a highly regarded design leader of the day, was certainly not a snob about the use of large-scale graphics, as many premier architects of the time seemed to be. Another proposal

featured a large, blank building with a single, continuous sign canopy and an angled egg-crate grill supporting a ball. A sign "fin" or pylon was so disengaged from the facade that it appeared to be clipped on at an arbitrary point. With this design, Deskey seemed to forecast the future of signs, a time when sign structures would become increasingly independent from architecture until the two separated completely.

Becoming Figural: Distinctive Shapes and Physical Independence

Certain building types pushed the transition from the smoothly integrated sign and architecture of more urban conditions to a landscape of pieces, where the sign would eventually leave the surface of the building and become physically independent. Movie theaters, markets, drive-ins, filling stations, and some hotels needed either to advertise more aggressively or to cater most efficiently to the automobile. In some ways, these types paved the way to the future of commercial design: the suburban corridors of the 1950s, where signs stood at the roadside and buildings sat back from the thoroughfare, behind parked cars. The transition from enmeshed to independent graphics was especially well represented by buildings like that for Crenshaw Motors Ford (architect unknown, 1946), an automobile dealership in Los Angeles (see plate 11). At the rounded corner of this structure, a simple vertical extension of the parapet rose to make a place for a sign that would be high enough to address traffic. This aberration to the continuous roofline was visually united with rest of the building by way of fluid neon graphics. The vertical stroke of the letter *F* in Ford followed the curve at the crest of the parapet projection but also descended to link directly with the "baseline" of neon and lettering that ran along the top of the wraparound display windows. The surface of this building was thus tied carefully together despite the significant discontinuity in profile.

By the 1940s, storefronts with pylons or large vertical projecting signs became a common sight in America. What began as a relatively minor "fin" for signage on the urban storefront eventually grew in height and visual dominance. Some of these fins projected beyond the face of the buildings, beginning the evolution toward signs becoming fully independent and figural forms. Roof-mounted sign towers became so enormous that they sometimes descended all the way down, through the edge of the building, to the ground.

William and Hal Pereira's design for the facade of the Esquire Theater (1937) in Chicago provides a dramatic, high-style example of a vertical sign projecting as an independent but coordinated element (fig. 73). In this case, the architect cantilevered the sign panel with a carefully designed open steel grid, rather than simply an ad hoc series of connections mandated by engineering alone. Unlike many late-1930s buildings that were visually smoothed

(opposite) **Figure 67**
Sontag Drug Building (Norstrom and Anderson, 1935; altered), Wilshire Boulevard, Los Angeles, circa 1936. This early composition of solids and voids, of push-in and pull-out of building mass, prefigured the complex volumetric play of the 1940s.
SECURITY PACIFIC NATIONAL BANK COLLECTION / LOS ANGELES PUBLIC LIBRARY.

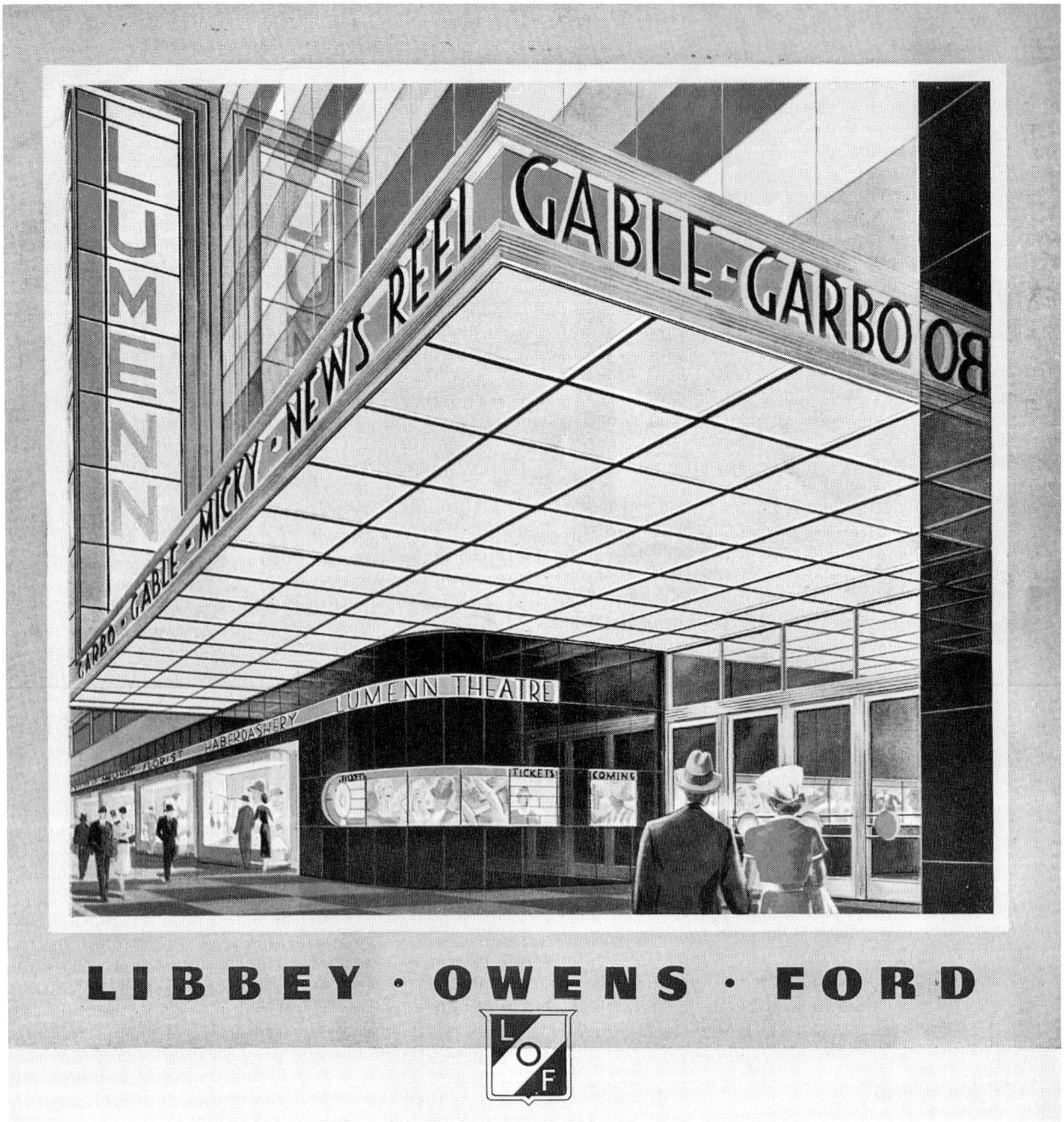

to appear as one continuous unit, this building was intended as a composition of articulated pieces. Other buildings with projecting, articulated sign fins included the Crest Hotel (Edward A. Nolan, 1941) in Miami Beach where the sign broke past the parapet and shot through a pergola on the roof, to be flanked by masts looking like inverted ski poles (fig. 74). Unlike the Esquire's sign, this vertical identity feature was connected to, if not continuous with, the skin of the building. For Marcus P. Miller's building for Chandler's Shoes (Los Angeles, 1938), the sign became completely independent of the parapet.

The effect was even more pronounced at his Conrad Building (1938), where a full sign tower rose out of the grouping of disparate forms visually woven together with a series of graphic bands.

Another significant example in the evolution of the independent sign structure was Raymond Loewy's design for Lucky Supermarket (San Leandro, 1945), which eventually was reproduced throughout California. Here, Loewy separated the sign pylon from the building altogether. Visually uniting the separate sign tower and building was a challenging assignment, as the curve of the vast arched roof was a closed, independent form. Loewy lightened the visual weight of the sign tower by punching three squares out of its mass, thus producing something of a graphic trademark. The fourth "square," at the tower's base, was also the entrance to the building. At Chicago's 1933 World's Fair, the Walgreen's Drug Company had proposed a suburban prototype with a slim, cylindrical sign tower mounted above the cylindrical building (Loebl, Schlossman & Demuth). A continuous canopy connected this structure with low-lying wings; it was a harbinger of the strip-architecture of the future, preparing visitors for the conveniences of suburban commercial design.[112] The cylindrical tower feature also recalled the synchronistic design development of drive-in restaurants in southern California.

From the late 1920s to the late 1940s, the schematic design for the ubiquitous drive-in restaurants of Los Angeles consisted simply of a round, or radial, building in the middle of an open lot, accessible to cars approaching from every direction. Typically, a sign tower was affixed to the middle of the roof. In the early years, the building was hexagonal, and the sign was a conventional rectangular add-on, supported on a skeletal steel base at the hub. By the mid-1930s, the basic design had been refined to feature a tall sign tower that stepped down to the roof. Within a few years, yet another

(opposite) *Figure 68*
Back cover of brochure for Libbey-Owens-Ford Glass Company (1937–38). Corporate collateral material advertised advanced design possibilities, pushing architects and business owners to stretch their imaginations and spend money. This particular image prefigured the ambiguity between inside and outside explored primarily in the 1940s and 1950s.
LIBBEY-OWENS-FORD GLASS COMPANY RECORDS, MSS-066, THE WARD M. CANADAY CENTER FOR SPECIAL COLLECTIONS, WILLIAM S. CARLSON LIBRARY, UNIVERSITY OF TOLEDO.

Figure 69
Page from *Visual Fronts* (Libbey-Owens-Ford Glass Company, 1943). This is a classic example of the new "open-front" approach to storefront design. To increase sales, store owners were encouraged to eliminate the front wall of the store visually, making it easier to lure customers inside.
COURTESY OF THE WOLFSONIAN–FLORIDA INTERNATIONAL UNIVERSITY, MIAMI BEACH, FLORIDA, THE MITCHELL WOLFSON JR. COLLECTION, XB1992.1494.

AMERICA DISCOVERS MODERNISM

refinement simplified the sign tower, which now became a slender post with stacked lettering (or in some cases, no lettering at all). The verbal identification was usually repeated at the edge of the cantilevered roof disk. Architect Wayne McAllister produced the first example of this step in the design evolution in 1935, with his Simon's Drive-in at Wilshire and Fairfax (fig. 75).[113] What was once a rather heavy and makeshift roof in earlier stages of development, now seemed almost to hover in the night like some unearthly airborne vehicle rising over a galaxy of taillights. Instead of a heavy masonry building, the space between roof and floor was mostly glass. McAllister cantilevered the roof out over the hoods of cars.[114] In addition to the bold lettering found on the sign tower, McAllister placed a basic pole sign curbside to advertise the business, so that patrons down the road could see it. In the early 1940s, the simple, circular drive-in grew in shape and complexity to accommodate new functions, like dining rooms and cocktail lounges with interior spaces. This meant the addition of a wing to the original hub, sometimes terminated by yet another hublike form with a vertical emphasis.[115]

In Miami Beach during the 1930s, architects devised a special form for hotels on corner sites, which presented a unique opportunity for tower signage well integrated with the architecture. The Essex (Henry Hohauser, 1938) and the Senator and Tiffany hotels (L. Murray Dixon, 1939) exemplified this type at its best (fig. 76). The rounded corner of each, facing Collins Avenue and the cross street, took advantage of both the horizontal movement of the building's long elevations and the vertical established by the implied cylinder at the street intersection, underneath the tower. The sign tower was

(below) *Figure 70* Proposal for updating Main Street, Niles, Michigan (Ketchum, Gina & Sharp, 1944). The underlying message from this complete presentation, with its large-scale graphics and angled, open-front glass entrances, was that the work was ideally placed in the hands of a single designer to coordinate and balance the look of the entire street.
ARCHITECTURAL FORUM (OCTOBER 1944), 110–11. REPRODUCTION COURTESY OF RYERSON AND BURNHAM LIBRARIES, ART INSTITUTE OF CHICAGO.

Figure 71

Grayson's (Gruen and Krummeck, circa 1945; demolished), Pasadena, California. One of several stores Victor Gruen designed for the chain, the design aggressively suggested a spatial interplay between inside and outside with a forecourt or exterior lobby that virtually scooped customers in from the sidewalk.

PHOTO BY MOTT STUDIOS. PUBLISHED IN EMRICH NICHOLSON, *CONTEMPORARY SHOPS IN THE UNITED STATES* (1945), 50.

AMERICA DISCOVERS MODERNISM

Figure 72
Proposal for the entrance of a bowling and billiards center, commissioned by Brunswick-Balke-Collender Company (Donald Deskey, circa 1945). With the tilted plane above and giant billiard ball shooting forth, the interior seemed to thrust aggressively outside to grab the patron's attention.
COOPER-HEWITT, NATIONAL DESIGN MUSEUM, SMITHSONIAN INSTITUTION / ART RESOURCE, NEW YORK.

located exactly at the center of the corner's radius. In most cases, the slender tower made a transition to the larger, rounded corner by way of a series of progressively larger drums or cubes. These neon rooftop beacons marked the skyline of lower Collins Avenue for many blocks and helped make the corner hotels competitive with those that were directly on the beach. Freestanding neon lettering that rested on the continuous stucco canopy over the first floor and its terrace entrance reinforced the tower signs at eye level.

The Shelborne Hotel (1940–41), a gimmick-free International Style composition by Igor Polevitzky and his partner T. Triplett Russell, presented a very different approach to sign integration (see plate 12). Placed upon the original tower, exactly the same width as the mass directly below it, was a sign composed of deep, freestanding, three-dimensional letters—finished in the same material as the hotel walls. With its dark, tropical shadows, the sign appeared to be a piece of the building, created out of the same substance. And yet the lettering, with its ribbon-thin face, rested lightly at the building's crest as if it had been lowered into place by a crane. It was both unified with the architecture and physically independent; it would thus seem to satisfy the International Style show curators' dictates for successful modern signage. This tower feature, along with a procession of similar neon identifications, aloft at night over the beach, welcomed new visitors as they arrived by causeway from the mainland.[116]

Architects of the late 1920s and early 1930s, especially in the more urban eastern United States, labored carefully to keep the sign feature and the facade knit together, not quite so independent of one another. Reconciling fins or towerlike sign features with a building facade required some finesse. The skyscraperlike beacon of Philadelphia's Midway Theater (Magaziner, Eberhard & Harris, 1929) stepped down to the two-story commercial building base just as the projecting sign descended in stages to the wide, oval marquee. The architect of the Embassy Theater (William

Figure 73

Esquire Theater (William Pereira and Hal Pereira, 1937; altered), Oak Street, Chicago. Although articulated as a separate piece, the vertical, projecting sign was an integral part of a large ensemble of hovering planes, boxes, and drum forms and played a key role in balancing the composition.
PHOTO BY HEDRICH-BLESSING, 1937.
COURTESY OF THE CHICAGO HISTORY MUSEUM, HB-04606.

Harold Lee, 1931) in Reading, Pennsylvania, provided a similar transition for the towering vertical sign by stepping the facade around the sign and resting the tower on a pyramid base that rose from the marquee (fig. 77). This same design logic eventually trickled down to small-town cinemas. For example, the vertical sign for the Capri (née Princess, 1948) in Shelbyville, Tennessee, was united with the canopy of the marquee by way of a cascade of neon steps (see plate 13).[117] The sign was designed and built by the Columbia Neon Company, working with Marr and Holman, the Nashville architectural firm assigned the task of reconfiguring the facade of an older theater building.

Movie theaters built in the late 1930s and early 1940s often had sign towers or fins visually stretching away from the buildings of which they were a part. The 20th Century Theater (Fred Stritzel, 1941) in Cincinnati provides one of the finest examples (fig. 78). Located on a central square in the neighborhood of Oakley, the theater with its sign tower was a landmark suitably scaled to the space in front of it. The tower terminated a three-story sine-wave facade wall, glazed with purple porcelain ceramic tiles. In Chicago, Kem Weber proposed several new (unbuilt) facade treatments for the RKO Palace Theater (1945), where the sign fin towered even higher—though in this case up the side of an existing building. In one scheme, an elaborate neon fin ran the entire height of the twenty-two-story building, yet still pushed past the roofline. A second fin, perhaps only half the height of the structure, carried the theater's name: it terminated in an L-shaped, asymmetrical canopy of light over the entrance.

Architect Jack Corgan designed a multitude of theaters in the South and Southwest during the late 1940s that featured dynamic sign fins and towers creatively engaged with building facades and massing compositions. The fin sign for the Hornbeck Theater (1947), in the town center of Shawnee, Oklahoma, was part of an otherwise flat composition; it slipped naturally into a groove in the dynamic, planar composition—and, like Weber's Palace proposal, projected well beyond the roofline. The sign tower for the May and the Will Rogers Theaters in Oklahoma City (both 1946) intersected the entrance pavilion or lobby, which was articulated distinctly from the auditorium. Located on suburban sites, both theaters were designed as assemblies of architectural pieces and forms, each part clearly communicating its function.

In 1945, demonstrating an even higher degree of architectural articulation, skyscraper architect Ely Jacques Kahn (Kahn & Jacobs) proposed several novel ideas for two movie theaters to be built along New York's Broadway between 45th and 46th Streets (see plate 14). Large-scale, colorful graphics would distinguish these structures: colored lights, bold patterns, and oversized movie posters. One concept was remarkable for its enormous sign fin that was the size of a full wall, thrusting forth from the auditorium and turning 90 degrees to become the unusual marquee.[118] Unlike the adjacent eight-story office block, this complex was daringly free-form, an intersecting group

(opposite) *Figure 74*
Crest Hotel (Edward A. Nolan, 1941), James Avenue, Miami Beach, Florida. Nolan designed the vertical projecting sign as part of the facade composition, thus making it more of a "fin" than an add-on.
PHOTO BY AUTHOR, 1996.

Figure 75
Simon's Drive-In Restaurant (Wayne McAllister, 1935; demolished), Wilshire Boulevard and Fairfax Avenue, Los Angeles, circa 1936. McAllister pushed the evolution of the radial California drive-in building type. First with Simon's and later with designs for many other such chains, he expertly blended the sign tower with the rest of the structure.
SECURITY PACIFIC NATIONAL BANK COLLECTION / LOS ANGELES PUBLIC LIBRARY.

of angular cubes, fins, and towers, bundled together with neon. The resulting composition was a very figural (foreground) object in contrast to the neighboring buildings whose facades continued the traditional (background) wall of the street. It was suburban in form, as if surrounded by plenty of open space.

The movie theaters of Los Angeles demonstrated the next step in the design evolution, of progressively more figural signs becoming visually independent from architecture while remaining visually coordinated to a whole. Architects in auto-oriented communities struggled with the assignment of merging two opposing forms: a tall, distinctive sign or tower feature for distant identification and a low-slung building of one or two stories, stretched out to address the ever-lengthening strip. The tower of the Leimert Theater (Morgan, Walls & Clements, 1931) was enormous in contrast to the single-story retail strip at its base. An ornamented silver metal mast or aerial with stacked neon lettering was placed at the top of the tapered stucco tower. Where the tower connected with the storefronts below, it stepped from vertical to horizontal with a religious flourish of ornament. Percy Parke Lewis's

Village Theater (1931) in the Westwood section of Los Angeles appeared to be just a tower—there was hardly a base at all except for its wrap-around marquee (see plate 15). This tower was both the literal sign (with neon at its crest) and the architecture (the entrance was through its base). The auditorium was connected to it only at one corner and was otherwise buried in the middle of the block and behind foliage. Lewis marked the Westwood branch of Sears (1936), an otherwise straightforward Spanish-colonial-style building, with a major rocketlike tower featuring a sign. The concentration of sign towers for movie theaters, gas stations, and grocery stores in this neighborhood was visible to drivers approaching Westwood from Wilshire Boulevard, and it served to distinguish the area visibly.[119]

In California, theater designer S. Charles Lee demonstrated great creativity and finesse with the way he linked identifying towers with their earthbound bases.[120] At the Academy Theater (1939) in Los Angeles, a corkscrew sign tower, visible from great distances, marked the location of the cinema. A spiraling fin descended from the crest of the tower, coming to rest at the back of the auditorium to help link vertical with horizontal. Breaking up the low auditorium mass visually, so that it resembled a bundle of drums, Lee mitigated the vast visual disparity between the tower sign and the bulk of the building. Each neon letter of the tower rested on a loop of the spiral. The graphics on the wide, bowed marquee were elongated to fill the space. Adept at both architecture and graphics, Lee was able to ensure harmony between the two in his composition.[121]

In Houston, by the late 1930s, tower signs and adjacent theaters had become fully independent of each other, linked only by style and other implied visual connections. W. Scott Dunne created a freestanding sign on the road as the primary identification for the Alabama Theater (1939), located in the new shopping district of the River Oaks neighborhood. A marquee of sorts advertising the current film fare was part of the curbside sign. On the theater facade, set back from the road with parking in front, was a more traditional marquee. In terms of functionality, the most significant sign was at the road. This phenomenon of erecting separate roadside signs for movie theaters eventually became the standard for off-street businesses.

Modernizing with or without Architects: The Coordinated Community and the Vernacular Individual

Leaders in the field of design pushed many of the bigger developments in commercial buildings and signs. But what of the smaller businesses with very small budgets for facade updates? Creating a new look for an old business often involved just the erection of a new sign. Since funds were often unavailable for whole storefront remodelings, there was little opportunity to integrate the sign with its site. Instead, signs with modest modern flourishes were applied in the conventional way: hanging or projecting from the facade or applied flush to the fascia area. In contrast to this ad hoc approach for identifying small businesses was a new trend to design small shopping strips with a consistent look from storefront to storefront. These highly controlled "centers," as they were sometimes called in promotional literature, often enforced uniform signage and consistent facing.

By the 1930s, the appearance of America's commercial strips, or "taxpayers," had changed significantly. Ornate projections and heavy pilasters no longer distinguished the bays of individual buildings. Now, the upper wall, or parapet, appeared to float above continuous glass display windows and entrances.[122] In the 1920s and 1930s, groups of stores along the street were often visually enhanced as an ensemble or at least marketed together as shopping centers.[123] The FHA actually encouraged a collective approach to Main Street improvements that might serve as the foundation for overall civic beautification and betterment.[124] The goal was to make a cluster of disparate storefronts appear as a visually distinguished unit. A single ownership or cooperative was better able to dictate how individual renters should maintain their structures.

Figure 76

Essex House Hotel (Henry Hohauser, 1938), Collins Avenue, Miami Beach, Florida, in 1938. One of several examples of the corner hotel type along Collins, the Essex demonstrated how a vertical sign tower could be visually reconciled with a building that emphasizes the horizontal.

COURTESY OF HISTORYMIAMI.

Both visual unity and distinctive design were employed to set some strip shopping centers apart from their weary-looking neighbors. For older building fronts, using pigmented structural glass or colorful glazed terra cotta to cover old and new facades was an effective means of applying vibrant, long-lasting color over an array of worn materials and inconsistent parapet profiles.[125] Despite, or perhaps because of, the exuberant new building skins, many centers confined graphics to a narrow zone that coincided with the location of the traditional fascia sign. A large, new taxpayer strip located at a major shopping hub in a northwestern Chicago neighborhood (Z. Erol Smith, 1935) was made visually cohesive with an elaborate skin, by Northwestern Terra Cotta Company, featuring a bold basket-weave pattern (see plate 16).[126] This new sheathing was so remarkable that the corner became a visual landmark, a special place along the seemingly endless grid of the city. The elaborate veneer, however, precluded the application of signs to the parapet area: no upper wall or projecting signs were permitted originally. All identities for businesses were relegated to the glass provided between neutral piers, making them the subtlest advertising in the neighborhood. Even the White Hut hamburger chain was shoehorned into one of these tight modules.[127]

Half-block or block-long shopping centers in the 1930s and 1940s frequently included an anchor store of some type—usually a food market or movie theater—that provided an essential architectural flourish. The anchor also served as a visual landmark with the opportunity it afforded for distinctive sign features that might rise above the others on the strip. Strict leasing rules or design authority given to a single person helped to pull these small retail centers together visually. Projecting signs were usually permitted only for anchor stores, and identities for smaller stores were often confined to a slim strip located over the display windows, creating a somewhat uniform appearance from business to business. In some cases, the owners and architects of new shopping strip buildings recognized the need for greater graphic freedom and thus permitted significantly larger upper wall sign area for graphics. The trademark lettering for chain stores increasingly mandated this visual variety. A block-long shopping center (Leichenko & Esser, 1942) with the Hillman's Pure Foods chain as anchor store in a north Chicago neighborhood demonstrated this design freedom (fig. 79). Only the major retailers at each end of the center were permitted projecting signs, but the chain stores occupying most of the space between were allotted generous wall space for their identities. The then-novel International Style architecture served to pull the ensemble together stylistically, and a continuous ribbon window functioned as a unifying link between design flourishes for the anchor store "bookends."

Several well-published retail innovations stimulated the concept of uniform signage.[128] General Electric advertised uniform electric signs for strip retail in the early 1930s. Sign panels of this type were especially suitable

Figure 77
Embassy Theatre (William Harold Lee, 1931), Penn Street, Reading, Pennsylvania, in 1943. The architect of the Embassy managed to design an especially convincing visual transition from the required vertical projecting sign to the horizontal marquee below it.
COURTESY OF THE HISTORICAL SOCIETY OF BERKS COUNTY.

Figure 78

20th Century Theater (Fred Stritzel, 1941; altered), Madison Road, Cincinnati. As the 1940s progressed, the sign towers of many theaters assumed more and more visual independence. In this example, it was a colossal pylon, with identity at one end and box office at the other.

PHOTO BY AUTHOR, 2006.

for suburban shopping centers with off-street parking and sufficient size to be major destinations. Three of the earliest such centers—the Park and Shop (Arthur Heaton, 1930) in Washington, D.C., a free-standing shopping center (Frederick A. Ackerman, 1931) in Radburn, New Jersey, and the Silver Spring Shopping Center (John Eberson, 1938) in Silver Spring, Maryland—offered large parking areas surrounded by retail establishments. The Park and Shop and the Radburn project were made noticeable by distinctive architecture—high dormer windows and cupolas—but the individual business signs were muted. The low-profile Silver Spring Shopping Center stressed modernity along its rambling length with a series of dark horizontal decorative strips above the shop windows and a uniform sign format. The distinctive vertical movie theater sign that bore the word *Silver* was the only major identifier on the entire site.[129]

By the time that Kawneer and *Pencil Points* magazine sponsored the competition for "The Store Front of Tomorrow" in 1943, the momentum among architects for radically controlling sign design had developed to such an extreme that the jury warned against overdoing it. The goal of the competition was to plan a group of stores rather than an individual storefront, and the site was a tabula rasa.[130] The judges, including Morris Ketchum Jr., Mies van der Rohe, and William Lescaze, praised efforts by entrants to unify the stores that they rendered with continuous canopies and common exterior lobbies, but they admonished some leading contestants against overcontrolling the graphics. "Too many restrictions will kill the tenant's business," the judges cautioned, with "harmonious but stiff" signs.[131]

The issue for commercial designers and architects to ponder during the 1940s was how to create unity without sacrificing individuality. Morris Ketchum's boast that his remake of Main Street was doing just this relied on the expert manipulation of a single architect. "Striking character has been given the separate stores, but through ingenious handling of the group plan adjacent facades play an important part in complementing and emphasizing each other." Convinced that postwar modernization must proceed on a community rather than individual basis, "the sponsors plan to develop a service which will make available designs for remodeled shopping centers, complete with re-planned stores, to groups of storekeepers all over the country."[132]

Signs created by an assortment of designers left too much to chance, according to Ketchum and his peers, so whole streetscapes or groups of stores must be designed all at once. This controlled variety was the antithesis of the traditional, democratic Main Street. But it appeared to be the only variety that many architects believed was suitable for America.

In complete contrast to such control, most Main Streets across the country evolved organically through the 1930s. It was a spotty rehabilitation along most of America's commercial thoroughfares: perhaps a single Vitrolite-covered bakery or tavern found along a street of otherwise nineteenth-century storefronts, some updated with projecting signs of porcelain enamel and neon. Bigger cities and towns more fortunate economically appeared more consistently up-to-date. The piecemeal modernizing was enough to make an impression on the knowing eye of Morris Lapidus, who traveled through the United States in the 1930s for his employer Ross-Frankel to install stores for chain retailers.

> The first pump-priming [of the economy by the government; i.e., FHA loans for storefronts] . . . took place in the southeastern part of the United States, and its effects were felt at once by Ross-Frankel . . . My first trip to Knoxville, Tennessee was in 1934. Main Street had not changed since the Civil War: farmers still brought their produce into town and backed up their horse-drawn wagons under covered sheds where housewives did their daily shopping . . . When I went back to install more stores in that city two years later, it had changed drastically. Gone were the farmers' wagons and their covered sheds. Fine, new modern stores lined Main Street.[133]

By the late 1930s, many of America's Main Streets were lined with a hodge-podge of buildings, both new and old. One block along Vine Street in Cincinnati, as photographed in 1939, was fairly typical, with its mix of late-nineteenth- and early-twentieth-century structures, randomly modernized from the fascia level down (fig. 80). Electric signs with opal glass letters hung above old painted signs—both secured with cables. Evidence of progress was the presence of two storefronts clad in dark structural glass and porcelain enamel. One had neon characters applied flush to the gleaming new surface, and on the other, narrow, streamlined lettering formed a unique logo.

The installation of new neon signs, rather than full facade rehabilitations, generally served to "modernize" many commercial streetscapes in the early 1940s. A striking projecting sign usually provided the biggest impact for the dollar. For some smaller towns, where the architecture was quite humble, the projecting signs lined up one after another, helping to define an otherwise poorly articulated street wall. The Main Street of Crane, Texas, for example, was lined with simple frame parapets enlivened by a jumble of hanging and projecting signs. In contrast to the rudimentary architecture, the somewhat chaotic wall of graphics contributed a sense of character and containment to a small Texas town (fig. 81). The exact design of each sign mattered little. The ideas may have come from Samuel C. Miller's *Neon Signs; Manufacture–Installation–Maintenance* or from an intriguing form on the back of a box of detergent, as suggested by one of the contributors to *Signs of the Times*. Most businesses and patrons only truly cared that there was plenty of neon light and a general look of prosperity.

Projecting signs had been fixtures on Main Streets for decades, but their use grew as the 1930s progressed. In towns that welcomed many newcomers, they communicated easily from afar and were thus well suited to the automobile. The growth in their size is partially explained by the aggressive promotion of the sign industry, which contended that it could help Main Street reclaim its prominence following lean economic times.

Trade books and articles in *Signs of the Times* introduced European design and the best of American signs to their readers, who pored over renderings and photographs of complex projecting sign examples. To generate better, more aggressive design work in America, designers such as Phillip Di Lemme and John Albright, among many others, published intriguing examples of abstract composition and streamline form.[134] Their stimulus eventually inspired work like the sign for the modest wiener shop, Original New York System (storefront, 1928; sign, early 1930s, Federal Sign Co.), in Providence, Rhode Island (see plate 17). Although the sign was not physically unified with the porcelain enamel facade, its angles and general shape were in sync with the angular window forms. Both sign and building were clad in porcelain enamel. Neon edging for the windows also served to link sign with storefront. Di Lemme and Albright's publications also directly inspired

Figure 79

Wallen Block (Leichenko & Esser, 1942), Devon Avenue, Chicago. This block-long structure was one of an increasing number of planned, coordinated shopping centers built within the urban grid of the city. Visual anchors like food markets and cinemas usually bookended such ensembles.

PHOTO BY CHICAGO ARCHITECTURAL PHOTOGRAPHING COMPANY, CIRCA 1944. COURTESY OF THE CHICAGO HISTORY MUSEUM, i61991.

the projecting sign for the Carlos Club in San Carlos, California (Coast Neon, Redwood City, 1947)—including its visual coordination with the long lines and circular window of the facade (see plate 18). Although easily perceived as an independent piece, projecting well beyond the parapet, it rested perfectly on a flagstone pier and referred to the simple geometries of the facade. Even the smallest business was able to order signs with modern flourishes. Some sign companies offered modern, up-to-date production-line sign designs that could be customized merely with the business' name. The basic sign for the Wilton Candy Kitchen (Cro Sign, 1946, Muscatine) in Wilton, Iowa, was likely straight from a catalogue or based closely on standard designs (see plate 19).[135] It was one of the few artifacts in the 1930s–1940s that served to update an otherwise nineteenth-century Midwestern Main Street.

As so-called neon benders became increasingly skilled, they were able to "draw" fluidly with light. Freed from the limitations of incandescent bulbs, sign designers could contour neon to almost any form. As a result of their mastery, projecting signs were now embellished with such details as art deco scrolls and horizontal speed lines. In addition to executing many purely graphic ideas in three dimensions, sign designers demonstrated their prowess in the art of neon illustration, creating neon-tube dragons, puppies, martini glasses, windmills, automobiles, cameras, and other fanciful shapes

AMERICA DISCOVERS MODERNISM

Figure 80

Commercial buildings and storefronts along Vine Street, Cincinnati, circa 1939. Most often, modern design arrived modestly along Main Street, without a rush of remodelings up and down the street. Here and there, business owners attracted attention merely by adding new signs made with neon or resheathing their storefronts with pigmented structural glass. Note the businesses Maly's Photos and Jackson's on this street corner.

COURTESY OF THE CINCINNATI MUSEUM CENTER.

and figures. Such illuminated illustrations, often elaborately animated, formerly had been confined to the rooftops of buildings in major cities. But by the middle 1930s, as more companies produced neon and prices came down, the medium offered elaborate displays to small businesses as well. The animated Bun'n Burger sign (Neon Products Signs, 1950) in Alhambra, California, exemplifies with what flourish a modest enterprise could present itself to the street. The neon was unusually well integrated with the architecture, but this is not surprising considering that the architect of the building was Walter Zick (1941), a prolific designer in Las Vegas during the 1950s, perhaps most famous for the fluid, neon-clad, Mint Hotel. With the 1950 graphic updating of the Alhambra facade by Neon Products, a "curtain" of pink neon filled the concave tower feature above the building's corner entrance; it alternated with an intricate neon illustration of a chef running with a burger on a plate. In 1941, Zick had placed the name in green neon on the edge of a convex canopy under the future location of the pink neon "curtain" and over the door.

Zick's concave entrance design easily accommodated, if not implied, some of the later neon additions. The design was visually resplendent, yet efficient and tightly coordinated; the graphics embellished the architecture, following its form and profile, and the architecture placed the focus on the signs (see plate 20).[136]

With his 1930 cover for *Vanity Fair*, French graphic designer Jean Carlu brilliantly expressed the fluid potential for neon, suggesting an aesthetic that the medium itself could define (fig. 82). With two curvaceous, interlocking faces drawn with light on this cover, Carlu demonstrated an abstract illustrative approach, where images were created with deft, unbroken strokes of light. Neon had its limitations: it was a continuous line, unless segmented with the use of blackout paint or hidden in a chase. In their zeal to please clients, American sign companies created far more literal illustrations in neon than did the French designer—at least as literal as the medium might allow.

Despite the advice and encouragement available in how-to books and *Signs of the Times,* many of America's commercial thoroughfares in the early 1940s were aesthetically incoherent, lined with structures and signs that tended to clash with, rather than to complement, each other. Industrial designer Raymond Loewy's "Cicero Sonnet" vividly captured the repetition, mediocrity, and convoluted graphic contrivances visible along a commercial strip leading to the airport: "For nearly an hour one sees nothing but the most dismal assemblage of blackened tenements, cheap stores, decrepit bars, and hamburger joints; literally hundreds of them, all alike, all splashing an orange or blue neon sign in a streaky window, or above a sad door. The signs were nearly all beer signs. I am haunted by the inevitability of this beer sign parade along the way . . . I am just drowsy, watching the signs go by."[137]

But the multitude of humble sign-only modernizations of the 1930s and 1940s provided an affordable upgrade for businesses that did not have the means to reface their establishments. The sometimes messy, but often vital, vernacular commercial landscapes created by the signs associated with this era are what dominated the public's view along the nation's Main Streets and highways. These signs, and the architecture beyond, were many generations removed from the high-style work presented in tonier architecture journals and original European work presented in trade magazines like *Signs of the Times* and *Architectural Record*. It may not have been a beautiful commercial landscape to some, and the prosperity that it attempted to communicate was often only skin deep. However, in many ways, this modest layer of design was a monument to America's survival, perhaps even its pluck, during a dangerous and discouraging period in history.

In the 1930s, the potential for great advances in American commercial design was both unusually powerful and tragically weak. On the one hand, there was an unprecedented rush of creativity and experimentation in European storefront design, which was rapidly documented and available for inspiration in books, architectural magazines, and sign company trade journals. On the other hand, by the time that this epiphany of European style, developed during the boom economy of the 1920s, reached the United States, the Great Depression had begun. There was little money available for architects and designers to fill American streets with equal visual excitement.

Fortunately, American corporations and the United States government were motivated to assist. The big illumination and building materials companies developed ambitious programs to lure customers back to stores. They realized that modernism could sell; something powerful and new was needed to pull shoppers back to Main Street as often as possible. The companies also worked to expand the vision of designers and architects so that they would use more new materials in their work. Expanding the architect's palette and canvas included showing him or her the great new ranges of materials produced, such as the rainbow of colors available for pigmented structural glass, like Vitrolite. Architectural journals and publications like General Electric's *Magazine of Light* showed how other architects were designing sign towers or arranging large swaths of color and three-dimensional lettering across two-story commercial building facades. By expanding the realm of the architect's creative work, boundaries were melted: between architect and sign designer and between architecture and sign. The 1930s thus became the decade of sign integration, where graphics were no longer mere afterthoughts but intricately a part of full artistic compositions.

The 1930s was also the decade that initiated an exploration of three-dimensional commercial design for its full potential. Commerce continued its expansion into suburban space, a momentum launched in full during the 1920s. Businesses like drive-ins and markets were among the first to offer opportunities for designing commercial enterprises in the round, as opposed to creating flat facades in urban locations. Signs that were limited to vertical fins in the city evolved to become, in suburban space, full pylons with increasingly tentative attachments to buildings. At the same time, buildings progressed from smooth, self-contained envelopes of space to structures with increasingly complex surfaces, with functional and decorative elements projecting out in all directions. Most important, the barrier between inside and outside was radically reduced, permitting customers to see deeply into store interiors and enter with unprecedented ease.

But the full design potential of the decade remained unexplored due to economic restrictions. Because storefront modernizing was, at first, so two-dimensional, sign companies, not architects, produced most of the updating. A new sign and a coat of paint is all that many businesses ever received during the Great Depression. Thus, sign designers ushered in small but significant streamlined features, glossy new materials, and neon lighting, even if it was

confined to small sign boxes that projected over display windows. These small bits of modernism were introduced both to dusty western towns with wood-frame false fronts, where there was little else but a Main Street, and to well-manicured county seats with brick and stone commercial buildings already more than fifty years old.

The sign designer's role, like the architect's, would eventually grow to include more facets of commercial design. During the 1930s, these artists received mixed messages about what was right; some articles suggested restraint, referencing images of European design, while others shared long lists of trusted design gimmicks. The potential for neon as a medium that would generate its own forms was still just being explored.

What set the 1930s and early 1940s apart from other periods of design was the attempt by many architects and sign artists to integrate graphics visually with building facades and storefronts. The poor economy had driven owners and developers to turn to designers as if they were scientists, a move subsidized by the government. Suddenly, the values of the creative force were pushed forward. Designers reconceived the streetscape as being

Figure 81

Main Street, Crane, Texas. The canopy of graphics, although somewhat chaotic, nevertheless contributed to a sense of scale and containment in a town just barely defined by its simple architecture.
PHOTO BY RUSSELL LEE, 1939. LIBRARY OF CONGRESS, PRINTS & PHOTOGRAPHS DIVISION, FSA/OWI COLLECTION, LC-USF34-33192-D.

VANITY FAIR

APRIL 1931
PRICE 35 CTS.
© THE CONDÉ NAST
PUBLICATIONS, INC.

JEAN CARLU

less the result of mere accident and more the consequence of careful planning. Instead of last-minute additions with awkward, skeletal fastenings, many signs were fashioned to be continuous with the skins of the buildings housing the businesses they identified. Signs may have reached for attention with towers or projections over the sidewalk, but the full thrust of each was tempered by its connection to the neutral line of a canopy, window edge, or doorway. During this same period, designers extended a great effort to present visually unified strips of businesses, small neighborhood shopping centers sometimes as long as a full block. The individuality of businesses, with potentially disparate, competitive visual identifications, was often suppressed in these strips; signs for supporting businesses were sometimes required to fit a template of size and color, while anchor stores were permitted great freedom. On the whole, these strips were at once vibrant and restrained, distinctive but harmonious.

All in all, the push for storefront design integration and communal unity during the 1930s and early 1940s did not straightjacket individuality; it merely regulated it. Updated streetscapes still provided plenty of visual stimulation, especially by theaters and markets. However, the free-market spontaneity of the 1920s was no longer associated with business vitality. Designers in the 1930s, armed with the unprecedented confidence that their clients had in them, aimed for a balance between individual and community. The realization of that goal may have been irregular, but it is the aim that was key because this idealism would not last. In decades to come, design would result primarily from unfettered capitalism and individualism along suburban highways or extreme control in the new regional shopping centers.

(opposite) *Figure 82*
Jean Carlu, cover of *Vanity Fair* (April 1931). The French designer created this simple illustration knowing the limits and benefits of the new medium of neon. By keeping the image abstract, the line of light could be continuous and the drawing given the power of an abstracted symbol or trademark.
REPRODUCTION COURTESY OF RYERSON AND BURNHAM LIBRARIES, ART INSTITUTE OF CHICAGO. CARLU / VANITY FAIR / CONDÉ NAST ARCHIVE.
© CONDÉ NAST.

Chapter 5
LANDSCAPES OF MORE AND LESS
CONSEQUENCES OF COMMERCIAL FREEDOM AND RESTRAINT, 1946–1964

AMERICA'S COMMERCIAL CORRIDORS showcased an unprecedented flowering of design exuberance during the twenty years following World War II. But this blossoming was accompanied by equally unprecedented strain and adjustment. Changes in shopping habits and demographics resulted in a shift of emphasis from urban to suburban shopping venues, threatening a "downtown"-oriented retail tradition of more than two hundred years. Merchants on Main Street responded with desperate attempts to outshine, or at least mimic, the scale and style of suburban retail design. Meanwhile, critics and high-profile designers lambasted the outrageousness of commercial signs and structures built for restaurants, motels, and stores, calling for a new aesthetic of architectural moderation and concise graphic symbolism. New technology in plastics caused a slow, steady decline of the artistic potential of neon design, a craft barely twenty-five years old. With the new plastic signs came an aesthetic of graphic containment, defined by the limits of the material and the requirements of an evolving corporate culture.

The end of wartime gas rationing, and the conversion of manufacturing plants from airplane production back to car production, created a new surge in automobile use in the late 1940s that would prompt rapid changes in America's commercial landscapes. Government subsidy of suburban home loans encouraged growth outside the traditional city limits. The opening of the Pennsylvania Turnpike in 1940 and Congress' authorization of the Federal Interstate System in 1956 spurred the creation of new superhighways. *Architectural Record* published special sections devoted to drive-in theaters, drive-in restaurants, and drive-through banks in 1946, 1950, and 1953, including the work of such architects as Wayne McAllister and John Lautner, revealing how important these new businesses and building types had become to the design professions.

The relatively unrestrained creativity of sign designers and architects characterized these postwar decades. More often, signs and buildings were physically independent of each other, permitting new design possibilities. The unconventional signs and trademark architecture across America resulted in large part from the influential design work of a few key individuals. Strip architecture and graphics were inspired by published images of this work or other references, like the shapes and compositions in advertisements and packaging. Most important, strip architecture and signage were developed to capture the attention of the jaded motorist from afar. Signs reached, lunged, and commanded, with implied kinetic energy in their novel graphic arrangements. By 1955, sign manufacturing soared to an all-time high in response to the growth of automobile-oriented businesses. As commerce increasingly spread to the strip, a new sign type, the pylon, emerged. During the 1950s and early 1960s, this figural, fully independent structure grew to enormous scale with progressively ambitious design.

During this period of unrestrained development and design, a new commercial ideal evolved. The planned regional shopping center, designed and controlled by a single force, was promoted as an antidote to the loose collection of structures and advertisements along the commercial corridor, considered offensive by architects, journalists, and a growing number of citizens. Leading designers and visionary developers felt there was a better model for commerce than the strip, which they viewed as a random manifestation of free enterprise. In its place they proposed something far cleaner and more predictable, a marketplace managed by a master. What evolved was a model Main Street where the visual expression of the individual was suppressed to the perceived benefit of the whole. The appearance of the center itself, rather than each business, dominated the customer's impressions.

Urban Update: The Transition to a New Commercial Landscape

The postwar surge of suburban development forced greater change on downtown and Main Street than anything over a century of almost constant design evolution had yet done. Competition between stores in the central business district and heavy promotion of design trends in trade magazines rapidly transformed many older retail corridors. The new open-storefront approach to design, broadcast through design journals beginning in the early 1940s, was joined by yet another modernizing strategy in the 1950s: covering outmoded commercial building facades with opaque or meshed metal panel systems. New sign technology, which employed formed acrylic panels illuminated from behind by fluorescent tubes, meant a push for the replacement of neon signs, as well as for any incandescent bulbs signs that remained from the first decades of the century. The National Electric Sign Association sponsored competitions in the late 1940s through the early 1960s that proved that urban sites continued to matter; more than half the programs for competition were established around existing retail locations. The 1950s offered the last opportunity for a creative mingling of graphics and architecture in an urban condition. The sprawling sites of suburban retail offered little opportunity for such design integration.

In 1956 the decision of the F. W. Woolworth Company to officially change its seventy-seven-year-old sign format prompted a four-page protest in *Architectural Record*.[1] On all new applications, the familiar composition of gold Roman letters set in a deep red fascia panel over the front display windows was being replaced by much larger, internally-lit, red plastic, sans-serif letters individually mounted directly on the building face (see plate 21). The distressed author of the article was Mildred Constantine, associate curator of graphic design at the Museum of Modern Art in New York. Her concern was an indication of how ardently the traditional sign was revered and how sign design in general was assuming new importance in America. Two years later, an article in *Landscape* praised the old Woolworth sign as "one of the few survivors from the good old days of well-mannered craftsmanship."[2] The authors of both articles cited the classical precedent for the old Woolworth sign—the Roman frieze or fascia—which led to a long-standing tradition where sign and architecture respectfully acknowledged one another.

Nineteenth-century sign design needed updating to twentieth-century conditions. To justify the design change, the Woolworth Company claimed that competitors had copied its classic format, a problem that had actually existed for decades. In truth, automobiles had created the need for a bolder, more flexible design approach. The old Woolworth's street identity was based on an urban sign tradition that had quickly become obsolete because of the increased speed of motorized vehicles. Fascia board signs like the traditional Woolworth's identity were underscaled, poorly located, and inadequately illuminated to serve the motoring public.

The new plastic lettering could be placed anywhere on the building's facade, at any scale, and on virtually any material or background color. For years, Woolworth's had been experimenting with new lettering on storefronts, including all kinds of new facing material and streamlined design features. Now, a new lettering style would be official. Woolworth's had finally succumbed to the inevitable.

In the late 1940s and 1950s, signs applied to older buildings in retail districts grew to disproportionate size for the scale of the nineteenth- and early-twentieth-century sites in order to address motorists increasingly used to the grand scale of things in suburbia. Well-publicized design competitions in the 1930s and 1940s had introduced large, upper-facade graphics, but with cash flowing after World War II, more businesses put this strategy to use.[3] Sign companies became more involved in facade rehabilitation work, especially after one of their heroes, Douglas Leigh, proposed covering the buildings around Times Square in 1954 with neutral, vertically ribbed, aluminum skins to serve as backgrounds for large-scale, corporate, promotional graphics. Leigh was one of the nation's premier sign designers, having achieved particular notoriety in the 1940s by creating the famous Camel cigarettes advertisement on Times Square, with an immense face blowing gigantic smoke rings out over traffic. He was also responsible for the on-premise sculptural signage for Bond Clothing (1948), which featured mammoth, three-dimensional male and female figures bookending a 120-foot-wide cascade of water on a base of neon lettering and a new zip.[4]

Radical updating of older storefronts—both sign and building skin—appeared essential if merchants wanted to stay in business downtown. The idea was reinforced over and over in the media and by word of mouth. The Providence, Rhode Island, City Plan Commission's 1959 master plan presentation, also known as *Downtown Providence 1970*, began by praising recent activity in refacing buildings. Blemishes in the business center required aggressive action, it suggested. At a speech presented to Providence businessmen, even the supervising architect

for historic structures of the National Park Service, Charles E. Peterson, revealed just how anxious the situation had become: "It is time . . . to begin correcting the mistakes before the cities become graveyards or ghost towns . . . 'Peterson's Law' . . . To tear down what is bad and save what is good."[5]

Downtown Providence 1970 presented illustrations of structures along Westminster Street as they might appear reclad in modular screen panels. Only buildings of highest historic integrity were to be spared this kind of modernization. And yet, sometime in the 1950s, the Wilkinson Building on Westminster Street in Downcity Providence (Stone, Carpenter & Wilson, 1887) was mummified from the bottom of the transom glass to the sill of the third story with decorative concrete tiles for a Lerner Shop. This modernizing move temporarily masked and distorted the classic base-shaft-capital composition of the building, with its careful proportioning. It created a heavy band that seemed to defy gravity, with only display windows below it to "support" the entire structure. A large script sign was mounted across this novel, textured concrete pattern. In 1955, the J. J. Newberry five-and-dime store completely covered the palatial, extravagant building in which it set up shop. The fine, French classical Providence Journal Building (Peabody and Stearns, 1906), located on a corner site, was cloaked with an exterior insulation finish material pulled right up to the eaves of its steeply dormered mansard roof (fig. 83).

Various cover-up stories were played out across America. In the 1950s and 1960s, sleek, light-colored slipcovering composed of metal panel systems was the preferred method for updating.[6] *Chain Store Age*, among several trade journals, illustrated just how affordable it could be for merchants to cover older structures with lightweight, standard, industrial aluminum siding. This was particularly attractive for chain stores, where a major cash outlay would be needed to update a long list of stores.[7] Buildings were reskinned across America, but the phenomenon was particularly pronounced in California, where entire blocks (if not complete towns) received updating.[8]

Newly covered upper stories often became blank slates for primary identities. By 1956, the proprietors of Murray's restaurant in downtown Minneapolis decided that the sweeping chrome canopy and large neon lettering above the entrance, added to the old facade when the restaurant opened in 1946, were just not enough to entice patrons (see plate 22). The heavy, Romanesque arches and piers of the upper facade were thus covered with porcelain paneling that served as a background for a giant, illustrated platter of a sizzling steak. The General Outdoor Advertising Company also added a three-story projecting sign.

What encouraged merchants to camouflage the original architecture along Main Street, besides a desire to look commercially vital or to keep up with the images presented monthly in *Chain Store Age*? The introduction of new building finishes to the postwar market at least partially explains this transformation. Aluminum was widely available in both sign manufacture and architectural finishes after World War II. The development of new, lightweight aluminum

(opposite) Figure 83
Providence Journal Building (Peabody & Stearns, 1906; altered), Westminster Street, Providence, Rhode Island. Buildings all over the country were cloaked in modern dress in the 1950s and 1960s as retailers on waning commercial corridors in old city centers attempted to appear vital. The degree of blandness in this particular "cover-up" was commensurate with the intensity of architectural embellishment on the original. The chains Newberry's and Thom McAnn followed Liggett's as the ground floor tenants.
TOP: PHOTO, CIRCA 1940. PERSONAL COLLECTION OF WILLIAM BURGIN.
BOTTOM: PHOTO BY WILLIAM BURGIN, 1983. COURTESY OF WILLIAM BURGIN.

alloys for the war effort, and a reduced market with the end of fighting, meant an aggressive new battle to get the material specified for new applications.[9] Metal storefront framing companies like Kawneer and corporations like Reynolds Aluminum and Alcoa promoted their new architectural products relentlessly through the late 1940s, the 1950s, and 1960s. Architectural magazines carried countless seductive advertisements for remodeling. In the mid-1950s, Kawneer promoted its new Zourite facing, which came in seven porcelain-fired colors. The Mahon and Reynolds Aluminum companies advertised corrugated sheeting, featuring storefront renderings by the likes of Morris Lapidus, a highly revered leader in retail design by this time.[10] Textures came in flush, ribbed, or fluted profiles. Alcoa offered increasingly creative patterns and modular units with bowtie or oval forms that snapped in place on channel systems.

While the aluminum industry targeted architects, sign companies were barraged by advertisements for porcelain enamel. This material, specified for decades for individual signs with durable, low-maintenance finishes and smart colors, was now promoted for its power to transform whole building fronts into signs. The product had proven itself already for use in individual signs. Companies like Seaporcel and Cherokee Porcelain Enamel were showing sign men how they could expand their business exponentially and move easily into territory architects claimed. As shown in full-page ads, sign men could sweep away the clutter of an accumulation of small signs and extraneous nineteenth-century architectural detail to erect multistoried walls of smooth or textured panels, finished off with creative lettering at several times the scale of the old signs.

Sign designers increasingly became "architects" for storefronts. Encouraged since the 1930s by trade publications like *Signs of the Times*, as well as the momentum generated by the glass company architectural competitions of the 1930s, sign designers were primed to move beyond the very limited area allotted to sign fascias. By the 1950s, sign company designers were routinely encouraging business owners to let them sketch up new ideas for entire storefronts. It made great business sense for both parties: the sign companies expanded their market, and the business owners received one-step facade remakes. Examples of the work of sign companies working alone or directly with contractors ranged from the bland, and mostly blank, metallic simplicity of new facades for the J. C. Penney Company, with straightforward acrylic sans-serif lettering—to the elaborate three-story slipcover-as-billboard for Dimling Candy in Pittsburgh, complete with sweeping script lettering and a candy illustration in an acrylic light box (Pittsburgh Outdoor Advertising Co., 1953) (see plate 23).

At the same time, promotions from the plastics industry, with its tough new acrylics, bombarded architects and sign designers alike. Again, a material that had become familiar for use in smaller applications, like individual signs or decorative lighting, was now advertised for much bigger projects. Plastics companies showed architects, by example, how to create entirely illuminated commercial facades and encouraged them to take sign design into their own hands. Handsomely illustrated how-to booklets were made available. At the same time, acrylic companies persuaded sign companies to tread into the territory of architects. Rohm and Haas, with its Plexiglas, went so far as to put together a "Storefront Renewal Program" kit for direct mail persuasion. Sign companies that identified storefronts in need of updating could send handsome promotional leaflets, included in the kit, to the behind-the-times business owners.[11] Rohm and Haas had one of the biggest advertising budgets in trade magazines like *Architectural Record* or *Chain Store Age*, regularly buying full or double-page space to promote its product, often in color.[12]

Chain stores such as J. C. Penney's, Uhlman's, and Dollar General Store had an increasing impact on the look of the average Main Street and by midcentury were leaders in covering older buildings. Unless Penney's built its own store on Main Street, which it often did, this national retailer was one of the most consistent in the use of upper-story slipcovering. The Penney's and the Woolworth on Main Street in Niles, Michigan, were the only buildings on the block that completely covered their old facades with metal slipcovers in the 1950s. Regional department store chains like Uhlman's and Peebles created the same look in countless small towns. They often took over local stores and eventually covered the upper floors. Among the national five-and-dimes, J. J. Newberry's was the most aggressive for completely covering the facades of its Main Street stores with metal facing. The slipcovering along South Main Street in Bryan, Ohio, completed by Uhlman's and Newberry's, covered roughly one half of this long block along the courthouse square for more than a decade. Parts of the block, which consisted of brick buildings from the 1860s through 1880s, were camouflaged for almost thirty years. Modernizing Main Street in this period was not limited to covering outmoded building facades. Often, original building features and ornament were damaged or removed. In Redwood Falls, Minnesota, J. C. Penney moved into the old Philbrick Dry Goods building (1886) on Washington Street some time around 1960, removing the peaked parapet and all the gothic gingerbread from the cornice (fig. 16). In effect, the building was decapitated.

Slipcovering older buildings with simple envelopes of flashy new material often provided such a grand opportunity for large-scale graphics that major projecting signs were often deemed unnecessary. Nevertheless, places like Chicago were famous, during the 1950s, for the creation of some of the largest projecting signs ever produced. These cantilevered graphics were often designed for smaller businesses such as cafes or camera shops, as well as for major companies. They grew during this period—not so much vertically, as they had during the 1920s, but horizontally, stretching the full width of the sidewalk. They reached out to each driver who came to the center of town from the suburbs, where patrons were used to large graphics designed to be visible from a great distance. These signs certainly dwarfed anyone walking underneath them.

Since the 1920s, projecting signs everywhere had grown from basic trapezoids with ornamental flourishes "breaking out of the box" to assume unique

Figure 84

Oyster Bay Restaurant sign (designer and date unknown; demolished), West Baltimore Street, Baltimore. Post–World War II signs for urban businesses were often designed at highway scale, dwarfing pedestrians. The speed generated by the alteration of city center streets to one-way traffic may have served to stimulate such creations.
PHOTO BY CRONHARDT AND SONS, CIRCA 1958. COURTESY OF THE MARYLAND HISTORICAL SOCIETY, 1982.2.41.

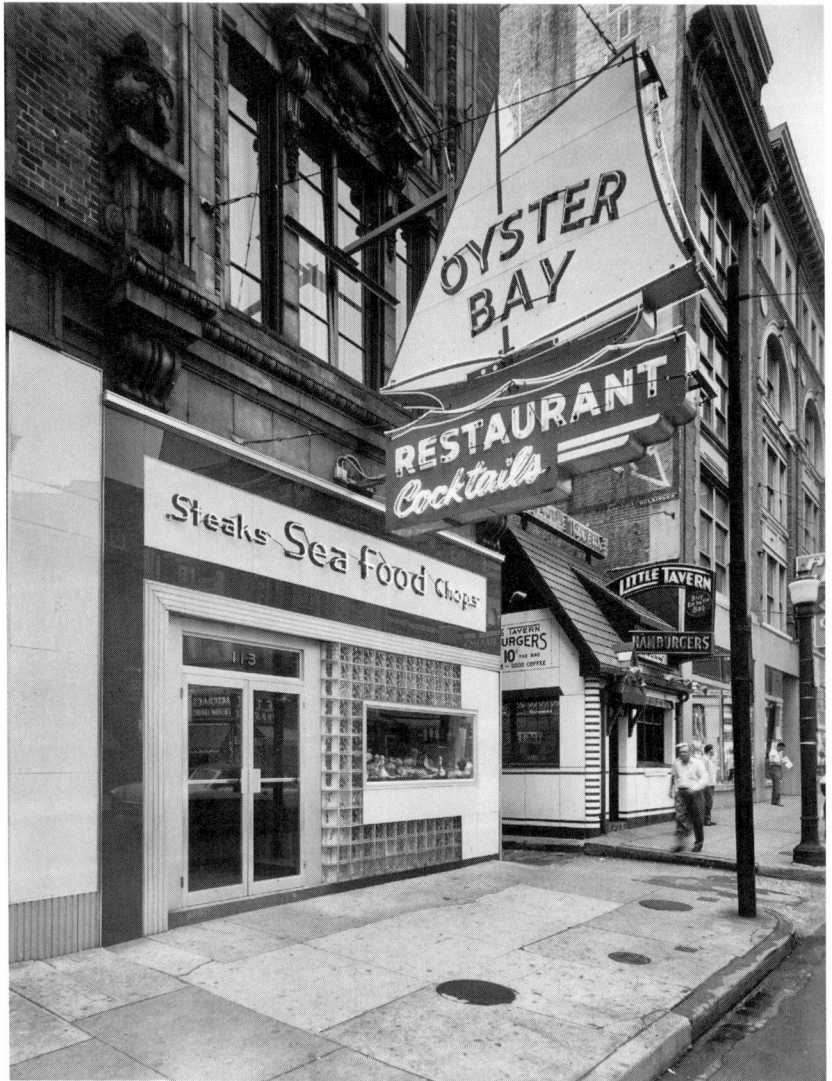

and distinct silhouettes. Such custom, complex forms had once been affordable only for the most prosperous businesses. The simpler, earlier, rectangular signs did not shout (as loudly) their independence from (or disrespect for) the perpendicular lines of the buildings. Photographs taken after World War II along key corridors in many American cities show gigantic projecting signs hovering over the heads of pedestrians (fig. 84). Similarly, by the late 1950s, Canal Street in New Orleans had extensive signage that projected horizontally over the sidewalk, scaled the heights of storefronts, wrapped around building corners, hung out on posts from window lintels, and towered over rooftops on superstructures. It was so saturated with neon that the architect and critic Peter Blake chose a view of Canal Street as the first incriminating image in his 1964 book *God's Own Junkyard* (fig. 85). On Canal Street, and on many other streets across America, the scale and number of projecting signs became so vast that buildings were completely obscured in long views down urban thoroughfares. It often appeared that the street had become a passageway defined by messages.

The new scale of graphics and the slipcovering of older buildings with metal and plastic filtered quickly down to the Main Streets of smaller towns. Through the 1950s and 1960s, Corben Furniture and then Sell's Furniture, on Myrtle Avenue in Monrovia, California, presented a large, angled fin sign overlapped by individual squares—one for each letter of the word FURNITURE (fig. 86). It stretched from the display windows up past the extended parapet. At the crest of the fin was the name *Sells* in channeled script neon, the top half of the lettering projecting beyond the solid edge of the facade. This was no mere projecting sign; it was architecture by default, adorning an otherwise blank facade. It was also an enormous graphic, considering the unassuming scale of the building and the narrowness of the street. The simple facade, exuberant sign, and retail interior (architect and sign company unknown, 1956) covered and replaced an old picture house from 1919.

Figure 85
Canal Street, New Orleans, circa 1961. Architectural critics like Peter Blake condemned the supposed graphic atrocities accumulated along Canal Street, contrasting that view with the visual solace of campus settings like the University of Virginia.
CHARLES L. FRANCK STUDIO COLLECTION AT THE HISTORIC NEW ORLEANS COLLECTION, 1979.325.987.

Figure 86

Myrtle Avenue, Monrovia, California, looking north, in 1970 and in 2007. Early-twentieth-century structures were reclad in the 1950s, making graphics the dominant visual elements instead of windows and cornices. As of the 1970s, instead of *urbs in horto,* many cities seemed to aim for *hortus in horto* (garden in a garden), softening buildings with rusticated materials and often hiding them behind profuse plantings. Signs seemed to be the greatest offenders to this image and were thus reduced to being minor indexes instead of advertisements. **TOP:** CITY OF MONROVIA, COMMUNITY DEVELOPMENT DEPARTMENT, 1970S SIGN SURVEY. **BOTTOM:** PHOTO BY AUTHOR, 2007.

The evolving facade of Chicago's United Artists Theater offers a bold example of the change in urban signage between the 1910s and the 1950s (fig. 87). Built in 1921 as the Apollo (Holabird & Roche), the theater's first sign was modest. Individual letters under twelve inches high were fastened independently over the base of the four columns engaged to the theatre's rounded corner, above the entrance. The headliner was in much larger letters wrapped over the columns but still respectful of the building's design. Around the corner to the left, a projecting, rectangular sign—just over one story in height—caught the attention of the distant trolley rider. In 1927 when architect C. Howard Crane helped convert it from a stage theater to a movie palace, he replaced the corner lettering with an elaborate marquee sign that spanned the full width of the sidewalk yet corresponded closely to the stone frame around the engaged corner columns. Far to the left, a new, vertical blade sign—ten stories high—required a superstructure support on the roof, which was several stories high itself. By the late 1950s, the rather self-contained, boxy marquee was replaced by White Way Sign's composition of cubes, horizontal bands, and script lettering that completely obscured the corner columns of the building. Though a curvaceous freestanding series of illuminated graphic verticals vaguely acknowledged the old stone columns behind, the cubic message board merely collided with them. If the new sign elements corresponded in some fashion to the existing architectural features, they also seemed to break free of the building.

The facade of the Federal Theater in Denver was also updated during the 1950s; the flamboyant tailfin of the new marquee was intended to deflect one's gaze from the original glazed terra-cotta parapet sign set back between the twin towers of the original building (architect unknown, 1920) (fig. 88). The original sign was designed for the pedestrian and streetcar rider. The new marquee sign, with its projection out toward the curb and sweeping script lettering, was surely aimed at the motorist.

The open-storefront concept spread slowly from big cities in the 1940s to small towns in the 1950s, a momentum aided by the dramatic model provided by Ketchum, Gina & Sharp's 1944 revision of an entire block in Kawneer's home town of Niles, Michigan.[13] Similar projects were published regularly, providing inspiration and guidance to architects across the country. By 1953, the *Niles Daily Star* reported that the momentum of modernizations had reached a peak for the town, after several years of store upgrades.

Competitions sponsored by the National Electric Sign Association (NESA) fueled enthusiasm among sign designers to address the entire storefront, a sweeping change that eventually trickled down to many smaller towns.[14] But it had taken at least a decade for sign companies to take the initiative. The winner of the first NESA competition in 1946 produced a modest two-dimensional refacing of a small storefront. The competition work became progressively more expansive from this date, to the point where sign companies regularly sketched

Figure 87
Apollo/United Artists Theatre (Holabird & Roche, 1921; demolished), Randolph Street, Chicago. A relatively modest projecting sign originally identified the theater by name at far left, and a rooftop sign advertised the current film with immense, changeable illuminated letters (TOP). Alterations in 1928 replaced the small projecting sign with a gargantuan vertical sign that extended so far past the building that it required a complex rooftop support system (MIDDLE). A canopy marquee from 1927 was added at the base of the corner colonnade, but was swung left to meet Randolph Street, the primary entertainment corridor. In the 1950s, a new information board (White Way Sign Co.) was fastened awkwardly to the face of the colonnade, and a sweeping marquee wrapped the corner (BOTTOM).
TOP: PHOTO BY THE CHICAGO ARCHITECTURAL PHOTOGRAPHING COMPANY, 1930. DAVID R. PHILLIPS COLLECTION. MIDDLE: PHOTO BY CHICAGO ARCHITECTURAL PHOTOGRAPHING COMPANY, 1928. THEATRE HISTORICAL SOCIETY OF AMERICA. BOTTOM: PHOTO BY J. SHERWIN MURPHY, 1957. COURTESY OF THE CHICAGO HISTORY MUSEUM, i61992.

up three-dimensional graphics and revised architectural features for storefront remakes.

Heath and Company, a sign firm formed in Los Angeles in the late 1940s, inspired many followers. In Wayne Heath's hands, the entire storefront became a sign, subject to the same compositional discipline on display in the signs he created on poster board while a sign painter with Beverly Sign Company in Chicago. When Heath went beyond small-scale to big-picture and dazzled his clients with the full potential of their storefronts, he had a distinct advantage over the more timid proposals of the competition. Canadian designer Peter Horsley and others, regularly published in *Signs of the Times*, also pushed for sign designers to expand their canvas to include entire storefronts (fig. 89). Horsley drew plans and elevations to illustrate what kind of conversions savvy sign companies could produce with elaborate new canopy signs and expanded, less formal, exterior lobbies. Despite his imaginative, extensive graphics, however, the designs rarely displayed the graceful fluidity of the retail work of architects like Morris Lapidus and Victor Gruen. Horsley had a tremendous grasp on the possibilities for signs in three dimensions, but he demonstrated uncertain skill in spatial dynamics. The sign and its expansive canopy still appeared to be applied to a flat storefront. The integration of interior and exterior remained primarily in the hands of architectural designers.

A few architects joined Lapidus, Gruen, and the firm of Ketchum, Gina & Sharp in their attempt to bring graphics and architecture together into a single, sweeping whole. These designers were conspicuous, considering that most architects of the time increasingly shied away from sign design; since World War II and the decline of beaux-arts training, lettering was no longer included in most architecture school curricula. Taking their cues from points made by Philip Johnson and Henry-Russell Hitchcock in their book on the International Style, most American architects proposed discreet lettering that had some sort of physical separation from the building. Making a bold step in the other direction, a few dedicated storefront designers exploited an expanded use of glass, deeper spatial penetration beyond the traditional storefront line, and a looser sense of where the sign began and ended. Even firms such as Skidmore, Owings & Merrill engaged in commercial sign design, offering some surprisingly playful sign solutions for storefronts. In their 1946 proposal for the Toffenetti Restaurant in Chicago, they placed a blank wall where second-story windows would normally be and hung individual letters from a slim canopy that looped out from the edges of the facade so that each figure floated freely over the sidewalk below (fig. 90). This was technically a projecting sign, yet unlike others of the type, it related directly to the revised facade design. Physically articulated and distinct from the architecture, this lettering solution followed the tenets for good design Johnson and Hitchcock had established. It demonstrated that designers could be creative and "correct" at the same time.

Figure 88

Federal Theatre (architect unknown, 1920; altered), Federal Boulevard, Denver, Colorado. Built without a conventional marquee sign, the Federal was originally identified by glazed terra-cotta panels between its twin towers. This was deemed too discreet in the 1950s, when a large finned feature with lush script neon lettering was thrust out toward traffic.

PHOTO BY AUTHOR, 1993.

Other examples of sophisticated, inventive storefront design integration by architects were spread across the country. Whereas sign designers tended to wrap building fronts with graphics, weaving neon into new skins over old facades, architects preferred to articulate the graphic element, to visually disengage or make the sign distinct from the building while keeping it very much a part of the composition. The White Tower Restaurant (believed to be by Victor Lundy, 1959), at "Five Points" along Main Street in Sarasota, Florida, was a mere wedge of glass and a slim roof with tapered edges (see plate 24). Lundy placed decorative graphics for the business on horizontal panels that fit simply, at varying heights, between the verticals of the storefront framing. On the roof, the supports for the individually lettered panels spelling out *White Tower* were a continuation, above the canopy line, of this framing. The sign thus visually connected to, yet rose free from, the building system.[15] An incongruous but clever landmark feature also identified the business from the roof: a giant letter W and T sat in an immense rocking chair with a chef's toque on top (later addition, designer unknown). In Jackson, Mississippi, architect N. W. Overstreet fashioned a unique solution for integrating a true projecting sign with storefront architecture while keeping it physically disengaged. The Princess shoe store (1952) lured customers with an asymmetrical face of dark marble, a racy angled hood, a deep exterior lobby, elegant compressed neon lettering, and a single, cantilevered steel beam that thrust a seven-foot-square sign out over the heads of pedestrians (fig. 91). This was no mere sign box but the facade logo repeated twice in freestanding letters, once for each direction. The lettering was fastened at the base or top of the cantilevered support, depending on the direction. A series of cantilevered glass display boxes lined the lobby approach as one neared the glass doors. Lundy, Overstreet, and others showed architects that graphics could assume the prominence needed for the age and be articulate soloists and respectful ensemble performers simultaneously.

Figure 89

Design for Central Camera, Wabash Avenue, Chicago (General Outdoor Advertising Co., 1950). Winning new contracts usually meant presenting evocative renderings to prospective clients; sign companies were constantly pitted against each other and required talented artists on staff or brought in as consultants.

ARCHIVES OF THE AMERICAN SIGN MUSEUM.

Figure 90
Study for Toffenetti Restaurant, Monroe Street, Chicago (Skidmore Owings & Merrill, 1946). Simple, relatively discreet, yet playful and inventive, this concept aimed to please both advertiser and design critics.
ARCHITECTURAL RECORD (SEPTEMBER 1946), 113. REPRODUCTION COURTESY OF RYERSON AND BURNHAM LIBRARIES, ART INSTITUTE OF CHICAGO.

Development on the suburban strip mirrored and magnified this aesthetic predilection for keeping the sign element visually distinct. There was little motivation for visually integrating sign and architecture in suburban spaces, where these elements were scattered across vast sites.

(opposite) Figure 91
Princess Shoe Store (N.W. Overstreet, 1952; demolished), Jackson, Mississippi. This building represents a rare case in America where an architect conceived a projecting sign to be an essential, fully integral element in the composition of a storefront. The designer also created an unusually open exterior lobby, and the sign helped suggest that the inside space continued out to the sidewalk.
PHOTO BY JOSEPH MOLITOR, CIRCA 1953. JOSEPH W. MOLITOR COLLECTION, AVERY ARCHITECTURAL AND FINE ARTS LBRARY, COLUMBIA UNIVERSITY.

Dis-Integration by Design: Separating Sign and Architecture

The vast open space available in suburbia and the speed of the automobile brought the eventual disengagement of the primary sign from the building where business was conducted. Since the 1930s, buildings beyond the confines of urban sites were taking on more distinctive figural shapes. Signs became larger and more important for capturing the fleeting attention of motorists. Once parking moved up front, and buildings were pushed back from the road out of immediate view, signs assumed even more visual importance. Disengaged from the building completely, they took their place at the roadside. But before that leap was made, in the late 1940s, the primary sign remained tenuously anchored to the building. Designers no longer labored to make sign and architecture the smooth visual unit produced in the 1930s. Graphics were created to reach traffic; buildings reflected separate design agendas. Some buildings became signs in them-

210 *Signs, Streets, and Storefronts*

selves, assuming trademark forms, but increasingly they assumed more muted forms, allowing the sign to be the star of the show. Reyner Banham explains the evolution of the major, independent sign as a result of the growing division between what he calls the rational, functional shell and the fantastic garnish. The Bullock's Wilshire store (1929) was identified for many of its patrons by its eye-catching tower, a feature that grew out of the intricate, vertical detailing that covered the massive building. Contrast this to the arresting corner cylinder feature of the May Company on Wilshire, "chopped back" into a relatively plain box building. By 1959, the plain box shopping center building receded behind fields of parked cars and was advertised by a showy, structural tour-de-force at roadside, its only function being to support illuminated symbols.[16]

In the hands of some designers, the disengagement between sign and building was subtle in the immediate postwar years. Though pieces were clearly articulated or independent, there was great care given to visually unifying the whole. In the design of a Von's store (Arthur Froehlich, 1949) in Los Angeles, a series of six fins (one of which was made a sign) appeared to be thrusting forward, out into the street, from the interior of the great box that housed the store (fig. 92). Though articulated as individual, angled planes, they were united by the placement of a slanted roof across their tops, so that the roof and fins suggested a single volume intersecting or pulling out from the greater box. The entire architectural composition was ambiguous, appearing simultaneously as individual pieces and a suggested whole. The angles and sweeping scale were clearly designed for speed.[17]

The evolving disengagement of sign from architecture could also be seen at the drive-in food stands of this period. The classic cylindrical drive-in structure of the 1930s and 1940s was eventually squared off and stretched out toward the road because of a vastly increased patronage and new architectural aesthetics. Though the stand was always in need of a curbside sign, the primary identification remained on the roof until the 1950s. At this point, new drive-in restaurants were putting all of the parking up front, and the primary sign was often forced to leave the roof entirely. Its separation from the building allowed it to occupy the place once reserved for the secondary signage at the curb, yet it often remained leashed to the building by a long canopy or shed that provided ordering stations protected from the elements.[18] In Lexington, Kentucky, the Las Vegas–sized Parkette Drive-In sign (Ruggles Sign Company, 1957) stood in dramatic contrast to the humble metal sheds around it where customers were served (see plate 25).[19] In this case, the connection between sign and shelter was tenuous at best. The sign was the major, independent design element, overshadowing everything else on site. The relatively humble building where food was prepared receded completely. In other examples, the canopy linking sign to building was a feature unto itself, sometimes a sine wave or zigzag profile, outlined in neon. The enclosed structure rarely was distinguished with a noticeable, independent form.[20]

(previous page) Plate 1
Flamingo Colony Motel sign (designer unknown, mid-1950s; demolished), Sarasota, Florida. Place-reinforcing icons like this sign once lined the Tamiami Trail, created in the 1920s as the entrance corridor and automobile gateway to the resort city.
PHOTO BY AUTHOR, 1985.

(top) Plate 2
Publix Market (circa 1965; altered), College Park neighborhood, Orlando, Florida. The facade of this grocery chain, repeated across the state, was a powerful example of what architect Robert Venturi would call a "decorated shed," not unlike the far more celebrated Stardust Hotel in Las Vegas.
PHOTO BY AUTHOR, 1997.

(bottom) Plate 3
Butler's Café (architect and date unknown; altered), Covington, Kentucky. Residential building types have a long history of being modified for commercial use by opening up the ground floor with more glass for display and affixing a simple sign band just above the transom level. In this case, the visual intensity of neon alone is enough to identify it as a business, regardless of the actual verbal message.
PHOTO BY AUTHOR, 1994.

Plate 4

West Butler Street, south side of Courthouse Square, Bryan, Ohio. Structures built from 1860 to 1880, replacing frame buildings constructed since the town's founding in 1840, defined the commercial streetscape of this Midwestern town. Their fine detail and remarkably consistent proportions and rhythm of windows led a team of architects from Ohio State University in 1976 to propose that all distractions like signs be eliminated.

PHOTO BY AUTHOR, 2005.

(opposite) Plate 5

Tavern facade with Schlitz beer trademark (Frommann & Jebsen, 1903), Chicago. This early example of sign integrated with architectural design identified one of a vast network of bars the Schlitz Company owned across the city. Each was unique.

PHOTO BY AUTHOR, 2005.

Plate 6

Music Box Theatre (Louis I. Simon and White Way Sign, 1929), Southport Avenue, Chicago. The identifying vertical sign was designed and affixed—awkwardly off-center—after the building's completion. Its scale relates more to the scope of the street than to the building itself. Neon eventually replaced bulb lighting.

PHOTO BY AUTHOR, 2005.

(top) Plate 7
Kress store (Edward F. Sibbert, 1939), East Houston Street, San Antonio, Texas. Perhaps the most distinctive design in the chain of unique storefronts for Kress was this mixture of late Art Deco and early streamline moderne with Spanish mission revival style, which produced fins for lettering that grew out of the architecture. In most of the other stores, the Kress identity was flush on the surface of the building.
PHOTO BY AUTHOR, 1993.

(bottom) Plate 8
PSFS Building (William Lescaze and George Howe, 1929–32), Market Street, Philadelphia. The neon at the building's crest followed International Style dictates for being a good sign: it was articulated as a separate piece and distinct from the architecture.
PHOTO BY AUTHOR, 1998.

Plate 9

Three Ocean Drive hotels (Henry Hohauser and L. Murray Dixon, 1938–41), Miami Beach, Florida. These facades, like many created for commercial buildings across America following the 1935 *Designs to Modernize Main Street* competition, were perhaps more graphic than architectural.

PHOTO BY AUTHOR, 2006.

Plate 10
Albion Hotel (Igor Polevitzky and Thomas Triplett Russell, 1939), Lincoln Road, Miami Beach, Florida. This otherwise smooth, curved streamline moderne building accommodated many projections. Two such elements that extended beyond the basic building envelope became signs on the roof. Polevitzky was exceptionally comfortable designing verbal identity as part of his compositions.
PHOTO BY AUTHOR, 1997.

Plate 11
Crenshaw Motors Ford (architect unknown, 1946; demolished), Crenshaw Boulevard, Los Angeles. Fluid graphics served to unify the sign tower with the rest of the building.
PHOTO BY AUTHOR, 2000.

(opposite) Plate 12

Shelborne Hotel (Igor Polevitzky and T. Triplett Russell, 1940–41; Morris Lapidus, 1957), Collins Avenue, Miami Beach. The towers along Collins Avenue took the longstanding tradition of placing hotel identification on the rooftop and turned it into an art. The Shelborne's sign was one of the most graceful and beautifully integrated with the architecture.

PHOTO BY AUTHOR, 1996.

Plate 13

Capri/Princess Theatre (Marr & Holman and Columbia Neon, 1948), East Depot Street, Shelbyville, Tennessee. The Capri presents a simpler example of how a vertical projecting sign—the preferred, longstanding method for cinema identification in the United States—could visually transition to a horizontal, marquee base.

PHOTO BY AUTHOR, 1996.

Plate 14

Proposal for cinema complex, Broadway, New York City (Kahn & Jacobs, 1945). Sign panels, fins, and large-scale graphics dominated this ambitious, unbuilt scheme; architect Ely Jacques Kahn understood the necessity of advertising to fill theater seats and was very comfortable designing in the commercial realm.

KAHN & JACOBS COLLECTION, DEPARTMENT OF DRAWINGS & ARCHIVES, AVERY ARCHITECTURAL AND FINE ARTS LIBRARY, COLUMBIA UNIVERSITY.

Plate 15

Fox Village Theatre (Percy Parke Lewis, 1931), Broxton Avenue, Los Angeles. Although many theaters built by Fox in southern California in the 1920s and 1930s featured towers as identifying features, the Village took the prize.

PHOTO BY AUTHOR, 2006.

Plate 16

Commercial building (Z. Erol Smith, 1935), Belmont Avenue, Chicago, in 1935 and in 2006. The remarkable, glazed terra cotta applied as a smooth skin to this otherwise simple commercial strip was almost purely graphic, yet it offered no natural place for automobile-scale signs. The later image shows the inevitable spread of signs beyond the original limits set by the architect.
TOP: COURTESY OF THE CHICAGO HISTORY MUSEUM, i62149.
BOTTOM: PHOTO BY AUTHOR, 2006.

(opposite) Plate 17

Original New York System (architect unknown, 1927; Federal Sign Company, circa 1933), Smith Street, Providence, Rhode Island. Although not literally blended, the sign and the facade were unified through style and materials.
PHOTO BY AUTHOR, 2007.

(opposite) Plate 18
Carlos Club (Irving Caster and Coast Neon, 1947), El Camino Real, San Carlos, California. The simple, curved geometry of both facade and sign served to link the two visually.
PHOTO BY AUTHOR, 1999.

Plate 19
Sign for Wilton Candy Kitchen (Cro Sign, 1946), Cedar Street, Wilton, Iowa. The simple neon sign fastened to this basic, two-story false front—along with the neon edging inside the windows—served as an affordable way to electrify, and modernize, a facade from another century.
PHOTO BY AUTHOR, 1993.

(opposite) Plate 20

Bun 'n Burger (Walter Zick, 1941; Neon Products Signs, 1950), Main Street, Alhambra, California. A 1950 updating to the original streamline moderne design applied pink neon like paint to the contoured wall above the entrance, supplying a suitable architectural curtain to the performance of a new neon cartoon mascot. The script lettering over one window (to left) was also a midcentury addition.

PHOTO BY AUTHOR, 2007.

Plate 21

F. W. Woolworth store, Winchester, Indiana. The mammoth F. W. Woolworth Company chain, established in 1879, quickly developed a trademark appearance for its signs, a distinctive look that was eventually copied by competitors. Extended, gold, Roman lettering on a red fascia panel helped to identify the retailer quickly to anyone familiar with the business.

PHOTO BY AUTHOR, 1993.

(opposite) *Plate 22*

Murray's Restaurant (1946; General Outdoor Advertising Co., 1956), Sixth Street South, Minneapolis. Newly covered upper stories often became immense, blank slates for identification and promotion. Once seen in downtowns everywhere, facade remakes like this have become a rare sight in the early twenty-first century. Often the buildings have been restored and their original facades (both the great and the ordinary) exposed once more.

PHOTO BY AUTHOR, 2005.

Plate 23

Dimling Candy Company (circa 1870s; Pittsburgh Outdoor Advertising Co., 1953), Liberty Avenue, Pittsburgh. Dimling's Candy covered two buildings dating from at least the 1870s and transformed the entire facade into a graphic advertisement. This midcentury facade cover was in turn demolished and the original facades restored in 1997.

PHOTO BY AUTHOR, 1992.

Plate 24

White Tower Restaurant (believed to be by Victor Lundy, 1959; demolished), Five Points, Sarasota, Florida. Articulated graphics animated what was basically a Miesian commercial building. All was carefully integrated with the fenestration system module, except for the "wild card" use of the mascot trademark on an overscaled rocking chair (probably added later).

PHOTO BY JOSEPH JANNEY STEINMETZ, CIRCA 1960. REPRODUCTION COURTESY OF THE SARASOTA COUNTY HISTORY CENTER. PERMISSION COURTESY OF LOIS DUNCAN STEINMETZ ARQUETTE.

Plate 25

Sign for Parkette Drive-in (Ruggles Sign Company, 1957), East New Circle Road, Lexington, Kentucky. A towering example of the physically independent pylon sign type that developed so rapidly in the 1950s, this identifying graphic was built on the scale of Las Vegas signs, despite the extremely humble buildings that served the business.

PHOTO BY AUTHOR, 1994.

Plate 26

Rooftop signs for Caribbean (Harry Lanza/Allied Sign Company, 1957) and Bel Air (Jack Driscoll/Ace Sign Company, 1957) motels, Ocean Avenue, Wildwood Crest, New Jersey. Often as sweeping or angular as the inventive architecture beneath them, the signs of the Wildwood community were distinct and figural—not the carefully integrated graphics of Miami Beach.

PHOTO BY AUTHOR, 1994.

Plate 27

Chips Restaurant (Harry Harrison, 1957), Hawthorne Boulevard, Hawthorne, California. Googie compositions often included angled roofs (visually supported by little more than glass) and sign supports that pierced or slid right through them.

PHOTO BY AUTHOR, 2007.

Plate 28
Sign for Davies' Chuck Wagon Diner (designer unknown, circa 1965), West Colfax Avenue, Lakewood (Denver), Colorado. This sign, with its neon-illustrated cowboy, contributes generously to the regional history of the area. It is scaled for the road and not the small diner building it advertises.
PHOTO BY AUTHOR, 1998.

(opposite) Plate 29

Sign for Simon's Western Wear (Electrical Products, circa 1950; demolished), Central Avenue, Albuquerque, New Mexico. The loss of this sign, with its Western iconography and intricate craft, created a great deficit in the character of this special tourist corridor.

PHOTO BY AUTHOR, 1993.

Plate 30

McDonald's building (Stanley Meston, 1952/53) and sign (J. P. Kinnikin, Dexter & Company, 1961), Lakewood Boulevard, Downey, California. The sign was a towering mutation of the design Meston created as a prototype to be used by all franchisees. The jump in scale was probably in response to increased competition in the eight years since the original sign was built, as well as the growth in sign size everywhere in suburban United States, most especially in southern California.

PHOTO BY AUTHOR, 1999.

(opposite) Plate 31
Portfolio of signs by Billy ("Mac") Teague (circa 1960), Oklahoma City and surrounding area. This prolific designer, one of many creative mid-American sign crafters of this era, was endlessly inventive using a small kit of design parts—launching and weaving atomic orbs, sharp triangles, and Mondrian grids, to arresting effect.
COURTESY OF MAC TEAGUE.

(left) Plate 32
Balyeat's Coffee Shop, East Main Street, Van Wert, Ohio. The neon sign is mirrored today in the recently exposed Vitrolite of the neighboring business (see fig. 109). The sign remains a beacon along Main Street, once an alignment of the Lincoln Highway, and is prominent alongside another landmark, the tower of the old county courthouse.
PHOTO BY AUTHOR, 1995.

(right) Plate 33
Commercial enterprises along St. Charles Avenue, near Canal Street, New Orleans. At least three layers of history are on display in this image: the original buildings from the 1830s, cast-iron balconies from the 1860s, and neon signs from the mid-twentieth century.
PHOTO BY AUTHOR, 1994.

(top) Plate 34
Smitty's Men's and Boys' Wear, Vine Street, Cincinnati. The book *Street Graphics* attempted to create more appealing streetscapes by limiting the number and size of sign elements. This business would likely have been a perfect nightmare for the authors, yet it vitalizes the street.
PHOTO BY AUTHOR, 1994.

(bottom) Plate 35
Milwaukee Avenue, Chicago. Although designated as a historic resource by the city, this commercial corridor is recognized for its architecture only. The historic signs receive no special protection, although they contribute greatly to individual storefronts and the character of the corridor as a whole.
PHOTO BY AUTHOR, 2006.

(top) *Plate 36*

Sign for Margie's Candies (Acme-Wiley Sign Co., 1954), North Western Avenue, Chicago. This locally beloved landmark identifies a major intersection of three streets. The neon serves as necessary ornament for an otherwise blank building.

PHOTO BY AUTHOR, 2005.

(bottom) *Plate 37*

All Star Donuts (1928) and sign (circa 1951), Chestnut Street, San Francisco. A neighborhood beacon that cuts the fog, this sign warms an otherwise chilly location of low-rise stucco buildings. Although unrelated in design to the building it marks, it is well suited to the corner site and to the street scale.

PHOTO BY AUTHOR, 1998.

(top) Plate 38
Sign for Pat's Steak Sandwich (Ajax Sign Company, 1952; removed and restored), Ridge Avenue, Philadelphia. Along with basic modifications to the ground floor, the sign is what transformed an otherwise residential building into a place for business on the corner. The neon and porcelain enamel graphic continued to mark the neighborhood and reinforce the city's culinary identity for many years, even after the business was gone.
PHOTO BY AUTHOR, 1994.

(bottom) Plate 39
Laura's Fudge (ABS Sign Company, 1950), Wildwood Avenue, Wildwood, New Jersey. Although the building is not completely covered by neon, the graphics physically define this place after dark, as they do along the town's boardwalk and the boardwalks that line much of the Mid-Atlantic Shore. Such high artifice exists in extreme contrast to the summer season simplicity of the architecture and yet seems at peace with it, perhaps because of tradition.
PHOTO BY AUTHOR, 1998.

Two early drawings for the McDonald's franchise prototype demonstrated how, in the early 1950s, American roadside design was in a state of transition. Designers were uncertain as to where to place the greatest visual emphasis. Should it be the roadside sign or the graphics on the building? The final rendering for the McDonald's prototype, produced in 1952 by architect Stanley Meston and his assistant Charles Fish, showed what would eventually be used for construction: the now-famous golden arches, tilted roof, and red-and-white tile walls. For this proposal, the designer balanced the scale and visual emphasis given the independent roadside sign in contrast to the building set back from the road. But earlier that same year, an advertisement for enlisting franchisees included the illustration of a design that was never constructed. It showed all the major graphics placed on a round building, following the long-standing tradition established by drive-ins throughout southern California in the 1920s and 1930s (fig. 93). The original company mascot, Speedee, was pictured on the roof of a modified cylindrical drive-in stand, and the word HAMBURGER was spelled out in giant letters around the edge of the canopy.[21] The phrase "We have sold over 8 million" went on the canopy as well. Unlike the later rendering, which was used for construction, this early advertisement showed no roadside sign. The newer rendering acknowledged a new traffic pattern that came with self-service and fell in step with businesses everywhere that placed a major, independent sign along the roadside.

The separation of sign from architecture was not always the result of expanding sites, vast scales, and an emphasis on quick coast-to-coast identification. For example, the exuberant neon signs of Wildwood, New Jersey, were rarely integrated with the motel architecture. As in south Miami Beach, another vacation environment scaled to both pedestrian and motorist, Wildwood's signs and lodgings were pushed close to the sidewalk (due to constrained sites). Yet in Wildwood, the lettering did not rest on horizontal overhangs or climb fluted stucco towers. Instead, the resort town's signs were typically located on poles at curbside right next to the buildings or mounted on skeletal roof superstructures (see plate 26). The signs simply did not connect to the architecture in the seamless way demonstrated in Miami Beach, even though building and sign were both positioned snugly next to the sidewalk.[22] Since much of Wildwood was developed in the mid-1950s (more than a decade later than Miami Beach's classic art deco blocks), the balance between pedestrian and motorist was, by this time, tipped in favor of the motorist. The signs of Wildwood were designed to be seen from afar, mounted on roofs and on poles, like signs along a highway. They were proportionately larger than those in Miami Beach, and they were often mounted perpendicular to the streets. The architecture of Wildwood, too, was designed to attract attention from afar, unlike the hotels of Miami Beach, which were smoothly contoured to fill every inch of their urban sites. Rakishly angled glass, ramped rooflines, and daring cantilevers broke free from the straightjacket that might have been imposed by the grid of streets. Signs and buildings appeared as a carnival of free-form pieces. The focus on suburban design in the media may have powerfully influenced Wildwood's designers, many of whom never received formal architectural training.

It is easy to see why sign and architecture physically diverged at Las Vegas, given its generous open spaces, but why at Wildwood, with its compact sites and buildings so close to the curb? Although space was at a premium in Wildwood, the motels often tried to supply a minimum of off-street parking with a partial setback for the buildings; sometimes this mandated a pylon sign. Or perhaps because of the modest budgets for the Wildwood motels, little effort was made to integrate sign and architecture. But there is an aesthetic issue worth considering. Wildwood's motels exemplified the trend in the 1950s to separate the various parts of an architectural design in new buildings, including the signs. An emphasis on contrast and variety, seen in the work of even the most respected architects and designers of the period, often resulted in exaggerated distinctions between elements of a design composition. The effort, in the 1940s, to allow elements of a composition to appear as ensembles of parts—as opposed to visually blending them together or cloaking them under streamlined skins in the 1930s—had now fully evolved.

Postwar architecture was designed with an acute appreciation of articulated pieces: panels or walls were often joined to vertical supports or roofs with small but significant reveals (discreet visual gaps) between the parts. The reveal was often nothing more than a shadowed indentation that highlighted the joint between assembled pieces. Post–World War II architecture often celebrated a contrived complexity. The architecture of the late 1940s and 1950s expressed a love of technology and structural exhibitionism that the teachings of the Bauhaus in the 1920s had inspired. A clear expression of materials and parts was often more important than communicating a building's purpose or how to enter it.

This new aesthetic, which was also characterized by an efficient spareness, was disseminated through professional architecture journals and popular magazines such as *House Beautiful*. These publications presented countless examples of interiors devoid of unnecessary furniture; architecture was the true focus of

Figure 92
Von's Market (Arthur Froehlich, 1949; demolished), Western Avenue, Los Angeles. The angled fins suggested the speed of motoring customers. This big box business seemed to pull interior space out toward the road with its striking entrance.
CHAIN STORE AGE (JULY 1948).
REPRODUCTION COURTESY OF UNIVERSITY OF CHICAGO LIBRARY.

Figure 93

Advertisement seeking franchisees for the first McDonald's Self Service Drive-In (1952). In 1952, the McDonald's Company made a seismic shift in its restaurant design, from the classic radial California drive-in building that was slightly modified for walk-up traffic—with traditional roof-mounted identification—to the now famous, squared-off stand flanked by golden arches. The new design was a more suitably space-age building, distinctive enough to serve as a trademark, with a coordinated sign that sat closer to the road to advertise directly to motorists.

COURTESY OF JIM HEIMANN.

attention. The open space and large glass walls that were characteristic of this architecture were analogous to the large areas of white space seen in the high-style graphic design of this period. Covers for *Arts & Architecture* by designers such as Ray Eames were often collages of seemingly disparate pieces: unrelated organic forms or images clipped from newspapers or magazines intuitively arranged in harmonious compositions.[23] Much of Eames's work, and that of the Swiss designer Herbert Matter (who often collaborated with Ray and Charles), was derived from collage. This was a medium of expression that showcased the artist as an assembler of images, someone who put pieces together. Thus, like much of the architecture of the period, the work of the collage artist was an assemblage of parts.[24]

Postwar design was characterized by contrast. Images of historical artifacts and motifs were often juxtaposed with modern, abstract shapes. Flat areas of pure color served as foils to reproductions of stock photos, vintage engravings, or woodblock prints. Graphic designers like Lester Beall and Paul Rand often contrasted smooth and coarse objects, using both type and images (fig. 94). According to Rand, "By contrasting the type area and emphasizing the margin . . . [the typographic designer] reinforces, by contrast, the textural quality of the type."[25] There was an architectural counterpart to this graphic design approach. Architects such as Paul Rudolph and Frank Lloyd Wright placed rough planes of stone or brick against smooth ones of glass, marble, or wallboard. Against the precise geometry of a George Nelson coffee table, an interior designer might place a primitive African carving. Charles and Ray Eames often contrasted forms that were smooth and round with those which were sharp and fine, exemplified

CONSEQUENCES OF COMMERCIAL FREEDOM AND RESTRAINT   **215**

Figure 94

Print advertisement for Disney, Hatmaker (Paul Rand, 1947). Contrast and simplicity were key in midcentury design of all kinds. In this example, the graphic designer juxtaposed basic geometric shapes in color against intricate black-and-white vintage drawings. Generous blank space (the white, in this case) also served as an improved setting for appreciating the product on display.
REPRODUCTION COURTESY OF YALE UNIVERSITY LIBRARY, MANUSCRIPTS AND ARCHIVES. COPYRIGHT, MARION SWANNIE RAND.

by the curvaceous fiberglass shell chair, with its wiry, angular "Eiffel Tower" base.[26]

The architectural firm of Armet and Davis used the aesthetic of articulated pieces, collage, and contrast to exaggerated effect in commercial design for the masses. Best known for their "Googie"-style coffee shops in the Los Angeles area, they borrowed the look established by such prestige designers as the Eameses and architect Frank Lloyd Wright.[27] Yet, unlike the respected architectural compositions of the period, which displayed a structural logic, Armet and Davis seemed to ignore gravity. Their work was more like graphic design rendered in three dimensions. Heavy roofs floated freely in space with vertical "supports" that seemed to slip through rather than connect in a convincing manner. Enormous vertical signs pierced roofs, contrasting sharp spears and starbursts with the thick, floating slabs (see plate 27). Sign letters sometimes rested on individual supports connected tenuously to the edge of the roofs, recalling Skidmore, Owings & Merrill's Toffenetti Restaurant.

Freestanding signs assumed increased importance as the 1950s progressed. They now established the character and nature of a business, in addition to advertising its virtues. They were also burdened with responsibilities that a sequence of features for businesses in urban sites, like window signs and display windows, had once addressed. The speed of the automobile required this compression of information because a driver's gaze was pushed forever forward, and every second counted. There was no time to discover fragmented messages in a succession of layers and at a variety of scales, as a pedestrian could downtown. Both heraldic and informational communication appeared simultaneously in a single sign unit.[28]

By 1950, the pylon sign became the full focus of the sign designer; it was no longer an adjunct element on a business site. One of the most innovative, adventurous leaders in the sign design field was George F. Meyers, of General Outdoor Advertising, who published countless ideas for pylons in *Signs of the Times* during the 1950s. One of his first pylon designs was published in 1950 for a fictitious automobile dealer. The composition was a collection of disparate, mostly triangular shapes that overlapped loosely (fig. 95). The designer made no attempt to stack elements or lock them together in a tight ensemble; they merely floated, visually, and assembled in a seemingly random manner. In the late 1940s, most of Meyers's work was confined to urban signs, but even these seemed ready to slip away from the buildings to which they were attached. They angled away from the storefronts, reached out from their solid perches. More and more, Meyers used complex shapes instead of orthogonal elements, which were still popular with his contemporaries. Somehow his groups of disparate elements, which were so freely, intuitively assembled, had a real visual logic and balance.

George F. Meyers and equally prolific Peter Horsley appeared monthly in *Signs of the Times* through the 1950s and were given full pages for their artwork each time. These pages dominated the magazine visually because of their size and the rich, dark tones of charcoal and ink rendering. Meyers's work was also published in two large books in 1946 and 1956, as well as in a set of twenty-four-page volumes Sylvania Electric gave away to its customers. Such ideas were bound to show up in neon across America.

In the late 1940s and early 1950s, the new California partnership of Heath and Gorsich also made a name for itself by producing creative pylon compositions of hovering forms, often more complex than the paper ideas published by Meyers. Partner Wayne Heath's 1952 design for the Hula Hut Restaurant, a landmark in the Pico Rivera district of Los Angeles, was a jumble of large-scale, free-form quadrilaterals (fig. 96). Most early pylon signs in America included a major solid vertical element to connect the composition to earth; at Heath and Gorsich, this was often an angled fin form, as rakish and arbitrary for its task as

Figure 95

Design concept for a pylon sign (George F. Meyers, 1950). The unique, tapered forms in this composition were gathered loosely, intuitively, displaying little of the structural logic or bottom-to-top stacking of forms that architectural firms later employed when designing their own pylon signs. Meyers was a major influence in the growing trend toward pylon or freestanding signs.
SIGNS OF THE TIMES (FEBRUARY 1950).
COURTESY OF SIGNS OF THE TIMES.

were fins on automobiles. The Hula Hut sign, and other designs that followed it, seemed to challenge gravity with supporting elements that tapered away to nothing as they reached the ground. Many of these compositions leaned precariously to one side, suggesting a sort of kinetic energy. Lee Klay, art director of the subsequent partnership, Heath and Company, had a regular column in *Signs of the Times* that often ran several pages, with large photographs. It was a virtual advertisement for his and Wayne Heath's work.[29]

The new design propensity for pylons narrowing at their bases was displayed even among the lesser-known winners of the 1951 competition sponsored by the National Electric Sign Association, ushering in a trend that would last almost the entire decade. One of the most creative examples of this formal type was erected in Cincinnati for Frisch's Mainliner Restaurant (Quehl Sign Company, 1956), near the city's old airport (fig. 97). The outside edge of one trapezoidal element of the sign was defined by the speed trail (in lights) for a scale model of a plane, with spinning propellers, incorporated into the pylon.

By 1953, the visual heaviness of the often soft-cornered, contoured pylons of the early 1950s was swiftly being replaced by sharper corners and slimmer panels. Instead of major overlaps between panels or pieces, sign elements had space between them, emphasizing their visual independence and implying movement or energy. George F. Meyers's rendering of a service station pylon sign in 1952 for *Signs of the Times* demonstrated the rapid transition from rounded, heavy forms of the tail end of the streamlined era to the lighter, crisper design evolving in the mid-1950s (fig. 98). The small graphic panels holding the business identity were supported on a pair of thin, needle-shaped posts, one bent to point toward the business. This was quite unlike the bundle of curvaceous, triangular forms of 1950, bunched loosely together and supported by a heavy,

Figure 96
Design sketch of pylon sign for Hula Hut Restaurant (Wayne Heath/Heath & Gorsich, 1952; demolished), eventually constructed on East Whittier Boulevard, Pico Rivera, California. The visually unstable, potentially kinetic designs of Wayne Heath influenced sign designers across America, as the freestanding pylon sign became the standard means of suburban identification.
SIGNS OF THE TIMES (OCTOBER 1952).
COURTESY OF SIGNS OF THE TIMES.

Figure 97

Pylon sign for Frisch's Mainliner Restaurant (Quehl Sign Company, 1956), Wooster Pike, Cincinnati. With its classic pylon tapered base and sweeping angled line suggesting movement, this sign was made unique with a three-dimensional plane complete with whirring propellers.

PHOTO BY AUTHOR, 1994.

tapered base. Tubelite Neon featured an example of this new aesthetic in a full-page advertisement in 1957 with a giant compressed arrow as the "spear" for a collection of pieces; this became a popular formal type, influencing the design of hundreds of signs, such as the elegant pylon for the Skyliner Motel in Stroud, Oklahoma (fig. 99).

As signs became taller, the supports became slimmer and the panels or pieces smaller or lighter relative to the entire composition. The sign support was often given its own aesthetic. By the mid-1950s, sign designers were becoming more structurally and sculpturally adventurous. George F. Meyers explored sign base forms that were heavily influenced by the work of Japanese-American sculptor Isamu Noguchi, designer of a famous coffee table produced from 1947. For a home furnishings store, Meyers proposed a sharply angled pylon intersecting with the cantilevered roof of the showroom he designed himself.

Meyers's volumes published by Sylvania included clever, sometimes animated, storefront signs with neon illustrations of animals and people. Peter Horsley's many pages in *Signs of the Times* also presented myriad possibilities for neon illustration. Projecting sign compositions included a pair of neon legs, a stylized man in a top hat, a painter climbing a ladder, swooping curves, kidney shapes, boomerangs, and spirals. Some of the drawings were for very modest signs, no more than a novel shape and some creative lettering. These blueprints were eventually built exactly as drawn or were produced with minor alterations, filling retail streets all over America. Sign companies across the country invented their own original animated graphics, filling the roadsides with pictures as well as words (see plates 28–29). In addition to his published work, Horsley was paid by sign companies across the country to produce drawings for the purpose of impressing prospective clients. The little extra out-of-pocket cost to hire Horsley and other big names may have given these companies the needed edge to win an especially important contract.[30]

Meyers, Horsley, Heath, and others published heavily in *Signs of the Times* had a great impact on the look of the strip in just a few years' time. Due to increased competition in the industry and the availability of leasing, more and more businesses could afford to indulge in ambitious signs. Designing for the roadside required that investment in signage. After World War II, motels across the country enhanced their roadside appeal with new neon graphics at curbside. Old motor courts from the 1920s and 1930s were given facelifts, not always by modernizing the modest buildings but by lavishing attention at the point of sale: the highway. A glamorous neon palm tree might serve as advertisement for lodging units that looked like lakeside cabins from Indiana. Sometimes the domestically styled office structure might be brought up-to-date with a sweeping, angled porte-cochere appendage, but most often the sign was the only new investment necessary—especially at night, when the road's edge was defined solely by light. Before the advent of corporate lodging chains, the motel advertised primarily to one-time clientele, customers completely unfamiliar with the territory. Therefore, motels relied heavily on their signs to advertise and identify, burdening them with extra information to impart to the stranger. This was the only shot the business had at luring customers new to town, patrons beyond the range of local newspaper advertising, and this need to reach out visually often set motel signs apart from the architecture on the sites. At the Royal Host Motel in Denver, for example, a vertical stack of individually lettered acrylic panels with a neon crown for its base advertised a building that was crisp, restrained, gridded, and thus architecturally correct for its time, according to the images presented in trade journals of the era (fig. 100). Although the design of the panelized sign perhaps drew inspiration from the building's distinctive framework, its scale, its incongruous iconography and name, and its lavishness were a response to its intended audience more than they were fitting for the business itself.

The Holiday Inn sign (known inside the company as the "Great Sign") was the most dominant and ubiquitous example of the commercial sign as a freestanding monument: again, lavish in contrast to the sleek, modern aesthetic of the architecture. First erected in Memphis in 1952, at a height of fifty feet, the

Figure 98

Design concept for a pylon sign (George F. Meyers, 1952). Comparing this drawing with fig. 95, which preceded it by only two years, reveals a significant design evolution. The shapes joined together were slimmer and sharper, suggesting a greater sense of movement.
SIGNS OF THE TIMES (NOVEMBER 1952). COURTESY OF SIGNS OF THE TIMES.

(opposite) Figure 99

Skyliner Motel sign (Tuny Monday, circa 1959), West Main Street, Stroud, Oklahoma. Among pylon signs, this was a particularly popular design type: the immense, compressed arrow with stacked lettering. Many motels had a version of this at one time, but this example was particularly clean and direct.
PHOTO BY AUTHOR, 1993.

original design (Cummings & Company, Nashville) was not drastically altered until the 1980s. The first sign was a sizeable investment of $13,000, with 1,500 feet of neon and 500 bulbs. It involved a high degree of handcraft, considering it would be built from scratch again and again all over the world. By 1960, a separate department in the company was devoted to the care and promotion of these signs nationwide. The sign unified a chain comprised of many different building designs across the country. It was also the only part of the typical Holiday Inn complex that was consistently visible at night, when many patrons made their lodging choices.

McDonald's permitted some experimentation with its new pylon sign design, even after Ray Kroc launched the national roll-out of the chain. Eight years after their 1953 opening, the franchisees of the Downey, California, stand replaced the original sign with a towering mutation of the concept most franchisees had used for construction since 1952 (see plate 30). Instead of the relatively compact sign contained by a gentle parabolic arch, seen in the original concept,

the new Downey sign included a much taller arch—dramatically compressed—with a long sign box cantilevered precariously from the top. Rendered in neon, the company's mascot, Speedee, marched toward the end of this horizontal element as if it were a diving board. Only the word HAMBURGERS was spelled out on this cantilevered piece. The detailed information, including the name *McDonald's* and the number of burgers sold, was modestly included near the base. This Downey sign, created by J. P. Kinnikin, Dexter, and Co. around 1961, was unique and site-specific. It addressed a particular suburban intersection, and it anticipated competition that was just beginning to grow around the stand. Restored in 1996, this sign can still be seen at great distances by motorists. Such a major identifying feature was increasingly seen as a necessity in the seemingly endless gridded development of the area.[31] A significant early example of a commercial graphic as an independent monument, the sign is clearly more important than the architecture of the hamburger stand. Though later franchisees followed the original Meston and Fish rendering more closely, their signs were also stand-alone monuments.

The largest and most independent of the new suburban signs were those that identified shopping centers. These were monuments in every sense of the word, acting as landmarks not only because of their sheer size but also because of the design virtuosity often on display. The 1959 NESA competition for a shopping center pylon was the apotheosis of 1950s sign design. It was the first time that the organization had chosen such a sign for the challenge. Unlike many previous competitions, this neutral context was free of most restrictions or references: the sign would be floating freely in a pool of Pontiacs and Impalas. The entries singled out for honors in 1959 were sculpturally ambitious. They were also especially sharp, fine, and visually energized. All of them reflected a love for distinct pieces rather than the smooth blending together of parts that was identified with the streamline era. The judges chose designs that emphasized articulated letters and shapes rather than the fluid, inventive, script neon lettering of the early 1950s. Single sign panels had been fragmented to pieces, reduced in size and increased in number, stealing the show with creative shapes and arrangements. This evolution was largely the result of the transition from graphics rendered in molded neon tubing to flat areas of back-lit acrylic. The winners of the 1959 competition displayed a disparate range of ideas, from space age references to colonial modern (fig. 101). One design might be described as a wipeout of surfboard shapes and spiky boomerangs, all circling around what appeared to be a giant sparkler. Another featured three narrow spindle or toplike shapes belted with Saturn rings and hoisted on tall rods of unequal length above simply lettered panels. Other entries included a tower of planets and sputniks—a shish kebab of space-age iconography and nervous energy.

This aesthetic of pieces, celebrated with abandon in the NESA competition, filtered its way through cities and small towns across America. The visual elements of the signs inspired by this look were increasingly light, fine, and

Figure 100
Royal Host Motel (architect and sign company unknown, circa 1959; building altered, sign demolished), East Colfax Avenue, Denver, Colorado. The relatively simple, orthogonally oriented sign related to the straight lines of the building. It was not the boomerang extravaganza typical of its time, and yet its articulated pieces were very much in sync with the era. The automobile pictured, although curvaceous and seemingly anachronistic, was actually exactly contemporaneous.
PHOTO BY AUTHOR, 1998.

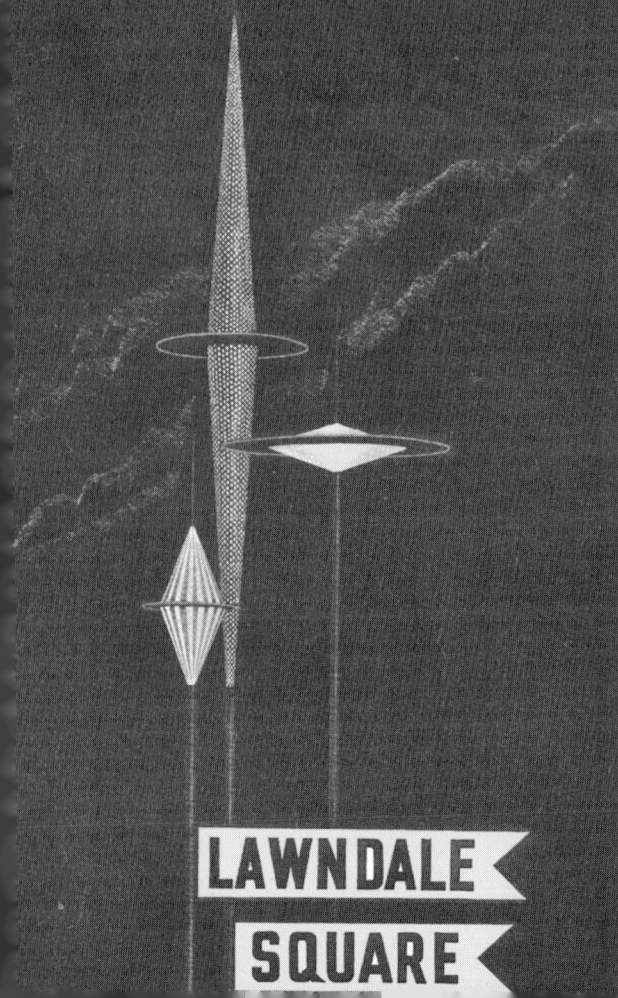

LAWNDALE SQUARE

SHOPPER'S mall

sharp; the compositions were energized by variety of form, novel juxtapositions, and virtual (if not actual) movement. This new look spread quickly. A pair of elongated shields and a tower of small spheres identified the El Camino Restaurant in Socorro, New Mexico. Scotty's Hamburgers (1964) in Bismarck, North Dakota, hoisted a series of variegated "flying saucers" into the sky, above playful, elongated lettering in neon. In Oklahoma City, Billy ("Mac") Teague was just one of America's newly energized, postwar sign designers, creating roadside landmarks for increasingly vast open spaces and low-slung buildings. As designer, owner, and salesman, he generated a limitless portfolio of energetic arrangements, assembling elongated triangles, "atomic" spheres, jutting diagonals, and piercing supports for an astounding variety of markers along the highway (see plate 31).[32] Leading designers like Wayne Heath and George F. Meyers had inspired sign crafters across America to design lighter, to arrange small pieces of information with a visual verve—and hopefully with a clear sense of hierarchy and not simply optical stimulation.

Signs of the Times stressed design originality because clients needed to have their signs stand out from the pack. A 1964 article encouraged designers to watch television to generate ideas. It also recommended that sign designers roam supermarkets or drug stores for examples of package design that might provide inspiration.[33] *Signs of the Times* articles written about the Seattle and New York world's fairs in the early 1960s bubbled with enthusiasm over novel forms and new ideas discovered while touring the exposition architecture, displays, and shows. The fantastic shapes and original juxtapositions were published to fuel ideas for future sign design.

Sign designers became increasingly important to fabricators of electric signs, although a formal training was often unnecessary or unavailable. Sign companies competed for work by preparing often expensively rendered design proposals on spec. Securing business was not unlike participating in a series of informal design competitions, with clients free to choose whoever impressed them the most with free sketches. Such a system may have contributed heavily to increased exuberance in sign design, especially during the 1950s. The combined force of competition—between sign companies to win a contract and between signs along the road to win the business of patrons—often led to the boldest, and sometimes most outlandish, designs. The best professional background, many in the sign industry would agree, was to have extensive experience as a "show card writer." These artists carefully produced, with paint and airbrushes, the custom-designed boards employed to advertise movies and merchandise on site. The task of creating a show card required an agile mind capable of generating hundreds of different design ideas.

Formal training was available to the most motivated sign crafters. Among the most highly regarded establishments were the Grand Central Art School in New York City and Chicago's Institute of Lettering and Design. Informal training might include the many available correspondence courses or careful study

(opposite) **Figure 101**
Selections from the 1959 National Electric Sign Association competition. Articulated pieces and kinetic arrangements distinguished this definitive moment in the evolution of postwar sign design. The assignment was to create an appropriately monumental landmark for a large shopping center, to be erected in a vast field of parked cars.
SIGNS OF THE TIMES (APRIL 1960).
COURTESY OF SIGNS OF THE TIMES.

of the work published in books, magazines, and pamphlets.[34] *Signs of the Times* also produced regular articles on lettering, introducing new alphabets like Beton Italic or Cavanaugh Modern Condensed. Many new lettering styles were ushered in and old ones rediscovered in the 1950s. Extra-bold, heavily serifed alphabets, extra slim and compressed lettering, and brush stroke and script styles provided the contrast and novelty so revered at the time.[35]

Trade publications had a powerful impact on the way the commercial thoroughfare would look. Since most American sign design was still produced by artists with little or no formal training, *Signs of the Times* was a major source for many of their ideas. The signs illustrated in this magazine were, in turn, influenced by graphic design journals and architectural publications, as sign design was a three-dimensional medium that lay somewhere in between the other two disciplines. The better efforts of leading designers to integrate sign and architecture would therefore be filtered and cropped by successive steps of media exposure and interpretation on their way to stimulating the sign shop designers. As a result of this trickle-down path of information, and a market-driven obsession for the novel and eye-catching, many roadside signs became objects that related to little or nothing on their sites.

Reduction and Control: Reining in Exuberance and Centralizing Design Power

The new commercial landscape of the suburbs was unfamiliar, disorienting, and increasingly unpopular in the press. There were no recognizable layers of history, no new signs on well-known buildings or corners, no old landmark signs that had marked places for years. Most of the strip had been built from scratch on areas that had recently been farmland or minor commercial enterprises such as produce stands or early food stops for long-distance travelers. This land had been transformed, seemingly overnight, into what many saw as a carnival of neon and novel architectural forms. For a 1959 article in *Fortune*, Saul Steinberg produced a cartoon that pictured an outlandish landscape defined by elaborate motel signs and comic building flourishes (fig. 102).[36] It was a clever exaggeration of the impression that many held of the strip. Although motorists found suburban shopping to be convenient, no one was particularly proud of the strip's appearance. Once peripheral and subordinate to the old town center, the strip slowly became the new Main Street in the 1950s and 1960s. As it increasingly assumed a central role, and for some became the everyday face of the community, it received growing scrutiny from citizens, journalists, and academics.

During the 1950s, suggestions for roadside improvement were often purely the result of aesthetic opinion—although some critics, who searched for clarity in the clutter, had quick and efficient recognition of the desired destination as their primary goal. What was unclear, or not discussed by many critics, was whether the reduction of the perceived chaos would result in a landscape

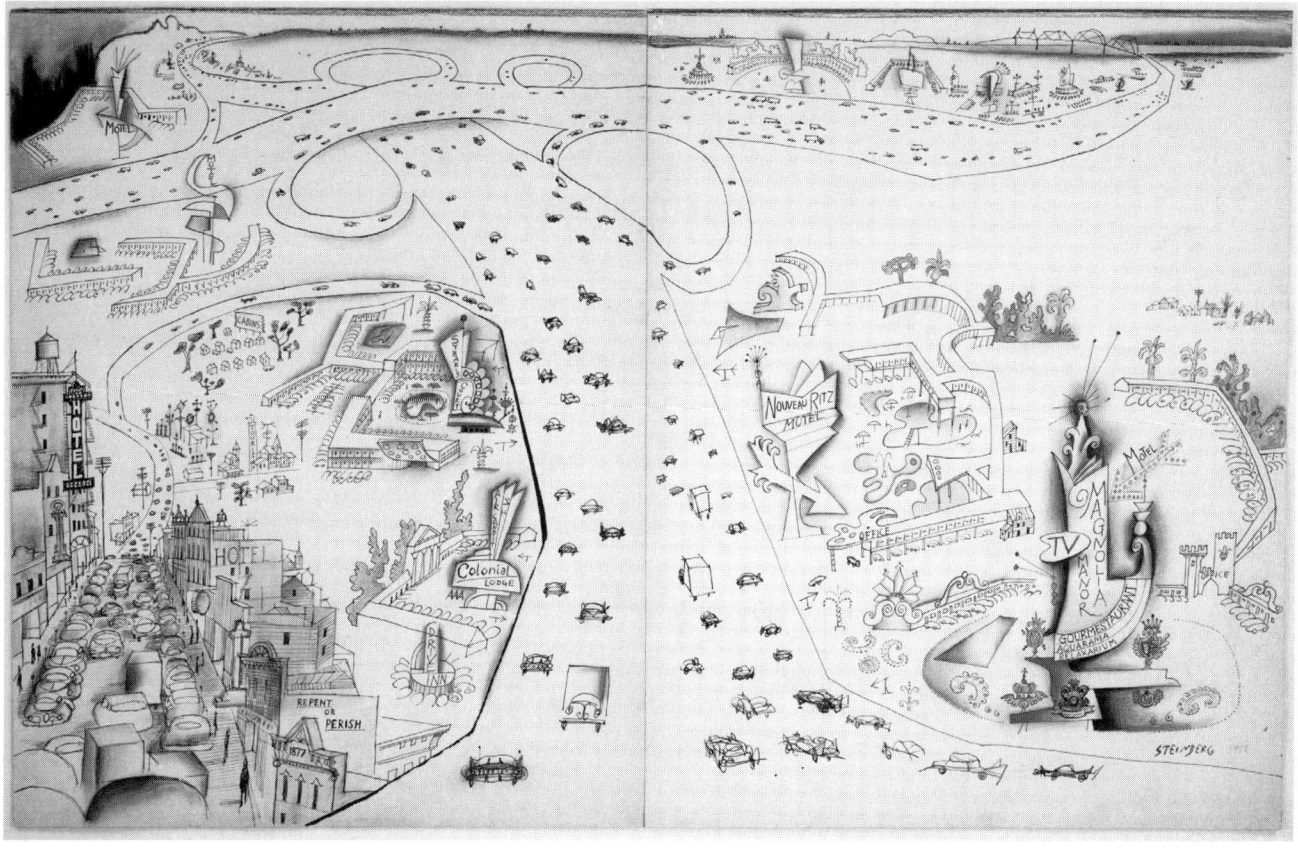

that was more understandable, useful, or meaningful. By the end of the 1950s, change would come. Growing corporate ownership of commercial enterprise, as well as development of increasingly ambitious shopping centers, would bring the much-desired constraint and control. The change from neon to acrylic-faced signs and limited new sign legislation would also play roles in the "simplifying" of the strip. But the aesthetic motivation was perhaps the greatest, and it was part of a larger effort in design to clean things up, reaching from the spare new look of residential interiors to simpler advertising.

While the commercial landscape was being saturated with neon-enhanced graphics during the 1950s, leading graphic designers were attempting to rid print-media graphics of their excess. This movement influenced graphic design in the United States and, eventually, some sign design as well. The immigration of avant-garde European designers to this country, which started during the 1930s, began to have its greatest impact after World War II. The most significant aspect of this influence in graphic design was a new emphasis on the visual over the verbal, on abstraction over the literal. French designer A. M. Cassandre's work for the Chicago-based Container Corporation of America turned the conventions

Figure 102

Saul Steinberg, Untitled, 1959. Ink, colored pencil, and pencil on paper, 27 1/8 x 44 in. Steinberg lampooned the aggressive development of the commercial strip—specifically the burgeoning roadside lodging industry—mirroring with humor the complaints made by the design elite of the time and the growing concern of the general public.

ORIGINALLY ACCOMPANIED "THE MOTEL FREE-FOR-ALL," IN *FORTUNE*, JUNE 1959, 120–21. PRIVATE COLLECTION. © 2010 THE SAUL STEINBERG FOUNDATION / ARTISTS RIGHTS SOCIETY (ARS), NEW YORK.

of advertising upside down. In one 1937 ad, he employed a dominant visual element and only a few words. This was quite a novelty in a period in which slice-of-life stories with long, "grey" columns of type persisted in advertisement design.[37]

By the late 1940s and early 1950s, sophisticated American graphic designers were putting more and more white space in their work. An open field of white permitted the free play and interaction of individual graphic elements. It was a design strategy that had gained great favor in Europe during the 1910s through the graphic work of the Futurists and the members of the de Stijl movement. American advertisements had traditionally been saturated with information and ink. In their clutter they were not unlike the old interiors full of heavy furniture, dull colors, and bric-a-brac that postwar architectural trade journals and homemaker magazines were attempting to purge. By the late 1950s, large, simple photographs and a restrained use of type were the norm in the editorial layouts and many of the advertisements in popular magazines.

America's new graphic design was more than simply a novel aesthetic. Despite the fanciful appearance of much of the work, it was guided by a serious discipline. In 1947, graphic designer Paul Rand published *Thoughts on Design*, a book that was influential at a time when commercial art had not yet received much respect. In it, he praised the work of the Shakers and explained that the role of the advertising designer was to unify elements and eliminate superfluities. Hans Schlegere later claimed that Rand "belongs to the very small group who are keeping gadget-ridden advertising from becoming an end in itself."[38] Ladislav Sutnar, another leader in postwar American graphic design, claimed that every design solution required a logical structure and should not simply be the result of spontaneous improvisation. For him, the function of graphic design was to communicate ideas as efficiently as possible.

Many critics and designers argued that American sign design needed a radical change. Novelty and originality were highly prized in the market-centered culture of the United States. Competition and postwar prosperity were creating a landscape of confusion: too many words and little sense of hierarchy. Roadways and city streets were a jumble of messages, all competing to be heard above the others. Critics pleaded for the nation to clean up sign communication. From the mid-1950s to the mid-1960s, periodicals including *Architectural Record, Landscape,* and even *Signs of the Times* proposed that symbols begin to replace the plethora of words that had accumulated on roadside signage. In *Architectural Record,* Ladislav Sutnar explained how preliterate Americans had relied primarily on symbols and pictures to identify establishments.[39] Carved or painted icons, such as a red horse for the Red Horse Tavern, provided brilliantly simple identification. *Signs of the Times* speculated that the new medium of television had made Americans more attuned to quick visual expression.[40] Victor Gruen, the architect known as the father of the modern shopping mall, suggested that this new restraint might only be possible with an architect in charge: "The architect will reach his greatest effectiveness not alone when he heeds and fulfills the demands of his client concerning signs, but also when he can analyze the true needs of the owner and tastefully interpret them—often by means other than signs; as by symbols, colors, shapes, etc."[41]

Symbols for national chain businesses were becoming increasingly familiar to anyone with a car. Shell Oil's scallop shell (which dates from 1904), the Texaco Star (from 1903), and the Mobil Oil Pegasus (from 1931), were a few examples. A description of a cross-country road trip in Vladimir Nabokov's novel *Lolita* reveals how these signs were seen, by the late 1940s, as common icons in the American landscape: "We had stopped at a gas station, under the sign of Pegasus . . . she had found the toilet occupied and had crossed over to the sign of the conch in the next block."[42]

These well-known symbols were lost in a tangle of words and images along the roadside. Since they addressed strangers unfamiliar with what they had to offer, signs for local businesses were forced to incorporate more words and images than did the national chains. The idealized landscape of simple symbols critics proposed in the 1950s only started becoming a reality once corporate-owned chains and franchises began to dominate the roadside. These businesses were presold by mass-media advertisements; Americans did not require much more information along the roadside than the name or symbol of a chain. After the first appearance of name-brand gasoline stations across the United States in the 1910s, chain food establishments, specialty services, and discount stores were also being developed.[43]

There was a growing tendency toward abstraction and simplicity in trademark figures such as the Mobil Pegasus. More important, according to the design historian Philip Meggs, it was not the appearance of the symbols themselves that had been revolutionized but the consistency with which symbols were applied to products, packaging, and signage, as well as the care given to the design of all these promotional elements. Each single piece was seen as contributing to the consumer's complete image of a company.[44] Elliot Noyes, IBM's design director in the late 1950s, claimed that the corporation wished to promote an up-to-date image of itself. "We are not looking for a theme," he wrote, " but for a consistency of design quality which will, in effect, become a theme."[45] Over the years, advertising had been used to cultivate brand loyalty; in the new self-service retail environment, the sale had to be clinched before the customer entered the store. Visual identity had become critical to a product's success. The graphic designer became a highly respected image specialist who could plan and coordinate an entire visual system for a corporation. In 1959, an entire issue of *Print* magazine was dedicated to corporate identity, a clear indication of how very important it had become.

Paul Rand emphasized the goal of timelessness when simplifying and abstracting trademarks. In the late 1950s, he designed the IBM and Westinghouse corporate identity programs. To be functional over a long period of time, Rand said, a trademark must be reduced to styleless, elementary shapes. It should be flexible enough to be used in many applications. In 1960, the design firm of Chermayeff & Geismar took the radical step of eliminating the Mobil Pegasus and designing a type-only identity for the corporation, just as Rand might have prescribed. Set against the otherwise blue logotype, the "O" was now emphasized in red, a circle suggesting a wheel. But the new simplicity was not without its critics. The *Harvard Business Review* in 1958 warned that the typical new corporate identity "negates the complexity of the modern diversified corporation."[46] By the late 1960s, modern architecture, too, would be criticized for its extreme reductivism.

The simple new corporate identities typical of the early 1960s could be more easily reproduced in sign form than could the complex graphics of the previous period. This was especially critical when it came to the mass construction of chain service stations, restaurants, and markets. The new corporate identities were not generated with neon in mind. They were the creation of designers whose primary experience was with printed media. Using corporate trademarks as sign art was in sync with a radical change in sign technology at the time, which involved screening images on plastic sheets that were illuminated from behind by fluorescent tubes. New photographic-reproduction methods could easily enlarge a tear-sheet logo to the required size for a sign, eliminating most hand drawing and creative work.

The change from neon to plastic began slowly but was clearly under way right after World War II. As early as 1949, a *Signs of the Times* article asked, "What Will Plastic's Place Be in the Signs of the Future?"[47] A year later, *Business Week* ran a story about how fruitful and painless the switch from neon to plastic had been for two Ohio sign companies.[48] By the mid-1950s, many sign companies could no longer assure a neon tube bender that he would have forty hours of work per week. Yet the disappearance of neon from commercial thoroughfares did not occur as soon as plastic sign facing gained acceptance. For one thing, neon remained in use, even after it "disappeared," since it continued to supply the light source behind plastic for sign features that were not contained within simple, orthogonal boxes. Department store signs, for instance, often consisted of script-lettered logos that were enlarged to a grand scale; the plastic facing merely camouflaged the newly unfashionable neon. Eventually, fluorescent tubes, a cheaper light source developed in the late 1930s, would illuminate many plastic-faced signs.

Advertisements in *Signs of the Times* after the war indicated how forceful that push for the use of acrylic in signs would be. In 1948, the plastics giant du Pont ran a full-page advertisement with a photograph of a new Sunoco sign in acrylic, touting low maintenance and an even distribution of illumination. A ribbed texture to the plastic face recalled the horizontal bands of neon that were once on the face of the Sunoco sign but were now hidden or eliminated. The coupling of du Pont and Sunoco was a vision of the future, in which corporations ruled the roadside. That same year, however, other formidable companies such as General Electric and Sylvania were still touting neon tubing in full-page black-and-white ads.

By 1956, elaborate two-page color advertisements demonstrated how commercial America had already been changed. "Wherever you go . . . you see big names . . . in signs of . . . Plexiglas," they boasted over a twilight photo of internally lit acrylic trademarks. The signs and storefronts for Sears, F. W. Woolworth, and Gulf Oil pictured in one full-spread photograph showed not only how technology had changed but also how corporate giants had begun dominating the night skies with quickly recognizable symbols and very little, if any, extraneous signage. Through the late 1950s and the 1960s, four-color, elaborately produced, double-page advertisements for Plexiglas appeared in virtually every issue of *Signs of the Times*, and full-page ads ran in every issue of *Chain Store Age*. Each unique ad managed to suggest reasons for making the switch to plastic and ways to increase business with the new technology.

Despite the big-money push for change, the disappearance of neon from sign design was surprisingly gradual.[49] Corporate chains tended to favor more acrylic because of low expense and ease of production compared to the careful handcrafting required by neon. Signs that were to be replicated many times could be more efficiently produced with screened graphics on vacuum-formed acrylic sheets. Yet through the 1960s and later, major chains, such as Marriott and Holiday Inn, continued to use exposed neon and porcelain enamel backgrounds.

Scorn for contemporary commercial development grew increasingly loud as the 1950s progressed; by the early 1960s, it seemed almost unanimous but for a few soft voices. *God's Own Junkyard* decried the desecration of the American landscape with some particularly vivid and incriminating pictures. Author Peter Blake, one-time curator of architecture and design at the Museum of Modern Art and soon-to-be editor-in-chief of the *Architectural Forum*, was in a position to influence many. His technique was to set up pairs of photos, comparing what he considered to be good landscapes with bad ones. One might argue that his complaint was weakened by choosing to juxtapose such disparate examples as Canal Street in New Orleans with the Lawn and Rotunda at the University of Virginia. After all, this was comparing a marketplace to a revered learning institution. His overall message, however, reinforced the disdain that many had already developed for the American commercial environment. Blake's intent was to show how new development was undermining a meaningful visual hierarchy—one that favored important institutions like church and government.

A volume of commercial design, published by *Progressive Architecture* in 1956, exemplified the disappointment that many design critics felt for the American roadside:

>It is horrifying to realize that the majority of buildings in this category . . . have so little distinction that even real estate journals . . . would not publish them. It is in this one particular field of construction that our sense of responsibility for the beauty of our country is at its lowest ebb. Ugliness surrounds us. Garish signs, competing in primary colors to the point of mutual extinction, vie with each other in size and frantic activity. As we go by, all blends into a swimming mass of clashing red, white, and yellow symbols. A giant dripping white mountain of stucco ice cream squats near a fake windmill, while a life-size airplane competes with the thousands of bare bulbs of a used car lot.[50]

Photographs of the few examples of commercial architecture the folio editors found acceptable were cropped to exclude signage. Images of storefronts included no street context whatsoever. Another folio, published in *Architectural Record* in 1952, displayed the same limitation. A store for Cargoes Inc. (Skidmore, Owings & Merrill) in San Francisco was identified merely with a large letter "C" on a banner, hung from the ceiling on an all-glass storefront. Apparently, these stores were conceived as perfect, isolated monuments, unspoiled by their neighbors. Richard Snibbe, the editor of the 1956 folio, encouraged architects to minimize signage and suggested, "The character of the architecture is such that a sign is not necessary at all or perhaps a lovely piece of sculpture suggestive of [an owner's] wares will be used in place of a sign."[51]

Although the outcry against commercial chaos was gaining force during the 1950s, some writers showed a true respect for signs, particularly for what signs offered to architecture and the street. This appreciation offered a wide range of perspectives, ranging from a superficial regard for the sensory delights offered by signs to a deeper understanding of the contribution they made to placemaking and identity. In a 1958 article in *Landscape,* John Maas condemned the "sleazy confusion" of modern-day signs but expressed delight for the "sparkle of a lighted city."[52] Many writers of the period acknowledged that signs had the potential to improve what they saw as the blandness of modern architecture. As James S. Hornbeck, *Architectural Record* senior associate editor, wrote in 1956: "There is the chance for tasteful form, texture, color, material, play of light and shade—the possibility of enriching, through contrast, the flat severity and modern regularity of much contemporary work."[53]

By turning his focus away from aesthetics, architect and planner Kevin Lynch was one of the few voices of the period expressing appreciation for these artifacts. His studies, in fact, revealed them as important landmarks and placemakers, helping people create mental maps of the city and the potentially disorienting suburbs. Through interviews, Lynch discovered that people recognized commercial signs as part of an informal pattern or regular system and rarely as mere visual clamor.[54]

Others, however, focused on the perceived street blight. Control was a key concept in the proposals for improving commercial America. Christopher Tunnard, director of Yale's graduate program in city planning, was one of several critics who expressed their aversion to the commercial landscape while also providing a possible solution. In his 1963 book, *Man-made America: Chaos or Control?*, he critiqued landscapes at the urban fringe, "the present-day 'wasteland' of the design world, where professional talent has so far been conspicuous by its absence."[55] Because it offered a framework of order that afforded flexibility, the planned shopping center was Tunnard's solution to the problem. For him, people unfamiliar with aesthetic principles had made too many aesthetic decisions at the urban edge. Land-use specialists, financial institutions, and maintenance organizations were defining suburbia. In contrast, according to Tunnard, the planned shopping center was a cohesive landscape, the design of which could be controlled in its entirety by an architect.[56]

Despite his appreciation of the value of the strip, J. B. Jackson arrived, to some degree, at the same conclusion shared by the bitterest enemies of signs: the shopping center presented a very attractive model for the future of commercial growth. Jackson was a cultural geographer who began a lonely early defense of much of the commercial development others progressively condemned. But he also approved of the gathering of various commercial enterprises into a contained marketplace and marveled at how, like a small community, they could be subjected to certain self-imposed controls.[57] What probably pleased him most was that this balance of freedom and restraint could be achieved in the private sector, avoiding the growing and deadening tide of urban improvement that had as its seeming goal the "sterilization of the roadsides." Jackson was speaking, it must be made clear, of smaller groupings of establishments, not the major regional shopping centers that would eventually be created by architects like Victor Gruen.

The federally subsidized Linda Vista Shopping Center near San Diego (1944) was one of the first schemes proposed as an antidote for America's increasingly random commercial development. Completely restrained, with minimal signage, this retail facility presented an alternative to what was familiar to most Americans. Its architect, Whitney Smith, boasted that "instead of garish storefronts and a raucous discord of signs, there are the order and peace of an early village green."[58] According to the California historian Kevin Starr, this center anticipated what could be achieved in suburbia, "almost on the level of utopian statement."[59] This was a government-sponsored project, and it remained to be seen whether or not such a design ideal could survive under purely market-driven conditions.

The high-minded goals of the Linda Vista Shopping Center had precedent in several projects dating back to at least the 1910s. Lake Forest's Market Square and Kansas City's Country Club Plaza were two of the more famous examples

Figure 103
Broadway Store (Albert B. Gardner, 1940), Colorado Boulevard, Pasadena, California, circa 1940. The corner feature and sign for the 1947 Broadway store at the celebrated Broadway-Crenshaw Center in Baldwin Hills were much the same as those created for this chain's earlier stores.
COURTESY OF THE NATIONAL ARCHIVES, 111-SC, BOX 692, 329538.

of controlled design and restrained commercial features. What they did not include were off-street parking and private, contained common areas—features that would become commonplace as the planned regional shopping center evolved. In the 1930s, both Park and Shop (1930) in Washington, D.C., and Silver Spring Shopping Center (1938) in Maryland offered generous (and at the time, novel) spaces in front of their storefronts for off-street parking. Shop signs were wall-mounted only and relegated to a limited panel size and specified location. Highland Park Shopping Village (Fooshee and Cheek, 1931) in Dallas, though draped in historic forms and ornament, was advanced in another way, as it was one of the very first shopping centers to be oriented around a courtyard (there were actually two, and they accommodated automobiles).

After World War II, the scale and ambition for planned shopping centers progressed rapidly. The design for the Broadway-Crenshaw Center (1947) in Los Angeles, which received a great deal of press, straddled the line between past and future. The project was immense by comparison with earlier planned shopping centers, and it broke precedent by bringing together two major department store anchors and a long list of well-established chains. Its main facade was conventionally placed flush to the public sidewalk, and a public road segregated the two anchors from each other. At the corner of Crenshaw Boulevard and Santa Barbara Avenue, the lead destination, the Broadway store, was marked with a tower composed of progressively narrower cylinders—almost like a compressed birthday cake—from which a sign fin projected (fig. 103). This method of identification, a visual strategy dating from the late 1920s, was borrowed from many of the movie theaters of Los Angeles. Such architecture and graphic integration would fall quickly by the wayside in the late 1940s. The Broadway-Crenshaw Center was also somewhat novel by offering two facades: one to the street and one to the vast parking lot "behind" the bank of stores. Neon lettering along the parapet of the "back" of the Broadway store greeted customers from the parking lot. In the future, designers increasingly would turn attention to store entrances directly from off-street parking lots; these would soon be the primary means of arrival—at least until the enclosed shopping mall was developed. The signs for the smaller stores at the Broadway-Crenshaw Center were not the cautious plaques seen at earlier planned centers, including Linda Vista. They varied widely in location, scale, and material down the block, but all were wall-mounted, nonprojecting signs, unlike the identities for many of the stores downtown.[60] They were not designed to be seen from down the street at an oblique angle, but across a vast open space, in pure elevation.[61]

Other leading centers in the late 1940s and early 1950s would maintain strict limits on the signs of individual stores.[62] Ernst Payer's 1948 L-shaped center for Euclid, Ohio, permitted signs of any width or illumination as long as they were confined to the top of the parapet. In this center, even Howard Johnson's was forced to comply with a common look by reducing its standard signage to neon lettering alone and removing all traces of colonial design from its proposed facade.[63] Morris Ketchum's Shopper's World (1951) in Framingham, Massachusetts, only the second regional, planned shopping center to have a mall space surrounded by retail, limited store signs to small panels attached to the edge of the common canopy or arcade signs mounted underneath the overhang. For a time, canopies such as this provided new shopping centers with a dominant common architectural feature that was intended to suppress individuality. Eventually, other common features, including elaborate interior mall landscapes, would make manifest the central control of the single owner and master architect for these centers, a force that never existed on Main Street.

Victor Gruen and his contemporaries sought to create restful atmospheres within the new, high-profile, planned regional shopping centers, to remove customers from overreaching signs and noisy traffic yet provide enough choreographed liveliness to stimulate activity. This was the next step in the development of the shopping center. As businesses increasingly turned primary storefronts inward toward common spaces and away from automobiles, the exterior of the new shopping center became progressively mute. Instead of distinctive architecture, Gruen looked to a grand massing of structures to provide an imposing impression of the shopping center to those walking or driving by.[64]

Figure 104

Environmental graphic features of Northland Center (Alvin Lustig, 1954), Northwestern Highway, Southfield, Michigan. Lustig's coordinated graphics program, along with sculpture by others, brought character and life to a very chaste ensemble of buildings. It also guided the patron through a vast, and potentially disorienting, landscape.
COURTESY OF ELAINE LUSTIG COHEN.

A major advance in post–World War II shopping center design was, arguably, suburban Detroit's highly acclaimed Northland Center (1954). Its design was a collaboration between Gruen and the graphic designer Alvin Lustig. Though Gruen himself was an able sign designer, he probably sought Lustig's assistance because of the scale of the project and the comprehensive graphic wayfinding program it required. Lustig, in turn, had proven himself to be a successful architect of interiors besides being one of the country's foremost graphic designers. It was unique in America to find high profile, commercial signage created by such an illustrious graphic designer.

At Northland, Lustig designed all common signage, from the water tower symbol to the wayfinding sign system. The Northland graphics were praised for being bold, yet controlled. The shopping center's main identifying symbol, a large sign structure in the parking lot, was a significant departure from the typical montage of boomerangs, kidney shapes, and flashing arrows that characterized the majority of strip signage at this time (fig. 104). Lustig had carefully considered the crisp, orthogonal architectural aesthetic of Gruen's buildings. His design was light yet powerful, contrasting a network of simple modern frames against the intricate starburst of Northland's logo trademark. Though this sign was highly disciplined, Lustig gave it a surprising energy and playfulness by weaving, intersecting, and rotating the elements in relationship to each other. In many ways, the sign was a monumental piece of modern sculpture.[65]

With the signs he designed for all of Northland's common spaces, Lustig seemed to be playing a thoughtful but clever game with a kit of parts: stacking panels and letters, enlivening chaste typefaces with color, and energizing ordinary sign poles with stripes. His work displayed the playfulness of Charles and Ray Eames's children's toys and the design discipline and structural virtuosity that impressed serious architects. Lustig prided himself on using richer typefaces than the potentially anemic Futura or Helvetica lettering many architects favored for their polite neutrality. Lustig chose the lettering at Northland, especially the extended Clarendon typeface with its heavy serifs, because it had the strength necessary to complement the large, plain surfaces of the architecture.

Lustig's groundbreaking work at Northland ushered in a series of regional centers whose signs were designed by well-educated graphic designers. In 1956, *Architectural Record* devoted over thirty pages to the work of these experts, including Elaine Lustig, Ladislav Sutnar, and the directors of graphic departments in the architectural firms of I. M. Pei and Victor Gruen.[66] This exemplary work existed nationwide, providing models of what was hoped could replace the clumsy and often illegible signs cluttering the roadsides, which were designed and produced by sign fabricators. The editors also hoped it would improve the inept graphics produced by architects untrained in lettering and distracted by other design obligations.

The sign work of well-schooled graphic designers like Alvin Lustig was both visually stimulating and logical. The primary regional shopping center

Figure 105
Design of primary identification for Mondawmin Center (Alvin Lustig, 1955), Liberty Heights Avenue, Baltimore, Maryland. The parking lot signs for the new regional shopping centers were true landmarks, veritable monuments. Unlike the work of sign companies, these sculptures displayed a design logic informed by a reverence for connections.
COURTESY OF ELAINE LUSTIG COHEN.

identifications at roadside easily qualified as monuments. Unlike the signs of the average merchants on the strip, these were relatively restrained compositions that reflected a relish for the aesthetic of articulated pieces and visual contrast. Designers often inserted panels into open structural grids or set letters on individual panels to collectively spell out the name of the center. There was usually plenty of open or "white" space between the pieces.

Comparing the signs for the highly regarded regional shopping centers Mondawmin (Alvin Lustig, 1955) in Baltimore or Valley Fair (Gruen Associates, 1956) in Santa Clara Valley, California, with common contemporary signs from the strip reveals a fundamental difference in design approach (fig. 105).[67] The same pronounced contrast was visible when comparing them to even the most lauded contemporary graphics of the sign industry, most especially the 1959 NESA competition for shopping center signage (see fig. 101). Suburban commercial strip signs from the 1950s could be described as intuitive compositions of dissimilar pieces, randomly overlapping to create a pleasing and stimulating visual whole. Organic shapes were in abundance on the strip, but the contemporaneous regional shopping center signs were composed exclusively with perfect circles and 90-degree orthogonal shapes. Gravity seemed nonexistent on the strip, as one found plenty of large signs, with questionable balance above, tapering down to narrow bases at grade. Design elements did not connect so much as they slipped past each other. In contrast, the work from the offices of Lustig, Pei, and Gruen displayed a certain basic architectural logic of construction. Northland's main parking lot sign consisted of lettered panels supported by open steel frames. The compass rose trademark rested carefully, its points lined up precisely with the intersection of the two frames.

How well these primary identifications communicated was another matter. The designers of Gruen's and Pei's offices favored abstract patterns over the illustrations that some strip businesses might have used to indicate quickly the nature of their services or products. The regional shopping center signs were landmarks, memorable and readily distinguishable from the neighbors. They were identities only and did not serve as the visually descriptive, if not verbose, advertisements that common strip signs provided. What they sometimes offered, other than occasional structural histrionics, were trademarks or symbols of the kind that corporate chains were refining for individual businesses. Northland's compass rose complemented the directional name of the center. Mondawmin's abstract symbol incorporated the shape of the *M* into a starlike feature element. Such trademarks were easily adapted to shopping bags, letterheads, and newspaper advertisements. They communicated little more than a name, which was sometimes obscured by clever graphic games.

Unremarkable today, but taken quite seriously at the time, were Northland's rules for all tenant signage. No sign could be more than four feet tall. All signs had to be flush-mounted to the storefront with no flashing illumination. Each design had to be reviewed by the shopping center owner.[68] Gruen understood that if the architectural frame of repeating bays and neutral piers was visually strong enough, then the latitude for individual expression by the stores could be greater.[69] This was not the severe reductivism of early centers like Linda Vista and Shopper's World; there was a balance between restraint and the expression permitted by extra wall area. Malls all over the country soon adopted Northland's sign format. The center was heavily published and highly influential. It came midway in a decade during which shopping center growth in the United States ballooned from 100 to 3,700 facilities.[70]

The planned regional shopping center was a design utopia where the excesses of the strip were to be purged. But the reduction in flourishes also brought a reduction in the amount of information communicated. Individual stores were often identified by name or a unique logo within the new complex, but graphic information about the type or character of business was stripped away as merchants were confined to the neutral bays of rentable space, their signs strictly controlled. Moving from Main Street to the mall, the tenant sign was no longer an advertisement but increasingly a rather pragmatic verbal or symbol-oriented identification. The merchandise itself was to assume the role of primary advertisement, especially now that it was behind glare-free glass or no barrier whatsoever. Attractive patterns and textures often appeared at malls in place of the informative images found on downtown signs. In renderings of the proposed storefronts for the Roosevelt Field Shopping Center (1956) by I. M. Pei and Associates in East Garden City, New York, the type of business often remained unidentified, leaving only the name of the business, such as Cook's or Venus (fig. 106). The emphasis on interesting patterns for the awning fabrics,

Figure 106

Proposed storefronts for the Roosevelt Field Shopping Center (I. M. Pei and Associates, 1956), East Garden City, New York. Unlike the newer signs of Main Street or the suburban strip, these graphics were limited to wall locations, with placement and scale strictly regulated. Sufficient visual variety would supposedly be achieved through awning patterns and typeface choices.
ARCHITECTURAL RECORD (SEPTEMBER 1956), 250–51. REPRODUCTION COURTESY OF RYERSON AND BURNHAM LIBRARIES, ART INSTITUTE OF CHICAGO.

which overwhelmed the modest sign lettering, may have indicated a greater desire by the master architect to charm than to identify successfully.

Sometimes this emphasis on aesthetics and visual stimulation assumed new extremes. Edward Larrabee Barnes, a prominent Harvard-educated architect of the period, once proposed a shopping center where all the walls would be made of white stucco and all the signs would be raised white letters. Ostensibly, his intent was to place emphasis on the merchandise, but his primary motivation was an improved appearance of the stores. For this project in Houston, to be known as Neiman Marcus Center, Barnes subordinated everything to an architectural ideal.[71] According to him, the white-on-white scheme still permitted a play of shadow and light. Useful communication would be secondary in importance. Victor Gruen spoke, by contrast, about a new, fairer strategy for signs: "It is important that the individual characteristics and expressions of the participants not be suppressed but, on the contrary, encouraged. It is, however, equally important that a strong denominator be created to tie the individual enterprise into a homogeneous unit. These two aims appear to be divergent, but skillful planning and design can reconcile them harmoniously."[72]

Victor Gruen has been credited by some with striking the right balance between severe restraint and design freedom in signage and storefront design. His formula for tenant sign area and design limitations at Northland won him praise. In contrast to most other shopping center designers, he was unwilling to force graphics to be an overly regulated afterthought, perhaps because he himself had done a good deal of sign design for individual specialty shops during the 1940s. Gruen's schooling in Europe, where the lines between the various design professions were often blurred, made him ideally suited to address all facets of shopping center design. He was part urban designer, part architect, and part graphic designer.[73]

Despite his ability to create vibrant new marketplaces, it might be said that Gruen and his contemporaries filled the common spaces with delightful but meaningless colors and shapes. Gruen's all-new shopping landscapes were disconnected from everything that had previously held meaning for local residents, with no traditional landmarks or well-known signs, nor was there the accretion of details that reveal the history or meaning of a place. Instead, the common spaces of his malls were filled with whimsical structures. "In every court or mall a delightful piece of modern sculpture attracts the eye," one journalist cooed.[74] Gruen intended that the staggered arrangement of courts, terraces, and short malls around the central anchor store feel like the picturesque jumble of streets in a European city. A 1954 article on Northland ominously cited a sure sign of the center's success, "The most frequent comment by shoppers: you wouldn't know you were in Detroit."[75] Just three years later, J. B. Jackson offered this opinion of Gruen's earliest triumphs: "What bloodless places these shopping centers are! . . . Art shows indeed! It strikes me that some of our planners need to acquire a more robust idea of city life. Perhaps I do them an injustice, but I often have the feeling that their emphasis on convenience, cleanliness, and safety, their distrust of everything vulgar and small and poor, is symptomatic of a very lopsided view of urban culture."[76]

Jackson was distressed that these new "marketplaces" automatically rejected anything from outside, limiting their clientele to the middle- and upper-middle-classes and avoiding messy but potentially vital minor businesses like lunch counters, taverns, Laundromats, and market stalls. In contrast to the planned regional shopping centers, Jackson described a phenomenon that he observed in every community, something he called "the Strangers' Path," that visually loud part of town devoted to the outsider, the transient, marked by a profusion of signs (for the uninitiated). When he first wrote about it, the Strangers' Path began at the bus or train depot, but less than a decade later, one could make a case that it also began at the superhighway exit. From that point, following Jackson's logic, it could be traced along an informal route from the "squalor" of service stations and truck facilities at the cloverleaf, down the strip, toward the most "respectable" or "fashionable" retail district: arguably, the mall. The path and the planned regional shopping center were almost polar opposites. Instead of the irregular profusion of signs aggressively trying to address and inform the visitor, one encountered a staid regularity purged of anything new or uncertain.

In 1955 one of the most popular commercial spaces in the United States opened; it had been created by people who understood what Gruen referred to as "atmosphere," the concept that guided him in the creation of many artificial landscapes.[77] Disneyland's Main Street USA offered a romanticized version of a typical small-town business thoroughfare, the kind of place that was already suffering from suburban competition all over the country. Disneyland was later criticized for creating an overly cleaned-up version of real Main Streets and influencing small towns everywhere to replace existing signs with small, painted, flush-mounted signs of consistent size and location. In truth, Disneyland offered a vast range of sign sizes and types—many of them electrical and mounted in a wide variety of places on its Main Street buildings. This was hardly the relative uniformity of signage seen at one of Gruen's malls. However, the sign locations and characteristics were all preconceived simultaneously by a single team of designers (eventually designated by Disney as Imagineers) who were well aware of the collective picturesque effect of the signs and their interaction with the architecture. Walt Disney no doubt appreciated Gruen's work and his ability to control large environments. He was known to keep a copy of Gruen's 1964 book *The Heart of Our Cities* on his shelf.[78] Gruen's public pronouncements against billboards on Ventura Boulevard in Los Angeles's San Fernando Valley were not unlike Disney's well-known complaints against the commercial clutter that grew up around Disneyland after it opened. It was ironic that this "clutter" was merely the midcentury version of the turn-of-the-century commercial exuberance enshrined on Disney's Main Street USA. The message Gruen and Disney seemed to be broadcasting was "The only good variety is controlled variety."

Whereas Disney built a carefully controlled, scenographic interpretation of a disorderly past, Seattle's Century 21 Exposition of 1962 presented a future of what might be labeled *controlled chaos*, displayed in its Signs of the Future exhibit. Renderings for the exhibit, published before the fair opened, showed a multilevel commercial landscape of elevated, freeway-scaled walkways and signs suspended at a multitude of heights and locations. Simple arrow signs and corporate symbols commingled with attractive larger, nonverbal panels depicting city skylines, architecture, and rural landscapes (fig. 107). This was a landscape designed primarily for the automobile. The individual signs, artistically suggested in the published drawing, avoided the overabundance of words to be found on 1962's suburban strip. The message may easily have been that if you make the signs more efficient, and fewer in number, the view can include more than just signs. Nevertheless, there was a kind of kinetic energy on display. This was a twentieth-century picturesque landscape to be explored at great speed: quick stimulation with little need to linger.[79]

The Seattle fair, as a whole, was more organized and contained than the Signs of the Future exhibit might lead one to think. It reflected, above all, the new enthusiasm for the shopping center. Here, however, the principles at work in suburban shopping centers were placed in an urban context. The plan of the fair was integrated with the existing street grid on the edge of Seattle's central business district, and the overall appearance of the fair was given a Gruen-like coherence by supervising architect Paul Thiry. A cohesive sign system directed visitors at the fair, and the fair commission provided most exhibition buildings. The result was almost mall-like. The Century 21 Exposition was a huge hit with both the public and architectural critics, as might be expected in a society that had embraced the suburban shopping center.[80] In direct contrast, the exuberant, free-market individualism of the corporate pavilion designs at the 1964 New York World's Fair was universally panned.

By the mid-1960s, the new commercial ideal presented by the regional shopping center was losing its luster. Many of the principles that had been so novel or well employed in the early centers were forgotten, abused, or overused. Control alone was not a sustainable design approach, for sterility could result. Arbitrary aesthetic choices did nothing to prevent disorientation and often did little to prevent boredom. In 1962 the preeminent commercial developer James Rouse lamented that too many shopping center identifications were inappropriately designed and their entrances anemically indicated; they were never the significant portals to grand spaces they should be. But closer to the heart of the matter, "Despite the emphasis on convenience and design—or perhaps because of it—the centers have become oppressively out of scale with people. The huge parking areas, the massive factory-like buildings, the enormous unbroken spaces, the *(opposite) Figure 107* Proposal for "Signs of the Future" Exhibit (Paul Thiry, FAIA, 1959), Century 21 Exposition, Seattle. In this rendering, the roads that America had committed to building with the Federal-Aid Highway Act of 1956 were envisioned as soaring through a landscape of succinct symbols scattered picturesquely among views of architecture and trees. These abbreviated verbal messages were what design critics for years had been pushing to replace an overabundance of messages that blotted out all else. ARTS & ARCHITECTURE (DECEMBER 1959), 13. REPRODUCTION COURTESY OF RYERSON AND BURNHAM LIBRARIES, ART INSTITUTE OF CHICAGO. PERMISSION COURTESY OF DAVID TRAVERS.

storefronts and signs all add up to a big project imposed on a community rather than a warm and friendly market place growing out of the community."[81]

Had the marketplace been taken out of the marketplace? Were the new commercial utopias just commodities instead of the community centers many of their planners had hoped they would be? Perhaps too many of the efforts to clean up commercial streets and roadways had lost sight of the nature of the subject being reformed. Corporate control and big business had certainly manifested themselves on the new landscape of the suburbs. But what was being advertised by the new, improved signage—the wares of business or big business itself? One thing was certain: individual ideas and individual ownership were quickly disappearing from the American commercial landscape.

The decrease in visual connection between sign and architecture along the suburban commercial thoroughfare resulted from a physical separation but also from a new aesthetic that placed high value on visual contrast and articulation. Neighborhoods, individuals, and locations, once effectively marked or acknowledged by a hierarchy of commercial signs in urban centers, had few corresponding markers in suburbia, resulting in a growing sense of placelessness. The new signs communicated both more and less information, compared to those in urban centers. Each pylon or pole sign was loaded with more visual stimulation but conveyed less of the important indirect messages that marquees, wall signs, or projecting signs telegraphed through their placement, context, and other characteristics.

The planned regional shopping center, as a replacement for the sprawl of suburban commercialism, brought additional losses. The growth of corporate ownership of smaller businesses along the strip compounded these losses. Sign craft declined with decreased use of exposed neon. Communication suffered with fewer elaborate illustrations and distinct forms. Freedom and individuality of design were the most obvious sacrifices.

The new corporate design of the strip and the rise of the regional shopping center offered one clear gain: control. What garnered increased appreciation in publications and community meetings was a "correct" aesthetic, a clean, predictable look that could only be achieved under the master hand of a well-indoctrinated designer or a firm set of rules. This aesthetic, though it was no particular style, was one of restraint. But it was also one of limited visual variety that was only acceptable if created by experts. The goal of the contrived, picturesque chaos of communal banners and novel sculptural features was primarily optical stimulation. Communicating useful information became a secondary, if not coincidental, aim.

Some critics have charged that the leading architects and designers of the postwar period placed too much emphasis on superficial variety. A few have even claimed that design of the period had variety and contrast as its principal aim. The interplay between delicately patterned wallpaper and a rough stone wall

was cited as a critical design issue in *Contemporary,* a book by Lesley Jackson, which examines the priorities of postwar design.[82] In his 1984 book, *The Decorated Diagram,* Klaus Herdeg analyzed the influence of professors who came from the Bauhaus to teach Harvard architecture students in the late 1940s. He accused the Harvard-trained architects of producing irresponsible architecture and leading a nation of designers toward meaningless design. In the Harvard studio projects of such architectural leaders as Paul Rudolph, Philip Johnson, I. M. Pei, and others, "we can perceive the seeds of formalism, in the pejorative sense as the term is commonly being used, that is, connoting the employment of forms for purely literal and superficial reasons such as visual variety. Formalism in this sense implies a total non-recognition of the multiplicity of meanings a form may have."[83]

According to Herdeg, students were asked to provide visual variety as an end unto itself in matters of building and site arrangement, as well as in the choice of patterns, textures, and roof forms. In 1962, Lewis Mumford had decried the desire among modern architects for architectural originality, disregarding the inner purpose of buildings. This growing design perversion included, according to Mumford, "the utilization of sensational methods of construction merely to produce equally sensational forms, which have no purpose other than that of demonstrating the esthetic audacity of the designer."[84]

Marcel Breuer, one of the leaders of the Bauhaus who fled Germany for Harvard in the 1930s, designed a modern house with a butterfly roof, which was put on exhibit in the courtyard of the Museum of Modern Art in 1949. Herdeg criticized Breuer's use of such a distinct form for the roof, a design gesture that he deemed meaningless in terms of giving information about either the use of the spaces beneath the roof, the nature of the structure, or any poetic intent on the part of the creator.

During the 1950s, roadside signage and the popular architecture of coffee shops, bowling alleys, and other commercial buildings commonly employed eye-catching forms to appeal to a mass popular audience. Sometimes these forms successfully communicated important messages, either directly or indirectly. Sometimes they just contributed to confusion. Considering that they were influenced by the publication of a great deal of content-empty design work from many so-called design leaders of the day, it is not surprising that sign designers—often practicing without any formal design education—would create equally meaningless designs. Boomerang shapes, appearing almost like arrows, sometimes pointed away from the businesses they were meant to advertise. Rounded, organic figures were used as backgrounds for such technical businesses as automobile repair. A variety of different shapes were exploited merely to attract attention. The abstract butterfly shape of the Bel-Air Hotel sign (Jack Driscoll, Ace Sign Company, 1958) in Wildwood, New Jersey, offered no more legitimate a message about the purpose of the building than did the butterfly roof on Breuer's house at the Museum of Modern Art (see plate 26). Ambiguous and potentially confusing forms like these seemed questionable when they appeared in signs, which were by nature intended as clear devices of communication. Though signs are meant to stimulate action and identify content, such an overemphasis on stimulation often obscured identity.

Not all of the leading post–World War II designers were motivated primarily by content-empty aesthetics. Ladislav Sutnar and Paul Rand pleaded for design logic. Clarity, hierarchy, and flow distinguished their work from that of many other well-educated designers. In order to help rid sign communication of its excess, inefficiency, and confusion, many respected critics and designers called for well-designed symbols to be used to identify the businesses of the strip.[85]

It was believed that good taste and good planning would transform the commercial corridor for the better. The growth of corporate-owned businesses, with their need for consistent, easily reproduced identities, addressed the call by critics and the public to reduce the graphic overload of individual enterprises. Requests for replacing a perceived clutter of words with easy-to-read symbols and trademarks was made possible through nationalized advertising campaigns that familiarized customers with businesses through electronic and printed media. Almost three decades of neon was rapidly being replaced by the new technology of back-lit acrylic sign boxes. Tougher new local codes would fuel the transformation. In the decades to come, urban commercial corridors would be stripped down considerably of their messages, looking perhaps less cluttered but also progressively more blank—especially to those not well acquainted with the new businesses through television.

Chapter 6
REDISCOVERING MAIN STREET
RETRENCHMENT, REPAIR, AND REINVENTION, 1965–2010

FOLLOWING WORLD WAR II, societal and economic changes altered America's commercial corridors—its Main Streets and its suburban strips alike. The shake-up began when "downtown" business owners realized they were losing market share to their suburban counterparts. Initially, this led to efforts to imitate the layout, appearance, and amenities of the new shopping centers in order to woo back customers. Years later, downtown business owners decided, instead, to stress what made Main Street appealingly different. Owners of businesses along suburban corridors faced their own challenges, including stringent new zoning codes and unpredictable changes in popular taste. The creative splurges and resultant exuberant designs that had animated both urban and suburban landscapes soon seemed passé.

Retrenchment characterized much of the 1970s, as Americans recoiled from the perceived excesses of the previous decades, and protecting the earth's ecology and historic assets became more important. On Main Street, this often meant peeling away superficial facades that had been applied to older commercial structures. The excesses in scale and visual novelty of the sign industry came to a halt beginning with the federal government's attempt to limit or ban billboards from the new interstate system. The sign industry had for years promoted a clear distinction between offsite and onsite advertising, but this did not quell citizen ire about signs in general. The passage of the Highway Beautification Act in 1965 gave the antisign movement tremendous momentum for further legislation aimed against business signs and overly exuberant architecture. The new attitude was "enough is enough," and soon new legislation imposed unprecedented limits on the size and number of on-premise signs.

After the about-face of retrenchment, it was necessary to repair much of the damage wrought by the explosion of postwar commercial growth. Many communities realized that restored and rehabilitated historic commercial buildings attracted customers. History became marketable. Soon, whole streets and towns were renewed to their presumed historic appearances. As early success stories accumulated, organizations like the National Trust for Historic Preservation's Main Street Center were formed to assist communities in their revitalization and marketing. Rehabilitation was also necessary to connect historic neighborhoods to new development and to replace some of the losses where misguided urban renewal demolition left voids in otherwise continuous streetscapes.

The word *reinvention* probably best captures the range of effort put forth to make commercial corridors appear vital as they aged during the latter decades of the twentieth century. The first and most radical strategy was closing commercial streets in town centers to automobile traffic and turning them into pedestrian "malls." In some instances, the creators of suburban shopping centers directed this reinvention; these were the very people who had successfully drawn crowds away from the old corridors. Some streets were not closed but heavily landscaped with trees, benches, and banners just the same. They became, in effect, more rural. Decades later, many loosely developed, rambling suburban corridors were replanned and rezoned to be more densely developed and tightly structured—and thus more urban, more like Main Street.

Facade Stories: Preservation Policy and Unmasked History

During the 1950s and 1960s, many nineteenth-century buildings along the Main Streets of America were covered completely, or in part, by what is now commonly termed a "slipcover." This often involved the installation of modern metal paneling systems in various textures and designs over older storefronts, or entire commercial buildings, in order to hide what was considered decrepit or out-of-date. (For more on this phenomenon, see chapter 5.) This slipcovering was not merely a masking of the old but an attempt to revitalize commercial enterprises with a bright new look and more suburban-scaled graphics. By the late 1960s, slipcovering had become a common method of *muting* the nineteenth-century commercial building, of cloaking its perceived design excesses. No longer a bright new background for over-scaled graphics, by the early 1970s, slipcovering had become akin to shrouding.

In some communities, like Niles, Michigan, once home to the Kawneer storefront systems company, which manufactured such slipcovering material, the cover-up in 1972 began just above the display windows and ran up to the crest of the parapet. It also continued up and down the block, masking preexist-

Figure 108

Presentation of proposed resheathing of Main Street, Niles, Michigan (1972). Shadowform, a Kawneer wall system with a smoked bronze finish, was proposed for a block in Niles, the hometown of this powerful manufacturer of storefront systems. Plans for coordinating a cover-up of an entire block of older facades with modern finishes had begun in the 1940s, but this was the first time the full program was implemented.

COURTESY OF DONNA OCHENRYDER COLLECTION.

ing variety in windows and architectural materials. The Kawneer product used for this refacing was called Shadowform. Discreet, uniform signs were placed just above the display windows, on the new surface, mimicking the standardized system of signs in many suburban shopping centers. This new, smoky bronzed material covered over most upper-story windows (fig. 108). Shadowform was also applied to portions of blocks on the south side, thus having a major effect on the character of the town. Most of the north side of State Street had been effectively covered by the early 1970s. In the 1990s, about thirty years after the Philbrick Building in Redwood Falls, Minnesota, was shorn of its elaborate cornice and projecting parapet in the cause of slick modernizing, the second-story windows were filled in and painted the brick color of the rest of the building, since the upstairs apartment was no longer rentable. The unifying paint scheme and cornice severance was an attempt to wipe away all the surface ornament and economically modernize the structure. At this same time, the storefront on the first floor was covered with dryvit and most of the display windows reduced in size (see fig. 16).

In general, slipcovering in the 1970s tended to be dark, with minimal graphics. Rough-finished wood siding and shingles offered another means of updating the look of Main Street. It was another way of rejecting the slick look of the 1950s, using earth colors and coarse materials to suggest a respect for ecology. Often these materials were applied to new framing and plywood to create mansard-shaped canopies. Many of the nineteenth-century buildings on both sides of Main Street in Van Wert, Ohio, were covered with cedar paneling or shakes, flush with the facades; some were painted, and some were left to weather naturally. In 1979, the black Vitrolite installed in the late 1930s to modernize Balyeat's Coffee Shop was covered with brick and a shake-covered mansard canopy (fig. 109 and

Figure 109

Commercial storefront layers, 100 block north, East Main Street, Van Wert, Ohio. Two original, nineteenth-century facades were modernized in the 1930s with black structural glass and then modernized again in the 1970s with brick and wood shingles (partially removed from one business to reexpose the Vitrolite).
PHOTO BY AUTHOR, 2005.

RETRENCHMENT, REPAIR, AND REINVENTION

Figure 110

Patterson's Department Store (1867), South Main Street, Findlay, Ohio, circa 1948, in 1949, and in 2007. In the first of several architectural updates (LEFT), the increased affordability of glass and availability of steel structural members made the generous glazing and bay windows possible. During the twentieth century, department stores increasingly relied on artificial illumination, and windows could assume a quasi-functional role. In this case (MIDDLE), a meandering "ribbon" window provided the modernizing flourish. Eventually, the building was cocooned in a thick coat of stucco (RIGHT), making it seem to recede visually rather than attract attention, as it once did.

LEFT, MIDDLE: MAE HUSTON LOCAL HISTORY RESOURCE CENTER, HANCOCK HISTORICAL MUSEUM, FINDLAY, OHIO.
RIGHT: PHOTO BY AUTHOR, 2007.

plate 32). This Vitrolite finish had been installed as a continuous new surface across the first-floor facades of two older buildings that housed Balyeat's and the music store next door. Decorative silver striping and sign lettering were set flush into its glimmering surface. The large, projecting neon sign, designed and erected by Herring Neon Sign of Lima, Ohio, for the first owner of the restaurant, had remained almost unchanged since it was first erected. It outlasted three different storefront designs, spanning more than seventy-five years—a beacon of sorts, on the old Lincoln Highway through town.

The resheathing or covering of commercial buildings did not end in the late 1970s even although some businesses were at that time being liberated from their mummification. Where slipcovering continued in the late twentieth century, stucco often replaced aluminum as a cover-up material of choice because of its low cost and the fact that owners desired neither a slick modern nor a rustic appearance when "improving" their buildings. For example, the building that housed Patterson's Department Store in Findlay, Ohio, was completely covered in stucco in 1984. Its display and upper-story windows were each reduced in

size by as much as 70 percent. A smooth coating also covered the cornices at the first floor and building crest, as if the material had been spread over everything like cake icing. The original Patterson's building, constructed in 1867, had been updated several times in just over a hundred years (fig. 110). For an ambitious late-1940s remodeling, a meandering, cantilevered ribbon window was located in an otherwise blank facing material that was fastened over the original grid of tall, arched windows. It emphasized the new auto-age vogue for horizontality, reinventing a facade that was constructed with very vertical proportions. The stucco covering closed up the windows, as natural light had been deemed intrusive for department stores. It is ironic that this building's facade, which was visually opened up from top to bottom with glass in the early twentieth century for three floors of display windows, would be closed up again before the century was over.

Covering over original buildings continued into the early twenty-first century. In 2003, while Niles, Michigan, was engaged in its "Big Brown Take Down" project—carefully removing the dark slipcovering that had shrouded

Figure 111

Main Street, Buffalo Lake, Minnesota. The buildings along this corridor were united visually with a common metal sheathing installed in the mid-2000s. Distinct roof profiles maintain some level of variety. This unusual treatment was the result of a choice by downtown business owners, not a municipal mandate.

PHOTO BY AUTHOR, 2007.

RETRENCHMENT, REPAIR, AND REINVENTION

Main Street for decades—tiny Buffalo Lake, Minnesota, was recladding most of its commercial buildings with grey metal siding.[1] Buffalo Lake achieved instant visual unity along the length of the town's Main Street with its light-colored slipcovering material (fig. 111). A few modest brick buildings were not covered, however, and the hardware store owner permitted the old corbelled brick cornice to project above the new sheathing of his building. Some of the siding material was applied only to gables or upper facades, often with creative new profiles— easy places to apply signs. Despite inconsistencies, Buffalo Lake comes across as a freshly clad metal town. In many ways, it appears as an uncontrived twenty-first-century frontier village, quickly assembled, with elaborate false fronts.

By the time the first generation of slipcovering in the 1950s, with its boldly colored aluminum facing and multistoried, script-rendered store signs, evolved into the muted earth hues and rustic cladding materials of the 1970s, the notion of unrestrained capitalism had lost its shine. A big about-face on signs led to a miniaturizing and standardizing of the graphics. Corporate identities, when they appeared on Main Street, were rendered in vacuum-formed, internally illuminated acrylic sign boxes. As the economy of Main Street shrank and more modest businesses filled empty storefronts, the investment in signage became no more than a painted panel or a silk-screened awning. These underscaled, slightly old-fashioned storefront identifications often seemed in conflict with the massive, slipcovered wall above. Niles demonstrated perhaps the most blatant example of this clash of identities: delicate, uniform lettering, individually mounted at the bottom of the dark bronzed Shadowform frame, was replaced, by the 1980s, with an assortment of random, temporary-looking signs. Irregular acrylic sign boxes and brightly colored bullnose awning signs were fastened to the bronzed screen in a variety of locations. All variety now lay in the signage, not the architecture.

Ada Louise Huxtable once wrote that the modernization of storefronts "has been completely successful as a building products sales campaign and as an architectural and neighborhood assassination."[2] A community-sponsored architecture school reevaluation of the urban design of Bryan, Ohio, peeled off the town's extensive slipcovering in stages in 1975. But the bland Uhlman's metal front remained in place until 1997. The Newberry's cover-up in Providence was removed in 1978, when the chain left town. The solid "blanket" covering the Providence Journal Building, one of the city's most elaborate historic structures, was removed in 1984. Yet in Niles, Michigan, the slipcovering remained in place until the early 2000s partly because some locals perceived it as being part of the town's heritage as the one-time headquarters of the Kawneer Corporation. Niles was by no means the last community to begin stripping away downtown cover-ups.

By the late 1960s, a few building owners and communities began to explore a potentially fruitful alternative to covering up older commercial buildings as a means of appealing to shoppers. Fixing up or restoring individual structures or storefronts aided business, surely, but doing so for an entire street was exponentially more rewarding.

The historic preservation movement in America had begun with the restoration of individual buildings like Mount Vernon (1858), but it evolved to include whole districts, such as Charleston, South Carolina (designated in 1931 as the nation's first protected local historic district). Eventually, advocates formed the National Trust for Historic Preservation (1949), and its list of nationally designated buildings and districts attracted attention in the media, which in turn stimulated more designations and local efforts to protect, restore, or rehabilitate. The National Historic Preservation Act (1966), a federal mandate that created state preservation officers and thus localized power for preserving historic buildings, also created the National Register of Historic Places. This legislation was close on the heels of the well-publicized demolition of New York City's famed Penn Station in 1964, an event that seemed to mark the end of the public's tolerance for wholesale destruction of revered places, even in the cause of urban renewal.[3] In Charleston, the earliest efforts toward restoration were lavished on residential structures. It would be many years before eyes turned toward the slowly degrading commercial structures along King Street.

Cities like Charleston and New Orleans may, indeed, have been leaders in America's preservation movement, but they were not in the vanguard when it came to Main Street restoration. That honor goes, instead, to several smaller and more obscure communities like David City, Nebraska, and Medina, Ohio, where the earliest efforts at recognizing and marketing historic architecture were sometimes only skin deep—at least at first.[4] In the mid-1960s, the small-town modern architecture mecca of Columbus, Indiana, attracted attention for hiring an architect to devise a plan for its Main Street that showcased its vintage stylistic identity.[5] The leaders of Albia, Iowa, recognized the worth of the town's historic fabric in the early 1960s. This value was not so obvious at the time; buildings around the courthouse square looked so worn and dark that a columnist for the *Des Moines Register* claimed that Albia was one of the dirtiest towns he had ever seen.[6] The decline of the local coal industry had taken its toll, along with absentee ownership of the many two-story commercial buildings that surrounded the square. In 1962, the Albia Area Improvement Association was formed. In 1967, its efforts were combined with that of Robert Bates, CEO of one of the town's banks, but formerly an interior decorator to the stars of Hollywood, who had returned to his hometown. The result was called "Operation Facelift."

A "face-lifting" process in Albia began with proposed improvements drawn up for each storefront by an architectural firm from nearby Ottumwa. Robert Bates advised on colors and decorative accents. The Albia Area Improvement Association paid for all design services, but owners were responsible for all rehabilitation costs. The local banks offered generous loan terms. Improvements were kept between $200 and $6,822. In many cases, the work was just repainting. The innovation of the time was picking out minor architectural details—like a panel of raised brick or a line of trim in a window hood—with contrasting paint colors, which called attention to the decoration and ornament of the facade.[7]

Historical accuracy was not the goal with the improvements; helping the buildings gain value in the eyes of town citizens had greater worth at the time. This would eventually lead to more thorough restoration work in decades to come. Bates's decorator flourishes included additions like lacey, second-story cast-iron balconies borrowed from New Orleans, mansard awnings, and paneled shutters to enframe windows that had never before been shuttered. Bates and Ottumwa architect Stephen M. Stoltz were also generous with coach lights and contrasting paint trim. The color palette was pastels and coordinating dark tones. Bates admitted it was "all poetic license."[8] Nonetheless, the original architecture was respected for the most part, and in many cases, facades were merely cleaned or repaired, and brick was exposed instead of painted.

Neon was forbidden in the newly improved Albia, the logic being that it did not belong in a Victorian town.[9] Projecting signs were removed from around the square, but merchants continued to cover the transom zone with much of their wall signage, thus forfeiting the extra daylight afforded by the original Luxfer prism glass. The traditional fascia zone was the preferred location for signs, although it, alone, did not permit the scale of lettering that had become commonplace in the 1950s and 1960s. On most of these rehabilitated commercial facades, fluttering with architectural flourishes everywhere, there was little, if any, room remaining for a sign.

The novelty of Operation Facelift brought a barrage of publicity for Albia. Travel magazines and newspapers gave nearly full pages to accommodate photographs. Town boosters sent a before-and-after slide show on a tour of the state to other, hopeful towns and published a handsomely designed booklet explaining how Albia's rejuvenation had come to be. Such comprehensive self-promotion of town history and beauty as an example for others (and as a stimulus for tourism) recalled Santa Barbara in the 1920s and 1930s. Even the *New York Times* revealed a fascination for this small town (population approximately 10,000 in 1970) that decided to showcase its history rather than camouflage it. As architecture critic Ada Louise Huxtable stated: "Albia's buildings have been neither false-fronted nor Williamsburged. There has been minimum sneaky 'colonializing' or touches to make Victorian 'respectably' fake-Federal. There may be some over shuttering, but it is tasteful. The important thing is that the buildings are looked at with fresh and appreciative eyes for what is really there . . . Many a restoration has gone wrong at the ground floor in the 20th century. Albia's shops and services are strictly commercial and contemporary in use, as they should be."[10] Ultimately what distinguished Albia in Main Street history was that it bucked the trend to slipcover and instead refocused on its historic fabric. As Huxtable wrote, "We are just learning that art is in Main Street as well as in museums. These are America's hidden assets, Kawneer-covered on every business block."[11]

Unlike Albia's dramatic transformation from dour and cluttered to bright and beautiful, Bryan, Ohio's improvements would develop more slowly—one building at a time. Yet the plan for Bryan was comprehensive, far-reaching, and rapidly developed. The proposed improvements would not be the result of sketched suggestions by a decorator and an architect but of tough rules conceived by a team of academics. Motivated by civic pride and the threat from the 1974 opening of K-mart on the south side of town, the chamber of commerce and the Bryan Development Corporation took action to spare Bryan's thriving historic center from decline. In 1975, the city invited members of the Ohio State University Department of Architecture to study their courthouse square for its potential. This study emphasized the ensemble and was as much a planning and urban design study as an architectural one. Each building was appreciated for being vernacular and ordinary. The introduction to the guidelines published as a result of the Ohio State work emphasized that "it is only when the entire square is *viewed as a whole* that its architectural significance becomes readily apparent."[12]

The goals of the study were aesthetic in nature but driven by a desire to maintain property value. The design team emphasized that it did not wish to turn the town into a museum. There should be no replications of historic originals where there were gaps in the streetscape or buildings of low architectural value. Underlying all suggestions was a desire to return the appearance of each street around the square to a scale appropriate to a pedestrian or slow-moving vehicle. Building proportion, scale, and rhythm from element to element, storefront to storefront, were emphasized. The team stressed a balance between unity and variety. Despite the striking harmony and limited range of building dates, according to the streetscape facade analyses, thsere was much visual variety around the square, so it was now a matter of imposing the right amount of unity. Bryan's leaders made certain that the work received generous press coverage, an indication that they knew they would need to rely on outsiders to keep the old core vital. Albia had arrived at the same realization a decade before.

A design analysis of Bryan's square revealed major obstructions to the unity desired. As the studies revealed, most of the buildings that lined Bryan's courthouse square were built within a period of ten to fifteen years (see plate 4). Showcasing this unique consistency was paramount. First among the perceived problems was the major visual camouflaging of these historic facades by slipcovers of metal and wood paneling and by "oversized" signs, both projecting and wall mounted. The new guidelines suggested that all original brick walls should be exposed and if a painted surface was unavoidable, earth tones were recommended. In contrast to the pastels and contrasting dark tones of the palette in Albia, Bryan's trim paint was to be consistently white. Most other features were to be white or dark brown.

A major eyesore, the study revealed, was the mid-twentieth-century-business sign. Signs appeared to disturb the unifying rhythm of the upper-story windows around the square. Backlit acrylic signs and neon were deemed incompatible with the materials of the original Victorian architecture. Projecting signs were considered the most offensive for their size and irregularity. Only one year after the guidelines were published, the city of Bryan mandated compliance with the suggestions made by the Ohio State team, granting a five-year amortization period for nonconforming signs. The architectural guidelines remained only suggestions, however, and were never made prescriptive.

The guidelines and ensuing code banned projecting signs outright. All wall signs (now the sole identification) were relegated to the traditional, minimal location of the fascia board above the display windows, with a maximum allowable vertical dimension of two feet. Lettering could be up to one foot in height. All such signs were to be mounted in a manner to produce a level baseline from one to the next, building to building. All sign backgrounds were limited to a single background color: dark brown. To balance unity with variety, which was one of the stated goals, the choice of lettering styles and color were left open. The only major features to bring noticeable variety to the square were awnings and banners, the latter being perceived as the ideal substitution for projecting signs, as they offered "a desirable touch of excitement and variety without creating visual chaos." In principle, this was not unlike the contrived variety that Victor Gruen proposed for many of his public spaces: dashes of color strictly guided by a master hand, or in this case, a code.

Enthusiasm for change in Bryan brought some striking results; some were close on the heels of the study, and some occurred only years later. With the code requiring the elimination of all projecting signs, a sign dealer gave the town a bargain price for removing the offending graphics; twenty-eight signs came down in one fell swoop.[13] Brick buildings once painted white were changed to brown with white trim. Slim sign panels were lined up carefully. The next most noticeable change on the square came in 1997 when removal of the immense slipcovering on the east side of the square was finally complete, and the original block-long brick street facade was fully exposed for the first time since the 1960s. The elimination of these great visual blocks permitted the remarkable rhythm of windows and the original proportions of facades to be appreciated.

Towns like Bryan and Albia offer some instructive examples of the results of strong community control. Albia's historic enhancement was as much the product of the aesthetics of the mid-1960s as Bryan's plan revealed the values of the eco-friendly, toned-down 1970s. Both towns showed zeal in scraping away visually intrusive business signs, with particular disdain for the projecting sign.

The wholesale removal of old signs or reduction in their size for historic town centers may have appeared extreme at the time, but such actions revealed a growing bias against signs in the preservation movement. Publications of the late 1970s and early 1980s reveal how preservation policy encouraged this design prejudice. Careful restoration revealed the qualities of the original commercial architecture, long hidden or neglected, but often this occurred at the expense of decent, useful, and historic signs. The accumulation of signs was a layer of history that may have required some thinning out, but in many cases, the new enthusiasm for historic "authenticity" led to an obliteration of anything but the base layer, the earliest artifact.

Although the National Trust, the National Park Service, and the American Planning Association may not have commended the destruction of projecting signs, these institutions initially made little effort to halt the purging of vintage graphics. At times they even seemed to endorse it. In 1982, the National Park Service not only revealed a trend but also seemed to adopt it as policy: "In examining historic streetscape photographs, one is struck by the number of signs—in windows, over doors, painted on exterior walls, and hanging over (and sometimes across) the street. While this confusion was part of the character of 19th century cities and towns, today's approach toward historic signs tends to be much more conservative. Removal of some signs can have a dramatic effect in improving the visual appearance."[14]

Historic signage was endangered by the muted or absent defense of its virtues. Although Americans increasingly revered preservation in the late twentieth century, preservationists continued to judge historic signs of all kinds for their temporary aesthetic merits rather than their historic value. Expansive, permanent loss of these signs has been the result. Opportunities to restore nineteenth- and twentieth-century commercial landscapes accurately, with a sense of the profusion and scale of historic lettering, were lost during the 1980s and 1990s. Signs were everywhere in the late nineteenth century—on large projecting planks, in parapets, painted broadly across any available wall space—and yet most restored nineteenth-century towns were rendered graphically blank. By the twenty-first century, most city governments preferred that signs merely index the historic commercial environment. They should no longer advertise with a flourish. Most of the early literature on the restoration of Main Street emphasized the architecture so emphatically that signs were of peripheral interest, except for how they might contribute to the general character of the neighborhood in choice of materials and lettering style. How a sign might be an important element in a facade composition, in the identity of a street, or as an essential determinant in the potential success of a business, seemed to be of little concern. "Don't obscure significant architectural detailing with large, applied signs—old or new. Remove old offenders in the process of rehabilitation. New signs should be designed in a size and style compatible with the historic building. New hanging signs may be appropriate for historic commercial buildings if they are of a scale and design compatible with historic buildings."[15]

In some guidelines published in the 1970s and early 1980s, the desired compatibility suggested between sign and architecture seemed to endorse a peaceful coexistence between the two. But accompanying drawings and photographs often showed no signs at all, or provided a historically inaccurate subordination of graphics. The 1978 National Trust publication *Main Street: Building*

Improvement File illustrated many examples to make a case for an extreme reduction in sign space for Main Street businesses. For a typical nineteenth-century commercial building, it established a preference for signs confined to the fascia board. All projecting signs were deemed interruptive to facade features, too large and modern to be desirable. This was not stated outright but powerfully implied by the way such graphics were left out of storefront illustrations or reduced to a scale impossible to decipher except by the most determined pedestrians. One example singled out as admirable for its "subtle" signs actually displayed no signs whatsoever. This document, reproduced for distribution as late as 1995, continued its influence into the twenty-first century as indirect support for any council whose preference it was to remove all projecting signs and reduce wall signs to a very modest single panel.[16] The late-twentieth-century taste for recessive signage appeared in publications produced locally and federally. Cities like Charleston and Chicago, for instance, produced case study books with a strong antisign bias that illustrated and analyzed facades in order to guide future improvements.[17]

By the late 1980s and early 1990s, the National Trust, the National Park Service, the American Planning Association, and a few state agencies made a genuine effort to be more inclusive in their advice on graphics, though the full range of their communications remained inconsistent on the matter. Sign diversity on Main Street became more acceptable. Two of the earliest publications that claimed value for old signs came from Oklahoma and California in the late 1980s. The *Oklahoma Sign Design Guidelines* began by stating that a business sign "is the most visible advertisement a store or office can have." Oklahoma reasserted the importance of this much-maligned contribution to the street. In other words, a sign's value was not merely as an index to the environment (or something that may merely add a degree of character to a neighborhood), as claimed by such influential publications as *Street Graphics* (1971) (see below for more about *Street Graphics*). The Oklahoma guidelines went on to claim that "historically, downtown has been filled with a rich variety of signs." "Consistent quality, rather than uniform materials or standardized placement, relates the signs to each other ... It is a popular belief that the back-lit, neon, or lighted signs are not appropriate for a renovated area. This is not true ... it would be wrong to remove all neon signs in the name of beautification or design uniformity."[18]

A statewide sign grant program actually supported sign improvement and restoration in Oklahoma, encouraging creativity in new graphics and care in the restoration of old signs. In 1987, the National Trust's *Main Street Guidelines* acknowledged the damage done from coast to coast by treating signs merely as visual obstructions. "Members of the business community, in their zeal for visible improvements, may create a campaign that results in the imposition of a single treatment for all signs in the area. Well meaning citizens may successfully lobby for legislation that bans certain historic sign types or materials altogether. Even when the motivation for such campaigns and ordinances is to clean up downtown rather than mandate uniform sign treatments, the result can be visual sterility that diminishes the district's appeal."[19]

Peter Phillips's breakthrough planning advisor service (PAS) memo of 1988 and Michael Auer's respectful preservation brief for the National Park Service in 1991 both encouraged a new appreciation for the value of historic signs. Far from labeling signs as mere indexes to the commercial landscape, as 1971's *Street Graphics* had done, Auer wrote of signs' rich contribution to streets and neighborhoods. Although his focus was on historic signs, much of what he wrote suggested a careful consideration for new signs as well: "Signs speak of the people who run the businesses, shops, and firms. Signs are signatures. They reflect the owner's tastes and personality. They often reflect the ethnic makeup of a neighborhood and its character as well as the social and business activities carried out there. By giving concrete details about daily life in a former era, historic signs allow the past to speak to the present in ways that buildings by themselves do not. And multiple surviving historic signs on the same building can indicate several periods in its history or use."[20]

By documenting the developing municipal trend of designating signs as either historic or visual landmarks, Peter Phillips reversed years of denigration. His PAS memo was one of the earliest policy documents to suggest that there was enormous value in older signs. Signs were not just to be accommodated but protected with specific action. The publication cited places as diverse as Rockford, Illinois; Pasadena, California; Manhattan, Kansas; Baltimore; and Dallas, which had created ordinances to identify and protect historic signs. The means for designation in these communities included a list of possible criteria, which varied from city to city.[21]

Rather than merely deride signs, some preservation leaders realized that graphics could be tools for reestablishing a unique sense of place for communities that had been overwhelmed with bland, oversized corporate identities. Preserving local, historic signs and creating new signs with key materials, contributing themes, and proper scale could nurture towns' local character. Ronald Lee Fleming of the Townscape Institute and Mary Means of the National Trust's Main Street Program were among the first to champion the concept of strengthening local identity. Fleming wondered why, with so many Americans yearning for a sense of place, the country was still victimized everywhere by big decision-makers like government and corporations, which "have evidenced through carelessness or deliberate design a lack of respect for the integrity of our landscape."[22]

Preservationists like Fleming and Means encouraged a more careful stripping away of the storefront materials and signs that had accumulated on the first floor—up to a point. Their goal was not to enshrine each building as a museum piece but to enhance and nurture real working towns, places with local character and successful local businesses.[23] According to them, memorable architectural features, iconographic elements like sculpture that held meaning for the community, and civic and commercial signs could all establish or strengthen a sense of place if they were designed distinctively and made of materials with character. In 1980, after a three-year pilot program involving three historic town centers in the nation's heartland, Mary Means established the National Main Street Center through the National Trust, with a system that balanced the business world with design and preservation.[24] Eventually, towns and cities across the United States benefited from its guidance in their efforts to return to historic appearances and become economically vital once again.

As early as the 1980s, several national and regional publications revealed this new philosophy of acknowledging, accommodating, or even celebrating layers of history on Main Street. This approach to restoration and facade alteration was attributable, in large part, to the Secretary of the Interior's Standards for rehabilitation and preservation, published in 1977, which stated, "Most properties change over time; those changes that have acquired historic significance in their own right shall be retained and preserved."[25] The National Park Service preservation brief on storefronts reinforced this viewpoint in 1982: "In evaluating whether the existing storefront is worthy of preservation, recognize that good design can exist in any period; a storefront added in 1930 may have greater architectural merit than what is replaced. In commercial historic districts, it is often the diversity of styles and detailing that contribute to the character; removing a storefront dating from 1910 simply because other buildings in the district have been restored to their 1860s appearance may not be the best preservation approach."[26]

Mike Jackson of the Illinois Historic Preservation Agency included signs as one of these layers: "Many 20th century signs clash with the typical 19th century mainstream image that many preservationists hold dear . . . this is where we challenge the preservationist theory that everything should be harmonious and should have the same integrity and be of the same generation. Instead, we argue for complexity and contradiction, for layers of history, one generation after another."[27]

One of the best examples of layered history in a commercial context is to be found in New Orleans. Ornate cast-iron galleries from the 1860s and later were often added to relatively discreet buildings from the decades bracketing the 1830s. Mid-twentieth-century neon signs supplied yet another important layer, helping to establish the rich atmosphere that was incorporated into the works of writers like Tennessee Williams. Signs for enterprises like Kolb's Restaurant and the Pearl Oyster Bar on St. Charles Avenue near Canal Street (buildings erected 1835, 1840, and ca. 1890) demonstrated great variety in design and location (see plate 33). Considering the variety in the heights and details of the cast-iron porches, this graphic array might be said to be in sync with the character of the street.

Layered history appears in a few unexpected places. Among Staunton, Virginia's careful nineteenth-century facade restorations, thoughtfully coordinated paint colors, and severely muted signage are a few surprising mid-twentieth-century storefronts. A 1940s first-floor makeover of a modest early-nineteenth-century building consists of black porcelain metal panels and a 1980s retro neon sign located where the fascia would have been. This building revealed several layers of history at once. Down Beverley Street, and carved out of the base of the otherwise very solid Hoover House Hotel (T. J. Collins, 1893-94) is an example of the open-storefront trend in retail design—initiated among leading commercial architects like Morris Lapidus in the 1940s but only commonly practiced on Main Streets in the 1950s. Its very open exterior lobby was created by deeply angling the display window to the door, set considerably back from the sidewalk.[28] A cantilevered showcase box projected from a marble wall. When this new storefront was created, individual ribbon letters rested on a small ledge just above the big open display lobby, and the rest of the old hotel was covered over in a slick, stuccolike material. In recent years, the upper stories were uncloaked, and the midcentury storefront was permitted to remain below. The modern sign, however, was lost during the uncovering of the upper facade. In its place, a dainty painted plaque was hung on a curlicued bracket fastened to a cylindrical modern column. Yet another layer of history and taste was permitted to remain in place, whether or not the present town council found it suitable or appropriate.

These midcentury anomalies do not immediately appear to fall in step with the mostly conservative approach that Staunton has taken in facade revitalization. The majority of the city's buildings are from the nineteenth or early twentieth century, and the storefronts and signage are muted in an attempt to respect that period. Rehabilitation work is carefully considered, and it is generously spread through an old city core that is graced with many good buildings, both humble and ornate. Many stores in the old business district of Staunton appear to be without signs when seen from a reasonable distance. Most signs are subtly placed on awning valences, configured into stained glass panels in transoms, or painted on small wooden panels hanging from brackets. No internal illumination is permitted by code in the business district. The wall sign area allowed by frontage in Staunton is one of the lowest in the nation, though not uncommon, at one square foot per linear foot. The outright ban on all projecting signs, imposed since 1972, was terminated in 2002; now each proposal is reviewed for appropriateness. The historic preservation commission examined vintage photos of Beverley Street and acknowledged that history provided precedent for projecting signs of great variety. The National Park Service required restoration of the neon rooftop sign of the Stonewall Jackson Hotel, refurbished and reopened in 2005, upon the owner's application for preservation tax credits. The sign, mounted on the tallest building in Staunton, has served since 1924 as a beacon to visitors and a lantern of sorts to locals. It continues a nationwide tradition for hotels to display roof signs as landmarks for newcomers to town.

In the twenty-first century, the Sell's Furniture Building in Monrovia, California, is unrecognizable compared to how it appeared in the 1950s–1970s with its giant fin sign (fig. 86). A clay tile shed roof projects from the low-profile, stuccoed parapet front. A small, sandblasted sign hangs over the entrance. Wood sandblasted signs, conspicuously introduced to Monrovia in the 1970s, are still permitted in town, although they are not encouraged. Some stretches of Myrtle Street, Monrovia's original commercial corridor, are lined with an almost continuous band of fabric awnings in a variety of muted colors and variations in profile. Only discreet white letters on the valences identify the different businesses along this stretch. Since the 1970s, signs have been regulated to "minimize their tendency to compete excessively with each other and with the desired character of the town." A scheme was generated to mitigate architectural individualism as well. No two buildings with two different architectural styles could adjoin each other without an intermediate three-foot-wide vertical flat surface extending the full height of the structure to act as a transitional element. This neutral pier requirement recalls the restrictions of many enclosed shopping malls. Myrtle Street has been generously greened over in recent decades with plantings intended to soften the architecture, create shade, and delight the eye—making the corridor more park-like and decidedly less urban. Review boards and committees have been charged with overseeing central Monrovia since the mid-1970s. In contrast to this overall muting, in 2000 the municipality successfully lured a multiplex cinema complex to its Main Street. Built with a facade that harks back to movie theaters of the 1920s and 1930s, the new building is a beacon of modernity on an otherwise arcadian passage.

Despite conservative preservation planning policy in Staunton and Monrovia, these towns have allowed important exceptions to their rules. Both cities have discarded many of the accumulated artifacts of the twentieth century, removing layers of history, yet each now sees the benefit of leaving well enough alone at times. Staunton has saved common, everyday storefronts of the mid-twentieth century, even as it has carefully maintained or restored the original eighteenth- and nineteenth-century appearance of upper stories. Monrovia has recently permitted marked visual exceptions to the rigidly safe visual policies that have ruled its Main Street for many years. In all cases, these exceptions to narrow visual regulation open the door to future exceptions, permitting an accretion of history to line the principle thoroughfares.

Altering an Image: Edited History and Lost Neighborhoods

Although many cities had obvious historic charm and easily conformed to the handsome nineteenth-century image that was first promoted by preservationists, others struggled with less palpable qualities and minimal resources. Some were faced with indiscernible identities, others with the pressure of aggressive standardized development. The old center of Ontario, California, for example, faced continuing decline in property values and something of an identity crisis. Due to the exceptional width of the central boulevard laid out by town fathers, as well as an emphasis on plantings in the wide median, Ontario was missing the sense of urban enclosure experienced on most main streets. Many buildings were only a single story high, and most were not built in the traditional Victorian style commonly found on Main Streets east of the Mississippi. Commenting on the history and late-twentieth-century condition of Ontario, architectural critic Reyner Banham stated a belief that the city had far too much plant material and too little brick and stone. "The general impression is that the citizens of Ontario built a 'garden city' and left out the 'city' part, urban homesteaders imposing their ideal of suburbs without urbs in the pattern of Greater Los Angeles almost before it had begun to take shape."[29]

By the late twentieth century, the leaders of Ontario were trying to strengthen the fragile urban core by encouraging development, and in so doing they took a few creative risks. They decided on a very historically inclusive approach to restoration and development. The design guidelines developed by the Arroyo Group of South Pasadena, and adopted by the city in 1998, seized on the variety of eras represented on Euclid Avenue, the city's formal commercial street. The planners realized that in restoring buildings and infilling along Euclid Avenue, no single style should dominate. In order to strengthen the image of each period of architecture, to give it real presence and not permit the streets to become a nondescript hodge-podge, the planners identified three distinct architectural subdistricts along the retail corridor, each recognizing the predominant period of design in that area. This included the historic turn-of-the twentieth century subdistrict, as well as those for the 1920s-1940s and the 1950s, periods just beginning to be recognized as having value. The guidelines were written to address each of the three time periods, for both architecture and sign design, so that no single, blanket set of rules would force uniform conformance.

The new guidelines were some of the most sensitive in the United States for respectfully considering the accumulation of history. Layers of history were not just permitted on a case-by-case basis; they were encouraged by policy. Ontario's guidelines called for "historically designated" and "significant" buildings to be restored according to the history and documentation for those buildings individually, regardless of the subdistrict in which they were located. But for all structures labeled as "context buildings" (as well as new infill), design should conform to the parameters described for the subdistrict of that particular site. Signs should follow accordingly.[30]

Reconciling a reverence for the town's 1950s Googie architecture with the need to strengthen Ontario's urban presence might seem like an impossible assignment, considering that this particular design period was antiurban by nature. The one building along Euclid Avenue that might truly be identified as Googie possessed a tilted, irregular roof slab, typical of the style, but in this case it was attached to a wall that was continuous with the common storefront line of the rest of the block (fig. 112). It was a useful, hybrid model to emulate. However, most of the city's 1950s buildings along Euclid Avenue were not Googie at all;

they were solidly urban, built right up to the sidewalk, with no architectural feature that broke away from the norm. The city treated these as no less valuable or authentic for the era than the celebrated Googie style the guidelines singled out for attention. Often these buildings were asymmetrical in composition, spare in detail, and wrapped by ribbon window panels. In order to strengthen the distinguishing image of the 1950s along its primary corridor, Ontario's guidelines borrowed from both its Googie and its conservative examples when it came to signs. Instead of the classic Googie pole sign that merely poked through or intersected the roof, the city permitted a jauntily clipped-on appearance for signs, allowing identities to be mounted at the edge of a zero-setback building, at roof level, in order to project both up and out.[31] This gave them something of the character of a freestanding object.

Like Ontario, many older communities throughout the country struggled to keep their well-established commercial corridors from collapsing. Although most Main Streets in America faced hard times as the suburbs drew business away, some were particularly hard hit. Roseland, Illinois, and 125th Street in Harlem present two poignant examples. Each is on the fringe of one of America's largest and most prosperous cities (Chicago and New York). Each, in its heyday, was one of the metropolitan area's busiest retail hubs. But in their striving to rise again to prosperous times, they were threatened with losing their character completely. The sense of place that had developed organically over decades was at risk of being lost in just a few years.

Roseland's decline began slowly after World War II with the general lack of reinvestment in urban areas. Chicago's 1953 "Perimeter Plan" was established to help older shopping corridors compete with outlying centers.[32] Combined with the national trend for older retail centers to suffer in the 1960s and 1970s, Roseland was doubly hit due to a dramatic change in demographics. From 1960 to 1980, the population changed from Italians, Swedes, and Lithuanians—with an African-American component of 23 percent—to an all-black community. And along with this change came less spending.[33] By the late 1970s, all the major stores along Roseland's core retail corridor, Michigan Avenue between 110th Street and 115th Street, had closed. This loss included major grocers and department stores, as well as the long-established Gately's People's store, a regional phenomenon complete with departments for groceries, hardware, apparel, music, and jewelry, topped off with a full-service soda fountain.[34] The next four decades ushered in new plans and new leaders. A series of planning conferences produced lists of neighborhood needs and desires but very little action.[35]

The facades of Roseland's core of early-twentieth-century commercial buildings had been camouflaged, like those all over America. But whereas most cities had completed the process of peeling off this often maligned layer of signage, plywood, and aluminum by the 1990s, Roseland was still accumulating additional layers that disguised the original facades. The old South End Chamber of Commerce Building (Burtar & Gassmann, 1903), with its Second Empire arched stone parapet, had been covered at the first floor with black-pigmented structural glass in the 1930s. In 1963, a concave mesh screen covered the whole upper portion of the building, the vertical edges defined by elongated sign panels that spelled "J-E-W-E-L-E-R." By 2000, the modern, concave front was sheathed with a giant vinyl photograph of a black male model, advertising the clothing to be found within (fig. 113). In the 1970s, the national retailer Payless Shoes attached a dark bronze slipcover system over the entire upper facade of the building vacated by a former five-and-dime. The old Woolworth building next door, once a brick facade but slipcovered in the 1950s, was later covered with solid panels painted bright yellow, with giant orange lettering that spelled "SUPER SALES." The painted graphic soon flaked off in the sun. This showy facade, in disrepair, and others like it, did not present the kind of image that would lure black middle-class shoppers back from the nearby malls.

In 2006, a new grant-based facade improvement program was introduced locally, offering grants for up to 75 percent of construction costs, funded by tax increment financing. This financial support permitted the upgrading of old signs as well. The program, combined with a new planning initiative, promised to launch a new era for Roseland, even as South Michigan Avenue faced its toughest retail years yet. But despite the potential for improved storefronts, the local city

Figure 112

(Former) Walter's Coffee Shop (Harry Pierre Woodman, 1959), Euclid Avenue, Ontario, California. Although Googie buildings typically were built as "sculpture-in-the-round," exuberant compositions to be seen from all sides in the open suburban landscape of southern California, sometimes one encounters examples that conform surprisingly well to urban sites.

PHOTO BY AUTHOR, 2009.

RETRENCHMENT, REPAIR, AND REINVENTION   **271**

alderman proposed a scheme that called for the demolition of most of the old structures along Michigan Avenue and replacing them with new zero-setback structures offering larger open floor areas, hoping to accommodate national chains by sparing them the trouble of conversion.[36] The threatened vintage buildings were not in themselves remarkable, but as a whole, they presented a notable, largely intact historic streetscape at a consistent scale. Less notable Main Street architecture was being lavished with attention in other places in America. After years of little progress in Roseland, leaders felt obliged to show dramatic changes, and the national chains that were so desired might find the conversion of older buildings into larger floor plates an undesirable expense. Some in the community felt it was time to move on and reach out to the big corporations rather than just wait passively.

The neighborhood around 125th Street in New York City, Harlem's primary commercial corridor, struggled for many years with race relations, economic woes, and big plans for bringing back a vitality lost from a thoroughfare that had both local and national historic significance. In 2007, when the first major change to the area's zoning since 1961 was proposed, citizens protested that the neighborhood would be altered beyond recognition. They felt that new development was already rapidly eroding the long-established sense of place on 125th Street and that altering the zoning would hasten this process. This was a neighborhood with an almost mythically powerful reputation.[37] The American Planning Association announced in 2007 that 125th Street had been selected as one of its first Great Streets, due in part to its history of maintaining "a strong identity through periods of tremendous population growth and infrastructural strain, disinvestment, and urban renewal."[38] But residents perceived 125th Street as rapidly being transformed into a generic All-American strip, turned over to big chains like the Disney Store, Old Navy, Nine West, and Krispy Kreme Donuts.[39] Others argued that there must be change, perhaps even dramatic change, for the street to remain vital.[40]

The buildings of 125th Street were largely unremarkable when viewed individually, but seen as a whole, this architecture had great value. City historians have singled out for reverence a few good buildings, even great buildings, but the real value of the street is in the plethora of modest vernacular commercial structures. In many ways, the street has changed very little in one hundred years, except for the declining condition of its structures. Most of the buildings are from the 1880s and 1890s, including some remarkably intact residential tenements. Few buildings suffered radical alterations in the 1950s and 1960s; rarely were cornices removed or whole facades slipcovered with metal or stucco.[41]

For the most part, the business signs on 125th Street today are the same in size and placement as they were over seventy years ago. The only big change is a substitution of internally illuminated awning signs, with bullnose profiles, for the bulb and neon panels once seen over display windows.[42] Along 125th Street, as in most of New York, neon is now a rare commodity. A notable surviving example is the M & G Soulfood Diner at Morningside Drive. Both 125th Street in Harlem and Michigan Avenue in Roseland continue, in the early twenty-first century, to be haunted by big projecting neon signs left behind by department stores long closed.[43]

The patchwork of brick and stone buildings and their modest signs along the eastern half of 125th Street contrasts dramatically with the aggressive gloss of new development along the western half (fig. 114). The large, horizontal expanses of glass on the elevations of Harlem USA, a 275,000-square-foot urban shopping center developed in the late 1990s, create a scale and finish fundamentally different from that of the older buildings with their closely spaced, vertically oriented windows in masonry walls. Mimicking the colossal advertisements behind the glass of Harlem USA, older buildings nearby are covered on upper stories with outdoor advertising boards. The immense vinyl photographic posters, stretched tightly over the facades of older structures, shroud buildings like the cast-iron

(opposite) Figure 113

Commercial buildings along east side of South Michigan Avenue, between 111th and 112th Streets, Roseland (Chicago), Illinois: 1927 versus 2005. The streetscape of Roseland, like that of many other communities that experienced great growth after 1910, was heavily influenced by streetcar and automobile. Second stories, when they existed at all, were generously glazed and often used for display. Although some communities have been removing their slipcovers from building facades for decades, others continue to rely on them to stimulate business. This has become increasingly affordable with the advent of large-scale, flexible vinyl graphics. *Connotative* design communication (refined architecture associated with better businesses) is often overwhelmed by the *denotative* (big signs).

TOP: PHOTO BY NELS O. LARSEN, 1927. PUBLISHED IN BILL STACHMUS, RON NIETUPSKI, BETTE KOOISTRA, MARIO AVIGNONE, AND PAUL PETRAITIS, *ROSELAND, THE GOLDEN YEARS: A PICTORIAL PRESERVATION OF MEMORIES* (1984), XXXIX. PERMISSION COURTESY OF BETTY JO PURVIS.

BOTTOM: PHOTO BY AUTHOR, 2005.

Picher Building, one of the last of its kind this far north in Manhattan. Nearby, the standard-issue, extra-wide, train-shed arch of an Old Navy store is the best that corporate America appears to offer 125th Street, as a token historic look, although foreign to the scale and proportions of neighborhood buildings. Hoping to tie in to the spectacle of Harlem USA, owners and tenants reclad their smaller, locally operated stores in one-story taxpayers with shimmering new materials and supersized acrylic-faced electric lettering in primary colors.[44]

New York City's planning department stressed that the new zoning was created to maintain the scale of the street wall by establishing real height and setback limits where there were few or none. The city mandated a set minimum percentage of glass at ground level, based on historic precedent for retail. The aim was to engage the street with the activity seen inside, to allow no solid, dead street walls. The possibility of too much glass had not been addressed.

Because of the new up-zoning for increased density, and because so few historic buildings are protected in this area, at least half of 125th Street could be radically altered within a few years. Only four buildings along the corridor have the city's landmark designation.[45] Unless historic designation is given to more buildings, or at best an entire district, there is little incentive for preservation. Fortunately, the zoning was not altered much on some sections of the street, often those with the best-preserved buildings. This brings less pressure for development. Other sections, however, will be powerfully affected by changes, especially at the extreme east and west ends of the street. The humblest vernacular buildings are most at risk. The new code set building envelope limits only and did not define the scale or the upper story appearance of infill or replacement buildings, so important to the rhythm and texture of the street.[46]

The new zoning encouraged, with building height incentives, the growth of existing entertainment enterprises located along 125th Street and the creation of new venues. Electric marquees were permitted—if not required—to identify these places. But the code was not rewritten to permit or encourage super-scaled graphics on the upper elevations of buildings along 125th Street. In other words, 42nd Street would not be replicated in upper Manhattan, as some had once proposed.[47] Change could be big, nevertheless. The historic street's resiliency, cited by the American Planning Association, may not prove to hold out for another generation.

Reimagining Main Street: Spotlighting Fountains, Trees, and Banners

During the mid-to-late 1950s, the threat of suburban competition called for action—some sort of decisive strategy to avert the increasing decline downtown. Ambitious plans were supported, in large part, by urban renewal funding from the federal government. Title I of the Housing Act of 1949 kick-started the "urban renewal" program that would reshape American cities. The act provided federal funding to municipalities to cover the cost of acquiring areas of cities perceived

Figure 114

Harlem USA (Skidmore, Owings & Merrill with Simmons Design Group, 1998–2000), 125th Street, New York City. Much of the new retail development on 125th Street does not acknowledge the historic materials and scale-defining elements of the nineteenth-century buildings that presently make up most of the corridor.

PHOTO BY AUTHOR, 2008.

to be slums. *Urban renewal* was a phrase popularized with the passage of the 1954 Housing Act, which made these projects more enticing to developers, by among other things, providing mortgages backed by the Federal Housing Authority.[48] A 1957 conference, Main Street 1969, which architect Victor Gruen chaired, attempted to address the potential force, both good and bad, that had been unleashed on cities by the then-recently authorized federal highway program. This was another federal impetus to altering the traditional downtown.[49]

Specific proposals for pedestrianizing Main Street began to appear as early as the mid-1940s, although it was not until the mid-1950s that real momentum developed. Early schemes by firms like Victor Gruen and Ketchum, Gina & Sharp explored how to make old town centers more appealing by removing traffic from Main Street. These proposals introduced principles that would be promoted for years to come: creating ample, shared, off-street parking behind stores, and smoothing traffic flow with a loop of circulation on existing roads around the ensemble.[50] Some of the earliest proposals included Gruen's 1943 plan for revising the center of Syracuse, New York, and Ketchum's 1946 concept for Rye, New York. The schemes relied heavily on generous continuous canopies applied to existing storefronts. These and nearly uniform signage, store to store, were created with hopes of smoothing out visual irregularities along the developed promenades. As in many of the Gruen's later proposals, a new civic center would often anchor one end of the ensemble.[51]

Cities from coast to coast were troubled by the potentially bleak future of downtown retail business. Although Kalamazoo, Michigan, retail was healthy in the mid-1950s, local businessmen were concerned about falling property values. In contrast, downtown Providence, Rhode Island, already suffered from a vacancy rate of 7 to 9 percent in the late 1950s. The city was very quiet on weekends and had already lost several of its motion picture theaters. Nothing on the scale of a regional suburban shopping mall would be built in the Providence market area until 1968, however. Nevertheless, outlying, local, neighborhood shopping centers were already draining downtown's primary corridor, Westminster Street, of its life. In contrast, State Street in Chicago was beginning to suffer the effects of the continuous spread of retail to the suburbs. Park Forest Plaza, one of the first major regional shopping centers in the United States, opened in 1949, with Marshall Field's first post–World War II branch store. State Street had showed a steady decline in sales every year since that opening, reaching its lowest point as early as 1964.[52]

Plans to keep business strong in the town centers were often ambitious and proactive. In the mid-1950s, Chicago's Greater State Street Council and the city produced a parking study that revealed the need for seven facilities located around the periphery of the Loop, costing $15.5 million.[53] The parking structures were designed by architects like Alfred Alschuler, who aimed to create elevations comfortable alongside some of the newer commercial buildings. The council arranged for the repaving of State Street and the replacement of the turn-of-the-century streetlights with space-age, hydralike fixtures that offered four times the illumination. Stimulated by the improvements in the streetscape, merchants made facade alterations and interior upgrades. Montgomery Ward joined the trend toward suburbanizing by removing classically inspired terra cotta ornament and resheathing its building in concrete.[54]

In 1953, the Chicago Plan Commission proposed, as a first step in a series of improvements for the central business district, that the stores along the east side of State Street be linked by second-level enclosed bridges, forming a continuous passageway through the buildings. The stated goal was to address the congestion of people and automobiles in the street; there was no lack of shoppers on State quite yet. Separating modes of transport—pedestrians from cars, and cars from trains—had been a goal of city planners and futurist dreamers since the late nineteenth century. The elevated "State Street Promenade," proposed by the Chicago Plan Commission, was an opportunity to put a new face on State Street, however indirectly. This was a street in the sky, a public passageway through existing stores, that required new interior corridor facades for well-known buildings like Marshall Field's, Carson Pirie Scott, and Wielboldt's department stores. There would be sidewalk cafes and television and news theaters. This unrealized proposal was the precursor to the sky-bridges eventually built in downtown Minneapolis, a pedestrian system that proved powerfully influential to many cities across the country.

Subsequent schemes for improving State Street were aimed at the entire corridor. The idea of addressing Chicago's congestion by pedestrianizing the existing street, on ground level, was first suggested as early as 1947 for other shopping hubs in the city.[55] By 1957, Chicago was inundated with grand schemes for State Street. Like the Promenade, the "State Street of Tomorrow," presented by the Jaycees in 1957, envisioned a pedestrian landscape one level above vehicular traffic. This time, however, the shopper was not confined to bridges; a vast, continuous, open-air plane of parklike design was available to pedestrians above the old State Street. The sides of the buildings depicted along the street in the rendering were glass curtain walls—featureless and sign-less, except for the iconic electric identity of the Chicago Theatre (Rapp and Rapp, 1921). Such a dramatic facelift for the street was intended to provide "modern, sweeping architectural changes."[56] Other schemes were published regularly, including one presented by real estate mogul Arthur Rubloff, who controlled most of the property along State Street's nearby competition, North Michigan Avenue. Rubloff proposed a $10 million makeover that featured a "median" of new one-story buildings running down eight blocks of State Street.[57]

Pomona, California, and Springfield, Oregon, are considered by many to be the first cities to test the idea of a pedestrianized Main Street, with temporary street closings.[58] Other early experiments with pedestrianization included the "Downtown Futurama" experiment for Fort Worth, the "Miracle Mile" event for Des Moines, and other tests from Boston to Waco, Texas.[59] Most experiments were basic street closings with temporary exhibits and wheeled-in shrubs and flower boxes.

Nineteen fifty-nine was the year of the pedestrian mall in America, as trials seemed to be cropping up everywhere, accompanied by relentless media coverage.[60] One temporary mall that captured an inordinate amount of publicity was at Adams Street and Madison Avenue in Toledo, Ohio, a layout designed by the local chapter of the American Institute of Architects. The media's focus on Toledo was likely due to the length of the study (a total of 37 weeks over 1959 and 1960) and the decision to base it in a city with a significant population (318,000 in 1960). The success of the Toledo mall, however, was deemed shaky. Critics noted America's obsession with this concept and warned that no simple, single answer was going to solve the impending crisis.[61] "What started as an apparently dramatic design for one Central Business area . . . has succumbed to the old foe of inflexibility and overselling. A worthy symbol has been transformed into a stifling, mechanical recipe. A flame has become half-baked and overdone. A preconceived pattern has replaced creativity related to studied requirements.

What appears aesthetic [in] an artist's rendering has been substituted for ground-level interests, the bird's-eye view for the human's."[62]

The first permanent, urban pedestrian malls in the United States, east and west of the Mississippi, were in Kalamazoo, Michigan (1959), and Pomona, California (1962). The mall established along three blocks of Burdick Street in Kalamazoo was part of a comprehensive plan by Victor Gruen to give longevity to the downtown. Gruen had been responsible, in large part, for America's fever for pedestrian malls by introducing the idea of pedestrianizing public thoroughfares as part of his well-publicized plan for the center of Fort Worth, Texas (1955).[63] In contrast to Gruen's overwhelming credentials in retail and urban design, the creator of Pomona's mall, Millard Sheets, was a celebrated California painter and architect and native of the Pomona Valley.

In Victor Gruen's proposal, both the street and architectural elevations were altered; Millard Sheets's designs, as realized, were confined to embellishing the street passageway itself, although some owners took the initiative to slipcover old facades once the mall work had begun. A few of Kalamazoo's flat-topped, classical revival buildings were included in a new cityscape designed by Gruen which was composed primarily of folded plate (or zigzag) roofs and glass curtain walls (fig. 115). Like many modern architects, Gruen contrasted texture and scale, old and new, to dramatic advantage. A few new canopies appeared here and there, unifying groups of structures. Sheets directed some of the finest sculptors and muralists in California for the mall project in Pomona. The long, straight stretch of nine blocks was broken up visually by a series of regularly spaced, three-foot high stone planters, as well as by recessed areas with foun-

Figure 115
Rendering for proposed Burdick Street Mall, Kalamazoo, Michigan (Victor Gruen Associates, 1959). Gruen and his contemporaries generally contrasted rough with polished in design. In this instance, the leader of the mall movement also juxtaposed select older buildings with new structures worthy of the space age.
VICTOR GRUEN ASSOCIATES, *KALAMAZOO: 1980* (1959), 27. COURTESY OF THE CITY OF KALAMAZOO DIVISION OF RECORDS MANAGEMENT, RESEARCH, AND ARCHIVES.

tains, sculpture, and seating. Projecting signs were not initially banished from either mall. Both malls were opened with incredible press coverage and renewed confidence in the city center.

Plans for redeveloping the downtown shopping district in Providence by the City Plan Commission were almost as comprehensive as those proposed for any Gruen project. The master plan for Downcity, as the old, nineteenth-century commercial core was known, was published in 1961 in the lavishly illustrated *Downtown Providence 1970*. The principle was basically the same as Gruen's strategy: strengthen the retail core, surround it with a smooth-flowing traffic loop coordinated with ample parking nodes, and wait for the impending construction of the national interstate system to hook up to this local system. Unlike Kalamazoo, Providence already suffered from a severe lack of off-street parking, so the plan proposed immediate construction of garages. These parking facilities appeared frequently in the renderings of the proposed streetscapes (although not on the proposed pedestrian mall) as structures with retail space at the base, and a screened midsection. Spare, slab "cornices" (or multiple vaults, which were in vogue at the time) served to terminate these multifunction structures at their rooflines (fig. 116). The intention was to insert modern buildings only when necessary, often with setbacks, creating small plazas. The same variety of spaces Victor Gruen proposed were valued by the planners in Providence.

The proposed mall, along Westminster and Matthewson Streets, would be given a new face with the insertion of a new department store and selective refacing of older buildings with decorative aluminum screens and brise-soleils. Older buildings classified as "good" in the city's structures survey would be left as they

Figure 116
Rendering for proposed alterations to Weybosset Street, Providence, Rhode Island (1960). No "stick-out" signs were permitted to clutter the street, but select historic buildings chosen for their quality were allowed to remain.
PROVIDENCE CITY PLAN COMMISSION, *DOWNTOWN PROVIDENCE 1970* (1961). COURTESY OF THE RHODE ISLAND HISTORICAL SOCIETY.

were, creating a certain variety along the street's elevations, just as in Gruen's proposals. "Stick-out," or projecting, signs were not to be a part of this variety. Their irregular and sizeable profiles, perceived as cumbersome along the street perspective, would be erased and replaced by "a row of dignified 'flat' signs."[64] The dominant visual element along this shopping thoroughfare was now to be the row of angular, idiosyncratic streetlights positioned down the center of the street. As a sidebar to this regal scene, the city planners gave Providence an outlet for more wanton eye-candy and casual divertissements; an entertainment district was planned for a small side street, where projecting signs and architectural curiosities would be placed on display to create special character. The concept called for a petite gaslight district, with random roof signs, sailors, beatniks, and Chinese lanterns—a sort of anti-Disneyland but with almost the same degree of control over the contrivance, via very crafty codes. This calculated chaos was, in truth, not all that different from Main Street USA in Anaheim in its attempt to charm with novelty and picturesque arrangement.

The mall was completed in 1964, but by the late 1970s, all of the department stores in Providence had closed or were soon to disappear from Westminster and surrounding streets. An infusion of cash from federal sources made a major facelift possible. Noted graphic designer Malcolm Grear brought history back to the street without aping its forms. Historic artifacts, like a standing clock, were enframed or acknowledged by the positioning of newer elements. Porcelainized graphic panels were screen printed with old photographs, allowing the street itself to be read like a book.

Chicago's State Street Mall was one of the latest of the major American pedestrian malls to be built, with a price tag of over $1 million. It opened to the public in 1979, just as Providence completed its first remake of the Westminster Street mall. Chicago's mall was the result of years of proposals and careful monitoring of the apparent "successes" of malls elsewhere in the country.[65] Despite many negative reports on the ability of pedestrian malls to sustain improvements in retail sales or slow the loss of shoppers to the suburbs, the city refused to let the concept die. An experiment conducted on Madison Avenue in New York City in 1971 was of particular interest to Chicago planners, although the results were deemed "less than positive," or ambiguous.[66] Four years before it was built, Pulitzer Prize–winning architecture critic Paul Gapp of the *Chicago Tribune* deemed the proposed mall as more harmful than helpful.[67]

There was very little delight built into the State Street Mall. In part, this resulted from the stated emphasis on transportation. It was not a true pedestrian-only mall, since many of the city's bus routes were channeled down its length. A wall of buses, thus, visually segmented the space reserved for people. This pedestrian space was rather blank-looking, providing none of the amenities of Kalamazoo or Pomona, like fountains and sculptures and seating. The State Street Mall was a victim of the time in which it was finally conceived. The first urban pedestrian malls in the United States were established during the early 1960s, when value was still placed on novelty, variety, textural changes, and color. Fountains, sculptures, and mosaic tile murals gave human scale to the architecture and landscape amenities when the Pomona and Kalamazoo malls were created. When Chicago's mall was planned, modernism had fully entered its spare, brutalism stage. The dominant visual elements on State Street were the heavy-framed shelters for stairs and escalators to the subway. The wispy-thin tree specimens placed here and there would not be of the proper scale for this grand street for years to come. State Street was dominated by department stores, which traditionally offer lengthy and discreet, if not monotonous, architectural elevations to the street. They provided little visual diversion from the stark public realm. The unwelcoming mall suffered a steady decline in patronage from the start.

Unfortunately, the signage along State Street was increasingly perceived as excessive in the years after the completion of the mall. The criticism focused on the west side of State Street and, in particular, Block 37, the notoriously downscale group of buildings Mayor Richard Daley Sr. earmarked for redevelopment and eventually demolished. The west side of State Street was populated primarily by small shops, which, unlike the department stores across the street, used aggressive signage. Paul Gapp lamented its tawdriness: "Here, in the heart of Chicago, is blight by neon, plastic, fake brick, rock'n'roll, cheap merchandise, cheap food—and sex. It extends along the west side of State between Randolph and Harrison. Slowly but persistently, it is spreading. Nobody seems to know how to stop it. The Great Street is beginning to look like one of those before-and-after ads for acne remedies: clean and attractive on one side—pitted, pimpled and pockmarked on the other."[68]

A sign ordinance created by the State Street Council in the early 1980s intended to rid the mall of many of its "oversized" signs. The stated belief was that these signs were not in keeping with the "quiet atmosphere" desired.[69] Shoppers, however, complained that the mall was too barren, too noisy, and too cheaply done. The refined image the council wanted was not high on their list of suggested improvements. Even architect Harry Weese said that State Street had been "mauled."[70]

After an initial flush of increased sales, most city street malls never lived up to their billing. Many were serious failures within only a few years of the opening celebrations. Pomona's mall was one of the first major casualties and one of the hardest hit. After a precipitous decline, Pomona's mall struggled for years, eventually evolving into a bohemian enclave and an antiques row.[71] For other cities, a series of superficial remakes slowed the decline, at least temporarily. Kalamazoo's mall remained stable longer than expected, especially considering that the city never followed through on Gruen's master plan for a system of ring roads, parking structures, and massive redevelopment around the core.

(opposite) Figure 117
Crocker Bank Building / Saks Fifth Avenue (Arendt, Mosher and Grant, 1960; Cearnal Architects, 1998), State Street, Santa Barbara, California. The city's Architectural Board of Review permitted modernism to mix with historic motifs. In this case, the barrel tile roof did most of the work of anchoring the building regionally, if not locally. The city's Historic Structures Ordinance of 1960, strengthened in 1977, required that all new or modified structures be compatible with the thick-walled, small-windowed look of the 1920s Spanish revival architecture, hence the dramatic transformation of the 1990s.
TOP: *NOTICIAS* (WINTER 1971). COURTESY OF THE SANTA BARBARA HISTORICAL MUSEUM. BOTTOM: PHOTO BY AUTHOR, 2007.

The street was reopened to auto traffic in 1997, with elaborate new environmental graphics depicting regional history and geography. But the departure of the department stores did not bode well for a thriving retail future.[72]

Many cities considered alternatives to the fully pedestrianized mall. The semi-mall was born. The traditional right-of-way of the commercial thoroughfare in America was bare concrete from one side of the street to another. But if Main Street provided trees, flower plantings, and benches from storefront to curb, the transformation would suggest that this was not merely a passageway of expeditious errand running but a place for looking and lingering. It could be both path and place, in other words. Such an investment also communicated to the public that the thoroughfare had been reborn, was new. Thus began America's obsession with streetscape embellishment. It was not altogether different from the White Way movement of the early twentieth century.[73]

One of the most dramatic image alterations played out in Santa Barbara, California. In the early 1960s, community leaders were motivated to add attractions to the pseudohistoric streetscape of the city's primary commercial thoroughfare, Calle Estado, knowing that serious suburban competition was imminent.[74] This required, above all, shoring up the Spanish-Adobe image that had been established during the 1920s. Between that time and the 1960s, a certain bold twentieth-century commercialism had crept on to State Street, making its appearance a little less unique compared to Main Streets elsewhere. The Architectural Board of Review, reinstated in 1947, had controlled the quality of development along the street but permitted modernism to mix in with the purely historic look created by the architects of the 1920s. Patterned concrete screens and ribbon windows were in abundance, as opposed to the rough stucco and arches of the 1920s. Large, angled script signs of neon and acrylic swept across upper facades in place of small, black, pin-mounted letters or diminutive, wooden plaques hanging on curling wrought-iron standards just above doorways. A vertical, projecting neon sign advertising "Chop Suey" was one of several of its kind along lower State Street, contributing little to the city's Hispanic appearance.

Santa Barbara's highly marketable image was threatened. The first step in its reinstatement was the creation of a historic district, El Pueblo Viejo, which was formed to preserve the central core of Santa Barbara in 1960, protecting the genuine eighteenth-century structures and the faux Spanish of the 1920s. Budget limitations eventually prevented the full pedestrianizing of State Street proposed in 1964, but the rich embellishments planned for the proposed grand "paseo" were implemented to coexist with automobile traffic. What Santa Barbara eventually achieved was a partial "malling," of sorts, with patterned paving, coves for seating, and generous plantings.

During the 1970s, following this upgrade of the public realm, a new generation of Hispanicizing began, renewing the civic spirit of the 1920s. This transformation was virtually mandated by the Historic Structures Ordinance of 1960, which was established with the creation of the historic district and strength-

RETRENCHMENT, REPAIR, AND REINVENTION   283

ened considerably with a new ordinance and interpretive guidelines in 1977. It required that all new or modified structures be "compatible" with the early-nineteenth-century California adobe and Monterrey revival styles and the Spanish revival look of the 1920s. Walls were required to suggest heavy masonry construction, with light-colored stucco the preferred finish.[75] Alterations to existing structures often went far beyond direct code requirements. Flat-fronted basic commercial buildings were refronted with blind arches, and light, modern buildings made heavy with stucco (fig. 117). The 1977 guidelines also required signs in the district to be compatible with the pseudohistoric architecture. This meant no internal illumination; no plastic, steel, or aluminum; and no lettering taller than ten inches. As the green landscaping matured, State Street increasingly appeared as a unique, hybrid creation. It was both urban (with the bright white architecture of arid Spain) and rural (with a lush, dark canopy of trees and vines that often camouflaged much of the architecture and recalled the Spanish Caribbean). Thus, it followed no single historic precedent, least of all State Street (Calle Estado) as it appeared before 1920.

In the 1980s, it became apparent that a new intervention was necessary to keep shoppers in central Santa Barbara. After years of research and struggle and several false starts, the city agreed to plans for a new open-air shopping center, or mall, inserted behind a screen of historic facades along Calle Estado (El Paseo Nuevo, 1990). It was spatially linked to another, much earlier open-air passageway, the old Paseo (James Craig and Carlton Winslow, 1922-24). Little harm appeared to have been done to the city's original "Main Street," and patronage increased for all.

Fifteen years earlier, cities like Reading, Pennsylvania, and Redlands, California, attempted ambitious new schemes hoping to integrate major new mall developments with their old retail corridors, but the results might be termed ham-fisted in comparison. Redlands demolished everything on State Street west of its major central cross street, Orange, gutting most of its downtown in order to create a conventional suburban mall near its old shopping streets. Thus, a field of parking lay as a barrier between the old and the new, the planning department fretting for years as to how this gap could be bridged. In contrast, Reading proposed that its new, enclosed mall would be developed dead center in the heart of town, filling in a portion of Penn Street immediately next to Penn Square; parking would be located in structures contiguous with the new buildings. The disheartening lack of business on Reading's large, open square may have appeared exaggerated because of the sheer scale of the place, and it may explain in part why the city decided to locate the development as infill in contiguous public space. These vast right-of-ways, the street and the square, were laid out in 1748 by Nicholas Scull and William Parsons and were inspired by London's formal residential squares, as well as the Holmes Plan for Philadelphia, published by William Penn in 1683. Even the subsequent construction of a courthouse and market stalls in the square, both demolished in the nineteenth century, failed to fill the vast open space adequately.

By the early 1970s, a plan was developed with $15 million in federal funds to build the double-level enclosed mall from 6th to 8th Streets along Penn Street, partially filling up the city's primary public thoroughfare just slightly to the east of the square. The proposed structure spanned from street wall to street wall. Penn Square itself would remain an open plaza, eventually to be sculpted with an ambitious streetscaping scheme, bringing in fountains, trees, and seating (as well as parking). The new, enclosed mall was unusual, as it incorporated a series of atria or squares open to the elements. The scheme was actually part of a multiblock plan for urban renewal. Superblocks had been proposed for downtown Reading since the early 1960s, eliminating the "wasted space" given to the streets. The urban mall scheme was never realized due to a failing economy. Even the ambitious relandscaping of the open square, and design guidelines for merchants, failed to prevent a swift decline of the city center.

As the Reading schemes show, the potential danger to cities was permanently filling the public realm with what amounted to a private endeavor, however public its market amenities may have been described. Arcades in America as well as Europe were rarely if ever placed inside the public right-of-way. Architectural roadblocks to the continuous, open grid of streets in the United States were usually permitted only for important civic structures like courthouses, railroad stations and civic entryways (as in Denver or New York City), or a Board of Trade (an essential Chicago and regional institution). At least 25 percent of the facades along Reading's primary street would have been hidden or defaced had the enclosed mall been built, and a major thoroughfare blocked and filled in. The proposal of this mall displayed disrespect for the principles of planning as William Penn established them. However, to its credit, Reading never went as far as Redlands, California, did, demolishing nearly a third of its city center to make way for a mall development. Plenty of unnecessary demolition occurred nevertheless.

The idea of bringing a major infusion of new retail into a struggling city center was turned into a major success story in the 1980s by developer James Rouse, with his festival marketplaces. Rouse's inventive formula made him the urban pied piper du jour across America, as Victor Gruen had been in the 1960s with his redevelopment schemes that included pedestrian malls. Both Gruen and Rouse were leaders in the development and building of suburban malls in the 1950s, yet both turned around and aimed to save what the regional shopping center was killing. Both had grand visions for future communities, laid out in books or fully realized. As in Gruen's projects, Rouse employed a certain contrived gaiety in his urban retail centers, generated by colorful banners, strategic plantings, kiosks, and the like.[76] But unlike the congenially designed modern sculpture and zigzag roofs nestled among vintage buildings in Gruen's schemes,

Rouse's chief architect, Benjamin Thompson, restored and put to new use ailing historic structures or designed new buildings that echoed historic types that could handle the vast retail program (like glass train sheds, warehouses, or nineteenth-century fair pavilions). The Faneuil Hall Marketplace project in Boston, his first great success in this genre, involved the careful refurbishment of three blocks of warehouses built in 1826 in order to house new restaurants, small shops, and push-cart vendors—all contiguous with the namesake, brick civic structure reconfigured by architect Charles Bulfinch in 1806.

For large cities, empty of life after the workday, the formula was an instant success; but for smaller or mid-size cities, like Richmond or Toledo, the projects were partially vacant within a year or two, and eventually shut down. A major new urban marketplace by Rouse and his architect opened almost every year of the 1980s, but by 1988, the mania came to a halt. Architectural critics had never been particularly kind to Rouse's schemes. Of Harborplace in Baltimore, an editor of *Progressive Architecture* claimed that the buildings "are a mash of clichés—high tech, antique store, postwar modern, 19th century band shell and pavilion-by-the-sea—not well reconciled to each other nor resolved in themselves . . . Atlantic City's boardwalk with a touch of Disneyland."[77] For many, these enclosed pavilions of retail, no matter how sensitively related to their sites for the time, eventually appeared to be quasisuburban follies. The controlled, air-conditioned envelopes of space were often bypassed by pedestrians more interested in the vagaries of the now-bustling, nearby, public streets, once perceived as so threatening and dark less than thirty years earlier.

By the end of the 1980s, plans were still afoot in Chicago, Providence, and other major cities, to restore their once-thriving retail corridors to the glories of the past, but with more historically oriented strategies. Preservationists had established greater presence in city planning departments, and interest in marketing history had increased significantly since the 1970s. Long gone were ambitious plans for multileveled traffic and slick, glass-roofed downtown streets. In 1989, Providence undid its 1964 pedestrianizing of Westminster Street. The closing of the city's last two department stores in the early 1980s indicated that the original mall design was not enough to keep interest very high, and the upgrade in 1978 had not proved significant enough. This time, the street was accentuated with old-fashioned lampposts and ornate gratings around the trees, mimicking history, rather than referencing it as Malcolm Grear had done.[78]

In 1995, six years after Providence returned both automobiles and nineteenth-century streetscape details to its Main Street, Chicago did the same. Skidmore, Owings & Merrill designed the $30 million State Street makeover. This ambitious project included replacing the heavy, much-maligned, modern subway entrance pavilions with gracefully curving entranceways inspired by City Beautiful architectural features from the turn of the twentieth century (the subway was actually built in the 1930s). The new lampposts were copies of those removed from State Street in 1958.[79] Perhaps the city's only misstep with regards to returning history to State Street—and it was big—was the complete demolition, in 1989, of the entire block across from Marshall Field's, the notorious Block 37. This often-mourned loss was the delayed end to Chicago's limited urban renewal efforts in the Loop. The removal, however, suited the plans of many to clean up the "down-market clutter" of certain parts of the western side of State Street.

During the 1980s and 1990s, Providence and Chicago both developed sensitive guidelines for new construction and signs along their celebrated Main Streets. Each city required buildings to present a transparent storefront to the street.[80] Massing was to relate to adjacent structures. In both cities, common building datum lines like the cornice and base were to be acknowledged on the new buildings.[81] Along Westminster Street in Providence, this was particularly important, as the many historic buildings lining the corridor had remarkably consistent two-story bases demarcated in various ways. Along State Street, the application of the principle was more sporadic.

There was an ironic logic in scale operating in the sign limits developed in the 1990s for Westminster Street and State Street. The new code for State Street, with its broad 116-foot right-of-way, continued a policy initiated back in 1907, of forbidding projecting signs (except for theaters and restaurants). In contrast, Westminster Street in Providence, with its narrow forty-foot right-of-way and many tall buildings, once again permitted projecting signs. The city, in fact, allowed them to extend up to six feet, with a generous sign face area limitation of forty-eight square feet. These previously maligned graphics were now encouraged along this narrow street.[82] Contrived graphic history, like hanging plaques or sign shields inspired by the eighteenth century, was actively discouraged. Neon signs were permitted by variance only, however, although Providence's Downcity Design Review Committee encouraged the unique in sign design. A revolving fund was available for up to $5,000 per sign in design, fabrication, and restoration costs. Wall signs on both Westminster and State Streets were permitted to be the same two square feet per lineal footage of street frontage. No roof signs were permitted in Chicago, where they could be easily viewed from the generous space between buildings, yet they were welcome in Providence, where it would be difficult to see them from the street.[83] Chicago encouraged sign panels within the fascia, lintel, or spandrel, and not to expand beyond.

The scale of State Street and the flatness of the facades seemed to cry out for large signs to animate the great space. Projecting signs would seem to be particularly appropriate; they were permitted on Randolph (with its higher concentration of theaters), but not on State. To compensate for this limitation, from the 1920s to the 1970s, buildings along State Street were embellished with generous electric wall signs that extended up to the fourth floor of building elevations (when such square footage was still permissible). On some building corners, individually mounted lettering would be stacked vertically for as many as six to eight stories. This signage grew in density over the decades, as more and more advertising was added, until business dropped off in the 1970s. Because the

scale and height of buildings along State Street varied widely, one to the next, a "band of neon" created a sort of visual continuity from block to block. Located along the lowest three stories of the buildings lining the west side of the corridor, neon signage created an electric datum, unifying architecture with wildly inconsistent architectural bases.

State Street in the early twenty-first century is visually hushed compared to its glory days, despite the return of business and investment. In contrast to the large compressed neon lettering of Alschuler's 1937 design for the Kitty Kelly store, fitted carefully into the base of a four-story glass-block window, but long gone, the new tenant was identified by a temporary banner and acrylic-faced lettering that was one-sixth the height of the original sign. The big red letters for Woolworth (Shaw, Metz & Dolio, 1949), once spaced along the smooth stone facade of the building when the structure was built, were replaced with small square sign panels confined to the space over each door, advertising the Foot Locker with a corporate logo.[84]

The streamlined modern commercial structure designed by Alfred Alschuler in 1936 for Benson & Rixon clothiers had lost its continuous, curving metal band that served as a base for metal ribbon letters. Over the new, heavily squared-off base for the building, one that covered the once fully glassed-in storefront, McDonald's placed a slim acrylic sign panel, an attempt to create a fascia sign where there was never a fascia (fig. 118). The new, narrow openings to the restaurant interior were covered with red awnings, each with a yellow corporate "M." Mounted at the third-floor level, over the still extant curving ribbon windows was a miniature version of a vertical electric sign with a form borrowed from the 1910s or 1920s, edged in incandescent bulbs. This sign type was traditionally mounted so as to project from a building, but in this case, it was mounted flush, like a wall sign. The awnings and the sign were no doubt meant to be a nod to the early twentieth century, a vague bid to fall in step with the faux antique public realm features of the latest incarnation of State Street. But they were incompatible with the design of the building and woefully inaccurate, if they were actually intended to appear historic.[85] The sign was remarkably out of sync with the scale of the building, and, most especially, the street.

Main Streets across America were altered drastically during the final decades of the twentieth century. Some were transformed into pedestrianized malls, and some had enclosed malls forced on them. First they were modernized with slick design and then historicized with relics of an often-borrowed past. Some were overcontrolled by rules, and some were put into harm's way by inappropriate design direction or lack of historic designation.

The matter of striking the right balance was revealed in the differences and similarities of the philosophies held by Victor Gruen and urban activist Jane Jacobs. Gruen was the master designer, the controller supreme, who only permitted design spontaneity if it was planned. Jacobs celebrated the fortuitous and organic. But there were shades between their extremes. Gruen welcomed a

(opposite) Figure 118
Benson & Rixon Company Building (Alfred Alschuler, 1936; altered), State Street, Chicago. The curved, flowing nature of Alschuler's original design (fig. 60) was ignored for a 1960s makeover on the ground level. The subsequent tenant, McDonald's, continued the trend of squaring off and filling in. The underscaled vertical sign, applied flush (as no such sign in history had ever been fastened), was a token gesture to the street's cinema history, most notably as home to the still-extant Chicago Theatre.
PHOTO BY AUTHOR, 2005.

certain variety of old and new signs along his malls. The streets were not scraped bare when he marched in with his renderings. And Jacobs applauded the early attempts by Gruen and others of enlivening streets with variety and detail by incorporating arcades, kiosks, cafés, and flowerbeds. Such features were a welcome novelty at midcentury, when most architects were designing sparer and sparer environments.

Gruen's aim is revealed by a quotation from his 1964 book, *The Heart of Our Cities:* "What makes the appearance of the city superior? We may get a clue to the answer by observing the few spots still left in some of our cities to which tourists and visitors flock. Most visitors to New York will go to Greenwich Village in spite of the fact that there is hardly an outstanding structure there. What the tourists seek and admire is what they call 'atmosphere,' which, when one digs deeper, is found to be the result of small-grained variety and diversity."[86]

Gruen was enamored of the superficial effects of an environment, while Jacobs appreciated something deeper in the diversity of a place. From Jacobs's viewpoint, the signs of a streetscape might have delighted the eye, but they also communicated something about the identity and use of a neighborhood or business. For her, a bend in the street created spatial identity and psychological closure, whereas Gruen might have seen such a phenomenon primarily as an interesting diversion or a tool for increasing sales by focusing attention. Gruen and most of his contemporaries thought they could easily re-create the general excitement enjoyed in urban spaces of Greenwich Village or Europe by hanging mobiles, planting flowers, or forming a small court by removing a building. He would permit diversity, but only under the control of one master designer or creative team. The vitality that Jacobs valued was possible only with many designers. For Gruen, the streetscape was not defined by the multifaceted, community-owned walls of the street but by the common elements owned and controlled by the mall developer or by the city. The contribution of the tenant or merchant to placemaking was small in his estimation. The question of how much central control was right for Main Street would persist for decades to come.[87]

Controlling Commercial Chaos: Scrutinizing Signs, Re-Forming the Strip

The scrutiny of, if not outright hostility toward, development along Main Street and the strip, which began as early as the 1950s, came to full force in the mid-1960s. The challenges to commercial excess were no longer coming only from progressive critics in professional journals. By the late 1960s, this momentum led to a crackdown in zoning codes. A wholesale removal of signs ensued, followed by a reduction of perceived architectural excesses. Decades later, a prescriptive vision for an improved commercial corridor began to replace the negative, reductive legislation. Communities made plans to strengthen the physical presence of commerce instead of hiding or eliminating it.

Signs were primary targets in the 1960s. Restrictions on business signs, city to city, varied widely. Many cities had little legislation regarding signs, although some had established limits in size and location as far back as the turn of the twentieth century. A survey conducted in 1964 by the American Planning Association for central business districts revealed that Portland, Oregon, had no restrictions whatsoever. Indianapolis required only that the height limit for signs be held at twenty-four feet. San Francisco limited projecting signs to a generous 75 percent of the sidewalk width and established a forty-foot height limit for ground-mounted signs. Sign design was left relatively unrestrained. Neither city placed a limitation on sign area. New York and Baltimore, however, permitted no more than three to five square feet per lineal foot of frontage. By 1970, this range was leaning toward the high side compared to the national average.[88] In extreme contrast, Chicago, in 1964, allowed twenty-four square feet of sign area per lineal foot of frontage, and Philadelphia, fifteen square feet. In 2010, cities typically limited wall signs from one to two square feet per lineal foot of frontage in neighborhood commercial districts, with four square feet per foot the allowance permitted for all combined signage for any one business throughout the city. The limit for projecting signs varies widely.

The 1954 United States Supreme Court case of *Berman v. Parker* gave local governments the authority to broaden their evaluation of public welfare to include aesthetics as a legitimate object of police power. Many civic efforts to improve appearances, up until then, were devised by using codes established to maintain health and safety for the community—the only way at this point to avoid court hassles over constitutionality. The door was finally open for restrictions based on public taste: "The concept of the public welfare is broad and inclusive... The values it represents are spiritual as well as physical, aesthetic as well as monetary. It is within the power of the legislature to determine that the community should be beautiful as well as healthy, spacious as well as clean, well balanced as well as carefully patrolled."[89] This made possible a major shift in public policy. It also pushed urban renewal into high gear. Municipalities could now eliminate what was perceived as harmful to the image of their streets.

In 1972, Staunton, Virginia, demanded the removal of all projecting signs on the recommendation of the consultant hired by the city to develop a revitalization plan.[90] Only one year of amortization was granted before all such signs were to be removed. Nearly two hundred signs were demolished almost overnight, some being finely crafted in neon and porcelain enamel.[91] This was a big about-face for a community whose code in the 1960s had permitted projecting signs as large as sixty square feet, extending up to five feet over the sidewalk, and required all neon and electric signs to be lighted every day except Sunday from thirty minutes past sunset until 9:30 p.m.[92] Staunton's new wall sign limit was two square feet per linear foot of frontage, among the lowest in the nation.[93] The city decided that projecting neon signs were not in keeping with the old-fashioned image desired for the center of town. By 1984, this sort of bias was reinforced by national organizations such as the American Planning Association, with regular publications like planning advisory service memos: "Signs that hang over the sidewalk can be counterproductive to business because they often obscure individual buildings and interrupt the harmony of the street. Removal of these signs can be an easy and dramatic step toward revitalizing the district."[94] The memo went on to explain that "occasionally, even a well-designed projecting sign, in good condition, may be retained for its artistic or historic value." Although this message offered a hint of the respect that vintage signs would eventually receive, the mixed message ultimately provided enough support to fuel an effort nationwide to rid the streets of the clutter allegedly caused by projecting signs.[95]

Charleston, South Carolina, and Pasadena, California, offer a valuable comparison on how one might address accumulated layers of history on commercial facades. The cities share a similar evolution of historic preservation and Main Street revitalization since the late 1960s.[96] The Main Streets of both communities were locally and nationally designated. But here the similarities end. In general, Charleston's approach to signage is far more conservative to that of Pasadena. Following sporadic enforcement of a 1947 ban on projecting signs along Charleston's King Street, the ordinance was restated in 1962, giving five years for compliance.[97] Eventually, hundreds of old neon signs came down; only a handful remained. Since that time, signs along King Street in Charleston have been relegated almost exclusively to the traditional fascia zone, and most are nonilluminated. Despite this apparent regularity, the Architecture Review Board considers each storefront on a case-by-case basis. A large mortar-and-pestle shaped neon sign, fabricated for the Tellis Pharmacy in 1960, provides one of several significant exceptions to this restrictive visual pattern. Thanks, in part, to the projecting bay window of the Eastlake-inspired building to which it is anchored, the giant sign extends out over the full width of the sidewalk.

Pasadena took a gentler, more inclusive approach to signs, but it had some good reasons to do so. It was, of course, a much younger city, the result of a boom in the late 1880s and the California car culture that blossomed in the 1920s. Many of the facades along a key stretch of Colorado Boulevard were updated in 1929, due to a major street widening, with bold art deco motifs. The right-of-way along the street was also significantly broader than that of Charleston's King Street, thus making ample space for projecting signs. The 1979 design guidelines for Old Pasadena defined the core commercial stretch of Colorado Boulevard as being oriented to both pedestrian and automobile. The leadership of Pasadena Heritage saw projecting signs as less visually intrusive than were many wall signs on the city's historic facades.[98] Even as early as the 1970s, Pasadena worked hard to prevent the city from become quaintly historic. Features from the 1880s, the 1920s, and the 1990s are visible simultaneously in the newer city. Pasadena was one of the first municipalities to create an ordinance respectfully recognizing historic signs from the twentieth century, excusing designated vintage signs from regulations restricting height and size. This was not permission by exception, as in Charleston, but permission as a form of honoring and encouragement.[99]

Chief among the boosters for signs nationwide was architect Robert Venturi, who studied the value of signs and symbols in both ancient and modern landscapes. He began this study in his 1966 book *Complexity and Contradiction in Architecture* and investigated advertising graphics more thoroughly and literally in 1971 with *Learning from Las Vegas: The Forgotten Symbolism of Architectural Form*. Although Venturi examined the power and value of signs per se, his ultimate concern was how people read the landscape via forms and symbols. Less celebrated but extremely valuable was the work of Ian Nairn, an editor and correspondent for architectural journals in England, who roamed the American landscape and observed relationships between buildings, signs, and trees, paying careful attention to sequences of perception. The arbitrary elimination of all projecting signs in places like Bryan, Ohio, and Staunton, Virginia, would have been problematic in his eyes:

> The courthouse, already apprehended as a whole, is continually having a fan dance performed in front of it by the overhanging signs. This is admirable, and there is a double counterpoint, both visual and intellectual, in the confrontation of "Maymie's Café" and "Montgomery County Loans" with the august symbol of county justice in the background. In the countryside these things would be (and are) abortions, caused by the meeting of incompatible strains. In a town street they are in their natural place, and to suggest moving them, as the people of Kalamazoo want to do in their pedestrian mall . . . would be disastrous, a confusion between tidying up a town and preserving its character. They are not necessarily the same thing at all. Some parts may need tidiness, some may thrive on chaos: as in life, there is no one law for everything.[100]

Signs on the strip also energized writer and cultural critic Tom Wolfe. He was dazzled by the electric, kinetic showmanship. But like Venturi, he perceived that signage, often well integrated with the architecture of auto dealerships and restaurants, imparted useful information even as it titillated the senses. He called what he was seeing "electro-graphic architecture." Many of the spectacles that Wolfe described were, in Venturi parlance, "decorated sheds," ordinary buildings made extraordinary with layers of (often) symbolic visual elements—literally readable architecture for the twentieth century. Some were dazzling monuments providing no shelter but plenty of stimulation and very direct messages.

> Los Angeles commercial artists have unified the concept [of "designing for the eyes of people moving"]. They don't just add the lighting. They combine lighting, graphics, and building structure in a single architec-

> tural form . . . They convert the building itself into one vast electrical advertisement . . . The structure itself takes on the hyperbole of advertising.
>
> Here is an electric Buick sign I saw on El Cajon Blvd. in San Diego, near the Route 395 freeway . . . Each letter of Buick is on a baroque rocket . . . The lights work in a series . . . In phase 2 the rockets light up orange and yellow . . . They shoot off red jet flames . . . They take off to the left . . . A terrific rush of light shoots up the main stem there, the big parabola . . . It explodes in the crazed atomic nucleus at the top . . . The sign is 105 feet high, 11 stories up in the air, in other words . . . It's insane! . . . It's marvelous![101]

For Wolfe, this art was more vital and exciting than the work of highbrow artists like Dan Flavin or Robert Rauschenberg. But would architects and critics like Venturi, Nairn, and Wolfe, out of the mainstream, be able to persuade America that these raucous illuminated graphics were worth celebrating, were worth saving from demolition?

A 1971 book called *Street Graphics*, by William R. Ewald and Daniel R. Mandelker, became a major threat to the sign industry and a counterforce to the renewed enthusiasm for neon. The stated principle of the book, with its systematic method for controlling signs, was to reduce the profusion of information in the commercial environment. "Imagine the change in the view of America if signs and billboards spoke to us separately instead of screaming at us en masse."[102] The authors' goal was to make business graphic communication succinct, efficient, and therefore more effective. Although the authors stressed that creativity was in no way to be hamstrung by this system, they perceived business signs primarily as indexes to the commercial environment and not as advertisements to potential customers. However, graphics could be "an important expression of a community's culture . . . The blending of individually expressive graphic designs . . . helps create a sense of place."[103] The authors also claimed that self-policing by business did not work to keep signs under control, nor did regulation based on street frontage. Limiting signs this way might reduce overall area, but it would not reduce the number of signs. After all, they argued, the problematic visual clutter was caused by an overabundance of parts and pieces (see plate 34).

This new system of sign regulation was based in large part on limiting these very pieces of information. The *Street Graphics* system reduced to ten the number of items (symbols, logos, syllables, etc.) permitted for each business. Complex geographic shapes were counted as points against this limit. This was a potential strike against creativity, which in combination with the spread of corporate design, did not bode well for the unique or ambitious in sign design. The book did not, however, literally suggest the elimination of projecting signs from the streets of America; that coast-to-coast purging was mostly the result of long-established biases in popular taste. The strategy of *Street Graphics* was merely to thin them out, to reduce the excess; to this end it advocated a lengthy sixty feet between each projecting sign. This in itself was, of course, a prescription for a great deal of destruction—considering that most storefronts were approximately twenty-five feet wide. Wall signs were granted 40 percent of the signable area.[104]

Ewald and Mandelker were enamored with the signs they had seen in Europe, both antique and modern, and this led to their enthusiasm for judging signs on a case-by-case basis, as was done overseas. The *Street Graphics* book began with a survey of simply worded wall signs and basic projecting artifacts, symbols, and panels. European corporate symbols and highly crafted renditions of the initials of shop names were sometimes the only identifications for stores or cafés. Wall signs were composed of one or two words, elegantly scripted or lettered. Most of the examples presented were electric; there was no obsession with "ye olde public inn" or scenic eighteenth-century wood and wrought iron "shoppe" signs. Photographs of projecting signs were, in fact, abundant. Each photograph carried but a single word or an attractive trademark. This Kodachrome portfolio of sign heaven was contrasted later in the book with black-and-white drawings of sign hell. Paired with each simple sketch that depicted graphic clutter—the "before" example, in other words—was the inevitable "after" view, the same scene improved by the application of the principles espoused in *Street Graphics*. In one set of drawings, twenty words scattered on eight different panels were replaced, in the improved example, with a single sign panel carrying only three words. Stacking the deck, the authors overloaded the "before" pictures with dark tangles of telephone poles and power lines. Trees and shrubs were thrown in to sweeten the "after" sketches. What more persuasion could the civic-minded wish?

The authors of *Street Graphics* implied that the best-looking towns were those under the control of an elite minority rather than the majority. The wisdom of a central committee or master architect would guide success rather than leaving things up to the chaos of organic development, a physical manifestation of many voices. It was an arresting proposal at the time, one in which a laissez-faire government approach by midcentury had replaced the progressive trends of the early twentieth century. The organized, visually repressive sign systems of suburban shopping centers had been the forerunner of this new comprehensive approach to sign control.

Because the publication and distribution of *Street Graphics* was made possible by the U.S. Department of Housing and Urban Development (HUD), the Urban Land Institute, and the Landscape Architecture Foundation, it received great respect, but also well-deserved scrutiny. Among the book's critics were psychologist Karen E. Claus of the University of California, San Francisco, and legislative consultant R. James Claus.[105] A major concern of the Clauses was the potentially unequal effect such a system would have on businesses. Large businesses could simply adjust their media mix to offset the loss from the new signage regulations. Small retailers, however, could afford no other medium than signs to advertise their presence to potential customers. Not only did the on-premise sign deliver a high degree of advertising reach and frequency, but it did so for pennies per thousand customers compared to dollars for other media.[106]

Concern that *Street Graphics* was being made available by agencies like HUD, and anticipation of a drastically altered commercial landscape, led to a sign summit of sorts in 1976. Officiated by HUD and conducted in Chicago, the Urban Signage Forum welcomed a wide range of speakers, including representatives from various sign organizations, small business owners, urban designers, preservationists, marketing experts, planners, and architects. Gary E. Rhoads, an attorney familiar with sign legislation and legal compensation, stressed the scale of the impending loss of livelihood to small business with a clampdown on signs: "Perhaps there is no public policy that can equalize the opportunity of large corporations and independent businesses, but it is possible to allow small businesses the chance to compete. The influence of large corporations is more apparent every year."[107]

Dr. Edward J. Mayo, professor of marketing at the University of Notre Dame, emphasized that small business could not exist without signs. According to him, 85 percent of a business's primary effective trading area received exposure to the on-premise sign of a business; in comparison, newspaper advertising could reach only 53 percent and television only 14 percent of that market. This meant that a sign cost a business only 20 cents per thousand potential customers versus $932 per thousand for television.[108] The point was a critical one in an age when television was rapidly defining the commercial landscape. With corporate chain businesses presold to the customer through television advertisements, the question was how could small business compete without a chance to appeal to and inform the customer on site (many, for the first time). The emphasis in the *Street Graphics* system, that signs were primarily for indexing the commercial environment, revealed how slanted it might be toward big business.

Steven Izenour of Venturi, Scott Brown, and Associates tried to explain the importance and value of automobile-scaled signs along the highway and in the traditional business center—the very signs threatened by aggressive legislation. "The fact is that the car isn't going to go away . . . It's going to be generating signs. It's going to have to be something we are going to have to deal with, no matter what our problems become . . . The urban street has [also] always been a loaded thing . . . It's always been a streetscape that has traditionally had a layering of many years of architecture and many different eras of signs, and this is what gives vitality in our eyes to the urban street."[109]

But Ronald Lee Fleming directly challenged Izenour's stance: "The celebrators of the plastic, commercial environment, Venturi and Brown, became academic apologists for the corporate visual 'rip-off' of America. Their talk about pluralism in America, which would 'promote a rich variety of attitudes and techniques' as opposed to more elitist European cultures which established more tasteful systems of design control, appears condescending. Does their advocacy protect the identity of New Orleans, Galveston, Baltimore, Santa Fe, or Plymouth, Massachusetts against the ravages of the Kentucky colonel?"[110]

Fleming and Thomas Lutz, assistant director of the National Trust's Midwest office, made a case for protecting and reinforcing the character of individual places. Each feared that the proliferation, if not excess, of corporate identification would smother the historic and unique sense of place for towns and neighborhoods everywhere. They explained that business signs could contribute powerfully to civic character rather than just detract from it. Some signs could be designed in traditional forms or carefully themed; if modern, they could be sensitive to the context in terms of scale, at the very least.[111] Fleming even defended "the small-scale locally crafted neon signs of the 1940s" and explained, "craft arts can be more easily nurtured by developing sign codes which give merchants incentives for symbol signs, using local materials and relating their signage to the architecture of the buildings."[112]

The impact of *Street Graphics* on most cities was indirect but powerful. Unlike the code proposed by Ewald and Mandelker, which required policing the count of the number of "items" at a business and basing the area of signs on the speed of the corridor, most municipalities proportioned sign area and number on street frontages. This trend lasted through the turn of the twenty-first century. The introduction of the *Street Graphics* system did, however, encourage cities to rethink their fragmented and inconsistent codes. With alleged evidence that drivers were limited to the amount of information they could process effectively and safely, even towns with no history of sign legislation became convinced it was time to do some graphic housekeeping. *Street Graphics* was published one year before Staunton, Virginia, required all projecting signs to be removed and four years before the same was done in Bryan, Ohio. Fifty years of sign craft came down in a thunderclap in many cities at about this time. And though *Street Graphics* did not directly propose the elimination of this sign type, the suggestion that corridors be thinned of their graphic clutter provided the excuse needed to destroy the much-disfavored neon.[113]

Reforming the increasingly random-looking post–World War II strip development of America's major retail arteries became an obsession by the mid-1970s. Commercial architecture of the strip, especially for chain businesses, was restrained during the period because of the need to standardize design in a climate of widely varying, but increasingly limiting, municipal codes. Instead of the glare of plastic and chrome structures with attention-getting design, business went under wraps of used brick and wooden shingles.[114] But signs continued to reach for attention. With escalating architectural restraint, commercial buildings pulled back from the street, behind vast parking lots. This placed the sign even more in the spotlight, giving it almost exclusive responsibility for luring customers. New design extremes developed for signs. Interstate interchanges were marked by loose collections of mile-high corporate logos on spindly posts, floating so far off the ground on such minimal supports that they

Figure 119

Lincoln Highway (Route 30), Breezewood, Pennsylvania. Interstate exits are marked by nests of familiar corporate logos and bland architecture. Often the signs reach to the clouds to be seen far enough in advance of the off-ramp.

PHOTO BY AUTHOR, 1992.

seemed like kites on strings (fig. 119). Shopping center signs increasingly presented lists of stores and indecipherable logos at curbside, making these signs like enlarged pages from a telephone directory. In the 1970s and 1980s, the signs of the strip began to face the same scrutiny aimed earlier at urban signs and strip architecture.

Municipalities addressed the ungainly look of the strip in at least two ways. One method involved ruralizing the strip, much as many Main Streets had been the recipients of aggressive natural landscaping programs, and by moving signs down to the ground on stone and brick bases. The other means of improving the strip was through the opposite approach, urbanizing it. The extent of this effort usually involved building more densely and bringing the loosely arranged buildings of the strip back to a common line at a sidewalk.[115]

Several communities, including Guilford, Connecticut; Staunton, Virginia; and Redlands, California, created special overlay zoning districts at the turn of the twenty-first century in order to encourage development along the entrance corridors to look more like Main Street and less like an interstate. This meant borrowing design parameters from the town center, to some extent. The vision for improving the strip included enforcing a spatial likeness to Main Street, while in some cases looking to the architectural forms and iconography from the early highway (rather than the more recent, corporate corridor). Perhaps the primary wish of these towns was to make these corridors more pedestrian friendly. The new guidelines associated with the overlay zoning called for careful consideration of features like porches and porticoes and the banishment of unfriendly blank walls. Rooflines required variety instead of the monotony of flat parapets. The potentially large building form of suburban stores was to be broken into smaller masses. In order to create a sense of containment along the road, setbacks were considerably reduced from the suburban norm, and parking was to be moved behind new buildings whenever possible. Vast parking lots in front of existing stores were to be filled, in part, with new business structures, built right up to the sidewalk.

Redlands, California, was among the earliest communities in the United States to benefit from such zoning. The community redesigned a suburban-looking strip between the interstate exit and downtown State Street to blend with the older historic fabric. Since Redlands had demolished half of its downtown in the mid-1970s to make way for an enclosed mall, it was important to keep the fragile island of urban character that remained around State Street from being overwhelmed by suburban sprawl. The street wall of Orange Street, a former "suburban" strip that served as a gateway to the heart of Redlands, was strengthened with two-story commercial buildings and tall one-story buildings built flush to the sidewalk (fig. 120). The buildings were unique, hybrid inventions, pedestrian-friendly in scale and architectural details but auto-oriented as well. They were designed to be experienced in the round, with back and front entrances. In this way, they were reminiscent of the suburban corridor buildings of the late 1920s and 1930s, when urban building design began to accommodate the automobile. Tower features were included at corner sites to solidify the edge of the block and provide landmarks from afar. Although the new street wall was not consistently solid, as on Redlands's State Street (because of the need for parking between buildings), trellises, arcades, and garden walls spanned the gaps between building fronts whenever possible.

The nearby sprawl development that threatened Guilford's old town center around its public green was also reformed to improved effect. In this case, the intruder was a highway with a long history, the Boston Post Road, or Highway 1—a path that had been rerouted in the 1920s away from the Guilford Green, which it once circumvented along its east-west alignment.[116] In 2000, the citizens of Guilford decided it was time to evaluate the character of the Boston Post Road to determine how to control future development. Urban designer Andres Duany praised the effort, saying, "It's remarkable that your strip is worth saving, because it is. And it's remarkable that you are trying to save it."[117] Could the old center continue to endure the pressure of modern commercial growth so near to its doorstep? Input from public workshops led Guilford planners to develop a set of guidelines that called for greater density and more traditional architecture along the length of Highway 1. The intention of Guilford's new guidelines was to codify and reinforce successful existing architectural massing, sign design,

(opposite) Figure 120
Orange Street, Redlands, California. The former strip development connection between Interstate 10 and the town center has recently been rezoned to produce more urban commercial structures, built up to the sidewalk. These buildings (top photo) are both car-friendly in back and pedestrian-friendly in front, and they segue to the older buildings of the town center (far right in top photo and full frame in bottom photo).
PHOTOS BY AUTHOR, 2007.

and spatial relationships between road and building for the designated zones along the old highway. Based on this information, the aim was to create new parameters for the less-admired sprawl-like areas of the road. This would hopefully produce a successful urban-to-rural transect or visual transition. The new plan for the highway articulated three districts, according to changing density and design. The segment closest to the old town center with its public green was composed largely of older residences that had been converted to commercial use. Similar conversions had occurred around the Guilford Green. This special segment of the highway was named the Post Road Village Zone. Nowhere along the Post Road were off-the-shelf trademark buildings to be permitted.

The existing signs of the Post Road Village Zone were close in form and materials to the signs found around the Guilford Green: small wooden panels mounted on wood posts or hanging from posts, gallows-style. This was a sign type that had been borrowed from England and employed throughout the American colonies. It was a type found usually, but not exclusively, outside of city centers in England, since it required more room. In New England, it was used in both village and countryside. Around the Guilford Green one could find post-mounted signs as well as those hanging from building facades on ornate brackets, the latter being the more appropriate for an urban context. This mix of sign types was not uncommon for the roads and spaces of New England villages and the crossroads towns of the Southern colonies, which were quasi-urban when compared to the cities of Europe (or even the tight, densely built small towns of Pennsylvania). The rural, freestanding gallows sign type may be seen as most appropriate for the Post Road as it nears the town center, as it is less urban than Guilford's rather densely developed edges around the green.[118] Guilford's new guidelines encourage the creation of such signs for the road and recommend that they be constructed only of high quality, natural materials.[119]

Staunton, Virginia's 2008 ordinance creating overlay districts for entrance corridors differs from Guilford's guidelines by requiring building design to be based on more recent precedent. The guidelines cited not the urban buildings of the old town center as models but buildings developed along the old highway entrance corridors from the early 1900s through the 1950s, which addressed the automobile. Planners chose these examples because they were friendly to both pedestrians and motorists and often used ingenious methods to address changes in grade. Although they were not typically urban in form, if properly sited with minimal setbacks, they could still create a sense of enclosure along the road. They would help establish "Staunton's unique cultural and historic characteristics."[120] One of the design reference models was an old country store, chosen for the way it established a transition from street to interior with its porch and recessed entry door. A grocery store from the 1950s was cited as exemplary because it was located close to the sidewalk, provided a strong transitional zone at the front, and supplied parking behind and to the side of the structure; it also included a modest tower feature, which made a separate sign structure

Wright's Dairy-Rite

20¢ BURGERS

Wright's DAIRY-RITE

CURB SERVICE

COLONEL SANDERS' RECIPE
Kentucky Fried Chicken

"SPECIAL"
2 BURGERS
29¢

Dimensions and annotations:
- 13'
- 5'9"
- 15"
- 2'8"
- 3'6"
- 7'
- 25'
- CHASING BULBS 11 WATT
- 3'6" & 15" LETTERS, SINGLE TUBING
- 10" LETTERS SINGLE TUBING
- 10" — SINGLE TUBING
- 6" & 10" LETTERS PAINTED ON WHITE PLEXIGLAS
- CHANGEABLE LETTER PANEL TO ACCOMMODATE 4 ROWS OF 6" LETTERS
- PRESENT BASE

1" SCALE
by STANFORD & INGE Inc.
ROANOKE, VA.
R.A.E.

unnecessary. Another example from the 1950s was Wright's Dairy Rite, a popular drive-in restaurant near the edge of Staunton's downtown. The composite building accommodated both cars and walkers, with covered pull-in spaces with speaker menus set to the side and an enclosed structure sited near the sidewalk for pedestrian arrival and indoor eating. The freestanding neon pylon sign (Stanford and Inge, Roanoke, 1961) was cited as a model example of the use of neon and roadside imagery in the community (fig. 121).[121]

Two other cities helped to build on the neon and automotive heritage of their entry corridors. Both Pasadena, California, and Sarasota, Florida, worked to redevelop roads characterized by loosely defined, anti-urban sprawl, with vast front parking lots and buildings in a multitude of scales, shapes, and locations in relation to the road. In Sarasota, the old highway into town was called the North Tamiami Trail, also known as Highway 41. In Pasadena, it was East Colorado Boulevard, some of the final West Coast miles of old Route 66. Like Guilford and Staunton and many other American cities, these communities envisioned the corridors as pedestrian friendly, with minimal setbacks, shared rear and side parking, and prominent architectural features marking street corners. But because of each city's automobile-oriented heritage, there was a hybrid vision for the roads. They would be urban spatially, but the buildings would be a mixture of the suburban and urban in form. Since the old highways in each community were several miles long, it was proposed that the collective sense of place be segmented into identifiable "nodes," or "sub-areas," for the purpose of establishing places of individual distinction. A unique sense of place would be fostered at each node, based on nearby institutions and local history.

Pasadena's 2003 Specific Plan for East Colorado Boulevard emphasized the auto heritage of the old highway into town, even as it called for pedestrian-oriented buildings located close to the sidewalk. The design guidelines specified streamlined modern forms from the 1930s and 1940s, as well as the oblique angles and iconographic signs of the 1950s—three decades often considered as the best years of old Route 66. In the new buildings and sign designs, the city encouraged take-out windows at the sidewalk, plenty of neon, and pylon signs integrated with the architecture. The urban yet auto-friendly buildings from the 1930s and 1940s were perhaps the most appropriate models for this hybrid environment, as they often offered ambitious neon sign towers and pylons incorporated into the design of buildings that were located close to the street. Fortunately, the Los Angeles area offered some of the best examples from this era in the United States. In contrast, roadside features from the 1950s tended toward being more isolated objects, freestanding in open space.[122]

Sporadically marking the length of East Colorado Boulevard in the 1940s were buildings with pronounced sign features and towers, ready models for urban-suburban commercial design. The Broadway department store (1940) featured a tall, compressed "wedding-cake" corner tower with a carefully integrated sign fin that pushed up just beyond its height (see fig. 103).[123] Aside from

(opposite) **Figure 121**
Design for Wright's Dairy-Rite sign (Stanford & Inge, 1964), Greenville Avenue, Staunton, Virginia. The city of Staunton has recently recognized this sign and the modest commercial structure it advertises as potential models for future development along entrance corridors.
COURTESY OF SHIRLEY WRIGHT MCKEE.

its showy, figural tower, the Pasadena Broadway store was a basic, urban, background building, built right up to the sidewalk. Farther down Colorado Boulevard from town center, the slab pylon and tower signs built for Troll's Hardware (1945) and Jack's Food Town (1946) demonstrated how to incorporate vertical, auto-friendly identifying features with modest, horizontal, pedestrian-friendly buildings. The Van de Kamp's windmill tower (1943), flanked by Dutch gables, once rested at the sidewalk's edge; its base featured windows with generous, welcoming awnings—a pedestrian-friendly feature mixed with auto-oriented advertising imagery.[124] If the city had chosen to emphasize the 1930s and 1940s (a more pedestrian-friendly era than the 1950s) for the look along its old Route 66, it had these ready prototypes available.

But as indicated by the design guidelines, Pasadena planners demonstrated a preference for the latter period. Photographic examples published by the city included monumental sculptural pole signs that advertised buildings pushed back from the street—images borrowed from other communities. The challenge before developers was to reconcile the automobile-oriented design of the 1950s—known for its architecture fully conceived in the round—with the pedestrian-friendly continuous street wall of the early-twentieth century. Fortunately, Pasadena's own history includes precedent where this seemingly impossible compromise was very nearly reached. Gwinn's Restaurant and Drive-In (Harold J. Bissner and Harold B. Zook, 1948), a Pasadena institution, provides a very worthy example (fig. 122).[125] The modernist architectural composition of horizontal planes hovering over glass pressed tightly up to the property line. A trellised canopy continued from the one-story building along the sidewalk and out toward the parking lot, located to the side of the restaurant. This feature prevented the building from appearing as an isolated structure surrounded by cars and suggested at least a partial wall along the street. Vines and shade screened the parking lot. A slab pylon sign provided the necessary identifying feature and single vertical element anchoring the visual arrangement. Several midcentury motels, and even the local Denny's, where Googie designs have been made almost urban, provide other good examples for the city.[126]

The writers of the guidelines went out of their way to promote creative solutions for future signs, especially those inspired by the 1950s, for which size and location bonuses were offered. The city's special creative sign permit process (2005) encouraged graphics that did not fit within straightforward code parameters; review by the director would ensure quality.

For the North Tamiami Trail in Sarasota, the Innovation41 study of 2006 was perhaps the first city-sponsored proposal to acknowledge the entire corridor's heritage as a place of cultural and architectural merit. The trail had suffered years of physical decline since most of the north-south traffic that once energized the corridor was rechanneled to Interstate 75 in the 1980s. The Tamiami Trail was constructed in the 1920s as a convenient automobile route from Tampa south and east to Miami, hence its name. During the 1930s and 1940s,

motels were built along the northern entrance to the resort town, along this new corridor. But the real growth came in the 1950s, which brought a more exuberant layer of design to the once modest, domestic-looking accommodations—with creative neon graphics and rakishly angled porte-cocheres applied to the original motel buildings. Due to the application, in the 1980s, of a complicated series of residential (rather than commercial) zones along the length of the North Trail, reinvestment during this period was poor, and serious decay set in. Despite the city's new historic sign ordinance, established in 1989 with hopes for prolonging the life of vintage signs threatened with noncompliance, most of the old neon had disappeared by 2000. Crime and prostitution had begun to plague this old commercial strip. In the 1980s and 1990s, a serious effort was made to clean up this image, especially for the benefit of the universities and colleges that dotted the length of the North Trail, and careful studies were made for urbanizing the corridor with minimal setback development. The old motels were not part of this new vision.

Along with the goal of redeveloping the image and identity of Sarasota's North Trail was an effort to urbanize the corridor, much as Redlands and Pasa-

Figure 122

Gwinn's Restaurant and Drive-In (Harold J. Bissner and Harold B. Zook, 1948; demolished), East Colorado Boulevard, Pasadena, California. For a city searching to reconcile automobile- and pedestrian-friendly design for future development along a historic corridor, this commercial structure offers a surprisingly good model.

PHOTO BY J. ALLEN HAWKINS, CIRCA 1960. COURTESY OF THE PASADENA MUSEUM OF HISTORY.

dena were creating zero-setback streets out of former sprawl. It was not the intention of the 2006 plan to transform the trail into Main Street. Instead, the study called for a series of concentrated nodes, usually developed around key cross-streets. Each of the nodes and mile segments of the Renaissance Trail received a locally meaningful name and distinct iconography. Environmental graphics, special street furniture, and new lighting were to be installed to help create place and reinforce the branding. Marketing schemes and coordinated promotional material would be developed as one of the earliest priorities. Among the various places identified along the trail was an area with a concentration of the kind of old motels that used to thrive up and down the entire length of the corridor.[127] This area was singled out as being worthy of preservation and reinforcement. It was identified as a particularly marketable feature of the Renaissance Trail.

> While this section of the corridor is the most "damaged" by the poor reputation of the older motels, it is those very motels that represent the heritage and particular marketing strength of the Corridor. With the shift in hotel demand from seniors to a younger, "hipper" crowd, there is the opportunity to utilize the better-designed, vintage motels as a "hook" for re-capturing the lodging market in this area and for enhancing opportunities for conference and other venues relating to area institutions . . . Restoring some of these motels will both serve the identified need for hotels for area visitors and create a retro ambiance that will attract certain tourists.[128]

For each node along the trail, a form-based code was recommended to define the building envelope for new development and to regulate urban design. The motels required plenty of pull-in space and parking, and all of their signs were freestanding pylons or pole mounted. Aiding the effort to urbanize the trail was the fact that many of the old motels were laid out with L- or U-shaped plans, with one leg reaching all the way out to the sidewalk. As in Pasadena, the auto-friendly and the strictly urban in design would be asked to coexist.

America's decades of indulgence (the 1950s and 1960s) led to decades of repentance, of trading one extreme for another. In place of fantastic architecture on the strip and brightly colored, overscaled signs with metal resheathing on urban commercial corridors, the 1970s ushered in muted earth colors and an unseasoned respect for historic architecture. Corporations and government wrestled for control of the commercial corridor. Most prominent was the increasing influence of corporate advertising. The spread of corporate trademark buildings and graphics had an obvious impact on the strip.[129] At the same time, building owners in the old town centers were persuaded by metal panel manufacturers to create an up-to-date appearance and cloak their old buildings. Before the century was over, these same cover-ups were pulled back down. Another important development in this period was the increasingly blurred distinction between architect and sign designer when it came to storefront design. Architects became graphic designers and vice versa, thanks in large part to corporations looking at every possible angle for expanding sales opportunities.

To compensate for years of automobile congestion and the perception of visual clutter, Main Streets everywhere were stripped of traffic and, in many cases, projecting signs. An idealized urban environment, the pedestrian mall, was born. Victor Gruen's presentation drawings seemed so clean and yet so lively; their appeal was obvious. Civic leaders were seduced, despite questionable feedback in the early years. The focus of design, once storefronts were simplified with slick, attractive skins and interesting textures, was not on the street walls but on the common space between, which was filled with free floating sculpture, randomly placed fountains and trees, and curvilinear pathways and paving. Much of this lushness was brought in to ruralize what was traditionally urban.

Just as the momentum for malling was picking up, America's fledgling preservation movement fanned out from a few revered historic sites to small towns across the map. This new appreciation for old buildings included respect for the collective whole, for entire streets and districts, and was quickly seized upon for marketing potential. The emphasis was on architecture, on the purest, oldest layer beneath all the updates from the nineteenth and twentieth centuries. To most amateur and some professional preservationists, this meant that electric signs were in the way, dismissed en masse as cluttering the view of the historic facades. Only after a great deal of removal did some come to see that these signs were a legitimate product of the auto age. The signs were mostly nondestructive appendages attempting to bridge the gap between centuries and keep businesses vital. Oddly enough, the newly revered nineteenth-century buildings dated from a time when design could be as exuberant (in its own way) as architecture was in the 1950s. Late-nineteenth-century signs were somewhat comparable to those of the mid-twentieth century, assuming a multitude of shapes and locations. But reviving Main Street often meant reconceiving history, cleansing it of the truth in an attempt to appeal to present-day taste, to customers who were weary of clutter. As the historic preservation and Main Street revival movements matured, layers of history were treated with increasing respect, although it was still difficult for most civic leaders to appreciate historic signs.

The goal, after all, was unity and harmony, with a little variety tossed in. There was much talk of balancing the consistent with the creative, but the scales were tipped. Although it might be seen as an extreme example, Bryan, Ohio, presented to many the ideal of consistent vintage architecture and regimented signage—characteristics so successful in suburban shopping centers, the competition. Restoration in many other cities revealed a striking timidity, a desire to be handsome, correct, and inoffensive. A simple publication called *Street Graphics* lent enormous support to suppressing signs and emphasizing building facades and trees. Its authors also joined designers like Victor Gruen in calling for "planned serendipity." Banners became all the rage, uniform advertisements for the street and neighborhood activities (not directly for businesses), dashes of color on increasingly conventionalized urban thoroughfares. The focus shifted away from the individual, toward the whole, with enormous control given to the master architect or single voting body.

Growing municipal control replaced extreme individualism. Giving so much power to a single, controlling body left history completely vulnerable to the aesthetic biases of a single generation. Once the many thousands of projecting signs were removed from commercial streets, there was no getting them back. Since many businesses in the 1920s through 1940s could only afford a new sign when it came to updating appearances, that loss meant that traces of at least one entire generation were wiped out at the whim of a consultant or bureaucrat. Eliminating the huge variety of signs, both projecting and those perceived as overscaled for the space above display windows, was a questionable move, especially in the name of preservation. Many of the architectural details revealed by cleansing the buildings of signs were never intended to be examined in such detail.

Even today, there continues to be a danger of putting the future of the street into the hands of the few rather than the many. As Peirce F. Lewis observed in 1975, "If we justify historic preservation on grounds of cultural memory, it is obviously necessary that the preservation be truthful and by that I mean the whole truth, or as close to the whole truth as we know how to come."[130] In 1984, Joseph S. Wood went even further: "Unfortunately, the present practice of historic preservation, especially in pursuit of tax incentives, too often encourages . . . conceit by invoking preconceived ideas of aesthetic and functional purity. When preservation commissions carry out architectural-design review, for instance, predetermined universal standards of preservation are necessarily imposed. The result of contrivance, whether it is a consequence of design review or simply of historicist notions, is a pseudoplace, a place that stands for something that never existed."[131]

Since then, the revitalization of historic commercial streets in America has begun to allow layers of history to coexist. The preservation press did not encourage this trend early on, but its published advice evolved to be inclusive of more aspects of historic fabric. Although the 1930s storefront has been acknowledged as having historic value, the open storefront of the 1940s and 1950s has yet to receive equally thoughtful consideration. This lack of appreciation may be due, in part, to the way many an older building was carved away at the base in order to make room for open retail frontages.

Appreciation and protection for the way historic signs mark place and neighborhoods of people in the endless, potentially indistinguishable city grid have also been growing. According to preservationists and historians, more could be done. Few, perhaps, would deny the power of the Blumstein sign in Harlem, marking the place where black citizens gained new respect along 125th Street. Yet this landmark is just one example of many important commercial city graphics that are unprotected, unsurveyed, and unacknowledged. Although historically designated with much fanfare in 2008, Milwaukee Avenue in Chicago is celebrated for its commercial architecture, which dates up through the 1920s.[132] Its many remarkably designed and crafted midcentury neon signs contribute a valuable layer to this many-layered commercial district, yet little exists to encourage their maintenance or restoration. There is no outright protection against demolition of signs, yet all artifacts along this corridor are to be considered when approval is granted for any changes to a site (see plate 35).[133]

Continuity between past and present is finally being realized. New sign codes across America encourage larger graphics and projecting signs if they are high in craft. In many places, the strip is being reformed to be more like Main Street in architectural form and spatial organization, yet it also celebrates the iconography of its true highway heritage. Perhaps, some have paused to consider, Main Street should be a bit more like the strip—visually less polite. New criteria are being evaluated for where signs are too many, and where they are too few. When they were shorn of their "overscaled" signs in the 1970s, small businesses could no longer compete with franchises and their seemingly unlimited advertising budgets. Main Street was rendered into a recreation space and not a serious contender for everyday business. The more that businesses there were prevented from advertising as they once had, the more Main Street was forced to surrender its traditional role and become something new. With the strip becoming more like Main Street, there are indications that Main Street is now being reinvigorated with a balance between sign and architecture. It is being informed by the strip as well as by its own past. It need no longer be an island. There is great potential for increased connection between the old commercial corridor and the new.

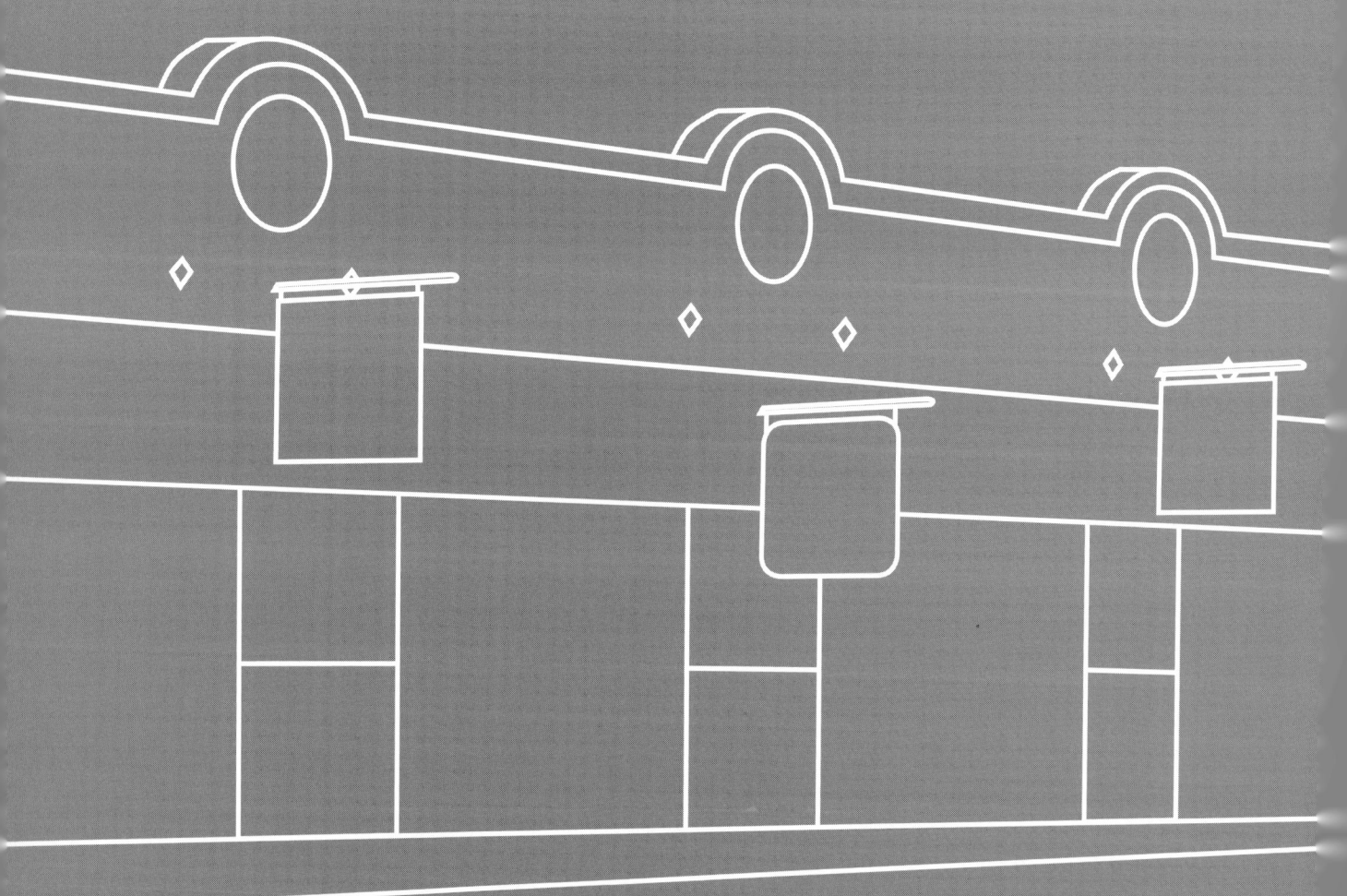

Conclusion

EACH OF THE FOUR FORCES SHAPING Main Street and the suburban strip—customer, advertiser, designer, and technology—has taken its turn dominating the others as the American commercial landscape has evolved. However, a special tension or charged dynamic has always existed between the four, keeping them in balance, fighting yet feeding each other. This is especially apparent between pairs of forces. For one, a powerful relationship has long existed between designer/architect and advances in technology (including the corporate forces that pushed for their use). In many cases, designers aimed to achieve purely aesthetic improvements that were merely made possible by new technology, not inspired by it. In contrast, technology sometimes took the lead, suggesting possibilities that either were not yet conceived by creators of signs and architecture or were low in their priorities. An early and significant development in storefront design occurred because of the increased availability, in the mid-nineteenth century, of large pieces of glass, which permitted easier display of goods from within the shop. In this case, technology served a practical need. Later, the increase in glass in commercial facades kept architects searching for suitable stylistic and compositional solutions. The introduction of affordable electric incandescent bulbs launched a whole new sign industry in the early 1900s, yet proved a horror for sign artists, who had great difficulty reconciling luminous points with the fluid, elegant, thin and thick strokes of good lettering and the swirling aesthetic of the period. Soon, electric animated signs became possible, and designers fully exploited the potential of electricity with advertising possibilities unimaginable in the 1880s.

The versatility of new materials like pigmented structural glass, neon, and glass block greatly expanded the freedom that European modernism brought to the scale and location of lettering, lighting, and decorative finishes. As designers proposed increasingly open storefronts to encourage sales, glass companies invented more sophisticated framing systems to accommodate the trend. Conversely, corporations marketing the use of the new materials, like Libbey-Owens-Ford and General Electric, employed aggressive programs for expanding their use during the Great Depression, especially on sales-stymied Main Streets beyond New York and Los Angeles. They pushed the imaginations of designers through generous media exposure of design advances. Through advertisements, these same companies encouraged sign companies to enter the business of storefront design, shifting the responsibility for the look of many businesses from school-trained architects to job-trained sign designers and manufacturers. Neon's proliferation in the 1930s fundamentally altered the appearance of electric signs, permitting continuous, fluid, and intricate lines of light instead of the coarse figures suggested by arrangements of bulbs. Some sign artists used neon as they might an ink pen or pencil, incorporating elaborate detail in lettering or images. A few sign designers and graphic designers recognized the limitation of the medium and made it a strength by drawing in light with a few deft, sweeping neon lines that suggested a figure rather than literally illustrating every feature.

Another duality of forces worth examining is customer versus advertiser. The advertiser was the business owner and aggressor, attempting to lure the customer through sign and storefront appeal, along with the architecture of the building housing the business, and its strategic location. The customer, as recipient and target of the information placed on display, evaluated the worth of these artifacts. In the first decade of the twentieth century, the customer became active as citizen, assuming the responsibility of being a watchdog against the materialized boosterism of the advertiser. Early-twentieth-century progressives leaned on municipal governments to reign in the apparent free-for-all on the streets of the city: signs placed on every imaginable surface. The struggle between an ideal vision of the city (muted, harmonious, communal) and its actual condition (brash, individualistic) was represented in the stark contrast between the classical regularity of the World's Columbian Exposition and the first electric advertising sign erected in public space, which blinked on a hotel rooftop in blue, green, and red lights. Both debuted in the same year, 1893.

During the early 1900s, tension existed not only between citizen and advertiser but also between citizen and citizen. Civic reformers ran up against small town boosters promoting improvements for their Main Streets. Though each group shared the goals of civic betterment, with improved roadways and lighting, the White Way zealots had improved commerce as their ultimate aim and welcomed every electric sign proposed, in order to help give Main Street an extra glow for customers passing through town.

In the 1920s, the advertiser appeared to dominate the commercial landscape. Signs and commercial architecture became equally exhibitionistic, and few communities succeeded in doing much more than to attempt control of advertising. One notable exception, Santa Barbara, engineered a vision of what a city should look like rather than merely what it should not. Citizens assumed power over advertisers in this community, reconfiguring their average-looking Main Street to become Calle Estado, a pseudohistoric Spanish passage.[1] The city's success in municipal image-making and control was then paraded through the national press as a civic model and tourist destination. Santa Barbara's muted wooden sign plaques and ornate iron standards were codified as the only appropriate way to advertise in a Spanish village. The city eschewed the contemporary technology of electric bulbs. Elsewhere in America, signs and architecture responded to the speed of customers in automobiles. Buildings became more horizontal, even as they borrowed from historic styles. They also often assumed trademark forms for easy and appealing identification.

In the 1950s and 1960s, a period notable for virtually unchecked suburban development, advertisers stretched the limits. During this time, both sign and architecture assumed particularly conspicuous, flamboyant forms, building freely on open land and attempting to lure customers with unprecedented spectacle and scale. Pylon signs, increasingly separated from the businesses advertised by oceans of parking, became the primary advertising feature on many sites. They assumed most, if not all, of the responsibility of identifying and luring. The size and exuberance of these signs grew as traffic increased, streets were widened, and competition attempted to outdo neighboring enterprises.

In the 1960s and 1970s, all four of the forces that shaped the commercial corridor were at work, though the designer and customer rose to new power—as reform was the order of the day. Critics led the charge, which the public quickly embraced, against the disorder and accelerating scale of architecture and signs in town centers and on the strip. Designers forced a proactive change in the look of the corridor, led by an aesthetic born from the spare, clean lines of modernism. Architects such as Victor Gruen proposed major visual alterations to Main Streets everywhere, with harmony as their aesthetic goal and a contrived variety overlaid for visual stimulation. The street walls where advertising once dominated the view were muted, as signs were removed and the spotlight placed on sculpture and banners in communal space, the street. Exponential growth of chain businesses and franchises during this period ushered in an era of simplified corporate trademarks as signs—as opposed to unique figures and copious wording. Advertisers were changing tactics. Vacuum-formed plastics served this reductivism with easy mass production; logos designed for print were graphically reproduced at any scale for corporate site identity. This new technology also served the growing reform movement, as elaborate neon signs were replaced by smaller, simpler panels and the source of illumination was hidden according to tough new legislation. This was an era of control, of publications like *Street Graphics*, a reaction to the laissez-faire exuberance of the previous decade. Citizen zeal to reform the commercial corridor of its perceived excesses quickly grew to overshadow other forces as the century drew to a close.

Although technology and the will and vision of the designer had a powerful hand in the creation and evolution of places like Bryan, Ohio's courthouse square and Sarasota's Tamiami Trail, ultimately it was the customer and advertiser who determined the staying power of commercial facades, storefronts, and signs. The advertiser or business owner determined whether a storefront was up-to-date enough to lure in the required number of customers. Elaborate brick structures replaced simple wood frame commercial buildings in the 1870s and 1880s in places like Bryan. In the 1930s, slick new finishes like Vitrolite and porcelain enamel panels brought fresh appeal to the first-floor storefronts of many of these buildings; larger, more elaborate signs also replaced transom-level windows of Luxfer prism glass. In the 1960s, both upper and lower floors of commercial facades were covered with new skins and even larger graphics. But then, in 1975, a team of consultants scrutinized Bryan's courthouse square as a whole and developed a strict set of guidelines and laws that determined what would stay and what would go around the square. This was a radical shift of power away from individual business owners who had, for more than a century, made incremental design alterations that collectively created the ever-evolving streetscape. The aim of the new plan was to create visual harmony, something that would instill civic pride and stimulate business. The vision was not unlike that for the new pedestrian malls of the 1960s: storefront regularity with an emphasis on common amenities like street furniture and green landscaping. Most of the accretions of history, the layers of design and advertising that had accumulated, were swept away by the aesthetic of a single generation. The sanitized version of the square, and the rules that created it, continue to this day.

In Sarasota, after decades of the advertiser building up the neon appearance of the Tamiami Trail, the customer stepped in to "clean up" the "overload." As with many strips throughout America, legislation developed in the 1970s and 1980s that determined the size and shape of business signs, as well as the location and form of many motels and shopping centers. This was not so much a vision as it was a checklist of what was to be avoided. Roadside artifacts from many decades that did not conform to the new limits were deleted. Many vintage signs that exceeded square footage allotments or setbacks could not be repaired or reused; they had to be replaced. Tough limits on setbacks and floor areas constrained modification of existing motels and restaurants. The advertiser had very little say. The temporary disrepair of this historic corridor led to such drastic code restrictions that the city had, in effect, removed the incentive to invest in property; in so doing, it exacerbated the very visual decline that was to be avoided. A generation of neon craftsmanship disappeared, replaced by graphics that often required little creativity—just a bit of computer composition, digital compression of type to fit the sign panel.

Over the course of more than two hundred years, the American commercial thoroughfare has been in a constant state of evolution. During this long history, business signs and commercial architecture alternated between being independent of each other and being physically united. Their mutual proximity was the direct result of the rural or urban character of the context. In the early nineteenth century, as a commercial building type evolved from neutral or residential structures in growing urban centers, graphics applied directly to the building replaced the once freestanding post or gallows-type sign. Signs proliferated by the mid- to late nineteenth century, covering all exposed surfaces of buildings that housed merchants and places of hospitality. Signs were painted on or fastened to almost every conceivable location. By the end of the century, architects and designers created increasingly elaborate building ornament and signs, generating a great tension on the commercial facade, a struggle for space. This was exacerbated by the expansion of glazing on the facade. By the 1920s, signs and buildings grew in scale and showiness, each awkwardly conceived as an autonomous creation. With the arrival of outside influences during the 1930s, American designers were creating signs and buildings as holistic, fully integrated artifacts. However, to satisfy customers accustomed to the convenience of the automobile (and its spatial requirements), sign and architecture separated once more in the 1950s. The independent signpost of the early nineteenth century had, in a sense, returned, though in a different guise. This independent graphic, with increased responsibility for communicating the nature and character of the business due to the simplification of roadside architecture, remains with us today.

Context is key in understanding sign, street, and storefront. For more than a century, architects have been encouraged to consider designing signs or, at the very least, to make places for them on the facades they have designed. Sign artists, in turn, were encouraged to get to know the buildings on which their designs would be placed. Though such care was not always exercised, the mere attempt to achieve some sort of harmony reveals a true awareness on the part of professionals that signs were not isolated artifacts. Graphics and architecture are perhaps best understood as part of a design continuum along the corridor, with each addressing—to some degree—both commerce and aesthetics, individual and community. The market encouraged business identification to be loud and plentiful; civic responsibility called for a certain decorum and playing by the rules, even if such rules were not codified or enforced. Signs have evolved in response to many forces but always in relation to architectural developments and the scale of competition along the street. When the architecture of the commercial building and storefront receded, graphics often pushed forth (as in the early nineteenth and late twentieth centuries), and when architectural invention flourished and urban centers were strong, business identification temporarily became constrained in scale (around the turn of the twentieth century) before expanding in a new form. In certain eras, like the 1920s, both graphic and building facade were pushed to extremes in size and ornamentation.

Commercial design in the 1930s illustrates how balanced and interdependent sign and site could be. During this period, architects and designers made an enormous conceptual leap by no longer drawing a line between graphic and building. Signs were contoured and placed so as to appear continuous with canopies and openings, or facade compositions were primarily graphic in nature, excluding traditional features like columns and entablatures (elements that evolved from structural need). Business identifications may have been exuberant at times, especially with the design freedom possible on suburban sites, but they were most often expertly leashed to a grander visual scheme. During the 1930s, architects and designers assumed greater power. They presumed that a storefront could be much more than a decorative display with an advertisement applied as an afterthought. Under the control of an able designer, a sign could be a component of a greater scheme. Industrial designers and architects examined each commercial assignment for its potential efficiency and beauty. Although the new aesthetic may have appeared arbitrary at times, its novelty served to persuade customers that there was something new to see. The shift in the way graphics were perceived and used in the 1930s greatly elevated the significance of signs. Designers acknowledged their potential beauty, even as they functioned as advertisements. Although this era of design may seem idealistic and inapplicable to today's suburban landscapes, it calls attention to the potential for balance of scale and visual coordination. It also demonstrates most vividly the need to consider both graphic and architecture together when making alterations to any feature of historic properties.

Vintage architecture and historic signs were beginning to regain favor across America by the late 1970s and 1980s, appreciation of the latter being the most recent. At first, the restoration of original commercial facades meant demolishing later additions, including many valuable signs. But vintage graphics have increasingly become revered. In 1989, Sarasota enacted its Landmark Sign Ordinance, providing businesses with the opportunity to designate older signs and mitigate tough code requirements. Since the American Planning Association's PAS memo of 1988, which outlined ways to protect historic graphics, municipalities have designated signs across America and given incentives to maintain and protect them. In 2006, a rare surviving example of a large-scale, single-arch McDonald's sign (circa 1962, Pine Bluff, Arkansas) was added to the National Register of Historic Places. In 2007, San Diego's Historical Resources Board turned down a new development because it would "block the 'postcard' view of El Cortez Hotel's iconic red sign from Balboa Park."[2] The sign on the tower's crest was intentionally created as a beacon to travelers when the hotel was built in 1927 and remains an icon for the city. Due to their high level of craft, unusual scale, and key placement, these signs were deemed significant for being true landmarks in their neighborhoods.

Many other signs across the country that serve as identifying features for specific neighborhoods or key locations remain unrecognized in this fashion. Distinctive signs for businesses on street corners are particularly valuable as markers of place in the potentially endless, disorienting grid of the American city. In his description of eighteenth-century Philadelphia, landscape historian John Stilgoe credits corner taverns with creating a system of landmarks in the potentially bewildering sameness of the city.[3] With these taverns came their unique icon signs. A balance of the unique and the constant has long helped to guide and give historic meaning to the ever-growing American city. In Chicago, today, the expansive neon sign for Margie's Candies (Acme-Wiley Sign Co., 1954), sweeping around the corner of a major intersection, dominates the nearby, anonymous franchises (see plate 36). Even a relatively modest projecting sign like the one for All Star Donuts in San Francisco's Marina District serves as a neighborhood beacon, an orienting device especially valuable on foggy mornings (see plate 37). The remarkable porcelain enamel roof sign for Pat's Steak Sandwich in Philadelphia (Ajax Sign Company, 1952) was in sore need of restoration and landmark status for years. Although the business advertised was long gone, the sign continued to mark the neighborhood and reinforce the city's culinary identity (see plate 38).[4]

While traveling the pre-interstate U.S. 40 across the United States at midcentury, novelist George R. Stewart recognized the importance of signs in Western towns, where the architecture was modest and recent compared to that in the East. These towns were highly dependent on the road for their commerce. Although the landscape has changed radically in the ensuing years, signs continue to dominate, if not define, many Western towns visually. Of Roosevelt, Utah, Stewart wrote, "A future historian, deprived of other evidence, could reconstruct much of the life of this town from the signs displayed along both sides of the block. Two hotels, two cafés, and a grill indicate its preoccupation with the traveler . . . The Architecture—low, flat-roofed, undistinguished—offers little that is outstanding, but is fully characteristic of its time and place. The hotel is carrying on, though in a modest way, the old false-front tradition of the early cow-town."[5]

Signs in ethnic neighborhoods are particularly valuable graphics in the public realm. The languages appearing on signs, and distinctive modifications sometimes made to basic commercial architecture, establish the presence of a distinct community. Some very well-known examples would be the Chinatowns of San Francisco, Los Angeles, and Chicago, which were marked for the general public and the tourist in the 1920s and 1930s with Anglo-Asian architecture (often designed by Caucasians) and flamboyant signage. The abundance of signs helps to establish a festival atmosphere conducive to buying and having a meal. Cities like San Francisco consider the vintage signs in Chinatown (and other recognized districts) as character-defining features of the neighborhood and exempt them from limitations in size and placement required by new codes.[6] The signs in Chinatown, unlike the architecture, are genuine, representing actual individuals who once worked, or continue to work, on site. For other neighborhoods, ones populated primarily by only one or two cultures, the language alone, in graphic form, identifies the residents; the architecture is hardly modified. In many cases, the current inhabitants have occupied the area for only a few years. Inexpensive signs and ephemera like posters can serve efficiently and inexpensively to establish place for new communities.

As of the turn of the twenty-first century, historic graphics have become increasingly recognized for their powerful contribution to reinforcing a sense of place. In some cases, an abundance of signs itself is essential in establishing the character of a community. In many seaside communities with their traditional boardwalks and amusements, the abundance of neon and incandescent bulb signs on rooftops or simple parapets mixes easily with the casual, painted

(opposite) **Figure 123** Cunningham's Drug Store (Robert Bierly, 1954) and Merchant's National Bank (Louis Sullivan, 1914), Fourth Avenue, Grinnell, Iowa. A dramatic aberration from the rhythm, style, and materials of the rest of the street, the midcentury Cunningham's building appeared doomed when the original business folded in 2003. However, recent thinking by preservationists appears to be more inclusive, even in towns ruled by very tight sets of guidelines, and the building, although somewhat altered, continues to be adaptively reused.
COURTESY OF THE DRAKE COMMUNITY LIBRARY, GRINNELL, IOWA.

frame buildings (see plate 39). There is a lightness and playfulness to both sign and architecture. In many cases the signs are, in fact, far more substantial than the architecture. In contrast to this exuberance, the signs of many interior New England towns, modest in scale and materials, also speak volumes about the nature of the communities. As cities and villages have faced the pressures of growth and the anonymity of corporate businesses, their leaders have progressively recognized that it is essential to preserve distinctive neighborhood features in order to maintain individuality.

Movie theater facades, which are usually dominated by signs and marquees, often provide a visual anchor for a neighborhood, a glowing hearth for the street at night. Sometimes the name of a cinema identifies place directly, if it alludes to cross streets nearby, the town name, or a community historical figure. Unfortunately, many current municipal codes, the product of 1970s and 1980s reductivism, prevent the creation of such assets today. Either the nature of these signs far exceeds square footage allowances per business, or setback requirements for off-street parking preclude the creation of facades butting sidewalks and overhanging marquees. In 2003, a devoted local group raised funds for a facade restoration and cinema expansion for the Strand Theatre in Grinnell, Iowa. A miniaturized re-creation of the old vertical sign was based on photographs of the original, but the projecting marquee, designed by local architect Dan Tindall and sign company Image First, was an invention of the twenty-first century, inspired by marquees from the 1940s. Creating this marquee required not just a variance (which was not permitted by code) but rewriting the sign ordinance to accommodate the nonconforming scale, proportion, and lighting of this proposal.[7]

The threat to historic signs must be considered alongside the continuing threat to storefronts and facades. Although nineteenth-century commercial architecture has long been revered in America, fine examples from the twentieth century are often overlooked or underappreciated. State offices of the National Trust's Main Street Center bemoan the fact that this occurs routinely. Kennedy Smith, former director of the National Main Street Center, blamed this on the fact that much of the early literature from the National Trust and other preservation-minded organizations focused most of its attention on nineteenth-century buildings and streetscapes.[8] Some of the earliest success stories came from towns in New England and the Northeast, where buildings were older than most in the rest of the country and new signs were patterned after those in vintage engravings. This led to a belief that the rest of America should look this way in order to have historic legitimacy. Many assumed that elaborate Italianate cornices and window hoods were required for a marketable vintage appearance. Sign codes and guidelines for communities west and south of these better-known historic Eastern communities tended to favor nonelectric storefront signs, even though many of these towns were barely established before the time that electricity became a common municipal amenity.

Western Oklahoma provides just one of many examples where the original, regional commercial architecture was underappreciated until recent years. Known as "Plains commercial" buildings, these structures are noticeably horizontal compared to the vertical proportioning of the typical business building found in town centers of Ohio or Connecticut. Often only a single story in height, they present the most basic parapet to the street, the profile undulating up and down in steps only a single brick or two high. Ornamentation is often provided by a basic graphic pattern stretched across the full width of the structure, a decorative flourish frequently repeated building to building. These structures were erected during an era when the automobile was swiftly becoming the conveyance of preference, and speed meant longer streets, wider storefronts, and less ornament and fuss per foot of frontage. Many towns in the state were created during oil boom years, when the country seemed in a rush to accommodate the motorcar, so these design characteristics seem highly appropriate.

Historic legitimacy and value need to be considered for commercial architecture that may not conform to preconceived notions of history. The building and sign for Cunningham Drugs (Robert Bierly, 1954) in Grinnell, Iowa, seem a wild contrast to the conservative late-nineteenth-century structures around them (fig. 123). All too easily, they could have been deemed by twenty-first-century preservationists as unfit for the historic look of the town and completely disrespectful of their highly revered neighbor, Louis Sullivan's Merchant's National Bank (1914).[9] Enforcement of Grinnell's Downtown Design Guidelines (2002) has brought a remarkable consistency to the town center; many commercial buildings are trimmed with the same dark green and tan paint and have color-coordinated awnings. Signage is subtle; most consists of small lettering on awning valences and fascia boards.[10] The Cunningham building is quite unique in this environment. It is only one story tall, with a flat roof slab that projects over the sidewalk and a rakishly angled fin sign with (at one time) large, script neon lettering. Instead of continuing the street wall, the architecture emphatically punctures the otherwise consistent roofline of the corridor.[11] When Mr. Cunningham closed the original business, it may have seemed an opportune time to rethink the use of the site. But community memory of afternoons spent at Cunningham's lunch counter stirred up such affection that the building was spared demolition.[12] "Right" or "wrong" though the building may be for its neighbor or the street, it appears to be spared from destruction, at least until the judgment of the next generation. The structure is as much sign as it is architecture; isolating the angular sign from the building and evaluating its square footage based on a rectangular template was a setup for failure. Yet, typical of most city ordinances, this is precisely what happened. Ultimately, it was necessary for the city of Grinnell to grant special permission to the new owner in order for the fin to continue in use as a sign. The town guidelines prohibit illumination except by "dim internal lighting," so the original neon look was forbidden for new businesses in the building.

Many other commercial buildings and storefronts across America face demolition or unsympathetic alterations—a large number because they have not yet been recognized as historic. In many cases, the graphics are carefully linked to the architectural composition. The Lenox Lounge, just off 125th Street in Harlem (1939), displays a remarkably intact, inventively detailed 1930s storefront, with burgundy Vitrolite, nickel detailing, and original period lettering at the fascia and around the doorframe (fig. 124). In 1999, the facade received a costly renovation. Unfortunately, few buildings on or immediately around this famous corridor are protected, through local historic designation, from the whims of future development. The Lenox Lounge remains as vulnerable as its less jewel-like neighbors, except for the zeal of its present owners. Miami Beach has long recognized the importance of protecting both architecture and graphics from this same era. However, graphic defacement of buildings from the 1930s and 1940s along State Street in Chicago reveals the need for knowledgeable leadership in that city to

(opposite) Figure 124
Lenox Lounge (architect unknown, 1939), Malcolm X Boulevard, New York City. This is one of the increasingly rare, intact American "storefront" designs from the 1930s, designed with every element coordinated, as if it were a streamlined appliance or a machine. In many cases, these first-floor, applied facades are not historically designated even in a major city like New York.
PHOTO BY AUTHOR, 2009.

CONCLUSION **521**

educate, advise, and provide incentive for suitable improvements informed by (though not necessarily mimicking) history. Commercial buildings from more recent decades still await meaningful recognition and protection. Better known and highly regarded, but still at risk, are the Googie-style coffee shops of southern California and the motels of Wildwood, New Jersey. A critical mass of the character-defining "doo-wop" signs and motel buildings in Wildwood, with their rakish angles and jet age or tiki imagery, have been demolished since 2002, despite the surge of appreciation for their worth by academics, locals, and the national media, just prior to the turn of the millennium. No local preservation ordinance was in place to protect them from a boom economy and an insatiable market for condominiums.[13] There are smaller, less heralded counterparts to these examples from coast to coast where historic commercial architecture and signs are disappearing quickly. A vast number have been lost already, their relatively brief existences barely documented in photographs.

The new obsession for protecting historic signs and architecture from the late nineteenth and early twentieth century should not blindside communities from permitting new signs of distinction, or new commercial buildings that respect both pedestrian and motorist, to be created. There is great opportunity for continuity between past and future, even with new technologies emerging. As some communities recode the Tamiami Trail and other pathways into town so that they segue in a more respectful fashion into highly ordered town centers, it may be time to examine what those urban centers should be and what they should look like. Controls on the core might be relaxed gently in years to come, just as the parameters for the strip become more numerous and demanding. As those limits shrink on older town centers, it may be possible for the advertiser to once again express the potential of new design and technology. The presence of the individual will not be quite as suppressed as it is currently in many communities. Perhaps most important, in the future, we will see more layers of history permitted to overlap, to be on display simultaneously, allowing the presence of many owners and many eras to be read as one walks or drives down the street.

Notes

INTRODUCTION

1. The focus of this section of the introduction is on the northern portion of the Tamiami Trail, which runs through the city of Sarasota and continues south. The Tamiami Trail is a highway constructed in the 1920s to link Tampa and Miami, hence its name.

2. The *decorated shed* is a term coined by Robert Venturi in his 1972 book *Learning from Las Vegas*. It refers to architecture that is otherwise plain but has symbols (and ornament) applied to it in such a way that they always remain distinct from the architecture. This is quite unlike "duck," or mimetic, architecture, where the building is created in the form of a symbol. Venturi used the term *duck* in reference to a relatively famous Long Island roadside stand where poultry was sold. In the case of the Publix buildings, one side of the simple structure was saturated with advertising and ornament, meaningful symbols and mere "eye-candy." It was unusually animated with information and visual stimulation for a grocery store. See Robert Venturi, Denise Scott Brown, and Steven Izenour, *Learning from Las Vegas: The Forgotten Symbolism of Architectural Form* (1972; revised ed., Cambridge, MA: MIT Press, 1977), 89, 90; Tom Wolfe, "Electrographic Architecture," *Architectural Design* 39 (July 1969): 380–82.

3. Pressure from civic groups and business leaders has led many communities to adopt restrictive codes to control signs. One municipality often simply borrows these codes from the next, with little analysis as to the local vision for the commercial landscape (except for getting rid of "sign excess"). Often, town leaders consider a flawed or inappropriate sign code better than none at all. Since signs in the commercial landscape so closely reflect the public's changing interests, needs, and desires, they also supply the focus of much public debate.

4. To better understand and appreciate the subject of this book, it is necessary to dispel years of confusion that have led many to hold a bias against signs of all types. The significance of on-premise commercial signs has been diminished through the years by indiscriminately lumping them in with outdoor advertisements, like billboards, and condemning them as a blight on the landscape. In present-day parlance, a sign has loosely come to be understood as any kind of graphic in the built environment, be it an advertisement, a shop identification, or a set of directions. Because of this broad and vague definition, it has become necessary in the sign trade and in government planning to attach the term *on-premise* to the word *sign* to distinguish a graphic that is physically attached to the location of a business from all others that are not. The focus of this book is exclusively on the commercial on-site or on-premise sign.

5. Peirce F. Lewis, "Axioms for Reading the Landscape: Some Guides to the American Scene," in *The Interpretation of Ordinary Landscapes: Geographical Essays*, ed. D. W. Meinig (New York: Oxford University Press, 1979).

6. *The Oxford English Dictionary*, 2nd ed. (Oxford: Clarendon Press, 1989) defines a sign as "a characteristic device attached to, or placed in front of, an inn . . . or shop, as a means of distinguishing it from others or directing attention to it; in later use commonly a board bearing a name or other inscription, with or without some ornament or picture." The earliest use of the word *sign* is to identify an enterprise on site. So context is key to meaning. Etymologically, *sign* comes via the Old French *signe*, from the Latin *signum*, meaning "mark." See John Ayto, *Dictionary of Word Origins* (New York: Arcade, 1990). The earliest documented use of the word in print was in 1467, in the tradesmen's book, *English Gilds*: "That no person sille none ale out of his place, but he have a signe at his dorre." See Robert E. Lewis, ed., *Middle English Dictionary: Plan and Bibliography Supplement* (Ann Arbor: University of Michigan Press, 1984), 852. Most, if not all, appearances of the word in print over the following four hundred years refer to shop signs or to signs hanging in front of inns or alehouses. From the fifteenth century, sign has been associated with place.

7. Venturi began to establish value for signs and symbols in the built world with the publication of two books, *Complexity and Contradiction in* Architecture (New York: Museum of Modern Art, 1966) and *Learning from Las Vegas*. One important exception to this publication drought on the subject is *Signs in America's Auto Age: Signatures of Landscape and Place* by John A. Jakle and Keith A. Sculle (Iowa City: University of Iowa Press, 2004).

    J. B. Jackson lectured and wrote essays in the journal *Landscape*, beginning in the 1950s. "It would be hard (though not impossible) to exaggerate the extent of this blight," he wrote in one. "But still we must give these roadside establishments their due. They are entitled to their day in court, and so far, they have not had it. Many have experienced driving for hour after hour across emptiness—desert or prairie—which was not blemished by highway stands. How relieved and delighted one always is to finally see somewhere in the distance the jumble of billboards and gas pumps . . . these are very welcome sights, and even the commands to EAT, GAS UP, GET FREE ICE WATER AND STICKERS, have a comforting effect"; *Landscapes: Selected*

Writings of J. B. Jackson, ed. Ervin H. Zube (Amherst: University of Massachusetts Press, 1970), 57. Jackson also described the value of "the stranger's path" through town. This was the route that began at the train depot, bus station, or highway. Basically, it was lined by businesses that catered to the outsider or visitor and was marked by the boldest signs, unmannered and undiscriminating. To Jackson, "The path . . . has the prime function of introducing new life to the city, of bringing the city into touch with the outside world," while, naturally, also bringing the rural stranger into touch with the city; "The Stranger's Path," *Landscape* 7 (Autumn 1957): 14.

8. Paul Groth, "Frameworks for Cultural Landscapes Study," in *Understanding Ordinary Landscapes,* ed. Paul Groth and Todd W. Bressi (New Haven: Yale University Press, 1997), 3.

CHAPTER 1. *The Making of Main Street: Transformation and Invention on the Commercial Frontier, 1700s–1899*

1. Sylvia Doughty Fries, *The Urban Idea in Colonial America* (Philadelphia: Temple University Press, 1977), 40–43, 48–50, 79–94, 138–39, 152–53; Joseph S. Wood, *The New England Village* (Baltimore: Johns Hopkins University Press, 1997), 14–15, 44, 89; John R. Stilgoe, *Common Landscape of America, 1580 to 1845* (New Haven, CT: Yale University Press, 1982), 43–57; Edwin B. Bronner, *William Penn's "Holy Experiment": The Founding of Pennsylvania, 1681-1701* (New York: Temple University Publications, distributed by Columbia University Press, 1962), 61; Albert Cook Meyers, ed., *Narratives of Early Pennsylvania, West Jersey and Delaware, 1630-1707* (New York: Charles Scribner's Sons, 1912), 242–44; Jean R. Soderlund, ed., *William Penn and the Founding of Pennsylvania: A Documentary History* (Philadelphia: University of Pennsylvania Press, 1983), 82–85, 204–6.

2. Wood, *New England Village,* 98–133. The full "encampment" observation is as follows: "A village, with its scattered white houses, often reminds one of an encampment, with its white tents, that tomorrow morning, at the sound of the bugle, will be struck, and disappear"; N. H. Chamberlain, paper on New England Architecture read before the New England Historic Genealogical Society, Boston, September 4, 1858. Describing early-nineteenth-century New Haven, architectural historian Vincent Scully wrote, "Around the Green, each house stood free on its plot of ground, defining the central open space as ships moored around it, not as a wall. The concept of the row house was resisted in such towns . . . The major definition of space was eventually to be accomplished by trees"; *American Architecture and Urbanism* (1969; revised ed., New York: Henry Holt, 1988), 30.

3. Wilbur Zelinsky, "The Pennsylvania Town: An Overdue Geographical Account," *Geographical Review* 67 (April 1977): 131, 133–37, 144–45; Peirce F. Lewis, "Small Town in Pennsylvania," *Annals of the Association of American Geographers* 62 (June 1972): 338.

4. In the 1760s and 1770s, most Williamsburg taverns added one-story piazzas across their fronts, along the street, which served as open reception spaces. Also, tavern plans were reworked in the second half of the eighteenth century to accommodate more specialized activities. The best taverns, like the Raleigh and Wetherburn's, added private dining rooms, billiard rooms, and bar rooms for their customers. Carl Lounsbury (Senior Architectural Historian, Colonial Williamsburg) in discussion with the author, March 5, 2008, and in an e-mail message to the author, September 21, 2009.

5. Cecil A. Meadows, *Trade Signs and Their Origins* (London: Routledge & Kegan Paul, 1957), 2.

6. *The Book of the General Laws for the People within the Jurisdiction of Connecticut* (1673) quoted in Margaret C. Vincent, "Some Suitable Signe . . . for the direction of Strangers' Signboards and the Enterprise of Innkeeping in Connecticut," in *Lions & Eagles & Bulls: Early American Tavern and Inn Signs from the Connecticut Historical Society,* ed. Susan P. Schoelwer (Princeton, NJ: Connecticut Historical Society in association with Princeton University Press, 2000), 38.

7. Johann David Schoepf, *Travels in the Confederation [1783–1784],* trans. and ed. Alfred J. Morrison (Philadelphia: J. Campbell, 1911), 2:4.

8. However, these classic signs were not the only method of identifying a place of hospitality. "It is not always the custom to hang shields before taverns, but they are easily to be identified by the great numbers of miscellaneous papers and advertisements with which the walls and doors of these publick houses are plastered; generally, the more of such bills are to be seen on a house, the better it will be found to be." Ibid., 2:30.

9. Stilgoe, *Common Landscape,* 97; Wood, *New England Village,* 96, 116; Louise Andrews Kent, *Village Greens of New England* (New York: M. Barrows, 1948), 53.

10. Phillip D. Zimmerman, "Reading the Signs: An Object History of Tavern Signs from Connecticut, 1750-1850," in Schoelwer, *Lions & Eagles & Bulls,* 30. The importance of signs in the eighteenth century was revealed in the respect given to the profession of sign painting in the colonies. According to William Williams (1721–91), a British portraitist and scenery and sign painter who emigrated to America in the 1740s, signs in eighteenth-century Britain served as "the nursery and reward of painters, for great sums were expended on these ornaments, and the best artists of the age employed in executing them." See Susan P. Schoelwer, "Introduction: Rediscovering the Public Art of Early American Signs," in ibid., 9. Many sign painters were also coach and carriage painters and often earned handsome fees for the decoration of military standards. See Nancy Finlay, "Lions and Eagles and Other Images on Early Inn Signs," in ibid., 64. William Hogarth was known to paint a sign or two under the pseudonym Hagarty, and he displayed his fascination with signs by foregrounding them in many of

his drawings. Often, the signs he included contributed to the message he wanted the work to convey. He served on the hanging committee for at least one early exhibition of signboards, in 1762. See Fritz Endell, *Old Tavern Signs: An Excursion in the History of Hospitality* (Boston: Houghton, Mifflin, 1916), 139, 156, 212. Benjamin West, the first American-born artist of note, is known to have painted at least two signs before leaving the colonies for England in 1759. He trained under William Williams. Thomas Cole, founder of the Hudson River school, painted signs and stage scenery in the early 1820s in Steubenville, Ohio. See Schoelwer, "Introduction," 9.

11. Endell, *Old Tavern Signs*, 97.
12. Meadows, *Trade Signs*, 3, 25.
13. Endell, *Old Tavern Signs*, 271.
14. Kathryn A. Morrison, *English Shops and Shopping* (London: Yale University Press, 2003), 42.
15. Maury Klein and Harvey A. Kantor, *Prisoners of Progress: American Industrial Cities, 1850–1920* (New York: Macmillan, 1976), 71.
16. Vincent, "Some Suitable Sign," 48.
17. Ibid., 50.
18. Ibid., 51–52.
19. James D. Kornwolf, with the assistance of Georgiana W. Kornwolf, *Architecture and Town Planning in Colonial North America* (Baltimore: Johns Hopkins University Press, 2002), 23; Hugh Morrison, *Early American Architecture: From the First Colonial Settlements to the National Period* (New York: Oxford University Press, 1952), 92.
20. Richard V. Francaviglia, *Main Street Revisited: Time, Space, and Image Building in Small-Town America* (Iowa City: University of Iowa Press, 1996), 12, 18.
21. The tavern was mentioned in the *Town Records* in 1738, and the sign was mentioned in 1746. See Samuel Adams Drake, *Old Boston Taverns and Tavern Clubs* (Boston: W. A. Butterfield 1917), 67, 114.
22. Ann Smart Martin, "Commercial Space as Consumption Arena: Retail Stores in Early Virginia," *Perspectives in Vernacular Architecture* 8 (2000): 201–18.
23. Ann Smart Martin and Mark R. Wenger, "The Restoration of Williamsburg," 2006, www.history.org/history/teaching/enewsletter/volume4/july06/restoration.
24. Richard Longstreth, *The Buildings of Main Street: Guide to American Commercial Architecture* (Washington, DC: Preservation Press, 1987), 16.
25. In other words, the *open* garden and piazza—the private spaces—were given a solid, protective face. The opposite held true for the *solid* building, which was given an open, glass face. Robert Stockton (architectural historian and adjunct professor in the History Department at the College of Charleston), e-mail messages to the author, March 25–27, 2008.
26. See Lewis, "Small Town in Pennsylvania," 330.
27. There are many exceptions to this generally stated trend. Woodstock, Vermont, for example—an exceptionally prosperous town—focused commercial development in one area off one end of its common. This concentration of construction, in the mid-nineteenth century, was as dense and continuous as that in any Midwestern or Mid-Atlantic town its size. Many New England towns benefited from large commercial blocks developed to house multiple businesses. In Woodstock, it was the Edson Block and its immediate neighbors, part of a continuous strip of two-story commercial structures. Elsewhere, the long blocks would sit as distinct pieces, surrounded by space, in the loose arrangement of buildings around commons and greens. In Grafton, Massachusetts, it was the Wheeler Block (1806), followed by the Warren Block (1862). In Barre, Massachusetts, the amalgamation of buildings known as the Jenkins Block (1855) would serve multiple tenants and help bring a decidedly more urban element to the town center.
28. Johann Friedrich Geist, *Arcades: The History of a Building Type* (Cambridge, MA: MIT Press, 1983), 37; Morrison, *English Shops and Shopping*, 25.
29. Morrison, *English Shops and Shopping*, 22.
30. Ibid., 41.
31. Scully, *American Architecture and Urbanism*, 80; Robert Venturi, Denise Scott Brown, and Steven Izenour, *Learning from Las Vegas: The Forgotten Symbolism of Architectural Form* (1972; revised ed., Cambridge, MA: MIT Press, 1977), 13, 18.
32. Eric C. Stohr, *Bonanza Victorian: Architecture and Society in Colorado Mining Towns* (Albuquerque: University of New Mexico Press, 1975), 61–65.
33. Longstreth, *Buildings of Main Street*, 16.
34. Klein and Kantor, *Prisoners of Progress*, 129.
35. Jan Nash, "Iowa's Main Street Commercial Architecture," National Register of Historic Places, Multiple Property Documentation, Iowa, National Register #64500811, E8.
36. Carole Rifkind, *Main Street: The Face of Urban America* (New York: Harper & Row, 1977), 57.
37. Lewis Eldon Atherton, *Main Street on the Middle Border* (Bloomington: Indiana University Press, 1954), 4–7.
38. Nash, "Iowa's Main Street," E2–3.
39. Charles Dickens, *American Notes for General Circulation* (1842; reprint, ed. Patricia Ingham, London: Penguin Books, 2000), 34.
40. Ibid., 81.
41. Peter Nicholson, *Encyclopedia of Architecture: A Dictionary of the Science and Practice of Architecture, Building, Carpentry, Etc. . . .* , ed. Edward Lomax and Thomas Gunyon (New York: Johnson, Fry & Co., 185–?), 15, 204, 413; Russell Sturgis, *A Dictionary of Architecture and Building: Biographical, Historical, and Descriptive* (New York: Macmillan, 1901–2), 1:145, 682; 2:14, 155; Cyril M. Harris, ed., *Illustrated Dictionary of Historic Architecture* (1977; reprint, New York: Dover, 1983), 141, 210, 235.
42. Nathaniel Dearborn was the author, and he included such lettering as Sign Painter's Roman, block letters, Old English, German text, and Jewish and Greek alphabets. See Charles

Louis Henry Wagner, *Wagner's Blueprint Textbook of Sign and Showcard Lettering* (Boston: Wagner School of Sign Arts, 1926), 90–91.

43. Charles L. H. Wagner, *The Story of Signs: An Outline History of the Sign Arts from the Earliest Recorded Times to the Present d'Atomic Age* (Boston: MacGibbon, 1954), n.p.

44. The popularity of glass on the commercial facade was reinforced by the significant reduction in awning heights late in the century. This corresponded in time with the creation and adoption of Luxfer prismatic glass tiles, which fit in the transom area above the display windows. First marketed in 1896 by the Radiating Light Company of Chicago, these tiles significantly increased the amount of light that could penetrate the typically deep and narrow interior spaces of commercial establishments. They were applied in a tight grid between the fascia and display window; the top of the awning was situated just below them. When the awning was sloped less severely, it became difficult to see graphics that were placed on the apron, or top. Since potential wall space was "stolen" from the storefront to accommodate the prism glass, and no new solid, sign-bearing space was provided anywhere else, sign makers found themselves increasingly frustrated. See Dietrich Neumann, " 'The Century's Triumph in Lighting': The Luxfer Prism Companies and their Contribution to Early Modern Architecture," *Journal of the Society of Architectural Historians* 54 (March 1995): 24.

45. Dickens, *American Notes*, 34.

46. Many other projecting signs in urban America, by contrast, borrowed from a sign-design tradition that dates back to medieval London. The custom of hanging an enlarged representation of an object over the sidewalk to identify a shop or hospitality establishment continued on the streets of towns as diverse as Milwaukee and Charleston. Giant umbrellas, top hats, and beer steins communicated clearly what was to be found beyond the facade.

47. Longstreth, *The Buildings of Main Street*, 31; Nash, "Iowa's Main Street," E17–21.

48. Miller, *Inland Architect and Builder* 17 (January 1885): 140.

49. *St. Paul and Minnesota's Pioneer Press*, November 23, 1884, quoted in Larry Millet, *Lost Twin Cities* (Saint Paul: Minnesota Historical Society Press, 1992), B9.

50. Margot Gayle and Carol Gayle, *Cast-Iron Architecture in America: The Significance of James Bogardus* (New York: W. W. Norton, 1998), vii; Carl W. Condit, *American Building Art: The Nineteenth Century* (New York: Oxford University Press, 1960), 30–31.

51. Gayle, *Cast-Iron Architecture*, 221–22.

52. Many, if not most, department stores of the turn-of-the-century built their presence in the community as a public institution might, choosing to avoid grand signs. Their often discreet identifications no doubt established an air of higher quality than did the more flamboyant signs of smaller neighbors. These enormous stores had worked for years to become household names and were already so well known in their neighborhoods that signage in scale with the enormity of their buildings was seen as a potential, if not gross, redundancy.

CHAPTER 2. *The Great Blight Way: Electricity and Reform from Main Street to City Center, 1900–1917*

1. According to one published contemporary account, the first electric sign advertised Admiral cigarettes and was erected at Broadway and Fifth Avenue in New York City in 1893, with the second, for a summer resort at Manhattan Beach, Long Island, following shortly thereafter. See "Electrical Display Advertising," *Signs of the Times* 14 (November 1910): 3. However, another account has it that the first electric sign was the one for the summer resort and that its date was May 1892; placement was on the uptown wall of the old Cumberland Hotel at Twenty-third Street and Broadway. See S. N. Holliday, "Through the Years: With Electrical Advertising on the Great White Way," *Signs of the Times* 68 (May 1931): 30–31, and Clarence B. Lovell, "Broadway Blazed Its First Electric Sign Just Thirty Years Ago," *Signs of the Times* 41 (May 1922): 14. Tama Starr and Edward Hayman's comprehensive account of electric advertising and family businesses dates the first sign to July 1892 and notes that the Edison General Electric Company erected it. See Tama Starr and Edward Hayman, *Signs and Wonders: The Spectacular Marketing of America* (New York: Doubleday, 1998), 55.

2. Bayrd Still, *Mirror for Gotham: New York as Seen by Contemporaries from Dutch Days to the Present* (New York: University Press, 1956), 188.

3. "Shop Fronts a Maze of All Kinds of Advertising Signs," *Chicago Daily Tribune*, November 27, 1898.

4. Many of these new graphics were off-site advertisements.

5. See, e.g., "Electric Signs in Muskogee," *Signs of the Times* 14 (November 1910): 23; "Fort Dodge, Iowa, Boasts a Sign Lamp Per Capita—America's Brightest, Busiest Streets," *Signs of the Times* 36 (July 1917): 18, and "Introducing Electric Signs: How They Were Popularized among the Business Men of Meridian, Mississippi," *Signs of the Times* 14 (November 1910): 20.

6. *(Guilford, CT) Shore Line Times*, June 11, 1908.

7. *Signs of the Times* 2 (October 1906): 1.

8. In addition to this popular type, there were other options that were frequently encountered in the early days but did not prove to have longevity. They included "punch out" signs, which consisted of a sign cabinet, internally illuminated by bulbs, with the sign face perforated by tiny tabs or awl points punched through the metal face—creating the effect of miniature light bulbs. The graphics of these signs were composed by these points of light but also with a sparkly, painted sign surface employing glass smalts. Other signs were built with internally painted, opal-glass faces or milk-glass graphics exposed through custom-cut openings in otherwise solid metal faces.

9. William S. Reid, *Signs of the Times* 2 (November 1906): 4.
10. It may have been a fortuitous effect or the result of immediate design influence, but the reduction of many signs to mere symbols at the turn of the twentieth century coincides immediately with the powerfully simple graphics on display at that time in the posters and advertisements of Lucian Bernhard (or possibly Ludwig Hohlwein, or the Beggarstaff Brothers in England). Bernhard's work relied solely upon the potent form of the product pictured and an absolute minimum of type. Although the German designer did not immigrate to the United States until 1923, it is possible that his effect may have been felt through immediate publication of his work worldwide. More likely affecting the work of American sign artists was the lingering effect of history and the memory of early sign traditions in Europe and the United States, which turned to images in place of words.
11. According to historian and sign artist Charles L. H. Wagner, there was at least one sign painter's manual—authored by A. P. Boyce and published in 1875—in wide circulation during the nineteenth century. However, it is difficult to discern how influential it may have been in the far reaches of America. See Charles L. H. Wagner, *The Story of Signs: An Outline History of the Sign Arts from Earliest Recorded Times to the Present "Atomic Age"* (Boston: Arthur MacGibbon, 1954), 94.
12. Other manuals included *Elements of Lettering and Sign Painting, Prepared for Students of the International Correspondence Schools* (Scranton, PA: Colliery Engineer, 1899); Sydney Hackes, *David's Practical Letterer: Instructions in Commercial Lettering with Brush and Pen* (New York: T. Davids, 1903); Charles L. S. Strong, *Detroit School of Lettering*, series of 10 booklets (Detroit: Detroit School of Lettering, 1905); A. Ashmun Kelly, *The Expert Sign Painter: A Book of Reference Designed for the Use of Practical Sign Painters and Letterers* (Malvern, PA, 1911); and Charles L. S. Strong, *Strong's Book of Designs* (Detroit: Detroit School of Lettering, 1910).
13. J. H. Van Dyne, "Sign Painting in New York City: Metropolis Now Divides Honors with Other Cities," *Signs of the Times* 13 (September 1910): 25.
14. William Goltz, "Electric Sky or Roof Signs," *Signs of the Times* 1 (July 1906): 7.
15. George Williams, "Electrical Publicity—A Talk with Those Interested," *Signs of the Times* 5 (December 1907): 9.
16. Stanley Harris, "Electric Sign Suggestions and a Sketch Idea," *Signs of the Times* 32 (June 1916): 20.
17. C. Matlock Price, "A Renaissance in Commercial Architecture: Some Recent Buildings in Uptown New York," *Architectural Record* 31 (May 1912): 449-69.
18. W. S. Wright (Flexlume Sign Company, Buffalo, NY), "Architect Protects His Client by Co-operating with the Electric Sign Manufacturer," *Signs of the Times* 36 (June 1917): 21.
19. "Praises Posters," *Architectural Record* 31 (April 1912): 447.
20. Longstreth, *The Buildings of Main Street: A Guide to American Commercial Architecture* (Washington, DC: Preservation Press, 1987), 68-75.
21. This subject is addressed comprehensively in Bernice L. Thomas, *America's 5 & 10 Cent Stores: The Kress Legacy* (New York: John Wiley & Sons, 1997).
22. Early theaters often named themselves "museums" in order to appear more respectable to the middle class and thus counteract any misgivings members of the public might have about patronizing such establishments. Phineas T. Barnum is often credited as the man who first developed the marketing concept of entertainment cloaked in the guise of education. His earliest theatres (known as Barnum's American Museum and Barnum's New American Museum) opened in 1841 and 1865, respectively. Other early theaters, such as New York's Olympia (J. B. McElfatrick & Son, 1895) and the Hippodrome (Frederick Thompson, 1905), had signs that were selectively confined to the arch, defined panels on the facade, or some sort of configuration over the portico.
23. Motion-picture theaters required large-scale electric signs to lure customers, and it was no easy task to integrate such enormous graphics with architectural compositions. Historical styles presented questions of proportion and established forms. The modest Dreamland (1907) in Portland, Maine, New England's first purpose-built movie house, incongruously combined a broad arch with a Belgian stepped gable, but the Jacobean facade panels and detailing generated a full-width sign frame that connected well with the windows and roofline features. More ambitious was the Liberty Theater (c. 1909) in Los Angeles, where the sign maintained its physical independence above the parapet, giving it the scale of a rooftop advertising spectacular. Unlike off-site advertising, this sign worked closely with the architecture, following the arched cornice and fitting neatly around a statue mounted at its crest.
24. "Novel Electrical Display on Rialto Theatre Attracts Both Eye and Ear," *Signs of the Times* 32 (June 1916): 26.
25. Peter B. Wight, "The Transmutation of a Residence Street: Michigan Boulevard, Chicago," *Architectural Record* 27 (April 1910): 285-93.
26. Journals such as *Architectural Record* were still discussing the phenomenon of the auto showroom district in the late 1920s. Auto showrooms, one article claimed, tend to create new districts. Then, once six to seven auto establishments emerge, a bank is bound to follow. "Technical News and Research: Featuring Store Buildings," *Architectural Record* 65 (June 1929): 583-606.
27. Bellamy's vision of the year 2000, devoid of the chaos of the city of the 1880s, was a call to action for peaceful self-socialism of the capitalist order, the medicine that might heal the full organism of the city. After *Uncle Tom's Cabin* and *Ben Hur*, *Looking Backward* was the most popular book of the late nineteenth and early twentieth century, printed in the millions. Bellamy clubs sprang up all over the United States and included social workers, farmers, businessmen, and housewives in their ranks. See Erich Fromm in the introduction to Edward Bellamy, *Looking Backward: 2000-1887* (1888; reprint, New York: New American Library, 1960), v-vi, and

John L. Thomas, *Alternative America: Henry George, Edward Bellamy, Henry Demarest Lloyd, and the Adversary Tradition* (Cambridge, MA: Belknap Press of Harvard University Press, 1983), 262–63.

Bellamy's book was a natural model for the progressive movement. Where the progressives faced corrupt government, he described a benign entity looking out for the well-being of the citizens. Where they faced a cacophony of advertising messages, the streets of his imagined Boston in 2000 were restrained and lined with statuary. "Nowadays . . . there is no destination of the surplus wealth so popular as the adornment of the city, which all enjoy in equal degree," said host Dr. Leete to the book's protagonist, Julian West (18). What better philosophy to match the goals of the City Beautiful movement? In Bellamy's Boston of 2000, the physical manifestation of competition (i.e., advertisements) did not exist, nor was there need of them since competition was eliminated as a great waste. Julian marveled how most of the city that he saw before him was new—and yet there were no stores. Indeed, it was explained to him, there was but one store per city quarter, and it was identified in a very subtle manner. "There was nothing in the exterior aspect of the edifice to suggest a store . . . There was no display of goods in the great windows, or any device to advertise wares . . . Nor was there any sort of sign or legend on the front of the building to indicate the character of the business carried on there; but instead, above the portal, standing out from the front of the building, a majestic life-size group of statuary, the central figure of which was a female ideal of Plenty, with her cornucopia" (45). At his return back to Boston of the 1880s, advertisements confronted him everywhere, covering "the walls of the building, the windows, . . . the very pavements, everything in fact, save the sky" (206).

Ebenezer Howard admitted to swallowing Bellamy's book whole. Inspired by Bellamy's communal stores, Howard's great glass arcade for shopping, called the Crystal Palace, would obviate an accumulation of signs and individual commercial buildings with their variety of styles and heights. The vast structure would run around a central park and civic center with its public buildings (the city hall, theater, museum, library). But this was not to be a communal supply house run by the state, as in Bellamy's society. The great public markets would be operated by individuals who paid tolls to the municipality for the space they occupied, being free from municipal control except on a few points. As long as a tenant gave satisfaction to the town, no direct competition would be allowed in. See John L. Thomas, *Alternative America*, 360, and Ebenezer Howard, *Garden Cities of To-Morrow* (1902; reprint, ed. F. J. Osborne, Cambridge, MA: MIT Press, 1965), 96, 98.

28. *Signs of the Times* 14 (November 1910): 18.
29. *Architectural Record* 31 (April 1912): 447.
30. "Offensive to the Public Eye," *New York Times*, September 8, 1910.
31. Harry F. Lake, "The Billboard Nuisance," *American City* 3 (August 1910): 219.
32. *New York Times*, July 7, 1910.
33. *New York Times*, January 9, 1909.
34. *New York Times*, March 25, 1911.
35. *New York Times*, December 17, 1899; July 8, 1910; March 24, 1911; April 5, 1914.
36. William H. Wilson, *The City Beautiful Movement* (Baltimore: Johns Hopkins University Press, 1989), 85.
37. Charles Mulford Robinson, *Modern Civic Art; or, The City Made Beautiful*, 1st ed. (1903; reprint, New York: Arno, 1970), 125. Citations, unless noted, are made to this edition.
38. Charles Mulford Robinson, *Modern Civic Art; or, The City Made Beautiful*, 3rd ed. (New York: G. P. Putnam's Sons, 1909), 159–60.
39. Charles Mulford Robinson, *The Improvement of Towns and Cities; or, The Practical Basis of Civic Aesthetics* (New York: G. P. Putnam's Sons, 1901), 79–80, 87–88.
40. Robinson, *Modern Civic Art*, 151–53.
41. Robinson, *Improvement*, 91–93.
42. Gregory Gilmartin, *Shaping the City: New York and the Municipal Art Society* (New York: Clarkson Potter, 1995), 139.
43. Starr and Hayman, *Signs and Wonders*, 27.
44. Stanley K. Schultz, *Constructing Urban Culture: American Cities and City Planning, 1800–1920* (Philadelphia: Temple University Press, 1989), 35–36, 47–48, 57, 75.
45. Frederick C. Howe, *The Modern City and Its Problems* (New York: Charles Scribner's Sons, 1915), 68.
46. Raymond B. Fosdick, "Big Billboards in Big Cities," *American City* 7 (December 1912): 512–14.
47. Gilmartin, *Shaping the City*, 147; "Smash Road Signs and Win Medal," *New York Times*, June 9, 1912.
48. "Call for Artistic Signs: Directors of Municipal Art League-Plan Crusades," *Chicago Daily Tribune*, December 8, 1903.
49. "City to Inspect Signs: Stirred to Action by Fatality During Recent Gale," *Chicago Daily Tribune*, January 5, 1906.
50. "Rid State Street of Monster Signs," *Chicago Daily Tribune*, September 2, 1907.
51. "Chicago 'More Cultured' but Dimmer," *Chicago Daily Tribune*, May 16, 1909.
52. "At a Loss to Bar Fifth Ave. Signs," *New York Times*, July 9, 1910.
53. This was another way for cities to get around the codes. If the scaffolding to support the signs could be eliminated, the signs would have to come down, too. One wonders about the honesty of the statements made by these municipal improvers about liking the signs but hating the supports. "New Electric Signs Offending the Eye," *New York Times*, September 10, 1910.
54. Frank Koester, *Modern City Planning and Maintenance* (New York: McBride, Nast, 1914), 26.
55. Davis quoted in David Nasaw, *Going Out: The Rise and Fall of Public Amusements* (New York: Basic Books, 1993), 7.
56. William Archer, *America To-Day: Observations and Reflections* (New York: Charles Scribner's Sons, 1899), 45.

57. Booth Tarkington, *The Gentleman from Indiana* (New York: Doubleday & McClure, 1899), 329.
58. Ibid, 4.
59. Grinnell, Iowa's primary streets were paved in 1909. For Bryan, Ohio, it was 1912. Even communities on the south side of Chicago, such as Englewood and Roseland, were not paved until after 1900.
60. Tarkington, *Gentleman from Indiana*, 2.
61. Sherwood Anderson, *Poor White* (1920; reprint, Whitefish, MT: Kessinger, 2004), 15
62. Dreiser wrote this description during his 1915 journey from New York City to his hometown of Terre Haute, Indiana; *A Hoosier Holiday* (1916; reprint, Bloomington: Indiana University Press, 1997), 272.
63. Sinclair Lewis, *Main Street; The Story of Carol Kennicott* (New York: Harcourt, Brace, 1921), 416.
64. *Staunton (Virginia) Spectator and Vindicator*, January 19, 1912; April 26, 1912.
65. "Big Vote Favors Paving—Bryan Gets Improvement," *Bryan (OH) Press*, March 28, 1912; "Prospect Good for Highways," *Bryan (OH) Press*, April 4, 1912.
66. Mark J. Bouman, "Luxury and Control: The Urbanity of Street Lighting in Nineteenth-Century Cities," *Journal of Urban History* (November 1987): 12-13.
67. In 1901 more than twenty-five thousand gas street lamps still operated in Chicago. Two years later, an order was placed for the extinguishing of 40% of the gas street lamps in the city's outlying districts; budgetary reasons were cited for this move. Electric lights were preferred in the business districts, however, leaving gas lighting to predominate in residential areas. *South Chicago Daily Calumet*, March 20, 1901; July 10, 1903.
68. Until the public accepted the necessity of a uniform and well-designed system of ornamental street lighting, progressive merchants installed, at their own expense, groups of streetlights. Some states created laws that permitted the creation of assessment districts for the purpose of taxing abutting property. Publications such as the *American City* advised municipalities that they should avoid the accumulation of uncoordinated lighting efforts. See L. A. S. Wood, "The Adequate and Attractive Lighting of City Streets," *American City* 25 (July–December 1921): 466.
69. In communities that regulated signs, electric signs were permitted to be larger than painted signs, thus providing incentive to light up the street by any means possible. Major electric additions to the street were the cause of much excitement, and in most small towns (and many well-established cities) the recipients of much appreciation. In some cases, the favor was courted, or even orchestrated, by the merchant. See, for example, "All about That Big New Electric Sign on Calhoun Street," *Fort Wayne Journal-Gazette*, October 12, 1922.
70. C. E. Varney [Meridian Light and Electric Company], "Introducing Electric Signs," *Signs of the Times* (November 1910): 20.
71. E. M. Jenison, "Fond du Lac's Great White Way," *American City* 7 (September 1912): 246.
72. Advertisement, *Signs of the Times* (May 1906): 4.
73. Harold L. Platt, *The Electric City: Energy and Growth of the Chicago Area, 1880–1930* (Chicago: University of Chicago Press, 1991), 101.
74. "Electric Lights in Los Angeles," *Signs of the Times* (November 1910): 18; "Salina Street, Syracuse, New York: A Noteworthy Example of America's Brightest and Busiest Streets," *Signs of the Times* (May 1917): 7; H. H. Skinner, "Sign Lighting in Providence," *Signs of the Times* (November 1910): 21; L. D. Gibbs, "Illuminated Advertising," *Signs of the Times* (November 1910): 25.

CHAPTER 3. *Visions and Velocity: The Expansive Age of the Automobile, 1918–1928*

1. Sinclair Lewis, *Babbitt* (1922; reprint, New York: Bantam Books, 1998), 161.
2. Gary Dean Best, *The Dollar Decade: Mammon and the Machine in 1920s America* (Westport, CT: Praeger, 2003), 63, 66.
3. The motion-picture palaces accommodated great numbers of patrons at affordable prices. George Rapp, a leading movie palace architect, once boasted, "Here is a shrine to democracy where the wealthy rub elbows with the poor." Palace decorator Harold Rambusch was quoted in *American Theatres of Today* as saying, "In a sense, these theatres are a social safety valve in that the public can partake of the same luxuries as the rich." Journalist Lloyd Lewis explained that the movie palace provided an alternative world, one richer, more romantic, and far more democratic than the mundane worlds that the picture palace customers inhabited on the outside. See David Naylor, *American Picture Palaces: The Architecture of Fantasy* (New York: Van Nostrand Reinhold, 1981), 31, and David Nasaw, *Going Out: The Rise and Fall of Public Amusements* (New York: BasicBooks, 1993), 239.
4. Naylor, *American Picture Palaces*, 31.
5. Ben M. Hall, *The Best Remaining Seats: The Story of the Golden Age of the Movie Palace* (New York: C. N. Potter, 1961), 106–9.
6. Ely Jacques Kahn, "Ziegfeld Theatre, New York: Joseph Urban and Thomas Lamb, Architects," *Architectural Record* 61 (May 1927): 385–86.
7. Charles E. Thompson, "Toledo's Electrical Advertising Growth Is Result of Specialized Effort," *Signs of the Times* 55 (March 1927): 44.
8. Enormous vertical signs appeared on smaller nontheater commercial buildings as well. At the corners of several branches of Wieboldt's department store in Chicago, for example, were signs as high as the five-story structures themselves. Wieboldt's, because of its market position as a more affordable department store, was somewhat unique among stores of this type for using such grandly scaled

signing. As stated earlier, department stores in general opted for more discreet identifying graphics due to their power in the community, already being well known and well advertised.

9. "New North Side Theater Completed: Turn on Big Sign," *Chicago Daily Tribune,* August 16, 1925.

10. H. F. Voorhees, "Mammoth Electric Dominates Chicago's White Way," *Signs of the Times* 49 (April 1925): 38.

11. Howard McLellan, "Electric Signs Constitute Best Form of Theatre Exploitation," *Signs of the Times* 41 (May 1922): 54.

12. R. W. Sexton and B. F. Betts, *American Theatres of Today* (New York: Architectural Book Publishing, 1929), 2:9–10.

13. Writing in the *New Yorker* in 1933 about the design of Radio City Music Hall, Mumford claimed, "Ten years ago, I observed in the Freeman that some day an architect would be bold enough to design the electric sign and metallic awning as the chief decorative motif of a theatre's façade... At least Reinhard & Hofmeister, the architects, did not at first design a Greek temple and then wake up and find to their great surprise that it was necessary to cut into the front with an awning and an electric sign." Lewis Mumford, "The Sky Line: Two Theatres, January 14, 1933," in *Sidewalk Critic: Lewis Mumford's Writings on New York*, ed. Robert Wojtowicz (New York: Princeton Architectural Press, 1998), 93.

14. "Striking Spectacular Electric on Front of New Volkmor Shoe Store," *Signs of the Times* 45 (November 1923): 30. The term *lamp* was preferred to the term *bulb* in sign industry parlance, though the two words refer to the same thing.

15. Kauffer often expressed disappointment at the reluctance of Americans to accept the bold simplicity of modern design. "If in comparison to other countries, America necessarily exaggerates, then it is the country that ought to accept the modern poster, for it does the same thing in order to be seen and felt." Edward McKnight Kauffer, "Poster Designers Are Incompetent Says New York Poster Artist," *Signs of the Times* 40 (February 1922): 17–18; Mark Haworth-Booth, *E. McKnight Kauffer: A Designer and His Public* (1979; reprint, London: Victoria and Albert Museum, 2005). In his article, Kauffer cited for American readers, at a relatively early date, the qualities and strategies needed for effective poster (and sign) design:
    - visibility from a distance
    - power to arrest attention
    - simplified structure
    - contrast and color for emphasis
    - resist a slavery to realism
    - geometrical patterns and shapes are powerful
    - contrast by means of isolation

16. A brief description, in the *Chicago Tribune,* of a building to be erected on the city's South Side in 1921 suggests how Alschuler casually intertwined the exotic and the mundane. Indirectly, it also revealed how commonplace these exotic motifs had become: "Plans for a two story structure in the Mexican style of architecture... by Architect Alfred Alschuler.... [T]he upper floor will be devoted to an unusually elaborate café, possibly in the Hindusian style of architecture, similar to the Bulldog and Whistle. There will be six first floor shops, with the corner possibly given over to a drug store." Al Chase, "Plan $175,000 Café and Shops for Woodlawn," *Chicago Tribune,* November 24, 1921.

17. Richard Longstreth, "J. C. Nichols, the Country Club Plaza and Notions of Modernity," *Harvard Architecture Review* 5 (1986): 120–35. Nichols aimed to avoid the "unattractiveness" of the streetcar commercial strip by asserting style and control. The Spanish architectural motif was, in part, chosen because it had the potential to rise above the generally plain "flat tops" of the common strip with towers and other flourishes. The Spanish motif was also seen as ideal for generating a festive atmosphere that would enhance merchandising efforts. Stucco and tile as surfaces were appealing because of the relatively low cost.

18. Charles H. Cheney, "Ten-Million-Dollar Loss Due to No Building Code," *American City* 33 (October 1925): 373.

19. National Committee for Restriction of Outdoor Advertising, *What Attracts the Tourist to Your Town* (New York: The Committee, n.d.).

20. Two powerful, disparate forces combined to facilitate the transformation of Santa Barbara's public face in the 1920s. One of these was the presence of an unusually high concentration of talented designers and skilled reformers; the other was a fortuitously timed earthquake. Among the visionaries determined to reform the city visually by "Hispanicizing" it were Bernhard Hoffmann and Pearl Chase, who cofounded the Community Arts Association. This organization, dedicated to the physical and cultural improvement of Santa Barbara, oversaw the activities of related groups and boards. For example, the Plans and Plantings Committee closely monitored all matters of civic aesthetics, from billboard control to design competitions. Adhering to democratic principles, committee members urged the city to create the City Planning Commission and the Architectural Advisory Committee, which, in turn, successfully recommended creation of an architectural review board.

21. T. Mitchell Hastings, chairman, Santa Barbara Architects, Architectural Advising Committee, to Mr. Abram Garfield, First Vice President, American Institute of Architects, Santa Barbara, August 12, 1925, Santa Barbara Community Arts Association. See also Pearl Chase, "Bernard Hoffmann—Community Builder," *Noticias* (Santa Barbara Historical Society), Summer Bulletin 1959.

22. *(Santa Barbara) Morning Press,* March 6, 1928. See also Plans Committee of the Community Arts Association, *Honor Awards: Civic and Commercial Architecture in Santa Barbara and Montecito in the Years 1928–1929* (Santa Barbara, 1929).

23. Kevin Starr, *Material Dreams: Southern California through the 1920s* (New York: Oxford University Press, 1990), 279.

24. Sinclair Lewis, *Main Street: The Story of Carol Kennicott* (New York: Harcourt, Brace, 1921), 130–31.

25. "Santa Barbara; The Case for Unified Architecture," *Architectural Forum* 59 (July 1933): 84. See also Winsor Soule, "The

New Santa Barbara," *American Architect* 130 (July 5, 1926): 1–10.

26. Walter Prichard Eaton, "The Beautiful Town an Earthquake Built," *Charleston (WV) Daily Mail, Syracuse Herald*, and others, June 3, 1928.

27. Seymour I. Toll, *Zoned American* (New York: Grossman, 1969), 193; Robert M. Fogelson, *Downtown: Its Rise and Fall, 1880-1950* (New Haven, CT: Yale University Press, 2001), 168.

28. Toll, *Zoned American*, 201.

29. "City Planning and Zoning Accomplishments," *American City* 38 (April 1928): 110.

30. Mark S. Foster, *From Streetcar to Superhighway: American City Planners and Urban Transportation, 1900-1940* (Philadelphia: Temple University Press, 1981), 70.

31. Lewis Mumford, "Botched Cities," *American Mercury* 18 (October 1929): 143–50; Toll, *Zoned American*, 256. In 1939, Roosevelt believed that decentralization would result in some manufacturing inefficiency but would reduce costs of governing and providing services. In the 1930s, freeways would be constructed or were planned for Los Angeles, New York (the Westchester Parkway system), Detroit (which planned to spend more on freeways than on the proposed subway), and Chicago (which had an equal commitment to superhighways and the new subway construction). See Foster, *From Streetcar to Superhighway*, 143, 165.

32. Edward D. Hartman, "A Proposal to Zone the Lands along the State Highways of Massachusetts," letter to the editor, *American City* 38 (March 1928): 159–61; Catherine Gudis, *Buyways: Billboards, Automobiles, and the American Landscape* (New York: Routledge, 2004), 212.

33. "Bans 'White Lights' in 5th Av. Region," *New York Times*, March 12, 1922.

34. As code enforcement pressured compliance on 34th Street, the Electrical Board of Trade, which represented this key commercial corridor, issued a statement claiming that sign limits altered the appearance of the street in a positive way. Emboldened by their success, Fifth Avenue merchants next proposed the elimination of projecting signs from all side streets surrounding Fifth Avenue, between Sixth and Park Avenues from 35th Street north to 59th Street. The Broadway Association responded by vowing to fight the growing encroachment upon its territory. It was one powerful Manhattan commercial corridor pitted against another—one representing no-holds-barred capitalism and the other, a community of ostensibly cooperative and refined citizens.

35. A. D. Seymour Jr., "The Hanan Shoe Stores," *Architectural Forum* 40 (June 1924): 264.

36. "Electrical Board Backs Store Signs," *New York Times*, February 20, 1927.

37. Ibid.; "Sees 'Confiscation' in Curb on Shop Signs," *New York Times*, May 8, 1929.

38. "City Seeks to Bar All Unsightly Signs on New Wacker Drive," *Chicago Daily Tribune*, July 17, 1926. In 1923, the Chicago Auto Trade Association was shown plans by the Chicago Plan Commission for vast projects to widen streets, extend boulevards, eliminate jogs, and straighten the river so that auto traffic could be conducted with convenience. See James J. Flink, *The Car Culture* (Cambridge, MA: MIT Press, 1975), 164.

39. Pasadena's 1928 sign ordinance was highly specific with respect to allowances for sign projection from building facades. For example, a sign whose height as measured from the sidewalk was greater than eight feet but up to twelve feet could project no more than twelve inches. For a sign whose height was greater than twelve but less fifteen feet, the projection was limited to thirty inches. And so on. The code also addressed, in detail, freestanding signs, which were becoming increasingly commonplace in the 1920s (especially in California). By contrast, the ordinance enacted in Reading, Pennsylvania, in 1927, did not address pole signs specifically (they were lumped in with billboards, as was common nationally early in the century); only height was limited. Reading permitted all projecting signs to extend up to six feet from a building, no matter the height or clearance, though there was a minimum clearance from the sidewalk of twelve feet. Reading continued to encourage the erection of electric signs (as opposed to simple painted signs, for example) by limiting projection to signs that helped light the street. Pasadena Ordinance no. 2692, City of Pasadena, California, 1927, 1–11; Reading Pennsylvania Municipal Code 1927, Chapter 14: "Signs and Billboards," 554–59.

40. "Where the Sign Ordinance Is Weak, Sign Conditions Are Poor," *Signs of the Times* 42 (September 1922): 65; W. W. Bell, "No Posting on Highways Says Ass'n to Protect Poster Interests," *Signs of the Times* 45 (September 1923): 14.

41. Bill Dorsey and Tom Swormstedt, "A History of 20th Century Sign Industry," *Signs of the Times* 203 (May 1981): 5.

42. Sam Kamin, "Sign Designers Now Recognized," *Signs of the Times* 62 (June 1929): 38.

43. C. A. Atherton, "Electric Signs of the Future Must Make Sales: Their 'Good Will' Days Are Over," *Signs of the Times* 41 (August 1922): 46; M. Luckiesh, *Light and Color in Advertising and Merchandising* (New York: D. Van Nostrand, 1927), 254; Kauffer, "Poster Designers Are Incompetent," 18. Kauffer, a celebrated poster designer, condemned the clutter of most advertising of the day: "The sentimental printed sheet which manifests itself in the pretty picture with a 'human interest' story . . . Examples of these efforts to pander to the great public are shown in the brainless-looking mother caressing a celluloid infant, the family doctor pointing a finger at you." The city is not like these slice of life advertisements; its "voice is sharp; motors scream and life is of a rapid-transit order. Let us go—we are there; let us do—it is done."

44. Gudis, *Buyways, Billboards, Automobiles*, 79.

45. C. A. Atherton, "Associating the Article, the Idea and Sale in the Public Mind with Electric Signs," *Signs of the Times* 44 (June 1923): 45.

46. "Now Just What Is Store Front Advertising and What's Its Relation to Signs?" *Signs of the Times* 44 (June 1923): 51.

47. In one, a rocking chair outlined in incandescent bulbs sat above a square frame with electric channel lettering and moved back and forth. In another, a man shown in profile from the waist up, appeared to tip his hat. Business owners had been displaying animated signs with complex contours since the advent of electricity in signs, but now elaborate devices were available to a wider audience at more affordable prices. A more basic design advance of the 1920s was the evolution from simple vertical signs to compound shapes that could incorporate more words and images. For example, a basic vertical sign box might now be shaped like the letter T, modified with scrolls and swashes. Despite the efforts of *Signs of the Times*, most signs produced in the 1920s resembled those produced a decade earlier—if not before that. Sam Kamin may have called for simpler lettering, but the designs he chose to accompany his articles were replete with nineteenth- and early-twentieth-century ornamentation. J. N. Halsted, revered among sign painters and designers, also published sign designs with elaborate panel shapes, scrolled edges, and dated art nouveau forms and details. Halsted confidently claimed, "There are three classes of art that are adaptable to modern applications more than any others: Chinese, Moorish, and Egyptian." In his column "Sign Suggestions," which appeared regularly in *Signs of the Times*, E. L. Koller, director of Art Schools International Correspondence Courses, frequently included photographs showing large projecting signs with curvaceous frames and intricate iron supports, many extending fully from shop front to curb.

48. A few designers were, however, beginning to emphasize simple imagery by emulating historic signs from previous centuries. They were especially influenced by the styles of historic Andalusian Spain, Tudor England, and colonial America; the result was a profusion of wooden hanging signs throughout the nation. Their appearance coincided with increased automobile travel into the countryside, in search, ironically, of America's more bucolic past. One issue of *Architecture* magazine featured a multipage portfolio picturing eighteenth- and nineteenth-century inn signs along with new signs suggestive of the past. *Signs of the Times* ran a page of sketches of new wooden signs based on the old forms; they were intended to identify roadside businesses, points of interest along a highway, or the entrance to a village. Some were faithful copies of original inn signs, while others were clever takes on the spirit of older signs and vintage graphics. A few included jigsaw-cut silhouettes of human figures engaged in various quaint, old-time outdoor activities; incongruously, several of these involved an automobile. In 1923, *Architectural Record* published several pages of signs identifying Jones State Beach and the town of New Rochelle, New York, with each example employing silhouetted human figures supported on posts or curling, wrought-iron standards. Silhouetted sign forms along roadsides became highly popular during the 1920s, especially for identifying older neighborhoods or helping confer a sense of place on new developments. This instance of sign reform signified a reaction against new technology and the proliferation of exotic styles. "Portfolio: Current Architecture," *Architectural Record* 54 (September 1923): 253–63; "Road Signs from the Sublime to the Ridiculous That Are Read by the 13,000,000 Atour," *Signs of the Times* 45 (October 1923): 16; "Artistic and Harmonious Roadside Signs Are Suggested for Town Betterment," *Signs of the Times* 51 (October 1925): 6–7; "Commercial Sign Design: Group III," *Signs of the Times* 70 (March 1932): 30; "*Architecture*'s Portfolio of Hanging Signs," *Architecture* 66 (July 1932): 47–61.

49. Ralph Green, letter to the editor, *Signs of the Times* 45 (October 1923): 90. Green was a sign designer.

50. Dana Somes, "Recent Shop Fronts in New England," *Architectural Forum* 40 (June 1924): 251.

51. Sam Kamin, "Sign Designers Now Recognized," *Signs of the Times* 62 (June 1929): 63.

52. Fogelson, *Downtown: Its Rise and Fall,* 181, 198.

53. Richard Longstreth examines the development of the market thoroughly in his important book, *The Drive-In, the Supermarket, and the Transformation of Commercial Space in Los Angeles, 1914–1941* (Cambridge MA: MIT Press, 1999). See also James M. Mayo, *The American Grocery Store: The Business Evolution of an Architectural Space* (Westport CT: Greenwood, 1993), 169.

54. Aldous Huxley, *After Many a Summer Dies the Swan* (1939; reprint, Chicago: Elephant Paperbacks, 1993), 4–11.

55. Chester H. Liebs, *Main Street to Miracle Mile: American Roadside Architecture* (Boston: Little, Brown, 1985), 48–49.

56. The early years of design development of the White Castle chain demonstrated most revealingly the pure power of building-as-sign. Design experimentation throughout the 1920s led to many stylistic changes, from the crude faux-stone literalism of the earliest store built in castle form in 1921 through the stylized, glazed brick, vaguely art deco castles of the late 1920s. By 1930, the company had returned to architectural literalism, with more fanciful crenellation and a far more pronounced corner tower. After years of legally challenging the White Tower Company with plagiarism (building design, slogans, business methods, even the exact shape of the burger), it had become time to make the corporate trademark more distinct and unique. The little sandwich shop was now far more elaborately ornamented with Middle Age turrets, a look that was closely inspired by Chicago's famous Water Tower, a gothic revival fantasy design from 1869. It was necessary for the building to work harder at being a sign, to be quite literally a "white castle," and not merely a tower of white. It is also significant to note that the lettered sign shrank dramatically in size from a full wall sign in 1921 to a small panel above the windows by the end of the decade—but the name *White Castle* replaced *Hamburger* in prominence. Despite the subtle visual emergence of the trademark name, the owners of this rapidly growing business discovered, for a time, that the architecture was still going to do most of the talking. The lettering was reduced in scale just as the corner tower gained true

prominence. The once token tower feature of 1921 had become a sparkling eye-catcher by 1931. It is surprising that the tower on neither version carried the sign, though this might be the obvious location for one. By the late 1920s, the competing chain, White Tower, began to experiment with large, projecting signs attached to the towers, a move that would more effectively address the increasingly auto-bound patron, as well as distinguish this business from all other "pretenders." Eventually, White Castle did the same. Such a move indicated the urgency, in the motoring age, to broadcast identity clearly and from a great distance. It also revealed that a graphic better communicated from afar than did architectural nuances. See Paul Hirshorn and Steven Izenour, *White Towers* (Cambridge, MA: MIT Press, 1979).

57. Reyner Banham, *Los Angeles: The Architecture of Four Ecologies* (New York: Harper & Row, 1971), 94–100.

58. Bernice L. Thomas, *America's 5 & 10 Cent Stores: The Kress Legacy* (New York: John Wiley & Sons, 1997), 6.

59. One particular sign type created perhaps the most effective graphic continuity for chain-store identification in the early years of the automobile. So-called raised-glass letter or opal-glass signs offered chain businesses special advantages over exposed-bulb signs. Typically, they were used to identify gasoline filling stations and drug stores, many of which were associated with corporate chains. To create raised-glass letters, a void in the form of the graphic character or trademark was cut out of sheet metal. A sheet of opal- or milk-glass was melted to curve down into this void, thus making a projecting letterform. The formed letter was then placed behind a metal mask or facing to block out (or black out) the area without graphics, allowing only the projecting letter to glow with light. When illuminated from behind, the opal-glass design glowed on a black background. Although smaller businesses continued to rely on rudimentary exposed-bulb electric signs, corporations and chains favored raised-glass signs because they could display unique, complex graphics for trademarks, picture images, and distinctive letterforms. Sign companies such as Chilco, Opalite, and Opalume created distinctly fluid signs and also produced preformed letters for the commercial assembly of more modest signs. The downside of raised-glass signs was that they cast less light than did exposed-bulb signs. Since many municipal codes favored signs that created more ambient light for Main Street, the raised-glass variety was treated with more restrictions (as a form of disincentive to owners for installing them). This sign type was restricted to projecting only half as far from a building facade as could exposed-bulb signs. Such limitation, combined with greater cost, severely reduced the potential spread of its use. "Early Replies to Signs of the Times Electric Sign Survey Show Gain," *Signs of the Times* 54 (October 1926): 55; "Nedelman . . . ," Signs of the Times 53 (May 1926): 36; Matthew Luckiesh, *Light and Color in Advertising and Merchandising* (New York: D. Van Nostrand, 1927), 242.

60. John A. Jakle and Keith A. Sculle, *The Gas Station in America* (Baltimore: Johns Hopkins University Press, 1994), 42.

61. K. Lönberg-Holm, "Technical News and Research: The Gasoline Filling and Service Station," *Architectural Record* 67 (June 1930): 576–77.

62. "Identifying National Agencies with Standard Electric Signs," *Signs of the Times* 50 (July 1925): 36.

63. Many such competitions were conducted throughout the United States. In 1926 H. Roy Kelley of Los Angeles designed a gas station for a Miami neighborhood that won first prize in a national competition that included New York society architect Dwight James Baum as a juror. A colonnade temple of sorts, with barrel-tiled roofing, provided a drive-through for motorists and essentially hid the service bay. The sign—a small parapet band—was fully integrated with the roof. The New York Arts Center and the American Civic Association of Washington conducted another set of competitions in 1928 for designs addressing a refreshment stand combined with a gasoline station: "Beauty in the Gas Age," *New York Times*, March 24, 1928.

64. Ibid.

65. Lönberg-Holm, "Technical News," 576–77.

66. Also in 1922, the Atlantic Refining Company of Pennsylvania erected several ornamental stations that would, according to a report in the *American City*, "minister to the needs of its customers, and at the same time serve as an advertising medium for its product, combining the function of service and the quality of beauty in approximately equal proportions." Designed by the Pittsburgh firm of W. G. Wilkins, these buildings were constructed of terra-cotta and tile. See J. F. Kuntz, "Greek Architecture and Gasoline Service Stations," *American City* 27 (August 1922): 123.

67. "Editorial Comment: Symbolism in Architecture," *American Architect and the Architectural Review* 124 (July 1923): 42; *Rutven (IA) Free Press*, September 7, 1927.

68. Sinclair Lewis, *Free Air* (New York: Harcourt, Brace, & Howe, 1919), 191. This novel also describes the variety of buildings along Main Street and the lack of consistent sheathing materials: "The entire business district of Schoenstrom consists of Heinie Rauskukle's general store, which is brick; the Leipzig House, which is frame; the Old Home Poolroom and Restaurant, which is of logs concealed by a frame sheathing; the farm-machinery agency, which is galvanized iron, its roof like an enlarged washboard . . ."

69. Gary B. Coombs and Phyllis J. Olsen, *Sentinel at Ellwood: The Barnsdall-Rio Grande Gasoline Station* (Goleta, CA: Institute for American Research, 1985), 8–13.

70. "Appearance of Santa Barbara County Service Stations Win Awards," *Santa Barbara Daily News*, April 20, 1934; "Service Stations of City Emphasize City's Beauty," *Santa Barbara News-Press*, May 26, 1929.

71. See Eaton, "Beautiful Town," 12; Gudis, *Buyways*, 180; and Edward D. Hartman, "A Proposal to Zone the Lands along the State Highways of Massachusetts," letter to the editor, *American City* 38 (March 1928): 159–61.

Eventually, corporations joined with individual leaders working on a national level, such as Elizabeth Boyd Lawton, who published extensive surveys of unsightly roadside conditions, to fight this problem. In 1924, a coalition of some forty organizations formed the National Roadside Council to serve as a clearinghouse for antibillboard efforts. That same year, Standard Oil placed an ad in six hundred newspapers announcing that it would remove all signs from scenic areas, and the company's California operation sponsored a contest to select the best photographs depicting defacement of the landscape.

72. Flink, *Car Culture,* 156; Warren James Belasco, *Americans on the Road: From Autocamp to Motel, 1910–1945* (Cambridge MA: MIT Press, 1979), 144. By 1923, there were 13 million motor vehicles in use in the United States, or one to every eight persons. This vast number was having a major effect on the landscape. See "Road Signs from the Sublime to the Ridiculous," 63.

73. Belasco, *Americans on the Road,* 131, 134, 137, 140, 169.

74. Daniel M. Bluestone, "Roadside Blight and the Reform of Commercial Architecture," in *Roadside America: The Automobile in Design and Culture,* ed. Jan Jennings (Ames: Iowa State University Press for the Society for Commercial Archeology, 1990), 175–76. This condition might be considered, conceptually, a crude or highly vernacular version of the decorated shed—most apparent when the profusion of signs was literally covering the meager buildings, rather than merely deflecting the view away from the structures.

75. Sinclair Lewis, *The Man Who Knew Coolidge: Being the Soul of Lowell Schmaltz, Constructive and Nordic Citizen* (1928; reprint, Freeport NY: Books for Libraries, 1971), 230.

76. H. I. Brock, "At the Sign of the Gas Pump—Inns of Today," *New York Times,* September 4, 1938.

77. There is still a distinction to be made between the mimetic architecture of the dog-shaped Barkie's Café and the Barnsdall-Rio gas station, a beacon of sorts, enveloped with signs. This distinction was established by Robert Venturi as the *duck* versus the *decorated shed.* But like the nineteenth-century American false-front, both involved a degree of exaggerated presence, and both communicated primarily via the building's envelope rather than via projecting signs. The building's skin offered a greater percentage of communicating area than noncommunicating area. See Jim Heimann and Rip Georges, *California Crazy: Roadside Vernacular Architecture* (San Francisco: Chronicle, 1980), and Karal Ann Marling, *The Colossus of Roads: Myth and Symbol along the American Highway* (Minneapolis: University of Minnesota Press, 1984).

CHAPTER 4. *Sign as Storefront: America Discovers Modernism, 1929–1945*

1. Alison Isenberg, *Downtown America: A History of the Place and the People Who Made It* (Chicago: University of Chicago Press, 2004), 129, 135–51.

2. Van Doesburg to Oud, February 24, 1930, Foundation Custodia, Paris, in Ed Taverne, Cor Wagenaar, and Martien de Vietter, *J. J. P. Oud: Poetic Functionalist, 1890-1963: The Complete Works* (Rotterdam: NAi Publishers, 2001), 341.

3. Ely Jacques Kahn, "A Modern European Shop and Store," *Architectural Forum* 50 (June 1929): 789. Other journals made equally compelling cases for paying attention to what was coming forth from Paris. *Architectural Record* stressed that sign lettering on Parisian storefronts was used as a major design element, contrasting it to lettering in America, which was praised only if discreet—if it was mentioned at all; William Dewey Foster, "Some Modern Paris Shop-Fronts," *Architectural Record* 65 (June 1929): 534. *American Architect* actually decried the paucity of good design in Paris, except for the city's great storefronts; Samuel Chamberlain, "In Search of Modernism: Concerning the Dearth of Material in France for the Inquiring Reporter," *American Architect and the Architectural Review* 131 (January 20, 1927): 71–74.

4. Oscar P. Cleaver, "What We Can Learn from Europe in Electrical Advertising Practice," *Signs of the Times* 71 (June 1932): 14.

5. "Old-World Sign Art," *Signs of the Times* 69 (September 1931): 23.

6. Cleaver, "What We Can Learn," 13.

7. Gerrit Rietveld's design for a men's furnishing shop was remarkable for its three-dimensionality. A corner location permitted the architect to allow perpendicular sign planes to slip past each other and for the cube of display glass to rotate. He thus broke the corner site open, pushed past the confines of the standard building line of the street, and revealed a set of new, solid pieces rather than just fresh skin applied to old. This was an important early step toward breaking the barrier between inside and outside for retail design. Other influential, commercial examples of European modernism include Robert Mallet-Stevens's Alfa-Romeo auto dealership (Paris, 1927), the Czech Avion shop (1929), and the Odeon shop (1929). Each composition boldly broke the shiny skin of its facade and projected graphics beyond the building surface. The simplicity and purity of the Doral shop by Siégel (1931) was notable for its simple banded opal-glass sign backlighting, which was continuous across the entire facade and ascended the full height of the parapet. All of these designs were a major improvement from the simple add-on projecting signs of the early 1920s in America, which were supported awkwardly with rods and chains, designs that had no relationship with the business facades. Most solutions were comprehensive, fluid, and architecturally organic.

8. "The necessity of producing something entirely different from anything previously created has naturally given to most of the buildings and exhibits a spectacular character. Nothing in the exposition, or very little, is of an unobtrusive character. Yet most of the violences are rational and in no sense shock one's idea of the artistic. While 'modern art' as displayed here never whispers and frequently does shout, it must be said that occasionally it sings." W. Francklyn Paris,

"The International Exposition of Modern Industrial and Decorative Art in Paris: II General Features," *Architectural Record* 58 (October 1925): 371. See also "Architecture Displays Its New Ideas, " *New York Times*, January 31, 1926. The immediate trickle-down effect of the Paris design exposition in America came through corporate pavilion design, an intermediate step before the visual trends proffered abroad took root in more permanent displays like storefront design. See, for example, Marrion Wilcox, "The Crane Company Exhibit Building, Atlantic City, New Jersey," *Architectural Record* 59 (February 1926), 102.

9. Walter F. March, "The Problem in Designing Modern Shop Fronts," *American Architect* 133 (June 20, 1928): 783-92. March stated, "The exterior [of the store front] is now called upon, in its general design and in its details . . . to serve as a very valuable and permanent advertising feature." In March's mind, dynamic window display areas were key to this goal. Along with many examples from Europe, March cited two from the United States. A store for Lucky Strike in New York by William Van Alen employed bold graphics and large, round windows, one of them wrapping around the corner. A John Ward shoe store in New York by Richard Haviland Smythe featured a double-height glass arch entrance ornamented by graphic silhouettes of shopkeepers and patrons. Architect Smythe's advanced work for John Ward had been featured in the *American Architect* a few years earlier: the extensive bowed display windows of this store on Broadway were virtual drums of pure glass, acting as visual supports for the tall fascia with its distinctive (and then quite novel) neon lettering. "Interior Architecture: A Unique Shop," *American Architect* 130 (July 5, 1926): 31-32.

10. Foster, "Some Modern Paris Shop-Fronts," 535.

11. So-called ribbon lettering was a subtle graphic approach, designed to be as continuous with the storefront as the metal frame that held the display glass in place. There was usually no visible source of illumination for this type of sign. The front face of each letter consisted of the fine, sharp edge of a metal strip that was perhaps three to five inches deep, curved and bent to create the desired shape. Holabird & Root and Vahan Hagopian (with his London Character Shoe Store) used this kind of sign with great success in the early 1930s, establishing a look that seduced a great many American architects and sign designers. Louis Allen Abramson's black Carrara glass front for his Longchamps Restaurant design (New York City, 1939) bore ribbon lettering with coordinated curving ribbon railings below. In the mid-1930s, the firm of Sobel and Drielsma redesigned several storefronts in Chicago with black granite and ribbon lettering backlit by frosted-glass panels. Continuous horizontal ribbons extending past the edge of the granite by several inches secured the lettering and helped to suggest a visual continuity for the facade.

12. *Signs of the Times* reported to its readers on the Russian display at the Florence International Exhibition, which, though pushed to the side in the exhibition area, captured the writer's attention: "Their simple, effectively designed cartoon posters . . . have been mighty factors in wielding the iron chain the government of Lenine [*sic*] has woven about the minds of Russia's great masses of illiterate peasantry." Manuel Rosenberg, "Bolsheviki Posters Rival the American Art at Florence International Exhibition," *Signs of the Times* 42 (November 1922): 29, 36.

13. Among IIT's graduates were several key Miami Beach architects (including Albert Anis and Roy F. France) and the prolific theater designer S. Charles Lee of Los Angeles.

14. "Lettering as an Element of Store Design," *Architectural Record* 67 (February 1930): 144.

15. See, for example, the many illustrations of sign and building front merged together in the June 1932 issue of *Signs of the Times;* Cleaver, "What We Can Learn," 13-14.

16. In the late 1930s, the head designer or "sketch artist" of one of Chicago's leading sign companies looked to a local sign company, owned and operated by Germans, that specialized in show cards. He also turned to the exceptionally creative and impermanent promotional work of the Balaban and Katz theater sign shop, whose artists could somewhat afford to experiment and stay on the cutting edge. In addition, newly published books on lettering offered guidance in novel letterforms. Robert Hunterford (designer for Beverly Sign Co. during the late 1930s, 1940s, and 1950s), in discussion with the author, December 2009.

17. R. J. Polittzer, "The Poster in Austria," *Signs of the Times* 64 (January 1930): 29. Joseph Binder was credited in the article as the best known Austrian advertising artist. A great wave of immigration during the late 1930s brought many designers to America. This list included Joseph Binder, Jean Carlu, Herbert Matter, Alexey Brodovitch, Walter Landor, Mehemed Fehmy Agha, Will Burton, George Giusti, Albert Kner, Alexander Liberman, and Allen Hurlburt. Designer William Golden credited designers like Agha and Brodovitch with changing the status of the profession in America by demonstrating that the designer was not merely a craftsman but could think. See R. Roger Remington and Barbara J. Hodik, *Nine Pioneers in American Graphic Design* (Cambridge, MA: MIT Press, 1989), 56, 60.

18. Jesse Newton Halsted, *Modern Ornament and Design* (Cincinnati: Signs of the Times, 1927), 48.

19. B. W. Holland, "Layout . . . the 'Soul' of the Show Card," *Signs of the Times* 64 (January 1930): 52. Historian James Fraser explains that American advertising art never quite made the conceptual leap European advertising did. Stylized realism, as opposed to stylized symbolism (the domain of European design), was as avant-garde as the outdoor advertising industry in America would get. Though Fraser referred specifically to billboards and the like, this same claim could be applied rather accurately to business signs. See James Fraser, *The American Billboard: 100 Years* (New York: Abrams, in Association with OAAA, 1991), 79.

20. Philip B. Meggs, *A History of Graphic Design,* 3rd ed. (New York: John Wiley and Sons, 1998), 13. Remington and Hodik, *Nine Pioneers,* 49, 70, 75-76. Besides the major exhibition

it held on the International Style of architecture (1932), the Museum of Modern Art presented shows on the Bauhaus, installed by Herbert Bayer (1938) and on the U.S. government's Rural Electrification Administration (1939), which included posters by Lester Beall.

21. "The Designer's Job," *Signs of the Times* 71 (July 1932): 15.
22. "Signs and Buildings," *Signs of the Times* 74 (May 1933): 43.
23. Horace Ginsbern, "In Store-Front Displays . . . Harmonious Design Is Still the Modern Advertising Force," *Signs of the Times* 77 (July 1934): 11.
24. H. H. Magdsick, "Electrical Advertising for Prosperity Avenue," *Magazine of Light* 1 (November 1930): 24.
25. V. S. Klein (Art Director, Electrical Products Corp., Seattle), "The Designer's Job in Creating Today's Sign Advertising," *Signs of the Times* 71 (July 1932): 16.
26. "Wrinkled Face of City Lifted," *Los Angeles Times*, November 30, 1930.
27. Arthur Millier, "Building for Our Age," *Los Angeles Times*, April 27, 1930. Richard Neutra was also turning heads at this time with his earliest residential work in Los Angeles, including the Jardinette apartments (1928) and the Lovell House (1929). Henry-Russell Hitchcock commented that Neutra's Hollywood apartments were quite as fine as the best modern work being published at the time (which was mostly to be found in German magazines, according to the architectural historian). See Henry-Russell Hitchcock Jr., "Foreign Periodicals," *Architectural Record* 64 (December 1928): 537.
28. In 1926, for the Leah-Ruth Shop, Schindler attempted to update an older commercial building with a radical, abstract diagonal lattice screen. His design for Lindy's no. 1 (1932) featured a continuous pergola across the front of the restaurant connecting with freestanding letters constructed the full height of the building. The vast graphic appeared to be scaled for reading at great speed and distance from an automobile, though it is questionable whether or not this was literally the intention. Kem Weber also designed for the automobile with his proposals in 1934 for drive-in restaurants (made with students at the Art Center School (then in downtown Los Angeles).

    Kem Weber was lauded in America as early as 1928 for his furniture design at Macy's First Exposition of Arts and Trades, and *Architectural Record* reported extensively on his major store design (inside and out) for Sommer and Kaufmann (San Francisco, 1930). Despite its enthusiasm for the store's interior, the journal correctly noted that the "lettering above the entrance is not easily read, whereas lettering at the top of the façade is not readily seen." Weber had created a handsome multistoried window screen, flanked by stone, that terminated with a sign at the crest—a graphic well integrated with the architectural features but apparently too subtle to identify the business adequately. "Weber's Design Show," *Los Angeles Times*, February 24, 1929.

    Weber's projects for Paramount Studios (1932–34) and his longtime client Barker Brothers Department Store were exuberant and fluid, creatively integrating bold, easily identifiable graphics with architectural features. One rendering for a Paramount movie set revealed an unusually advanced concept for signage: a curved, projecting canopy (with freestanding dimensional letters along its edge) was cantilevered continuously above a similarly shaped display window. By interrupting the rigid wall of the street with such plastic fluidity, Weber anticipated the inside-outside "open storefront" that would dominate retail structures of the 1940s and succeeding decades. Sometime between 1930 and 1932, Weber wrote this unpublished piece that he titled "The Shop," in which he acknowledged the importance of graphics to storefronts: "Advertisement—lettering—signs—electric light—effects—reflections—movements and other attractions hitherto superimposed upon the classical architectural efforts of our storefronts have now become the basis for storefront design—copies of classical columns, pilasters, cornices and antique stone structures are replaced by designs evolved from modern steel and concrete construction and advertising necessities are the means of enrichment, variation, and character." Kem Weber, "The Shop" (unpublished paper, ca. 1930–32, Architecture & Design Collection, University Art Museum, University of California, Santa Barbara).

29. "Prosperity Avenue Sells Its Wares with Light, Character, and Charm in Architecturally Coordinated Signs," *Magazine of Light* 1 (November 1930): 27. More refined establishments like the McCreery and Company men's shop (Starrett and Van Vleck, 1932) in New York contrasted bursts of modern ornament in nickel against plain expanses of black marble. The symmetrical, stepped design was devised to cover a single arch that once defined entrance for this store. It radically updated the fussy turn of the twentieth-century storefront with its classical design and details. Many other delicately ornamented storefronts were created in the late 1920s and early 1930s. Among the many examples, Brownley's Confection Building (Porter and Lockie, 1932) in Washington, D.C., is worth noting. The facade suggested a parted curtain in the way that metal ornament framed the entrance and display window; the store name, spelled out in script, appeared above this richly textured decoration as a subtle metal-on-metal relief. Such lush detail, though confined to limited areas, was often employed for jewelry stores and women's apparel shops. As early as 1930, *Chain Store Age* described the process a men's furnishing retailer underwent to make the leap to modernism. Executives had researched modern design across the country for the design approach to take while creating three West Coast stores. They finally decided to follow "the modern architectural trend" "in principle," avoiding color and decorative extremes. The choice of facade design might be described as close to that of certain modern storefronts in Vienna. The choice was praised for establishing a clear relationship with the graphic design style of the company's advertising. See Frederic H. Moore, "We Decide to Go Modern," *Chain Store Age* 6 (April 1930): 64.
30. According to Urban, "The trouble with our [U.S.] modern architecture . . . is that too much of it is piecework, without

sufficient conformity to one general design. If a building is to reflect the efforts of artistic planning, it must be harmonious to the minutest detail . . . [The architect] must sketch, plan, and consult on every detail, and the more expert he is in all related fields, the more unity he will achieve." See Arnold Aronson, *Architect of Dreams: The Theatrical Vision of Joseph Urban* (New York: Miriam and Ira D. Wallach Art Gallery, Columbia University, 2000; distributed by University of Washington Press); Carter Randolph, *Joseph Urban: Architecture, Theatre, Opera, Film* (New York: Abbeville, 1992); Frank Cady, "Joseph Urban Excels Because He Doesn't Specialize," *Brooklyn Eagle Magazine,* March 30, 1930.

31. Stage design was a profession that later included such industrial designers as Norman Bel Geddes, Raymond Loewy, and Henry Dreyfuss.

32. By the early 1930s, the Vienna Secessionist ornamentation popularized by Joseph Urban (as well as highly decorative art deco design) was supplanted by a minimalist, modern style in advanced commercial design. This was best exemplified by his proposal for an unbuilt theater (1931), flanked on each side by a series of stores that zigzagged in plan, leading to the smooth front face of the auditorium, marked at its crest by the word *Camera* in large, deep, aluminum, Futura letters outlined in red neon. See Irvin L. Scott, "A Motion Picture Theater for a Suburban Town in New York: Joseph Urban, Architect," *Architectural Record* 70 (August 1931): 111–14.

33. Other retail designs by Dorwin Teague, commissioned by Pittsburgh Plate Glass in 1935 and 1936, directly influenced facade drawings by sign designer Philip Di Lemme, which were published in trade journals and used by art departments everywhere. His work was compiled and published in a single book as copyright-free reference in the 1980s. See Philip Di Lemme, *American Streamline: A Handbook of Neon Advertising Design* (New York: Van Nostrand Reinhold, 1984).

34. "Exteriors—in 1931," *Chain Store Age* 8 (January 1932): 30.

35. "Three 'London Character Shoe' Stores: Vahan Hagopian, Architect," *Architectural Record* 67 (February 1930): 139. See also L. M. L., " 'Individual' Store Fronts Retain Family Semblance," *Chain Store Age* 6 (February 1930): 55–56. The Newark store was recognized as a significant contributor to commercial design evolution in a special issue of the *Architectural Forum* dedicated to the "Design Decade." "Design Decade," *Architectural Forum* 73 (October 1940): 217–320.

36. All three storefronts were clad in unpainted aluminum panels, the bolting at the edges being part of the aesthetic. Two stores shared recessed, "flat" lettering with a brass finish, as well as a stepped border of internally illuminated amber glass. The writer reviewing the London Character Shoe store designs in *Chain Store Age* stressed, "It is no longer necessary for one store of a chain to look exactly like another . . . To use all opportunities, [the architect] may find it necessary to make some distinct variations in the design, without losing the likeness to the other stores of the chain." The writer recognized the value of design progression from store to store: "A steady growth of ideas is maintained, keeping the chain at all times well abreast of progress in store design." L. M. L., " 'Individual' Store Fronts," 55–6.

37. In the same year that he created the heralded London Character Shoe stores, Vahan Hagopian designed his first A. S. Beck Shoe store, on Fifth Avenue, a project also given exceptionally generous press. *Architectural Record* claimed that the distinctive design was free of arbitrary decoration: "There was no deliberate attempt to achieve a startling or 'modernistic' architecture." "The A. S. Beck Shoe Store: V. Hagopian, Architect," *Architectural Record* 65 (June 1929): 543. All pattern and form was the result of a direct scheme to lead the eye deeper and deeper into the entrance arcade and then the length of the store interior. The architect's strategy was a system of display-case step-backs and converging lines, a forced perspective with a major focal point. Both ceiling and floor of the entrance appeared like ziggurat arrows aimed at the front door. In addition to the editorial pages devoted to this store, its design was featured in several advertisements, including one for the engineers and contractors. For one example, see *Chain Store Age* 5 (November 1929): 92. The step-back or zigzag display window strategy was also employed for the Wise Shoe shop on Fifth Avenue. *Chain Store Age* titled its coverage of this design "Modernism Did It" and stressed how display area was vastly increased. The journal seemed to be selling the new style as a means of achieving practical advantages, since its design appeal was not yet proven at this early date. "Modernism Did It," *Chain Store Age* 5 (February 1929): 71. For more on the A. S. Beck designs, see Vahan Hagopian, "Shops and Stores for Modern Merchandising," *Architectural Forum* 58 (January 1933): 69–72.

38. Morris Lapidus, *Too Much Is Never Enough* (New York: Rizzoli, 1996), 96. Lapidus's first employer, design firm Ross-Frankle, maintained a long-standing contract for designing the storefronts for the Mangel's chain, which spread quickly to large- and medium-sized cities, thus making Lapidus's ideas for graphics very influential. Each storefront for Mangel's was slightly different—though certain features, like the rounded sans-serif lettering, established a consistent trademark. The Jacksonville, Florida, store (early 1930s) integrated a projecting vertical sign with the facade composition in the manner of Mallet-Stevens and his Alfa Romeo showroom of 1927.

39. In the 1930s, when the chain store was making remarkable inroads on Main Street, *Chain Store Age* stated, "For special reasons some chains are still standardizing their stores. In the larger number of instances, however, the tendency is to change the pattern and thus to take full advantage of the many new developments in building materials which are constantly occurring." See "1939 Store Design Influenced by New Materials," *Chain Store Age* 15 (November 1939): 11. On the issue of chain store design consistency, Victor Gruen would later contribute the following: "It is not necessary that [all stores of a chain] be alike as eggs in a basket. In fact, the advantages of individual locations are likely to be lost

by complete standardization of stores ... Devices by which varied stores in a chain may be made identifiable at a glance include the following: basic color schemes, distinctive and somewhat uniform signs, trademarks and certain common architectural features. It is necessary only that stores of the same chain be made to look like members of the same family: they need not appear as identical twins." Victor Gruen, "Achieving Flexibility in Individual Units without Losing Chainwide Identity," *Chain Store Age* 23 (July 1947): 18. Yet another voice encouraged standardization, warning that customers who found themselves in unfamiliar surroundings might bypass a chain that was right under their noses because it lacked tied-in identity. W. L. Nichols, "Standard Fronts Are Called Vital," *Chain Store Age* 23 (July 1947): 47. See also "Modernized Chain Stores 1937 Models," *Chain Store Age* 13 (Administration Edition, November 1937): 21-24; "Standardizing Store Modernization," *Chain Store Age* 11 (Administration Edition, June 1935): 15; and Godfrey M. Lebhar, "The Story of the Chains: 1925-1950," *Chain Store Age* 26 (Silver Jubilee Edition, June 1950): 14-26.

40. It was done in the fashion of the André Hunebelle Paris shop front (published in *Architectural Record* in 1929). Winold Reiss—a designer, illustrator, and artist—is credited for the interior design of this store and may very likely have contributed to the storefront design.

41. The crisp white planes in this composition, and most especially its horizontality, might be said to fall in step with the Dutch De Stijl movement. But other Dutch work of the time emphasized horizontality as well. American architecture journals often published examples of work from Holland in the late 1920s, which served as appropriate inspiration for an increasingly motorized America. "It seems impossible to reconcile many of the exaggerated forms that are so manifestly becoming stylistic in equal degree to any tradition of the past. Horizontal lines, in contrast to the usual vertical accents of Gothic or Renaissance architecture, become so positive that one is conscious of an almost abnormal fear of the vertical line. The flatness of the Dutch landscape can hardly account for such sudden and universal agreement and it is far more likely that there is some purposeful decision—a recall of our own Frank Lloyd Wright." Ely Jacques Kahn, "The Architect's Library: Nieuw Nederlandsche Bouwkunst (vol. II)," *Architectural Record* 62 (July 1927): 77-78.

42. Henry-Russell Hitchcock and Philip Johnson, *The International Style: Architecture since 1922* (1932; reprint, New York: Norton, 1966), 73.

43. Ibid., 74.

44. Francis M. Falge (Nela Park Engineering Dept., General Electric), "Architectural Sign Lighting Developments," *Signs of the Times* 71 (July 1932): 20.

45. G. R. LaWall, "There's No Saturation Point in Electrical Advertising Sales," *Signs of the Times* 88 (January 1938): 14; Reed Clement, "Five Elements of Electric Sign Design," *Signs of the Times* 71 (June 1932): 27.

46. Falge, "Architectural Sign Lighting," 20.

47. Ibid.

48. Sign professionals in the 1930s consulted venerable industry standards dating from the late 1920s and before, including A. Ashmun Kelly, *The Expert Sign Painter: A Book of Reference Designed for the Use of Practical Sign Painters and Letterers* (Malvern, PA: 1911); W. A. Heberling, *Basic Lettering* (Chicago: Wallbrunn, Kling, 1922); Charles Wagner, *Blueprint Textbook of Sign and Showcard Lettering* (Boston: Wagner School of Sign Arts, 1926); Jesse Newton Halsted, *Modern Ornament and Design* (Cincinnati: Signs of the Times, 1927); Duke Wellington, *Theory and Practice of Poster Art* (Cincinnati: Signs of the Times, 1934); and H. C. Martin, *1000 Showcard Layouts* (Cincinnati: Signs of the Times, 1928). As useful as these publications might have been, however, they rarely focused specifically on sign design. Instead, they offered either general principles of design or examples of lettering styles and decorative flourishes executed in paint and/or gold leaf.

49. Another patent restriction severely slowed neon development in this country. Progress in luminous tubing had begun as early as 1856, and it leapt ahead in 1904 when D. McFarland Moore produced the first luminous tube sign installation for a hardware store in Newark, New Jersey. But with its incandescent bulb industry threatened, General Electric ensured the failure of McFarland's effort by buying his patents—even though the life of his tubes was severely limited. It remained for Mr. Claude, from France, to both assist and restrain the further progress of neon. Rudi Stern, *Let There Be Neon* (New York: Abrams, 1979), 16-27; William W. Anthony (President, Federal Sign Co.), *Signs of the Times* 198 (September 1976): 65.

The transition from bulb signs to neon design increased in velocity in the very late 1920s. As late as October 1927, articles in *Signs of the Times* claimed "Neon Will Soon Dominate as the Light of the World, Says Authority." But in March of that same year, at a New York sign company trade show sponsored by an electric company, only one neon-capable company was presented, despite participation by fifty-seven companies (although not all were electric). However, in California (the leading edge of the neon movement), in autumn of that year, one company secured a contract to install neon tubing to outline the roofs of all gas stations belonging to the Standard Oil Company "from Tijuana to Vancouver." Suddenly in 1928, full-page advertisements for neon signs appeared for the first time in *Signs of the Times*. Originally, the designs for signs using the new technology were the same as those for bulb signs; designers had not yet begun to explore the fluid potential of the medium. Neon red and mercury blue were the only colors used in the first U.S. neon sign, in Los Angeles in 1923. Fluorescent colors in a rainbow of hues and tints were made available in 1935 but were not widely available until 1938. See "Neon Tube Sign Industry Flourishing along Entire Pacific Coast," *Signs of the Times* 57 (November 1927): 58, and "There's Big Money in the Neon Business for You," *Signs of the Times* 59 (July 1928).

50. H. C. Martin, *H. C. Martin's Modern, Money-Making Ideas for Showcard Artists, Sign Writers, Screen Process Artists, Window Display Managers, Poster Artists, Letterers, Students (Book Three)* (Orlando, FL: H. C. Martin Press Press, 1935), n.p.

51. V. S. Klein (Art Director, Electrical Products Corp., Seattle), "The Designer's Job in Creating Today's Sign Advertising," *Signs of the Times* 71 (July 1932): 15.

52. Ibid. Architects in America suffered in the same way that sign designers did when it came to selling the public on the new European look in design. William Lescaze, who suddenly shot to stardom in 1932 with his PSFS tower in Philadelphia and its large but simple neon sign at the crest (all done according to the rules delineated by Hitchcock and Johnson), had slaved in America on dispiriting projects after emigrating from Switzerland in 1920. He was rather startled at how such a vibrant nation could be so behind-the-times, considering that the "new style" in Europe had been developing steadily in various forms since the 1910s. Once in America, he worked as a draftsman of several conservative school buildings and even designed a few Chinese restaurant interiors. He initiated his own furniture design work to prevent himself from falling into complete despair before things began to change for him in 1930. Lorraine Welling Lanmon, *William Lescaze, Architect* (Philadelphia: Art Alliance Press, 1987), 23-29.

53. Otto Teagan quoted from "World's Fair Weekly" in "Chicago's Exposition: Its Influence upon Sign Art and Design," *Signs of the Times* 74 (June 1933): 11. For other design commentary about the exposition, see Harvey Wiley Corbett, "The Significance of the Exposition"; Joseph Urban, "The Color of the Exposition"; Paul Phillipe Cret, "The Festive Stage Setting"; Ely Jacques Kahn, "Close-up Comments on the Fair"; and Albert Kahn, "A Pageant of Beauty," all in *Architectural Forum* 59 (July 1933): 1-31; Benjamin F. Betts, "Reflections on A Century of Progress," and Arthur F. Woltersdorf, "Carnival Architecture," both in *American Architect* 143 (July 1933): 9-20; Douglas Haskell, "Mixed Metaphors at Chicago," *Architectural Review* 74 (August 1933): 47-49; Henry H. Saylor, "The Century of Progress Exposition," *Architecture* 68 (August 1933): 63-68; and Clarence W. Farrier, "The Gadgets: Shelters, Flags, Decoration," *Architectural Record* 73 (May 1933): 363.

54. Quoted by H. C. Martin, from an article in *Advertising Arts*, in *Signs of the Times* 74 (July 1933): 26.

55. "Chicago's Exposition: A Source of Inspiration and Ideas for the Sign Industry," *Signs of the Times* 74 (May 1933): 14.

56. "Sign Art at the World's Fair," *Signs of the Times* 74 (July 1933): 9.

57. Neon's successful emergence in the United States, once the Claude patent expired in 1932, folded in well with the trend toward integrating signs with building design. And it coincided perfectly with the opening of A Century of Progress.

58. Lenox R. Lohr, *Fair Management: The Story of A Century of Progress Exposition: A Guide for Future Fairs* (Chicago: Cuneo, 1952), 99.

59. Christopher Innes, *Designing Modern America: Broadway to Main Street* (New Haven, CT: Yale University Press, 2005), 105.

60. "What's New at the Fair," *Signs of the Times* 77 (July 1934): 8. Neon was still a rather new medium for sign illumination in America when the fair was in its planning stages.

61. Ibid.

62. "Chicago's Exposition," 14. Just a year after the fair closed, the highly influential graphic artist H. C. Martin began a series of books that revealed a giant leap in style from what he published in 1930. The fair also had a tremendous "trickle-down" effect, through the 1930s and early 1940s, on amusement park design. These parks were commercial thoroughfares of a different sort. The same principles of salesmanship or showmanship as that practiced at the exposition or on Main Street were necessary here. Individual concessions, both food establishments and attractions such as rides, faced small "midways," squares, or commons. These businesses confronted new guests every day, and each needed urgently to sell its offerings, considering the small window of time available for making an appeal to the customer. A flamboyant threshold, or gate, often beckoned customers to enter these special precincts, so yet another appealing sign was needed.

In the 1930s, amusement parks across America received significant updating from their original design features, which typically dated from the turn of the twentieth century. Just as on Main Street, new visuals were necessary to convince patrons to part with cash they could barely afford during such trying economic times. Coney Island's Luna Park entrance gate received a creative new look that altered a classically symmetrical composition to become quite asymmetrical and modern. Other parks such as Palisades Park, Washington, D.C.'s Glen Echo Park, and Pittsburgh's Kennywood received partial or complete facelifts during the 1930s. Richard Crowther's inventive, seductive gateways, ticket booths, and loading stations at Denver's Lakeside Park (another park created around 1900) incorporated new graphics seamlessly with the altered or new architecture—even when the lettering was enormous. The Auto Skooter lettering was an inflated version of the ribbon lettering first attempted on Parisian storefronts of a decade before, blown up to the scale of a world's fair advertisement. The cove-lit, stacked lettering of the Cyclone station combined graphic features from the Chicago fair and the new movie theater towers. These elaborate structures were fully three dimensional, like many of the corporate buildings at A Century of Progress, even though their locations along plazas and pathways put them into service as the definers of space, like the facade-oriented buildings of Main Street.

63. Hugh M. G. Gordon, "Color, Yes—But Architecture? A Century of Progress Criticism," *Architect and Engineer* 20 (August 1933): 21-23.
64. "The Chicago Century of Progress Exposition, 1933," *Architect and Building News* 134 (June 1933): 392-97.
65. A giant stucco boy and his Radio Flyer wagon also greeted children at the Enchanted Island amusement area. American motorists of the time were rather accustomed to mimetic architecture such as this, encountering inhabitable ice cream cones and three-story root beer barrels at roadside stands. The Nash and the Crane pavilions, unlike the Havoline and Radio Flyer icons, were a good deal more than mere inflated versions of the product sold or promoted on site. The product, whether enlarged or actual size, was part of a novel and distinctive composition. In all cases, this was architecture as sign, a clear identity or message broadcast without the need of symbols to denote or explain. In the future, corporate architecture like that for McDonald's would work even more effectively as a sign, with the support of media advertisement and familiarity.
66. "Products and Practice: Architectural Porcelain Enamel," *Architectural Forum* 66 (May 1937): 457.
67. "Modernize Main Street," *Architectural Forum* 63 (July 1935): 51-62; Gabrielle Esperdy, *Modernizing Main Street: Architecture and Consumer Culture in the New Deal* (Chicago: University of Chicago Press, 2008), 84, 86-87, 100.
68. "Dress Up Store Fronts, Plea to Upper Clark St.," *Chicago Daily Tribune*, February 8, 1931; "Retail Merchants Urged to Renovize," *Better Housing*, March 5, 1935, 3.
69. "Gayety Advised for Store Fronts," *Washington Post*, March 22, 1936.
70. Lynn Hardesty, "Store Fronts in Bright Hues Gain Popularity," *Washington Post*, April 10, 1938.
71. Kenneth Kingsley Stowell, *Modernizing Buildings for Profit* (New York: Prentice-Hall, 1935), 11. For good examples of the many before-and-after stories presented in professional journals, see Frederick M. Feiker, "The Meaning of Modernizing," *Architectural Forum* 58 (January 1933): 1-2, and examples following, 34-69; see also Louis C. Stone, "The Economics of Modernization," *Architectural Forum* 58 (January 1933): 80-84.
72. Stowell's book presented Chicago's Blue Danube Grill (Gordon Gundling, 1934) as a sterling example of what design could do for business. Publications presenting makeovers like these had an immediate and often direct effect across America. The Sunshine Inn in Reading, Pennsylvania, for example, was an almost exact duplication of the Blue Danube. The simple but effective design, easy to re-create, featured a neon sign that curved into an entrance vestibule cased in milk-glass light panels.
73. Ginsbern's many configurations of the basic design for Hanscom Bake Shops were documented in several design journals, both architectural and graphic. Among the publications were "Store Fronts and Show Windows," *American Architect* 147 (December 1935): 60-71, and Horace Ginsbern, "In Store-Front Displays," *Signs of the Times* 77 (July 1934): 11.
74. The *Magazine of Light* (1930-1970s) was preceded by the journal known as *Light* (1923-29).
75. For example, see A. L. Lyman, "'Light Incorporated' Exemplifies Modern Store Lighting," *Magazine of Light* 2 (April 1931): 30.
76. The *Magazine of Light* featured several articles about drive-in restaurants, with all exterior surfaces—columns to roof—illuminated from within. Luminous Structures, Inc., of Los Angeles was the pioneer of this glowing architecture. It may have taken a cue from hamburger chains White Castle and White Tower, which had pioneered brightly lit restaurants, albeit illuminated indirectly by floodlighting. Most of these projects were three dimensional, conceived as visual landmarks, and not the typical fare of Main Street. Glowing pylons towered, lettering floated, and planes visually disengaged themselves from other planes. The company president of Luminous Structures advised: "All examples illustrated would be fabricated of steel, porcelain, glass and light. You will note that we refer to light in the same way that we refer to steel. Unless light is thought of as part of the materials which go into the job as steel and concrete, the designer or architect has not the proper frame of mind to successfully conceive a true luminous structure." Edward D. Neale, "Styling Luminous Advertising in 1934," *Magazine of Light* 3 (Year End 1933): 22-23.

    Local electrical companies actively supported General Electric's promotion of the use of illumination. A General Electric entity, the National Electric Light Association's Committee on Electric Advertising existed to encourage central power stations nationwide to increase the use of their product through more extensive lighting. The *Magazine of Light* profiled local power companies that creatively boosted their sales. In one instance, the lighting sales department of the Gulf Power Company introduced backlit (silhouetted) lettering into the design of a modernized, freestanding auto showroom.
77. By the 1920s, such elaborate formations included what was known as the fishbowl vestibule—a free-floating, full-height glass display case at the entrance, encircled by public space for browsing without entering the store proper. For an example, see *Chain Store Age* 26 (June 1950): 35.
78. In its 1930 catalogue, Newmanco presented several design renderings of window frames with the symmetrical stepping and angles associated with the Paris design exposition of 1925. One was particularly striking: an asymmetrical storefront composition with a soffit stepping down to a doorframe that was crisscrossed by an abstract pattern suggestive of mullions. The shop name covered the width of the structure, its large, fine, angular lettering intersecting the sign frame at both top and bottom.
79. Advertisement in *Chain Store Age* 6 (May 1930): 58.
80. PPG primarily promoted Carrara glass for interiors until 1934, when the product suddenly appeared in a multitude

of advertisements for storefronts. Vitrolite was given a sudden boost around this time as well, when L-O-F purchased the smaller company in 1935 and placed it in the limelight with the Modernize Main Street program.

81. By 1930, other companies—such as Portland Cement—were also looking into the future. The strip storefronts and automobile showrooms proposed by this manufacturer were relatively advanced architecturally but graphically conservative. The one-story storefronts illustrated in promotional literature were modules of a series, minimally ornamented but up to date, with subtle fluting between shops and minimalist ribbed friezes or fascia bands. The proposed sign panels, if they were shown at all, were merely token, and barely adequate from a distance. Too often the company's sign designs, like those still being created by most American architects, focused on ornament at the expense of communication. Sign companies would often have to apply workable signs over these subtle design features later on, once it was discovered that few could read what was there, let alone be drawn by it. In some cases, the companies would build large metal suspension structures on the roof behind the parapet in order to suspend or project a sign that was suitably sized and perpendicular to traffic flow and speed. Such add-on signage was geared to the automobile age, suggesting a need to explore design potential. An automobile dealership built by Portland Cement was elaborately faceted in the art deco fashion, yet the signs were applied sometime after the building was completed, in a manner completely divorced from the building's features and rhythm. The faceting of the building, however modern, provided no natural place for a flush sign, let alone a projecting one. The entrance tower seemed as if it begged for a sign. Such oversights seemed especially irrational considering this example was a building erected to sell motorcars.

82. In 1935, the Federal Housing Administration expanded its 1934 National Housing Act to guarantee loans of $50,000 for modernizing commercial properties.

83. *52 Designs to Modernize Main Street with Glass* (Toledo, OH: Libbey-Owens-Ford Glass Company, 1935), 4–5.

84. Such broad exposure was bound to influence Main Street facade updating significantly, by stimulating work and guiding design. The journals included *Architectural Record*, which coordinated the effort, *Pencil Points, Architectural Forum, National Real Estate Journal, Drug Topics, Progressive Grocer, Apparel Arts,* and *Gasoline Retailer*. See "Forum of Events: Winners in Modernize Main Street Competition," *Architectural Forum* 63 (October 1935): 78–81, and "Modernizing Main Street: Selected Designs from The Record's Competition," *Pencil Points* 16 (October 1935): 501–19.

85. Kenneth Stowell, who guided *Architectural Record* in the production of the competition, actually discouraged deeply projecting signs and display windows. Stowell, however, encouraged holistic facade design incorporating signs and windows.

86. "Building Boom Gathers Force across Nation," *Washington Post,* August 8, 1935, 20.

87. PPG marketed their complete storefront package under the name Pittco. In contrast to the ideal timing of the Pittco system, L-O-F was not able to introduce a corresponding package until 1937, with the introduction of Extrudalite, an aluminum display-glass framing system that combined with Vitrolite's structural glass and the company's clear plate glass to compose entire storefronts. PPG was also advanced in its ability to offer its own financing, titled the Pittsburgh Time Payment Plan, as early as 1936—an offer to streamline the loan process experienced with the federal government. Gabrielle Esperdy covers the coordination between the glass companies and the FHA program thoroughly in *Modernizing Main Street,* 108–12, 133.

88. Their charge was to evaluate how well the competing architects used glass in their storefront designs. The judges awarded one of the top honors to the firm of Pioso and Peterson for its sober facade created for the William Hahn Company. The simplicity and scale of the facade was its prime appeal, as well as its generous use of glass. On the upper stories was a single multistory window, with letters spaced at regular intervals across it.

89. It is interesting to note that this flashy new facade on State Street replaced another major icon along the street, the Orpheum Theatre, with its two-story arched entrance. Designed by the preeminent architectural firm of Holabird & Roche in 1907, the theater was the last of the first wave of cinemas in the loop, although this building was not a true nickelodeon. The Orpheum was originally a spacious and rather resplendent vaudeville house, which made the switch to movies within two years of its construction.

90. The product was first available for architectural specification in 1935. Chicago's A Century of Progress exposition introduced the public to a glass block product in the design of the Owens Illinois building, a structure completely composed of the material. A stepped glass block tower rose between two glass block wings, a massing almost duplicated six years later for the Glass Incorporated Building at the 1939 World's Fair in New York, where three glass companies shared one structure.

91. See "National Cash Register Building Miami Florida," *Florida Architecture and Allied Arts* (1941): 49. Four years after the introduction of Insulux, Owens-Illinois launched a competition challenging architects to explore creative ways of using this novel glass block product. Not surprisingly, the most successful entries were those in which glass block made up most of the elevation. By the 1950s, a new product was available to architects wishing to illuminate the entire fronts of stores. For example, Rohm and Haas, the manufacturer of Plexiglas, promoted storefronts created by leading store designers like Morris Lapidus, with his luminous facade for the Holly store, in Baton Rouge, Louisiana. Corrugated white translucent Plexiglas, backlit by neon, had a similar look to one of the most popular patterns of glass block.

See advertisement, "When a Store Needs Personality... Plexiglas Comes to the Front," *Architectural Record* 108 (August 1950): 197.

92. See Robert P. Stockton, "King Street Building a 'Cinderella Story,'" *(Charleston) News and Courier,* November 19, 1979.

93. Around this same time, signs in cities such as Chicago had become particularly grand in scale, both projecting and those mounted flush with the building skin. The entire three-story fronts of the structures that housed Hirsch Clothes and the Jack Lord store, near the intersection of Belmont and Lincoln Roads, were basically immense, square signs. The Leo Ross facade, on State Street, consisted merely of the store's distinctive vertical logo, rendered two stories high in reversed channel neon; behind these letters was a blank, flat background.

94. One of the earliest was *Original Sign Designs Featuring Store Front Advertising* (Ohio State Conference of Signs and Pictorial Artists Local Unions, 1941).

95. In 1935, Alschuler designed several options for a Woolworth's store, at State and Adams Streets in Chicago's Loop, which demonstrated great sophistication in creating suggested layers of form while maintaining a continuity of surface. These prepared the architect well for his later work for the Grant's chain. Drawings for the Woolworth's project are located at the Chicago History Museum.

96. John McAndrew, ed., *Guide to Modern Architecture: Northeast States* (New York: Museum of Modern Art, 1940), 49.

97. See Robert A. Fash, "For Departmentalized Merchandizing," *Architectural Record* 95 (April 1944): 109. Other retail chains attempted subtler solutions for weaving together building skin and graphics. At the Hecht Company warehouse on New York Avenue in Washington, D.C., continuous ribbons of thin, opaque wall material appeared to hold in place the glass block "cylinder" suggested at the corner, as if they were rubber bands. The glass block "crown" at the top of the corner reinforced the idea of a cylindrical structure that might otherwise appear continuous with the glass-block ribbon windows. So there was a clever tension between possible perceptions: a smooth, continuous building envelope or a grouping of masses. Darkened glass block squares along a straight section of ribbon window spelled out the company name. Although such subtle signage was lost on most pedestrians or motorists at street level, it exemplified the American tradition of specifying minor graphics for major buildings, such as department stores. More important, this graphic approach illustrated the emphasis at this time for smoothing away potential interruptions of a perfect surface. Eric Mendelsohn had earlier established such a tension between a continuous whole and pieces pushing to be free with his Schocken department store in Stuttgart (1928), which in turn is often credited as being inspired by Louis Sullivan's store for Schlesinger & Meyer in Chicago (1906). In Stuttgart, the volumes were less in a tenuous balance, however, as the corner piece was pulled forward considerably and the sign certainly had a three-dimensional, physical identity of its own. In America, by the very late 1930s and early 1940s, the design pieces, including signs, were increasingly breaking away from the building mass.

98. Gene Burke and Edgar Kober, *Modern Store Design* (Los Angeles: Institute of Product Research, 1946), 8.

99. "Postwar Cigar Store-Haberdashery; Design Gives Spaciousness to Small Site," *Architectural Forum* 81 (October 1944): 113.

100. Malcolm Erb (Pittsburgh Plate Glass Company), "Modernizing the Smaller Store" in National Retail Merchants Association Store Management Group, *Planning the Store of To-Morrow,* compiled by Store Management and Sales Promotion Divisions of the National Retail Dry Goods Association (New York, 1945), 29.

101. "Store Designers Don't Suffer from Tradition Fixations—Thank God," *Pencil Points* 25 (August 1944): 40.

102. The leap toward more open fronts could also be seen by comparing advertisements by Libbey-Owens-Ford in the late 1930s to those of the early and middle 1940s. For example, the advertisement on the inside front cover of the November 1930 issue of *Chain Store Age* featured a wide expanse of clear glass, but under a conventional, solid fascia zone. Even the bulkhead was solid and rose to waist height. The ad on page 51 of the July 1944 issue, in contrast, featured a triple-height facade of glass, which eliminated any semblance of a solid wall. The fact that the focus was now on remaking the entire building facade, rather than just recladding one or two stories, revealed the radical nature of the change.

103. "Remodel Main Street, Niles, Michigan," *Architectural Forum* 81 (October 1944): 101–12.

104. In the same year as the Niles project, 1944, *Chain Store Age* and *Architectural Record* collaborated by inviting the firm of Ketchum, Gina & Sharp, architect Morris Lapidus, and others to explore the possibilities for effective postwar commercial design. The definite lull in construction during World War II led several journals to initiate an exploration into store design for the postwar years, recognizing a need to advance beyond the status quo and to address the growing backlog in required remodeling. The result was a section of *Chain Store Age* devoted to "Tomorrow's Chain Stores." Ketchum proposed a radical remake of the classic five-and-ten-cent store, with its traditional fascia sign. In this proposal for the H. L. Green Co., the upper stories of the preexisting commercial building disappeared and the entire front was replaced with glass, recessed approximately fifteen feet from the common storefront line, creating a generous arcade. Six-foot letters were individually fastened across the full width of the glass front. An aggressively sized horizontal projecting sign cantilevered out from the overhanging slab roof. With this project, alongside the Niles work, Ketchum confirmed that he was not against generously scaled graphics, as long as they were manipulated by an able architect. "Tomorrow's Chain Stores; Tomorrow's Variety Store," *Chain Store Age* 20 (April 1944): 13.

105. Morris Ketchum claimed that horizontal or vertical projecting signs had advertising value, but if they were not used

with restraint, too many signs would cancel each other out. Like Lapidus, he was enamored with the possibilities that graphics offered if carefully considered with the design whole. In his work he often employed even large-scale graphics. His scorn appeared to be directed at stores that used too many individual signs—a perceived clutter of graphics. Morris Ketchum Jr., *Shops and Stores*, Progressive Architecture Library (New York: Reinhold, 1948), 170.

106. Kawneer also published free booklets, available to customers upon request, that promoted Ketchum's modern store design; Ketchum, *Shops and Stores*.

107. "Trade: Store Block," *Architectural Forum* 73 (October 1940): 294.

108. Lapidus, *Too Much*, 110.

109. Morris Lapidus, "The Retail Store and Its Design Problems," *Architectural Record* 97 (February 1945): 96–109.

110. Grayson's expanded at a time when most businesses put improvements on hold, as the war had put powerful limits on access to building supplies. The Grayson's locations described above were in urban locations, but the chain also located a great many stores on automobile strips. This required a shift in strategy, with features like sixty-foot towers to be seen from afar, and appealing, accessible (glass) rear entrances for parking in back. See "How Main Street Stole Fifth Avenue's Glitter," chap. 2 in M. Jeffrey Hardwick, *Mall Maker: Victor Gruen, Architect of an American Dream* (Philadelphia: University of Pennsylvania Press, 2004), 48–71. For an example of literature written to introduce the how-to's of the open front, with good coverage of Grayson's Seattle, see Dr. Louis Parnes, *Planning Stores That Pay: Organic Design and Layout for Efficient Merchandising* (New York: F. W. Dodge Corp., 1948). For coverage of Grayson's and other work by its designers, see "Recent Work by Gruenbaum, Krummeck, & Auer," *Architectural Forum* 75 (September, 1941): 191–97.

111. Perhaps it was indebted to S. Charles Lee's Tower Bowl sign of 1941, in San Diego.

112. Drive-in markets and early shopping strips were some of the earliest projects to explore the effectiveness of tall, slim tower signs. The Mesa Vernon Drive-In Market (George J. Adams, 1929) featured the simplest of vertical elements—merely a prolonged cube with the word *market* scrawled vertically up its side in neon. See "Store Buildings," *Architectural Record* 65 (June 1929): 603.

For the many Sears, Roebuck stores that Chicago's Nimmons, Carr & Wright and others designed in the late 1920s and 1930s, the corner architectural tower became a trademark feature, as memorable and identifiable as any consistent advertising graphic. This was important in establishing a presence, as these stores were not contiguous with established shopping hubs. The towers served like beacons for distant motorists. In the 1930s, the Sears architects deftly incorporated lettering with the architectural detailing of each tower to establish the company's identity, but the distinctive corner tower feature alone would effectively communicate the brand to anyone familiar with Sears stores. For Chicago's A Century of Progress exposition, Nimmons, Carr & Wright designed a windowless tower on a long horizontal base, something of a distilled architectural trademark, a logo or diagram in three dimensions. At the same time, Sears announced windowless stores for the future of department store retailing with its new site in Englewood, near the fair, where the tower played a key role in creating visual interest. This tower powerfully marked the intersection of 63rd and Halsted Streets, the hub of the second greatest business center in metropolitan Chicago, one of the rare instances in the early roll-out where a Sears, Roebuck store was placed in a tight urban context, among other stores. The tower feature would rather suddenly fade from the plans for Sears stores in the 1940s, especially with the Pico Boulevard, Los Angeles, and Wisconsin Avenue, Washington, D.C., locations. See "Without Windows: Sears Discards Precedent to Gain a Functional Store Interior," *Architectural Forum* 62 (March 1935): 207–11; "No Windows: Sears Roebuck & Company Risk $1,500,000 on a New Type of Store Building," *Architect and Engineer* 120 (February, 1935): 35–38; and most especially Richard Longstreth, "Sears, Roebuck and the Remaking of the Department Store, 1924–1942," *Journal of the Society of Architectural Historians* 65 (June 2006): 238–79.

Filling stations also employed sign towers of all descriptions—features deemed necessary since the customer was rarely moving at the casual pace of a pedestrian and therefore required effective visual identification from afar. A somewhat common approach to identifying filling stations was to erect an extreme sign tower—a vertical spear on an otherwise modest, low-level structure. Engineer Milton Nigg built a station for Signal Gas (1939) on Wilshire Boulevard that borrowed the vertical strategy of drive-in restaurants and movie theaters in Los Angeles. In this case, however, the sign tower appeared as truly independent of the horizontal building on which it rested. An ingenious set of circles arranged in the fashion of a traffic signal served as the graphic to stop traffic and lure customers. At a Shell station in St. Louis (1937), a tall, fluted sign tower rose from the end of a wedge-shaped building located on a site created by the intersection of three streets. The tower actually served double-duty as a chimney, and codes mandated its height relative to a neighboring multistory building. "Service Stations," *Architectural Forum* 66 (February 1937): 91. For another remarkable design of a Shell station, where the building serves as an internally illuminated sign, see A. L. Powell, "A Gas Station in Glass and Color," *Magazine of Light* 3 (second Summer issue, 1934): 24.

113. Chris Nichols, *The Leisure Architecture of Wayne McAllister* (Salt Lake City UT: Gibbs Smith, 2007), 82.

114. Vertical sign towers assumed many forms as architects explored distinctive ways to stack letters, but most remained very narrow and tall. One of the earliest instances of a slim, illuminated tower employed as a primary identifying feature was incorporated into the design of the Century Grille at the Chicago World's Fair of 1933. At about this same time,

Kem Weber led students at the Art Center School (then in downtown Los Angeles) to explore design possibilities for this building and sign type, and an illuminated tower featured prominently in several of the proposals. See "Special Building Types: Roadside Diners," *Architectural Record* 76 (July 1934): 56. A tall neon tower marked Bertrand Goldberg's North Pole ice cream store (1938) in River Forest, Illinois, but the business identification was confined to lettering at the roof's edge. The illuminated tower, like many in California, acted as a sign despite the absence of lettering.

115. The once freestanding circular drive-in restaurant was partially but firmly embedded in a greater orthogonal building mass by the mid-1940s, as revealed by a building type study. See "Drive-In Restaurants and Luncheonettes: *Architectural Record*'s Building Types Study Number 117," *Architectural Record* 100 (September 1946): 99–113.

116. The signs of the other Collins Avenue towers, marking at least one new hotel built each year during the 1940s, could be seen from the long approach from the mainland to the beach. The hotel, as a building type, had a long history of advertising its identity from afar by placing an illuminated sign on the roof. This served well as a landmark for strangers unfamiliar with local geography. It also served as an outthrust welcome. The Miami Beach hotels of the late 1930s and early 1940s continued this tradition as they competed for attention. What was new here, however, was the design integration. No massive iron support structure marred the roof; each identity was as smart and seamless as a monogram on a bathrobe. The full name or initials of the hotels were most often located on a modern turret that crested each building. After dark, the signs were advertisements with lives of their own, competing for attention as the crowd returned each season.

117. A series of neighborhood theaters designed by Walker and Eisen for the United Artists chain (in Inglewood, Pasadena, Long Beach, and other locations) featured a central vertical sign fin flanked symmetrically by faceting that tapered down to the marquee. The designer of the Highland Theater (Myrtus A. Wright, 1939) in St. Paul, Minnesota, approached the challenge of making a design transition from vertical sign tower to horizontal marquee in a novel way for American theaters, by creating an asymmetrical, Bauhaus-inspired composition.

118. William Lescaze proposed a similar upswept marquee, taking a turn at ninety degrees to become the primary identification for motorists. See "Theater: William Lescaze, AIA, Architect," *Pencil Points* 25 (August 1944), 49.

119. Chicago's Southtown Theater (Rapp and Rapp, 1932) had two towers: a relatively short one that stepped down into the facade over the entrance and another, far taller, structure that stood independently at the curb next to the front parking lot. The 200-foot-tall sign tower, constructed by the Lu-mi-nus Sign Company, had vertical lettering on each face. Located a block away from the new windowless Sears store, at 63rd and Halsted Streets, it was a Chicago landmark for many years and was commonly featured as an icon in newspaper advertisements for the cinema.

120. For a full account of the life and work of S. Charles Lee, see Maggie Valentine, *The Show Starts on the Sidewalk: An Architectural History of the Movie Theatre, Starring S. Charles Lee* (New Haven, CT: Yale University Press, 1994).

121. When architect Timothy Pflueger renovated the New Mission Theater (1932) in San Francisco, he made little effort to visually tie the new tower to its base via form. There was transition from tower to base, but no stepped connection as with many other theaters of this date. Instead, the architect created a sense of unity by means of graphics rather than architecture. A horizontal banding pattern on the tower served as a link to the horizontal base below.

122. The modest commercial work of E. L. Robertson, Albert Annis, and Harry Hohauser in Miami Beach vividly illustrated the progression toward simplicity. Robertson's 1934 storefronts on Washington Boulevard had fluted buttresses that emphasized urban verticality around each glass bay. Solid walls or pilasters between tenants carried some of the zigzag ornament up through the parapet. By 1936, one of his simple storefront strips along Washington Boulevard instead emphasized the horizontality of the strip by eliminating these full-height verticals. Henry Hohauser designed several storefronts in 1936 that consisted almost entirely of display glass; horizontal lines at the parapet underscored this feature. For a long strip of storefronts along Lincoln Road, Albert Annis created, in 1940, a blank wall above the continuous display glass, which was sliced horizontally by a thin glass block ribbon that ran its full, multistore width. But Annis's visual spareness did not encourage the intrusion of a variety of signs, and the architect did not identify a panel where signs were welcomed. There was also no accommodation in any of these designs for projecting elements—fins, for example—that might support signs.

123. The term *shopping center* was originally applied in advertisements to identify well-known hubs or concentrations of retail activity owned by various individuals in urban locations, but it became increasingly associated with groups of shop fronts owned or coordinated by a single entity and visually fashioned to appear as a single unit. Newspaper articles and books encouraged owners or potential investors, in the early 1930s, to extend their Main Street makeovers by including as many stores as possible into the new refacing. This was an economic strategy, in part—why have a decrepit or empty storefront next to one brilliantly updated? It would harm sales. Better to control more street frontage or work collectively with neighboring owners or retailers. "Briton Offers New Shopping Center Ideas," *Washington Post*, August 25, 1940; "Modernizing Puts Business on 63rd Street," *Washington Post*, February 9, 1936; Kenneth Kingsley Stowell, *Modernizing Buildings for Profit* (New York: Prentice-Hall, 1935), 164.

124. Federal Housing Authority, *Community Campaign: How Your City Can Get the Greatest Benefit from the National Housing*

Act: A Suggested Plan for Organizing Your Local Campaign under the Better Housing Program (Washington, D.C.: Federal Housing Administration, 1934), 20.

125. The sales force for Vitrolite, for example, approached groups of tenants and building owners to present renderings of how a remade building front might look (another example of the aggressive sales strategy of the glass companies). Color and continuous line were key to making the strip appear harmonious while giving each storefront distinction. Sometimes an array of storefront colors would be visually held together merely by keeping the signs confined to the same band area, the top of the colored glass consistent from one store to the next. For others the color was consistent across a long facade, from business to business. *Glassic* (Libbey-Owens-Ford internal newsletter), Toledo, Ohio, July 1939.

126. *Architectural Record* noted in 1929 that volumes and articles on modern architecture were revealing a radical change of appearance growing from a new kind of building material. In this case, the journal cited structural steel and concrete. But the point it was trying to make was that American architects were substituting flat lines of different colors in place of pseudostructural members such as buttresses and pilasters. The availability of pigmented structural glass in the 1930s permitted this trend to expand to the point that ornament became fully independent of any reference to architectural order. Color flowed freely on the surface of new buildings. This example in Chicago demonstrated how radical this freedom could become. See Arthur W. Colton, "The Architect's Library: Book Reviews," *Architectural Record* 65 (February 1929): 205.

127. The White Hut chain borrowed from the success of the White Castle and White Tower chains by employing bright white sheathing to distinguish the business from dining establishments of spurious hygiene. Originally the look of White Hut shops was a direct copy.

    For another strip of retail, across the street, a newspaper advertisement proclaimed the grand opening of the Belmont Center in 1941, including a two-page illustration of the new look for an old corner. In the drawing, everything appeared as if it was modern and new, yet a uniform sign system of modestly scaled, vertical projecting signs camouflaged what was basically an amalgamation of old two-story commercial buildings. New graphics were an economical way of creating a new image, especially important in the 1930s. In this case, an appealingly uniform new center was proposed by severely limiting the shape and placement of signage. Advertisement, *Chicago Daily Tribune,* October 12, 1941.

128. Earlier, arcades had been a notable manifestation of uniform signs, though quite limited on American soil. Large buildings, such as skyscrapers, were another place where regular, regulated bays of signage, restricted to spaces specifically designed for identification, seemed a natural. General Electric, in advertisements in the 1920s, promoted illuminated, standardized panels for tall buildings. And yet, examples of such uniformity were somewhat rare. Unlike the small shopping centers in outlying, low-level districts, the skyscraper was rarely, if ever, a retail destination with an identity of its own, made more attractive with a well-known anchor. It was just as rarely given added presence through advertisements as such a destination. It most cases, skyscraper retail was limited to a series of specialty shops and restaurants. In a quite a few instances, a theater might be the primary tenant in such an office building, but its effect as a visual anchor was limited. Unlike suburban theaters, sign and marquee alone identified the urban cinema. It was one of many signs of similar scale and did not establish a profile on the horizon as a figural building with a glowing identity in the otherwise blank horizontality of suburbia.

129. See "Drafting and Design Problems: Neighborhood Shopping Centers," *Architectural Record* 71 (May 1932): 325–30. This trend to minimize signs visually is documented in plenty of examples published up until the war. See, for instance, "Building Types: Community Shopping Centers," *Architectural Record* 87 (June 1940): 99–120.

130. Locating the site on a blank slate and setting the program for a group of stores revealed the mindset of the mid-1940s: architects and developers were progressively more fixated on suburbia and concerned with establishing visual harmony in a land where it was perceived that chaos was growing, with the random design and placement of new commercial buildings.

131. But the message from the jury was mixed; tenant signs for the winners of the second and third prizes displayed uniform lettering of extremely small scale placed discreetly along the narrow confines of canopy edges or tucked tightly over door frames, barely visible. In contrast, the first-prize winner was praised for establishing a limited variety in his graphics by placing signs of heterogeneous lettering directly above or below the canopy edge. Freestanding display cases with lettering also served to identify stores, winning praise for their potential flexibility in advertising. *Reports on Two Architectural Competitions; Sponsored by the Kawneer Company, Niles, Michigan* (Niles, MI: Kawneer Company, 1943), 4, 9.

132. "Remodeling Main Street, Niles, Michigan," *Architectural Forum* 81(October 1944): 101.

133. Lapidus, *Too Much*, 94.

134. See especially Philip Di Lemme, *Luminous Advertising Sketches* (Cincinnati: Signs of the Times, 1935). This book was quite popular and was reprinted with additions in 1953 and 1984 by Signs of the Times and Van Nostrand Reinhold.

135. The simple rectangular or strip signs of the past eventually assumed greater complexity of form, even for smaller businesses; it was common to see C-shaped signs, T-shaped signs, and I-shaped signs with horizontals at top and bottom. Some sign companies offered standardized, though elaborate, designs through catalogs, thus making neon signs affordable to smaller businesses. These signs were extremely accessible, priced to sell, with few decisions to make—choose your

design and select from a short list of key words with fixed sizes and prices.

136. Zick's building dates from 1941, with only modest, but smoothly integrated, dimensional letters faced in neon, resting on the canopy over the door. In 1950, Neon Products Signs added the script-lettered sign on the side wall, the curtain of neon, and the animated chef running with his burger. Although architect Zick may not have been directly consulted for this addition in 1950, his building was designed in such a manner that invited display. The concave entrance was almost a stage, a focal point for attention.

137. Raymond Loewy, *Never Leave Well Enough Alone: The Personal Record of an Industrial Designer* (New York: Simon & Schuster, 1951), 338.

CHAPTER 5. *Landscapes of More and Less: Consequences of Commercial Freedom and Restraint, 1946–1964*

1. Mildred Constantine, "The Woolworth Story," *Architectural Record* 120 (September 1956): 263.
2. John Maas, "Images and Letters," *Landscape* 8, no. 2 (Winter 1958–59): 3.
3. Upper stories were used less as services moved to the suburbs along with the former residents of the urban area. In many cases, store owners agreed to forego the rental from the upper floors in order to be able to install continuous, multistoried metal skins up the facades of buildings. For fire department access to the then-blocked upper stories, the designers of these new facades incorporated shadow boxes with decorative designs stacked up the front. Dominic Campanella, "Unifying the Façade," *Chain Store Age* 24 (July 1948): 32.
4. Of particular note was Leigh's plan to unite two historic Broadway theater facades, the Astor (1905) and the Victoria (opened in 1908 as the Gaiety) behind a skin. Douglas Leigh's contribution to the world of signs and publicity is, in itself, a worthy subject for a book. Animation was often key to his work, be it smoke rings blown from a giant painted face or cartoons broadcast on a vast matrix of bulbs (a first-generation JumboTron of sorts, using new technology dubbed Leigh-Epok). This book does not emphasize New York and Times Square—material very worthy, but addressed at length in other books, including Darcy Tell, *Times Square Spectacular: Lighting Up Broadway* (New York: Smithsonian Books: Collins, 2007), and Tama Starr and Edward Hayman, *Signs and Wonders: The Spectacular Marketing of America* (New York: Doubleday Business, 1998).
5. "Cities Urged to Right Architectural Errors," *Providence Sunday Journal*, March 30, 1958.
6. Preservationists often use the term *slipcovering* to refer to the refinishing of a building facade with a new material, especially if the cladding is loosely applied, as with metal panel systems. This is often such a loose application of sheathing that it is not unlike pulling a piece of fabric over the original facade.
7. One example given was part of a smaller chain of department stores, each outlet with a long, multistory building facade under consideration. A "colorful and modernist effect" was achieved with a mere $6,000, plus $2,000 for the new sign lettering. The entire endeavor was accomplished "at cost in line with rent." See "Low-cost Exterior Remodeling," *Chain Store Age* 34 (July 1958): A38.
8. In Ontario, California, e.g., the two-story masonry buildings from the turn of the twentieth century that lined several blocks received new facades sometime in the 1950s. For one building, the second-floor elevation was made to visually float over the storefronts below, like an independent panel; a four-sided frame edged the entire "panel." The old windows were made to appear as a continuous ribbon window (per Le Corbusier) by putting textured panels laterally between the existing openings and framing this entire horizontal band as one piece. The new facade for Fallis' department store unified a group of disparate facades with one plain, blank covering; giant lettering crossed it diagonally to claim the composite structure as one whole.
9. To meet the voracious wartime demand for strong, lightweight metals, the U.S. government subsidized the expansion of the industry's productive capacity. The production of aluminum increased by more than 600 percent between 1939 and the peak year of 1943. Even before the conclusion of the war, industry executives were concerned with developing new markets to absorb the expanded capacity. Alcoa held a monopoly on the manufacture and sale of aluminum and was ready and able to purchase the factories the government had built with public money during the war. However, the Justice Department initiated an antitrust action designed to break Alcoa's monopoly. Encouraged by the government, the R. J. Reynolds Tobacco Company and the Kaiser Company quickly established independent aluminum companies. See Dennis Doordan, "Promoting Aluminum: Designers and the American Aluminum Industry," *Design Issues* 9 (Autumn 1993): 46.
10. In the 1950s, both Alcoa and Reynolds created styling and design or market development departments. Industry designers distributed informative literature and samples, visited design offices to demonstrate new developments, invited outside designers to visit aluminum production facilities, and publicized innovative uses for the material. Ibid., 47.
11. One particular two-page advertisement for this crafty system presented a series of cartoon panels that showed Mr. Keen, "the sign salesman who lives up to his name," as he discovered a potential target. Following the instructions in the kit, Keen wins the order, leaps for joy in the glow of the dazzling new facade, and finally speeds off in a car much fancier than the one shown in panel one of the sequence. "This Storefront Renewal Program . . . Courtesy of Your PLEXIGLAS® Supplier . . . Can Increase Your Sales, Too!" *Signs of the Times* 167 (August 1964): n.p.

12. Color was still relatively rare in such trade journal advertisements of the early and middle 1950s. Plexiglas advertisements featured tag-lines or slogans such as "Gives distinction to your signs . . . to your place of business" or "Whether your store is old or new, Plexiglas makes it modern."

13. Ketchum's ideas and advanced design philosophy for retail was advanced in Kawneer's promotional literature of the period. For example, see Kawneer Co., *Machines for Selling: Modern Store Designs* (Niles, MI: Kawneer, 1946); *A Plan for Modernizing Main Street* (Niles, MI: Kawneer, 1945).

14. The concept of expanding the sign area to the entire storefront or building facade was not new, of course. It had been promoted heavily at least as early as the Vitrolite architectural competition of 1935 and by *Signs of the Times* in the early 1940s.

15. Signs and architectural features were articulated as distinct elements of a cohesive design composition. Victor Lundy was one of the most celebrated architects of a group that came to be known as the Sarasota school of architecture. Lundy's studies at Harvard in the 1940s were under Walter Gropius, founder of the Bauhaus. The school's appreciation for the graphic arts as well as architecture may have influenced the cohesive design package Lundy delivered for the White Tower chain. Work from Sarasota received a great deal of attention in the press during the 1950s; it was known for its articulation of parts, clean lines, and elegant use of new materials and technology. Lundy designed a wide range of building types in Sarasota during the 1950s and was equally adventurous with churches and schools. His novel technology and expressive forms were seen as exuberant departures from the norm even in the innovative architectural community of Sarasota. His Galloway Furniture store (1959) on a highway south of town was a round glass building with a structural core like a tree trunk. The White Tower (1959) was independent and expressive as well, with its all-glass walls and unique signage. But it was built on Main Street and conformed carefully to its tight site. There were no setbacks or signs on poles spearing rakishly angled, overhanging roofs as one might have seen if a California "Googie" architectural firm (like Armet and Davis) had been given the commission. See note 27 below for definition of Googie.

16. Reyner Banham, *Los Angeles: The Architecture of Four Ecologies* (1971; reprint, Berkeley: University of California Press, 2009), 93–102.

17. See "Store Modernization Review," *Chain Store Age* 24 (July 1948): 18. Individual planes and volumes were more clearly articulated in the design of Milliron's, designed by Gruen and Krummeck (1949) for the Los Angeles community of Westchester. The low-slung, block-long stretch of the main facade was dematerialized by a series of fins or thin buttresses, which cast deep shadows. Several display boxes, individually roofed, were affixed to these ribbed walls, thrusting merchandise out towards the road; these were perhaps the most motorist-oriented display windows designed to date. A three-story sign slab terminated this long wall, making an architectural exclamation point. See "Roof Parking Modifies Store Layout," *Architectural Record* 106 (August 1949): 130–31; "Something New in Stores," *Architectural Forum* 90 (June 1949):105–9.

18. This transition is well represented in "Drive-In Restaurants and Luncheonettes: Architectural Record's Building Types Study Number 117," *Architectural Record* 100 (September 1946): 99–113. See especially "Rectangular Drive-In with Non-Glare Front" by Hardison, Rhoda, and Moist, Architects, 103. See also "Building Preview: Drive-In Restaurant," *Architectural Forum* 83 (November 1945): 162–63. See the citation below regarding Harvey's Broiler in Downey, California.

19. This unusual sign cost all of $10,000 at the time of its construction, indeed putting it in the company of Las Vegas signs. It stands 30 feet tall and is approximately 400–500 square feet per side.

20. Las Vegas design history presents an important evolution of the physical and visual separation of sign and building. Early Las Vegas hotels were identified with primary neon sign features linked directly to the main buildings of each site. For later hotels, the primary signs would move out to the road, leaving the buildings, as growing front parking lots placed increased distance between these buildings and oncoming motorists. The slim pylon for the Flamingo (1946) was architecturally balanced against a sleek, modern, flat roof. The Thunderbird Hotel (1948), the Desert Inn (1952), and the Sahara (1952) each had identifying neon icons placed on heavy, central architectural towers. Each business had a secondary, low sign with a changeable message board at the road's edge. A significant physical break between sign and architecture came with the completion of Wayne McAllister's Sands Hotel (1952). In this example, the primary sign was at road's edge, a significant structure in its own right. Composed in the materials and design language of the hotel's porte-cochere, the main sign had become an independent piece of three-dimensional graphic design. By the 1960s, the primary sign of each hotel was always the one at the edge of the road. This sign gained altitude rapidly. In 1962, the architect of the Dunes Hotel had designed a primary sign to tie handsomely into the porte-cochere, but the hotel management snubbed the idea and insisted instead on siting the largest sign yet erected in Las Vegas (at 180 feet high) out at the road's edge. From the late 1940s to the early 1960s, the exterior architecture of these hotels had become progressively more modern and spare and less evocative of the exotic locales suggested by the hotels' names, leaving it up to the sign to create an image, establish a theme, or generate atmosphere. For a full education on the vast topic of Las Vegas architecture and sign history, see Alan Hess, *Viva Las Vegas: After-Hours Architecture* (San Francisco: Chronicle Books, 1993), and Charles F. Barnard, *The Magic Sign: The Electric Art/Architecture of Las Vegas* (Cincinnati: ST Publications, 1993).

21. Architect Meston had worked for Wayne McAllister, the man responsible for Simon's, the exemplary California circular

drive-in from the 1930s—along with other drive-ins like Herbert's, Robert's, and Van de Kamp's: all radial in plan or featuring a circular tower feature. See Alan Hess, "The Origins of McDonald's Golden Arches," *Journal of the Society of Architectural Historians* 45 (March, 1986): 62.

22. Sometimes a tight space for parking was made available between hotel and sidewalk. But space for pool and auto was most often pushed to the side rather than placed up front, which would require a major setback.

23. Some of the best graphic designers of the 1940s and 1950s contributed to *Arts & Architecture,* the journal which became the voice for better modern design in a variety of disciplines under the leadership of publisher John Entenza. Ray Eames, wife of architect, industrial designer, and filmmaker Charles Eames, designed many covers for the magazine.

24. Charles and Ray Eames demonstrated how postwar American design offices could be as interdisciplinary as the Bauhaus. Lines between professions could be abandoned or at least a firm could gather many kinds of design professionals under one roof. Deborah Sussman, one of the leading environmental graphic designers of the past forty years, spent many years working at the Eames firm. Certainly the title of one of the celebrated architectural journals of the period, *Arts & Architecture,* attests to an ideal of interdisciplinary sensitivity.

25. Paul Rand, *Thoughts on Design* (New York: Wittenborn, 1947), 110.

26. The elaborate structural base of this iconic design from 1951 resembled the exaggerated superstructure supports for some of the signs of the period.

27. According to author Alan Hess in his book *Googie Redux: Ultramodern Roadside Architecture* (San Francisco: Chronicle Books, 2004), the origin of the name *Googie* goes back to 1949, when architect John Lautner designed the coffee shop Googie's, which had very distinctive architectural characteristics. Googie's was located at the corner of Sunset Boulevard and Crescent Heights in Los Angeles. The architecture was typically influenced by car culture, the space age, and the atomic age, originating from southern California in the late 1940s and continuing approximately into the mid-1960s. The types of buildings that were most frequently designed in a Googie style were motels, coffee houses, and bowling alleys. Googie features include upswept roofs, curvaceous, geometric shapes, and bold use of glass, steel, and neon. Googie was also characterized by space-age designs that depict motion, such as boomerangs, flying saucers, atoms, and parabolas. Architectural compositions in this style or fashion often seemed to defy gravity, with heavy, sculptural roof slabs supported by fine spears and glass; columns often continued right through roofs, supporting nothing, but perhaps becoming signs. The Los Angeles–based architectural firm of Armet and Davis was one of the most prolific in design of this type.

28. The heraldic aspect of sign communication is that which is designed to attract the attention of the viewer. The heraldic and informational aspects of sign communication are described in Robert Venturi, Denise Scott Brown, and Steven Izenour, *Learning from Las Vegas: The Forgotten Symbolism of Architectural Form* (1972; revised ed., Cambridge, MA: MIT Press, 1982), 87.

29. Sign aficionados often credit Wayne Heath with spreading the concept of "panelization" with the work of his firm. *Panelization* refers to compositions of distinct shapes that serve to organize a great deal of information. Heath developed his skills as a designer while working as a show card painter for the Balaban and Katz theater empire, and as a sign painter with Sealander and Swanson and at Beverly Sign Company. In 1947, he headed west from Chicago with his new partner, and formed Heath and Gorsich in Los Angeles, making the leap from painted to electric signs. Heath's early experience creating posters and painted signs had prepared him well for the compositional possibilities of electric signs. The panels or shapes used to help organize and prioritize type in paint also served to arrange the message desired in lights.

30. Ray Quiel of Quiel Brothers Sign Company, in discussion with the author, July 1, 2008.

31. Just over two miles away, another major, super-scaled graphic provided the area with a significant landmark, the electric sign for Harvey's Broiler drive-in restaurant (Paul B. Clayton, 1958). In this case, the sign was fully responsible for *making* place as well as *marking* it. The building was little more than a long, low, flat slab roof hovering over the pavement, with floor-to-ceiling windows spanning the gap. The sign was notable for the immense, loose, cursive word "broiler," rendered in neon and mounted on a cantilevered beam that seemed to project out over the street. This startling effect was heightened by a bend in the long straight road (Firestone Boulevard) just as one neared the restaurant, which permitted the sign to be a focus on axis for many blocks upon approach. The restaurant was rebuilt after unlawful demolition by a previous owner and opened again to the public in 2009 as Bob's Big Boy Broiler. Although not an example of a sign as a major, independent monument, this sign was conceived to take advantage of its unique site and remains a true landmark. Like many drive-ins of the era, the roof reached out to the road and provided an opportunity for the architect to design an identity that responded to the long horizontal base that a roof can supply for a graphic.

32. With no formal training in design or the technology of his medium of plastic and neon, he relied on his intuition and his experience as a painter of show cards. Teague never entered the NESA competitions, but he was inducted into the Oklahoma Sign Manufacturer's Hall of Fame, only the second ever to be so honored. Mac Teague and Sam Teague (son), in discussion with the author, January 15, 2010.

33. According to Lucian Howze, art director at Stanford and Inge, in Roanoke, Virginia, a sketchpad full of thumbnail sketches collected during these studies could provide a convenient library of on-hand solutions that would be ready when the next client walked in the door. Lucian H. Howze, "Designing

Electric Signs, Part IX: Thumbnail Sketches," *Signs of the Times* 167 (June 1964): 57.

34. George F. Meyers, Peter Horsley, Don Sturdivant, Bill Boley, and H. C. Martin were well represented on the bookshelves of sign crafters—the last three for expertise in lettering and showcard design.

35. Ephemeral print work in magazines by highly regarded designers like Paul Rand and Alexy Brodovitch was highly accessible and at least indirectly influential to sign designers crafting artifacts that would remain in the landscape for years.

36. "The Motel Free-for-All," *Fortune*, June 1959, 120–21. For a vivid verbal description of the "longitudinal metropolis" of highway businesses, see Bernard DeVoto, "The Easy Chair: Motel Town," *Harper's*, September 1953, 45–48.

37. Phillip B. Meggs, *A History of Graphic Design* (New York: Van Nostrand Reinhold, 1983), 368.

38. Yusaku Kamekura, ed., *Paul Rand: His Work from 1946 to 1958* (New York: Knopf, 1959), 14.

39. Ladislav Sutnar, "Commercial Symbols in Architecture," *Architectural Record* 120 (September 1956): 257–61. See also "Display Art: The Trend to Symbolism," *Signs of the Times* 141 (October 1955): 58–61.

40. "Display Art: The Trend to Symbolism," 58–61.

41. Victor Gruen, "Architect Gruen States the Challenge That Graphic Design Presents," *Architectural Record* 120 (September 1956): 246.

42. Vladimir Nabokov, *Lolita* (1955; reprint, New York: Knopf, 1992), 224.

43. Corporate symbols and trademarks were not only part of a reform movement for roadside graphics but for roadside architecture as well. As early as the 1910s, in response to public demand, Standard Oil of California had undertaken a campaign to clean up and beautify its stations. See Daniel M. Bluestone, "Roadside Blight and the Reform of Commercial Architecture," *Roadside America: The Automobile in Design and Culture*, ed. Jan Jennings (Ames: Iowa State University Press for the Society of Commercial Archeology, 1990), 179. A new Mobil gas station built in the mid-1950s in Anaheim, California, held a large three-dimensional Pegasus aloft on one of four masts that supported hanging roofs. Published in several journals, the design was praised by the *Architectural Forum* because it "eliminated the building" and let the signs do the work. "A Handsome Gas Station," *Architectural Forum* 107 (August 1957): 118–19. This would probably have pleased J. B. Jackson, who expressed hope in 1956 that signs would assume increased responsibility for distant eye-appeal and allow the architecture to calm down. John Brinckerhoff Jackson, *Landscapes: Selected Writings of J. B. Jackson*, ed. Ervin H. Zube (Amherst: University of Massachusetts Press, 1970), 68.

44. Meggs, *History of Graphic Design*, 425–29.

45. Pierre Martineau, "Sharper Focus for the Corporate Image" (abridged from *Harvard Business Review*, November–December 1958), *Print* (May–June 1959): 25.

46. Ibid., 23.

47. Bill Dorsey and Tod Swormstedt, "1950-1959," *Signs of the Times* 203 (May 1981): 23.

48. "Neon Signmaker Goes into Plastic," *Business Week*, June 10, 1950, 52.

49. Acrylics faced no big hurdles, such as the patent challenges of the late 1920s that had slowed the change from incandescent bulbs to neon. But the use of fluorescent tubes, which would eventually go hand-in-hand with the use of plastic sign facing, may have initially been perceived as a design straightjacket. Illumination by fluorescent tubes limited sign shapes to simple trapezoids based on standard tube sizes and regular tube spacing. By the early 1960s, most signs were a mix of acrylic and exposed neon. Acrylic trapezoids often provided a solid framework around which freer shapes or script lettering in neon could be arrayed. Changeable message boards for theaters and motels were a natural application of acrylic and fluorescents.

50. Richard W. Snibbe, *A Photographic Record of 100 Selected Designs for Small Commercial Buildings Executed within the Last 20 Years* (New York: Reinhold, 1956), 2. Snibbe was later responsible for an ambitious 1962 redesign proposal for 42nd Street between Seventh and Eighth Avenue, sponsored by the Broadway Association. The scheme aimed to homogenize the perceived existing chaos and seediness with a double-height glass front running down both sides of the street. An arcade on the lower level permitted a second-level terrace for pedestrians, with visually coordinated bridges spanning the six-lane street. All business signs were to be homogenized, too, being arcade identities of standard format. The old theaters, located behind this new front, would be marked by standardized vertical, projecting signs. Context was a vague, grey background. Tell, *Times Square Spectacular*, 137–38.

51. Snibbe, *Photographic Record*, 3; see also Caleb Hornbostel, "Store Design: Architectural Record's Building Types Study Number 188," *Architectural Record* 111 (July 1952): 149–78.

52. Maas, "Images and Letters," 4.

53. James S. Hornbeck, "Signs & Symbols in Commercial Architecture," *Architectural Record* 120 (September 1956): 242.

54. For an article printed in *Landscape* magazine, Kevin Lynch conducted a series of interviews with pedestrians in a particular commercial neighborhood of Boston. Kevin Lynch and Malcolm Rivkin, "A Walk around the Block," *Landscape* 8, no. 3 (Spring 1959): 32. See also Kevin Lynch, *The Image of the City* (Cambridge, MA: MIT Press, 1960).

55. Christopher Tunnard and Boris Pushkarev, *Man-made America: Chaos or Control? An Inquiry into Selected Problems of Design in the Urbanized Landscape* (New Haven, CT: Yale University Press, 1963), x.

56. Even the exuberance of Times Square in New York City was seen as something that could be made better with a master plan or organizing idea. In 1955, a design studio led by Jose Luis Sert, then dean at Harvard's Graduate School of Design, offered a solution to the perceived chaos of Times Square. After appearing in the *Architectural Forum*, the proposal was

published again in Mildred Constantine's *Sign Language,* which heralded worthy examples of contemporary sign design, primarily from Europe. The proposal included a vast three-dimensional space-frame as a "neutral" matrix for panels of advertising. The frame itself, which bulged and projected into the spaces of Times Square and towered somewhat arbitrarily at points above it, became the true star of the show. In relatively muted contrast, the individual signs conformed to standard panel sizes. A gridded bank of revolving cubes was also intended for advertising messages but appeared to be primarily about color, motion, and visual variety rather than communication. In the rendering, only patterns were shown on the faces of the cubes—not messages. "Could This Be Times Square Tomorrow?" *Architectural Forum* 103 (August 1955): 106–12; Mildred Constantine, *Sign Language for Buildings and Landscape* (New York: Reinhold, 1961).

57. Jackson, *Landscapes,* 71.
58. Whitney R. Smith, "No Cars on Main Street," *Better Homes and Gardens,* January 1945, 23.
59. Kevin Starr, "The Case Study House Program and the Impending Future: Some Regional Considerations," in *Blueprints for Modern Living: History and Legacy of the Case Study Houses* (Cambridge, MA: MIT Press, 1989) 136.
60. "Retail Trade: Broadway Opening," *Time,* December 8, 1947, www.time.com/time/magazine/article/0,9171,934176,00.html; "Service Traffic Confined to Underground Tunnels," *Architectural Record* 106 (August 1949): 127; "Broadway-Crenshaw Store, California," *Architectural Record* 103 (April 1948): 10, 12, 14.
61. With its vast parking lot, which was perceived (from certain approaches) to be in front of the stores (rather than behind as was common before World War II), the Broadway-Crenshaw Center provided a model or template for the common suburban shopping center that began to appear in America's suburbs during the 1950s and 1960s. This California harbinger was much larger than its coast-to-coast progeny, but the basic characteristics were intact: large parking in front, a predominance of chain (rather than locally owned) stores, and freedom in sign lettering and size as well as a limitation to wall- or parapet-mounted graphics. A flurry of trade journal articles ushered in the era of the planned shopping center, whether neighborhood-sized or regional in scale. See "One-Stop Centers Continue Growth," *Chain Store Age* 22 (September 1946): 23–24; Bruno Funaro and Geoffrey Baker, "Shopping Centers: *Architectural Record*'s Building Types Study Number 152," *Architectural Record* 106 (August 1949): 110–35; "Shopping Center Round-Up," *Chain Store Age* 26 (July 1950): 26–29; S. O. Kaylin, "The Planned Shopping Center," *Chain Store Age* 30 (May 1954): 13–19; "New Ideas in Shopping Centers," *Chain Store Age* 26 (June 1954): 39–45. In Charleston, South Carolina, for example, a ring of such centers appeared in the middle to late 1950s along the primary corridors that led out of the old city center—especially as bridges were improved crossing from the peninsula to outlying communities and narrow two-lane highways were widened. "Ashley Span Approaches Take Shape" *Charleston Evening Post,* March 19, 1959; "1,400 Parking Spaces Painted," *Charleston Evening Post,* September 16, 1959; "Belk's to Open West Ashley Store," *Charleston Evening Post,* January 15, 1954; "New Shopping Center Opens," *Charleston Evening Post,* May 1, 1959.
62. Gruen and others explained that because mall managers controlled the competition, sign design could relax from the exuberant forms seen on the strip when a business was located in a shopping center. Since a shoe store, for example, wasn't cheek-by-jowl with other shoe stores, its signs needn't shout. Funaro and Baker, "Shopping Centers," 111; Victor Gruen, "What to Look for in Shopping Centers," *Chain Store Age* 24 (July 1948): 66.
63. Trained in Europe (under Josef Hoffman in Vienna) and at Harvard with Gropius, Ernst Payer was clearly one of Cleveland's most important early modern architects. His public buildings throughout Cleveland are an important part of his legacy, including the Medusa Portland Cement corporate headquarters in Cleveland Heights; his public libraries in Cleveland, Cleveland Heights, and Orange; and the Crawford Aviation and Auto Museum at the Western Reserve Historical Society. See "40 Stores," *Architectural Forum* 88 (May, 1948): 93–148; Nina Freedlander Gibans, "Cleveland Goes Modern: Designs for the Homes 1930–1970," www.architectureofcleveland.com/html/gibans_essay.pdf (accessed April 1, 2010).
64. Speaking in 1948 about a major shopping center that he proposed for Los Angeles, Gruen claimed, "The arrangement of the buildings . . . will give an imposing impression of the shopping center to those walking or driving by on the main boulevards . . . The tower-like warehouse would . . . form a monumental landmark for the department store and for the entire shopping center." Gruen, "What to Look for in Shopping Centers," 22.
65. See "Architecture and Sculpture: The Northland Regional Shopping Center," *Arts & Architecture* 72 (May 1955): 21–23; "Northland Shopping Centre, Detroit, Michigan," *Royal Architectural Institute of Canada Journal* 33 (June 1956): 227–31; "Centre commercial 'Northland,' Detroit, États-Unis," *L'Architecture d'aujourd'hui* 30 (April–May 1959): 38–39; "Northland: A Regional Shopping Center for Detroit, Michigan," *Michigan Society of Architects Monthly Bulletin* 28 (March 1954): 33–43.
66. "Commercial Buildings: Signs and Symbols" (special section), *Architectural Record* 120 (September 1956): 242–72; see also "Building Types Study: Buildings for Retail," *Architectural Record* 119 (March 1956): 205–27.
67. Among the many articles that cover the subject of monumental shopping center signs, see especially, "Landmark Identity for Shopping Center," *Signs of the Times* 157 (January 1961): 37; "61-Foot Pylon Offers Outstanding Readability," *Signs of the Times* 152 (August 1959): 56; and John Crerar Reid, "Height Draws Attention in Suburban Area," *Signs of the*

Times 137 (July 1954): 27. For Mondawmin Center, see "A Break-Through for Two-Level Shopping Centers," *Architectural Forum* 105 (December 1956): 114-26; "New Thinking on Shopping Centers," *Architectural Forum* 98 (March 1953): 122-45.

68. "Northland: A New Yardstick for Shopping Center Planning," *Architectural Forum* 100 (June 1954): 106. But for all its novelty, Northland's tenant signage was, in essence, a controlled updating of the traditional fascia sign of Main Street. This sign type had the fine scale of mid-nineteenth-century architecture in its heritage. In the 1950s, Gruen and his contemporaries were enforcing an updated version of this primary business sign type with their own system of neutral piers and regular bays of retail frontage. Had F. W. Woolworth known that the pedestrian-oriented shopping mall was on the horizon, its relatively modest gold-on-red sign might have been saved and continued for decades to come.

    Historian Alison Isenberg concurs with this perception of a conceptual circling back to a previous scale and homogeneity for the American commercial corridor. See Alison Isenberg, *Downtown America: A History of the Place and the People Who Made It* (Chicago: University of Chicago Press, 2004), 198-99. During the progressive era, in the early twentieth century, municipal housekeepers aspired to make modest but transformative improvements in order to achieve a dignified, unified Main Street corridor. The tendency for commerce to advertise with loud signs was reined in wherever possible, and a consistent urban infrastructure of rhythmically spaced, decorative lighting poles was placed along newly paved streets and sidewalks, muting individuality. Then, everything changed during the Great Depression, which warranted individual initiative and novelty in order to stimulate Main Street sales. The freedom initiated during this period was further exploited in the 1950s. But early shopping center design during the 1930s and 1940s pointed the way to the future, with modesty and regularity the order of the day.

69. "The aim of the shopping center designer . . . is to create an overall architectural framework, simple and strong enough to hold together the grouping of stores as a unit. The more successful the architect is at creating character and strength, the greater will be each tenant's latitude for individual expression." Gruen limited storefront height to a generous fourteen feet, making it "possible for every one of the tenants to build attractive fronts which expressed their individual merchandising characteristics." Victor Gruen, as told to Henry Goldstein, "The Chain's Stake in Planning the Center," *Chain Store Age* 30 (May 1954): 38-39.

70. Witold Rybczynski, *City Life: Urban Expectations in a New World* (New York: Scribner, 1995), 206.

71. Edward Larrabee Barnes, "Control of Graphics Essential to Good Shopping Center Design," *Architectural Record* 131 (June 1962): 164-65. A similar obsession with sensual satisfaction and the effects of light and shadow (perhaps overriding the need to communicate clearly) could be seen in architectural journal articles of this period. See, for example, Robert Lepper, "Corruption, Opportunity, and an Approach," *Architectural Record* 120 (September 1956): 268-71.

72. Victor Gruen and Larry Smith, *Shopping Towns USA: The Planning of Shopping Centers* (New York: Reinhold, 1960), 140.

73. Gruen deplored the climate of specialization that he believed was ruining American cities. "Many . . . claim . . . that architecture should be solely concerned with the design of the individual structure and that the responsibility for the shaping of the man-made and man-influenced environment belongs to others. This view, in my opinion, lies at the root of the trouble and is the reason for the presently prevailing confusion of our profession." Victor Gruen, *The Heart of Our Cities: The Urban Crisis: Diagnosis and Cure* (New York: Simon & Schuster, 1964), 156.

74. M. Jeffrey Hardwick, *Mall Maker: Victor Gruen, Architect of an American Dream* (Philadelphia: University of Pennsylvania, 2004), 135.

75. "Northland, A New Yardstick," 103.

76. John Brinckerhoff Jackson, "The Stranger's Path," *Landscape* 7 (Autumn 1957): 11-15, quoted in *Landscape in Sight: Looking at America*, ed. Helen Lefkowitz Horowitz (New Haven, CT: Yale University Press, 1997), 27.

77. Gruen wrote about the pleasurable effect of picturesque spaces and details in 1964: "What makes the appearance of the city superior? We may get a clue to the answer by observing the few spots still left in some of our cities to which tourists and visitors flock. Most visitors to New York will go to Greenwich Village in spite of the fact that there is hardly an outstanding structure there. What the tourists seek and admire is what they call 'atmosphere,' which, when one digs deeper, is found to be the result of small-grained variety and diversity." Gruen, *Heart of Our Cities,* 170.

78. Karal Ann Marling, ed., *Designing Disney's Theme Parks: The Architecture of Reassurance* (New York: Flammarion, 1997). The book may have influenced the functional stratification of the Magic Kingdom in Orlando, with its underground service corridors.

79. "Century 21 Exposition, Seattle, Washington" *Arts & Architecture* 76 (December, 1959): 10-13; James T. Burns Jr., "The Architecture of Century 21," *Progressive Architecture* 43 (June, 1962): 49-62; "Seattle Votes for Architecture," *Architectural Record* 130 (August, 1961): 102-4; "Seattle Fair," *Architectural Forum* 116 (June, 1962): 94-103; "A Tour of Century 21 with Paul Thiry," *Architectural Record* 131 (June 1962): 141-48; Superficially, the exhibit recalled Brownjohn, Chermayeff, and Geismar's exhibit for the United States at the Brussels World's Fair of 1958, except that it offered less variety in type of sign, shape, and scale. As Philip Meggs wrote about the Brussels exhibit, "The scale and character of the American urban environment was presented . . . expressing the vitality and spirit of the city"; Meggs, *History of Graphic Design,* 435. At the Signs of the Future exhibit in Seattle, the scale of everything was more inflated and

enveloping than the miniature landscape created in Brussels. On closer inspection, the Brussels display was fundamentally different. The designers abstracted and fragmented the graphics of the city, arranging the pieces in a three-dimensional composition that, a decade later, would surely have been labeled pop art. As attractive and exciting as the display may have been, the sign pieces offered little more than visual stimulation. The graphics were pleasing forms rather than meaningful symbols. Little to no relationship between sign and site existed. The Seattle exhibit presented full signs displayed in great abundance, located as if along a roadway or highway. The Brussels exhibit seemed to reflect on the chaotic charm of the waning urban landscape, while the Seattle exhibit presented the new energy of the growing suburban strip—with high hopes that it could be made better. The Brussels exhibition was remarkable in its forthright appreciation of material that was routinely snubbed by all. Not until the publication in 1972 of Robert Venturi, Denise Scott Brown, and Steven Izenour's *Learning from Las Vegas* would "found" graphics be publicly enshrined on such a scale. In contrast to the focus on form and visual stimuli at Brussels, their work analyzed commercial design for what it could teach us about design communication and spatial layering.

80. In contrast, many considered the 1964 New York World's Fair a disappointment, if not a failure. This was in no small part due to the freedom given to participating corporations in the design of their individual pavilions. Chicago's 1933 A Century of Progress exposition had foreshadowed the design individualism of the strip. The New York fair of 1964 expanded this freedom. Critics feared that design chaos would ensue when they learned that fair president Robert Moses had rejected the recommendation of the original design board to house all exhibits in a single structure.

    Though it was not contained in a single building, the 1939 New York World's Fair had enjoyed a certain design harmony lacking at the 1964 fair because of the construction of communal exhibition buildings throughout the site. Aside from statuary, the Unisphere, and buildings inherited from the previous exposition, the 1964 fair was virtually at the mercy of free-market corporate America for its appearance. Though the general public's opinion of the fair's design is unclear, its growing intolerance for visual disharmony at the time was revealed by the popularity of *God's Own Junkyard*, published the same year. During the second year of the fair, Lady Bird Johnson's Highway Beautification Act was enacted to clear outdoor advertising from America's freeways. Though these events were not directly related, they were indicative of the building momentum, throughout America, against commercial clutter in the mid-1960s.

81. James W. Rouse, "Must Shopping Centers Be Inhuman?" *Architectural Forum* 116 (June 1962): 106.
82. Lesley Jackson, *'Contemporary': Architecture and Interiors of the 1950s* (London: Phaidon, 1994), 113.
83. Klaus Herdeg, *The Decorated Diagram: Harvard Architecture and the Failure of the Bauhaus Legacy* (Cambridge, MA: MIT Press, 1983), 79.
84. Lewis Mumford, "The Case Against 'Modern Architecture,'" *Architectural Record* 131 (April 1962): 159–60.
85. It can be argued that reducing signs to corporate symbols and trademarks, however well designed, favored chain businesses over those that were unique and local. Corporations could afford to spend millions in television and newspaper advertisements; small businesses couldn't hope to compete with such expenditures. Each corporate symbol or chain trademark on the strip represented a mammoth development campaign. In effect, much of what used to exist downtown—from the cleverly animated neon figures to the verbally descriptive messages—disappeared from the streets and highways to "reappear" on television sets everywhere as commercials. See chapter 6.

CHAPTER 6. *Rediscovering Main Street: Retrenchment, Repair, and Reinvention, 1965–2010*

1. The reasons were twofold. On one side of the street, there were incentives from the local economic development association. A tornado severely damaged the other side in 2003, and it needed to be rebuilt economically. Connie Kottke (Buffalo Lake Economic Development Association) and Tammy Almich (owner, Main Street Market) in discussions with the author, April 8, 2008.
2. Ada Louise Huxtable, "Albia, Iowa, Has Lesson to Teach City," *New York Times*, October 24, 1971.
3. For more on the preservation movement in the United States, from its earliest moments, see William J. Murtagh, *Keeping Time: The History and Theory of Preservation in America*, 3rd ed. (Hoboken, NJ: John Wiley, 2006), and Max Page and Randall Mason, eds., *Giving Preservation a History: Histories of Historic Preservation in the United States* (New York: Routledge, 2004).
4. David City, like Albia, managed a superficial paint-up and fix-up to the veneer of its Main Street. Medina, Ohio, created a themed facelift of its historic courthouse square, assisted by well-known industrial designer and local, Gene Smith. Corning, New York, was another of the earliest towns to market a historic appearance for its Main Street. In this case, a force of nature aided the town: Hurricane Agnes indirectly delivered a windfall of federal support. The Corning Glass Company, headquartered in the struggling town center, footed the bill for the Market Street Restoration Agency, providing top-quality designers, like Norman Mintz. Mary Means (creator of the National Main Street program and former vice president of the National Trust for Historic Preservation), email to author, March 7, 2010.
5. It is somewhat surprising that Columbus, a city that had rapidly gained notoriety for its modern buildings by celebrity architects, would restore rather than replace its old town

center. Columbus's fame for modernism was well established by the mid-1960s. In 1942, Eliel Saarinen had designed the First Christian Church, the very first example of the "modern" postwar architectural style in Columbus. In 1957, the president and chairman of Cummins Engine Company, the town's major industry, hired Eero Saarinen to come to Columbus to design his home. The president then established a program where the Cummins Foundation would pay the architect fees for any project in town if the client hired an architect from a foundation-compiled list of architecture firms, which included only the crème de la crème of America's modernists.

6. Dave Johnson (president of Albia Industrial Development Corporation and trustee of the Robert T. Bates Foundation), in discussion with the author, July 31, 2007, Albia, Iowa. The grayness of the town was in large part the result of soot from the local coal-burning power plant. It had a significant impact on the appearance of commercial buildings maintained by off-site owners.

7. After the mid-1990s, Albia's restoration program benefited from the largesse of Robert Bates, who bequeathed financial support for the Bates Foundation. This entity purchased 25 percent of all courthouse square frontage and offered grants for the next, more comprehensive level of preservation work. The historic preservation board of Albia reviewed projects on a case-by-case basis during this period. Projecting signs were permitted to extend three feet, and the maximum area for all signs of a single business was a flat figure, independent of the width of the storefront, as it was in many communities of the United States. Johnson discussion, July 31, 2007.

8. *Winfield (Kansas) Daily Courier*, May 5, 1982.

9. Jim King (board member, Monroe County Historical Society), in discussion with the author, July 31, 2007, Albia, IA.

10. Huxtable, "Albia, Iowa."

11. Ibid.

12. The Ohio State University Department of Architecture, *Guidelines for Aesthetic Enhancement of the Downtown Environment of Small Mid-Western Public Square Centered Towns with Case Study Applications to Bryan, Ohio* (Columbus, 1976), 1.1; emphasis in original.

13. Tom Voigt (vice president/general manager of the Bryan Publishing Company), in discussion with the author, June 13, 1998, Bryan, OH.

14. H. Ward Jandl, *Rehabilitating Historic Storefronts*, Preservation Brief 11 (Washington, DC: Technical Preservation Services, National Park Service, U.S. Department of the Interior, 1982), 10.

15. Ibid.

16. However, this same publication made a case for variety in signs, supported by a single image of a vintage drug store.

17. Charleston's study of thirty-six buildings for its King Street Facade Program (1982) included critiques of streetscapes and individual buildings. Charleston merchants, prohibited from erecting projecting signs since the 1940s, compensated by mounting large wall signs that intruded from the fascia into the transom zone. The facade program proposed the reduction of all these signs to fit into the narrow fascia area for each storefront. The reduction of signage proposed for commercial buildings and streetscapes in Chicago by the Landmarks Preservation Council of Illinois seemed extreme, but this may have been due to the size of the city's existing signs. The authors of *Neighborhood Commercial Design Guidelines* (1983) recommended removing all projecting signs, no matter the size, materials, or degree of craftsmanship. Wall signs that extended from the heads of display windows to the sills of second-story windows were to be removed as well. Many stores in the improved version, or "after" example, were identified merely with discreet lettering on the valences of fabric awnings. Others were granted a portion of the frieze or fascia area, where individually pin-mounted letters were placed. Visibility of such signs by motorists would most likely have been difficult.

"Guide all signage decisions by remembering that the building itself is the best sign . . . A sensitively rehabilitated, well-maintained building is the best advertisement for a business' attention to detail and the quality of its products and services." Wallace Rappe with Emily J. Harris, *Neighborhood Commercial District Design Guidelines* (Chicago: Landmarks Preservation Council of Illinois, 1983), 4. This message also appeared in Planning Advisory Service, American Planning Association, PAS Memo 84-2 (February 1984), 1, a reprint from chapter 3 of *Neighborhood Commercial District Design Guidelines*. Signs hanging over a sidewalk, Rappe maintained, "can be counterproductive to business because they often obscure individual buildings and interrupt the harmony of the street." If projecting signs were to be used, they would have to be small and coordinated with surrounding buildings and signs. Just how to coordinate a sign with its surroundings was left up to interpretation and imagination.

18. Oklahoma Department of Commerce, *Oklahoma Sign Design Guidelines* (Oklahoma City: Oklahoma Department of Commerce, 1986), 11, 15. See also Janice Pregliasco, *Developing Downtown Design: Guidelines* (Sacramento: California Main Street Program, 1988), 24. This California publication has been used as reference by other states, such as Iowa's Main Street Program.

19. Norman Mintz, *Main Street Guidelines: Signs for Main Street* (Washington, DC: National Trust for Historic Preservation, 1987), 3. The publication proceeded to reexamine the way signs were approached in most communities and suggested that stating sign intent in an ordinance was better than merely listing limitations.

20. Michael J. Auer, *The Preservation of Historic Signs*, Preservation Brief 25 (Washington, DC: Technical Preservation Services, National Park Service, U.S. Department of the Interior, October 1991), 1.

21. The following possible thresholds were itemized in the memo. Each city with a historic sign ordinance had incorporated some of these criteria into its list, and in most cases,

only a certain number of the suggested thresholds were required to be met:
- A sign must be of exemplary technology, craftsmanship, or design for its era.
- A sign must be at least 15 years old.
- A sign must be of historic significance to the city.
- A sign must possess unique design or character.
- A sign must be a civic landmark, of great scale, and visible from a great distance.
- A sign must be integrated into the architecture of the building to which it is attached.

Peter H. Phillips, PAS Memo (November 1988), p. 4.

22. Ronald Lee Fleming quoted in U.S. Department of Housing and Urban Development, *Proceedings of the Urban Signage Forum, April 22 and 23, 1976, Chicago, Illinois* (Washington, DC: U.S. Government Printing Office, 1976), 386.
23. Ibid., 97.
24. The four-point approach of the National Main Street Center is organization, promotion, design, and economic structuring.
25. The standards were originally published in 1977 and revised in 1990 as part of the federal regulations; *Code of Federal Regulations,* Department of the Interior, title 36, part 67.
26. Jandl, *Rehabilitating Historic Storefronts,* 4–5, 11. Because storefronts are particularly susceptible to alteration in response to changing marketing techniques, it is worthwhile to find visual documentation from a variety of periods to have a clear understanding of the evolution of the storefront. Removal of later additions that contribute to the character of the building should not be undertaken.
27. Mike Jackson, "Storefronts of Tomorrow: American Storefront Design from 1940 to 1970," in *Preserving the Recent Past 2,* ed. Deborah Slaton and William G. Foulks (Washington, DC: Historic Preservation Education Foundation, 2000), 84, 89.
28. *Exterior lobby* or *arcade* were terms used to describe increasingly large areas "carved out" of the display area in the front of a store which permitted shoppers to wander in past the front plane of the store, or common sidewalk line, without actually opening a door. This deep recess, once modest at the turn-of-the twentieth century, rapidly grew to include sometimes as much as 20–30% of the depth of a store's footprint.
29. Reyner Banham, *Los Angeles: The Architecture of Four Ecologies* (1971; reprint Berkeley: University of California Press, 2000), 150.
30. Ontario's two best buildings from the 1920s to the 1940s—the Art Deco First National Bank building (1928) and the streamlined modern Blue Seal Laundry building (1940)—were used as models for new construction in that subdistrict. The guidelines highlighted features such as a cylindrical corner tower placed at the corner of a building, at a street intersection, an idea borrowed from the laundry, now a restaurant, as desirable for this subdistrict. This model demonstrated an efficient weaving together of horizontal and vertical, as the parapet line of the predominantly horizontal building corresponded with the first of the staggered, subtle setbacks going up the side of the tower. Though wall signs for the turn-of-the-century subdistrict were relegated to the traditional fascia area, graphics for the 1920s–1940s subdistrict were to be a set percent of the feasible "placement area" on the facade—the largest, uninterrupted flat panel. Vertical, projecting signs were also deemed appropriate for this era, but no established area limitation was set. In common to all subdistricts were what was called "pedestrian-scaled projecting signs." The guidelines allowed a surprisingly small area for these signs, considering the vast dimension of Euclid Avenue. If one took Reyner Banham's comments about Ontario to heart, one might conclude that this was a space that might benefit enormously from more urban animation in the form of substantial buildings and signs—it was a landscape that needed more artifact and less nature.
31. This compromise actually had a local precedent, as similar signs could be seen on many of the more conservative buildings from the 1950s elsewhere in southern California. However, to accommodate popular taste, the scale of the new signs was reduced from the originals.
32. Shirley Lowry, "Vision 'Dream' Center by 1956 at 63rd-Halsted," *Chicago Daily Tribune,* April 8, 1954.
33. Melaniphy & Associates, *Chicago Comprehensive Neighborhood Needs Analysis; Roseland Community Area* (Chicago, 1982), 2:18. See also P. J. Bednarski, "The Other Michigan Avenue, a World Away from Water Tower Place; Roseland's Strip Struggles with Change," *Chicago Sun-Times,* July 30, 1989.
34. Ledall Edwards (executive director, Roseland Business Development Council), in discussion with the author, July 23, 2007, Roseland, IL. See also Bednarski, "Other Michigan Avenue."
35. Chicago Department of Planning, *Roseland's Plan for the 1990s: A Vision for a Thriving Community* (Chicago, 1990). The city's facade improvement program led to only a few upgrades. Sporadic funding plagued the program. The 1998 strategic plan was similar to many other such plans across America with its identification of a historic district, a plan for an infusion of natural landscaping, hard streetscaping improvements, and a small park to replace the unstable Gately's Department Store Building. Roseland considered its potential to rise again by luring back its broad base of middle-class African American homeowners who had avoided the historic center of Roseland because of the unwelcoming character of the old retail corridor.
36. Alderman Anthony Beale (9th Ward, City of Chicago), in discussion with the author, April 28, 2008.
37. Giving this street part of its power was its association with entertainers like Ella Fitzgerald and James Brown, whose careers were launched at the Apollo Theatre, and with Malcolm X, Rev. Adam Clayton Powell Jr., the National Black Theatre, and the Congress of Racial Equality.
38. American Planning Association, "Harlem's 125th Street Named One of 10 Great Streets in America," October 2, 2007, www.planning.org/newsreleases/2007/ftp10020717.html.

39. Timothy Williams, "City's Sweeping Rezoning Plan for 125th Street Has Many in Harlem Concerned," *New York Times*, February 21, 2008; Maria Luisa Tucker, "Zoned Out," *Village Voice*, December 4, 2007; Alan Feuer, "In This Record Store, Time Itself Is Warped: 125th Street Marches On, but Older Rhythms Haunt a Harlem Storefront," *New York Times*, March 3, 2003.

40. The thought of change and new ownership reminded everyone of the tensions that had remained high along this corridor since the 1920s regarding whose neighborhood it was, anyway. There had been a chronic problem among white-owned businesses (which historically dominated the street) in not hiring blacks. As late as the 1960s, some stores hired no African Americans whatsoever, and protests ensued. Before the 1930s, many stores refused even to serve black customers. A study by the Mayor's Office in 1978 reported that Harlem was largely owned and controlled by outsiders and that a system of pure economic colonialism extended into every moneymaking endeavor that touched the life of a resident. The tension reached a peak again in 1995, when a white-owned clothing store was perceived as muscling out a black-owned record shop for expansion space; the protest led to a blaze and five dead. About this same time, the ongoing conflict between black street vendors and white store owners led to the removal of the vendors to 116th Street. However, local black-owned businesses claimed the vendors were a problem as well. See Robert D. McFadden, "A Shopping Trip, a Protest, and Lingering Questions: Death on 125th Street," *New York Times*, December 17, 1995; Cathy Connors, "Vendors Seek to Return to 125th Street," *(New York) Amsterdam News*, January 6, 1996.

    For many years, changes along 125th Street had been eyed with suspicion. A proposed up-zoning for a fourteen-story tower along West 125th Street in 1971 led the only African American member of the City Plan Commission to express concern that the street might become a canyon of office buildings (even though this particular proposal had a black developer behind it). See Peter Freiburg, "125th St. Future Debated," *New York Times*, November 18, 1971. In order to alleviate tension and concerns about alienation, the city formed Community Advisor Committees to participate in the discussions for the development of the street.

    All through the 1980s and much of the 1990s, long-awaited plans for a major shopping complex and an international trade center to serve as economic anchors suffered false starts. Finally, in the late 1990s, Harlem USA, a 275,000 square foot urban shopping center complete with cinemas, was built on the west end of 125th Street—the site targeted for such a development for twenty years. It required a cash infusion of $300 million dollars from federal, state, and city sources. On Malcolm X Avenue (aka Lenox), a ten-story tower was erected in 2002 with more national retail in its base and yet more cinemas. A new full-service supermarket (the first to be built in three decades) anchored the slow-starting east end of 125th as of 1999, forcing the closure of six local stores.

41. In the 1910s and 1930s, however, several four- and five-story brick tenements or wood-frame houses were demolished to make way for one-story taxpayer units, a commercial type that continues to have a strong presence at the turn of the twenty-first century. These structures appear to have the loudest signs and most aggressive businesses. A *taxpayer* is defined as a building, often temporary, which yields a minimal return on investment, usually little more than covering real estate taxes. Such buildings were usually modest investments. They just marked time until land values went up and the land could be resold. Some taxpayer strip commercial buildings are, naturally, notable for their economy of design and construction.

42. New business in the 1980s and 1990s brought the far more affordable awning signs to 125th Street; it was a graphic option useful to many modest businesses across America. Yet here it appears as an almost universal rule. Long street elevations of buildings from the late nineteenth century are given virtually continuous "bases" of these signs, butted end to end. There is a wide variety of color from storefront to storefront, but the graphics are basic and unremarkable. The awning signs rarely stray above the second story windowsill, thus permitting building facades to be seen fully, even where decay has set in. Here and there, a projecting entrance canopy or showy parapet sign singles out a particularly ambitious business—especially east of Park Avenue and on side streets.

    In 1978, the Harlem Development Corporation hired a consultant to propose storefront improvements for 125th Street. The firm predictably targeted a perceived "chaos" in storefronts and graphics, recommending that there be strict unity among signs within each "parent building." It did not, however, suggest that there be uniformity along the entire street. In a rough, ad hoc sort of way, this proposed sign modesty is visible today nevertheless, though signs rarely align. The variegated awnings, with their slightly random locations up and down, give the street much of its present-day visual vitality, but it is a gentle variety. Recently built structures require sign uniformity along building elevations, a condition that would certainly please the Harlem Development Corporation. The only true jarring moments along 125th Street are where large, glass-clad modern structures have been inserted. This may become the look of Harlem, as big money pours in. The city preservation department has adopted no plans or programs to prevent such a change.

43. Blumstein's (Robert D. Kohn and Charles Butler, 1923), with its four-story streamlined modern neon sign on 125th Street, closed in 1978, its first floor turned over to several small businesses. Gately's People's store in Roseland, with its exuberant, rakishly angled, navy blue porcelain enamel sign, closed one year later. The Blumstein's sign is as much a landmark on the street as the city-protected sign and marquee for the famous Apollo Theatre. The Blumstein's sign marks a major turning point in Harlem's history. This is where the "Buy-Where-You-Can-Work" campaign, begun by the Rev. John H.

Johnson in 1932, led to the hiring of blacks on a street that had shunned them except as customers. "As Blumstein's goes, so will go 125th Street," Johnson said. See Christopher Gray, "How a Black Boycott Opened the Employment Door," *New York Times,* November 20, 1994. In Roseland, the Gately's People's graphic was without peer on its quiet corridor. It marked the center of what was once Chicago's third largest retail hub and is still a beloved neighborhood. Both buildings and their signs are threatened: in New York because of the pressure of development and in Chicago because of lack of the same. Both neighborhoods are at risk because little support for historic preservation exists there.

44. The lettering of the signs was the result of digitalized type being extended or compressed on the computer beyond its design limits and then rendered up large in metal and plastic. It is probably more pronounced on 125th Street because of the immense scale of all new design. Some type fonts are designed as compressed typefaces and can be further compressed digitally without making the "thin" strokes appear as thick as the "thick" strokes, a condition which is visually unnatural for serifed type. Even more extreme, noncompressed typefaces are often compressed digitally to such an extent that the fonts appear even more unnatural, if not illegible. Because signs are now often designed by artists or technicians who have not been trained in the principles of lettering that were once mastered while hand-drawing as an apprentice, such distortions often occur.

45. Elisabeth de Bourbon (director of communications, NYC Landmarks Preservation Commission), email to the author, April 8, 2008.

46. Even some of the most architecturally and historically valuable buildings appear to be prime targets for developers, like Blumstein's and the Koch department stores. A proposal for the Victoria Theatre (Thomas Lamb, 1918), close neighbor of the Apollo, sites a 317,570 square-foot mixed-use complex, with a tower five-times the height of the original facade, immediately behind the original, historic elevation. This may be one of the lucky buildings; despite the tremendous jump in scale, at least something is saved.

47. Gov. George Pataki, whom many credited for supporting the new development in Harlem, once expressed a desire to see the new rules that had energized 42nd Street in the 1990s be applied to 125th Street. See Greg Thomas, "Pataki's Man in Harlem," *Village Voice,* January 28, 2003.

48. The urban renewal effort gained powerful momentum in 1954 by soliciting the concern of the general public through a major publicity campaign launched by the American Council to Improve Our Neighborhoods (ACTION). Founded in the same year, this organization drew its members from a cross-section of influential Americans. Popular Magazines like *Family Circle, Life,* and *Better Homes and Gardens* carried stories inspired by ACTION Press Releases.

49. Subsequently, the Housing and Community Development Act of 1974 established the Community Development Block Grant program (CDBG), which began in earnest the focus on redevelopment of existing neighborhoods and properties rather than demolition of substandard housing and economically depressed areas. This financial source traditionally supplied, on a municipal level, such efforts as facade improvement programs. Urban improvements were also supported by more local funding, including tax increment financing, where debt issued to pay for projects was financed by future gains in taxes. Local assessments, usually of the business owners directly benefiting from improvements, also provided the funds, in many cases, for street repairs, mall infrastructure, and urban landscaping or "streetscaping."

50. Ketchum, Gina & Sharp would eventually make a name for itself by designing Shopper's World in Framingham, Massachusetts, one of America's first shopping centers with a central, though not enclosed, mall space. See *A Plan for Modernizing Main Street* (Niles, MI: Kawneer Company, 1945).

51. "New Building for 194X," *Architectural Forum* 78 (May 1943): 69-70; "Shopping Center," *Architectural Forum* 85 (August 1946): 78-79; "Redevelopment Plan for Grand Haven," *Architectural Record* 103 (February 1948): 92-97; "Syracuse, N.Y." *Architectural Forum* 78 (May 1943): 71.

52. JoEllen Goodman, "State Street Seeks Salvation," *Crain's Chicago Business,* May 19, 1980, 11.

53. Greater State Street Council Press Releases, *Chicago Daily News,* August 21, 1957; "Nine Garages for City of Chicago Make a Frontal Attack on Parking Problem," *Architectural Record* 115 (March 1954): 153-56.

54. Christian Laine, "State Street Face-lifts Mar City Landmarks," *Chicago Sun-Times,* July 8, 1980.

55. W. N. Sutherland, "Toledo Mall Plan Studied as City Traffic Solution," *Chicago American,* August 10, 1959. These hubs included the busy Belmont/Lincoln/Ashland intersection and the 63rd and Halsted center in Englewood.

56. "Plan to Beautify State St. Unveiled," *Chicago Daily News,* October 8, 1957.

57. According to this proposal, everything would need to be designed by an architectural commission under a master plan. Arthur Rubloff, "New Mall for State Street Unveiled" (press release, Chicago, September 26, 1957), 1-4. By the early 1960s, the visions included such features as massive roof structures covering the prime eight shopping blocks of State Street, with glass-covered bridges that spanned the street and housed restaurants. Increasingly, in the proposals, the public realm was becoming the show, with the irregularity of signs and variable commercial architecture smoothed away. See Dale Morrison, "Roof over State Street Urged as Shoppers Lure," *Chicago Daily News,* May 2, 1962.

58. Robert M. Hyatt, "Pomona's Dream Comes True," *Westways* (Auto Club of Southern California, Santa Ana, CA), November 1962, 15.

59. Donald Lutes, *The Downtown Mall* (Dallas, TX: Central Business District Association, 1959), 2:48. Lutes was an architect and planner and president of the Springfield, Oregon, Planning Commission.

60. See, for example, "Modernizing Main Street" and "Modernization: Key to Downtown Revival," *Chain Store Age* 34 (February 1958): 21–29, and "Kalamazoo's Permanent Mall: 'Psychological Shot in the Arm,'" *Chain Store Age* 36 (October 1960): E31–E33.

61. "Toledo's Experiment," *Chicago American*, August 6, 1959, 18.

62. Seymour Stillman, "The Downtown Mall: Magic or Madness," speech presented at the Downtown Development Session of the National Retail Merchants Association's 48th Annual Convention, Hotel Statler, New York City, January 13, 1959, reprinted for the *Chicago Daily News* idea packet. See also Lutes, *Downtown Mall*, 48: "A WORD OF WARNING—The shopper's mall brings with it no magic. It will not solve the problems of the traffic-pedestrian separation, parking, proper business location, or commercial area rehabilitation. But it will—if these other aspects of the problem are solved as part of a total plan—contribute to the bold and dramatic touch necessary to revitalize downtown."

63. For an efficient article presenting Gruen's persuasive case for the creation of both planned, regional suburban shopping centers and replanned city centers, see "Retailing and the Automobile: A Romance Based upon a Case of Mistaken Identity," *Architectural Record* 127 (March 1960): 192–210. This article also shows Gruen's burgeoning portfolio by this date and his rapid development of authority in this realm, a mere six years after the completion of Northland. Gruen's concept is explained more at length in Victor Gruen and Larry Smith, *Shopping Towns USA: The Planning of Shopping Centers* (New York: Reinhold, 1960). Since this all came to the public's attention with the buzz surrounding Gruen's plan for Fort Worth, Texas, see "Typical Downtown Transformed," *Architectural Forum* 4 (special reprint, May 1956).

64. Providence City Plan Commission, Urban Renewal Administration Housing and Home Finance Agency, *Downtown Providence 1970: Downtown Providence Master Plan Project, A Demonstration Grant Study* (Providence, RI, 1959), 58; "That Unsightly Forest of Stick-Out Signs Should Go," *Providence Journal*, May 23, 1955.

65. A 1973 article in the *Architectural Forum* by esteemed urbanist Jaquelin Robertson had made a very persuasive case for the auto-free transit-way and for improving cities by designing good streets and pedestrianizing. Robertson, the former director of New York City's Office of Mid-town Planning and Development, was then a fan of what he had seen in Minneapolis—that is, until the proliferation of skyways siphoned people off the public streets. In 1975, the managing director of the State Street Council said that the mall in Chicago had always been primarily viewed as a means of traffic control and that its aesthetic benefits were considered secondary.

66. "Chicago Officials Study Mall Success in Other Big Cities," *Chicago Tribune*, July 11, 1971. See also Vincent Butler, "N.Y. Weighs Success of Closing Madison Avenue to Boost Sales: Mall Plan Weighed by New York," *Chicago Tribune*, May 17, 1971.

67. Paul Gapp, "Merchants Optimistic: State Street's Got a One-Way Future," *Chicago Daily Tribune*, October 18, 1975.

68. Paul Gapp, "Planners Eye the Wild Side of State Street," *Chicago Daily News*, January 8, 1986.

69. Robert Enstad, "State Street 'Sign Pollution' under Attack of Mall Council," *Chicago Tribune*, April 24, 1980. See also Greater State Street Council's board of directors minutes, executive committee meeting, June 25, 1982:

> It was determined that a sign ordinance structured to address future signage was of primary importance to the future environment of the area . . . There appeared to be a consensus that the traditional character of State Street should continue to be reflected in the uniqueness of present and future physical and aesthetic presentation. Any new ordinance should be restrictive enough to control flagrant abuses and permissive enough to encourage creativity and innovation. With the Council's continued aggressive efforts to enhance the business environment of downtown, specifically the State Street Mall, it is believed the majority of signage considered visually polluting will disappear. Space users of the future will probably cooperate with the Council in its efforts to maintain the overall architectural ambience of the area.

70. Frederick C. Klein, "Downtown Chicago's State Street Mall Fails to Revive Area Stores, Disappointing Many," *Wall Street Journal*, May 9, 1983.

71. Located in a region dense with communities competing for the retail dollar and an especially mobile population assisted by a network of new freeways, its chances for survival were slim. In the late 1960s, after the opening of the especially convenient Montclair Plaza regional mall, just five minutes away, Pomona's share in the retail pie slipped worryingly. The growing vacancy rate called for some desperate measures. By the mid-1970s, the nine-block stretch that once boasted ninety stores had just a handful remaining. In 1970, the *Los Angeles Times* reported that one block of Pomona's mall was being reconfigured as a "colorful, festive 'Mexican village'" to stir up sales. In the mid-1990s, two large graphic archways in Victorian style marked the entrance to either the Arts Colony or Antique Row on either side of the traffic artery. But the carnival colors and festivity these monuments suggested actually identified a street that was silent a great deal of the time. "'Mexican Village' Proposed on Pomona Mall," *Los Angeles Times*, November 15, 1970.

72. By the early 1990s, this district of four blocks was looking tired and sales were declining. Up and down the street, where neon projecting signs, like the fin for J. C. Penney's, had once soared up past rooflines, there were only modest wall signs and polite directories. A struggle ensued over whether to reopen the mall to automobile traffic, with one side claiming that to do so would be tantamount to "removing the stars from Old Glory." Finally, in 1997, a major, $4 million, ten-point plan developed by a consultant led to the

73. In the late 1960s, the town of Carroll, Iowa, took comprehensive steps to modernize its Main Street, even though it was not immediately threatened with suburban or regional competition. The two primary business streets, Main and Adams, suffered the effects of absentee ownership and empty second floors. One of the town's two department stores, J. C. Penney's, was threatening to pull out of town. The mayor was quoted as saying that the "downtown area looked like hell." Unlike Albia's approach of fixing up existing buildings and marketing its history, Carroll's civic leaders practically reinvented its central business district from the ground up. Armed, in 1967, with over $2 million in federal funding for urban renewal, plus over $700,000 from the city, they purchased and demolished forty-eight buildings and relocated ninety-three businesses. Several large modern structures were built for the displaced retail, including the old cinemas. No one raised strong opposition to the project, despite the fact that almost half of downtown Carroll was replaced or altered significantly. Once complete, the praise overflowed; the executive vice president of the Carroll Chamber of Commerce gushed, "It's the most successful urban renewal project in the country!"

The changes to Carroll were significant. A substantial brick and bronzed metal arcade was erected as a "screen" along the faces of the buildings that remained, linking them to new, one-story construction, lined up with the originals. Flared, cantilevered concrete "umbrellas" towered above the arcades in a variety of locations, in one case to link the midblock entrance of a new, enclosed mall of shops, buried behind an arcade, to an older interior arcade across the street. All of the old signs were removed, replaced by uniformly shaped arcade signs mounted under the roof of the new sidewalk coverings. Gordon Gammack, "Carroll Boosted by Renewal, Farms, Industry," *Des Moines Sunday Register,* September 30, 1973; Art Neu (state senator of Iowa from 1967 to 1972, lieutenant governor of Iowa from 1973 to 1979, mayor of Carroll from 1982 to 1985) in discussion with the author, March 1, 2008; *Carroll: The Progress Continues! Mayor's Corridor of Commerce Task Force Interim Report to the Carroll City Council* (June 10, 1992), 6.

74. La Cumbre Plaza, a suburban shopping center with off-street parking, opened in late 1967. It was located far north on State Street. Early that year, more than 50 percent of the 142 property owners along six blocks of State Street signed a petition to create an improvement district to be called Downtown State Street Plaza. Bert Willard, "Over 50% Signup for New District," *Santa Barbara News,* June 4, 1967.

75. Santa Barbara Landmarks Committee, *Guidelines: El Pueblo Viejo District, Santa Barbara, California* (1987; City of Santa Barbara, 1995), 4, 6, 7, 29, 38, 42.

76. In 1958, Rouse built one of the first enclosed shopping centers, in Glen Burnie, Maryland. (He is even credited with first calling them "malls.") Like Gruen, he wrote a treatise on his beliefs about urban planning, *No Slums in Ten Years.* Rouse then went on to successfully establish a town based on his principles—Columbia, Maryland—with a central retail component. Rouse's architect, Thompson, was quoted as saying that the secret to their business success in retail development, in large part, was "individual proprietorship, with immense, chaotic variety." See Richard Zoglin, "The Urban Renewer: James W. Rouse (1914–1996)," *Time,* April 22, 1996; "Living: He Digs Downtown," *Time,* August 24, 1981; James W. Rouse and Nathaniel Keith, *No Slums in Ten Years, A Workable Program for Urban Renewal* (report to the commissioners of the District of Columbia, 1955).

77. "Roundtable on Rouse," *Progressive Architecture* 62 (July 1981): 100–106; Robert Campbell, "Evaluation: Boston's 'Upper of Urbanity'; Faneuil Hall Marketplace after Five Years," *AIA Journal* 70 (June 1981): 24–31; William Marlin, "Building Types Study 510: The Case for Design Quality in Today's Marketplace," *Architectural Record* 162 (December 1977): 81–128; "Down to the Sea in Shops: South Street Seaport, New York City," *Architectural Record* 172 (January 1984): 98–107; Jennifer Stoffel, "A Downtown Cleveland Mall Adjusts to Setback," *New York Times,* December 31, 1989; Bernard Stamler, "Rough Sailing for the South Street Seaport," *New York Times,* March 29, 1998; Francis Marrone, "Reconsidering South Street Seaport," *New York Sun,* August 28, 2008; Robert Campbell, "Two Urban Drawing Cards Are Now in Limbo," *Boston Globe,* December 21, 2008.

78. Downcity Providence endured the opening of Providence Place (1999), an urban mall intended to bring new life to the old central business district. Unfortunately, it was not placed close enough to Westminster Street to offer much of the intended customer spillover. Discussions among the developer and planners in the 1990s aimed at preventing the new center from being too much of an islandlike magnet—too isolated and too internalized. But the pathway between Providence Place and Westminster Street was awkward, and the enormous, enclosed urban mall building was deemed by many as too unwelcoming to the pedestrian, a citadel with little true connection to the street; Nora Lockwood Tooher, "Mall Entrance Remains Sticking Point," *Providence Journal,* May 23, 1997; Nora Lockwood Tooher, "Mall Design Favors Drivers over Walkers," *Providence Journal,* March 7, 1999; Ariel Sabar, "Providence Place: Will It Become the New 'Town Square'?" *Providence Journal,* July 25, 1999.

Providence leaders fretted for years over the lack of connection between the new enclosed urban mall and the old retail corridor several blocks away. A sky bridge was eventually built to link the mall and the hotel and convention center, the latter being a potential joint along a path from the new retail to the old. But the move, an indirect/non-public link at best, just disappointed critics more. Trying to connect a private, enclosed mall to an existing public street proved difficult for Redlands, California, as well, almost twenty-five years earlier. The barrier in Redlands was a sea of parking between the suburban-style mall and old State Street; in

Providence, it was unwelcoming, highway-scaled streets to cross. A movie theater appeared to be one possible answer for pulling Downcity Providence closer to the new development. An agreement with the developer of Providence Place required that the city be assisted in building a small movie theater complex somewhere in the Westminster Street area. A charette conducted by urban designer Andres Duany revealed the opportunity to create a large vertical tower and sign to mark the new theater and serve as a beacon down Matthewson Street from the Convention Center. This visually enhanced passageway could become one of the threads for weaving the large-scale new construction, which was already a chain of structures, to the old spine of activity, Westminster Street. Since many leaders in Providence wished, at the beginning of the twenty-first century, to develop Downcity as an entertainment district, there was a clear alignment of possibilities. Thomas Deller (planning director, Providence, Rhode Island), in discussion with the author, January 8, 2008; Duany Plater-Zyberk and Company, *Connecting and Completing Downcity Providence, Rhode Island* (City of Providence, 2004), 18–19.

79. The Greater State Street Council had been calling for the revamp of the mall since at least 1987, when it offered a comprehensive proposal that suggested segmenting the long shopping district along State into three subareas with identities of their own, including an entertainment hub, a retail hub, and a cultural hub. This Skidmore, Owings & Merrill makeover was primarily cosmetic, but the street was evolving already into segments by the mid-1990s, especially since Randolph Street to the north had been reinforced, with city help, as an entertainment district. Student dorms and university uses were filling the vacant department stores to the south, and shopping was beginning to thrive again, in between.

80. In Chicago, this meant that 75% percent of the first floor, located between 2½ and 8 feet from the sidewalk (grade), was to be glass (70% in Providence). Chicago's guidelines strongly advised a height minimum of four stories (or 55 feet) for new buildings on State Street. In Providence, the requirement was a three-story minimum.

81. *City of Providence Code of Ordinances*, Article V: Special Zones, Section 502: Downcity District (October 13, 2006).

82. Clark Schoettle (Downcity Design Review Committee and executive director, Providence Preservation Society Revolving Fund), in discussion with the author, January 4, 2008.

83. *Chicago Zoning Ordinance and Land Use Ordinance*, Section 17-12-1103, State Street (2007); *Providence Code of Ordinances*, Section 502.

84. Until 1996, enormous porcelain enamel sign panels for a men's clothier covered the mezzanine and second story of the celebrated Reliance building (D. H. Burnham and Company, 1890–95), also on State Street. The delicate gothic tracery on the building's skin was also sheathed in stainless steel. A comprehensive restoration was completed with great reverence in the mid-1990s, but it left the building virtually signless.

85. The drastic change in signage is also evident in the neighboring polished-stone corner building created for Bond's Men's Furnishings by architects Friedman, Alschuler, and Sincere in 1949. This building was, by the late twentieth century, lacking any signs to replace the large-scale neon graphics that were essential elements of the firm's composition for the multistoried building. The original, spare look of the Bond's store was half graphics and half architecture. Vertical sans-serif neon letters, placed on the roof, lined up with a six-story window panel; eight-foot tall neon letters were stacked vertically up and down the corner of the building; a diagonal, brush-stroke script rendered in neon swept across the otherwise blank wall along State Street. By the late twentieth century, no signage existed above the first story of this building. The original composition by the architectural form in 1949 would be prohibited by the radically toughened sign code for State Street, established in 2004. The new code forbade all roof signs and changed the permitted sign area from twenty-four square feet per lineal foot of frontage to a gross figure of four—a 600% reduction.

86. Victor Gruen, *The Heart of Our Cities; The Urban Crisis: Diagnosis and Cure* (New York: Simon & Schuster, 1964), 170.

87. See Jane Jacobs, "Downtown Is for People," *Fortune*, April 1958, 133, and *The Death and Life of Great American Cities* (New York: Random House, 1961). Jacobs once explained a different way of thinking about stores, which reveals the nature of her paradigm for the city. To her, shops and businesses were not something that could be left out of a neighborhood plan because of their potential visual clutter. "Planners and architects are apt to think, in an orderly way, of stores as a straightforward matter of supplies and services—commercial space. But stores in city neighborhoods are much more complicated creatures which have evolved a much more complicated function. They are a big portion of the glue that makes an urban neighborhood a community instead of a dormitory . . . The stores themselves are social centers—especially the bars, candy stores, and diners." Excerpted from "Urban Design: Condensed Report of an Invitation Conference Sponsored by Faculty and Alumni Association of Graduate School of Design, Harvard University, April 9–10, 1956," *Progressive Architecture* 37 (August 1956): 102. A copy of the article was kept in the library of the office of Victor Gruen.

88. The figure remained the same in New York City as of 2008.

89. *Berman v. Parker*, 348 U.S. 26, appeal from the U.S. District Court for the District of Columbia, no. 22 (argued October 19, 1954; decided November 22, 1954).

90. Donald J. Balzar (principal, Balzar and Associates, Roanoke, VA), letter to the City of Staunton, November 2, 1971.

91. William A. Bodkin (former zoning administrator, City of Staunton, VA) in discussion with the author, November 21, 2000.

92. *Staunton (Virginia) City Code*, Section 41-1: Signs (1964).

93. Record Minutes of the Planning Commission Meeting, City of Staunton, VA (February 17, 1972), 310.
94. PAS Memo 84-2, 2.
95. As late as 1999, *Main Street News* and other publications by national planning and preservation groups continued to fan these flames, though projecting signs may sometimes be *praised* on the same page. However reasonable these negative analyses and conclusions may have been, they provided justification for continued prejudice that might not have been reasonable in every context: "Treating the ground floor and upper facade as unrelated elements was another prevalent type of building alteration that grew out of the popularity of shopping malls and strip commercial areas. Brightly lit, oversized signs were plastered across the fronts of downtown buildings in the 1950s and 1960s. Large, plastic projecting signs also appeared . . . The signs were intended to attract the gaze of passing motorists, and, because most commercial signs were being manufactured for the shopping strip, the ones that worked best on the highway were installed downtown as well." "Main Street 101: The Elements of Good Storefront Design," in "Revitalizing Downtown," *Main Street News*, January 1999, 10–13.
96. A shift from merely marketing the history of King Street and Colorado Boulevard to preserving it came in 1971 and 1972, with the decision to launch official surveys of the historic assets along these historic corridors. In 1974, Charleston's first official preservation plan was developed. And in 1976, the Pasadena Heritage Commission was formed, the kind of intelligent force necessary to protect Old Pasadena from events like the construction of the Bank of America headquarters in 1974. The years 1978 and 1979 saw more important steps for preserving Pasadena: *A Plan for Old Pasadena* (a revitalization proposal that emphasized a real city instead of a quaint tourist curiosity), an urban conservation overlay (to stop demolition immediately, among other goals), and a set of design guidelines (to direct all the investment that was sure to come).
97. Jack Roach, "City Sign Law Enforcement Set," *(Charleston, SC) News and Courier*, March 29, 1972.
98. Susan Mossman (executive director, Pasadena Heritage), in discussion with the author, June 9, 2007.
99. Unfortunately, the old projecting neon signs were often the victims of the sign industry itself, which, in order to keep business humming, hastened the replacement of neon with internally illuminated, acrylic-faced signs, which were new in the 1950s and 1960s: "I want you to think with me about the great principle of obsolescence, because therein lies a vast replacement market we have thought little about and one to which we have given little or no concerted, cooperative or planned industry attention"; Joseph M. Jones (account executive, Walker and Co., Detroit), *Signs of the Times* 153 (November 1959): 46. "Zigzaggy neon jumping all over the place has been replaced with clean plastic areas quietly lit from behind and accented with brilliant colored panels . . . Now as we are turning the corner into the area of total design of the shop front, interior décor, as well as the corporate symbol and the theme structure, we are fortified somewhat with what we have learned from the neon and plastic era . . . restraint and discipline"; Phil Sessions (art director, QRS, Los Angeles), *Signs of the Times* 170 (May 1965): 60–61.
100. Ian Nairn, *The American Landscape: A Critical View* (New York: Random House, 1965), 48.
101. Tom Wolfe, "Electrographic Architecture," *Architectural Design* 39 (July 1969): 380–82.
102. Daniel R. Mandelker and William R. Ewald, *Street Graphics and the Law* (Washington, DC: Planners Press, American Planning Association, 1988), 2. Although this quote comes from a later edition than the 1971 original, the principles, goals, and most details remained the same for the later publication.
103. Ibid., 4.
104. According to the *Street Graphics* model code, projecting signs could extend up to one-third of the sidewalk width (or four feet, whichever was less) and could go no higher than the sill of the second-story window unless the establishment contained an auditorium or place of entertainment. What made *Street Graphics* potentially difficult for application was its insistence that certain sign types be sized according to the speed of traffic on the corridor in question. This relationship was based on a study that allegedly determined how much drivers could perceive effectively and safely.
105. The Drs. Claus began their critique of *Street Graphics* by explaining that the core feature of the book, limiting to ten the number of items of information for identifying each business, was based on an erroneous assumption about the limits of human perception. Apparently Ewald and Mandelker misquoted and misrepresented the Clauses' own work. According to the Drs. Claus, the questionable concept of information overload, as explained in the context of the *Street Graphics* system, had no place as a basis for an ordinance so potentially powerful. Karen E. Claus and R. James Claus, *Street Graphics: A Perspective* (Cincinnati: Signs of the Times, 1975), 22.
106. Ibid., 46–47.
107. "Presentation of Gary E. Rhoads, O'Donnell, Rhoads & Gerber; Subject: Sign Codes, Severance Damages, and Business Losses," U.S. Department of Housing and Urban Development, *Proceedings of the Urban Signage Forum, April 22 and 23, 1976, Chicago, Illinois* (Washington, DC: U.S. Government Printing Office, 1977), 70–79.
108. "Presentation of R. T. Anderson, Director of Marketing Research and Planning, National Advertising Co., and Dr. Edward J. Mayo, Professor of Marketing, University of Notre Dame; Subject: The On-Premise Sign: Economic and Social Values," *Urban Signage Forum*, 332–35.
109. "Presentation of Steven Izenour, Venturi and Rauch," *Urban Signage Forum*, 32.
110. The quotation continues, "Venturi and Denise Scott-Brown would have us believe that clutter represents vitality. More often it represents an expensive confusion which

penalizes each owner. Usually the most cluttered areas are in the less affluent places [with fewer controls]." "Presentation of Ronald Lee Fleming, Executive Director, Vision, Inc.; Subject: Signing Up for Quality: A Mandate for Visual Conservatism and Enhancement in America," *Urban Signage Forum*, 386–87.

111. "Presentation of Thomas J. Lutz, National Trust for Historic Preservation; Subject: Signage and Area Restoration," *Urban Signage Forum*, 239–40.

112. "Presentation of Ronald Lee Fleming," 385.

113. In the years to follow, many model codes would be written, but few, if any, were as fastidious and complete as *Street Graphics*. The National Park Service recommended that sign codes be flexible, that they be written from the standpoint of what was desired rather than what was detested. After publishing a revised version of Ewald and Mandelker's book in 1988, called *Street Graphics and the Law*, the American Planning Association released an alternative model code, by Eric Damien Kelly and Gary Russo, aimed at small and midsized communities. It took a far less complex approach to regulation, with simple maximum area thresholds and percentages, the suggested quantities being very generous compared to the national averages of the time. In order to avoid turning over unnecessary power to review boards, Kelly and Russo recommended that certain aesthetic criteria, like colors and materials, be stated specifically in ordinances or guidelines. The total area, they contended, was more important than the number of signs. And in order to lower the mounting height and reduce the accumulation of signs on building facades, they suggested incentives, like permitting wider signs at lower locations, rather than outright restrictions.

114. This particular transformation of architecture on the American strip is so well documented that it is not necessary to describe it in detail here. See Philip Langdon, *Orange Roofs, Golden Arches: The Architecture of American Chain Restaurants* (New York: Knopf, 1986), and Chester H. Liebs, *Main Street to Miracle Mile: American Roadside Architecture* (Boston: Little, Brown, 1985).

115. Sometimes this urbanizing effort meant an image change without a spatial reorganization. In 2003, the community of Carroll, Iowa, decided to tame Route 30, the old Lincoln Highway that streamed through the town center with the requisite Kmart, McDonald's, and super-drugstore. Carroll's leaders hired a landscape architectural consulting firm that delivered a plan to mark the highway, at the point where development trickled off to farmland, with impressive multistory brick towers on substantial stone bases. Such gateway features implied that a town of significant scale would be found ahead, with a solid, traditional urban core. Most of the town center received improvements that stripped away the suburbanizing features imposed in the 1970s. This transformation involved removing the continuous metal canopies that covered storefronts and the reinforced concrete "umbrella" entranceways on Adams Street. The uniform shop signage was also jettisoned.

116. The Boston Post Road was dotted with only a handful of roadside businesses until 1953, when the town's first shopping center was built. In 1958, the opening of Interstate 95, with its frequent exits, put more cars on Highway 1. In 1961 and 1971, progressively larger shopping centers were built. By the mid-1980s, retail business around the common had been drained of two drug stores and the local department store (which closed after a hundred years of service). In the 1990s, planners reacted to the developmental pressure by creating tough size limits on retail structures: a maximum of fifty thousand square feet. Wal-Mart, with its mandate for larger floor plates, found what it desired in Guilford only by moving into a building constructed before the limits were set. By the turn of the twenty-first century, the old retail center of Guilford continued to thrive, if only because it had a good hardware store, plenty of parking, and because there was no space on the strip available for Home Depot. See also Dolores Hayden, "Flying over Guilford," *Planning* 66 (September 1, 2000): 10; George Kral Jr. (town planner, City of Guilford, Connecticut), in discussion with the author, August 16, 2007.

Regarding the proposed Big Box Amendment in 1999, this editorial piece appeared:

> Imagine the future potential of Boston Post Road in Guilford: You pass little, village-like shopping plazas one by one. They all look the same at one point— colonial, white, and under a certain square footage. It's like living in some strange dream world based on conformity. [If the Big Box Amendment is passed,] Big Y Supermarket . . . will remain the only large grocery store in town. Why? Because zoning restricts any stores larger than half Big Y's size. No competition. And that means continued high prices. Want more competitive prices? You'll have to go out of town for that . . . Forget any larger-scale shopping area even the size of Shoreline Plaza. You see, the square footage of Fleishman's Plaza is the maximum allowed. Need a bigger store with more variety that is open past 6 p.m. and open on Sundays? Take your patronage out of town.

"Big Box Amendment Too Restrictive," *(Guilford, CT) Shore Line Times,* December 8, 1999.

117. Kyle Stock, "Is Guilford Part of the Suburban Nation?" *Shore Line Times*, March 7, 2001.

118. It may be useful for the reader, at this point, to consult the sign transect diagram, figure 7.

119. *Town of Guilford, Planning and Design Guidelines, Route 1 East, Boston Post Road* (August 2000). The guidelines are not mandates but are officially recognized by the town and referred to in the zoning code.

120. Planning and Inspections Department, *Entrance Corridor Overlay District: Design Guidelines for Greenville Avenue* (City of Staunton, 2008), 22, www.staunton.va.us/directory/departments-h-z/planning-inspections/entrance-corridor-

overlay-district. Each of the thirteen designated entrance corridors has unique resources and challenges and thus requires its own unique sense of guidelines. Basic principles, such as encouraging buildings to be set close to the road and made pedestrian friendly by way of form and amenities, are common to all. Each set of design guidelines is based on identifying and amplifying the unique strengths of the particular corridor, focusing on encouraging development that perpetuates, rather than erases, the existing character of each.

121. The design of the sign was influenced by the towering, angular sign for the Parkette Drive-In, located in Lexington, Kentucky.

122. See the Googie coffee shops of Armet and Davis as an example.

123. It was a copy of the corner feature built for the Broadway-Crenshaw shopping center in Inglewood.

124. The models to which I refer do not all remain intact; some have been demolished or modified. For example, the Broadway store exists as a reference only in photographs. The same is true for the Van De Kamp's windmill tower. The buildings for Troll's Hardware and Jack's Food Town are still in place, though the signs have been heavily modified; the original signs related to the architecture in a more instructive way and remain as reference only in photographs.

125. As a model, unfortunately, Gwinn's is available only in historic photographs. See "Two Restaurants in One: Gwinn's Restaurant, Pasadena, California," *Architectural Record* 104 (July 1948): 124–28, and *Motels, Hotel, Restaurants, and Bars: An Architectural Record Book* (New York: F. W. Dodge, 1960), 306.

126. Armet and Davis, the firm most closely associated with Googie architecture, provided yet another building from the automobile era that satisfies the city's need to be pedestrian-friendly. The firm designed a relatively modest Denny's restaurant for East Colorado Boulevard in 1964 that was placed close to the sidewalk and pushed parking to the rear. The structure was a modified version of most of the firm's now-famous Googie buildings, which were designed as sculpture-in-the-round, conceptually floating on open sites. Although the boomerang-shaped roof seems to float above the site, the overhang in front helps to define a slim strip of a garden between the front wall and the sidewalk. The pole sign may be independent in form, but its stem is physically linked to the roof edge and serves to define space at the sidewalk edge. Regarding other buildings as potential reference along East Colorado Boulevard, several local motels, like the Astro (1962), have walls that are snugly up to the sidewalk line. Although these windowless walls at first appear unfriendly to pedestrians, they are highly animated in profile and texture, with zigzag rooflines and rhythmically placed brise-block panels that soften their appurtenance. The signs, although rarely well integrated with the architecture, are pushed up front in the slim space between wall and sidewalk.

127. The team was actually a consortium of institutions and groups, including consultants Renaissance Planning Group, Inc., and Wendy Grey Land Use Planning; the City of Sarasota; Sarasota County; Manatee County; New College of Florida; University of South Florida, Sarasota-Manatee; the Ringling School of Art and Design; Florida State University Ringling Center for the Cultural Arts, and the Manatee Airport Authority, among others.

128. Renaissance Planning Group, *Innovation41: "Transforming Path into Place"* (City of Sarasota, July 2006), 31.

129. Due to the already large scope of this book, it did not appear to be reasonable to attempt to examine corporate franchise architecture in any depth. The subject has been well covered by others, including Philip Langdon, Jim Heimann, and Alan Hess.

130. Peirce F. Lewis, "The Future of the Past: Our Clouded Vision of Historic Preservation," *Pioneer America* 7 (July 1975): 9.

131. Joseph Wood, "Nothing Should Stand for Something That Never Existed," *Places* 2 (Fall 1984): 82.

132. This district extends, basically, from Paulina to North Avenues.

133. As of 2010, the issue of potentially preventing a historic sign from being altered or demolished had not come up during review. Signs along the designated stretch of Milwaukee Avenue must comply with standard Chicago sign code limits.

CONCLUSION

1. Santa Barbara was not the only community in the early twentieth century to engineer a historic appearance for its streets. Santa Fe is just one of several of the more exotic examples, which include many cities in Florida.

2. "Board Opposes Tower Near El Cortez," *(San Diego) Union Tribune*, May 26, 2007.

3. Stilgoe goes on to explain what an important role the tavern played in town life. It helped to define urban neighborhoods and nurtured a fellowship associated with smaller, more rural settlements. John R. Stilgoe, *Common Landscape of America, 1580 to 1845* (New Haven: Yale University Press, 1982), 97.

4. Concern for the sign's precarious state led to its eventual removal from the site. Fortunately, it was spared from demolition by historian and neon preservationist Len Davidson. Subsequently, the third-generation owner of Pat's Steaks contracted Davidson to make a replica to go on the roof at his stand at 9th and Passyunk; the project remains in limbo. Davidson has loaned the original crown (with neon as yet unrestored) for display to another local restaurant. He has loaned many restored signs to businesses, permitting them to be seen in public. As of the date of this book's publication, the original sign awaits the funds necessary for its complete restoration.

5. George R. Stewart and Erwin Raisz, *U.S. 40: Cross Section of the United States of America* (Boston: Houghton Mifflin,

1953), 225. The signs today along U.S. 40, as it crosses through the center of Roosevelt, are far less conspicuous than they were when Stewart visited town. When he made notes, many businesses were marked by significant, projecting neon signs. All that remains today is an old porcelain enamel Rexall sign and many modest painted business identities, most of them mounted flush with facades. The more prominent signs are those on the edges of town, a few blocks away. There, the tall but simple signs advertise businesses located in the most basic, generic commercial "boxes." When seen from afar, against the vast, flat land, signs like these undeniably have greater presence than similar markers in the East or West Coast, where trees and more developed infrastructure deflect focus.

6. Tim Frye (preservation technical specialist, NE Quadrant, Planning Department, City and County of San Francisco), in discussion with the author, March 31, 2010. Discretionary review for historic signs is triggered if the building to which it is attached is fifty years or older, or if the sign for the property is on the city's historic resources survey. Chinatown meets the requirements to be on the National Register of Historic Resources as a district, but it has not been officially designated. However, this recognition of historic resources, and the requirements of the California Environmental Quality Act, empower the city and county to consider signs—as well as buildings and streetscapes—on a case-by-case basis, where merited.

7. Jim Ramsey (president of Strand Theatre LLC), in discussion with the author, November 15, 2007.

8. Kennedy Lawson Smith (former director of the National Main Street Center), in discussion with the author, February 28, 2008.

9. The storeowner worried that the building and its sign would be judged harshly, even threatened, when the National Main Street Center director Kennedy Smith once visited Grinnell. But Smith praised the building for representing its era well and offering diversity to the street, encouraging its preservation. David Danforth (past president of Grinnell Main Street program and board member, Grinnell Renaissance), in discussion with the author, August 1, 2007.

10. Grinnell Renaissance, the new body that replaced Iowa's Main Street program for the town and provides funding for facade renovation, has the power to review many business facades for compliance with the Downtown Design Guidelines (2002). This set of suggestions was based on the Secretary of the Interior's Standards and is very similar to that of many communities motivated to preserve their historic appearance.

Grinnell's sign guidelines are a bit more specific and restrictive. Signs should "fit within the architectural details of the building they are placed upon. The building should frame the sign." Instead of suggesting that signs be merely compatible with the architecture and not obscure significant architectural details, per the National Park Service and the National Trust, the guidelines request that signs relate to architecture in at least materials, shape, or color. For example, a dark green awning placed above a window "could have trim to match the stone lintels of the building." Placement of signs is to be coordinated storefront to storefront. "Placing a sign higher or lower than adjacent signs may not increase readability, but instead creates visual confusion." The code, as opposed to the guidelines, permits a total sign area of two square feet per lineal foot of frontage, double that of Staunton, but still on the low side nationally.

11. Like many post–World War II commercial buildings on Main Street across America, this building has minimal barriers between potential customers strolling on the sidewalk and the merchandise awaiting within. This meant a maximum of glass, minimal bulkhead, and an angled entrance arcade. In contrast to this break in the otherwise continuous street wall of two-story brick buildings, each of Sullivan's banks gives an ordered closure to the irregular accretion of buildings that line the commercial blocks by "emphasizing the growing simplicity of rectangular masses that seem to rise from the grid of the street." Lauren S. Weingarden, *Louis H. Sullivan: The Banks* (Cambridge, MA: MIT Press, 1987).

12. Credit must also be given to Grinnell Renaissance and the developer Bill Knapp, an alumnus of Grinnell College, who recognized the building's worth during a reunion trip that brought him back to his alma mater from Washington, D.C. Danforth discussion, August 1, 2007.

13. The real estate boom of the 2000s on the eastern shore was particularly hard on Wildwood, just as its self-proclaimed doo-wop architecture and signs were gaining exposure and praise across the country, demonstrating that the community's midcentury, historic design was highly marketable. Unfortunately, despite the herculean efforts of the Doo Wop Preservation League, local preservation ordinances were not in place to protect existing buildings and signs, proving that appreciation is not enough. Market-rate condominium buildings replaced iconographic motel buildings, as mom-and-pop owners sought easier retirements. Wildwood's motels were placed on the National Trust's "America's 11 Most Endangered Historic Places" in 2006. To its immense credit, the community of Wildwood and the preservation league established sets of design guidelines—one for the boardwalk with its own character and one for the motels and business off the boardwalk—to help guide development. Proposals made for how existing motels could be enlarged to address the new market were attractive and accessible; the guidelines made very clear what it was about Wildwood that made it unique and how that character could continue to develop as the community grew. Some developers have employed the guidelines with respect.

Essay on Sources

THIS BOOK BEGAN MANY YEARS AGO as a photo-documentation of vintage business signs and their context, commercial architecture and streetscapes. Primary sources have informed the research from the start, a great many of them being historic photographs of commercial thoroughfares. In archives and libraries from coast to coast, small villages to major cities, I have collected images of Main Street and the highway into town. As the aim of the book became a narrative of the visual evolution of these places, the research grew to include understanding their histories. To better comprehend how and why change had occurred, I developed a focus on about thirty case study towns, investigating carefully the major and incremental changes along their streets, in landmarks of all kinds, and on the faces of buildings. The walls of my office and home were fully papered with photocopied re-creations of various Main Streets across the nation, each represented by several iterations of itself, era by era, decade by decade, as it changed over time. In addition to photographs of each town, I examined a century of local newspapers, Sanborn fire insurance maps, county atlases, old codebooks, design guidelines, planning proposals, and council meeting notes. These were housed in a variety of locations—everything from the dusty backroom filing cabinets of village historical societies, with little in the way of indexes or finding aides, to vast state archives vaulted in palatial strongholds with efficient digital organization. When I conducted most of the basic research for this book, little was available online; only at the tail end of the work did the easy resourcing of the new digital age emerge. However they were accumulated, the documents retrieved over the years helped me build an understanding of the evolution of commercial corridors and of changes in aesthetics and local laws.

An array of trade journals illuminated more than one hundred years of building design, technological evolution, and corporate promotional agenda. One particular resource was a standout: *Signs of the Times* has been the industry bible for sign designers and fabricators for more than a century, with no other resource having a run nearly as long. The journal thus had tremendous power to influence and deserved a special emphasis in my research. Over the years, it revealed design trends and mechanical minutiae, and its advertisements tell as much of a story as its editorial content. The best archive for these volumes is to be found at the offices of ST Publishing in Cincinnati, the home of the magazine since its inception in 1906. This is also the location for the American Sign Museum, an outstanding resource for sign media of every description. Along with signs on display spanning the twentieth century, the collection includes vintage design and technical manuals, sign company sales and collateral material, presentation drawings and renderings, and photographs. Other trade journals informing the history of design and technology include *Architectural Record*, the *Architectural Forum*, *Pencil Points/Progressive Architecture*, *Architect and Engineer*, *Arts & Architecture*, *Florida Architecture*, and *Inland Architect*. *Architectural Record* provides perhaps the most extensive coverage of commercial design, exploring building or business types, like the store or restaurant. It even devoted several large sections in the 1940s and 1950s to architecture of the road and highway. Other trade journals addressing the restaurant business, motion picture theater display, and retail (most especially *Chain Store Age*) reveal design trends, preferences for materials and technology, and the public's changing tastes.

Collateral material, sales brochures, and catalogues of major materials manufacturers also illuminate evolving technology and the growing power of large corporations like Newmanco, Pittsburgh Glass, and General Electric to influence the design of the commercial corridor. One of the finest archives for such material is the Hagley Library, near Wilmington, Delaware. This reservoir of material also includes the archives for industrial designer Raymond Loewy. Other sources for storefront material suppliers include the Ward M. Canaday Center for Special Collections at the University of Toledo for the records of the Libbey-

Owens-Ford Glass Company. Even small local libraries have been great sources for this type of material. Of particular note is the Niles Public Library in Niles, Michigan, for publications documenting products and promotions by the Kawneer Company.

As a guide to the progressive effort by citizen activists and small-town boosters alike to improve the look of Main Streets everywhere, one journal is particularly valuable. The *American City,* published from 1909 to the present, is a fount of information, with news of what was happening in the town next door or across the globe, ideal designs for everything from curbs to public comfort stations, and suggestions for the best spacing for street lamps and where to order the finest illumination for your own Main Street. Popular journals like *Fortune, Time,* and *Life* also provide a glimpse of the public's enthusiasm or disdain for signs and roadside businesses through the years. Issues of national interest can be traced in the newspapers of major American cities, like the *New York Times, Chicago Daily Tribune,* and *Los Angeles Times.* Eventually, the public acted through agencies and organizations like the National Trust for Historic Preservation, the National Park Service, and the American Planning Association. Their regular publications, like PAS (Planning Advisory Service) Memos and Preservation Briefs, and special guidebooks and materials provided to guide preservation efforts on a local level across the nation are available at the library of the American Planning Association in Chicago.

Although primary resources were the heart and soul of the work, many books and lectures by a broad range of authors guided and influenced the narrative and its conclusions. A selection of them, by no means a complete listing, follows. Since this study has always emphasized context in understanding individual signs and buildings, it has been essential to consider whole streets, one element connected to the next. Through lectures and publications, Carroll William Westfall, John R. Stilgoe, and Vincent Scully have given the work a grounding in hierarchies, how the village or city was formed, and what made it American. Stilgoe's *Common Landscape of America, 1580 to 1845* (New Haven, CT, 1982) should be the starting point for any understanding of the American landscape as the earliest European settlers formed it; *The Urban Idea in Colonial America,* by Sylvia Doughty Fries (Philadelphia, 1977), rounds out this understanding. Vincent Scully's *American Architecture and Urbanism* (New York, 1969) is also essential, basic reading. For understanding the principles and details of good street-making—the scale, the rhythm, and the relationships—one could hardly find anything as illuminating as Christopher Alexander, Sara Ishikawa, and Murray Silverstein's *A Pattern Language* (New York, 1977) or as informative and inspiring as one of the community charettes led by Andres Duany or Stefanos Polyzoides.

In the realm of meaning and theory in architecture and urban design, as they relate to the commercial landscape, the work of writer John Brinckerhoff Jackson has been especially influential. His clear observations, fresh insights, and lack of prejudice when considering what is often overlooked, dismissed, or scorned provide a beautiful model for documenting all landscapes. Whether considering picket fences, trailer parks, neon signs, or parking lots, Jackson found value that required careful consideration, unusual thoughtfulness, and a let's-try-it-on, gypsy spirit. The magazine he founded, *Landscape,* published his thoughts and sketches, which were collected in books like *The Necessity for Ruins* (Amherst, 1980) and *Discovering the Vernacular Landscape* (New Haven, CT, 1984). *Landscape* also presented the work of others who provided valuable insights for this book, including John Maas, Roland Rainer, and Grady Clay. Geographers and cultural geographers providing facts, insights, and methodological enlightenment include Peirce F. Lewis and Paul Groth. Writers who have made good cases specific to the value of commercial vernacular artifacts, like signs, include British architectural critic Ian Nairn, with *The American Landscape: A Critical View* (New York, 1965), and Tom Wolfe, with his short pieces on the dazzle and artistic merit of roadside neon. Nairn thoughtfully considered the power of graphic symbols and their appropriate placing in the city. The best-known voice to express enthusiasm for graphics and symbols in the landscape is, of course, architect Robert Venturi, especially with his book *Learning from Las Vegas: The Forgotten Symbolism of Architectural Form* (1972; revised ed., Cambridge, MA, 1977). But Venturi's work is important here not because it may be thought to enshrine the electric sign but because it explains how our landscapes are marked in various ways to be read or decoded. This happens with clearly denotative elements like signs and symbols but also with connotative architectural elements like tall classical columns or stone cladding on a Main Street facade, which may indicate, by association, the presence of a bank. Venturi's *Complexity and Contradiction in Architecture* (New York, 1966) made a powerful case for messy inclusiveness at a time when modernism called for exclusive purity. "Main Street is almost alright," his often-quoted aphorism, started here, and despite the slow acceptance of his points, Venturi's work made it possible for writers on the American commercial vernacular to be taken seriously.

Other theorists important to the work on these pages include British architectural critic Reyner Banham, who, as a flaneur on wheels, wrote about the sprawling city at length in *Los Angeles: The Architecture of Four Ecologies* (New York, 1971). Banham offered a new way of seeing; for example, he perceived Wilshire Boulevard as the true downtown, a linear city core. He stressed context when judging, an approach taken to heart for this book. Banham saw a valuable variety in Los Angeles where others observed only confusion. Shorter but no less valuable pieces by Banham include "The Missing Motel: Unrecognized American Architecture," *Landscape* 15 (Winter 1965-66) and "Towards a Million-Volt Light and Sound Culture," *Architecture Review* 141 (1967).

In the 1960s, urbanists Kevin Lynch and William H. Whyte examined how people experienced and behaved in the city and countryside. They were among the first to see beyond the subjective, swelling, aesthetics-based sea of criticism for urban streetscapes and commerce along the highway. Lynch considered how the street was marked and what visually helped citizens navigate their way through town, a paradigm that linked up well with J. B. Jackson's almost contemporaneous "The Stranger's Path," in *Landscape* 7 (1957). Important works by Lynch on this subject include *The Image of the City* (Cambridge, MA, 1960), *Signs in the City: A Study by Graduate Students of Urban Design in the Department of City and Regional Planning, Massachusetts Institute of Technology* (co-authored with Donald Appleyard and Sidney N. Brower) (Cambridge, MA, 1963), *The View from the Road* (with Donald Appleyard) (Cambridge, MA, 1964), and *Designing and Managing the Strip* (with Michael Southworth) (Cambridge, MA, 1974). Extremely useful on this same front is Grady Clay's *Close-Up: How to Read the American City* (New York, 1973). Like Lynch, William Whyte was greatly concerned with the visual approach, or entrance, to the city and believed in its potential to help one develop a sense of place. But, according to Whyte, the "huge things stuck up on stilts" that advertised roadside operators were anathema, blocking the way for this potential. His general push for reduced land waste, access roads for businesses divorced from scenic throughways, and clustering signs at information nodes ran counter to the beliefs of researchers like Drs. R. James and Karen E. Claus, who anticipated the trouble ahead for small businesses if their signs were restricted. Vital work by Whyte includes *The Last Landscape* (Garden City, NY, 1968), *Cluster Development* (New York, 1964), and *City: Rediscovering the Center* (New York, 1988). Jane Jacobs also based her conclusions on observation, but she was more subjective than Lynch or Whyte on patterns of use, submersing herself in street life. Her work emphasized the value of what existed already in the ordinary and everyday. Her seminal book, *Death and Life of Great American Cities* (New York, 1961), provides a crucial background for understanding the value of architectural scale and landmarks along streets and in neighborhoods. It is also a most persuasive argument for the corner store.

Authors addressing context and placemaking specifically include Ronald Lee Fleming, Ada Louise Huxtable, and Robert Bruegmann. Urban planner and preservation advocate Ronald Lee Fleming challenged Venturi and Steven Izenour's enthusiasm for large graphics in the 1970s, defending well-established communities against the visual intrusion of corporate architecture and highway-scaled signs. Both sides presented convincing cases. The report from the national sign summit, *Proceedings of the Urban Signage Forum, April 22 and 23, 1976, Chicago, Illinois* (Washington, DC, 1977), documents the debate well from all sides. Fleming is one of the first to prepare a visual history of Main Street and explain how storefronts evolved over time. Two especially valuable books by him include *Facade Stories: Changing Faces of Main Street Storefronts and How to Care for Them* (New York, 1982) and *Saving Face: How Corporate Franchise Design Can Respect Community Character* (Chicago, 1994).

Ada Louise Huxtable, writing in the *New York Times*, was one of the earliest serious commentators on architecture and urbanism to rally for the renewal of Main Street's historic assets. She was also an early fan of Robert Venturi's pluralistic aesthetic. She provides a wealth of insights over many years, often extending her focus well beyond New York. Like Venturi in the 1960s, Robert Bruegmann in the 1990s called attention to worth to be found in the unconventional; in this case, it was a new order developing at the fringes of suburbia. His material of value on this subject has been presented in several persuasive lectures, and his published essays include "The Corporate Landscape," *Inland Architect* 33 (September–October 1989), "The New Main Street" *Inland Architect* 34 (November–December 1990), and "New Centers on the Periphery," *Center: A Journal for Architecture in America* 7 (1992).

Turning specifically to the traditional commercial corridor, Carole Rifkind's *Main Street: The Face of Urban America* (New York, 1977) provides an ideal introduction. Richard V. Francaviglia's *Main Street Revisited: Time, Space, and Image Building in Small Town America* (Iowa City, 1996) offers a brief study of the formal evolution of buildings followed by an enlightening discussion of their relationship to town planning and space. Richard Longstreth, who has established a sterling reputation addressing commercial design and urban dynamics with a critical mass of books and journal articles, provides an essential foundation for this subject with *The Buildings of Main Street: A Guide to American Commercial Architecture* (Washington, DC, 1987), identifying compositional types.

Two major works by Longstreth examine the dispersal of business and entertainment from the old city core of Los Angeles to various suburban arteries and neighborhoods; specific though these may be to a particular city, they help us to imagine parallel developments in our own corners of America. Both *City Center to Regional Mall: Architecture, the Automobile, and Retailing in Los Angeles, 1920-1950* (Cambridge, MA, 1997) and *The Drive-in, the Supermarket, and the Transformation of Commercial Space in Los Angeles, 1914-1941* (Cambridge, MA, 1999) are essential reading. Longstreth emphasizes patterns of use and evolving spatial relationships over stylistic development in "What to Save? Midcentury Modernism at Risk" *Architectural Record* (September 2000) and "Sears, Roebuck and the Remaking of the Department Store, 1924-1942" *Journal of the Society of Architectural Historians* (June 2006).

The commercial roadside has garnered a generous amount of attention of late, but serious works remain small in number. Most of the better work has focused on building or business types. Chester Liebs's *Main Street to Miracle Mile: American Roadside Architecture* (Boston, 1985) is a classic, perhaps the closest thing to a survey in this genre, respectfully tracing the development of such roadside phenomena as the drive-in, the motel, and automobile showrooms—businesses that made the leap from town center to periphery. John Jakle and Keith Sculle deserve high honors for skillfully pursuing each business or building type, book by book. Armed with backgrounds in geography and history, and the paradigm of place-product-packaging for their studies, their work is not focused on stylistic or formal evolution but how and why these enterprises evolved. Their explorations, which include signs of all kinds along the road, the motel, the gas station, the fast food stand, and an analysis of changing land use in car culture, provide a thorough grounding in roadside history.

Alan Hess's *Googie: Fifties Coffee Shop Architecture* (San Francisco, 1986) and *Viva Las Vegas: After-Hours Architecture* (San Francisco, 1993) provided this author with the earliest sense that commercial design was still vital and valid for analysis so many years after Venturi's studies. Unlike many authors of serious books on commercial design, Hess examines style and form but also provides a rich contextual analysis. He presents visual appearance as a product of each unique city and era. A few other books are classics on highway-oriented design. They include Jan Jennings, ed., *Roadside America: The Automobile in Design and Culture* (Ames, IA, 1990), which contains a few key essays on the impact of the automobile on architecture and advertising; Warren H. Anderson, *Vanishing Roadside America* (Tucson, AZ, 1981); and Warren James Belasco, *Americans on the Road: From Auto Camp to Motel, 1910-1945* (Cambridge,

MA, 1979). Authors addressing specific phenomena of the commercial thoroughfare include Karal Ann Marling, with *The Colossus of Roads: Myth and Symbol along the American Highway* (Minneapolis, 1984)—most useful here because of insights into the impact of commercial imagery—and Catherine Gudis, *Buyways: Billboards, Automobiles, and the American Landscape* (New York, 2004), for background on the progressive movement to legislate roadside advertisements.

A few books have been written specifically about signs, but they tend to be focused on the nation's two most celebrated hubs of wattage: New York's Times Square and the Las Vegas Strip. The intent of this book has been to look beyond these highly scrutinized hubs. Nevertheless, though dense with details or anecdotes, these works have important histories to share, histories that play an key role in the development of iconography and technology elsewhere. Charles F. Barnard's *The Magic Sign: The Electric Art/Architecture of Las Vegas* (Cincinnati, 1999), Tama Starr and Edward Hayman's *Signs and Wonders: The Spectacular Marketing of America* (New York, 1998), and Darcy Tell's *Times Square Spectacular: Lighting Up Broadway* (New York, 2007) are three of the more useful publications.

In addition to the many archival resources for images of streetscapes taken over the past 150 years, books of photography are extremely useful when studying American commercial streetscapes. Many cities have been rather recently honored with books created to present pairs of photographs that show the changes to specific sites over the decades. These "then vs. now" books are quite enthralling, as the changes are often astounding. For more artful, even insightful, images from the many photographers who have prowled American streets and highways, one should pay particular attention to the work of photographers like Walker Evans, Russell Lee, and Arthur Rothstein.

The following sources are best organized by the specific chapters to which they primarily relate. Chapter 1, addressing everything up to the year 1900, is greatly aided by books like Kathryn A. Morrison, *English Shops and Shopping: An Architectural History* (London, 2003), perhaps the closest counterpart in England to my own work here. Aside from books cited earlier by Stilgoe, Scully, and Fries, *The New England Village* (Baltimore, 1997) by Joseph S. Wood is particularly enlightening on the formation of the earliest villages and commercial cores that eventually developed, as well as the role the tavern played. The formalism of Middle Atlantic urbanism (in contrast to the ruralist tendencies of New England), is addressed in Peirce F. Lewis, "Small Town in Pennsylvania," *Annals of the Association of American Geographers* 62 (1972), and Wilbur Zelinsky, "The Pennsylvania Town: An Overdue Geographical Account" *Geographical Review* 67 (April 1977). This is important for understanding the dynamic that influenced the shaping of towns as the nation spread west. John W. Reps, *The Making of Urban America: A History of City Planning in the United States* (Princeton, NJ, 1965), reveals the forces at play influencing town form in the eighteenth and nineteenth centuries. The basic evolution of towns is explained in Blake McKelvey, *The Urbanization of America: 1860-1915* (New Brunswick, NJ, 1963); Sam Bass Warner, *The Urban Wilderness: A History of the American City* (New York, 1972); and Maury Klein and Harvey A. Kantor, *Prisoners of Progress: American Industrial Cities, 1850-1920* (New York, 1976). Early descriptive books by visitors to America provide useful glimpses of towns and cities, from nascent Main Streets to the awe-inspiring lights of Broadway. In addition to Charles Dickens's *American Notes, for General Circulation* (London, 1842), highlights include Johann David Schoepf, *Travels in the Confederation, 1783-1784* (Philadelphia, 1911); William Archer, *America To-Day: Observations and Reflections* (New York, 1899); and J. Nelson Fraser, *America, Old and New: Impressions of Six Months in the States* (London, 1912). An abundant visual tour of middle- to late-nineteenth-century towns in America is provided by the indispensable work of visual artists and writers. John Warner Barber and Henry Howe, collected in many volumes organized geographically. An excellent primer on architecture of the period is James D. Kornwolf, *Architecture and Town Planning in Colonial America* (Baltimore, 2002). The history of cast-iron architecture is well documented in *The Origins of Cast Iron Architecture in America* (New York, 1970), a reprint composite of books from the nineteenth century by Daniel D. Badger and James Bogardus, and Margot and Carol Gayle, *Cast-Iron Architecture in America: The Significance of James Bogardus* (New York, 1998). On the subject of early signs, the following are full of valuable facts, but also many an anecdote or digression: Fritz Endell, *Old Tavern Signs: An Excursion in the History of Hospitality* (Boston, 1916), and Cecil A. Meadows, *Trade Signs and Their Origin* (London, 1957). For an extremely useful, well-written source for an understanding of colonial signs as artistic and civic phenomena—supplied with superb images—Susan P. Schoelwer, ed., *Lions & Eagles & Bulls: Early American Tavern and Inn Signs* (Princeton, NJ, 2000), is unsurpassed.

For chapter 2, on the early-twentieth-century city and the progressive and town booster movements, the Museum of the City of New York and the Chicago History Museum offer a magnificent collection of original drawings by the best architects of the time, along with miles and miles of photographic streetscapes for viewing. Robert A. M. Stern's series on the city, which includes *New York 1880: Architecture and Urbanism in the Gilded Age* (New York, 1999), provides another treasure trove of images, with a detailed and perceptive text. The views of the leaders of the City Beautiful movement are well represented in book form and include Charles Mulford Robinson, *The Improvement of Towns and Cities; or, the Practical Basis of Civic Aesthetics* (New York, 1901) and *Modern Civic Art; or, the City Made Beautiful* (New York, 1903), and Frank Koester, *Modern City Planning and Maintenance* (New York, 1914). William H. Wilson, *The City Beautiful Movement* (Baltimore, 1989), provides an excellent overview, and John Whiteclay Chambers, *The Tyranny of Change: America in the Progressive Era, 1890-1920* (New Brunswick, NJ, 1992), sets the bigger stage. A revealing study of civic goal versus reality and of the role of postcard views of Main Street is offered by Alison Isenberg, *Downtown America: A History of the Place and the People Who Made It* (Chicago, 2004). David Nasaw's *Going Out: The Rise and Fall of Public Amusements* (New York, 1993) is a superb study of how theaters, nickelodeons, and amusement parks were used and viewed by the public around the turn of the century; it is an important work for anyone analyzing facades and advertisements designed to lure an audience. James J. Flink, *The Car Culture* (Cambridge, MA, 1975), and John B. Rae, *The American Automobile: A Brief History* (Chicago, 1965), are valuable background reading for this chapter and those that follow.

Chapter 3, devoted to the architectural eclecticism and grandiosity of the 1920s, relies heavily on research into theater design. Classic books on the genre include Ben M. Hall, *The Best Remaining Seats: The Story of the Golden Age of the Movie Palace* (New York, 1961), and David Naylor, *American Picture Palaces: The Architecture of Fantasy* (New York, 1981). A superb survey, Craig Morrison, *Theaters* (New York, 2006), comes complete with many full-facade, vintage elevation drawings from the early twentieth century by Anthony F. Dumas. Another well-illustrated volume is *Cinema Treasures: A New Look at Classic Movie Theatres*, by Ross Melnick and Andreas Fuchs (St. Paul, MN, 2004). A wealth of theater photographs, design manuals, and advertising and marketing journals is available at the Theatre Historical Society's headquarters in Elmhurst, Illinois. Two journals that proved very illuminating include *Theatre Catalogue* (Philadelphia) and *Motion Picture Herald* (New York, with Better Theatre section included). Among many books worth noting at the society's headquarters, *American Theatres of Today*, 2 vols. (New York, 1929), proved especially valuable. If only for their wealth of images, the many books on the subject of local movie theaters are worth exploring. This includes Larry Widen and Judi Anderson, *Silver Screens: A Pictorial History of Milwaukee's Movie Theatres* (Madison, WI, 2007); Michael V. Doyle, *Boxoffice Open: Michigan's Small Town Movie Theatres* (Bloomington, IN, 2007); and David Welling, *Cinema Houston: From Nickelodeon to Megaplex* (Austin, TX, 2007). On the subjects of zoning, street congestion, and the expansion of the city during this era, the following are excellent resources: Mark S. Foster, *From Streetcar to Superhighway: American City Planners and Urban Transportation, 1900-1940* (Philadelphia, 1981); Seymour I. Toll, *Zoned American* (New York, 1969); Robert M. Fogelson, *Downtown: Its Rise and Fall, 1880-1950* (New Haven, CT, 2001); and John Nolen, *New Towns for Old: Achievements in Civic Improvement in Some American Small Towns and Neighborhoods* (Boston, 1927). At the Library of Congress Prints and Photographs Division, the collection of photographer Theodor Horydczak provides a streetside view of much of Washington from the 1920s through the 1950s. The Architecture and Design Collection in the University Art Museum at the University of California (UC), Santa Barbara, houses many impressive original drawings by the architects of that city, including George Washington Smith and Lutah Maria Riggs. Of greatest value are the drawings depicting how entire street blocks might appear when improved by Spanish colonial revival architecture and arcades. Useful material on Santa Barbara's reinvention can also be found in the Pearl Chase archive at the Department of Special Collections, Davidson Library at UC Santa Barbara, the Santa Barbara Trust for Historic Preservation, and the Santa Barbara Historical Society. The concept of strengthening a visual identity for a town, taken from local history, is addressed well in Chris Wilson, *The Myth of Santa Fe: Creating a Modern Regional Tradition* (Albuquerque, NM, 1997). Wilson's book highlights the manipulation of a city's image and was useful even though Santa Fe is not directly addressed in the final edit of my text. For the commercial work of prolific southern California architect Stiles O. Clements, one may turn to the Maynard L. Parker photographic archive at the Huntington Library, San Marino, California. The library is also a good source for images of Pasadena's roads and streets in the 1920s. On the subject of the automobile's influence on the city and early highway culture, Daniel M. Bluestone's "Roadside Blight and the Reform of Commercial Architecture," in Jennings, *Roadside America*, is particularly informative; also instructive is Belasco, *Americans on the Road*. The abundance of images in Jim Heimann, *California Crazy and Beyond: Roadside Vernacular Architecture* (San Francisco, 1980), helps to establish a mental picture of the evolving automobile landscape for this chapter and those that follow. The White Castle System Inc. Records at the archives of the Ohio Historical Society in Columbus are of great use in studying the early development of corporate iconography in architecture and advertising.

For chapter 4 and the spread of modernism in America, the earliest and most influential sources for European advances in design were publications by French designers and key American architecture journals. Among the many portfolios of work worth exploring are René Herbst, *Devantures, vitrines, installations de magasins à L'Exposition Internationale des Arts Decoratifs, Paris 1925* (Paris, 1928); Louis Pierre Sézille, *Devantures de boutiques: 48 planches* (Paris, 1927); René Herbst, *Boutiques et magasins* (Paris, 1929); René Chavance, *Nouvelles boutiques: Façades et intérieurs* (Paris, 1929); and Roger Poulain, *Boutiques 1931* (Paris, 1931). American magazines were quick to spot both the work itself abroad and its thorough documentation in portfolios. America photographer Thérèse Bonney was instrumental in disseminating this design style, through both her own images and those by others; for a collection of her work, see Lisa Schlansker Kolosek, *The Invention of Chic: Thérèse Bonney and Paris Moderne* (London, 2002). Another key influence during this early period was the *Magazine of Light*, published by General Electric from 1930 to 1953, with hundreds of images presenting design advances. For excellent reference books on expositions that propagated modernism, see Lisa D. Schrenk, *Building a Century of Progress: The Architecture of Chicago's 1933–34 World's Fair* (Minneapolis, 2007); Lenox Lohr, *Fair Management: The Story of A Century of Progress, a Guide for Future Fairs* (Chicago, 1952); and *Drawing the Future: Design Drawings for the 1939 New York World's Fair* (New York, 1996). Although not specific to commercial design, a filter of discipline came to Main Street via Henry-Russell Hitchcock and Philip Johnson, *The International Style: Architecture since 1922* (New York, 1932). A major compendium of fresh storefront ideas was supplied by the first key design competition of the 1930s, published as *52 Designs to Modernize Main Street with Glass* (Toledo, OH, 1935). This celebrated effort fathered many other such competitions sponsored by the makers of storefront materials, illumination, and advertising. All were well documented in trade journals of the period. A highlight of key books that spread the new commercial look in America includes Kenneth Kingsley Stowell, *Modernizing Buildings for Profit* (New York, 1935); Morris Ketchum Jr., *Shops and Stores* (New York, 1948); and George F. Meyers, *Electrical Display Dynamics: Modern Signs and Storefronts* (Cincinnati, 1946). Gabrielle Esperdy expertly addresses the powerful influence of corporations promoting their materials in *Modernizing Main Street: Architecture and Consumer Culture in the New Deal* (Chicago, 2008). Unfortunately, it was published just as I was finishing my final draft, but it is an invaluable resource for anyone interested in Main Street history or the economic recovery of the 1930s, and I recommend it heartily. For background on the changes in retail that were amplified by the stagnant economy of the 1930s, see Walter

S. Hayward, Percival White, and John S. Fleek, *Chain Stores* (New York, 1928), and Godfrey M. Lebhar, *Chain Stores in America, 1859–1950* (New York, 1952).

Chapter 4 looks frequently to auto-oriented design invention coming from Los Angeles. In *Endangered Dreams: The Great Depression in California* (New York, 1997) and *Material Dreams: Southern California through the 1920s* (New York, 1990), Kevin Starr displays the mind and eye of an architectural historian, even though he is out to address bigger issues. Also see David Gebhard, *Los Angeles in the Thirties, 1931–1941* (Los Angeles, 1989) and *Guide to Architecture in Los Angeles and Southern California* (Santa Barbara, CA, 1977); and *Kem Weber: The Moderne in Southern California 1920–1941* (Santa Barbara, CA, 1969). Gebhard founded the Architecture and Design Collection in the University Art Museum at the University of California, Santa Barbara, which contains a treasure trove of original drawings and writing by architects including Rudolph M. Schindler, Kem Weber, J. R. Davidson, Robert Vincent Derrah, and Marcus P. Miller. The books of Richard Longstreth, cited above, are essential reading for the Los Angeles of this period (as well as the 1920s). Other work on Los Angeles includes Maggie Valentine, *The Show Starts on the Sidewalk: An Architectural History of the Movie Theatre, Starring S. Charles Lee* (New Haven, CT, 1994), which showcases the astounding design work of one of the most prolific commercial designers in America during this period. For another major West Coast commercial design leader, see Chris Nichols, *The Leisure Architecture of Wayne McAllister* (Layton, UT, 2007). Richard Guy Wilson powerfully introduces the streamline aesthetic popularized in the 1930s in *The Machine Age in America, 1918–1941* (New York, 1986). Works by the industrial designers so key to economic recovery in the 1930s and 1940s include Norman Bel Geddes, *Horizons* (Boston, 1932); Walter Dorwin Teague, *Design This Day: The Technique of Order in the Machine Age* (New York, 1940); Raymond Loewy, *Never Leave Well Enough Alone* (New York, 1951); and Henry Dreyfuss, *Industrial Design: A Progress Report, 1929–1952* (New York, [1952]).

Chapter 4 also included exploration into the archives of the following institutions: the Chicago History Museum (for photographs—including the spectacular Hedrich-Blessing Collection—as well as books, collateral material on A Century of Progress, and documentation of the commercial work of architect Alfred Alschuler and the firm of Holabird & Root / Holabird & Roche); the University of Chicago Library (for the Century of Progress 1933–34 World's Fair Collection); University of Illinois at Chicago Special Collections (including more on the fair); the Wolfsonian Museum, Florida International University, Miami (for European storefront design publications, material on world's fairs, and drawings and photographs of Miami Beach hotels and commercial buildings); the Cooper-Hewitt, National Design Museum, New York (for drawings and photographs documenting the work of industrial designer Donald Deskey and photographs of Paris storefronts by Thérèse Bonney); the Avery Library Drawings and Archives Department at Columbia University, New York (for original drawings and photographs of the work of architects and designers including Winold Reiss, Ely Jacques Kahn, and Horace Ginsbern); the Whittington Collection, Special Collections, University of Southern California (for photographs of commercial arteries in Los Angeles by the studio of "Dick" Whittington); the Woodrow W. Wilkins Archives of the Historical Museum of Southern Florida, Miami (for the architectural drawings of Kiehnel and Elliott, photographs of the work of Igor Polevitsky, and documentation of the main commercial corridors of the area); the Ward M. Canaday Center for Special Collections at the University of Toledo (for the publications and advertising campaigns of the Libbey-Owens-Ford Glass Company); the archive of the Architecture + Design Department of the San Francisco Museum of Modern Art (for the drawings of architect Timothy L. Pflueger); and the Gottscho-Schleisner Collections (which offer documentation of commercial exteriors from the mid-1930s to the mid-1950s) at both the Museum of the City of New York and the Library of Congress Prints and Photographs Division.

Chapter 5, on the power of the suburban shopping center and the separation of sign and building in the 1950s, relies heavily on trade magazines as sources, since the power of the media to influence was intensifying at this time. It also turns to information gleaned from interviews conducted across the country with people active during this period as owners or designers at sign companies. Unfortunately, development outside of the old town center is poorly documented across the country: archives hold little information on local businesses located out on what was once the fringe of town. Therefore, early drive-ins, hamburger stands, strip centers, and the like are rarely found in photographic collections. Traditions of photographing all the employees of an enterprise standing in a row in front of a storefront appear to decline significantly after World War II. This is not to say, however, that none exist. Businesses were still in need of newspaper publicity on occasion, such as opening day; local archives are thus often essential. For work on the West Coast by more celebrated designers, the Julius Schulman archive at the Getty Research Institute in Los Angeles is invaluable, as Schulman captured the city's commercial growth over several decades. The Joseph W. Molitor Photographic Collection at the Department of Drawings and Archives at the Avery Architectural and Fine Arts Library, Columbia University, provides another survey of commercial work over several decades and several cities. Excellent references on graphic designers who influenced signs include Paul Rand, *Thoughts on Design* (New York, 1947); R. Roger Remington and Barbara J. Hodik, *Nine Pioneers in American Graphic Design* (Cambridge, MA, 1989); and Steven Heller and Georgette Balance, eds., *Graphic Design History* (New York, 2001). Phillip B. Meggs's *A History of Graphic Design* (New York, 1983) is the essential survey on the subject, useful to all chapters of this book. For an excellent introduction into the growth of coordinated graphics, see Pierre Martineau, "Sharper Focus for the Corporate Image," *Harvard Business Review* 36 (November–December 1958). For a good background on the era's commercial architecture, one should turn to Philip Langdon, *Orange Roofs, Golden Arches: The Architecture of American Chain Restaurants* (New York, 1986), in addition to Alan Hess, Chester Liebs, and the many books by the team of John Jakle and Keith Sculle, as cited above. Valuable literature from the period includes Louis X. Garfunkel, *Sandwich Shops, Drive-Ins, and Diners: How to Start and Operate Them* (New York, 1955), and Geoffrey Baker and Bruno Funaro, *Shopping Centers: Design and Operation* (New York, 1951). Lesley Jackson, *Contemporary: Architecture and Interiors of the 1950s* (London, 1994), offers an excellent text and strong visuals to explain the aesthetic of the era in general. The limitations of this aesthetic are exposed indirectly by Richard W. Snibbe in *Small Commercial Buildings: A Photographic Record of 100 Selected Designs for Small Commercial Buildings Executed in the Last 20 Years* (New York, 1956). Opposing approaches to seeing the commercial environment are provided by *Landscape* magazine during this period; Christopher Tunnard and Boris Pushkarev, *Man-Made America: Chaos or Control? An Inquiry into Selected Problems of Design in the Urbanized Landscape* (New Haven, CT, 1963); and Peter Blake's simplistic but revealing *God's Own Junkyard: The Planned Deterioration of America's Landscape* (New York, 1964). The work of Kevin Lynch, William H. Whyte, and Jane Jacobs, mentioned earlier in this essay, informs this chapter with key design philosophies of the period. George R. Stewart, *U.S. 40: Cross Section of the United States of America* (Boston, 1953), provides a far less biased view of the pre-interstate highway as it weaves in and out of town. This is one of many books addressing early cross-country routes—and one of the finest. A great deal more criticism of roadside phenomena appeared in designs journals of the day, too much to begin listing here. The proposed new suburban shopping aesthetic is presented in Victor Gruen, *Shopping Towns USA: The Planning of Shopping Centers* (New York, 1960); M. Jeffrey Hardwick, *Mall Maker: Victor Gruen, Architect of an American Dream* (Philadelphia, 2004); John Findlay, *Magic Lands: Western Landscapes and American Culture after 1940* (Berkeley, CA, 1992); and many articles in design journals, consumer magazines, and newspapers. The Browne Popular Culture Library at Bowling Green State University, in Bowling Green, Ohio, is an unequalled resource for ephemera documenting world's fairs (especially Century 21 in Seattle, upon which little is written), roadside businesses, and trends in popular graphic design.

Addressing the strategic alterations made to Main Street in the late twentieth century, chapter 6 greatly depends on primary source material collected in about thirty case study towns. This includes interviews with local planning officials, review of changing codes and guidelines, perusal of newspaper articles, and so forth. For insightful discussions of changes occurring in traditional town centers, see Daniel Lazare, *America's Undeclared War: What's Killing Our Cities and How We Can Stop It* (New York, 2001); Roberta Brandes Gratz with Norman Mintz, *Cities Back from the Edge: New Life for Downtown* (New York, 1998); Bernard J. Frieden and Lynn B. Sagalyn, *Downtown, Inc.: How America Rebuilds Cities* (Cambridge, MA, 1991); and Richard O. Davies, *Main Street Blues: The Decline of Small-Town America* (Columbus, OH, 1998). Victor Gruen's theories and influence are well presented in Victor Gruen, *The Heart of Our Cities; The Urban Crisis: Diagnosis and Cure* (New York, 1964), and Alex Wall, *Victor Gruen: From Urban Shop to New City* (Barcelona, 2005); as well as a plethora of articles in design and planning journals, consumer magazines, and newspaper articles. The nation's scorn for the perceived chaos of the commercial corridor and proposals to help tame it are found in a wide range of books, periodicals, and legislation. As a counterforce of reason to the eventual momentum that grew for sign destruction, the Drs. R. James and Karen E. Claus wrote the pragmatic but imperative *Street Graphics: A Perspective* (Cincinnati, 1975). This work responded directly to William R. Ewald and Daniel R. Mandelker, *Street Graphics: A Concept and a System* (Washington, DC, 1971), later revised as *Street Graphics and the Law* (Washington, DC, 1988), which had been held up as perhaps the most comprehensive path to improvement. Other systems to address signage include Eric D. Kelly, *Sign Regulations for Small and Midsize Communities: A Planner's Guide and a Model Ordinance* (Chicago, 1989). Analysis of existing codes and their worth is included in resources such as Leopold A. Goldschmidt, *Sign Regulation in the Central Business District*, Information Report no. 188 (Chicago, 1964). Of course there is no substitute for examining the codes of America's cities directly to see how they have changed over the years. Along with the ordinances of major cities like Chicago, New York, and Los Angeles, I found it necessary to study the legislation of the many smaller case study towns and cities that I grew to know while conducting research for this book. Beyond that work, in general, arguments for and against the onsite business sign can be found in architecture journals, landscape architecture journals, and periodicals ranging from *Landscape* to *Fortune* magazine.

I conclude this essay on sources by acknowledging works of fiction that offer perhaps them most vivid glimpses into the past available to us today. Beyond the obvious but no less useful *Main Street* (New York, 1920), by Sinclair Lewis, is other work by the author, including his road book, *Free Air* (New York, 1919), *Babbitt* (New York, 1922), *The Man Who Knew Coolidge* (New York, 1928), *Dodsworth* (New York, 1929), *Work of Art* (New York, 1934), and *Kingsblood Royal* (New York, 1947). All provide lively pictures of commercial thoroughfares, building facades, or grand movie palace architecture, showing how they were used or perceived by the characters in the novels. Booth Tarkington's *The Gentleman from Indiana* (New York, 1899) joins Lewis's *Main Street* in providing a memorable vision of the hope and disappointment associated with that central place. Sherwood Anderson's *Winesburg, Ohio* (New York, 1919) and *Poor White* (New York, 1920) illustrate how Main Street was occupied, especially at night, and what magic or despair it held. Theodore Dreiser's *A Hoosier Holiday* (New York, 1916), a factual account of a journey by a fiction writer, reads like a novel. The path is often harrowing, and entranceways into town—often welcoming with the small-town novelty of electric lights—seem light-years away from the bland, homogenized gateways experienced by travelers today. Aldous Huxley, *After Many a Summer Dies the Swan* (New York, 1939), and Vladimir Nabokov, *Lolita* (New York, 1955), both present roadside culture with an appropriate blend of awe and disrespect for the blank corporate icons, stupefying scale, hapless hyper-superlatives, and deadpan non sequiturs. I could go on and on to include writers like Raymond Chandler, John O'Hara, and many more. Fiction not only preserves past details of the street but also reveals its threatening or appealing ambiance and the ways people used commercial space and experienced or perceived store window displays, distant neon beacons, and theater marquees in the uniquely American landscape.

Index

THE LETTER *f* FOLLOWING A PAGE NUMBER DENOTES A FIGURE.

Academy Theater, Los Angeles, 179
acrylic sign boxes, 4, 6, 196, 200–201, 232–33, 262
Alabama Theater, Houston, 179
Albia, Iowa, preservation in, 259–60
Albion Hotel, Miami Beach, 158–59, plate 10
Albright, John, 157, 186–87
Alcoa (slipcovering manufacturer), 200
All Star Donuts and sign, San Francisco, 316–17, plate 37
Alschuler, Alfred, 92–93, 153, 156f, 157, 163f, 276
aluminum industry, building refacing and, 199–200
American Planning Association, 263, 264, 265, 291, 292, 316
animated signs, 52, 73–74, 101, 102, 220–21
arcades, 20f, 162–63, 267
arches, in theater facades, 59, 61f, 83, 84f, 85, 88
architects, signs and storefronts by, 11, 55–66, 162–63, 207–8, 311. *See also* modernism
Architectural Record, 85–86, 111, 123, 125, 151, 234; on signs, 60, 63, 68, 196
Armet and Davis, 216
A. S. Beck Shoes chain stores, 133
Atkinson, Frank, 53, 54, 54f
Atlantic and Pacific Tea Company signs, 52
Austin Automobile Company Showroom (1927), 102–3f, 104
automobile age (1920s): defining and protecting vision of place, 94–104, 115; design for space and speed, 104–14, 115; eclectic architecture and, 81–82, 91–94; movie theaters and, 82–90, 114
Automobile Club of New York, 73
Automobile Row, Chicago, 60, 63
automobiles, 10, 46f, 195; showrooms for, 50, 60, 63, 79, 102–3f, 104; signs separated from architecture and, 210–28. *See also* projecting signs
awning signs, 20f, 33
Aztec Hotel, Monrovia, Calif., 110

Bachelor's Men's Shop, Los Angeles, 128
Baltimore, 23, 286
Balyeat's Coffee Shop, Van Wert, Ohio, 253, 253f, 256, plate 32
Banham, Reyner, 110, 212, 268
Barber, John Warner, 18, 26
Barnsdall-Rio Grande gas station, near Santa Barbara, 112–13
Barre, Mass., 19f, 26–27, 26f, 27f
Bayer, Herbert, 122f, 124
Beall, Lester, 215
Bedell's women's clothing store, New York City, 133
Beer Street (Hogarth, 1751), 16f, 17
Bejach's Billiards' sign, 52
Bel-Air motel sign, Wildwood, N.J., 248, plate 26
Belasco Theatre, Los Angeles, 89–90, 93, 95f
Bel Geddes, Norman, 126, 145
Bellamy, Edward, 66, 71
Belluschi, Pietro, 138, 164–65
Benson & Rixon Company Building, Chicago, 153, 156f, 288f, 289
Berlin, Kopp & Joseph Shop in, 120f, 123
Berman v. Parker (1954), 291
billboards, 68, 70, 81, 166; regulations on, 67, 72–73, 113, 251

Binder, Joseph, 125
Blake, Peter, 202, 233
blight: civic visions and control of, 66–75; factors in development of, 49–50; sign integration with architecture and, 55–66; technological and international influences and, 50–55. *See also* Great White Way
Bogardus, James, 40–41
books, reference and instructional, 53, 139, 142, 186, 228
Boston, 23, 100, 286
Breezewood, Pa., interstate exchange, 298f
Breuer, Marcel, 248
Broadway Association, New York City, 100
Broadway-Crenshaw Center, Los Angeles, 236–37; Broadway Store, Pasadena, 236f, 303–4
Brunswick Sport Company, Deskey's designs for, 166, 169, 174f
Bryan, Ohio, 5–6, 7f, 26–27, 77; consistent architecture in, 31, 35–36, 314, plate 4; preservation in, 261–62, 307; slipcovering in, 201, 258
Buffalo Lake, Minn., sheathing in, 256–57f, 258
building codes, 73–74, 99. *See also* sign ordinances; zoning laws
Bull Dog and Whistle Restaurant, Chicago, 92f
Bullock's Wilshire store sign tower, 212
Bun'n Burger sign, Alhambra, Calif., 188–89, plate 20
Burnham, Daniel H., 57, 118
Butler's Cafe, Covington, Ky., plate 3
Butterfly Theater, Milwaukee, 60, 62f

C. A. Brandenburgh's Museum, Philadelphia, 59

375

Café de Unie, Rotterdam, 123
California Theatre, San Francisco, 60, 64f
canopies: of American theaters, 59, 61f; for signs, 157–58
Capri Theater, Shelbyville, Tenn., 177, plate 13
Caribbean motel sign, Wildwood, N.J., plate 26
Carlos Club sign, San Carlos, Calif., 187, plate 18
Carlu, Jean, 189, 193f
Carson, Pirie, Scott building, Chicago, 41
Carters' Corner, Bryan, Ohio (1870), 32f
Cassandre, A. M., 229–30
cast-iron commercial facades, 40–41, 42f
Castle Square Theatre, Boston, 59
cast-metal commercial facades, 37
Central Camera, Chicago, 208f
A Century of Progress, Chicago (1933–1934), 143–46, 153, 171
Chain Store Age, 148–49, 164, 165
chain stores, 110, 133–35, 147, 198f, 199, 201, 231, 313
Chandler's Shoes, Los Angeles, 170–71
Charleston, S.C., 77; commercial buildings in, 23–24, 25f, 31, 153, 154, 159f; preservation in, 259, 264, 292–93
Chase, Pearl, 97, 113
Cheapside (London street), 19–21
Chermayeff & Geismar, 232
Chicago, 77, 160–61f, 201; Alschuler's buildings in, 92–93, 92f; Belmont Ave. (1935), plate 16; building-as-sign in, 43, 45f; preservation in, 264, 309, 321–22, plate 35; sign ordinances in, 73–75, 100. *See also* Roseland, Ill.; State Street, Chicago; world's fairs
Chicago Plan (1909), 100
Chicago School, 41, 44f

Chicago Theater, 86
Child's restaurants, 134–35
Chinatowns, signs of, 317
chipped-glass signs, 38
Chips Restaurant, Hawthorne, Calif., plate 27
Cincinnati, Vine Street (ca. 1939) in, as hodge-podge, 186, 188f, plate 34
City Beautiful movement, 10, 66
Claus, Karen E. and R. James, 295–96
Clements, Stiles O., 93, 124
collage artists, postwar architects and, 215
Columbus, Ind., 259
commercial buildings: of early 20th century, 63, 65, 66f; evolution of signs for, 314–16; late 19th century, 35–38, 36f, 44–45; postwar finishes for, 199–200; universal sources for designs of, 29, 30f, 31; as urban design element, 8–9. *See also* automobile age; facade signs; stores and storefronts; strip retail buildings
Community Drafting Room (Santa Barbara architects), 94–95, 96
competitions. *See* design competitions
Connecticut, colonial inn sign laws in, 18. *See also* Guilford
Conrad Building, Los Angeles, 171
Container Corporation of America advertisements, 229–30
cornice, definition of, 32
cornice signs, 33, 34
court rulings, on sign regulations, 72–73, 79
courtyards, shopping center, 236
covering-up of buildings. *See* slipcovering
Crane, C. Howard, 85, 205
Crane, Tex., Main Street (1930s), 186, 191f
Crenshaw Motors Ford, Los Angeles,

169, plate 11
Crest Hotel, Miami Beach, 170, 176f
Criterion Theater, New York City, 83
Crown glass, segmented shop windows due to cost of, 33
Cunningham's Drug Store, Grinnell, Iowa, 319f, 321
Cushman's Bakery chain stores, 135, 154

David City, Neb., preservation in, 259
Davidson, J. R., 127, 128, 130, 130f
Davies' Chuck Wagon Diner, Denver, plate 28
decorated sheds, 5, 108–9f, 110
design competitions: for gas station and roadside refreshment stands (1927), 111; Kawneer- and *Pencil Points*-sponsored, 184–85; L-O-F-sponsored, 150–52, 150f; postwar, NESA-sponsored, 205, 207, 218, 224, 226f, 227; postwar, by sign companies, 197; PPG- and *Architectural Forum*-sponsored, 152
Deskey, Donald, 126, 152, 166, 169, 174f
de Stijl movement, 230
Detroit School of Lettering, 54
Dickens, Charles, 29, 31, 33
Dimling Candy, Pittsburgh, 200, plate 23
Disneyland's Main Street USA, 244–45
domestic architecture for commercial uses, 23–25; signs for, 9
Donahue Building, Los Angeles, triple-arched corner of, 104
Downey sign for McDonald's, 222, 224, plate 30
Dreyfuss, Henry, 126, 154
drive-ins, 190, 195; curb supermarket, 128, 130; restaurants, 171–72, 178f, 212–13. *See also* Googie-style coffee shops; roadside businesses
drum signs, 38, 40
duck. *See* mimetic architecture

Dyas Carleton Café, Los Angeles, 106, 106f

Eames, Charles and Ray, 215–16, 238
Eberson, John, 84, 90, 114
eclectic architectural styles (early 20th cent.), 81–82; of commercial buildings, 63, 65, 66f; of movie theaters, 82–90, 114; in private and public buildings, 91–94, 92f, 95f
École des Beaux-Arts, Paris, 124
Edison Building, New York City, 57, 58f
El Camino Restaurant, Socorro, N.Mex., 227
electric companies, 77, 78
electric signs: architect prejudice against, 56; civic reform groups on, 70; for Disneyland, 244; early use of, 44, 49, 50–51, 52; GE's promotion of, 140–41f, 143, 144–45, 144f, 148; growth in sizes of, 67–68; standardized, as logos, 111; uniform, for strip retail, 181, 184; for White Ways, 75–77. *See also* animated signs; neon signs; projecting signs, electric; sign ordinances
electrographic architecture, Wolfe on, 5, 293–94
Embassy Theater, Reading, Pa., 175, 177, 182–83f
English influence, 13, 17–26, 124
Esquire Theater, Chicago, 169–70, 175f
Essex House Hotel, Miami Beach, 172, 180f
Euclid, Ohio, shopping center, 237
Europe: experimental influences of, 118, 119f, 120f, 121–27, 122f; graphics integrated with architecture in, 56–57; progressives on civic improvements in, 70–71; shopping arcades in, 71–72
exotic architectural design. *See* eclectic architectural styles
Exposition Internationale des Arts Décoratifs et Industriels Modernes, Paris (1925), 123
exterior lobbies, 162–63, 267

facade conflict between architecture and signs, 35–47, 103–4
facade masking. *See* slipcovering
facade signs, 17, 20f, 21–22, 33–34, 40, 43–44, 101. *See also* upper stories
Fain's Carpet and Rug Store, Providence, 151–52, 152f
The Fair, Adams Street, Chicago, 43, 45f
false fronts, 28; signs on, 34–35, 35f
fascia: definition of, 32; expansion beyond, 122
fascia signs, 21, 31–33, 37, 38, 43
Federal Housing Administration loans, 146–47, 150, 180–81
Federal Housing Authority, 275
federal land grants, 29
Federal Sign Company, 78; Federal Sign System, 52
Federal Standard State Zoning Enabling Act (1924), 99
federal subsidies for shopping centers, 235
Federal Theater, Denver, 205, 208f
Fifth Avenue merchants, New York City, 35, 74, 99–100, 115
52 Designs to Modernize Main Street with Glass, 150f, 151, 154
filling station signs. *See* gas station signs
Findlay, Ohio, 254–55f, 256–57
fins, structural, 212, 214f. *See also* sign fins
Flamingo Colony motel, Sarasota, 2f, 3, plate 1
Flat Iron Arts Building, Chicago, 41, 43, 44f
Fleming, Ronald Lee, 265–66, 296–97
fluorescent tubes, 232

Ford Lunch, Ontario, Calif., 108–9f, 110
Fort Worth, Tex., Downtown Futurama for, 277, 278
Fox Village Theatre, Los Angeles, plate 15
frieze, definition of, 32
Frisch's Mainliner Restaurant, Cincinnati, 218–19, 220f
F. W. Woolworth Company, 110, 196–97, plate 21

gas station signs, 82, 106, 111–13, 115, 169. *See also* oil company signs
Gately's People's store, Roseland, Ill., 270
General Electric Company: modernism and, 127, 140–41f, 143, 144–45, 144f, 148; on neon signs, 233; on uniform electric signs, 181, 184. See also *Magazine of Light*
General Motors, 157–58
General Outdoor Advertising, 217
Ginsbern, Horace, 126–27, 147–48, 149
glass: for commercial display, 104, 128, 133, 146, 148; early sizes and types of, 33; pigmented structural, 118, 150–51, 181; technological advances in, 311. *See also* Libbey-Owens-Ford (L-O-F) Glass Company; Pittsburgh Plate Glass Company (PPG)
glass block (1930s), 153
God's Own Junkyard (Blake), 202, 233
Goodman Shops Building, Los Angeles, 105, 105f
Googie-style coffee shops, 216–17, 269–70, 271f, 304, plate 27
government policy. *See* sign ordinances; zoning laws
Grand Lake Theater, Oakland, Calif., 87–89, 88f
graphic design and graphic designers: consistent, for commercial chains, 110; for electric signs, 89, 90, 91f;

INDEX **577**

graphic design and graphic designers *(continued)*
    integrated with architecture, 54, 56–57; of late-19th-century signs, 38; modernism and, 124–25, 127; muted (1930s), 118; shopping center signs and, 238, 239f, 241. *See also* sign crafters and contractors

Grayson's stores, 166, 173f

Great Depression, 117–18, 146–53, 190–91

Great White Way, 68, 75, 100, plate 14; emulations of, 75–79, 89, 312

Grinnell, Iowa, preservation in, 318, 319f, 321

Gropius, Walter, 138, 164–65

Gruen, Victor: as architecture and design theorist, 207, 230–31, 243, 244, 275, 290; designs by, 166, 237–38, 241; Disneyland and, 244–45; pedestrianized Main Streets and, 278, 278f, 307–8

Guilford, Conn., 24, 27, 51–52, 52f, 65–66, 298–300

Gunning v. St. Louis (1911), 72–73

Gwinn's Restaurant and Drive-In, Pasadena, 304, 305f

Hagopian, Vahan, 133–34

hanging signs, 19–20, 40

Hanscom Bake Shops (chain), 147–48, 149, 149f

Harlem's 125th Street, 270, 272–74, 275f, 308–9, 320, 321f

Heath, Wayne, and Company, 207, 217–18

Henderson's Sign Painter (1906), 53, 54

Herbst, René, 118, 123

Herdeg, Klaus, 247, 248

Highway Beautification Act (1964), 251

Hi-Hat Restaurant, Los Angeles, 128, 130f

historic preservation: in Albia, Iowa, 259–60; as alternative to slipcovering, 258–59; antisign bias in, 10, 262–64; in Bryan, Ohio, 261–62; community control and, 262–63; community identity and, 265–66, 268–70, 317–18; Harlem zoning changes and, 272–74, 275f; layered history and, 253, 253f, 256, 266–68, plate 33; neighborhood rehabilitation and, 251; Phillips and Auer on, 265; summary of issues with, 316–22; vulnerable signs and buildings and, 321–22. *See also Street Graphics*

Hitchcock, Henry-Russell, 137–38, 165, 207

Hogarth, William, 16f, 17

Holabird & Roche, 41, 43

Holabird & Root, 135–36, 149

Holiday Inn sign, 221–22

Holmby Hall, Los Angeles, 93

horizontal signs, 21

Horn & Hardart, 132

Hornbeck Theater, Shawnee, Okla., 177

Horsley, Peter, 207, 217, 220–21

Hotchkiss Automobile Dealership, Paris, 119f, 123

hotels: independent signs for, 169; Las Vegas, 214. *See also* Miami Beach hotels

Housing Act of 1949, Title I of, 274–75

Housing Act of 1954, 275

Howard, Ebenezer, 66, 71

Howe, Henry, 18, 26

Hula Hut Restaurant, Los Angeles, 217, 218, 219f

Hunebelle (André) Glass Showroom, 121f, 123, 133

Huxtable, Ada Louise, 258, 260

icon signs, 17–18, 22

independent sign structures: articulated pieces in, 214–17, 225f; of drive-in restaurants, 212–13; evolution of, 162, 169–71, 169f, 175f, 210, 212, 214f; Holiday Inn sign in Memphis, 221–22; McDonald's experimentation with, 215f, 222, 224; by Meyers, Horsley, and Heath, 220–21; NESA 1959 competition and, 224, 226f, 227; pylon signs as (1950s), 217–20, 223f; for Wildwood, N.J., motels, 213–14

industrial designers, 118, 126, 154

informational signs on facades, 34

inn signs, 17–18, 34

International Style, 137–38, 165

interstate highway interchanges, 18, 297–98, 298f

Iowa, railroads and architecture in, 29

Izenour, Steven, 296

Jackson, J. B., 11, 235, 243–44

Jacobs, Jane, 289, 290

J. C. Penney's, slipcovering by, 201

Jefferson, Thomas, 13, 21

J. J. Newberry five-and-dime store, 199, 201

Johnson, Philip, 137–38, 165, 207

J. P. Kinnikin, Dexter and Co., 224

Julian Medical Building, Los Angeles, 159, 162, 167f

Kahn, Albert, 151, 152

Kahn, Ely Jacques, 85–86, 121, 124, 164–65, 177–78

Kalamazoo, Mich., 276, 278–79, 278f

Kansas City: Country Club Plaza, 93–94, 235–36; sign ordinances in, 100

Kärntner Bar, Vienna, 57

Kauffer, E. McKnight, 90

Kawneer (storefront systems company): design competitions and, 184–85; Niles, Mich., remodeling (1940s) and, 149, 165; Niles, Mich.'s

resheathing and (1970s), 252–53, 252f, 258; on postwar aluminum cladding, 200; Walden Book Shop design and, 148
Keck, George Fred, 136–37
Ketchum, Gina & Sharp, 165, 205, 207, 275–76
Ketchum, Morris, Jr., 165–66, 184–85, 237
Kinney's Shoes chain stores, 134
Kitty Kelly shoe store chain, 153, 155f, 289
Kodak showroom, New York City, 133
Koester, Frank, 71, 75
Krause Music Store, Chicago, 41
Kress Company, The, 59, 110, plate 7

Lake Forest, Ill., Market Square in, 42, 235–36
Lamb Tavern, Boston, 23
Lapidus, Morris, 134, 166, 185, 207
Las Vegas hotels, 214
Laura Lee store, Los Angeles, 128
Laura's Fudge, Wildwood, N.J., 318, plate 39
Learning from Las Vegas (Venturi, Brown, and Izenour), 293
legislation. *See* sign ordinances; zoning laws
Leimert Theater, Los Angeles, 178–79
Lenox Lounge, Harlem's 125th Street, 320f, 321
Lescaze, William, 151, 164–65, 185
letterforms and lettering: for fascia signs, 32–33; Hitchcock and Johnson on, 138; for Los Angeles shopping arcades (1920s), 106; manufacturers of, 53; modernism and, 123, 124–25; for movie theater marquees, 83; for PPG project (1944–45), 164–65; preservation in Bryan, Ohio, and, 262; progressives on, 70; in shopping centers, 181, 238; *Signs of the Times* on, 101, 228; types of, 54, 55. *See also* ribbon lettering
Lewis, Sinclair, 77, 82, 112, 114
Libbey-Owens-Ford (L-O-F) Glass Company, 150–52, 150f, 164, 170f
Linda Vista Shopping Center, near San Diego, 235
Lindy's restaurant, Los Angeles, 131, 132f
lobbies, exterior, 162–63, 267
Loewy, Raymond, 126, 135, 154, 171, 189
logos, 9, 110–11, 230–31, 238, 239f, 313. *See also* symbols; trademarks
London, 19–21, 29, 31, 33
London Character Shoe chain stores, 133–34, 135f
Longstreth, Richard, 23, 28, 57, 58f
Los Angeles: auto-oriented buildings in, 104, 105–6, 106f; eclectic architecture (1920s) in, 89–90, 93, 95f; electric signs by 1910 in, 51; modern European design in, 128, 129f, 130–31, 131f, 132f, 142; movie theater signs in, 178–79
lot sizes, National Land Ordinance (1785) and, 29
Lucky Supermarket, San Leandro, Calif., 171
Lundy, Victor, 208, 209
Lustig, Alvin, 238, 241

Maddux Air Lines office, Los Angeles, 128, 129f
Magazine of Light (General Electric), 123, 132, 148, 190
magazines, popular, 66–67, 81, 110, 228
Main Street: colonial era making of, 13–17; facade conflict on, 35–47; layered history of, 253, 253f, 256, 266–68, plate 33; pedestrianized, 275, 277–82, 305, 314; postwar designs for groups of stores on, 184–85; postwar transitions for, 196–210; signs separated from architecture of, 210–28; task-suited architecture designed for, 28–35; urbanizing rural for commerce on, 17–26; as visually chaotic (1930s–1940s), 186, 188f, 191f. *See also* automobile age; blight; historic preservation; modernism; shopping centers
Main Street: Building Improvement File (National Trust, 1978), 263–64
Main Street Guidelines (National Trust, 1987), 264–65
Mainstreet Theater, Kansas City, 86
manufacturing processes, 9–10, 311, 313
Margie's Candies, Chicago, 316, plate 36
marquee signs: among rural to urban sign types, 20f; for movie theaters, 60, 83–84, 114, 179, 205, 208f, 318; sign fins and, 177–78
May Company building: Cleveland, 57, 59; Los Angeles, 158, 212
May Theater, Oklahoma City, 177
McAllister, Wayne, 172, 195
McDonald's, 213, 215f, 222, 224, 288f, 289, plate 30
McFarland, J. Horace, 70, 73
McGraw-Hill Building, New York City, 137
Means, Mary, 265–66
Medicine Bow, Wyo., false-front sign in, 35f
Medina, Ohio, preservation in, 259
Merchant's National Bank, Sullivan's, 319f, 321
Meyers, George F., 157, 217, 219, 220–21, 222f
Miami Beach hotels: modernist facades of, 154, 158–59; of 1930s, 172, 174–75, plate 9, plate 10; preservation of, 321; sign fins on, 170, 176f; signs separated from, 213–14

Michigan Theater, Detroit, 86
Midway Theater, Philadelphia, 175
Midwestern towns, 19f, 26-27, 26f
mimetic architecture, 107
Minneapolis, White Way in, 77
Mint Hotel, Las Vegas, 188-89
Miralago Ballroom, Chicago, 136-37, 139f
modernism, 117-18; coordinated community and vernacular individual, 179-93; corporate concepts, competitions, and incentives for, 143-53; European design in America, 127-43; importing European integration, 118-27; open-front or open-storefronts concept, 153-169; signs and storefronts and, 10; sign shapes and physical independence, 169-79
Mondawmin Center, Baltimore, parking lot sign, 240f, 241
Monrovia, Calif., modernizing and restoration, 203, 204f, 267-68
Morgan, Walls & Clements, 90, 93, 112-13
motels: graphic enhancement of, 221; Sarasota, 2f, 3-4, plate 1; Skyliner, 220, 223f; Wildwood, 213-14, 248, 318, plate 26, plate 39
movie theaters: design styles (1920s), 81, 82-90, 114; evolution in design of, 50, 59-60, 61f; signs for, 169, 177-79, 318, plate 6, plate 13, plate 15; suburban, 104. See also marquee signs
Mumford, Lewis, 89, 90, 99, 248
Municipal Art Society, New York City, 68, 70
Murray's Restaurant, Minneapolis, plate 22
Museum of Modern Art, 125, 137-38, 157

Music Box Theater, Chicago, 86, plate 6
Muskogee, Mich., electric welcome arch for, 78

Nairn, Ian, 293, 294
National Cash Register showroom, Miami, 153
National Electric Sign Association (NESA) design competitions: in late 1940s, 196, 205, 207; in 1951, 218; in 1959, 224, 226f, 227, 241
National Historic Preservation Act (1966), 259
National Land Ordinance (1785), 29
National Park Service, 263, 264, 265
National Register of Historic Places, 259
National Trust for Historic Preservation, 259, 263, 264; Main Street Center, 251, 265-66, 318
neon signs: acrylic light boxes and, 232, 233, 248-49; bias against, 297; in Miami Beach, 154, 174; modernizing with, 166, 186-87; for movie theaters, 178; of 1930s, 145, 311-12; patent restrictions and, 142; plastics technology and, 195. See also electric signs; modernism
neon tube benders, 187-88, 232
New Amsterdam Theater, New York City, 59, 61f
Newark, Ohio, public square, 26f
New England: sign preservation in, 318; towns and town centers of, 13, 14-15, 18-19, 24-27; visual diversity in, 65-66
New Orleans, 202, 203f, 266, plate 33
New Theater, Staunton, Va., 56
New Theatre, B. F. Keith's, Boston, 59
New Theatre, Philadelphia, Pa., 59
New York City: animated signs in, 102; competition between architecture and signs in, 43; domestic

architecture for commercial uses in, 23; Edison Building, 57; electric signs in, 49, 52f; Great White Way, 68, 75, 100, plate 14; hierarchy of facade signs in, 30f; historic preservation and, 259, 272-74, 275f; modern European design in, 132-33; roof-mounted signs in, 74-75; sign ordinances of, 99-100; signs covering Trinity Building in, 33; streetlights in, 77; world's fair (1964) in, 227, 245; Ziegfield Theater, 84f, 85-86
Niles, Mich.: Big Brown Take Down (2003) in, 257-58; open-storefronts concept in, 205; remodeling proposal (1940s), 149, 165-66, 172f; slipcovering in (1970s), 201, 252-53, 252f
Northland Center, Southfield (Detroit), 238, 239f, 241-42, 243
Northwestern Terra Cotta Company, 181

Ohio State University Department of Architecture, 261-62
oil company signs, 110-11, 231, 232. See also gas station signs
Oklahoma, Plains commercial buildings of, 319
Omaha's sign ordinances, 100
Ontario, Calif., identity of, 268-70, 271f
open-front or open-storefronts concept: early American, 20, 28; modernist, 128, 130, 162, 165, 166, 171f; of 1940s, 196-210, 205. See also exterior lobbies
opera houses, 59
Original New York System wiener shop sign, 186-87
Orpheum Theater, Madison, Wisc., 86
outdoor-sign industry, 72. See also billboards
Oyster Bay Restaurant, Baltimore, 202f

Paradise Theater, Chicago, 90
parapets, with no space for signs, 67, 69f
parapet signs, 20f, 34, 34–35, 43, 60, 64f
Paris, design and designers (1930s) of, 118, 120f, 121, 121f
Parisian Bootery, New York City, 134
Park and Shop, Washington, D.C., 184, 236
Parkette Drive-In sign, Lexington, Ky., 212, plate 25
Park Forest Plaza, Ill., 276
parking lots: commercial design for, 212, 236; shopping center signs in, 237, 238, 239f, 240f, 297
Pasadena, Calif., 100, 102–3f, 104, 292–93, 303–4, 305f
Pat's Steak Sandwich sign, Philadelphia, 317, plate 38
Patterson's Department Store, Findlay, Ohio, 254–55f, 256–57
Pei, I. M., graphic designers for, 238, 241, 242–43, 242f
Penn, William, 13–14, 284, 285
Pereira, William and Hal, 169–70
Philadelphia: early signs in, 18–19, 21, 22f, 23; facade evolution in, 36–37, 36f; Penn's design of, 13–14; shopping arcade in, 71
Philbrick Dry Goods building, Redwood Falls, Minn., 201, 253
Phillips, Peter, 265
pier-mounted signs, 20f. *See also* pylon signs
pigmented structural glass, 118, 150–51, 181. *See also* Vitrolite
Pittsburgh Plate Glass Company (PPG), 152, 164–65
plastic signs, 195, 232. *See also* acrylic sign boxes
plate glass, 29, 33, 40
Plexiglas, 201
Polevitzky, Igor, 174, plate 10
police power, 72, 79, 99, 100, 291

Pomona, Calif., pedestrianized Main Street in, 277, 278, 281–82
porcelain enamel, 118, 146, 200
post- or pole-mounted signs, 17, 18, 20f, 34, 45, 106. *See also* pylon signs
postwar architecture, 214–16, 216f
Princess shoe store, Jackson, Miss., 208–9, 211f
Princess Theater, Shelbyville, Tenn., 177, plate 13
progressives, 10, 66, 70, 79, 312
projecting signs: building codes on, 73; electric, 51, 73–74, 99–100, 101; historic preservation and, 262, 291–92, 308; by Meyers and Horsley, 220–21; modernizing commercial streetscapes with, 186; motor vehicles' need for, 43–44; over pedestrians' heads, 201–3; for strip retail buildings, 67; uniformity in commercial buildings and ornateness of, 47; urbanization and, 21, 34; vertical, 86, 87f, 88, 128, 157. *See also* neon signs
property rights, 13, 70. *See also* sign ordinances; zoning laws
Providence, R.I.: makeover (1990s) of, 286, 287; master plan (1961) for, 279–80, 279f; New York System, plate 17; retail decline in, 276; shopping arcade in, 71, 72; slipcovering in, 197, 198f, 199
Providence Journal Building, 198f, 199, 258
PSFS Building, Philadelphia, 137, plate 8
Publix Market, Sarasota, 4–5, 4f, plate 2
pylon signs, 20f; of 1940s, enormity of, 169; separated from architecture (1950s), 217–20, 218f, 220f, 222f, 223f, 246, 313; for strip architecture, 195–96. *See also* independent sign structures; post- or pole-mounted signs

Quehl Company, 52
quick-read architecture, 107

railroads, 29, 45
Rand, Paul, 215, 230, 248
Rapp and Rapp, 86, 88
Reading, Pa., 41, 42f, 284–85
rebus signs, 18
Redlands, Calif., 284, 298–99, 301f
Redwood Falls, Minn., 37, 38–39f, 201
Reinhardt Theater, New York City, 132
reinvention of urban centers, 251–52. *See also* Kalamazoo, Mich.; Monrovia, Calif.; Pasadena, Calif.; Pomona, Calif.; Staunton, Va.
representational giantism, 107
Republic Steel (storefront manufacturer), 148, 149–50
restrictive codes. *See* sign ordinances; zoning laws
Reynolds Aluminum (slipcovering manufacturer), 200
Rialto (New York City movie theater), 60
ribbon lettering, 123, 133, 134, 135f, 136f, 174–75
Riggs, Lutah Maria, 94–95, 97f
roads, paved, 76, 77, 79
roadside advertising, 73, 113–14, 251
roadside businesses, 111, 113, 115, 221–22. *See also* drive-ins
roadside improvement: content-empty aesthetics of, 246–49; corporate identity symbols and, 230–33; design critics on need for, 233–34; Disneyland and, 244–45; individual ideas and ownership in, 246; Jackson on Stranger's Path and, 243–44; in 1950s, 228–30, 229f; planned shopping centers and, 235–43; Rouse on, 245–46
Robinson, Charles Mulford, 70, 71, 73
Rohm and Haas, 201

roof-mounted signs, 20f; automobiles and, 105–6; eclectic architecture and, 93; of movie theaters (1920s), 85, 86, 87f, 88; of 1940s, enormity of, 169; preservation of, 267; regulations on, 71, 73, 74–75

Roosevelt Field Shopping Center, East Garden City, N.Y., 242–43, 242f

Roseland, Ill., 43–44, 46f, 153, 270–71, 272f

rotary contact signs, 89

Rouse, James, 245–46, 285–86

row houses, commercial uses for, 23

Royal Host Motel, Denver, 221, 225f

rural sign types, 20f, 34

Russian constructivists (1930s), 124

Rye, N.Y., 1946 plan for, 275–76

Santa Barbara, Calif., 94–99, 97f, 115, 282, 283f, 284, 312

Sarasota: neon signs along Tamiami Trail in, 2f, 3–5, 304–6, 314, 316, plate 1, plate 2; White Tower Restaurant in, 208, plate 24

Sardi's, Los Angeles, 128, 130–31, 131f

Schindler, Rudolph, 127, 130–31

Schlesinger & Meyer department store, Chicago, 41

Schlitz Tavern, Chicago, 57, plate 5

Scotty's Hamburgers sign, Bismarck, N.Dak., 227

Scully, Vincent, 28

Sears, Roebuck stores, 179

Seattle's Century 21 Exposition (1962), 227, 245, 247f

Sell's Furniture Building, Monrovia, Calif., 203, 204f, 267–68

semi-malls, 282

Senator (Miami Beach hotel), 172

Shayne's Fine Furs of Chicago sign, 52

Shelborne Hotel, Miami Beach, 174–75, plate 12

Shopper's World, Framingham, Mass., 237

shopping arcades, urban, 71

shopping centers (malls): consistent look for, 180–81, 187f; criticism of issues with, 242–47; independent sign structures for, 212, 224, 226f, 227; parking lot signs for, 238, 239f, 240f, 241; planned, as blight control, 235–43; roadside improvement and, 228–29; signs and storefronts and, 10

Sidney, Ohio, courthouse square, 63, 65, 66f

sign craft, neon signs and decline in, 246

sign crafters and contractors, 11, 79, 227–28; painters, 32–33, 53–55, 83

sign designers: modernism and, 127, 145, 190–91; postwar, 194, 200, 207, 209f, 227; signs and storefronts and, 10, 311, 313–14. *See also* design competitions

sign fins, 169, 174f, 176f, 177–79, 190

sign industry (19th century), 38, 44–45

sign ordinances (regulations), 7–8; civic visions and, 66–75; destruction and debates on, 290–93; for shopping center tenants, 241–42; on sign styles and location, 99–100; in specific cities, 73–74, 282, 284, 304, 316, 321; *Street Graphics* and, 294–97. *See also* zoning laws

signs: as commercial chaos, 290–91; facade conflict with, 35–47; integration with architecture, 118–27, 314–15; preservation issues, 3–5, 262–66; separated from architecture, 210–28; task-suited architecture and, 28–35; urban design and, 8–9; White Ways of, 75–79, 89, 312. *See also* automobile age; blight; design competitions; Main Street; modernism; sign ordinances; *specific types*

Signs of the Times (trade journal), 51, 53; advertising in, 217, 219, 232–33; as design inspiration, 186–87, 189, 220–21; on design originality, 138–39, 227; electric companies and, 78; on electric signs, 52, 54–55, 56, 68, 111; launching of, 51, 53; on letterforms and lettering, 101, 228; on modernism, 121–23, 125, 126–27, 142; sign designer-architect conflict and, 103–4; on sign regulations, 101; on signs integrated with storefronts, 143–44, 145, 154; on symbols not words, 230

sign towers, 171–72, 177–79, 178f, 212

Silver Spring Shopping Center, 184, 236

Simon's Drive-in, Los Angeles, 172, 178f, plate 29

Skyliner Motel sign, Stroud, Okla., 220, 223f

slipcovering: in early 21st century, 256–57f, 257–58; in 1950s, 197, 199, 200, 252–53, 252f, plate 22, plate 23; process of, 196, 253, 256

smaller businesses, 147, 179–80, 295–96, 322

Smith, George Washington, 94–95, 96, 97f

Smitty's Men's and Boys' Wear, Cincinnati, plate 34

Socatch Bakery, Chicago, 136, 136f

Sontag Drugs building, Los Angeles, 162, 168f

Southern California Edison Company, 51

Spanjer Brothers of Chicago and Newark, 53

State Street, Chicago: electric signs (1920s) on, 73–74, 89; makeovers

of, 276–77, 280–81, 286–87, 288f, 289; preservation in, 321–22; sign-architecture competition along, 37, 40f
State Theatre, San Francisco, 64f
Staunton, Va.: antisign bias in, 56, 291–92; layered history in, 266–67, 268; overlay zoning district in, 298–99, 300, 302f, 303; predicting future cityscape of, 66–67
Steinberg, Saul, 228, 229f
"The Store Front of Tomorrow" competition (1943), 184–85
stores and storefronts: breaking facade plane in, 117, 128, 157–59, 162–63, 166, 190; combined commercial and residential, 23–24, plate 3; redesigns (1930s) for, 146–53; as urban design element, 8–9. *See also* commercial buildings; modernism; open-front or open-storefronts concept
Stough's Paint Store, Bryan, Ohio, 6, 7f
Strangers' Path, 244
streetcars, signs and storefronts affected by, 43–44
Street Graphics (1971), 264, 294–97, 307–8
streets, paved, 76, 77, 79
streetscapes, controlled, 71–72, 94–99, 97f. *See also* automobile age
strip retail buildings (taxpayer strips), 67, 69f, 85, 180–81, 195–96. *See also* shopping centers; *Street Graphics*
suburbs (suburbia), 99, 115, 117, 195, 276; signs separated from architecture and, 210–28, 246. *See also* shopping centers
Sullivan, Louis, 40, 41, 57, 67, 118, 319f, 320
Sun Drug Company, Calif., 110
Sutnar, Ladislav, 230, 238, 248
symbols, 52, 146, 230–31, 233, 248. *See also* logos; trademarks
Syracuse, N.Y., 53, 275–76

Tamiami Trail. *See* Sarasota
taverns, colonial, 16–17, 18, 19, 19f
taxpayer strips. *See* strip retail buildings
Teague, Billy ("Mac"), 227; portfolio of, plate 31
Teague, Walter Dorwin, 126, 133, 143
technology, signs and storefronts and, 9–10, 311, 313
television, influence on signs, 227, 230
Templeton, Mass., commercial evolution in, 27
terra cotta, 84–85, 89, 181
theaters, 132, 154. *See also* movie theaters; opera houses
three-dimensional signs, 20–21, 146, 164, 170f, 190
Tiffany (Miami Beach hotel), 172
Times Square, New York City, 102, 197
Toffenetti Restaurant, Chicago, 207, 210f
Toledo, Ohio, pedestrianized Main Street in, 277
towers, 105–6. *See also* sign towers
Townscape Institute, 265–66
trade journals, 53, 142, 151, 228. See also *Signs of the Times*
trademarks, 110–11, 115, 146, 241; for chain stores, 9, 135, 231–32, 248. *See also* logos; symbols
Trans-Lux Theater, New York City, 154, 158f
20th Century Theater sign tower, Cincinnati, 177, 184f

Uhlman's (slipcover material), 201, 258
United Artists Theater(s), Chicago, 205, 206f
University of Wisconsin, advertising research at, 101
upper stories, 33, 35–36, 197. *See also* slipcovering

Uptown Theater, Chicago, 87f, 88
Urban, Joseph, 85–86, 132, 145–46
urban renewal, 251, 259, 274–75, 285, 286–87, 291
Urban Signage Forum (1976), 296–97

Valley Fair, Santa Clara Valley, Calif., 241
van Doesburg, Theo, 118, 121
Vanity Fair, 189, 193f
Van Wert, Ohio, 253, 253f, 256, plate 32
Venturi, Robert, 5, 11, 28, 34, 110, 293
verbal signs, 22
vertical signs, 16f, 17–19, 53, 86, 87f, 88, 114. *See also* projecting signs
Vienna, Austria, 56–57
Village Theater, Los Angeles, 179
Visual Fronts (L-O-F Glass Company), 164, 171f
Vitrolite, 253, 253f, 256; Company, 150. *See also* pigmented structural glass
Volkmor shoe store sign, Cleveland, 90, 91f
Von's store, Los Angeles, 212, 214f

Wagner, Otto, 56–57
Walden Book Shop, Holabird & Root's storefront for, 135–36, 136f, 149
Walgreen's prototype, 171
wall signs. *See* facade signs
Weber, Kem, 127, 130, 131, 177
Western Union, Dreyfuss's storefront for, 154
Whelan Drugs, Fash's storefront for, 157, 164f
White Castle restaurants, 107
White Hut hamburger chain, 181
Wieboldt department stores, 52
Wildwood, N.J., signs in, 213–14, 248, 318, plate 26, plate 39
Wilkinson Building, Providence, slipcovering, 199
Williamsburg, Va., 13, 14–15f, 15–17, 23

Will Rogers Theater, Oklahoma City, 177
Wilton Candy Kitchen sign, 187, plate 19
window signs, 40
Wolfe, Tom, 5, 293–94
wooden swinging sign, 53
world's fairs, 49, 157–58, 312; Chicago (1933), 143–46, 153, 171; Seattle (1962), 227, 245, 247f
Wright, Frank Lloyd, 215, 216
Wright's Dairy-Rite sign, 302f, 303
W. T. Grant Company buildings, Alschuler's, 157, 163f

Ziegfield Theater, New York City, 84f, 85–86
zoning laws, 99, 113, 249, 298–300, 301–2f, 303. *See also* building codes; Santa Barbara, Calif.
Zourite facing, 200